Tony Cliff

In the Thick of
Workers' Struggle

Tony Cliff

In the Thick of Workers' Struggle

SELECTED WRITINGS
VOLUME 2

BOOKMARKS

London and Sydney

Tony Cliff: In the Thick of Workers' Struggle: Selected Writings Volume 2

First published 2002
Bookmarks Publications Ltd, c/o 1 Bloomsbury Street, London WC1B 3QE, England
Bookmarks, PO Box A338, Sydney South, NSW 2000, Australia
Copyright © Bookmarks Publications Ltd

ISBN 1 898876 85 1 (Paperback)
ISBN 1 898876 84 3 (Hardback)

Printed by The Bath Press, Bath
Cover by Ian Goodyer

Bookmarks Publications Ltd is linked to an international grouping of socialist
organisations:
Australia: International Socialists, PO Box A338, Sydney South
Austria: Linkswende, Postfach 87, 1108 Wien
Britain: Socialist Workers Party, PO Box 82, London E3 3LH
Canada: International Socialists, PO Box 339, Station E, Toronto, Ontario M6H 4E3
Cyprus: Ergatiki Demokratia, PO Box 7280, Nicosia
Czech Republic: Socialisticka Solidarita, PO Box 1002, 11121 Praha 1
Denmark: Internationale Socialister, PO Box 5113, 8100 Aarhus C
Finland: Sosialistiliitto, PL 288, 00171 Helsinki
Germany: Linksruck, Postfach 304 183, 20359 Hamburg
Greece: Socialistiko Ergatiko Komma, c/o Workers Solidarity, PO Box 8161, Athens 100 10
Holland: Internationale Socialisten, PO Box 92025, 1090AA Amsterdam
Ireland: Socialist Workers Party, PO Box 1648, Dublin 8
New Zealand: Socialist Workers Organisation, PO Box 13-685, Auckland
Norway: Internasjonale Socialisterr, Postboks 9226 Grønland, 0134 Oslo
Poland: Pracownicza Demokracja, PO Box 12, 01-900 Warszawa 118
Spain: Izquierda Revolucionaria, Apartado 563, 08080 Barcelona
United States: Left Turn, PO Box 445, New York, NY 10159-0445
Zimbabwe: International Socialist Organisation, PO Box 6758, Harare

This volume is one of a series devoted to the writings of Tony Cliff (1917-2000). Born in Palestine to a Zionist family, his development as a revolutionary Marxist was shaped by an extraordinary combination of influences. He came to hate all forms of oppression after witnessing the systematic exclusion of Arabs from Zionist society. Opposition to imperialism led to him being jailed by the occupying British power. He came to embrace Trotskyism when Stalin's disastrous international policies helped Hitler become German Chancellor in 1933.

Arriving in post-war Britain from an impoverished colonial country, Cliff was struck by the relative affluence here. This made him question the dogmatic followers of Trotsky who maintained the capitalist economy was collapsing. Above all, Cliff rejected their assertion that Red Army tanks, rather than workers' self-activity, could establish socialism in Eastern Europe. If the Eastern bloc was not socialist, and yet identical to Russia, that country was not socialist either. He concluded it was state capitalist.

This analysis preserved the central Marxist notion that workers' liberation (and therefore humanity's in general) comes from self-activity. This meant that theory and practice must be linked, which helped Cliff avoid the sterile abstractions of much of what passed for Marxism. Such insights guided him and others who formed successively the Socialist Review Group, the International Socialists and the Socialist Workers Party.

A wave of industrial militancy which peaked in the early 1970s enabled the SWP to intervene practically in the class struggle. The focus was in two areas: on rank and file action rather than union bureaucracy; and on the building of a revolutionary party which could offer political leadership in the fight for socialism.

The collapse of Stalinist regimes after 1989 confirmed the state capitalist analysis of 40 years before and cleared the way for the spread of the International Socialist Tendency in many countries.

Across seven decades of revolutionary activism, Cliff was a tireless writer and speaker who always combined theoretical rigour with practical action. We are pleased to be able to republish his writings, not as a monument to the past, but as tools to help build a future where humanity will no longer be threatened by the poverty, oppression, wars and environmental destruction that are inextricably part of capitalism.

Donny Gluckstein

Contents

Chronology 1945-2000   ix

Introduction   xvii

The Labour Party in perspective   1

Incomes policy, legislation and shop stewards
Introduction by Reg Birch   23
Preface   25
Why incomes policy?   28
Is it incomes policy or wage restraint?   35
Incomes policy and economic growth   42
George Brown's plan and George Brown's planners   54
The wages front   61
The dead weight of bureaucracy   67
Shop stewards and unofficial strikes   73
Anti-union legislation   92
The way ahead   100

Labour's addiction to the rubber stamp   123

On perspectives   129

The employers' offensive:
productivity deals and how to fight them
Preface   145
Why productivity deals?   147
The general characteristics of productivity bargaining   151
The sugar on the pill   157
A new wage pay system: measured day work   167
Greater flexibility in the deployment of labour   180
Job evaluation, grading and rating   201
Time and motion study and speed-up   210
Productivity deals and the threat of redundancy   220

Legal shackles on workers   231
The ideological offensive: production for what?   244
The role of the trade unions   261
Rank and file response   284
How to fight productivity deals   296

After Pentonville: the battle is won but the war goes on   329

1972: a tremendous year for the workers   335

Factory branches   339

Ten years on: 1969 to 1979   369

The balance of class forces in recent years   373

The state of the struggle today   423

In the balance   431

Change is going to come: but how?   437

Chronology 1945–2000

1945
End of war in Europe.
Labour government elected under Clement Attlee.
Nuclear bombs dropped on Japan.
George Orwell's *Animal Farm*.

1946
US and Canada lend Britain $5 billion.
Stalin, Churchill and US State Department start Cold War.
National Health Act.
Bank of England nationalised.

1947
Coal mines nationalised.
India and Pakistan become independent.
Tony Cliff arrives in Britain from Palestine.

1948
Foundation of the National Health Service.
British Nationality Act granted citizenship to inhabitants of the colonies.
Arab-Israeli war. Palestinians forced out of Zionist state.
Railways nationalised.
Labour shortages in Britain lead to immigration from West Indies and Indian subcontinent.
McCarthyism starts in US.
Tito breaks with Stalin.

1949
Britain devalues sterling.
NATO Pact signed by Britain.
Ireland Act recognises Eire as a republic.
Dock strike. Labour brings in troops..
Mao proclaims People's Republic of China.
Gas nationalised.
Berlin blockade splits Germany.
End of clothes rationing.
George Orwell's *Nineteen Eighty-Four*.
Stalin murders leadership of Hungarian Communist Party.

1950
Labour re-elected with tiny majority.
Dock strike.
Korean War.
Socialist Review Group founded.

1951
Steel nationalised.
Tory government under Churchill elected.
Britain conducts its first atomic tests on Monte Bello Islands, Western Australia.
Festival of Britain.
Defection to USSR of Burgess and Maclean.

1952
Stalin eliminates leadership of Czech Communist Party in anti-Semitic show trial.

1953
Death of Stalin.
East German rising.
Mau Mau activity in Kenya.

1954
Dien Bien Phu victory in Vietnam evicts French forces.
CIA-organised coup against elected government of Guatemala.
End of food rationing.
Landlord and Tenant Act.

1955
Tory government re-elected.
Anthony Eden succeeds Churchill as prime minister.
Hugh Gaitskell replaces Clement Attlee as leader of Labour Party.
Montgomery bus boycott launches civil rights movement in US.

1956
Kruschchev, leader of USSR, denounces Stalin's crimes at 20th Congress of Communist Party of the Soviet Union (CPSU).
Suez Crisis.
Hungarian uprising crushed by Soviet tanks in Stalinist revival.
John Osborne's *Look Back in Anger* performed at Royal Court Theatre.

1957
Harold Macmillan succeeds Eden as prime minister.
First stretch of motorway—Preston bypass.
Big shipbuilding and engineering strikes.
Sputnik, first space satellite, launched by USSR.

Crisis in Communist Party of Great Britain (CPGB) following Kruschev's speech and invasion of Hungary

1958
First Campaign for Nuclear Disarmament march.
London bus strike.
Race riots in Notting Hill.
Sterling becomes fully convertible.

1959
First TV coverage of general election.
Tory government re-elected.
First section of M1 (London-Birmingham motorway) opened.
Cuban Revolution.

1960
Labour leadership defeated on nuclear disarmament.
Harold Macmillan makes 'wind of change' speech to South African parliament.

1961
First British application to join the European Economic Community rejected.
National Economic Development Council (Neddy) formed.
'Pay pause' introduced by Tory chancellor.
Massacre at Sharpeville of protesters against South African pass laws.
Bay of Pigs CIA assault on Cuba defeated.

1962
Cuban Missile Crisis brings world to brink of nuclear war.
Commonwealth Settlement Act and Commonwealth Immigrants Act.
Algerian war of independence ends in victory.
War between India and China.

1963
Harold Macmillan resigns. Replaced by Sir Alec Douglas-Home as prime minister.
Harold Wilson makes 'white heat of technology' speech at the Labour Party conference.
Kennedy assassinated.
Sino-Soviet split (further weakens CPGB).
Greater London Council (GLC) created.
Beeching report on railways leads to big cuts.
Profumo scandal.
Beatles' first number one hit album.

1964
Labour government elected under Harold Wilson.
Lyndon B Johnson launches full scale war against North Vietnam.
President Nasser of Egypt takes Soviet aid to finish Aswan dam.

1965
March led by Martin Luther King attacked by racists in Alabama.
Black uprising in Watts quelled by 15,000 troops.
Rhodesian white colonialists secede from British rule in Zimbabwe (Unilateral Declaration of Independence).
Yorkshire miners' strike uses flying pickets for first time.
Founding of London Shop Stewards Defence Committee.

1966
Labour government re-elected.
Seamen's strike.

1967
London School of Economics occupation.
Sexual Offences Act brings limited tolerance of homosexuality.
Plowden report on primary education.
North Sea gas piped ashore.
Israel seizes Jerusalem and Sinai in Six Day War.

1968
Tet Offensive in Vietnam.
May Day revolt in Paris followed by general strike.
Commonwealth Immigrants Act.
Prescription charges reintroduced.
Civil rights march in Northern Ireland.
Mass anti Vietnam War demo in London.
Rising in Prague.
Socialist Worker starts.

1969
90,000 workers strike against Labour's 'In Place of Strife'.
Franchise extended to 18 year olds.
British troops sent to Northern Ireland.

1970
Pilkington strike (glass workers).
Tory government elected. Ted Heath becomes prime minister.

1971
250,000 demonstrate against Tory Industrial Relations Bill (twice).

Ford strike.
Decimal currency introduced.
Immigration Act.

1972
170,000 demonstrate against imprisonment of Pentonville Five.
Britain assumes direct rule over Northern Ireland.
Bloody Sunday in Derry.
Arrival of Ugandan Asians expelled by Idi Amin.
Miners' strike victory.
Local government reorganisation.

1973
1,600,000 strike against Tory counter-inflation policies.
Britain enters European Economic Community (Common Market).
Energy crisis. Three-day week.
School leaving age raised to 16.
US pulls out of Vietnam.
Allende overthrown in Chile by CIA-backed military coup.

1974
Miners' strike victory.
Labour government elected under Harold Wilson.
Guildford pub bombings.
Birmingham pub bombings.
Prevention of Terrorism Act.
Rent Act.
Portuguese Revolution.

1975
Social Contract established.
National Enterprise Board established.
Margaret Thatcher becomes leader of Tories.
North Sea oil pumped ashore.

1976
James Callaghan becomes prime minister.
Education Act extends comprehensive schools.
Right to Work Campaign.

1977
Firefighters' strike.
Grunwick strike.
Lib-Lab pact.
Anti-Nazi demo at Lewisham.

1978
100,000 on first Carnival Against the Nazis.
Winter of Discontent ran into 1979.

1979
Tory government elected under Margaret Thatcher.
Blair Peach killed by police on Southall anti-Nazi demonstration.

1980
First national steel strike since 1926 General Strike.
Bristol riots.
Solidarity strikes in Poland.

1981
Maze hunger strikes.
British Nationality Act.
Brixton and Toxteth riots.

1982
Falklands War.

1983
Tory government re-elected.
Neil Kinnock elected leader of Labour Party.

1984
Miners' strike begins.
Dock strike.
British Telecom privatised.
IRA bomb hits Tory conference.

1985
Miners' strike ends.
Tottenham riots.
Hillsborough power-sharing agreement (Ireland).

1986
Defeat of print unions at Wapping.
Westland affair reveals splits in Tory cabinet.
London stock exchange Big Bang.
British Gas and British Airports Authority privatised.

1987
Tory government re-elected.
Single European Act.

'Black Monday' on stock exchange.
King's Cross fire.

1988
Clapham rail disaster.
Salman Rushdie's *Satanic Verses* leads to fatwa from Iranian religious authorities.

1989
Tiananmen Square massacre in Beijing.
Fall of Berlin Wall.
Break-up of Soviet bloc in Eastern Europe.
Water industry privatised.
Convictions of Guildford Four quashed by Court of Appeal.

1990
100,000 demonstrate against the poll tax.
Margaret Thatcher replaced by John Major as Tory prime minister.
Strangeways prison riot.
Student loans introduced.
End of apartheid in South Africa.

1991
Gulf War.
Convictions of the Birmingham Six quashed by the Court of Appeal.
Gorbachev overthrown, collapse of Soviet Union and dissolution of CPSU.

1992
200,000 demonstrate against pit closures.
Tory government re-elected.
Pit closures follow election.
Black Wednesday. Britain forced to withdraw sterling from European Exchange Rate Mechanism.

1993
Break-up of Yugoslavia begins.
Council tax replaces community charge.
John Major and Albert Reynolds sign joint declaration on Northern Ireland.
Community Care Act.
Welling ANL demo against the Nazis.
Stephen Lawrence murder.

1994
Sudden death of John Smith, leader of Labour Party. Tony Blair elected leader.
IRA ceasefire.
Homosexual age of consent lowered to 18.

1995
Bosnian wars. Seige of Sarajevo.
Collapse of Barings plc after speculations by Nick Leeson.

1996
IRA ceasefire ends.

1997
Labour government under Tony Blair elected.
William Hague elected leader of Tory party.
IRA ceasefire resumed.
Sinn Fein joins peace talks.
Hong Kong handed back to China.

1998
Belfast agreement on Northern Ireland ratified by referendum.

1999
Elections to Scottish Parliament and Welsh Assembly.
Reform of House of Lords.
Kosovan war.
Seattle demonstration against the WTO.

2000
Blockade of petrol refineries by road hauliers and farmers in protest against cost of fuel.
Derailment at Hatfield leads to widespread disruption on the railways.
Tony Cliff dies on 12 April.

Introduction

Colin Barker

The second volume of this collection of Tony Cliff's writings focuses on the labour movement and the role of revolutionary Marxists in Britain. Here Cliff lived and was politically active from the late 1940s.

Marxism's core principle—that working class emancipation can only be won by the action of the working class itself—was always central to Cliff's Marxism, but with a crucial emphasis. Cliff's attention was always centred on the real working class, its forms of struggle and organisation, and the practical contradictions of its consciousness. Cliff combined intransigent revolutionism with the toughest realism.

Understanding the actual working class requires direct involvement in its struggles and its arguments. Marxists must be ready to learn, and to change their strategies and tactics, as the conditions of the class struggle change. Readers will not find Cliff offering any general philosophical theses about class consciousness. Rather, at each moment, they will find him insisting that working class practical consciousness consists of a struggle for ideas going on in its midst. Under capitalism workers' consciousness, struggle and organisation are riven with contradictions. Some workers always incline to militancy, others to conservatism, and between them is a majority pulled this way and that by the force of the arguments from either side. The balance changes from one situation or period to another, as does the practical meaning of militancy and conservatism. At each new development Marxists face the problem of assessing what the current balance is, where the key arguments are focused, and how socialists can best intervene. Thus the development of socialist theory and practice connects closely with an ongoing struggle inside the movement about how to organise and how to fight.

An effort to grasp the current balance of class forces is always Cliff's starting point. The assessment of that question shapes the others. How should socialists organise themselves in this period? Where do we stand in relation to the real movement? Who is with us, and who is near us? What is the balance of forces right now, a balance that necessarily includes ourselves? What can we do to move it? The way Cliff answers such questions—the truly vital questions of socialist theory—necessarily changes from period to period, as the nature of the situation changes. Always the *context* is decisive.

Cliff wrote the majority of the material in this volume between 1962 and 1985, in a very different setting from that of today. In the quarter century after the Second World War world capitalism experienced the longest continuous boom in its history, a boom sustained by high levels of arms spending across the global economy. Britain was a former world power in decline, its rulers torn between reform and conservatism. They needed to confront Britain's falling share of world production and trade, which implied upgrading and modernising British capital. But at the same time Tory and Labour governments alike sought to defend the tattered remnants of Britain's old imperial position, preserving costly military bases abroad, a higher level of arms spending than their European rivals, and the pound sterling as a reserve currency. Effectively, major institutional reform was ruled out.

On one question Tories and Labour were united. They must reduce working class strength. But in conditions of full employment this was a difficult project, for workers' bargaining power was strong. While union leaders might be persuaded—especially by Labour governments—to help contain militancy, British workers had developed a whole set of informal mechanisms for evading control by the union bureaucracy: unofficial strikes and other forms of industrial action, shopfloor organisation centred on shop stewards, and a variety of bargaining gambits (including 'wage drift', 'leapfrogging', 'coercive comparisons', 'protective practices', etc). If the ruling class was to reduce the working class's power of resistance, it must look for ways to refashion the very labour movement itself, to make it more pliable to capital's needs.

That labour movement was dominated by reformist politics, of the right (the Labour Party leadership and most trade union leaders) and of the left (the Communist Party and such groupings as that around *Tribune*). The revolutionary left was tiny and almost completely marginalised. However, reformist bodies exercised only loose control over their members: the Labour Party still had a fairly substantial left wing; within the unions informal and occasionally more organised shopfloor movements challenged the bureaucracies on practical issues of pay and conditions; and Communist Party industrial militants, after the Hungarian Revolution of 1956, were often open to discussion and joint activity. Movements such as the Campaign for Nuclear Disarmament (CND) and to a lesser extent the New Left could attract tens and occasionally even hundreds of thousands of people to their activities, creating a space to discuss socialist ideas. The level of (mostly unofficial) strikes was rising. The early signs of student radicalisation were appearing. New struggles against racism, and against British and US imperialism were developing. The early and mid-1960s were thus a period when new opportunities were growing for socialists.

In the 1964 election the *Economist* recommended a vote for Harold Wilson's Labour Party on the grounds that it was more likely to stand up to the unions. Wilson's government, elected in 1964 and again in 1966, certainly tried. Its efforts, which made it increasingly unpopular among workers, probably cost it the 1970 election. The Tories under Edward Heath took over, trying to use the law to control pay and unions, and provoking huge battles with major unions. But the effects of all this activity, by both Labour and the Tories, were not what had been planned—the level of industrial militancy rose, along with workers' self-confidence. Up to 1970 the number of strikes rose every year, while the following four years (under Heath's Tory government) witnessed some of the greatest labour battles of the 20th century, with workers (notably in the pits and the docks) achieving some powerful victories.

Labour returned in 1974, after winning an election in the midst of a national miners' strike. Now, while its general aims were unchanged, its methods were different. It sought to tie the union leaderships to it with a 'Social Contract', under whose terms the unions would police the workforce. When even the 'lefts' on the TUC (notably Hugh Scanlon and Jack Jones) supported the Social Contract, and promoted scabbing in strikes, the tide began to turn against workers. As unemployment rocketed, real wages fell, and Labour carried through some of the largest cuts ever in the welfare state. Labour prepared the way for Thatcher's Tory victory in 1979.

It was not until the 1980s that the ruling class could really begin to claim that it had, for a time, definitely pushed back working class militancy. It did so, eventually, in a series of set-piece battles against a trade union movement weakened by unemployment (which began to leave its deadly mark from the mid-1970s on) but above all by the poor generalship its own union leaders provided.

The books and essays collected here are thus produced at different points in an overarching wave of struggle, itself repeated in different ways in other major capitalist countries.

The first piece published here, on the Labour Party, comes from 1962. At that time the level of industrial struggle was low. The Tories had won the 1959 election on the slogan 'You've never had it so good—don't let Labour ruin it.' The last experience of a Labour government had been the Attlee government of 1945-51, which, for all its massive failings, was a famously reforming regime. It seemed axiomatic that Labour was the party of the British working class, attracting workers' votes even when it betrayed them. The roots of reformism ran far deeper than Lenin, for example, had allowed, and reformism's major political expression continued to be the Labour vote. Cliff's Marxist organisation, the Socialist Review Group, had no more than 60 members nationally. It just about managed to sustain a monthly paper and a new quarterly journal. For a tiny Marxist group, the Labour Party and its Young Socialists provided the only possible milieu, for there it could find some kind of combination of anti-Tories, industrial militants and CND supporters. Within and around the Labour Party socialists could enjoy some expressions of a militant 'do it yourself' politics, providing possible openings towards the principle of self-emancipation. Consistent propaganda could win some recruits to Marxism. Cliff makes an optimistic assessment of the potential of the situation in the early 1960s, noting how full employment has made workers more self-confident and daring, even though their struggles are highly fragmented. As yet Cliff's article foresees no alternative to the Labour Party as a place for expanding Marxist propaganda. He sees no opportunity to form a separate party, or even the embryo of one.

However, in changing circumstances Cliff's views altered. In 1964 and again in 1966 Harold Wilson's Labour Party won the election. While CND activity withered, and Labour Party internal life became increasingly moribund, rising workers' confidence manifested itself in strikes, most of them 'unofficial'. Many workplace disputes involved fights not over pay, but over issues to do with workplace control, with conditions of work and discipline. Cliff's group, now called the International Socialists (IS), turned towards the new opportunities.

The Wilson government deepened a policy trend initiated by the Tories—state-sponsored control over wage increases, or 'incomes policy'. Labour set up a Prices and Incomes Board under Aubrey Jones, a former Tory MP, and a Royal Commission on Unions and Employers under Lord Donovan, which finally reported in 1968. The ruling class was trying to control working class advances in a period of full employment, when the usual disciplines of unemployment had little purchase. They could not hope to *smash* the unions, but they could try to contain them, to limit them as expressions of working class power, and to co-opt them partly. The key instrument for doing this was the union bureaucracies. Industrial relations became especially 'political'.

In 1966 Tony Cliff and I wrote *Incomes Policy, Legislation and Shop Stewards*. Two aspects revealed the growing possibilities opening for the IS. The London Industrial Shop Stewards Defence Committee, led by IS members, published the work. And the book sold 10,000 copies, most of them to workers, themselves often Communist Party militants.

The book discusses the changing conditions of capitalism, notably the expansion of state intervention in economic life, but above all it analyses the condition and potentials of the workers movement. Workers through the boom conditions of the 1950s and 1960s made considerable economic gains, not so much through the 'official' action of their unions as through 'unofficial' action on the shopfloor, producing what economists termed 'wage drift'. Central to the rising militancy of the working class were the elected rank and file representatives on the shopfloor, the shop stewards. While the working class movement was as tied as ever to reformism, that reformism had a new aspect—it was 're-formism from below'. The upside of this situation was that workers' gains were dependent on local initiative, confidence and organisation rather than on distant and commonly right wing union leaders. Working class combativity paid off directly. The downside was that workers faced little need to generalise politically. The movement was paradoxically at once very fragmented and powerful. Industrial militancy could be combined with elements of racism, with social conservatism and so forth. There was a new 'do it yourself reformism', with the vital element that reforms were won through self-organised collective action. But it was still reformism, and it had its limits.

Roger Cox, an engineering worker at that time, writes:

Incomes Policy filled a vacuum among these militants, but not just as an academic explanation. Cliff's method of research was quite straightforward—he spoke with and questioned intensely many, maybe hundreds of militants. He would enquire about bonus schemes—how did they work? What was the relation of forces inside the factory? But above all, he asked what were the arguments being used in the daily struggles.

Because many of the militants were very confident and had never suffered a setback, they took too much for granted. He would confront them with questions that went to the heart of the matter. 'How do you fight redundancy?' 'Are incentive schemes good or bad?' In one case, interviewing a factory convenor, Cliff asked how the bonus scheme worked but the chap didn't know, despite having negotiated it! 'But this is madness,' cried Cliff. 'Not really—you see the management don't know either...' This was of course an extreme example, but Cliff's stress on the growing interconnection between events at workshop level and wider class struggle (which included the capitalist state) meant that *Incomes Policy* helped many militants confront their current problems.

This book also represents Cliff's transition from theoretician and commentator to a workers' leader. He was able to generalise from many sectional experiences and gained an insight into the movement that few individual militants could possess. He could see the strengths and also the limitations of the sectionalism that prevailed. The fight now was to build a party that could replace the CP as the natural home for the militant, but with revolutionary socialist politics.

Incomes Policy suggests that reformism's limits would be challenged by the politics of 'incomes policy'. The bosses wanted above all to tame the unofficial strikes and the shop stewards who led them. Shopfloor issues would become political. It was possible to envisage the growth of a new working class based socialist movement, rooted in workplace struggle. However, as experience would suggest, that vision was rather foreshortened. The politics of the movement were most certainly decisive, but there was no automatic link between rising militancy and revolutionary socialism.

Cliff's 1967 article 'Labour's Addiction to the Rubber Stamp' shows how far his emphasis had shifted from 1962. Parliament's irrelevance both in capitalist decision making and in workers' struggles for reforms was now the main focus. Social democratic parties were entering a new phase. No longer socialist parties, no longer even parliamentarian-reformist, they were increasingly parties that, in office, excluded the larger part of their MPs from significant decision making (which anyway occurred at the intersection of state, international finance and industry) and were more concerned with disciplining labour to the needs of state-monopoly capitalism than with their reformist representation.

The later 1960s saw dramatic shifts in opportunity for Marxists. The student movement exploded in tandem with the growing opposition to the Vietnam War. In Britain, for the first time, forces to the left of the Communist Party were able to develop an independent campaign against the American war, with revolutionary slogans. In France the student and anti-war movements provided the spark that ignited the extraordinary explosion of May 1968. When the response of many on the left was to engage in euphoric celebration, Cliff joined with Ian Birchall in writing a pamphlet combining intense enthusiasm with cool and sober analysis.[1] In his 'On Perspectives' article in 1969 he offered a summary account of the nature of the new period the French events had so dramatically disclosed. As familiar signposts disappeared, so did the value of old socialist routines. Openings for Marxist interventions were suddenly expanding very rapidly, even if the possibilities disclosed were not yet revolutionary. The working class and its forms of struggle were changing in ways that were still difficult to summarise with neat formulae. Socialists needed to capture the emerging new world in thought, so as to 'raise theory to the level of practice'. In the unknown and still emerging world of the late 1960s and early 1970s initiative and perseverance by revolutionaries were at a premium.

Cliff carried a large part of his 'On Perspectives' article across to a new piece (not printed here) he wrote in 1970, under the title 'The Class Struggle in Britain'.[2] Here he focused his sense of the emerging new world and its contradictions on the state of industrial class struggle, and in particular the matter of 'productivity deals'. Cliff had spent the previous year and more researching and writing *The Employers' Offensive: Productivity Deals and How to Fight Them*. Part of the research was undertaken by IS members who spent hours talking with leading shop stewards in a number of industries. The book itself proved to be an immense success among working class militants up and down the country.[3] Around 20,000 copies were sold, most of them to shop stewards in industry, often in bundles of anything between five and 50. Across Britain, Cliff and other IS members were able to speak to sizeable audiences of militant rank and file workers, some of whom were attracted to the IS group itself, laying the basis for the development of workplace-based branches.

Central to the book was the argument that employers were developing a new method of countering working class organisation. During the 1960s 'productivity deals' spread to around six million workers. Rather than attack trade unionism directly, the ruling class was crafting new strategies to persuade workers to sell their working conditions in return for pay rises. The union bureaucracies were actively promoting these deals, often involving senior shop stewards. *The Employers' Offensive* set out first to provide industrial militants with ideological arguments to undermine the appeal of such productivity bargaining, by showing the highly biased nature of the so-called 'science' underpinning the new schemes. It went on to offer a practical manual of advice on how best to resist the new employers' offensive. The book is thus deeply engaged with the details of workplace struggle, which it treats as a vital front of political engagement.

The ruling class was divided on the question of dealing with trade unions. One wing argued that it was better to follow the 'softly softly' approach of productivity bargaining, getting the unions to reduce their own powers voluntarily. Others argued for a 'tougher' approach, using the law. In 1969 Barbara Castle, then minister of labour, produced a white paper, 'In Place of Strife', proposing legal sanctions against strikes. It was withdrawn under protest. In

1970 the Tories under Ted Heath returned to government and introduced new anti-union laws, setting the stage for a series of major confrontations, with variable outcomes. In the summer of 1972 five London dockers were sent to Pentonville prison for picketing in defiance of the law. Flying pickets from the docks stopped the Fleet Street newspapers, and then spread the strikes across other branches of industry, compelling the TUC to threaten a general strike. The government was forced to back down. Cliff wrote 'After Pentonville', mapping the balance of class forces in the wake of this important working class victory.[4] As he pointed out, the weapons the ruling class was currently attempting to use—incomes policy, productivity deals, anti-union laws—were themselves conditioned by the strength of working class organisation. While rank and file militancy provided the core of that strength, it remained fragmented in structure and episodic in appearance. As a result, the union bureaucracy sometimes lost the initiative to rank and file organisation, but equally it often regained it, producing a heady mixture of successive victories and defeats. The need to build a revolutionary organisation that could connect up the rank and file, strengthening its capacity for action independent of the labour bureaucracy, was ever more apparent.

That theme obtained more concrete shape in the IS pamphlet Cliff wrote in 1973, *Factory Branches*. The IS group, which had succeeded in recruiting significant numbers of industrial workers, had started to build both workplace branches and rank and file groups across numbers of industries.[5] The *Factory Branches* pamphlet summed up what IS had learned up to then about the tasks of revolutionary organisation within and around workplaces.[6] As *The Employers' Offensive* had suggested solutions to militant trade unionists faced with productivity deals, the pamphlet offered advice to revolutionary workers' groups about how to organise, agitate and educate within workplace settings. In both cases the advice was based on a summing up of existing experience, explicitly aware that further developments in the struggle would teach new lessons.

In practice, most factory branches did not last long. The conditions of the class struggle became far less favourable after the re-election of a Labour government in 1974, even if it took some time for the new patterns to become clear. Labour dropped the Tories' *legal* attack on unions. Instead it worked to bind the union bureaucracies, right and left alike, to itself through the Social Contract. It relied on the union leaders to discipline rank and file initiatives. It started to reap the full fruits of the 'productivity deal' offensive. Not only did the government succeed in reducing real wages during most of the 1974-79 period, and in turning the tide of strikes in the employers' favour, but in key disputes 'left' union leaders actively promoted scabbing. The revolutionary left proved too weakly implanted to be able to defeat these offensives—the stronger force on the left, around the Communist Party, was too compromised by its association with the 'lefts' in the union leaderships to offer a serious alternative.

In 1979, after the election of the Thatcher government, Cliff offered a starkly new account of the balance of class forces. Where the *Factory Branches* pamphlet of 1973 had looked forward to a deepening of revolutionary influence within the working class, Cliff now suggested the union bureaucracy had partly succeeded in the task the Donovan report had set it. In industry after industry the fragmented and uneven but independently militant rank and file movement had been brought under control. This development was central to the British form of the 'downturn' that affected revolutionary socialism across Europe and North America.[7] Both in the article 'Ten Years On: 1969 to 1979', written immediately after the election, and then in 'The Balance of Class Forces in Recent Years', Cliff insisted on a realistic appreciation of the new tasks facing socialists. There had been an unstable contest within the working class movement between political generalisation and fragmented militancy. The outcome had not been a generalisation of industrial militancy to overcome fragmentation, but, rather, sectional militancy had declined thanks to the misleadership of the union bureaucracies, the Labour left and the Communist Party. Now it fell to the revolutionary left to defend the most basic of union slogans, which were now falling into disuse—solidarity, respect for picket lines, collections for workers in battle, and so on.

The longer of the two articles opens with page after page of detail about the downturn in working class combativity. There was a reason—many socialists at the time denied it. The division ran through the heart of the SWP (the new name for the former IS) over the question. Cliff's article was written partly in reply to a previous piece by Steve Jefferys, which ended by proclaiming expanding possibilities for building rank and file movements led by revolutionaries.[8] It was difficult for a generation of socialists who had grown up in a period of generally rising militancy and expanding hopes to make the shift to a new period, of defeat and retreat. Many socialists were—for the time being—lost in this period, either dropping into inactivity or joining the Labour Party in pursuit of a dream that some Labour left like Tony Benn, Ted Grant or Ken Livingstone would provide salvation.[9]

The employers' offensive was about to take an altogether tougher form. Thatcher's Tories inflicted a series of defeats on the British working class movement, taking on and beating major sections one after another. The problems identified earlier—sectionalism and fragmentation, weakness of socialist politics, strength of bureaucratic conservatism—now dominated. The union leaders retreated, failing to organise solidarity action. By the time of the 1983 TUC the right was crowing over the discomfiture of the Broad Left. The former was embracing 'New Realism' in the hope of talking to the Tories, while the left was in practice following behind while denying it. Each time the union leaders led a section of workers to defeat, the Tories grew more confident. In 1984 they felt strong enough to take on and beat the miners in the biggest mass strike in British history.[10]

In 'The State of the Struggle Today', Cliff attempted again to draw a map of the balance of class forces. Though the working class had suffered terrible defeats, he concluded, these were not on the scale of 1926. The Tories had won some serious battles, but they were far from easy victories. They had not driven wages down, despite the defeats and despite mass unemployment. Finding the correct balance was vital, for now most of the left was pushing either towards accommodation with the right or towards pessimistic passivity. With hopes of a leftward swing in the Labour Party absolutely dashed, many sections of the left fell apart. Everything may look terrible, Cliff urged, but that doesn't mean there's nothing socialists can do. The fact is that working class resistance is slowing the ruling class attack, and there is space for intervention by even a few thousand revolutionaries, if they are realistic and don't lapse into mere abstract propagandism.

The 1990s saw a new balance. Heavily defeated by a mass campaign against the poll tax, and increasingly deprived of credibility, the Tories became hugely unpopular. Very patchily and unevenly, workers' confidence began to rise again after the defeats of the 1980s. 'In the Balance', written in early 1995, tries to capture the character of working class recuperation, and to draw tentative practical conclusions. In terms of strikes, any such recuperation proved very slow, but popular anger finally swept the Tories from office in May 1997 to give Blair's New Labour a landslide victory.

It was in the immediate wake of that election that Cliff wrote the final piece in this volume. He began by observing how very few reforms Blair's new government promised. Given the low level of industrial struggle, Cliff's focus here lay on ideological issues. With popular expectations running far higher than Blair was prepared to deliver, socialist ideas could begin to enjoy a much wider appeal than for a long time. As always, the analysis of the pluses and minuses in working class consciousness led Cliff to conclusions about practice. At the time of his death in April 2000 he was following with fascinated enthusiasm the progress of the London Socialist Alliance's challenge to New Labour in the first Greater London Assembly elections.

Cliff's writings over 35 years and more are a journey of discovery about the British working class—its history, nature and potential—from a consistently revolutionary standpoint. His work—sometimes a little crude in its judgments, often amazingly perceptive—is unmatched as a body of writing about the British working class in the second half of the 20th century. Its strength derives from the combination of Cliff's practical engagement with day to day struggles, his ruthless realism, and his constant measuring of present day realities against a standard—the international proletarian revolution to whose future and reality his commitment never wavered. The period when Cliff wrote these pieces was also one when the International Socialists and then the Socialist Workers Party grew from a tiny group commenting almost entirely from the sidelines of class politics to become one of the largest and best known revolutionary groupings in Europe. Nobody played a more central part in that political development than Tony Cliff. As the group's capacity to intervene in politics grew, so too did the obligation to consider the effects of our own interventions. Cliff's writings reflect the fact that the organisation he helped to build and develop itself became a significant, if minority, part of the story of the British working class in the last part of the 20th century.

Notes

1   See 'France: The Struggle Goes On' in T Cliff, *International Struggle and the Marxist Treadition: Selected Writings Volume One* (Bookmarks, 2001), pp159-217.

2   It was published in N Harris and J Palmer (eds), *World Crisis: Essays in Revolutionary Socialism* (Heinemann, 1970). This article was republished under the title 'On Perspectives: The Class Struggle in Britain' in the volume of Cliff's writings published as *Neither Washington Nor Moscow* (Bookmarks, 1982), pp218-238, where it was mistakenly confused with the 1969 article.

3   The *Times* (25 March 1970) carried a half-page feature review under the title 'Militant's Handbook'.

4   There is a fine history of the period in R Darlington and D Lyddon, *Glorious Summer: Class Struggle in Britain 1972* (Bookmarks, 2001).

5   IS managed to build 40 factory branches and to expand attendance at industrial rallies from 700 in January 1972 to 2,800 in November 1973. C Harman, '1984 and the Shape of Things to Come', *International Socialism* 2:29 (Summer 1985), p68.

6   It is notable that throughout this pamphlet 'workers' are treated as overwhelmingly male, and most of the examples of organisation come from factories and the construction industry. Organisation among hospital workers is reported as notably difficult. How different the picture would be a quarter of a century later!

7   See also C Harman, 'Crisis of the European Revolutionary Left', *International Socialism* 2:4 (Spring 1979), pp49-87.

8   S Jefferys, 'Striking Into the 1980s', *International Socialism* 2:5 (Summer 1979), pp1-52.

9   The early 1980s saw a mood of 'super-optimism' affecting whole layers of the left, who argued that apparent left gains in the Labour Party reflected a real radicalisation among workers. See C Harman, '1984', pp82-83, for quotations from the *Morning Star*, *Militant* and *Socialist Challenge*.

10 There are good accounts of the miners' strike of 1984-85 in A Callinicos and M Simons, *The Great Strike* (International Socialism, 1985), and in C Harman, '1984', pp99-115.

The Labour Party in perspective

International Socialism (first series) 9, Summer 1962

Introduction

The aim of the present article is to try and discover what makes the Labour Party tick. The British Labour Party is unique among social democratic parties in its structure and embraces a number of contradictory phenomena. It has a membership of millions of workers throughout the country, and the allegiance of further millions—it is thus a mass party. At the same time it involves actively only a tiny minority of its supporters. Its base is in the industrial working class, but its leadership is a coalition of top trade union bureaucrats and middle class MPs. Its function is in the main that of an electoral parliamentary machine, but its spirit is that of industrial militants, rebel youth and Aldermaston marchers, whose central theme is not delegation of responsibility, but 'do it yourself'. Its thousands of loyal industrial militants expect—and get—hardly any help from it in their daily struggle against the boss on the factory floor. Its leaders are bound hand and foot to an ideology of class collaboration, and strive for Lib-Lab conformism, while its millions of rank and file supporters are grouped around shop stewards committees and trade union branches, the elements of the labour movement that capitalism cannot discipline and integrate completely into itself. Its ideology covers a wide spectrum, its facets tracing their origin to the oft opposing elements that fused to form it, from the socialist ILP to Lib-Lab trade unionists.

In a way the Labour Party is a replica of British capitalist society. Its oligarchy is centralised and its masses, while alienated and rebelling against the system, nevertheless still accept its main values. If the workers rejected all capitalist values—if they insisted on complete involvement in, and complete control and management of, their own affairs—the Labour Party hierarchy, as well as that of the trade unions, would be isolated. If, on the other hand, the class struggle did not break through to express itself in the party, the permanent tensions between the ranks and the leadership, between left and right, expressing themselves in recurring rebellions inside the party, would not exist.

The Labour Party is the political focus of the working class. But the class struggle and the political struggle do not necessarily run along parallel lines. While it is true that 'politics is concentrated economics', the two elements may not be complementary to each other, but substitutes or alternatives for each other. Labour Party history has a rhythm in which workers move towards political interest and activity not because the industrial struggle has reached a high level and the movement must go beyond it, but as a substitute for industrial struggle when the workers feel they are defeated in that field. At such times the political struggle, spurred on by defeat, will be modest and lacking in militancy. At other times there is a high level of activity in both political and economic fields; at yet others despondency and passivity prevail in both.

A first step to understanding the Labour Party's laws of motion is to know what the different and opposing forces within it are. The next is to see how they change in quantity, discover the points at which they alter in quality, and examine their mutual influence.

As the Labour Party is enmeshed in the life of millions, its development reflects the economic, social, ideological and political forces propelling the whole of British society. To a large extent, what makes the Labour Party tick is what makes the British people tick. We shall, therefore, in this article, have to give a potted history of the British labour movement, and analyse its structure and working. In doing so a certain isolation of elements will be necessary, and then to put them in perspective will involve some unavoidable repetition. It is hoped the reader will bear with this.

A dismal record of right wing reformism

In February 1900 the forerunner of the Labour Party—the Labour Representation Committee—was formed as the result of the coming together of hitherto Liberal-supporting trade union leaders and the socialist Independent Labour Party led by Keir Hardie; 353,000 trade unionists, or a little less than a fifth of the total at the time, joined. For them the move from Liberalism to independent Labour representation in parliament was a great step forward, as in the main they were radical Liberals with very little sympathy for socialism. On joining the Labour Representation Committee they did not change their ideology greatly, but merely expressed the need, on the basis of their experience over the past decade, for parliamentary representation to defend the rights of trade unionists then threatened by the government and the law. The new body declared its purpose to be the representation of working class opinion 'by men sympathetic with the aims and demands of the labour movement'.

The conference at which the decision was made gave short shrift to the attempt of the Marxist Social Democratic Federation to turn the Labour Representation Committee into a socialist organisation. The SDF wanted the LRC to declare that 'the representatives of the working class movement in the House of Commons' would form there 'a distinct party based upon the recognition of the class war, and having for its ultimate object the socialisation of the means of production, distribution and exchange'. However, Keir Hardie and the ILP, the architects of the Labour Representation Committee, were consciously ready for compromise and retreat. With only some 20,000 members in their party, they knew that a mass movement with a socialist programme was not possible at the time. Keir Hardie's retreat was smoothed over by the fact that he and the party he led were not Marxists or revolutionaries, but militant reformers who believed that one of the main, if not the main, arenas for achieving reforms was parliament. In order to get into it the maximum number of votes had to be won. This, in Keir Hardie's eyes, justified a compromise. And the extent of the compromise was decided by the level of consciousness of LRC and later Labour Party supporters, for great numbers of whom independent representation in parliament was a big step forward.

This was the first of a long series of compromises of varying magnitude made by Labour Party leaders with bourgeois liberalism. Keir Hardie's compromise made possible a step forward for the real mass movement—others did not, but fettered and retarded it. Gaitskellite revisionism comes into its correct perspective when viewed against their background. The traditional picture of the Labour Party drawn by many on the left is that of a socialist party with a glorious socialist record, betrayed only now and again by a MacDonald or a Gaitskell—a couple of aberrations in an immaculate story. A few illustrations will help to destroy this illusion:

> In fact, the history of the LRC is largely the history of political manoeuvres to reach electoral accommodations with the Liberals. That this often involved the support of 'moderate' Labour candidates in preference to socialist ones was something which the strategists of the LRC found it relatively easy to accept. After protracted and secret negotiations, MacDonald and Keir Hardie reached an understanding in 1903 with Herbert Gladstone, the Liberal chief whip, under the terms of which the Liberal leaders agreed to use their influence to prevent local Liberal opposition to any LRC candidate who supported 'the general objects of the Liberal Party'. In return, the LRC was to 'demonstrate friendliness' to the Liberals in any constituency where it had influence. Save for Keir Hardie, MacDonald's colleagues on the LRC had known nothing of the negotiations, nor did the labour movement at large know anything about the agreement after it had begun to operate in the constituencies. Indeed, both Keir Hardie and MacDonald denied that there existed any compact with the Liberals at either national or local levels.[1]

> Again the Parliamentary Labour Party did in fact act after 1906 as a more or less radical appendage of the Liberal Party in parliament.[2]

What contemporary militants thought of the Parliamentary Labour Party is clear from the words of Ben Tillett, of 1889 dock strike fame, when in 1908 he published a pamphlet with the suggestive title *Is the Parliamentary Party a Failure?* in which he denounced the parliamentary leaders as 'sheer hypocrites' who 'for ten and five guineas a time will lie with the best' and who repaid 'with gross betrayal the class that willingly supports them'.[3]

When the First World War broke out, Keir Hardie, who still has the reputation for pure, consistent socialism, wrote:

A nation at war must be united, especially when its existence is at stake. In such filibustering expeditions as our own Boer War or the Italian war over Tripoli, where no national danger of any kind was involved, there were many occasions for diversity of opinion, and this was given voice to by the Socialist Party of Italy and the Stop the War Party in this country. Now the situation is different. With the boom of the enemy's guns within earshot, the lads who have gone forth to fight their country's battles must not be disheartened by any discordant notes at home.[4]

The parliamentary atmosphere undoubtedly had a strong corroding effect on the socialist morale of Labour MPs.

David Kirkwood, one of the 'wild men', wrote later that, before he entered the House of Commons in 1922, he knew little of 'the Great Ones, the Powerful Ones, the Lordly Ones' but felt that 'they and the world they represented were crushing my fellows down into poverty, misery, despair and death'. When he entered the House, however, he found that 'it was full of wonder. I had to shake myself occasionally as I found myself moving about and talking with men whose names were household words. More strange it was to find them all so simple and unaffected and friendly.' Violently attacked over unemployment, Bonar Law 'showed no resentment', and expressed pleasure at hearing Kirkwood's Glasgow accent; denounced as a 'Uriah Heep', Stanley Baldwin, the Chancellor of the Exchequer, was gently reproachful and thus 'pierced a link in my armour that had never been pierced before'; and a Conservative member, having heard Kirkwood make a 'flaming speech' about the poverty of crofters in the Hebrides, told him, so the latter records in wonder, 'I could not vote for you, but I should like to help those men if I may,' and gave him a £5 note.[5]

Similarly, the former militant miners' leader, Robert Smillie, subsequently an MP, could write in 1924, 'In my young and callous days I was probably a little prejudiced in favour of my own class, and hot with resentment against those whom I regarded as their oppressors. But experience teaches, and I now know that a gentlemen is a gentlemen, whatever his rank in life may be, and may always be trusted to act as such'.[6]

The greatest depth of submission to their 'betters' was shown by the ministers of the first Labour government (1923-24). Thus, for instance, the minister of war, Stephen Walsh, was supposed to have told the generals, 'I know my place. You have commanded armies in the field when I was nothing but a private in the ranks'.[7] Another account has it that he opened the first meeting of the Army Council with the words, 'Gentlemen, always remember that we must all be loyal to the king'.[8]

J H Thomas, the new colonial secretary, was said to have introduced himself to the heads of departments at the Colonial Office with the statement, 'I am here to see that there is no such mucking about with the British Empire'.[9] Beatrice Webb describes a luncheon party at which 'we were all laughing over Wheatley—the revolutionary—going down on both knees and actually kissing the King's hand.' She also noted that ' Uncle Arthur [Henderson] was bursting with childish joy over his Home Office seals in the red leather box which he handed round the company'.[10]

A further chapter in the betrayal of the working class by the leadership of the Labour Party was recorded during the General Strike:

> When the railway workers struck in 1919 an elaborate emergency supply and transport system was worked out under the control of Sir Eric Geddes, at that time minister of transport. This system was not fully tested at the time, and in the following years it lapsed almost completely. In 1923 the task of reviving it was put into the hands of J C C Davidson, Chancellor of the Duchy of Lancaster. A groundwork had been laid, no more, when the first Labour government came to power, and Davidson, handing over to Josiah Wedgwood, asked him not to destroy what had been done... When the Labour government went out of office and Wedgwood handed over again to Davidson, he said, 'I haven't destroyed any of your plans. In fact I haven't done a bloody thing about them.' The plan remained a skeleton until Red Friday taught the government a lesson.[11]

These emergency supply and transport schemes were used a couple of years later to defeat the general strike.

On the eve of the government's preparation for a showdown with the workers, 'The leaders of the Labour Party seem to have been unaware of the preparations being made—or perhaps, of course, they silently approved of them'.[12] 'All of these leaders—MacDonald, Snowden, Thomas, Clynes, Henderson—were unequivocally opposed to the idea of a general strike... If they feared that defeat of the strikers would be a blow for Labour, they perhaps feared even more that a victorious strike would be a harder blow for the Labour leadership'.[13] On 29 April 1926, at a conference of trade union executives, Ernest Bevin, who was certainly no revolutionary, made 'a savage attack on the Parliamentary Labour Party for its cowardice in failing to make a statement in the House of Commons about miners' wages'.[14] A few days earlier the Labour Party leader, Clynes, declared that the strike would be 'a national disaster'.[15] So much for solidarity with the meagrely paid miners! 'MacDonald emphasised his respect for the constitution and his desire to see fair play and justice, loftily adding that "with the discussion of general strikes and Bolshevism and all that kind of thing, I have nothing to do at all".'[16]

One of the worst indictments of the Labour Party leadership is its behaviour towards the unemployed during the second Labour government (1929-31):

> In their evidence before the Blanesburgh committee on unemployment insurance in 1926, the TUC and the Labour Party had jointly proposed an increased scale of unemployment benefits of 20 shillings a week, with ten shillings for a dependent wife and five shillings for each child, and 'to that scale it adheres', *Labour and the Nation* had said. That these pledges would be fulfilled must have been the expectation of many who had voted for the return of a Labour government in 1929.
>
> However, when the government introduced its Unemployment Insurance Bill in November 1929, the bill was found to leave the unemployment benefit for

men at 17 shillings a week, and the allowance for each child at two shillings. Only the allowance of the wife was raised from seven shillings to nine shillings, and the benefits for unemployed juvenile workers were also slightly increased.[17]

Of the Parliamentary Labour Party of 288 members, only 32 voted against the bill. And the policy of the government towards the unemployed was confirmed at the Labour Party conference in October 1930 under pressure of the block vote (by 1,803,000 votes to 334,000). The number of insured workers unemployed, which was 1,164,000 at the time Labour took power, rose in July 1931 to 2,800,000! The Labour government even went so far, on the eve of its collapse, as to agree to lower benefits and increased contributions. The bill to this effect was passed through parliament with the support of Liberals and Tories, against the vote of left Labour MPs.

A first characteristic of any revolutionary is to wish to free himself from the prevailing bourgeois ideology. Neither the present leaders of the Labour Party nor their predecessors showed any inclination this way. The ideological sources of inspiration of the Labour Party leaders in the 'heroic' past were not Marxist, but bourgeois-liberal. The following is quite instructive:

> After the general election of 1906, W T Stead, the editor of the *Review of Reviews*, sent a questionnaire to the 51 Labour and 'Lib-Lab' members of parliament, asking them to set out what books they had found most useful in their early days. Of the 51, 45 replied. The most interesting feature of the answers, in the present context, is the paucity of books mentioned which are concerned with socialist theory. The answers of only two members, J O'Grady and particularly Will Thorne, both of the SDF, suggest any grounding in it. For the rest, their main intellectual influences appear to have been the Bible, and writers ranging from Shakespeare and Milton to Carlyle, Ruskin, J S Mill and Dickens.[18]

With such teachers, what wonder that Keir Hardie, in 1909, could describe MacDonald as 'the biggest intellectual asset which the socialist movement has in this country today'.[19] A review of the Labour Party leaders' record inspires amazement at the tenacity with which millions of workers continued to vote Labour, and the fact that no socialist party competing with the Labour Party managed to get the allegiance of the working class to any significant extent. On the contrary, after betrayal by the leadership, the Labour vote often increased. Thus after Black Friday (1921), when the miners were let down by the leadership and left prostrate before the mine owners, the Labour vote in 1922 was 2 million larger than in the general election of 1918. Again, after the demise of the first Labour government which had had such a pitiful record, the Labour vote in 1924 rose by well over a million above the previous election. The betrayal of the miners in 1926 did not prevent the Labour vote from rising in 1929 by nearly 3 million above the former maximum. After the bankruptcy of the second Labour government, with the main leaders of the party—MacDonald, Thomas and Snowden—joining the Tories in a National Government, the Labour vote declined radically by 1.7 million, but returned to the 1929 level in 1935.

While the leadership betrayed, the working people remained absolutely loyal.

This loyalty was rooted deep in the feeling that the Labour Party alone was the political organisation of the class. Without avowedly recognising the class struggle, the Labour and Conservative parties have become more and more congruent with the division of British society between Labour and capital.

The loyalty of the workers is of course affected by the policies of the leadership, and it could be broken if the betrayals went beyond a certain point. Their effect depends on a number of factors: first, the extent of the workers' feeling of being a class, if not with positive socialist aims at least with negative anti-boss attributes; secondly, the extent to which the workers' aspirations are limited to reforms in the framework of capitalism, and the extent to which these are realisable in the framework of the system, so that tinkering with capitalism by the Labour Party leaders does not come into headlong collision with their aspirations; thirdly, the extent to which the workers' desire for reforms flows into channels of parliamentary politics so that parliamentary reformism is relevant to it. By and large the leaders, while far from fully expressing the wishes of the rank and file, have not gone beyond what they would take.

Rhythms—economics and politics

Although no Chinese Wall separates the economic or trade union struggle from the political, one can find, over the 60 years of Labour Party history, recurring waves of change in emphasis between the two. To a considerable extent it was the failure of the trade union arm of the labour movement to deliver the goods single-handed that led millions to look for a political solution (1880-1900). And again, the disappointment with the latter led to a swing of the pendulum to the other side—emphasis on industrial activity with widespread political apathy (1906-21). The process was reversed again, this time with a declining curve of self-confidence and activity in both arenas, a process that went from 1922, with ups and downs, until the outbreak of the Second World War. After that the relation between the two arms underwent a variation. But that is to anticipate.

Until the late 1880s only a small minority of skilled workers were organised in trade unions. In 1888, however, the Miners' Federation (now the NUM) was established. Then in 1889 the Dock, Wharf, Riverside and General Workers' Union (now the TGWU) and the Gasworkers' Union (now the NUGMW) were founded, ushering in the New Unions which made the organisation of the unskilled and semi-skilled a permanent feature of British trade unionism. In the 1890s, however, the New Unions were struggling in rough seas for their very existence.

So long as only skilled workers were organised, the need for political action did not arise. The trade unions could rely on the skill of their members as a strong bargaining weapon. The New Unions were in a very different position. They were always, even in times of fair trade, subject to the pressure of the mass of unemployed. While scab labour was not a problem for the skilled workers, it was very much so for the newly organised unskilled. In the 1890s a strong offensive was launched by the employers against the dockers, seafarers and other sections, and all the New Unions lost heavily in membership by the middle of the decade: 'An important contributory factor to their decline was the worsening economic situation, and the growth of unemployment, after 1890'.[20] Strikes were broken by organisations of scabs, helped widely by the police and military:

> When, as from the middle years of the decade, the decisions of the courts began to echo the hostility of the employers and the prejudice of the politicians towards trade unionism, the working men found themselves in a world in which their accepted position was being rapidly undermined. Their last refuge was the law as enacted by parliament, and this, by judge-made decisions, was now being turned against them.[21]

The culmination of the attack was the Taff Vale decision of 1901, which made trade unions liable to heavy charges for any actions arising out of their activities:

> Inevitably the leadership of the trade union movement, however slowly their rank and file appreciated the position, were pushed into political action to remedy the situation by legislation. The strengthening of the Labour Representation Committee, the greatly increased independent labour representation at the general election of 1906 and the Trades Disputes Act of 1906 were the short term results.[22]

Thus from the practically pure trade unionism of the late 1880s and 1890s, the pendulum swung over to political action. But it did not stay long in this position.

Two decades of great effort on the part of the active members of the labour movement to establish an independent Labour Party produced disappointing results. The hope that the Parliamentary Labour Party would bring legislation shortening working hours and the establishment of a national minimum working wage for various industries was unfulfilled, while at the same time the urge for parliamentary activity became blunted as a result of the more favourable Liberal trade union legislation of the time. The Labour Party in parliament acted as the tail of the Liberal Party. Meanwhile the conditions of working people were deteriorating. 'The official figures show that whereas retail prices had risen by 16.5 percent from 1900 to 1913, wage rates had increased only 6.5 percent'.[23] This, accompanied by increased employment, encouraged a swift increase in trade union membership (from 1,972,000 in 1900 to 4,145,000 in 1914 and 8,334,000 in 1920). The success of the dockers', seafarers' and sweated trades strikes in London in 1911, as well as the relative success of the miners in 1912, also encouraged workers to look to industrial action. And the years 1910-22 saw widespread industrial unrest, almost every industry being affected. Strikes were fought with greater bitterness than ever before, and some of them threatened to paralyse the national economy. The war stopped the rising industrial wave for only a short time. Immediately the war was over large numbers of mass strikes occurred, and the four post-war years were (except for 1926) years of the most widespread industrial action. (The annual average of working days lost in industrial conflicts in the decade 1898-1907 was about 3 million, and in the years 1910-13 over 18 million. In the years 1919, 1920, 1921 and 1922, there were 36, 28, 82 and 19 million working days lost in industrial conflicts.)

But again this wave of industrial action broke on the rocks of capitalist resistance. The end of 1920 witnessed the beginning of a deep slump. In 1921 and 1922 the miners, the engineers and some other sections of the working class were routed in great industrial battles. (Engineers' wages were cut by as much as 16s a week in 1921, and then further after the lockout in 1922.) The employers' offensive against workers' standards continued during the long, widespread unemployment of the 1920s and 1930s. Trade union membership fell considerably (from 8,334,000 in 1920 to 5,522,000 in 1925, 4,804,000 in 1928, and 4,392,000 in 1933). The unions had to concentrate on the defence of wages, hours and working conditions. The unemployed could not look to industrial action to mitigate their hardships, and workers were very wary of taking industrial action under the prevailing conditions. Hemmed in as a class, the workers turned, with however dimmed hope, to the political wing of the movement.

A new swing of the pendulum occurred with the full employment brought about in the wake of World War Two and the radical mood of its aftermath.

Thus we see that radical changes in the economic and social routine, whether because of depression, rising prices or war, led to mass upsurges. There is no formula to explain why sometimes these led to purely industrial action while at other times they led to political action after labour was thwarted on the industrial field, while at others to both courses of action, and at yet others to apathy and passivity.

The stability and persistence of reformism

In spite of the Labour Party leadership's long record of opportunism, the influence of revolutionary socialist ideas in the working class is still quite small. We live in a critical period for civilisation. During the last half century humanity has suffered two terrible wars and is now living in the shadow of total annihilation. The present generation has witnessed mass unemployment and hunger, fascism and the barbarous murder of colonial peoples in Kenya, Malaya, Algeria and Korea. However, in the midst of these terrible convulsions, the working class of Britain, as well as of other countries of the West—the United States, Canada, Norway, Sweden, Holland, Denmark, Germany and others—shows a stubborn adherence to reformism, a belief in the possibility of major improvement in conditions under capitalism, and a rejection of the revolutionary overthrow of capitalism. Why is this so?

As long as some 50 years ago Lenin believed that British reformism had weak foundations. Lenin was without doubt the most important Marxist to define the roots of reformism. In 1915, in an article entitled 'The Collapse of the International', he explained opportunism, as he called it, thus:

> The period of imperialism is the period in which the distribution of the world amongst the 'great' and privileged nations, by whom all other nations are oppressed,

is completed. Scraps of the booty enjoyed by the privileged as a result of this oppression undoubtedly fall to the lot of certain sections of the petty bourgeoisie and
the aristocracy and bureaucracy of the working class.

How big was the section of the working class which received these 'scraps of
booty'? The answer: 'These sections…represent an infinitesimal minority of the
proletariat and the working masses.' And in line with this analysis he defines reformism as 'the adherence of a section of the working class with the bourgeoisie
against the mass of the proletariat'. The economic foundation of the small 'aristocracy of labour' is to be found, according to him, in imperialism and its super-
profits. An inevitable conclusion to his analysis of reformism was that a small, thin
crust of conservatism hides the revolutionary urges of the mass of the workers. Any
break through this crust would reveal surging revolutionary lava. The role of the
revolutionary party is simply to show the mass of the workers that their interests
are betrayed by the 'infinitesimal minority' of the 'aristocracy of labour'.

From this evaluation Lenin came to the following conclusion regarding tactics of communists in the British labour movement: 'I am personally in favour
of adhesion to the Labour Party on condition of free and independent communist
activity.'

These tactics could only be realised if the grip of reformism on the Labour
Party was so very weak that the communists could get in as an organised body,
and could easily expose the Labour Party leadership to the fighting masses who
really desired a revolutionary change.

The entire history of the Labour Party since that time shows the two assumptions to be totally unfounded.[24] The history of reformism in Britain, the
United States and elsewhere over the past half century—its solidity, its spread
throughout the working class, frustrating and largely isolating all revolutionary
minorities—makes it abundantly clear that the economic and social roots of reformism are not in 'an infinitesimal minority of the proletariat and the working masses', as Lenin argued.

During the 1930s, in the face of the deep world slump, unemployment and
fascism, it looked as if the foundations of reformism were undermined for good.
In that period and making a prognosis for the future, Trotsky wrote, 'In [the]
epoch of decaying capitalism, in general, there can be no discussion of systematic social reforms and the raising of the masses' living standards, when every
serious demand of the proletariat and even every serious demand of the petty
bourgeoisie inevitably reaches beyond the limits of capitalist property relations
and of the bourgeois state'.[25] If serious reforms are no longer possible under capitalism, then the knell of bourgeois parliamentary democracy is sounded and the
end of reformism is at hand. The war, as a sharpener of contradictions in capitalism, would, according to Trotsky, lead to the acceleration of these processes.

But the obituary was written too soon. War and the permanent war economy
gave a new lease of life to capitalism and hence to reformism in many of the
Western capitalist countries.

That its increasing dependence on the permanent war economy shows reformism's bankruptcy and the need for a revolutionary overthrow of capitalism

is true. Equally true, however, is the fact that this bankruptcy is not yet apparent to the mass of the workers through their daily experience.[26] So long as capitalism is expanding and the conditions of the workers are improving, and are seen to be able to be ameliorated within the framework of the present social system, reformism has stronger roots than revolutionary socialism. It was on this rock that the waves of political militancy beat time and again, whether within the Labour Party or without. A glance at the record will show that socialist parties outside the Labour Party made very few inroads into the labour movement. Thus, for instance, if parliamentary elections are used as a record of political influence: in 1922 the Communist Party put up seven candidates of which two were elected (one standing as an official Labour candidate); in 1923 they lost their two seats; in 1924 one member was returned; in 1929 none; 1931 none; 1935 one; 1945 two; 1950 none (with 97 out of 100 candidates losing their deposits); 1951 none; 1955 none; 1959 none. Undoubtedly members of the Communist Party have had quite a large influence on different sections of the labour movement at different times on the industrial front. They controlled, for instance, the National Unemployed Workers' Movement, had important positions in the AEU, NUM, ETU, etc, etc. But the political influence of the party as such was very small, as the election figures testify. Some 31 years after it was made, the prophecy of R Palme Dutt is not yet realised: 'The workers have lost confidence in the Labour Party, and seek elsewhere… The labour movement, the old labour movement, is dying. The workers' movement, the independent workers' movement, is rising'.[27]

The fate of the Independent Labour Party was sadder still. Its membership, which in 1932 after splitting from the Labour Party was 16,773, dropped to 11,092 in 1933, 7,166 in 1934 and 4,392 in 1935,[28] and today can be counted in hundreds (or tens)—it is quite inactive. To use parliamentary representation once again as a measuring rod of its influence, it held six seats in 1931, four in 1935, four in 1945, and none since.

Other socialist parties show a similar record. The Commonwealth Party established in 1942 managed to gain a fair amount of support in by-elections— winning two seats during the war in opposition to the 'electoral truce' of Labour with the Tories. It managed to get one seat in the 1945 elections, but shortly afterwards its leader, Acland, and other leading supporters joined the Labour Party. The Trotskyist Revolutionary Communist Party, which played quite an active role in a number of industrial struggles during the war, fared no better. The Communist Party managed to survive, despite the indifference of the mass of the workers in this country to it, largely thanks to its international connections which boosted members' morale. Between reformism and Stalinism, independent socialist parties have had very little chance of survival.

The rock of reformism proved impregnable to a number of internal oppositions, from the ILP which left the party in despair, to Cripps's Socialist League. In addition, a number of Labour youth organisations were suppressed or dissolved (1927, 1929, 1955).

The working class and politics

British social democracy is unique in that the trade unions are part and parcel of the political organisation.

The anaemia, apathy and bureaucracy prevalent in the Labour Party are an indirect derivation of the same diseases affecting the trade union movements. The Constituency Labour Party (CLP) is much less homogeneous than the trade union branch in social composition, which weakens class consciousness, even if the contours of the class and the party are generally congruent. 'Trade unionist consciousness', to use Lenin's term, grows spontaneously out of the soil of the industrial struggle and is much stronger among the activists in the branch and on the factory floor than among Labour Party activists. *Socialist* consciousness, on the other hand, can grow only through a grasp of the problems of society at large from the standpoint of the historical interests of the working class. And here the discussion in CLPs and trade union branches, finding their political focus in the Labour Party, is of central importance. The trade unions are, and are not, the Labour Party. The consciousness forged on the one anvil is in a way more advanced yet at the same time lower than the consciousness forged on the other. While militants in the unions attack political reformism from the left, there are other forces threatening it from the right— from the direction of non-political or business unionism. And the balance between the two results in nothing more definite than a directionless drift.

The first and most general factor causing apolitisation of the working class is the expansion of capitalism that has taken place over the last two decades. In a chaotic boom where different groups of workers in different industries and localities manage to squeeze out concessions for themselves, there is a strong trend towards fragmentation—ie away from class action.

Another factor is the rise of the white collar workers. Britain, like the other advanced countries, is witnessing a decline in the number of workers in basic industries, which are traditionally strongly unionised—notably coal mining and the railways—and a general decline throughout the whole economy in the importance of manual workers, while employment in service industries and in white collar jobs is increasing. In the US only 25 percent of the workers are now employed in manufacturing. In Britain and Sweden the ratio is about 40 percent.[29] In industry itself the proportion of staff is rising quickly. Thus, for instance, 'In ICI, to take just one example, the number of staff workers has risen by 45 percent in the last ten years and the number of manual workers by 2 percent'.[30] The immediate reaction of professional and white collar workers to trade unionism and especially to politically affiliated trade unions is, to say the least, cool. They think of themselves as belonging to the middle class, and have middle class aspirations. Thus the rise of the professions and their unionisation must have a blunting effect on the politics of the unions.

Another factor affecting the interest of trade unions in politics is the attitude of the government of the day. Many trade unions look to the connection with the Labour Party as an insurance against repressive legislation or government interference in their affairs. Hence the softer the Tory government in dealing with the unions, and the more access the latter have to the former, the less keen are they on their political association with the Labour Party.

As regards access of the trade unions to the government, 'No established right of access to the government was conceded to unions…until the Second World War… The long duration of the war and the much longer duration of economic problems encouraged its establishment'.[31] After the coming to power of the Tories in 1951 the trade union leaders showed no diminution of desire for access to the government and collaboration with it. Thus the general council stated, 'It is our longstanding practice to seek to work amicably with whatever government is in power and through consultation jointly with ministers and with the other side of industry to find practical solutions to the social and economic problems facing this country. There need be no doubt, therefore, of the attitude of the TUC towards the new government'.[32] 'Trade union leaders sat on 81 government committees in the year 1953-54, covering a wide range of subjects'.[33] The most prominent of these committees have been the two general advisory committees, the National Joint Advisory Council to the Minister of Labour and the National Production Advisory Council on Industry.[34] 'The Conservative government until 1955 appointed trade unionists to its consultative committees more than even the Labour government and a fair measure of informal consultation took place, too'.[35]

The trade unions have direct access to government departments, whatever the colour of the government. In 1946 Arthur Deakin could say, 'We have an open door in relation to all state departments, and are thus able to get our difficulties examined in such a way as would not have been possible with any other party in government'.[36] However, the situation has not changed since:

> The Conservatives preserved the system almost intact after 1951, although there is not the same familiarity of contacts with Conservative ministers as under the Labour government. While the TUC might not convince the Conservatives on many major economic issues, there was less difference on the everyday technical level. But the unions' views were heard. 'If I want to talk to the minister,' said a leading trade unionist in 1957, 'I just pick up that telephone'.[37]

In the past the trade unions often looked to parliament to protect them. Now, with their industrial strength much greater, they become more and more reserved about parliamentary intervention in certain fields, and above all in the field of wage negotiations:

> Arthur Deakin openly expressed this mood in 1953: 'Never be led into the mistake of supposing you are going to get an advantage by people asking questions in parliament affecting your collective agreements, conditions of employment and those things which are more properly dealt with by the union on the industrial level'.[38]

This is the reason why, 'once the spearhead of his union's industrial-political activity, the trade union MP now stands on the sidelines'.[39] This is also the reason why the unions send into the House of Commons only their Second Eleven.

A very important factor influencing the trade unions towards an apolitical stance is the decline in the importance of industrial legislation and statutory obligations on employers. Much of the early legislation occurred in the absence of unions or covered matters which unions were unable to tackle, such as workmen's compensation. Especially with the rise of fringe benefits in individual firms, the role of statutory obligations declined (although it is almost unnecessary to remark that Britain still shows little progress as regards fringe benefits compared with other countries, not only the United States, but even those in Western Europe).[40]

To add to the unions' disinterest in the political colour of the government is the fact that the Tory government is not more ready to use emergency powers and troops to break strikes than Labour in the past. As one student put it:

> The Labour government of 1945-51 always treated strikes seriously and anxiously, and intervened promptly, equipped with emergency measures. The Conservative governments since 1951, on the other hand, have been almost nonchalant in their treatment of strikes, despite some belligerent talk between them and union leaders. They have been less disposed to use emergency powers or troops.[41]

A whole number of other factors kept, and will continue to keep, alive the interest of the trade unions in politics. First of all, there is the increasing role of the government as employer The size of the civil service has increased. In 1914 there were 282,402 non-industrial civil servants. The number rose to 387,400 in 1939 and 635,700 in 1957.[42]

The government has become, through nationalisation, the largest industrial employer, employing more than $2^1/_2$ million people. Particularly since 1957 it has been using the boards of the nationalised industries to regulate wage standards in the economy as a whole. Under these conditions, the complete separation of economics and politics is clearly out of the question. As Cousins put it on the day the London bus workers started their strike, 'We are…not prepared to go backwards at the behest or instruction of a government not of our political feeling'.[43] He added that the London busmen were fighting the fight for all trade unionists. A few months later Ted Hill, general secretary of the United Society of Boilermakers, wrote:

> The Tory government has decided to declare war on the trade unions of this country in a more vicious way that any former government. It has decided to use its political power in purely industrial issues, and therefore the trade unions are free to use their industrial power in political issues.[44]

Secondly, the interest of the unions in politics cannot disappear altogether so long as the government continues in the role of regulator—now using the brake, now the accelerator—of economic activity. In case of a real slump it scarcely need be remarked that the politisation of the trade unions will be quick and far-reaching, especially as the years of full employment after the long and terrible mass unemployment of the 1920s and 1930s must have convinced millions that a slump is not an act of god, and that it can be cured.

Again a number of factors will make the workers unable to defend themselves with industrial means alone, and thus drive them to look for a political solution. First, there is creeping unemployment. Secondly, there are sectors of overcapacity of the productive machine.

Thus it is reported from the United States:

> In the year prior to negotiations with the steel union the corporations can—and do—load the warehouses. The union has to strike for six to ten months before management even *begins* to lose money. And what is true in steel is equally true in rubber, oil, auto, and all other mass production unions. The strike weapon, by itself, is no longer as paralysing as it was 12 or 15 years ago.[45]

As regards Britain, this is of course largely a song of the future (although the strike in BLSP fitted the model). But it is clear that labour's striking power under these conditions must be threatened.

It has been pointed out that the immediate effect of the rise of the white collar and professional workers and their unionisation was to dampen trade union interest in politics. But in the long run, the effect may well be exactly the opposite. With increasing automation, accompanied by an increase in the number of technicians and supervisors, the possibility of these people keeping the factory running during a strike will increase, a development that will paralyse the tendency of manual workers to rely on the industrial arm alone to improve their conditions:

> Frederick Pollack, a leading German authority on automation, even goes so far as to prophesy in his book *Automation* (New York, 1957) that in the new era the strike weapon will lose much of its effectiveness. And he gives as an example a 1945 strike of operating and maintenance workers at the atomic energy plants at Peducah and Oak Ridge. A handful of supervisory employees were able to keep up full-scale production during the three-day walkout because the plants are so highly automated.[46]

Of course, this again is mainly a song of the future in this country.

To the extent that trade union officials feel that the main battles have been won, and consider themselves part of the status quo, their interest in politics must be lukewarm, but there are counteracting forces. In summing up we can say that the relations of the trade unions to politics are much less clear than a generation ago. The picture can no longer be drawn with quick brush strokes. Now more meticulous details and careful shading and nuances make it up. Different and contradictory trends criss-cross one another.

Will the trade unions and the Labour Party separate? This question has been raised from time to time since the 1959 election defeat. The reasons are obvious. With Gaitskell appealing to the middle class floating voter, it is clear that the 'image' of the trade unions—alleged to be responsible for strikes, inflation, etc—is an embarrassment. The workers are presumed by the middle classes to take too large a share of the national cake. The party looks like an oligarchic organisation made up of both an irresponsible 'fanatic' left and tyrannical union bosses. All this damages the electorally valuable 'liberal' image. The trade unions are not even able to guarantee to deliver the votes of their members. So to many a party leader on the revisionist right the trade union connection is a wasting asset.

On the other hand, to many trade union bosses the political connection also does not look very advantageous, first because of above mentioned factors that reduce trade unionists' interest in politics, and above all because this connection seems to impede the attraction of white collar workers to the trade unions and especially the TUC. The election of a Labour government no longer seems to be the best, or a very important, way to serve the bread and butter interests of the union members. Some such thoughts seem to lie behind several pronouncements of George Woodcock, the secretary of the TUC. In April 1961 he wrote in *Red Tape*, the journal of the Civil Service Clerical Association, that the members of the TUC 'have been driven by circumstances to associate more with one party than the other two, but we are still an independent industrial organisation'. On 30 May 1961, speaking to the association's conference, he returned to this theme. 'We start', he said, 'as trade unionists, and we end as trade unionists. It would be wrong if we started on the assumption that it is the TUC's function to support one political party. In the trade union movement there are people of all parties, and people of no party'.[47] A few months later, appearing on television, he said, 'Trade unions are concerned with bread and butter issues', it was a mistake to introduce 'issues which divide us', and as for politics, they were relevant only if they 'spring out of your industrial experience'.[48] In other words, the trade unions should be political, but only in the sense that American trade unions are political—that is, they should help those who help them, but on such things as defence they should take no position.

The deeper the split in the Labour Party on broad political issues, the less do those who are set upon business unionism see any advantage in affiliation to it.

But anyone who visualises a complete break between the trade unions and the Labour Party, at least over the coming few years, will probably prove to be mistaken. As we have seen, although there are forces drawing the trade unions away from politics, there are others pushing in an opposite direction. Above all, so long as the old working class community, which can be seen in the mining village or dockers' areas, with their deep class loyalties, exist side by side with the more 'Americanised' modern working class, the process of separation of the trade unions from the Labour Party cannot be completed. However, the process of trade union withdrawal from politics will probably continue in the foreseeable future, notwithstanding the countervailing forces, and this will have a dampening influence on the party. The drift will continue. Of course this will change radically when capitalism is shaken by economic or social crisis.[49]

Challenge to reformism from the left

While reformism is being undermined from the right—from bourgeois influence which tends to dissolve the class content of the movement—other forces, connected with them, challenge it from the left. These are also rooted in the economic boom of the last two decades.

The vulgar 'Marxist' view sees in poverty only a cause for rebellion, and in reforms only a numbing of fighting ardour. Actually empty stomachs may lead not to rebellion but, especially if it is the stomachs of workers' wives and children, to submission. On the other hand, a full stomach may lead not to contentment, but to self-confidence and assertiveness. The British workers of the 1920s and 1930s had a much clearer feeling of belonging to the working class than at present, but this did not prevent them, misguided by the leaders of the TUC and Labour Party, from standing aside while more than a million miners and their families were starved into submission during the 1926 strike. Nor did hunger lead them to industrial action in support of the millions of unemployed. Threatened by unemployment themselves, they were docile and disinclined to act in solidarity with other members of their class.

Workers today are far more self-confident. They will not allow themselves to be pushed around. They go so far to resist the sacking of their mates, invading the prerogative of management regarding hiring and firing, fighting for an element of workers' control in the midst of capitalism. (How different to 1922, when the engineering employers fought the workers on the question of management prerogatives, and sacked thousands of shop stewards!)

Even the assertion of many workers that they are no different from the middle class is not only a negative, damaging element from the standpoint of socialism. No, workers declare thereby that they are not inferior to other people. The idea of 'the deserving poor' is gone—no more 'the rich man in his castle and the poor man at his gate', the idea that our ' betters' are born to rule.

With self-reliance comes also a much greater generosity of spirit, so clearly shown in the sympathy strikes of thousands of lorry drivers, dockers and engineers in support of the nurses' pay claim this May.

When it comes to wider social questions, again the workers show much more daring in facing up to issues than in the past. Hardly a worker thought that it was up to him even to take a position on the Boer War 60 years ago. Today a Gallup poll shows that 24 percent of Labour voters are for unilateral disarmament.[50]

But this great move forward is against a background of the general reformist ideology. Reformism is both in conflict with capitalism and accommodating to it. Its dual nature is a replica of the dual impact of expanding capitalism on the working class. Capitalism and modern industry, as Marx showed, unites the workers into disciplined armies. However, it also disciplines them to authority from above, whether from the employer or the Labour bureaucrat. The very strength of the labour movement that wrests reforms from the bosses, from capitalism, also makes it very conservative and resistant to the rank and file.

The different militant sections, whether workers on strike or Aldermaston marchers, etc are part of a large army struggling against the establishment and fighting capitalism. The fight against sacking is an element in the struggle for collective workers' control over production—CND is a movement for collective control over our lives. The partial struggle is part of the whole—that is, the struggle against the bomb is a struggle against the boss and vice-versa. But so long as capitalism is expanding, and reformism is the prevalent ideology in the working class, the partial struggles cannot be completely fused. If millions of workers are not ready for industrial action for political ends, the *actual* fusion of the fight against the boss and the bomb cannot take place. Without a working class unified in a revolutionary struggle, the tie-in between different sections of militants must remain weak.

The partial struggles also lack a unifying *political focus*. The militant industrial workers may rely on their own organisation on the factory floor to improve their conditions, while their involvement in trade union branch activity, trades councils and Constituency Labour Parties is very small indeed. Party activists are more involved in anti-Tory electoral activities than in anti-boss industrial struggles. Many of the Aldermaston marchers are neither in industry nor in the Labour Party. Above all, while the Labour Party and the trade unions remain deeply reformist, they cannot unite and channel revolutionary struggles directed against the capitalist order. One could describe the relation between the different militants in struggle as a number of interlinking circles with a very small overlap. Millions vote Labour, but only a minority are active politically. Millions are in the trade unions, but only a minority are militant. CND embraces only a tiny minority of trade union members and Labour supporters. So long as reformism keeps its strong hold on the labour movement, the fragmentation and lack of coordination between different sectors of the struggle against the establishment will continue. To the extent that there is, and can be, a political focus for all these segments, it is only in the left of the Labour Party.

One question raised again and again on the left over decades is the possibility of a split of the party into two separate organisations, the left moving out.

This is not on the cards. It is true probably nothing would make Gaitskell happier than that the left should leave. But the structure of the party, based as it is on the trade unions, is such that without the unions splitting the left would be out on a limb. The trade unions themselves are too strong, and have too much in common on bread and butter issues, to split for any issues of ideology (as the much weaker trade unions have done in a number of continental countries). Again, the British parliamentary electoral system must deter the left from splitting (and as yet politics is in the main on a parliamentary level). The sterility of the CP, ILP, etc must also serve as a warning.

If the left cannot, and should not, split from the Labour Party, is there any possibility of its taking over and transforming the party from a reformist to a revolutionary organisation?

The answer must be negative. The prevalence of reformist ideology in the mass base of the party makes its transformation into a revolutionary party inconceivable. Even if a conference passes good left wing resolutions, like Scarborough's unilateralist vote, the right wing is always able to mobilise to its support the mass of inactive, backward supporters. The reserves of the right are at present incomparably larger than those of the left. (Hence any election in the trade unions with a high poll ensures a right wing victory. Likewise ballots usually give a much worse right wing result than trade union conference decisions.)

The Marxists in the party would like to (a) make the right split from the party, or (b) compel it to submit to the democratic decisions of conference, and stop toying with Lib-Labism. Neither can be achieved in present conditions. The right, at the same time, would like (a) to make the left split from the party, or (b) to compel it to cut its connections with the rebel 'do it yourself' movements like CND which are independent of the bureaucratic machine. This, again, the right will not be able to accomplish. The left well knows that to split from the party is to commit suicide. It knows too that everything alive and pulsing in the movement is generated from those sections of it that are independent of the bureaucratic machine. The 'cancer' of unilateralism is too widespread in the labour movement generally, including a number of top officials in the trade unions, for surgery by Transport House to be successful. This does not mean that Gaitskell is not tempted to carry out such amputation, nor that the left should be careful not to play into his hands. The temptation for Gaitskell and Brown is particularly great, if they cannot cut off the big limbs—the Cousins, Horners, Russells—to compensate themselves with the small, like *Keep Left*.

The crisis in the Labour Party will go on. On the one hand, the pressure towards Americanisation of the labour movement, away from traditional reformism to Lib-Labism, and on the other the pressure towards unorthodoxy, militant, revolutionary activities will go on for years to come. There is a double crisis for traditional reformism, something that distinguishes the party at present from the past. And so long as there is no radical change in the objective conditions, ie in the economic, social and political environment in which the working class finds itself—as well as in the mass consciousness existing and inherited from the past—the crisis will go on, and the drift continue.

Given no major changes in the movement generally, what are the methods of work open to Marxists in the Labour Party?

They should keep the bridge open between the left inside the party, and the militants who cannot be assimilated and controlled by the trade union and Labour Party bureaucracy. In this connection the organisation of CND/Labour Party militants in factories and trade unions is of special importance. Papers serving the purpose of bridge-building are also of immense value—after all, there are many more militant party supporters in the factories than people who attend wards or general management committees.

Marxists should not set themselves up as a party or embryo of a party of their own. They should remember that the working class looks to the Labour Party as the political organisation of the class (and no doubt when a new wave of political activity spreads among the working class millions of new voters will flock to its banner and hundreds of thousands will join it actively). Marxists should never forget that consciousness of the aims of socialism on the part of the *mass of the workers* is a necessary prerequisite for the achievement of socialism.

Marxists should strive to unite with the centrist left in activity in defence of the traditional working class content of the party (as on the issue of Clause Four, defence of conference supremacy, etc) against right wing attack, trying to isolate the Lib-Lab revisionists.

Above all the Marxists should help to build bridges between the different sectors of the struggle, in industry, CND, etc, with the clear knowledge that political struggle is meaningless without a political organisation to channel it, and that the only party the working class in Britain thinks its own, with all its defects, is the Labour Party.

Notes

1   R Miliband, *Parliamentary Socialism* (London, 1961), pp19-20.
2   R Miliband, *Parliamentary*, p22.
3   R Miliband, *Parliamentary*, p28.
4   R Miliband, *Parliamentary*, p44.
5   R Miliband, *Parliamentary*, pp95-96.
6   R Smillie, *My Life for Labour* (London, 1924), p133.
7   R W Lyman, *The First Labour Government, 1924* (London, 1953), p106.
8   H Dalton, *Call Back Yesterday* (London, 1953), p147.
9   R W Lyman, *First*, p106.
10 M Cole (ed), *Beatrice Webb's Diaries, 1924-1932* (London, 1956), p2.
11 J Symons, *The General Strike* (London, 1957), pp23-24. On Red Friday 1925 the main unions backed the miners' stand against pay cuts and threatened a general strike. This forced the Tory government to grant a nine-month wages subsidy.
12 J Symons, *General*, p26.
13 J Symons, *General*, p40.
14 J Symons, *General*, p42.
15 J Symons, *General*, p115.
16 J Symons, *General*, p116.
17 R Miliband, *Parliamentary*, p164.
18 See *The Review of Reviews*, vol XXXIII (June 1906), pp568-952; R Miliband, *Parliamentary*, p33.
19 *1909 ILP Annual Conference Report*, p49. Quoted in R T McKenzie, *British Political Parties* (London, 1955), p345.
20 J Saville, 'Trade Unions and Free Labour: The Background to the Taff Vale Decision', in A Briggs and J Saville (eds), *Essays in Labour History* (London, 1960), p340.
21 J Saville, 'Trade Unions', p341.
22 J Saville, 'Trade Unions', p350.
23 B Pribicevic, *The Shop Stewards' Movement and Workers' Control, 1910-1922* (Oxford, 1959), p161.
24 For some 40 years the Communist Party repeatedly applied for affiliation to the Labour Party, but to no avail. The fact that at least to some extent the CP leadership's sectarianism on the one hand, and open dependence on the Kremlin on the other, made it easier for the right wing to reject the application is one thing. But to say that this was the only, or even the main, reason why they managed to do this is another. After all, Cripps's Socialist League did not manage to survive the persecution of the right.
25 L Trotsky, *The Death Agony of Capitalism* (1938).
26 From his view that any serious reforms in the framework of capitalism could not be achieved, Trotsky concluded that any struggle for reforms had an *immediate* revolutionary

potential. This was the essence of his Transitional Programme. That future reforms snatched by the workers would help stabilise capitalism was the last thing he would have said. Of course Trotsky's views on this point—at the time, they were shared by the present writer—were rational for the 1930s. However, they sound ridiculous when repeated parrot-wise in the 1950s and 1960s by those who publish his *Death Agony of Capitalism* without comment or criticism. Parrots have never made a revolution.

27 Quoted in H Pelling, *The British Communist Party* (London, 1958), p68.

28 H Pelling, *British*, p77.

29 M Shanks, *The Stagnant Society* (London, 1961), p71.

30 M Shanks, *Stagnant*, p71.

31 V L Allen, *Trade Unions and Government* (London, 1961), p12.

32 V L Allen, *Trade Unions*, p23

33 V L Allen, *Trade Unions*, p34.

34 V L Allen, *Trade Unions*, p35.

35 V L Allen, *Trade Unions*, p304.

36 M Harrison, *Trade Unions and the Labour Party since 1945* (London, 1960), p294.

37 M Harrison, *Trade Unions*, pp294-295.

38 M Harrison, *Trade Unions*, p295.

39 M Harrison, *Trade Unions*, p296.

40 See 'International Wage and Fringe Comparisons', *Trade Union Affairs*, Spring 1961.

41 V L Allen, *Trade Unions*, p128.

42 V L Allen, *Trade Unions*, pp71-72.

43 *Manchester Guardian*, 5 May 1958; V L Allen, *Trade Unions*, p206.

44 'November Circular to Members of the United Society of Boilermakers', in V L Allen, *Trade Unions*, p110.

45 S Lens, 'American Labour at Dead End', *New Politics*, Autumn 1961.

46 W Glazier, 'The Automation Problem', in C Cochran, *American Labour in Midpassage* (New York, 1959), p123.

47 *New Statesman*, 14 July 1961.

48 *New Statesman*, 8 September 1961.

49 The establishment of a Labour government, if followed by serious economic difficulties, resulting in a headlong collision between government and unions, may well accelerate the process of separation of the trade unions from the party. But in this case it will not lead to apoliticisation of the labour movement, but the opposite. However, this is at present speculation.

50 *Gallup Political Index*, Report No 9, September 1960.

Incomes policy, legislation and shop stewards

With Colin Barker, 1966

Introduction by Reg Birch

[Leading Maoist, former Communist Party militant, and top AEU official]

Here is a timely book which seeks to cut through the gibberish, pseudo-science and financial jargon attached to the 'City', industrial investment and finance, and above all the so-called incomes, prices and profits 'plan'.

In addition the authors have sought to evaluate the role and future of that much maligned worker, the shop steward.

Without doubt the first part does a great service to all workers, and I hope that the scholarly treatment will not put readers off. On the contrary, I urge them to read it carefully. A little perseverance to encompass the first page and you will find its simplicity, the refusal to write down, and the whole approach sound. It tears away the devices of so many writers on economics who consistently shroud the subject in such abstractions as to instil in the worker the conviction that this is not his subject, nor his business, but some special esoteric science, the preserve of the 'educated', the employers and the writers of the City page.

The whole question of 'incomes policy' has been discussed by some ad nauseam. That history will come to estimate that the plan is no plan at all, that it is nothing but a confidence trick on those who labour, is without doubt, but now that the 'experts' have all gone through the cerebral exercise there is the danger that the thing itself will come to be established by the indifference, passivity and, indeed, ignorance of the working class. If the workers are already sick of the matter, and they should be, then let them be assured they are going to be much more so, and of its effects in the future. To avoid this it is essential to understand it—given knowledge one will not be sickened but awakened to its dangers.

The book brings home that it is not more palatable to the working class to trade a Selwyn Lloyd pay pause for a George Brown warning light or a wages stop. Nor is it very original. Stafford Cripps tried and failed. It has been tried and is being tried in other European countries and has failed, and is failing thanks to the resistance of the organised working class. The notion is as old as capitalism and just as anachronistic.

It is in the second part that the book is not so well informed. I do not accept that the extension of shop stewards' organisations, their increase in number, will automatically lead to the development of a socialist movement. There needs to be politics—working class politics. This is not a question of being militant on economic demands within the factory or place of work alone, or of taking one's politics from the policies or utterances of the 'politicians', whether of right or left, but of the development of political aims by the working class, and of insisting that it is not a case of our supporting or adopting the policies of political parties but of their supporting the aims and aspirations of the working class.

On the question of so-called 'unofficial' strikes it is as well to remember that there is no special virtue in their being unofficial, that their designation thus is solely the business of the union concerned, ie the membership, and it is as well that this is so. It is not the business of the government, the employers or news media. Workers will wait a very long time before the employers will declare a strike official. Where a strike is said to be unconstitutional, in conflict with agreements entered into between the parties, it should be remembered that such agreements are frequently come about by virtue of strike action, that agreements are not the laws of the Medes and Persians, that they are frequently departed from by either side and are subject to amendment and revision. To argue that to incorporate no-strike clauses in agreements arbitrarily removes the possibilities of strikes or lockouts is to deny history. The conflict is there and will not be removed by wishful phrases.

The portion of this book dealing with shop stewards and workshop organisations is extremely timely. The attacks on them, which are after all the fruit of long industrial struggle and the natural development of a measure of democracy, are today unprecedented. An attempt is made here to explain the reasons for this campaign of lies and calumny being heaped against the unions and their officers in the workshops, the shop stewards. Space alone prevents a deeper exploration and analysis of the danger. The new threats of legislation, if unresisted, will rush us back to the Combination Acts. There was unprincipled abuse and pillorying of shop stewards and a cynical exploitation of this kind of McCarthyism introduced in the general election—a suggestion that the shop steward is some kind of monster tyrant strutting around the factory with a noose to hand to apply lynch law. There is a tyranny within factories, but it is imposed by the employer. It is a fact that a blacklist very much applies. It is a fact that in many factories every possible device is used to obstruct, delay and evade the operation of the trade unions exercising their functions. It is a fact that there are employers who deny trade union recognition altogether.

There is, paradoxically enough, a gentler tyranny imposed on the shop steward by some workers. Frequently he becomes their substitute for participation in the struggle themselves—they do sometimes see him as the substitute for their own militancy. There is a tendency at times for some groups of workers or an individual worker to exploit the best qualities in so many shop stewards, particularly the prime reason (in my opinion) why so many accept election to this union office. This is their unquestionable inability to accept injustice to their workmates, their desire to insist that they and their workmates shall be treated with dignity. In pursuit of this they are prepared to, and do, give up their leisure to devote many hours outside work time in dealing with the problems of industrial relationships. No employers devote anything like the time in this direction (perhaps this is just as well). But if the employers applied as much time to production they would undoubtedly have little left to bleat and whine about these dreadful people the shop stewards. Who knows, if they applied themselves to work a little more they might not even need to.

The workers do know that the average steward is ever ready to assist and represent them, and that this is continually done at the expense of the same steward applying himself to the daily task of maintaining his family and paying the rent. A survey of earnings of shop stewards, especially in the production field, where payment by results and piece-work obtains, would surely show that he takes out less on average than his workmate engaged on an identical worktask. That the workers are conscious of this is sometimes shown by their offsetting of the steward's loss of piece-work earnings through a shop fund. This is not general nor is it the answer. It is the steward's function to advance the just demands and aspirations of those who elect him, but equally it is imperative that the workers support and participate at all times in that struggle. Only thus can the maintenance of wages and working conditions be assured, let alone improvement be obtained in the present period.

The acceptance of this role can lead to the development of higher aims— socialist aims. It is especially important now for all workers to insist on no retreat, on their right to collective bargaining, on their right to trade unions unfettered by anti trade union legislation—to remember that the attacks on stewards today are truly an attack on the workers. The answer is to attack the attackers, no matter who.

We should thank the authors for their contributions whether or not we accept in toto the political conclusions. The serious research and selfless labour to produce this book is done without regard to any return or gain by them. It puts to shame so many organisations who should be doing just this. With all the lip service to modernisation (whatever that means) of the unions, we should be grateful that there are still volunteers.

Preface

It is doubtful whether any of the problems facing the labour movement of Britain in the 1960s is of greater importance than the two related questions of incomes policy and trade union legislation.

In this book we have tried to show how and why an incomes policy under capitalism must necessarily be an anti working class measure. In places readers may find some of the arguments a little complex and difficult on a first reading, but we feel it is important that all the arguments that have been put forward in favour of an incomes policy should be discussed in a book of this sort. As far as we could, we have backed up our statements with facts and figures that socialists and militants in the unions will be able to use in discussions with fellow workers.

Not many people will want to read the book right through in one go, so it might be useful to have a short summary of the book and what's to be found in each chapter. That way it will be easier to look up the different parts of the argument as they are needed.

In the first chapter we give some of the reasons for the growing importance of incomes policy for the employers. As capitalism has developed, it has changed its form a great deal, and some of these changes are explained in here. In particular the great monopolies with their vast plants have become more and more central in the economy, and this has altered the whole face of capitalism, and altered too the forms of the struggle between the workers and the capitalists. Incomes policy wouldn't have made sense at all in the capitalist Britain of the 19th century, or even as recently as the Great Depression of the 1930s. In Chapter One we show why it makes sense today, and why it has only recently come up.

In Chapter Two we look at the question, is it an incomes policy or is it really wage restraint? George Brown and the rest of the government all say that the incomes policy will be fair because it will apply equally to all forms of income. But this isn't true, and in this chapter we show why. Under capitalism profits can't be controlled. If you control wages under capitalism, profits will zoom ahead. That is what an incomes policy is supposed to achieve—wage restraint in the interests of better profits.

Chapter Three examines another argument that is often put forward in favour of the incomes policy: the argument that an incomes policy will contribute to economic growth. Here we try to show the assumptions that lie behind this argument, and to demonstrate how completely out of touch with reality those assumptions are. It isn't high wages that hold back economic growth, but the capitalist class themselves, the organisation of capitalist society, and the way that resources are wasted under capitalism.

Traditionally socialists have always talked about a socialist society as a society in which the economy will be planned. And many workers are confused by George Brown's National Plan, which we look at in Chapter Four. They think that, because there is some planning done in our society today, this must somehow be something to do with socialism. But it has nothing to do with socialism at all. There is such a thing as *capitalist planning*—indeed today, when capitalism is so vast and so complex, the capitalists *need* to plan ahead. Even the Tories (or most of them) believe in planning nowadays. And George Brown's plan is a capitalist plan—what is more, it is capitalists who help George Brown to operate it. It has nothing at all to do with socialism, for it is planning directed against the workers and their interests.

In Chapter Five we turn away from the questions of planning and the changing nature of capitalism to look at the way that workers win their wages. This is important because one of the main arguments that is put forward in favour of an incomes policy is the argument that if only the higher paid workers would stop demanding such large wage increases it would be possible to help the lower paid workers. To show that this idea is nonsense we examine the way that workers *really* win wages under capitalism, and the way that the struggles of the strongest and best paid workers help the worse off. In particular, we show how a growing part of a worker's wage packet nowadays is won through the struggle on the shopfloor instead of through national bargaining between the union officials and the employers' associations.

This brings to an end the part of the book in which we explain incomes policy, what it is and what it means. In the second part of the book we look at the way in which workers can best fight against incomes policy, and what form the struggle against incomes policy is likely to take. This is the general theme of the last four chapters.

Chapter Six is about the trade union brass. Nowadays, more than ever before, there is a struggle inside the unions as well as between the unions and the employers. For the union officials are becoming less and less the leaders of the workers, and more their foremen. As they are drawn into collaboration with the government, they become increasingly alienated from the rank and file of the unions. The unions are tending to become more bureaucratic in structure, and democracy in the unions is decaying. The lesson of this is very important—to fight against incomes policy successfully, workers will have to rely on their own strength and organisation, for the majority of the union bureaucrats cannot be depended on any longer.

Chapter Seven, therefore, is about shop stewards and unofficial strikes. It is the longest chapter in the whole book, for this is the most important question of all. We show how useless the official negotiation procedure is, and how most strikes these days are unofficial. The number of unofficial strikes is growing steadily, and unofficial strikes are the biggest problem the employers have. The strikes show that the workers today are stronger and more self-confident than ever before. Unofficial strikes are led by shop stewards, and it is clear that the shop stewards are becoming more and more important for rank and file workers. There are more shop stewards nowadays than ever before, and they are the natural leaders of the struggle today. But it would be foolish to try to idealise the shop stewards, and we end the chapter with an examination of the weaknesses and strength of their organisations. We hope that this section in particular will encourage workers and their stewards to try to develop and strengthen their organisations, and the links between the different factories and industries.

In Chapter Eight we look at the proposals for new legislation against the unions and especially against unofficial strikes. If incomes policy is going to work at all there will have to be new laws to control unofficial activities. This can only further widen the split between the rank and file of the unions and the officials, many of whom will unite with the government and the law courts to attack the shop stewards' organisations.

The last chapter is more general in scope. Here we move beyond the question of incomes policy to a wider discussion of the working class and the struggle for socialism today. Just as capitalism has changed enormously, so too the working class has changed, and in this last chapter we look at some of the changes, and the ways in which they can both weaken and strengthen the working class in the struggle for a socialist society. In particular, we look at the way the old ideology of 'reformism' has been weakened by the new conditions of the class struggle, because of changes that have taken place in the ruling class, the state and the working class. The book ends with a few comments on some of the most important next steps for the working class in Britain.

We hope this book will prove useful. For workers and socialists today, as always, there are three tasks in the struggle for socialism: studying the changes in capitalism and the working class; making propaganda among other workers; and organising for struggle. If this book can help at all in these three tasks it will have served its purpose —*Tony Cliff and Colin Barker*

Chapter One: Why incomes policy?

Over the last few years more and more publicity has been given to the question of 'incomes policy'. Labour Party and trade union conferences have debated it with great heat, the Tories were converted to 'incomes planning' in 1962, the present Labour government is convinced of the necessity for an 'incomes policy', and so on and so on. To understand why this question has become so important over the past few years we have to understand the changing situation facing those who own and control industry, the capitalist class.

The changing pattern of investment

Firstly, in present day capitalism the individual investments made by big business have grown enormously, both in size and in the time they take to mature. And at the same time the risks involved in the act of investment have also increased, because the pace of technological change is greater today than ever before. While it is true that the rapid advance of technology offers very high profits nowadays when investments are made in the right place, it is also true that the penalties for investment in the wrong place or at the wrong time are also much greater. Secondly, the threat of obsolescence (machinery, etc becoming out of date) has radically increased during the present technological revolution. Thirdly, the pressure of international competition is greater than ever, and has been made sharper still by the systematic lowering of the barriers to international trade since the early 1950s, notably inside the European Common Market and the European Free Trade Association,

Because of these developments it has become increasingly vital under contemporary capitalism for the typical board of directors to be able to plan ahead over a number of years with some degree of certainty and confidence. And thus planning has become very respectable with big business:

It is indeed characteristic of modern capitalist planning that the impulse to embark on the seemingly speculative enterprise of long-range prediction comes from the industries which find that they are compelled, because of the nature of the technology that they employ, to commit large indivisible blocks of capital to projects that will only pay for themselves after the lapse of several years.

Systematic economic analysis, preferably in collaboration with other industries similarly placed, whose decisions will also influence the outcome, is then the obvious way of reducing the risk. In Britain it was the steel industry which took the initiative in this field. The Iron and Steel Board, the public agency which had been set up in the early 1950s to supervise this industry, found that its attempts to guide the direction of steel investment, and to check whether its volume was adequate, required a close examination of trends over the economy as a whole. The third five-year development programme issued in 1961 was in some ways a pilot project for the full-scale planning operation on which the British government embarked with the establishment of the National Economic Development Council in 1962.[1]

As an illustration of the tendency towards the very long period before investments start to pay their way, the following recent example will suffice. In July 1965 the British Motor Corporation (BMC) took over the giant Pressed Steel Company for £33$\frac{1}{2}$ million. At the end of December 1965, partly to avoid being investigated by the Monopolies Commission, BMC sold the Pressed Steel factory at Linwood, near Glasgow, to the Chrysler-Rootes group. For this lone factory Rootes paid £14$\frac{1}{2}$ million. What matter here are the terms for payment—Rootes paid £3.6 million down, with a promise to pay another £2 million by the end of 1971. The Board of Trade is staking the other £8 million to £9 million (at an undisclosed but no doubt very favourable mortgage rate).[2]

As for the risk of equipment becoming out of date, we have only to remember the common saying in the United States that any aeroplane that exists is obsolete, and that many an aeroplane or missile is already out of date before it even leaves the drawing board. The same applies, even if not quite so dramatically, to other products. The huge British ICI combine provides a recent example:

> At Wilton on Teesside engineers from Kellogg International are putting the finishing touches to ICI's new 200,000 ton a year giant ethylene cracker. When it comes on stream in the spring it will be the biggest in Britain, and it is already scheduled as likely to close down next year, when the 450,000-ton super-giant being built by Lummus comes into operation. Some £7 million worth of gleaming hardware straight into mothballs waiting for demand to catch up—this is the alarming price of technical progress.[3]

ICI is Britain's largest manufacturing company, and the threat of obsolescence illustrated in the above example is expressed in the company's changing depreciation policy:

> The period of depreciation for equipment in ICI, which was commonly 20 years plus before the war, was reduced from 1950 onwards, when, according to the chairman, the company was 'beginning to think in terms of 15 years for new projects.

In the early 1960s this came down to 12 to 15 years, and more recently the average for new plant has come down to about ten years. For certain kinds of investment, where the risks of technical obsolescence are thought to be high, the amortisation period is down to five to seven years (information supplied by Paul Chambers, chairman of ICI).[4]

Also research takes a larger and larger place in production. According to the *National Institute Economic Review*, in 1959 the American aeronautics industry spent on research a sum equal to 35.7 percent of the value of its net production in 1958. The figure for the electronics industry was 36.5 percent.[5] Because of competition, research is shrouded in secrecy, and each firm is forced to spend huge sums of money on research that may well be obsolete long before it produces any results.

The long term nature of investment and the rapid pace of technological change impel large firms towards attempts at long term control over all aspects of cost—and particularly over labour costs. This is why the employers need greater predictability in their labour relations—wages, hours of work, grading, productivity—so that they can increase the area within which they can plan ahead in the working of their firms.

Another reason why the employers need an incomes policy is to be seen in the increasing unevenness between the conditions in different sections of capitalist industry in one and the same country. While industries with very fast rates of growth can easily afford relatively high wages demanded under full employment, other slower growing industries find it much more difficult to pay. The traditional capitalist solution, of leaving the problem to be solved by simple laissez faire (the rule of the jungle), would tear the ruling class apart today, in the modern conditions of very high concentration and centralisation of capital. In the present situation the solution that becomes necessary is one that involves state intervention to make sure that wages don't rise at a rate faster than the more backward industries can afford.[6]

International competition

Another factor making it vital for the employers to increase the predictability of their costs, and above all of their labour costs, is the increasing tendency for profit margins to decline. This is the effect of increasing international competition.

In the first decade after the war, when the rehabilitation of Germany, France, Italy and Japan had only just been achieved, it was quite easy for employers to put up prices when wages were increased. After all, the Employers' Federation that agreed to the wage increase was usually made up of exactly the same people as the trade association that determined prices. With world prices going up generally, until the late 1950s there was very little to prevent the employers from compensating for wage increases by putting up their prices, even in the field of exports. But as international competition increased, profit margins began to get squeezed. Take the case of the British engineering industry, which is responsible for a third of manufacturing employment in Britain, and for over half of all British exports—the following table shows the undoubted tendency for profit margins to decline:

GROSS AND NET PROFITS AS PERCENTAGE OF TURNOVER IN ENGINEERING[7]

	Non-electrical engineering		Electrical engineering	
	Gross	Net	Gross	Net
1954–55	14.8	12.9	14.0	12.2
1955–56	14.3	12.2	12.5	10.7
1956–57	12.6	10.5	12.5	10.2
1957–58	12.9	10.7	12.8	10.0
1958–59	12.4	9.9	11.4	8.4
1959–60	12.5	9.9	12.9	9.7
1960–61	12.4	9.8	12.6	9.2

R R Neild, too, found a decline in profit margins in relation to value added as a fairly general picture in manufacturing industry during the period.[8]

The problem of international competition is especially acute in the British economy. International competition has forced a squeeze on profit margins, but this squeeze threatens to become even tighter in an economy like the British capitalist economy which has large-scale troubles with its balance of payments. For in trying to solve the balance of payments problems, a succession of British Chancellors of the Exchequer have resorted to a system usually referred to as 'stop-go', which has meant forcing industry to work below capacity for an extended period, every four or five years. This has meant that unit costs in British industry have gone up too.

Indeed British capitalism has suffered under a double burden since the early 1950s: firstly Tory chancellors have operated stop-go policies that alternately released and shut off demand in response to the pressures of the balance of payments situation; and secondly there has been an enormous expenditure on armaments that devoured roughly half the amount available each year for investment. The result has been an economy that looked stable on the surface, but that grew at a rate lower than any other developed economy. From 1950 to 1955 the real national product per man-year in Britain grew by only 1.8 percent, and from 1955 to 1961 by only 1.6 percent. In other countries over the same period the figures were as follows: Germany 6 and 3.5 percent; France 4.3 and 3.5 percent; Italy 5.4 and 4.1 percent; Netherlands 4.4 and 2.6 percent; United States 2.8 and 1.4 percent.[9] And from 1954 to 1962 Britain's share of exports in world trade fell from 20.1 to 15.2 percent.[10]

At the same time, largely because of relatively full employment, workers' bargaining power has increased considerably. In many industries the employers have found themselves, without the disciplining sanction of unemployment, in a weaker position vis-à-vis organised labour than ever before. Up to the late 1950s the employers' main reaction to this situation was to make the best of it, giving way to the workers' demands wherever the only alternative was an extremely expensive stop in production, and passing on the higher costs in the form of higher prices. For the boom was on, and such a boom as never before.

Inflation was of course deplored, publicly, but as long as profit margins were maintained it was not felt as a real problem. But, as we have shown, international competition put a squeeze on profit margins, and with a semi-stagnant economy workers' bargaining power become more and more of a problem for the bosses. So at the end of the 1950s, and increasingly in the 1960s, state and industry together have sought to find ways to achieve the ultimate aim of any ruling class—a working class that knows 'its place' and keeps it, that demands no more than the iron rations offered by its rulers, and that is prepared to pay the costs of its rulers' mistakes.

The coming together of state and business in economic planning and its twin brother, incomes planning, has been made that much easier by the fact that the state has already become a central factor in the economy of the capitalist countries:

> Central and local government together employed 3 million people who earned 15 percent of all wages. The public sector as a whole was responsible for over 40 percent of all fixed investment and for as much as 50 percent of the building work done in the country.[11]

> In 1962 total public expenditure, including interest paid on the national debt, was equivalent to 44 percent of GNP. The ratio had varied but never fallen below 40 percent in the previous decade.[12]

The German, Japanese, French and Italian 'miracles'

The factors we have already mentioned made the British capitalists and their government anxious for an incomes policy, but they were further convinced when they made comparisons between their own performance and the 'miracles' of other capitalist countries, in Japan and in Western Europe. Remember how enviously Harold Wilson spoke during the 1964 general election campaign when he compared the British rate of growth with that of West Germany, France, Italy and Japan! Looking at these foreign economies, the secret of success for the employers was plain to see—wages there lagged behind profits more than they did in Britain.

In Germany during the early 1950s the fruits of rising productivity were channelled into business profits rather than into wages. The same happened in France in the late 1950s (after de Gaulle came to power)—real wages were held down for a number of years while profits soared. In fact real wages in France *fell* by 1 percent between 1958 and 1961, while production advanced rapidly. This of course gave the French capitalists a considerable competitive advantage in the international market—French exports benefited, as of course did profits. Similarly in Italy in the 1950s wages lagged far behind rising productivity, so that profits galloped far ahead.[13]

The logic of the Japanese economic miracle was much the same—there was a violent rise in profits compared with wages. Since the war, as a result, Japanese industrial production has risen at such a fantastic rate that by 1961 it was at least four times that in the mid-1930s. The average annual rate of growth of the Japanese gross national product has been estimated at 7 percent for the years 1953-59, and at 10 percent for the period 1955-60:[14]

> These conditions in the labour market lie at the root of Japanese progress. There has been an abundance of labour to meet the rapidly rising demand from the factories without provoking a steep increase in wages… In these circumstances it is not surprising that, while industrial productivity rose by 55 percent between 1955 and 1960, real wages rose by only 25 percent. Here is one of the main reasons for the massive industrial investment during recent years—gross investment has lately amounted to over 30 percent of the gross national expenditure—without which Japan's rapid progress would have been impossible.[15]

One very important cause of the lag of wages behind profits in these countries was the existence of a large reserve army of unemployed workers. West Germany was blessed with some 10 million refugees (from the part of former East Germany which is now in Poland, from the Sudeten zone of Czechoslovakia, and—some $2^1/_2$ million people—from East Germany). Italy got millions of new workers from the poverty-stricken south. In France rapid technological changes in agriculture freed millions to go to the towns, and the same happened on an even larger scale in Japan.

Also, in all these countries trade union organisation is much weaker than it is in Britain. Nor is this due only to the obvious pressure in the labour market of the reserve army of unemployed workers. In France only 2 million workers are organised into unions, and these unions are divided into three separate federations (Communist-controlled, Socialist-controlled and Catholic-controlled). In Italy there are also three federations of trade unions, while in Japan the history of the trade union movement since the war has been one of splits and divisions. Low union membership and a divided trade union movement obviously make workers' bargaining power much less of a threat to the employers, and wages suffer at the expense of profits.

Looking overseas at these various foreign 'miracles', the message for the British capitalists is very clear—if restrained wages can cause these 'miracles', then why shouldn't the British capitalists try to get themselves the same blessing?

Incomes policy as a substitute for the army of the unemployed

In the 'good old days' before the war the capitalists disciplined their workers, as Karl Marx noted, with the aid of a reserve army of unemployed. But since the beginning of the Second World War conditions of full, or nearly full, employment have existed in Britain, thus removing the threat of unemployment as a way of disciplining the workers. All the same, the idea of using deflation to create unemployment—so as to cut wage increases—has reappeared again and again among the ruling circles. Perhaps the most notorious example was that of Sir Stafford Cripps (Chancellor of the Exchequer in the first post-war Labour government) who stated in the Economic Survey of 1948 that the object of his policy was to increase the numbers of the unemployed by 50 percent in the course of the year by deliberately putting a damper on the building industry. At the end of 1947 there were 300,000 workers unemployed, and Cripps said that in order to get more mobility of labour their number would have to go up to 450,000 by the end of 1948.[16]

The same idea, that the economy needs a pool of unemployed workers, has been a recurrent theme in the *Economist* over the years. But, above all, the chief advocate of the idea has been Professor F W Paish, the main economic adviser to the Tory government over a number of years. Professor Paish's theories have received wide publicity, and have been rather uncritically accepted by many, including some socialists. Some discussion of them therefore seems worthwhile.

Paish's theory stresses the importance of running the economy with a certain margin of unused capacity. This he sees as a condition for growth without rising prices:

> It does not seem possible to put the necessary margin of unused capacity at less than 5 percent, which roughly corresponds to 2 percent of unemployment, and it may well have been higher, though not very much higher. We may probably put it somewhat within the range of 5 to 7 percent, corresponding to between 2 and 2$^1/_2$ percent of unemployment.[17]

Paish went so far as to calculate the exact changes in wages that would be associated with small changes in the unemployment rate.[18]

Unfortunately for Professor Paish, his calculations have been disproved by the facts of life. A level of unemployment somewhat above the level Paish considered necessary to contain wage rises was in fact sustained for a whole year—from the fourth quarter of 1962 till the third quarter of 1963—but wages still rose. And other countries had similar experiences. In some countries wages and prices rose quite rapidly when unemployment exceeded 5 percent and was often near the 10 percent mark. Thus in Italy, while the rate of unemployment outside agriculture was 13.4 percent (15.3 percent in the years 1950 and 1954), wage rates rose by 25 percent (1948-54). In Belgium the unemployment rates were between 11.3 percent and 7.6 percent in 1949-54, while wage rates rose by 30 percent (1948-54). As against Italy and Belgium, British unemployment from 1948 to 1954 was between 1.4 percent and 1.2 percent, and wage rates rose by 35 percent. The figures for Italy and Belgium show that not even an unemployment rate of 10 percent is sufficient to subdue the workers enough to stop the wage-price spiral.[19]

The wage-price spiral

Inflation—the wage-price spiral—is in fact the product of the class struggle under the conditions of modern capitalism, where there are only small or even no reserves of unemployed workers. On the one hand stands the capitalist class, organised in monopoly associations, and on the other hand there stands a mature and organised labour movement. Added to these two is a third agent of inflation, the capitalist state, which on the one hand has a permanent arms economy which tends to 'overheat' the economy, while on the other it is very afraid of the political consequences of mass unemployment in an advanced country with a strong labour movement.

Really the argument about *who* is responsible for the wage-price spiral is a meaningless one, although many professional economists have argued for years about whether the blame should be placed on rising wages that push up prices, or on rising prices that force the workers to try to increase their wages to keep up with the rising cost of living. But the fact of central importance is that workers and capitalists both try to increase their share of the national cake. The way the national cake actually gets carved up between them depends on the relative strength of the contending classes. Up to a point, of course, the wage-price spiral is satisfactory to the capitalists as a way of dealing with working class pressure for higher real wages and a bigger share in the national cake. The rising prices do cheat the workers of the extra purchasing power that they would otherwise have won. But of course the wage-price spiral also leads to a squeeze on profit margins when international competition becomes sharper, and it leads too to stagnation and relative decline in the whole national economy. Inflation has been doing what the reserve army of the unemployed did for capitalism in the past—keeping down the size of the workers' slice from the national cake—however badly this has turned out for the capitalists in terms of stagnation. Today the capitalists and their government hope that incomes policy will produce the same effect without the bad side effects of stagnation and decline. Thus practically all the Western capitalist countries have embarked on national economic planning and on an incomes policy—France, Italy, Sweden, Norway, the Netherlands, Belgium and Austria. De Gaulle's France is entering this year on its fifth five-year plan, while Italy has just started along the same road. All these countries have tried to some extent to implement a national incomes policy.[20]

Chapter Two: Is it incomes policy or wage restraint?

On 30 April 1965 George Brown told the Conference of Executives of Trade Unions, 'This is not just a wages policy but an incomes policy. It is not only just an incomes policy but a prices and incomes policy.'

In other words, he was at pains to argue, the incomes policy will be perfectly fair because it will apply equally to all incomes. In this chapter we shall discuss whether this claim has any truth.

Can profits be controlled?

There is a qualitative difference between wages and profits, in that wages are a necessary part of the costs of production while profits are not. Profits are a residue left over after production and sale, while wages are not. And wages are negotiated between two sides, while profits are not. All the talk about putting the same restraints on profits and wages, in fact, covers up the basic contradiction in any policy of *planning* of profits. This was very well expressed in an editorial in *DATA Journal* in June 1965:

> Wages and salaries are determined by negotiation and bargaining. Any changes in their magnitude are subject to discussion in advance of the changes being made. Profits in contrast are not subject to negotiation. An employer does not have to negotiate with his workers to secure an increase in profits.

Profits, moreover, are the motor of advance under capitalism and they act as the only reliable measure of how well an enterprise is doing. If the profit motive under capitalism is damped down, then economic growth will be damped down too. The *Statist*, a mouthpiece for business interests, pointed this out very clearly:

> It is precisely because profits *do* play a specific and essential role in a capitalist economy—in providing the finance for expansion, the inducement to invest and the stimulus to efficiency—that their control is such a hazardous, not to say impossible, operation.
>
> So long…as we maintain the capitalist rules of the game, so long as we continue to discard the idea of a total state planning, we must allow profits a high degree of flexibility.[1]

The same point was made by the management of the Dunlop Rubber Company, when it published 'Dunlop's Statement of Intent' in support of George Brown:

> *Profits for Security and Growth.* We are in a competitive business. Our success is measured by the profits we make. Augment them, be proud of them and recognise them as the fund which provides our security and the tools for our future success.

And Professor Paish put the argument against a profit freeze under capitalism in a nutshell: 'To try and peg profits would mean that every firm would be working on a cost-plus basis and would lose all incentive to keep down costs'.[2]

And if, instead of pegging profits directly, measures were taken to limit profits indirectly by imposing taxation on firms making high profits, the effect would be much the same:

> A high rate of profits tax has no effect on the inefficient firm which is only just managing to stay in business, while it increases the difficulty of efficient firms in obtaining the finance they need for expansion, both from internal sources and, very probably, the market. It also reduces the incentive to keep down costs, especially in the form of expenditures such as advertising, which may still be yielding some residual benefit to the firm after the tax, it may be hoped, is reduced or removed. No system could be better designed to slow down growth than one which keeps the inefficient alive, prevents the efficient from expanding, and reduces for everyone the incentive to keep down costs.[3]

Because profits are the locomotive of capitalist growth, it follows that the higher the rate of growth the more profits grow: 'Typically over the last decade, whatever the percentage increase in industrial output in any year, the increase in company profits has been nearly three times as great'.[4]

Profits rise most where industry is growing most, where industry is at its largest, where industry is most monopolistic. A statistical analysis by Ken Alexander and John Hughes, for the years 1948-59, shows an increase of nearly 60 percent in profit per unit of output in metal manufactures, chemicals, bricks and glass. In vehicles, 'other metal goods', food, drink, tobacco, and engineering and electrical goods the rise was about 40 percent. These industries typically have a small number of leading firms and a record of extensive collusion in price fixing. On the other hand, in textiles, clothing, timber, paper and printing there was either no rise or actually a fall in profits per unit of output.[5]

It is clear that a policy of levelling profits downwards under capitalism would produce industrial stagnation:

> The notion that company profits can be limited to, say, a 4 percent increase in line with the expected increase in national productivity is ludicrous. In any particular year the profits of any one industry, which may be recovering from a slump, will be advancing by, say, 50 percent, while the profits of another, which may be turning down from boom, will be declining by, say, 10 percent. To put an extra tax on profits which have risen through the greater skill of the management would be to tax and discourage efficiency. The Labour Party must accustom itself to the idea that the efficient profit-makers in a mixed economy are the pillars of the trading state. It is private enterprise which runs the export trade, which enables the nation to pay its way in the world and secure a surplus on its balance of payments. Sometimes it is the flamboyant business tycoon, drawing on an immense expense account, who is responsible for the most spectacular success in foreign markets. Wilson has got to make those businessmen feel that they can work with profit under a Labour government. And by 'with profit' I do not mean a meagre profit.[6]

Nor is any 'long-run' limitation of profits over a number of years possible. As long as a tiny section of the population owns and controls industry and therefore controls investment decisions, any attempt to 'control' profits would simply result in the owners and controllers of capital sending their money abroad, to sunnier climes. Any serious suggestion of control would lead to a complete shutting up of investment in Britain.

No. Profit is the lifeblood of capitalism. If you are allergic to profit then you just can't run a capitalist economy. Therefore as long as the Labour leaders are committed to such an economy they cannot and dare not harm or gag profits. A Fabian writer, J R Sargent, was really quite consistent when he argued that a Labour government should allow a *more unequal* distribution of income, in the interests of capital accumulation and a faster rate of growth. As he pointed out, if wages rose seriously compared with profits, the effect would be quite disastrous:

> As the share of wages continued to rise, and profit margins were further eroded, the lifeblood of capitalism would begin to run dry. Capital would try to flee abroad, and would presumably be checked by applying exchange control with the necessary severity. This done, businesses would gradually begin to close down, as there would be insufficient profit to induce them to replace their worn out assets.[7]

Prices control

Profits consist of the residue that is left from the selling price of a commodity after the costs of production have been deducted. So, to control profits, there must also be control of prices. In fact, however, to control prices is an extremely complicated, indeed an impossible task. First of all, price formation is a very intricate process:

> Price leadership, marginal selling, optimum product and price 'mixes', branding, scale economies, the concept of 'the contribution', and pioneer profit ideas are just a few among literally dozens of subtleties which can make price figuring among the most complicated arithmetic business gets involved in.

> What, ask the critics, will the review body make of complex price structures like organic chemicals and pharmaceuticals? Here they would find that at one end of the scale there are 'bread and butter' products that on paper make no profit at all (though because they are sold in big volume they make a useful contribution to research and other overheads) while at the other end are innovation products attracting pioneer profits of perhaps 100 percent or more on the apparent unit cost.

> How, too, will the 'wise men' find their way through the complexities of differential pricing? One example here is where a manufacturer sells, at vastly different prices, precisely the same product under his own brand label and as, say, a retailing chain's 'house' brand. Another common example arises when manufacturers 'load' the British prices to the maximum extent that the competition permits so that they can afford to operate at highly marginal prices in export markets.[8]

With prices so numerous and so complicated, how can a central body determine the 'right' profit per unit of output? This was precisely the problem the National Incomes Commission (NIC) met when it tried to discover how big profits were in the industries it was investigating. The NIC asked the employers if they would provide figures for turnover and profits, keeping the identity of the firms anonymous. The electrical contractors (NFEA) replied that they were very sorry, but they couldn't provide a sample of turnover and profits from their members and there was nothing else they could do to assist the commission beyond the written evidence already submitted.[9] The other employers the NIC tried to investigate made much the same reply.

It's true, of course, that in some cases the government might persuade a firm or an industry to hold down the prices of a particular product for a certain period, but these firms and industries can compensate themselves by altering the prices of other products. Since the typical firm today makes a multitude of different products, this is really very easy. One example will do. During the bakers' strike in November 1965 the employers, the Federation of Wholesale and Multiple Bakers, were holding down the price of bread for three months, by agreement with the Prices and Incomes Board. But, as the bakers' union complained to George Brown, while bread prices were held steady for a time, the prices of rolls, cobs and confectionery were being put up by as much as 50 percent in some places, and without reference of any sort to the Prices and Incomes Board.[10]

The Department of Economic Affairs has estimated that something like 3 million price changes are made each year, so it is hardly possible for the Prices and Incomes Board to keep track of them all. As for the government's proposed 'early warning system', this may help to delay price increases but, as the Confederation of British Industry suggested, it is unlikely to contribute very much to price stability. And the OECD Report of August 1964, discussing the problem of applying an incomes policy to non-wage incomes, came to the not very surprising conclusion that price controls were useful only as an emergency measure for short periods.

The 'profit equals dividend' trick

One way of selling the idea of an incomes policy to the labour movement is by pretending that dividends and profits are the same things, or that at least dividends make up a decisive portion of profits. Sir Stafford Cripps's wage freeze of 1948-49 was justified by using the 'dividend freeze' trick. And it's not uncommon today for apologists for the incomes policy within the labour movement to demand control of dividends as a fair bargain for the control of wages.

Wages are the payment that workers get for the sale of their labour power, but dividends *are not* the payment that capitalists get for their ownership of capital. The dividend is only part of the payment to the shareholder. If a worker gets a wage rise of 5s a week instead of 8s a week, the extra 3s are never collected up for him to draw at a later date. The wages that a worker loses he never sees again. But with a shareholder it's very different. If he gets a dividend of 5s out of a profit of 8s, the other 3s are probably transferred to investment and will come back to him as a capital gain a few years later. The dividend that the shareholder loses he does see again, in another form.

It is a central feature of the contemporary tax scene that the capitalist nowadays *prefers* capital gains to dividend income. Dividend freeze wouldn't suppress capital gains, but instead would make them even bigger: 'It is well known (indeed it is constantly broadcast by the financial press) that it "pays" a surtax-payer to select securities which have a low dividend yield but a high degree of expected capital appreciation'.[11]

What's more, in the case of successful companies, not only may the value of the shares (capital appreciation) be greater than the rise in dividends, but also it may be greater than the rise in profits as a whole, as represented in growth of company reserves from the continuous 'ploughing back' of undistributed profits.

Take the cases of Woolworths and Marks & Spencer. In February 1955 the market price of all the shares in Woolworths amounted to some £280 million, while share capital and accumulated reserves together came to only £39 million. Marks & Spencer's shares were worth £128 million, while their share capital and reserves came to only £20 million.[12]

A firm of London stockbrokers carried out a survey in 1959 which showed that the total value of six ordinary shares valued at £1,000 in 1913 had risen by 1 September 1959 to £73,840.[13]

Again, if £1 million had been invested on 1 January each year since 1919 in a representative group of 'blue chip' industrial equity shares and the gross income had been reinvested at the end of every year, the total value of the fund on 1 January 1960 would have been £646,330,000.[14] Yet again, 'It has been stated that £100 invested in 1951 in each of the following companies would have grown by May 1961 to these pleasing amounts: Jaguar, £3,098; GUS, £2,777; Legal and General, £1,744.[15]

'Never has so much money been made from property as in the decade 1949-59,' wrote Frederick Ellis, City editor of the *Daily Express*. He estimated that nine men had made a total net capital gain of £40,000,000 since the war. The Board of Inland Revenue statistics show that in 1957-58 there were only 2,600 people with incomes, before tax, exceeding £20,000 a year.[16]

Recently the *Economist* carried a study of the British tax system in the course of which it fully confirmed the above analysis:

> Briefly, the rich do not only have more money—they also make it multiply faster. Thus cash and fixed interest securities represent 45 percent of the wealth of individuals with less than £10,000, and equity shares only 5 percent. By contrast, equities represent 56 percent of the wealth of those with over £250,000, and cash and bonds only 22 percent. As a result, the average capital appreciation of the assets held by the wealthiest group, on this average composition, has been 114 percent between 1950 and 1964, while the assets of the £3,000-£10,000 group have appreciated by only 48 percent.[17]

It should be added of course that these figures refer only to the quite well off sections of the population anyway. Only 12.1 percent of the population have wealth invested of more than £3,000. The remaining 87.9 percent of the population undoubtedly saw their few pounds in the Post Office Savings Bank grow by even less than 48 percent.

Nicholas Kaldor calculated that if dividends had risen parallel with industrial production over the last few years—at a rate of somewhat under 3 percent a year—then there would have been an average annual increase in dividend payments of the order of £25 million to £40 million, while at the same time there would have been an average increase in the market value of ordinary shares of £500 million to £800 million a year.[18] This should make it clear that, even if wage rises were kept in step with the rise of dividends, they would be very much out of step with the rise in the value of shares in the market.

Will capital gains tax alter all this?

James Callaghan's capital gains tax won't alter the picture in any real sense. Even when capital gains tax is in full operation, it will—when taken together with stamp duty and death duties, the other two 'wealth taxes'—'still amount to a property levy of under 1 percent a year'.[19] For, quite simply, Callaghan's tax is not a tax on capital. A millionaire who improves his capital position after April 1965 is *not* liable to tax on his gains. He only has to pay the tax if he *realises* his extra wealth by selling his shares. But of course, precisely because he is a millionaire, he can very well afford not to sell, for he can live very nicely on his large income:

> It is not just that the wealthy are financially more sophisticated—they are also genuinely better placed to take risks, and need to keep a smaller proportion of their money unprofitably as a liquid reserve. The awkward fact is that any tendency towards a more even distribution of wealth in Britain is being counteracted all the time by these differences in its composition.[20]

The British rate of capital gains tax (30 percent) is only marginally above the rate that has existed in the United States over the last 30 years (25 percent)—and not one US millionaire has ended his life on the dole so far because of this! Indeed, one of the main effects of the Labour government's tax has been to push the value of shares up still higher because shareholders (to avoid the tax) are less willing to sell. Consider the example of the owner of six ordinary shares valued each at £1,000 in 1913 that we mentioned above. The value of his shares would have risen to £73,480 on 1 September 1959. If he had had to pay Callaghan's capital gains tax his wealth would have risen to 'only' £51,988, which is not too bad really!

Other bonuses for the rich

Nor is capital appreciation the only item on the profits side which the supporters of incomes policy quietly forget. There are also many 'fringe benefits' like expense accounts, trust funds, golden handshakes, tax fiddles, etc, etc.

As regards golden handshakes, a few examples will suffice:

> Some of the cases which received mention in the press in 1959 and 1960 included the following: Lord Portal £30,000 and Mr G Cunliffe £58,000 (British Aluminium takeover, *Economist*, 14 March 1959, p1001); Mr L Nidditch £40,000 (Ely Brewery and Jasper takeover, *Times*, 30 June 1960); Mr Perkins £30,000 (Perkins and Co, *New Statesman*, 7 February 1959); Mr Baron £29,237 (Carreras, *New Statesman*, 7 February 1959); Sir Frank Spriggs £75,000 (Hawker Siddeley, *New Statesman*, 14 March 1959); and Lt Col W H Kingsmill £60,000 plus annual pension of about £4,000 (Taylor Walker, *Times*, 22 June 1959).[21]

Colonel R W W Taylor, former managing director of Lang Pneumatic, received £40,000.[22] R Craig Wood, former managing director of the appliance division of Associated Electrical Industries, received £30,000.[23] Philip G Walker, former managing director of Reed Paper makers, received the huge sum of £124,000 in a golden handshake.[24] And Eric Morland, who served for only 26 months as managing director of Associated Fire Alarms, got a golden handshake of £20,000, or some £25 for every day of his 'service'![25] The reader should not forget that no tax at all is paid on golden handshakes...

As for expense accounts, it was estimated in 1955 that expenditure on spirits and imported wines on business accounts reached the sum of £33 million. A survey of London nightclubs and late-night restaurants showed that most of the bills for entertainment were paid by firms and not by individuals. As the *Economist* put it, 'Only Exchequer *largesse* paid directly via the tax-free expense account keeps the nightclub industry ticking at all'.[26] And Professor Titmuss tells us:

> Lord Kindersley...chairman of Rolls Royce, said that 'most of their cars were bought by companies'. Among employees and directors in the top 1 percent of incomes it appears to be a general practice to provide either cars for their own use or chauffeur-driven cars or car services from a company pool or rental system.[27]

To golden handshakes and expense accounts should be added endowment policies, education trusts and scholarships, non-contributory pensions, etc—most of which are allowable as legitimate business expenses and none of which find their way into the statistics on income distribution.

So even if George Brown's policy guaranteed that dividends didn't rise faster than wages, there would be no guarantee at all that profits as a whole would not rise much faster than wages. Also, even if the rate of growth of wages and profits *were* equal (which it couldn't be in fact), this would still not mean fairness, for the points from which the worker and the capitalist start are quite different. Three percent added to a weekly wage of £10 is nothing like 3 percent added to a profit of £1,000,000. Above all, the assumption that wages and other incomes should grow at the same rate means that the shares of different sections of society in the national cake are to remain the same. What a very conservative policy anyway!

But in fact, when incomes policy is referred to in discussions in the press, in parliament, etc, what is meant almost always is wages:

> There is no doubt that to most managements with whom I have discussed it, an incomes policy (they rarely mention the prices side) means an attempt to discipline the unions, especially at shopfloor level. It means an attempt to come to grips with constantly rising labour costs. And to some it suggests that the government have taken a hand to try to remove restrictive practices.
>
> Hardly an employer regards it as a means of introducing greater social justice into a chaotic wages and salary structure. Yet that is precisely how it is regarded by those trade unionists who support the concept.[28]

Chapter Three: Incomes policy and economic growth

In the first chapter we suggested some of the reasons for the growing respectability of the idea of planning among the capitalists. Planning has become a very popular activity in the Western capitalist countries, and of course a central place in this planning is given to incomes policy. Here we shall try to make clear the logic behind the ideas of the planners, by giving a picture of what it is that George Brown and his co-thinkers imagine will happen if they can only introduce an incomes policy into Britain. This can be represented by a diagram.

The basic assumption is that there is an intimate causal connection between each of the items in the diagram, and that one item inevitably leads into the other in a neat and beautiful chain. The diagram looks like this:

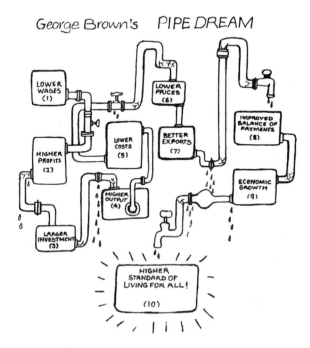

It's a beautiful picture, with each item running into the next one and all adding up to a better standard of living for everyone in Britain. The only thing wrong with it is that it is entirely useless. It's completely remote from the facts of life in capitalist Britain, and about as helpful in understanding reality as a chocolate machine would be in solving problems in higher mathematics. We will follow the argument stage by stage and point our some of the flaws.

Lower (or restrained) wages...higher profits... larger investment...higher output

The first link, between lower wages and higher profits, is true, on one condition: goods must not be sold at an undercutting price. In other words, surplus value must not only be produced but also realised. If, because there is a very high degree of competition, the capitalist can't sell at a profit, then this link won't hold.

As for the second link, it is one of the hoariest of legends that higher profits guarantee higher investments. In the actual conditions of British capitalism the relationship between profits and investment is very far from being as direct or as rational as that. Many British industries spend only a tiny proportion of their profits on investment. For instance, in 1955 the clothing and leather industries had net profits of £48 million, but they spent only £3 million on capital formation. The food, drink and tobacco industries spent only 10 percent of their net profits on investment. In metal manufacture, bricks, pottery and glass the figure was only 12 to 13 percent, and in shipbuilding, engineering and electrical goods it was only 15 percent.[1]

The Department of Scientific and Industrial Research revealed that the entire shipbuilding industry in 1958, with exports valued at £60 million, spent on research and development only 'about £282,000': 'The DSIR report on machine tools was hushed up even more, but one estimate is that the total spent on research in the whole industry, with an output valued at £150 million, is less than £1 million a year'.[2]

Indeed, the whole shipbuilding industry employed not more than 120 qualified men on research and development.[3] And investment in the shipyards between 1951 and 1954 didn't even cover the wear and tear in the industry—investment was about £4 million a year, while equipment written off as worn out, etc amounted to £9 million a year.[4]

The assumption lying behind this link between profits and investment overlooks not only the monopolistic organisation of industry and its effect on investment, but also the effect of government policies. In the recurrent balance of payments crises since the war—in 1947, 1949, 1951, 1955, 1957, etc, etc—one of the first things to be hit each time has been industrial investment. This, after all, is one of the causes of Britain's stagnation.

The third link in the chain, the assumption that higher investment must lead to corresponding increases in productivity and output, is even weaker. Some seven years ago Andrew Shonfield assumed that an investment in new manufacturing capacity worth £100 will probably produce at least £33 of additional output each year.[5] He even tried to support his argument by adducing figures to show that the rate could be still higher, quoting T Barna who calculated that the figure would be £45.[6]

However, the assumption that the national income will grow at a fixed rate associated with a certain rise in capital investment completely overlooks the question of the *rate of use* of capital investment. To have a lot of expensive machinery is one thing, but to use it at full capacity is quite another. The following table shows that the rate of use of capital investment varies quite considerably between Western capitalist countries:

ANNUAL AVERAGE RATE OF GROWTH (1950–60)[7]

	(1) Growth of GNP per employee	(2) Growth of capital stock per employee	(1) as a proportion of (2)
West Germany	5.0	4.6	1.09
France	3.9	3.0	1.30
Netherlands	3.6	3.5	1.03
United Kingdom	2.1	2.9	0.72

Thus in France every unit of investment gave an increase in the national cake almost double that in Britain.

Between 1957 and 1961 investment in Britain went ahead very quickly, while there was no acceleration in the growth of the national income. The ratio of the increase in capital to the resultant increase in output was one of 7.5 to one.[8]

The reason why a rise in investment does not lead inevitably to a corresponding increase in the size of the national product is to be found in the 'leakage' (or flaw) of unused capacity. If every machine installed in the factories were used to its capacity, then probably Shonfield's or even Barna's optimistic estimate would fit the facts. As it is, their estimates are just wrong. In the Institute of Economic and Social Research inquiry in 1963 into the mechanical engineering industry, only 6 percent of the firms reported that they had no spare plant capacity. On average the firms in the industry indicated that with the plant and equipment they already had they could increase output by some 22 percent. Firms in the motor vehicle industry could increase output by 15 percent.[9]

The best proof, perhaps, that there is no necessary connection between increased investment and corresponding increases in output lies in the fact that while the investment ratio in Britain rose rapidly and reasonably steadily in the post-war years (from 12.8 percent of the gross national product in 1950 to about 17.2 percent in 1963) industrial output did not show a parallel rise.

Higher output...lower costs...lower prices

The first link, between larger output and cheaper costs, is true. The second link, from cheaper costs to lower prices, would be true if we completely overlooked the existence of monopolies. Monopolies in fact play a major part in keeping prices high. It is important that this is understood in the labour movement, since high prices in Britain are often explained as due to rising wages. It is taken as self-evident by many that 'cost-push' resulting from trade union wage demands is at the root of the wage-price spiral that Britain has suffered over the last two decades, and is thus the cause of Britain's declining share in world trade. Thus the general council of the TUC, in the report recommending George Brown's incomes policy to the Conference of Trade Union Executive Committees, argued that 'the main reason why British exports lagged behind those of other countries was that incomes generally have grown disproportionately faster'.[10]

The facts, however, do not confirm this contention. Compared with its European rivals, Britain is certainly not suffering from greater wage inflation. Earnings in manufacturing industry have gone up half as much again in France and Germany, and twice as much in Italy. And as far as earnings per unit of output—in other words, wage costs—are concerned, the picture is the same, as the table on the next page shows.

In fact as the following chart, adapted from *DATA Journal* (June 1965), demonstrates clearly, British wages are at a generally lower level than among the main European competitors:

It is difficult, in view of these figures, to hold that British prices are high because of high wage costs. Thus it is extremely difficult to see much strength in the link between cheaper costs and lower prices.

Comparative wages: estimated hourly earnings of industrial workers, including social benefits, September 1964

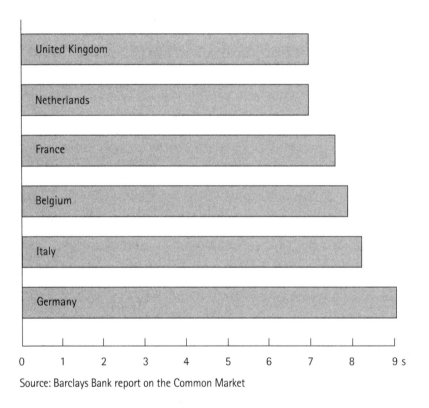

Source: Barclays Bank report on the Common Market

THE FIVE-YEAR MYSTERY (Source: NIESR. All figures are for manufacturing)[11]

	Percentage increase (1959–64) in:			
	Hourly earnings	Earnings per unit of output	Output per man hour	Exports (value)
Britain	35	13	20	28
West Germany	54	19	30	66
France	50	19	26	57
Italy	74	24	41	128
United States	15	4	20	53

Lower prices...better exports... improved balance of payments

The first link is partly true—but only partly. Selling abroad (like selling anywhere) is not only dependent on price, but also on other factors, like the quality of the goods being offered, the delivery dates that can be guaranteed, after-sales service, and so on. These are all matters of great importance to potential foreign buyers, and they are not necessarily connected with prices at all. As for the second link, between increased exports and an improved balance of payments, so much claptrap is talked about this that we need to go into this question in a little more detail. Britain has lived almost permanently in a balance of payments crisis (or the threat of one) ever since the Second World War. The years 1953, 1959 and 1963 were the only odd-numbered years in which there was no such crisis. But let's get the picture clear. Were these crises the result of Britain's failure to export enough?

The first thing that has to be said is that, while Britain's imports today are about five times bigger than before the Second World War, exports are eight times bigger. *Exports have grown faster than imports.*

In the first five years after the war there was a balance of payments deficit only in 1946-47, and a surplus thereafter. During the 1950s, a decade of supposedly chronic inflation, the deficit on the visible trade balance went down radically—from £302 million in 1938 and an average of nearly £250 million for 1952-54 to little more than £50 million for 1955-59.[12] If we take rising prices into account, the deficit on the balance of trade went down between 1938 and 1955-59 by as much as 90 percent. On present day prices, the pre-war adverse trade balance (£302 million in 1938) would today have amounted to some £1,000 million. Yet instead it has been only £50 million. If one excludes spending by the government abroad (mainly on military establishments, with which we will deal later), the years 1960-64 saw an average surplus in the current account of £260 million a year.[13]

'In the 13 years from 1950 to 1962 there were deficits on current account [and that includes expenses by the government abroad] in only four years, and there was an average surplus of £70 million'.[14]

In fact the numerous crises in the balance of payments were caused, not by deficits in the current balance of payments—which has become increasingly *healthy*—but by movements of capital out of Britain. As Thorneycroft said at the time of the 1957 crisis, when he was Chancellor of the Exchequer, 'Our problems therefore arise not so much as a trader but as a banker and overseas investor. Our difficulties are much more on capital than on current account'.[15] And Callaghan recently made the same point.

One authority summed the situation up very clearly when he said:

> The United Kingdom have exported capital on a scale never before equalled... official estimates for long term capital exports since the war yield an accumulated total of some £4,500 million. In monetary terms this was as much as the whole of the United Kingdom's overseas investments before the war (which of course had been accumulated over 100 years).[16]

In the five years 1960-64 the annual average export of private capital reached some £318 million.

The trend towards increasing exports of capital is inherent in the nature of modern capitalism. In the face of increasing international competition large companies are finding it more and more useful to establish subsidiary companies abroad. This is one expression of the growing conflict between the productive forces and the boundaries of the national state in contemporary capitalism. Thus in 1955 it was estimated that the sales made by subsidiary companies of US firms operating outside the United States were worth more than twice the annual volume of US exports.[17] The top 200 corporations in the US are said to derive a quarter of their incomes from foreign investments.[18] Similarly, large British companies like Unilever and ICI are finding it increasingly profitable to build subsidiaries all over the world.

While the export of capital worsens Britain's balance of payments position, its impact is made that much greater by the fact that nowadays the profits from the investments abroad are not brought back to Britain in the way they used to be. In the past the profits earned abroad were remitted regularly to the country from which the investment was made. But today, both at home and abroad, there is a tendency towards the reinvestment rather than the redistribution of profits. We have already said that the large shareholder nowadays tends to prefer profits in the form of capital gain to profits in the form of dividends, and the same is true of large companies with investments abroad. Today the majority of companies prefer to reinvest the profits from their successful foreign investments in overseas businesses—in line with the general tendency of 'ploughing back'—rather than to bring the money home.

How effective can controls on capital exports be?

It is altogether utopian to try to stop the export of capital under capitalism— in other words, as long as industry and finance are owned and controlled by a tiny minority. This is especially true of British capitalism, whose home market consists of only some 50 million people. The only thing a capitalist government can do to slow down the flow of capital abroad is to make the conditions for home investment more attractive to the capitalists:

> The only way to prevent the runaway of capital is by making Britain as attractive a place to the owners of capital as any possible alternative abroad. This at once sets pretty narrow limits to what the government can do about taxation, about social expenditure, about nationalisation, and a number of other major political issues. Here in fact is the vicarious reassertion of the political power of the owners of wealth.[19]

As long as industry is privately owned and as long as the commercial banks are privately owned there are many loopholes in any attempt that may be made to control the movement of capital. Those who have large sums of money which they wish to move abroad can do it quite easily, whatever the government of the time thinks is good for Britain.

Let's consider a simple example of how this can be done. If a car producer sells a car, say in Argentina, and the price of the car is £1,000, all he has to do is to write £950 on his invoice and arrange that, while the £950 is transferred to Britain, the other £50 will be salted away for him in a bank in Argentina. Or if an importer of meat buys £1,000 worth of Argentinian beef, all he has to do is to arrange for an inflated invoice of £1,050 to be sent to him—he sends off the money, and again the extra £50 is put away for him in Argentina. When we remember that Britain's foreign trade is worth some £10,000 million a year, it's easy to see that a 'mistake' of only 1 percent in pricing will mean a loss of £100 million to Britain. And a 'mistake' of a couple of percentage points can very easily go undetected. Ferranti made a mistake in its tendering for the Bloodhound Mark 1 missile and got 72 percent profit instead of the 7 percent that had been planned, and that mistake took many months to detect!

Or again, there is another way out to capital, through what might be called the 'Bahamas Gap':

> The Bahamanian tax structure is, to say the least, unusual. Government income comes from stiff import duties, and a $2 levy collected from each departing tourist. There is no income tax, capital gains tax, inheritance tax, or tax on real estate. Resident millionaires can invest their money in profitable ventures, such as property, without worrying about taxes. British firms can channel funds through Nassau offshoots, and use profits for overseas operations, without Mr Callaghan getting a look-in.[20]

The ease with which capital can be transferred out of the country explains how wealthy English people managed to stay on the French Riviera and spend thousands of pounds in the period when exchange control didn't allow you to take more than £25 out of the country. Probably every one of those tourists took his allotted £25 with him, but added, say, 25,000 shares in ICI or Shell. 'A man holding high and responsible office' in exchange control told Andrew Shonfield, 'Nobody but small fry takes any notice of exchange control'.[21]

The attitude of many City financiers was expressed in memorable terms by Mr W J Keswick (director of a merchant bank as well as of the Bank of England) in a letter he wrote to the Far East firm of Jardine Matheson of Hong Kong. Mr Keswick advised the firm to sell a substantial portion of its holdings of British government securities and to switch its funds to North American securities. He wrote, 'This is anti-British and derogatory to sterling but on balance, if one is free to do so, it makes sense to me'.[22]

Of course, as the government knows, even if exchange control did work perfectly, the prohibition or limitation of capital exports could only have a very detrimental effect on the working of the British capitalist economy. For if the Labour government were to impose an embargo on capital exports—making the idiotic assumption for the moment that this could be done without the nationalisation of industry and of the commercial banks—the capitalists' immediate reaction would be to go 'on strike'. In other words, they wouldn't invest at all, but would wait for a change of government and for the reopening of channels for the export of capital. After all, if one can get 30 percent profit on capital invested abroad, and only 15 percent on capital invested in Britain, it's still very worthwhile to wait for a few years to invest abroad. Besides, if the government allows that 15 percent profit on investment in Britain is quite fair and all right, why should it say there's anything wrong with 30 percent abroad?

Military expenditure abroad

As well as the capital exports leak, there is another leak of resources from Britain that has a very bad effect on the balance of payments. This is the expenditure in foreign currency on keeping British troops stationed abroad.

In 1934-38 the government's overseas expenditure amounted to £6 million a year. In 1956 military expenditure abroad, including the Suez operation, rose to £178 million.[23] In 1964 the cost in foreign currency of the military bases abroad was as high as £334 million.[24] This was divided roughly as follows:

OVERSEAS BASES, 1964[25]

	Uniformed manpower	Approximate annual cost (£ million)
BOAR (Germany)	52,000	85
Singapore & Malaya	32,000	100
Aden & Saudi Arabia	12,500	20
Gan (Maldives)	500	2
Bahrein	3,000	10
Cyprus	12,500	20
Other	16,500	53
TOTAL	129,000	290

It should be understood that the above table refers only to expenses in foreign currency. The total cost of keeping British troops abroad is a great deal larger. Thus, for instance, Denis Healey, Secretary of State for Defence, gave the cost of keeping British troops in Germany at £180 million in 1964,[26] while the cost in foreign currency amounted to only £85 million.

A few items in this expense account are worth noting: first, naval officers' flats in Gibraltar cost over £9,000 each to build;[27] second, 'an establishment of 115 dogs in Singapore (including 102 dog handlers) cost a total of £110,101 to maintain, or not far short of £1,000 per dog per annum'.[28]

The cost of keeping one police dog in Singapore 'to discipline the natives' is about the same as the cost of keeping five old age pensioners in Britain. Harold Wilson is right—socialism is about priorities!

'By 1968 an infantry battalion of the Rhine army will cost six times as much to equip as it did in 1963'.[29] What is true of the Rhine is equally true of our 'mission' east of Suez.

As long as Britain is dominated by big business, and as long as profits in the Middle East are a great deal fatter than they are in Britain, the keeping of troops there to defend 'our oil' is inevitable. And as long as big business dominates and the NATO alliance is its by-product, 'our role' east of Suez is justified.

Military expenditure damages the balance of payments in other ways too, quite apart from the direct spending of foreign currency on 'our' bases abroad. Firstly, military production has directly lost Britain certain overseas business which could not be fulfilled because the productive resources of the British engineering industry were stretched to the limit by arms orders. Secondly, it has had the more indirect effect of holding back investment and so has held back expansion of our industrial capacity, which would among other things have produced more exports. Thirdly, military production has monopolised certain of our scarce resources—particularly research and electronics—and this again has affected economic growth, including growth of exports. As *The National Plan* explained:

> As a nation we spend as much on defence as we do on industrial plant and machinery; appreciably more than we do on all durable consumer goods, from motor cars to TV sets, electric fires and furniture; and nearly 50 percent more than on publicly financed education of all kinds. The defence programme now uses some 35-40 percent of total national research and development expenditure and about one fifth of of the qualified scientists and technologists engaged in it.[30]

And, fourthly, the arms that are produced—particularly aeroplanes—depend in part on expensive imports of foreign materials and so cause an increase in the import bill.

Now, if capital flows out of Britain at the rate of £300 million a year, and another £350 million flows out in the form of military expenditures in foreign currency, these two items alone have to be balanced by exports worth £650 million a year. Actually, as exports have an import content of 20 percent, this figure is much higher, nearer £800 million. Thus British workers have to produce goods worth *more than £2 million a day* just to pay for these two items by themselves.

If the Labour government is not ready to do anything more than a spot of tinkering with the flow of capital exports, and is not ready to put an end to the cost of keeping British troops overseas, then there is no other choice. The Labour government can only strengthen the balance of payments by sacrificing the workers' standards to help 'our' export drive.

The international banking leak

Together with the two basic leaks, capital exports and military expenditure abroad, both of which cause radical instability in the balance of payments, there is a third factor which makes any sterling crisis worse once it starts. This is Britain's involvement in the international banking business, and it has aggravated the pressures to which the pound has become exposed.

Even before the crisis of November 1964 the British reserves amounted to only one tenth—actually slightly less than one tenth—of the value of Britain's foreign trade. And since the pound is an international reserve currency, it had also to cope with fluctuations in the trade of other members of the sterling area. By contrast the reserves of Germany, which does not have an international reserve currency, are about a quarter of the annual foreign trade, and those of the United States amount to about one half of foreign trade. Britain's role as an international banker has contributed enormously to its proneness to currency crises.

The movements of 'hot money' only add to the general instability, and the cost to the economy is incalculable:

> It is probably not going too far to say that the Bank's advocacy of bank rate excesses has cost the UK something like $2,000 million in additional interest payments on overseas debt during the past ten years or so—an amount closely approaching the sum we have to borrow from the IMF to survive the latest crisis.[31]

The indirect cost was much greater, though it is quite immeasurable. To defend sterling as an international currency, again and again a succession of Chancellors of the Exchequer have had to put their feet on the brakes—and the national economy has paid the price in stagnation.

More and more business circles have come to the not very surprising conclusion that British capitalism could very well do without the advantages of sterling as an international reserve currency:

> Our experiences during the past year may well be seen as endorsing the view that the UK would be better off if it were to withdraw from its international banker activities altogether and leave the job of meeting the world's need for a medium of exchange and all related tasks to others. And it is not without significance in this connection that, though a number of continental countries have been in a good position for many years to push out into this field, they have been careful to avoid doing so, taking the view that it was a game not worth the candle.[32]

However, getting out of the game isn't quite so easy. Firstly, as the same writer in the *Financial Times* put it, 'The business is so closely tied up with our sterling debts that such a retreat would be easier said than done'.[33]

Secondly, there are the vested interests of the City of London. After all, the City's earnings from its banking, insurance, merchanting and brokerage services reached an estimated £185 million in 1963.[34]

Thirdly, many of the industrial groups, like the great food processing and tobacco combines, with 15 percent of their input coming from imports and only 4 percent of their output being exported, side with the City as regards sterling.[35] In sum, to get sterling away from its international standing, when it has served British capitalism so well in the past, is extremely difficult. To do it would demand an upheaval of at least some strong citadels of power and privilege.

The factors leading to the great instability in the British balance of payments— capital exports, spending on armed forces overseas, and the position of sterling as an international currency—make for the heavy dependence of British economic policy on the international banking community. In Harold Wilson's language, there are 'the gnomes of Zurich'—only it should be remembered that some of the most powerful members of that eminent fraternity are also among the giants of the City of London. As Shonfield put it:

> We should recognise frankly that, having become so dependent on the mood and whim of foreign investors for the country's essential solvency, Britain has already lost control over a large part of her domestic policy. The brutal fact is that there are many things which the government might like to do, but dare not do at the moment because of the fear of the effect which they might have on sentiment abroad.[36]

The truth of this was driven home more recently. Thus, for instance, the *Financial Times* stated on 6 October 1965:

> As for the proposed early warning legislation itself, it is as well to be clear about the origins of this. It was, quite simply, the condition laid down by the international monetary authorities, and in particular by the United States Secretary of State for the Treasury, Mr Fowler, for the September support operation for sterling. Hence Mr Brown's unexpected and desperate dash to Brighton to see the TUC.

In conclusion, between the three items—lower prices, increased exports and improved balance of payments—there is a connection. They are not entirely unlinked. But unfortunately there are so many flaws that even quite a large wage restraint at the beginning of the process would have almost no impact at all on the balance of payments situation.

Improved balance of payments...economic growth...higher standard of living for all

Even if George Brown's incomes policy worked, and if after years of wage restraint the national cake did increase in size, who can guarantee that workers' standards would radically improve? It is only under exceptional conditions that the share of wages in the national income rises under capitalism (it did, briefly, in the period of the last war, though it soon fell back again), but it is always possible for the share of wages to fall. Indeed, there is an inherent tendency under capitalism for wages to do so. This tendency can only be prevented by vigorous trade union activity on the part of the working class. In the long run higher wages will always be passed on in the form of higher prices, to protect the rate of profit, but there is no 'countervailing tendency' in capitalism which pushes wages up together with higher profits or higher prices:

> A gain in their (the workers') real standard of living of nearly 44 percent in 11 years—3$\frac{1}{2}$ percent per annum compound—does not stand up against a rise of 200 percent (in real terms) in the value of equity shares which the owners of equity shares enjoyed, which was at the rate of 10$\frac{1}{2}$ percent per annum compound. And the workers never managed to win a larger share of the national income. Their share remained at a little over 42 percent throughout the Conservative regime.[37]

And this was a period, moreover, in which there was no 'incomes policy' to inhibit the workers' demands! Nor are things better under Labour in this respect:

> Britain was one of only four countries where workers' actual purchasing power decreased last year, according to a report by the International Labour Organisation published in Geneva yesterday. The others were Ireland, Hungary and South Korea. In industrialised countries generally, workers were more prosperous last year than ever before, says the report.[38]

And with international competition increasing each year, the distance between the sacrifice that the workers are asked to make now and the payment they are told they will get later is likely to grow even longer.

For socialists, of course, there is also a more fundamental question to be considered. An incomes policy that succeeds means a working class that is submissive, and that demands no more than its rulers offer. Such a working class, without spirit or fight, might crawl and quarrel for the crumbs beneath its masters' tables, but would hardly be likely to demand the whole loaf. However well fed, would such a working class be well placed to achieve its own emancipation? After all, there are many farmers who warm their cowsheds to get more milk, but we are still waiting to hear of the farmer who gives over control of his shed to the cows.

Chapter Four: George Brown's plan and George Brown's planners

A capitalist plan

An incomes policy is a central ingredient of George Brown's national economic plan. There is no space in the framework of the present book to deal adequately with the plan. We shall try only to point out its clear capitalist nature, the fact that its basis consists in raising capital investment (ie profit) compared with consumption (ie wages).

The National Plan is not obligatory, merely advisory. It is indicative. On the one hand it is a coordinated national market forecast, and on the other hand it tries to coordinate the activities of different industries within a total economic perspective.

The plan was composed as a result of assembling the replies to a questionnaire sent to firms and trade associations (none of whom would dream of telling the world that they would fail to raise production swiftly or that their export performance would be inadequate): 'Industries were asked what 25 percent national growth from 1964 to 1970 would mean for them'.[1]

Thus the industries' estimates used in the plan were not forecasts of what they expected to achieve, but hypothetical statements of what they could achieve given certain assumptions.

However, whether the plan is realised or not—and on the basis of the first 18 months of the Wilson Government, with production almost stagnant, one must be very gullible to believe Brown's hope that it will—its success depends above all on the close collaboration of the capitalists with the government. As was stated in connection with another plan, that in France:

> The first and indispensable condition for successful economic planning in the context of modern capitalism is confidence on the part of the business community in the seriousness of the government's intentions, as stated in the plan.[2]

> The large corporations, who are interested in planning as a means of reducing the uncertainties of investment and of achieving the orderly development of their markets, exercise their pressures too. The plan reflects, in large part, their ideas—or at least a compromise between their wishes and those of the officials responsible for government economic policy.[3]

> The planners make no secret of their belief in the iron law of oligarchy.[4]

George Brown's planning organisation is also, as we shall see below, dominated by representatives of big business.

To help realise an indicative plan, ie a non-obligatory one, which relies on changing the environment in which big business works, on persuading it to act as the government wants, there is no other way than that of giving financial inducement—to big business above all, seeing that their profits (and hence investment) rise relatively more quickly than wages (and hence consumption).

And this is the central theme of George Brown's plan. The priorities of the National Plan are made only too clear: 'Investment lies at the heart of the plan'.[5]

The plan visualises the following rise in investment over the years 1964-70:

Chemicals—1964 £190 million, 1970 £300 million.[6]
Iron and steel—1964 £58.85 million, 1970 £100 million.[7]
Mechanical engineering—1964 £124 million, 1970 £170 million.[8]
Electrical engineering—1964 £49 million, 1970 £65 million.[9]
Electronics—1964 £26 million, 1970 £37 million.[10]

Fixed investment in manufacturing rose by 2.4 percent a year from 1960 to 1964. The Tories' 'Neddy' plan wanted to raise this to 4 percent for the years 1961-66. But George Brown's plan wants to get it up to 7 percent a year![11]

On the other hand, the Neddy plan promised an annual increase in *consumption* of 2.8 percent per head of the population. But George Brown's plan promises a rise of only 2.4 percent a year between 1964 and 1970.[12] This target is only very marginally above the *actual* results for 1960-64—a 2.2 percent rise. The following table shows how very low Brown's targets for consumption are:

AVERAGE ANNUAL PERCENTAGE INCREASE IN CONSUMERS' EXPENDITURE[13]			
	1954–60	1960–64	1964–70
Food	2.0	1.6	1.3
Beer	2.1	2.7	1.7
Tobacco	2.4	0.6	0.5
Housing	2.4	2.7	3.1
Motors	15.2	15.6	7.4
Clothing	4.5	2.1	3.2

And what about good old Clause Four? The plan visualises the running down of the public sector compared with the private. Thus the plan for railways prophesies 'substantial progress…in implementing closure proposals'.[14] So employment on the railways will continue to go down swiftly, from 449,000 in 1960 to 390,000 in 1964, and to only 227,000 in 1970.[15] Similarly, in the mines the labour force will continue to decline, only at a more accelerated rate. From 1960 to 1964 the number of miners went down from 670,000 to 583,000, and this number is to be drastically cut to 409,000 in 1970.[16]

Other branches of state industry are to be axed too. Thus fixed investment in electricity, which rose annually by 13.2 percent in 1960-64, will rise by only 3.2 percent from 1964 to 1970.[17] Taking gas and electricity together, the figures tell the same story: 10.8 percent from 1960 to 1964, but 7.3 percent from 1964 to 1970.[18] The same tendency for public industry to be subordinated to private industry is shown in the changes in demand for capital engineering goods in the two sectors. The average annual percentage increase for private industry will rise from 5.4 percent in 1960-64 to 8.7 in 1964-70, but for public investment the figures show a reverse trend, from 9.9 to 4.4 percent.[19]

Pensions

During the 1964 election campaign Wilson, Brown, Callaghan and Co promised that if they were elected they would give old age pensioners a pension equal to half pay. Remember? Well, forget about it again. The plan states, in the most cynical and inhuman manner, 'An income guarantee would not contribute towards faster economic growth'.[20]

Of course, George Brown is quite right—a higher pension wouldn't contribute towards economic growth, for old age pensioners don't produce a thing. Actually, it would be better still to pay them a lower pension—the old people would get very cold without any fires at all, and they would have less food, and so we'd be rid of them that much faster, and the burden on the economy would be less…

The plan goes on to state:

From the studies so far undertaken, it is clear that radical changes in the pension arrangements are bound to take some time to carry out if they are to be soundly based to meet the needs of coming generations and if care is to be taken that the cost can be met without damage to the economy. Although, therefore, work is proceeding on a new pension scheme, it will not have any significant effect on expenditure up to 1970.[21]

So there we are. The pension arrangements would take such a long time to work out that only 'coming generations'—in other words, babies who aren't even born yet—can hope to benefit from them!

Defence expenditure

'Defence expenditure had been planned (by the Tories) to continue at about the same proportion of the national product'.[22]

But Labour are much more radical than the Tories—they plan to cut the defence budget from 7 percent of the national income to 6 percent, and to limit it to £2,000 million at constant prices.[23] Over the years 1964-70 they plan to raise total defence expenditure by about 6 percent, or about £115 million.[24] Scrap Polaris? Bring home the (expensive) troops from abroad? There's never a whisper of any such idea throughout the plan.

Profits and wages

There is one aspect of economic life about which the National Plan is strangely reticent. Throughout the plan there is a mass of rich detail on so many subjects. We are told, for instance, how much we are going to spend on beer, tobacco, travelling, entertainments and so on in different years in the future. But in all the wealth of detail there is not one single figure from the first page to the last on either profits or wages, or on the level of profits in relation to the level of wages. This omission is most revealing.

According to the plan there is to be a deliberate shift from consumption to investment. This can only mean that the plan rests on the unstated assumption that there will be a shift from wages to profits. That is why an incomes policy is so important to the plan. For the real significance of the incomes policy as a wages policy is that it is a very straightforward policy of wage restraint, in the interests of higher profits. In this way, it is assumed, Britain will have a little economic 'miracle' like the German, French, Italian and Japanese 'miracles' we described in the first chapter.

A democratic plan?

George Brown's plan was drafted on the basis of discussion with the management side of industry and on information supplied by business. Not even the Labour MPs, let alone the rank and file of the labour movement, were consulted about it. The first time the plan was discussed by the Parliamentary

Labour Party was on the morning of 3 November 1965—the eve of parliament's reassembly after the summer holidays, and some six weeks after the plan was published.

It's not surprising, of course, that the labour movement was not consulted, for Brown's plan is based on the subordination of consumption to capital accumulation, on the sacrifice of wages to profits, and on the neglect of the old age pensioners. George Brown's plan is a plan for the capitalists, not a plan for the working class, and as such it will have to be rejected and resisted by trade union militants and socialists.

The planners

To run a capitalist plan and its twin brother, a capitalist incomes policy, who could be more suitable than a bunch of business people? Look at the list of members of the National Board for Prices and Incomes (* denotes part time member):

The Rt Hon Aubrey Jones (chairman)
Former Tory MP.
Chairman Staveley Industries Ltd.
Director Guest, Keen and Nettlefolds Steel Co Ltd.

The Rt Hon Hilary Adhir Marquand (joint vice-chairman)
Labour MP 1955-60.
Former director International Institute for Labour Relations, Geneva.

Mr Duncan Dewdney (joint vice-chairman)
Managing director Esso Petroleum.

James Mortimer Peddie (Baron Peddie)
Director CWS Ltd.
Director Co-Operative Insurance.
Director West Norfolk Fertiliser Co.
Director British Luna Lamp Co.
Director Co-Operative Building Society.

Peter Edward Trench, CBE*
Former director National Federation of Building Trades Employers.
Director National Building Agency.
Runs his own firm of industrial consultants.

Robert Willis
Member General Council of the TUC.
General secretary (joint) National Graphical Association.

Jasper Frederick Knight*
Director Iron and Steel Board.
Director Chemical and Industrial Investment Co.
Director (Financial) Unilever Ltd.
Director Union Provident Trust Ltd.
Director Unilever NV (Dutch part).
Director Unilever Savings Bank Ltd.

Ronald George Middleton, DSO*
Partner in the legal firm Coward, Chance and Co.
Deputy chairman J H Sankey and Son.
Director Philip Morris and Co Ltd.
Director Sisalkraft Holdings Ltd.

Dr Joan Mitchell*
Reader in economics at Nottingham University.

It is nothing new, of course, for a Labour government to hand over planning to representatives of big business, as the experience of the 1945-51 government showed. Then big business itself administered the controls over business, as Rogow and Shore showed in their excellent study, *The Labour Government and British Industry* (Oxford, 1955). The following selection is drawn from their work.

The Chief Planning Officer, 1947-51, was Sir Edwin Plowden, a director of British Aluminium and two other companies. The Capital Issues Committee consisted of seven bankers, stockbrokers and industrialists plus one Treasury official, who, being the secretary, took no active part in the proceedings. The chief industrial adviser to the Board of Trade was Sir William Palmer, chairman of the British Rayon Federation. Most of the advisers and commodity directors of the Ministry of Food were representatives of business interests, paid by their firms. Unilever alone filled 90 posts in the Ministry of Food, 12 of them senior posts! A director of the Iron and Steel Federation headed the Steel Rearmament Panel of the Ministry of Supply, and the personnel of the various metals controls were drawn largely from the Non-Ferrous Metals Federation. The same story was equally true of leather, matches (the match controller even had his offices on Bryant and May's premises!), paper, footwear, hosiery, furniture, tobacco, alcohol, cotton, timber, newsprint, meat importing, clothing, sweets, nickel, tungsten, sulphur, etc, etc, etc. As long as business thought that controls were useful, business controlled the controls.

And when the capitalists had had enough of controls, they were extremely well placed to end them:

> Pressure to de-control industry, put upon the government by its advisers, was a factor of importance in the controls 'bonfire' of 1948-50. It was an unusual week in 1951 when the newspapers and periodicals did not feature a detailed criticism of the policy.[25]

The former controller of meat and livestock in the Ministry of Food attacked the bulk purchase of meat, the former London regional director of the Ministry of Works attacked building controls, the chairman of the Milk Marketing Board criticised government milk policy, the chairman of the Cotton Board criticised cotton policy, etc, etc.

Other parts of the present government's planning agencies tell the same story—business runs the planning:

NATIONAL ECONOMIC DEVELOPMENT COUNCIL ECONOMIC DEVELOPMENT COMMITTEES[26]

Industry	Chairman	
Building	Sir Jock Campbell	Booker Bros Mc Connell and Co Ltd (chairman)
Chemicals	Mr G H Beeby	British Titan Products Co Ltd (chairman)
Chocolate and sugar confectionery	Sir Joseph Latham CBE	Associated Electrical Industries Ltd (deputy chairman) Booker Bros
Civil engineering	Sir Jock Campbell	Board of Trade McConnell and Co Ltd (chairman)
Distributive trades	Mr H T Weeks	Industrial and Commercial Finance Corporation Ltd (director)
Electrical engineering	Sir Leslie Robinson KBE, CB	Finance Corporation for Industry (director)
Electronics	Sir Edward Playfair KCB	Formerly second secretary Westminster Bank Ltd (director)
Food processing	Sir Joseph Latham CBE	Associated Electrical Industries Ltd (deputy chairman)
Machine tools	Sir Steuart Mitchell KCB, CB	Shipbuilding Industry Training Board (chairman)
Mechanical engineering	Mr D A Dewdney	National Board for Prices and Incomes (joint vice-chairman)
Movement of exports	Lord Caldecote	British Aircraft Corporation (deputy managing director)
Paper and board	Sir Thomas Robson MBE, FCA	Price, Waterhouse and Co chartered accountants (senior partner)
Rubber	Mr J E Bolton DSC	Solartron Electronic Group Ltd (former chairman and managing director)
Wool textiles	Mr W H Mosley Isle FCA	Peat, Marwick, Mitchell and Co (former partner)

The only difference between this table and the situation between 1945 and 1951 is that the people are a bit more mixed up between industries. Naturally, other members of the councils are directly concerned with the particular industries. And if the chairman isn't actually from the particular industry, it is clear from the list that there is no fear that any of these 'planners' are likely to be hostile to business and its interests.

Probably the key appointment is that of Chief Industrial Adviser to the Department of Economic Affairs. This post has been filled by Mr Fred Catherwood, managing director of British Aluminium, who has been lent to the government for a period of two years by his company. His salary has continued to be paid by British Aluminium while he is in official employment. His main task so far has been that of organising the official side of the still embryonic industrial bodies, the Economic Development Committees ('little Neddies').

Chapter Five: The wages front

National wage negotiation and wage drift

Workers' earnings depend on two main factors—firstly, industry-wide bargaining between the national trade union or group of unions and the corresponding employers' organisation, and, secondly, bargaining within the individual firm. Generally speaking, national minimum rates are bargained on the national level, while at the local level negotiation takes place over such matters as piece-work rates and other forms of payment by results, additions to wage rates such as bonuses, and local rules and practices including the manning of machines and demarcation questions. Of course, this two-tier system of negotiating does not apply to all workers. Where there is only one employer, who fixes a standard rate of earnings for all workers in his employment —as in the public services, on the railways and buses, and in teaching—the two-tier system does not apply. Broadly speaking, the two-tier system applies to most of the private sector, with the exception of highly centralised areas like the banks.

Where there is only a one-tier system of negotiation, the national collective agreement must specify the actual pay received by workers quite closely.[1] Most of the 'wage drift' which we discuss below is generated in industries with the two-tier system of negotiation, but a two-tier system has a quite large, although indirect, impact on the one-tier system, because workers in one industry always compare their actual earnings with what workers in other industries are getting. This process has been called 'leap-frogging'. National bargaining in the two-tier system between the union or group of unions and the employers' organisation determines the national minimum wage for a particular industry. This is not necessarily what workers in that industry earn, however. Thus, for example, in 1964 the national standard time rate for an engineering fitter was £10 11s 8d, but actual average earnings for all fitters on time rate (excluding overtime) were £16.[2] The difference between nationally negotiated wage rates and actual earnings is called the 'wage drift':

Since 1948 the standard wage has fallen as a proportion of average wage earnings in most industries, while the importance of supplementary payments—the difference between the nationally negotiated wage rate and earnings (excluding overtime payments)—has grown. As a proportion of earnings, supplementary payments in manufacturing rose from about 19 percent in 1948 to about 26 percent in 1959.[3]

Although wage drift has played an increasingly important part over the economy as a whole since the war, it actually varies quite considerably between the different industries, to a large extent according to the strength and organisation of the workers in the different firms. The following table illustrates this:

ESTIMATED SHARE OF SUPPLEMENTARY PAYMENTS IN EARNINGS FOR A STANDARD WEEK, OCTOBER 1959[4]

Leather, leather goods and fur	13.9 percent
Food, drink and tobacco	14.5 percent
Paper and printing	17.8 percent
Chemical and allied trades	27.1 percent
Metal-using industries	27.4 percent
Metal manufacture	29.3 percent

In the building industry the wage drift is very large. Thus, while the three-year agreement signed recently offers builders an increase of 9$\frac{1}{2}$d an hour spread over three years, the actual bonus on building sites of London is very often about five or six shillings an hour.

Actually, the term 'wage drift' is a little misleading. It would be much better called wage *drive*, since it is the result of pressure from workers in the better organised industries and firms under conditions of full employment.

Now the impact of wage drift (or wage drive) on the general standard of earnings is much greater than it looks in the simple calculation of the proportion of wage drift in the nationally agreed minimum wage. This can be seen if we look at the *dynamics* of wage bargaining.

Let us assume that national negotiations gave a fitter a minimum wage of £5 a week, and that in a whole number of factories the wage drift amounted to another £1 a week. In the next round of national bargaining the pressure in *all* factories would be to raise the national minimum to £6 a week, and again the better organised workers would push ahead for a further wage drift, and so on and so on. In this way the most advanced section of the engineering workers would affect not only the actual wage drift, but also the national standard. Not only the 'ceiling' but also the 'floor' would be raised.[5]

And in industries where there is only one tier of negotiations, as on the railways, wages are affected by wage drift in other industries. The railwaymen demand wages comparable to the earnings of workers in other industries where wage drift has taken place. No driver of a railway engine would accept a wage similar to the nationally negotiated minimum wage for fitters, that is something like £11 a week. What he would want, and would get, would be something similar to the fitter's actual earnings, including both the nationally negotiated wage rate and the wage drift.

In some cases the causal chain works in the opposite direction. National wage rises are followed by changes in the earnings of various groups, so that other groups of workers will try to restore the percentage difference between themselves and those who got their wage rises through national negotiations.

Social justice: will an incomes policy help the lower paid workers?

George Brown and others have argued that if the workers who are in a stronger position would only forgo part of their wage rises, this would help the lower paid workers. In other words, the wage that the stronger workers give up by holding back on their wage claims will be given instead to the poorer section of the working class. This idea is accepted by many workers, who agree that incomes policy is a good thing in principle, even if they don't agree that it applies to themselves at present. But in fact the whole idea is based on a misunderstanding.

For instance, if BMC workers were to hold back on a claim for another £1 a week, would the management of BMC transfer the accumulated pounds they had saved to, say, the nurses, or would they transfer it into BMC's bank amount? We have only to ask the question to see what the answer is. In fact, the way that wages are won under capitalism is quite simple—workers in the strongest sections, in the technologically advanced industries, where they are best organised, win increases, and then the rest of the working class keep up by the simple process of comparing their own wages with those received by the strongest and best paid.

This is continually being shown to be true. Let us take, as an example, the recent case of the employees in the electricity supply industry. In May 1965 pay claims for the 50,000 white collar workers in the electrical supply industry were hinged on the improved pay and conditions that had recently been won by the manual workers in the industry. The existing three-year agreement that had been signed in January 1964 provided for an annual increase for the white collar workers of between 3 and $3^1/_2$ percent. But as the manual workers won more than this (in return for certain 'productivity' concessions), the white collar workers insisted on following suit, and threatened a strike on 22 June. The case was referred to the National Board for Prices and Incomes, which declared that the white collar workers' claim was not justified. It was, said the board, in conflict with the 'guiding light', especially since the white collar workers were making no productivity concessions:

We conclude, then, that a revision of the three-year agreement for the administrative and clerical staff would not be justifiable under the criteria set out in the white paper as justifying an exceptional pay increase. We conclude also that the concession for the lower grades to which the employers have agreed, though they have not been put into effect, go beyond anything that would be warranted by the criteria of the white paper.[6]

However, the pressure from the white collar workers was too great, and the board came to the conclusion that 'disturbance money' should be paid to them:

The basic problem with which we have had to contend is that in one and the same industry major changes in working practice have been secured from some categories of staff and that these changes have been compensated by considerable additions to pay, while the pay of workers from whom no major change is required is left unchanged. As a result there has arisen a sense of disturbance which the efficient working of this industry requires should be reduced.[7]

The result was an 8 percent salary rise—as 'disturbance money'. Once this was granted, the clerical workers in the gas industry began to feel 'disturbed'...

Or again, there is the case of the lowest paid workers, whose wages are fixed by the Wages Councils. There are some 3^1/$_2$ million of them—agricultural workers, workers in laundries, milk distribution, dressmaking, baking and many branches of the retail trade. Will restraint in making wage demands on the part of the well organised workers help and encourage these workers, who are in the main not organised, to join trade unions and thus help them to fight for better conditions? Of course not.

All past historical experience shows that with the general rise of wages, a rise which has been largely associated with the struggles of the better organised section of the working class, the differences within the working class have not increased, but on the contrary have declined considerably: '...the differential between skilled and unskilled grades, for example, which had stuck at around 50 percent for a long time prior to 1914, has by now been whittled away to 20 or 15 percent'.[8] (In other words, the unskilled worker's wage has risen from 50 percent to between 80 and 85 percent of the wage of the skilled worker.)

In fact, everything that raises the standard of living of the workers, skilled and unskilled alike, diminishes the differences between them. For this same reason differentials in backward countries, where workers have fewer rights and are much more downtrodden, are much greater than they are in the advanced, industrialised countries. This is shown clearly by the following table, which compares the wages of skilled and unskilled workers between the two world wars in Britain, an economically advanced country, and Romania, a backward country:

SKILLED WAGES AS A PERCENTAGE OF UNSKILLED[9]

	Britain	Romania
Pattern makers	131	200
Fitters and turners	127	210
Iron moulders	130	252
Plumbers	147	300
Electricians	152	182
Carpenters	147	223
Painters	146	275

Or again:

Typical rates for skilled men in Western-type industrial economies are 15 to 40 percent above those of labourers. In Africa and Latin America the typical skill differential appears to be from 50 to 150 percent, even when no racial element is involved. The average non-manual worker's salary was about three times the average wage in Egyptian industry, compared with a ratio of some two to one in Britain.[10]

The final blow, if it was needed, to the myth that incomes policy will act as an angel of social justice by helping the lower paid workers was given by Aubrey Jones when he refused any rise to the rail workers in January 1966. In his report the wages per standard week (excluding overtime) were given as follows: porters £10 18s; leading luggage room attendant £12 5s; second year guard £12 19s; qualified fireman £14 8s; qualified train driver £16 19s.[11] There was no suggestion, however, that more pay should be given to the wretchedly underpaid sections.

In fact it is best to see the different sections of the working class as standing on different wage escalators. The speed at which one escalator moves affects the speeds of all the others, and in the same direction. If one accelerates, so do the others. If one is held back, so will the others be. In other words, if the strongest and best organised workers hold back, the whole working class will be held back with them.

Effects of national negotiation on the general level of wages

We do not of course mean to say that only 'wage drift' determines the level of workers' earnings, and that national bargaining is of little importance. Nothing could be further from the truth. Local bargaining and national bargaining are the two legs on which workers walk, and a man with only one leg hardly walks faster or more strongly then a man with two. National negotiations do fix the 'floors' to earnings:

...but these 'floors' have the unique property that, when they are raised, the ceilings go up as well. An increase in wage rates secured by national negotiation will, in practically every case, raise levels of earnings throughout an industry, by however these levels may already exceed the levels of wage rates. National wage negotiation, although it is so largely concerned with the fixing of 'unrealities', is a powerful instrument for jacking up the entire edifice of earnings.[12]

And two other experts conclude, 'It seems clear that an incomes policy directed at wage rates would have a considerable effect on wage earnings'.[13]

Hence an incomes policy will have to aim at restraining both unions in national bargaining and shop stewards in plant bargaining.

Keynote settlements

The impact of national bargaining over wage rates is of particular importance in certain instances. In any year the size of national settlements—and thus of local settlements too—is conditioned to quite a considerable degree by the success or failure of certain key wage claims. There is a strong case to be made for the proposition that certain settlements in any one year determine (within limits) other settlements—these 'keynote settlements' set a trend which other employers then tend to follow, since workers deprived of rises that other workers are receiving naturally tend to become more militant (or 'disturbed', as Aubrey Jones put it). Sometimes this can be to the advantage of the unions, but sometimes it is certainly not:

> The small average size of subsequent wage increases in 1958 and much of 1959 seems to have been in large measure due to the psychological climate created by the failure of the bus strike. It is true that unemployment was rising throughout 1958, and this might have been expected to moderate wage increases anyway. On the other hand, retail prices rose rapidly during 1957 and the first half of 1958, and this might have been expected to make the unions more militant in their attempts to restore the real value of wages.
>
> It seems quite legitimate to infer from this that it may be possible to influence the size of keynote settlements, and hence of the succeeding wage round.[14]

And from what happened in 1958 it is clear how this 'influence' is exerted—by a deliberate government effort to defeat a strike. And if in 1958 the London busmen's wage claim was a 'keynote settlement', it seems that the recent government showdown with the railwaymen (in February 1966) was intended to serve exactly the same role. As the *Economist* put it:

> The only way to achieve an incomes policy in 1966 is going to be by outfacing the trade unions on some big national wage struggle, in the same way as Mr Amory and Mr Macleod achieved about 18 months of effective incomes policy in 1958-59 by outfacing Mr Cousins's London bus strike in May 1958.[15]

And in a similar vein a *Financial Times* editorial entitled 'Wage Policy On Trial' stated, 'With the railwaymen, the electricity workers and the dockers, the government will be forced to set an example'.[16]

As, however, the second base of workers' power is in the factory organisation, we shall now turn to the problem of the role of the shop stewards, and to the question of how the government, the employers and the trade union brass will attempt to deal with them in imposing the incomes policy.

Chapter Six: The dead weight of bureaucracy

Increasing centralisation in trade unions

In order to carry out an incomes policy—or wage restraint—it is first of all necessary to bring about great changes in the structure and function of the trade unions: 'The introduction of any sort of formal incomes policy would significantly affect the power, functioning and attitudes of the trade unions'.[1] In particular, since the size of individual wage bargains could not be left to individual unions and employers, the position of the TUC would have to be greatly strengthened. Trade union power would have to be centralised much more in the hands of the TUC, which would have to be able 'to speak for all and to enforce its word'.

> It will certainly mean the relegation of the present collective bargaining machinery to a secondary place in the structure since the crucial decision, of the size of the general increase for any one year, will be taken elsewhere... It also means that the central skill of many union leaders, that of negotiator, will be less important, with consequent effects on their general status.[2]

However, in return for this loss of function, they will perhaps be offered some compensations:

> It would probably require a number of the most influential and respected union leaders to take a step up from their position of union secretary to some higher position, perhaps in the government.[3]

Increasing collaboration with the state

With the centralisation of power in the TUC —a process already begun by the 'wage-vetting' scheme—there will be an increased need, if the incomes policy is to work, to draw the trade unions closer and closer to the machinery of the state. This closer association between trade union brass and state will be no new thing, however, but rather a continuation of a process that began a long time ago. In 1931-32 there was only one government committee on which the General Council of the TUC was represented, according to the TUC directory of committees. By 1934-35 the directory listed six such committees,[4] and the number has been increasing steadily ever since. The Second World War in particular saw a change in the relationship between the unions and the state:

No established right of access to the government was conceded to unions... until the Second World War... The long duration of the war and the much longer duration of post-war economic problems encouraged its establishment. Indeed, communications often moved in the opposite direction. Frequently it was the prime minister or one of his ministers who wanted to meet the trade union leaders.[5]

After the Tories came to power in 1951 the union leaders showed no desire to diminish their rights of access to the government or their policy of collaboration with it. Thus the General Council of the TUC stated:

It is our longstanding practice to seek to work amicably with whatever government is in power and through consultation with ministers and with the other side of industry to find practical solutions to the social and economic problems facing this country. There need be no doubt, therefore, of the attitude of the TUC towards the new government.[6]

Often, indeed, the policies of the union leaders expressed this relationship very well. Often their views were considerably closer to those of the Tory government than they were to those of many of the union rank and file, as a far from unfriendly commentator noted:

The TUC leaders, led by Deakin of the Transport and General, Tom Williamson of the General and Municipal, and Will Lawther of the Mineworkers, saw to it that the cautious and moderate policy which they had pursued under the Labour government was maintained under the Conservatives. Among other things, they ensured that resolutions denouncing all forms of wage restraint—such as were regularly submitted to Congress by the Communist-dominated unions—were voted down by adequate majorities.[7]

Despite the fact that the Conservative government had no 'emotional bonds' with the unions, the number of governmental committees on which the unions were represented rose from 60 in 1949 to 81 in 1954, and these covered a wide range of subjects.[8] The most prominent of these committees have been the two general advisory committees, the National Joint Advisory Council to the Minister of Labour and the National Production Advisory Council on Industry.[9]

Whatever the colour of the government, the trade unions have direct access to government departments. In 1946 Arthur Deakin could say, 'We have an open door in relation to all state departments and are thus able to get our difficulties examined in such a way as would not have been possible with any other party in government'.[10]

But the situation did not change once the Tories came to power:

The Conservatives preserved the system almost intact after 1951, although there was not the same familiarity of contacts with Conservative ministers as under the Labour government. While the TUC might not convince the government on any major economic issues, there was less difference on the everyday technical level. But the unions' views were heard. 'If I want to talk to the minister,' said a leading trade unionist in 1957, 'I just pick up that telephone'.[11]

This process of coming together between trade union leaders and the state can only be furthered by the development of incomes policy, which requires much more active collaboration from the union leaderships.

Increasing impotence of the TUC brass

The integration of the trade union leaderships into the state is one thing, but increasing their influence and impact on the state is quite another. The TUC undoubtedly seeks to be 'reasonable' in its dealings with civil servants and ministers but the power of its voice is remarkably small, for all the reasonableness and sweetness of its tones:

> The growing frustration experienced by the council can be seen from a study of the reports which its specialist committees make to Congress. Here one can read of the failure of the economic committee to influence budgetary policy; the production committee records its criticisms of government plans for high unemployment areas; and the education committee reports its unsuccessful attempts to secure the implementation of the Crowther report. But the decline in influence can be seen at its most tragic in the field of social insurance and industrial welfare, topics of great concern to the unions, where the General Council's past achievements have been considerable.[12]

Thus the TUC has failed to get the number of factory inspectors increased to a satisfactory level (in spite of a continuing high rate of industrial accidents), has failed to get concessions for the industrially injured, has failed to get compensation benefits standardised for those injured before 1948, etc. Many of these failures are nothing short of pathetic:

'Labour's National Health Act gave the minister power to provide appliances for the disabled. Consequently motor-tricycles were provided for those whose disability involved a loss of both legs. During the last few years specially adapted small cars have been designed for the use of the disabled, and they have been supplied, under the National Health Service, to the war disabled. Yet successive Tory ministers have refused to extend this provision to the industrially disabled. The TUC has pointed out that tricycles are less reliable than cars, and in cases of breakdown disabled men have been stranded for long periods... Despite the injustice and hardship caused...and the trifling cost involved, the representations of the TUC have had no effect.[13]

At the 1963 Congress, George Woodcock claimed proudly that the TUC had moved from Trafalgar Square to the committee rooms. The abject failure to gain any real influence in those committee rooms is only too clear. Organised force could have won cars for the industrially disabled in five minutes. There can be no doubt of the generous and sympathetic reaction that a call for industrial support for this claim would have produced from many groups of workers. But the TUC has long been cut off from the working class, and such a call to action today would be unthinkable.

Increasing bureaucratisation of the unions

That the top men in the trade unions are quite often knighted for their services to the nation is well known. Some of them are given posts on the boards of both nationalised and private industries, and of the Bank of England. Among the 35 members of the TUC General Council only one is a layman, ie not a full time official. And paid full time officials are coming more not only to control the TUC hierarchy but to man the lower echelons of the unions.

In the National Union of Seamen and the National Union of Boot and Shoe Operatives full time branch secretaries belong to a recognised grade of the hierarchy of officers with exactly the same privileges as other full time officers. There are many full time branch secretaries in the National Union of Printing, Bookbinding and Paper Workers, and in the National Union of General and Municipal Workers. The same applies also to the National Union of Miners.[14] Altogether the number of full time union officials reached the figure of 2,600 in 1959.[15] Since then, and especially since Wilson's coming to power, the drive to increase the number of full time officials in the unions has been hotted up. Take, for instance, the case of the ETU. At the biennial conference in May 1965 the ETU decided:

(1) To turn the executive council from a body of laymen to one of full time officials—and these new members of the executive council are to be elected every five years instead of every two (Rule 9).[16]

(2) Branch secretaries are to become full time officials (Rule 21).[17]

(3) At the same time the area committees which existed until the 1965 conference have been abolished. The area committees were composed of delegates from the different branches, and it was from these committees and not the executive council that the shop stewards got their authority.[18]

As Les Cannon, the ETU president, put it, 'The basic decision...was that we should abandon horizontal lines of organisation within the union, and replace these with the vertical structure'.[19]

One delegate opposing Les Cannon and his friends summed up the work of the executive council as follows:

> The executive council are calling for a full time executive council. This will mean that we will be electing the supreme policy-making body in the union for five years instead of for two years as at present. Not only will the executive council decide policy, but they will implement it and conduct all important negotiations. The individual executive councillor by virtue of that office will become the senior official controlling area officials in a large regional office. By judiciously recruiting branches and installing a full time branch secretary, this executive council devised structure, including their proposals to eliminate area committees, will ensure complete domination from the top on all policy questions, and national and district wage negotiations.[20]

In the AEU too a kite was flown at the national committee in June 1965 for turning branch secretaries into full time officials.[21]

The extent to which many officials in the unions are completely free of control from the members is clear from the fact that only a very small number of them have been removed by standing for re-election. Over a period of some three decades only 3 percent of them suffered this unhappy fate.[22]

The official's white collar and his briefcase, together with the fact that in most cases he does not have to face election, quite often give him a feeling that he is a member not of the working class but of the middle class. As one study based on interviews with hundreds of officials stated:

> We attempted to measure the feelings of trade union officials towards the social standing of the jobs by asking them to place their own jobs and the posts of the general secretaries in a list of 30 occupations according to what they thought would be 'the generally accepted view' of their social standing. The question was answered by 79 percent of the sample and, of these, 64 percent placed their general secretary's post as equivalent or superior to that of a medical officer of health or a company director, and 36 percent put it somewhere between a county solicitor and an elementary schoolteacher; 10 percent rated their own posts as equal to or above that of a civil servant (executive grade), 69 percent put themselves between a non-conformist minister and an elementary schoolteacher, and 21 percent somewhere below the schoolteacher.[23]

> Most full time officers rate themselves among the holders of middle class posts (and rate their general secretaries close to the top of a scale of social standing).[24]

Not surprisingly, very few trade union officials went back to the ranks after giving up their jobs, for whatever reason:

FULL TIME OFFICERS: SUBSEQUENT POST OF RESIGNED OFFICERS[25]	
Post in nationalised industry	48
Government post	25
Managerial post in private industry	14
Post in another union	11
Back to 'shopfloor'	13
Own shop or business	7
Labour Party post	4
Elected Member of Parliament	4
Post with other organisations	9
Other	9
Unknown	122
Total	266

Thus the trade union bureaucracy, rising above the rank and file membership of the unions, and feeling that it belongs to a group with a higher social status, hardly ever thinks of going back to the rank and file. To this degree it is alienated from those it supposedly represents.[26]

Decline of the union branch

An added factor contributing to the alienation of the officials from the rank and file membership is the fact that the trade union branch, once the cell that connected the rank and file to the union machine, has radically declined in importance over the past few decades. This decline of the union branches has been brought about by a whole number of irreversible forces. Firstly, as a great deal of collective bargaining has become more centralised, the local union branch has come to have little or nothing to do with the fixing of wages and general conditions. Secondly, the detailed working out of the way in which general national agreements are to be applied is being done more and more in particular establishments by shop stewards and works committees rather than by the branch. The only exceptions are those few places, outside the mining and steel industries, where the works and the branch do coincide. Thirdly, the function of the branch as a friendly society has largely disappeared as the state has come to play a more important role with regard to health, insurance and so on. Fourthly, the union branch used to be a social centre for talk and drink, but here too there has been a decline as more and more workers have come to work far away from home.

As the branch has declined, so organisations built on the basis of the branches like district committees and trades councils have declined too. In many big unions individual branches no longer send delegates to national union conferences or district committees, but are grouped together for the purpose of selecting a delegate. This weakens the branch, and the delegate representing several branches necessarily has less direct contact with those whom he is supposed to represent.

The union branch is the basic unit on which the higher levels of the trade union administration rise. The weakening of the branch is a further element—both as cause and as result—in the increasing centralisation of the unions, their bureaucratisation. If the decline of the branch is the result of the centralisation of capital and the centralisation of collective bargaining on a national level, this decline of the branch also accentuates the tendency towards centralisation. Lack of power and function for the branches breeds apathy among the membership at branch level, and apathy is the reverse of the coin of centralisation.

Pressure on the officials

Although a majority of the union officials are right wing in their political and union attitudes, and although they have sought to evade pressure from their members continually, they cannot entirely avoid this pressure, especially on the wages question. As a result, when the government has made demands on them they have generally dithered about, seeking to evade government pressures too, so as to avoid really concentrated fire from their members. It is only in this light that we can understand their response to George Brown's insistence on 'early warning of wage claims', which can only make national negotiations even more of a farce than at present, and the imposition of a 'wage-vetting' role on the TUC.

Chapter Seven: Shop stewards and unofficial strikes

Going through 'procedure'

The rank and file of the trade unions have to deal not only with the employers and the state, but also with the trade union bureaucracy. This, like the proverbial wheelbarrow, moves only as far as it is pushed and no further. And being a very rusty wheelbarrow, it takes a great deal of effort to make it move at all. The trade union bureaucracy sticks to procedure, in other words to formal agreements negotiated with the employers. Procedure dictates that when workers are in dispute with employers they should use all the constitutional rungs before they declare a strike.

Procedure is usually an extremely tortuous process, involving a number of stages: negotiation between local union officials and management; then negotiation between more senior union representatives and the district employers' association; and finally negotiations between national union officials and national employers' associations. In industries with joint industrial councils the final stage of negotiation may be at the council itself or else a committee of the council.

In engineering the process of procedure takes, on average, about three months. Quite often, if no agreement has been reached at the end of all the stages of negotiation, the entire process is begun all over again.

Not only is the process very slow indeed, but the number of cases that are resolved is tiny. Thus in 1959, for instance, of 147 cases involving the 1,300,000 manual workers in federated firms in the engineering industry that were sent to the central conference in York, only 14 were settled (23 were referred back, 42 were retained in the hands of the central authorities, in 56 cases a 'failure to agree' was recorded, and so on).[1]

It is hardly surprising to learn that in only a very small number of cases were strikes in the engineering industry 'constitutional', ie declared after procedure was exhausted:

CONSTITUTIONAL STOPPAGES OF ENGINEERING MANUAL WORKERS, 1953-62[2]

	Number of constitutional stoppages recorded
1953	4
1954	0
1955	0
1956	0
1957	0
1958	0
1959	3
1960	4
1961	7
1962	12

Thus over a period of ten years, in which there were literally hundreds of strikes in the engineering industry, the average number of 'constitutional' strikes was only three a year!

One of the nastiest features of procedure is that it is very discriminatory. Workers are not allowed to bring about a change in, say, wages or conditions until procedure has been exhausted, but employers are free to introduce changes in conditions, in speed-up, piece-rates, etc, and only after the change has been made can workers take them through procedure. Workers are not allowed to withdraw their labour until they have gone right through procedure. Employers are free to sack workers without going through procedure first.

Yet the York memorandum, with its 'provisions for the avoidance of disputes', still survives in the engineering industry after 50 years—and this after decades of sharp opposition to it among engineering workers.[3]

It is only on very rare occasions that official strikes take place before procedure has been exhausted. As a result, strikes are nearly always unconstitutional. But not only this—they are also nearly always unofficial.

Unofficial strikes

Outside the declining industries (coal mining and textiles) and to some extent the docks there has been an uninterrupted growth of strike movements over the past three decades, as the following table shows:

MAN-DAYS LOST IN SEVEN MAJOR INDUSTRIES[4]

	Annual average number of man-days lost through disputes (thousands)			Average number of man-days lost yearly in disputes per 1,000 insured persons		
	1930–38	1947–55	1956–64	1930–38	1947–55	1956–64
Docks	39.8	344.4	169.1	285	3,134	1,091
Shipbuilding and ship repairing	54.2	194.2	514.6	328	890	2,349
Coal mining	1,002.6	616.1	444.0	1,034	778	627
Engineering and vehicles	88.0	441.7	1,290.3	80	162	411
Construction	71.6	87.9	172.0	60	69	110
Textiles	1,504.0	21.0	27.1	1,311	22	30
Food, drink and tobacco	5.4	12.0	22.4	10	15	27

As one expert, Professor Turner, has noted:

If one takes…that five-year period up to 1961, one finds that the number of *workers* reported to have been involved in strikes is comparable with that in the five years of unrest up to and including 1926—the year of the General Strike itself—and that the number of separate *strikes* reported is very much higher than for any comparable period since figures first began to be systematically collected in the 1890s.[5]

And furthermore:

If one puts mining aside as the special case it is, the frequency of strikes for *all other industries* over the past few years immediately shows a very different aspect. And this is so marked that it is worth detailing. For ten years up to 1956 the reported annual number of stoppages fluctuated around 500 (which was also pretty similar to the rate for the immediate pre-war years). In 1956 itself it was 570, but the number then rose: in 1957 to 640; in 1958 to 670; in 1959 to 780; in 1960 to 1,180; and in 1961 to 1,220.[6]

Continuing the figures from the point at which Turner left off, we find:[7] in 1962, 1,244; in 1963, 1,082; in 1964, 1,456; and in 1965, 1,496. In other words, from 1956 to 1965 the number of strikes recorded by the Ministry of Labour nearly trebled.

Actually many strikes escaped the net of official statistics. Firstly, go-slows, overtime bans and cases of working to rule are not recorded in official statistics. Secondly, the number of actual strikes which have not been reported to the Ministry of Labour and thus have escaped being tabulated is very large, especially nowadays when strikes tend to be shorter in duration (see below). Thus, for instance, during an official inquiry into a dispute at the firm of Briggs Bodies in April 1957, the management complained that in the previous 18 months it had experienced 234 stoppages, but that of these only a dozen were reported in the press or recorded in official statistics. Similarly, early in December 1960 Ford claimed that it had had 57 strikes that year in its Dagenham plant, but that of these only ten had been publicly recorded.[8] And again, the shipbuilding employers estimated that in the first nine months of 1958 there had been 1,068 stoppages of work in their industry, although less than 100 of these were included in the annual statistics for that year.[9]

It appears that over the last year or so the tide of strikes has risen very sharply indeed. Thus, for instance, in the car industry the number of hours lost in strikes has been as follows:[10]

	1962	1963	1964	1964 (January–October)
BMC	2,943,232	1,684,643	1,942,727	5,003,573
Pressed Steel	454,732	199,605	76,424	881,432
Rover	246,178	140,861	282,975	412,327
STI	0	237,700	199,500	1,267,921
Rootes	223,003	45,933	88,963	85,967
Ford	793,011	34,201	76,997	185,905
Vauxhall	17	5,202	36,306	202,636
Jaguar	0	0	53,026	15,365

Of the strikes today the overwhelming majority are unofficial. On the docks:

> Out of 421 strikes since 1960, 410, accounting for about 94 percent of days lost, have been unofficial. This percentage of days lost through unofficial strikes is substantially greater than the corresponding percentages in a number of other industries involving heavy manual work, for instance shipbuilding (46 percent), engineering and vehicles (49 percent) and construction (36 percent).[11]

As regards the mines, 'Since 1926 there has been no nationwide strike sanctioned by the National Union of Mineworkers, and since 1939 every single dispute has been unofficial, unsupported by the National Union of Mineworkers'.[12]

Of the 498 strikes in the car industry in the first six months of 1965 only four were given official backing by the unions.[13] And the trend is for more and more of the strikes to be unofficial. Thus in 1936 and 1937, according to the Ministry of Labour, about one third of the strikes were official.[14] Today, according to the same source, the proportion has dropped to about one twentieth. And if account were taken of all the strikes which fail to get recorded in the ministry's statistics, then the proportion of official strikes would be even smaller. The small amount of support given to strikes and strikers by the unions is made very clear by the fact that the total amount spent by all unions on strike benefit in 1963 was £462,000, or about 11d per union member per year.[15] Death benefits were larger, at £1,011,000. Clearly union members get more from their organisations when they are dead and buried than when they are alive and fighting.

The impact of the few

To have a great impact it is not necessary for the number of workers on strike to be large. From an employer's point of view there is a relation between the capital/labour ratio (or 'capital intensiveness') of the firm or industry concerned and the cost of a strike. The greater the capital intensiveness of an industry, the more important it becomes, in order to cover the capital charges, to keep the plant running fully and continuously. Idle capital is a luxury which a capital-intensive industry can afford even less than it can afford idle labour.

It does not, of course, require a withdrawal of labour on the part of the entire personnel of a highly mechanised undertaking to bring the whole plant to a standstill. A strike by a relatively small number of key workers—for instance, forklift truck operators who remove finished products from the end of a production line—can cause the stoppage of a whole factory at a cost, in terms of lost production, which mounts to hundreds of thousands of pounds in a very short time.[16]

The impact of a strike by a quite small number of key workers is especially great in the motor industry, where the interdependence between large numbers of firms is very great indeed. Thus, for instance, BMC buys its components from no less than 4,000 different suppliers, and Standard-Triumph has 3,000 suppliers.[17] A strike in any of the supply firms or in the transport companies connecting them (or taking the cars away) can well lead to a standstill in the factories of the main car producer. This is illustrated clearly by the following short list of a few of the strikes that took place in 1965:[18]

	Factory	Strikers	Workers laid off	Lost output
17 January	Morris, Cowley	19	6,000 for 11 days by BMC	–
24 February	British Road Services	200 drivers	1,000 by BMC	–
April	Pressed Steel	Not known	6,400 for $2\frac{1}{2}$ weeks by Rootes	8,750 cars— £4$\frac{1}{2}$ million
28 May	Austin, Longbridge	300	5,000 by BMC	£2 million
15 June	Nuffield Bodies, Coventry	16 transport drivers	1,000 by BMC	–

August	ICT	Computer maintenance workers	2,000 for 2 weeks by Rootes	4,000 cars
August	Birmingham Aluminium Castings	80 die-casters	21,000 by BMC	£8 million
August	Sidgwick & Collings, Halewood	300 delivery drivers	5,000 by Ford	None—short time was imminent

Short but effective

On the whole the British working class is relatively so strong at present that the overwhelming majority of strikes are of very short duration, especially when we compare them with the strikes of the 1920s and 1930s. Then strikes were protracted, defensive struggles, often ending in defeat and demoralisation:[19]

	Number of workers involved (thousands)	Number of working days lost (thousands)	Average number of days per worker on strike
1914–18	3,159	26,460	8.4
1919–26	11,069	356,330	32.2
1927–38	3,669	38,950	10.6
1953–64	12,975	43,540	3.3

Thus the average length of strike in 1953-64 was less than one third of that in 1927-38, or about one tenth of that in 1919-26. (Of course, if we could take account of all the strikes that are not registered with the Ministry of Labour, the table would show a still more significant shift in the size of strikes.)

In the period 1919-26 the employers were on the offensive. Although the workers were on the defensive, they were very tough opponents, and thus the strikes were drawn out, often over weeks at a time. But a long series of heavy defeats and the crushing misery of mass unemployment finally demoralised the workers, and strikes in the period 1927-38 were both fewer and shorter. But today the situation is very different again: workers since the war have, although in a very fragmented way, themselves been on the offensive, and they have been confident and tough as perhaps never before. For one thing, for a whole generation they have known not one serious defeat, at least on any scale that can compare with the bitter and exhausting defeats of the 1920s.

It is no wonder that today the most perplexing issue facing management is 'labour relations'. It is a great deal easier for the bosses to calculate and predict the behaviour of inanimate machines than of people in a class divided society: 'It is hardly surprising that the Austin works manager used to spend 90 percent of his time on questions of industrial relations'.[20] And the same was true at Vauxhall too: 'The former vice-chairman, Sir Reginald Pearson, said that he spent between 60 and 75 percent of his time on labour matters'.[21]

Shop stewards

And who leads the struggle at plant level for improved pay and conditions? Who acts as the main organiser of the unofficial movement? Who spearheads the wage drift (or wage drive) strike? Who really worries the management? Above all, the shop stewards committees and similar rank and file committees. In the engineering industry shop stewards first appeared at the end of the 19th century, and during the First World War they became very prominent. The struggle that they led at that time culminated in the National Administrative Council of Shop Stewards in 1917, and in the fight for the 40-hour week in 1918-19.[22] By about 1920, with a rise in unemployment and an enormous offensive against the working class from the employers, the shop stewards' movement that had been born during the war was as good as wiped out. But in many individual factories shop stewards survived throughout the 1920s and 1930s, partly because their activities during and immediately after the war had forced the unions and the employers to recognise their existence in formal agreements. But as the trade position began to revive in the late 1930s a revival in the number of engineering shop stewards began: 'While the exact numbers are not known, the increase was indicated by the fact that the average payment to stewards for the four years 1935-38 was nearly three times as great as for the preceding four years'.[23]

During and since the Second World War national wage agreements have become more and more of a 'floor' for earnings, a general framework within which domestic plant-level bargaining, largely carried out by the stewards, has grown up. As we showed in Chapter Five, 'wage drift' has come to play an increasingly important part in the earnings of many British workers.

Some very interesting statistics relating to shop stewards in the engineering industry show clearly the acceleration in shopfloor representation over the past few years. In the eight years from May 1947 to June 1955 the number of AEU shop stewards in federated establishments rose by 24 percent, or about 2.8 percent a year. As against this, in the period from June 1955 to December 1961 the number rose by 39 percent, or some $4^1/_2$ percent a year.[24]

The total number of shop stewards in Britain is not known, and estimates vary widely. One source estimates them at about 90,000,[25] another at between 100,000 and 120,000,[26] and yet another at 200,000.[27] Shop stewards are characteristically to be found in large firms especially.

In small firms they are much more rare. About a half of all British trade unionists are covered by shop stewards' organisations, and this half is typically the best organised section of the trade union movement, and also often the most militant.

Workers are often much more involved in the elections of their shop stewards, and show more interest in stewards' work than they do in branch elections or branch activities. As we showed in the last chapter, there are a number of related reasons for the decline of the union branches. One estimate was that only about 4 percent of members of the TGWU attend union branch meetings. And according to another estimate, only one trade unionist in 20 takes anything like an active part in the life of his branch.[28]

In a research project from the University of Cambridge, 100 workers were interviewed at the Vauxhall factory at Luton, of whom 79 were members of trade unions (AEU or NUVB). Of these 79, only four said that they regularly attended branch meetings, and 57 said they never went at all. Only 36 of the 79 took the trouble to vote in the union branch elections (and NUVB ballot papers were actually taken onto the shopfloor for workers to fill in)—27 out of the 79 never voted at all. This apathy towards branch unionism was not, however, the whole story. There was a great deal more interest in shop unionism—66 out of the 79 regularly voted for shop stewards, and AEU shop meetings were attended by one man in every three. And many of the men who were interviewed spoke of discussions on trade union matters which they had had on the shopfloor either among their mates or with their stewards.[29]

Another survey showed that on average 53 percent of a steward's duties are concerned with discussions with members and other shop stewards (32 percent) and negotiations with management above the level of foreman (21 percent). Only 16 percent was spent on grievance dealings with foremen, 11 percent on forms of joint consultation, 8 percent on other meetings, and 6 percent each on rate fixing and correspondence.[30] Tony Topham has summed up the position of the stewards well:

> (1) We are witnessing a rapidly accelerating drive for worker representation on the shopfloor, which is displacing the concessionary management device of joint consultation. (2) The shop steward's constituency is of a size which renders him properly subject to democratic pressures from below—he is dealing with people who know the situation... (3) The steward's main role is concerned with issues arising directly between his constituents and management—his role in the union's machinery ('other meetings') is minimal.[31]

Those who support the idea of an incomes policy, too, have perceived the crucial role of the shop steward in bargaining, although the solutions they propose are exactly those which we are concerned in this pamphlet to counter:

> It is one thing for the TUC to sign the Statement of Intent, for the delegates to the Labour Party conference to cheer Mr George Brown's promises of a 'just incomes policy', but it is quite another matter for these sentiments to gain much support where it really matters, on the shopfloor... The measure of success with which the TUC and its member unions are able to win over the rank and file will depend either on the extent to which the former are able to impose their will or on how successful they are in persuading the shopfloor to follow their lead.[32]

The urge to control

Both the rise of the shop stewards' organisations and the number of unofficial strikes are symptoms (among other things) of the common aspirations of the working class—towards workers' control. Under capitalism the worker is a cog in the machine, with no say in the running of production, and no part in the creative organisation of his work. The growing number of strikes in Britain express the worker's rebellion against this subordination, this mutilation, limitation and alienation of his own creativity, only too clearly.

The situation is illustrated by an article that appeared in the *Economist* at the time of the Grimethorpe coal strike of August-September 1947, a strike that paralysed 63 collieries and cost 600,000 tons of coal. After 36,000 men had kept the strike going for three weeks in the face of strenuous attempts on the part of the NUM to get them back to work, the *Economist* wrote:

> The issue which is being fought out at Grimethorpe...can be summed up as a struggle between rationalisation and syndicalism. The argument over the extra working at the coal face appears to be merely the pretext for a showdown on whether control is to be exercised by an all-powerful board or whether the workers are to be given a measure of influence in the management of their own pits. Many miners expected nationalisation to result in workers' control. Instead it has resulted in a large bureaucratic machine leaving the individual miner face to face with the same managers... But the men have rebelled. They refuse to use the conciliatory machinery or to use the offices of the more remote union representatives. There seems to be no other explanation than that they wish to decide the issue for themselves.[33]

The urge for workers' control is becoming more stridently expressed in strikes, as the decline in the proportion of strikes over purely wage issues shows:

> In the 20 years of high employment from 1940 the proportion of strikes about 'wage questions *other than* demands for increases', and (particularly) about 'working arrangements, rules and discipline' rose remarkably—from one third of all stoppages to three quarters... One *could* say that these disputes all involve attempts to submit managerial discretion and authority to agreed—or failing that, customary— rules, alternatively, that they reflect an implicit pressure for more democracy and individual rights in industry.[34]

The TUC inquiry into 'Disputes and Workshop Representation' confirms for 1958-59 that the majority of strikes involve an issue of managerial authority.[35] It is only if one understands the deep urge to control, and to overcome the basic alienation of workers in capitalist production, that one can understand the 'folly' of workers who lose more money in waging a strike than they could possibly gain even if they won it completely. How else, too, can one explain the non-monetary causes of so many strikes?

A determination not to have the conditions of their work entirely dictated to them, a refusal to recognise what the capitalist press sometimes refers to as 'management's inalienable right to manage', and a simple assertion of their quality as human beings rather than as the dumb animals that capitalist production requires them to be much of the time constantly expresses itself in the struggles of workers on the shopfloor, whether they refuse the foreman the right to swear at them, resist speed-up, or deny that management has the right to decide how long a girl may spend in the lavatory.

Even in strikes for monetary causes, the rebellion against the basic alienation is never far from the surface. One writer put this very well:

> Wage claims are motivated much more frequently by *rebellion against working conditions* than by rebellion against the economic *burden of exploitation* borne by the labour force. They express an insistence *to be paid as highly as highly as possible for the time lost, the life wasted and the freedom alienated* as a result of working in such conditions. The workers insist on being paid as much as possible, *not because they put wages* (money and what it can buy) *above everything else*, but because, *as trade unions stand at the moment*, they can dispute the price of labour power with the employers, but not control over conditions and the character of the work.[36]

And in one of the very few detailed studies of a single strike, an American sociologist showed how a group of relatively backward, semi-rural workers expressed their resentment at increased supervision and tighter discipline by striking for a wage rise:

> To the extent that workers viewed the changing social situation in the plant as 'increased strictness', and most did, their reaction was influenced by their notion of what was causing these changes. In large measure, workers perceived these changes as economically motivated. As one worker said bitterly, 'They'll do anything to save a nickel.' In other words, 'strictness' was held to be due to the company's effort to save money at the worker's expense. In such a setting, a wage demand became a punitive retaliation—it was an effort, as one worker put it, to 'hit the company where it hurt—in the pocketbook'.[37]

The shop stewards' organisation as such is nothing but the expression of workers' urge to control their own destinies. In setting rules for the manning of machines, in insisting on safety standards, in demanding a say in the pace of work, in seeking control over overtime and shift work, the workers announce clearly that they are no passive cogs that management can push about as it will. Similarly the demand to control 'hiring and firing' (or at least to veto managerial decisions on this question), a demand that has led to innumerable strikes since the war, represents a challenge to the employers' authority at its most vital point.

In one and the same plant two opposed and quite contradictory powers—management with their foremen and workers with their stewards—face one another. The two camps put forward two opposing principles and sets of demands—the prerogative of authoritarian management versus the democratic self-expression of the workers.

It is true of course that this demand for workers' control is only partial, it is essentially *defensive*, it is fragmentary, and it is bound by the limits of the shop or the factory. But this demand for workers' control, a demand that is voiced in a thousand different ways every day that workers go to work, is the embryo of full working class control at every level of society, political and economic alike. For socialists it is the most important fact about modern industrial capitalism— for the 'bloody-mindedness' of workers, and the thousand and one ways in which they express their demand, implicitly and explicitly, for control over their own lives, is the embryo of workers' power, of socialism.

'Buying the rulebook'

Over the last few years there have been a number of 'productivity package deals'. These deals have been negotiated at a number of large plants in the oil, airways, electricity supply, chemical and metal industries, and to date as many as 20 have been signed. The most famous of them all, and the pioneer, was the 1960 agreement at Esso's Fawley refinery. A great deal was said at the time of the negotiations about the 'need to relate wages to productivity', the 'elimination of restrictive practices', and so on. But the central feature of this package deal was an effort by the management to buy out the rulebook in order to eliminate all the elements of workers' control, however limited, that existed in the refinery, and more specifically to cut the power of the shop stewards. This merits special attention, particularly as agreements of this sort are likely to spread further.[38]

The Fawley oil refinery near Southampton belongs to the Esso Petroleum Company and employs more than 2,000 workers. In 1960, after two years of negotiations between the management and the unions, a new package deal was signed that was quite unlike anything previously negotiated in Britain:

> Briefly, the company agreed to provide large increases in its employees' rates of pay- of the order of 40 percent in return for the unions' consent to certain defined changes in working practices that were hampering a more efficient utilisation of labour. These changes included some relaxation of job demarcations, the withdrawal of craftsmen's mates and their redeployment on other work, additional temporary and permanent shift working, and greater freedom for management in its use of supervision.
>
> The second, equally remarkable, feature of the agreements was their radical approach to the problems of systematic overtime—that is, overtime which, by being permanently maintained at a high level, had become built into the firm's wage structure, labour policy and work habits. By 1959 this had reached an average of 18 percent of total hours worked. Under the agreements management undertook to reduce this drastically over a period of two years and, among maintenance workers, to a stated target of 2 percent. The wage increases were to be given in five instalments, spread over the same period, so that they compensated for the dwindling overtime elements in the workers' weekly pay packets.[39]

The management's motives in seeking this agreement were twofold. They were anxious to increase the rate of profit on their operations, and they were equally anxious to curtail the power of the shop stewards in the refinery.

Esso is a wholly owned subsidiary of the Standard Oil Company of New Jersey, and during the second half of the 1950s the rate of profit in the US oil industry was being squeezed. The company was therefore concerned to cut its labour costs. As far as this objective was concerned, the agreements were a great success for the management. Although the figures given in the official account do not permit of any close analysis, management had no *financial* reasons to regret its 'initiative': 'The agreements, far from costing the company anything, showed a profit even in immediate terms'.[40]

Although the workers received quite large wage rises, the intensification of effort that was required of them by the package deal more than compensated the company. Labour costs per unit of output were reduced after the agreement. Productivity per worker increased by over 45 percent, while take-home pay went up on average by only 30 percent.

But in its attempts to curtail the power of the stewards the management was a great deal less successful. However much the package deal may have resulted in an increased rate of exploitation, it certainly did not diminish the role of the shop stewards. Far from it. Yet this was what the inner managerial group at Fawley had intended:

> They all cared, or came to care, about what they regarded as an abdication of responsibility on the part of management in labour relations. This had taken the form of allowing things to drift so that, by default, the initiative had passed increasingly into the hands of the shop stewards. The 'group' wanted management to manage, to use its authority purposefully with due regard for the human consequences of its decisions.[41]

Up to 1960 the existence of a large amount of overtime had strengthened the hand of the shop stewards, for they had maintained control over its distribution:

> It helped to bring about a shift in authority from the union delegates [full time officials] to the shop stewards. The full time officials had no say in determining the amount of this substantial part of the workers' pay packet. Their role was confined to the negotiation of rates. Moreover, here was a procedural aspect of industrial relations, the administration of overtime distribution, which was largely excluded from their control. Finally, overtime provided a convenient basis for a sanction which the stewards could apply—the rise in the fortunes of the unofficial movement among them coincided with the use of the overtime embargo.

The management intended that with higher pay, the abolition of overtime and the removal of 'restrictive practices' there would be a radical diminution in the power of the shop stewards. But things worked out completely differently: 'The shop stewards' influence on negotiations was enhanced'.[42]

The administration of overtime had been an important foundation of the stewards' authority in the workplace. With its reduction they had to find other outlets for their activities, and the Blue Book provided them. In submitting it to the unions, management was asking them to agree to an extension of its rights to act in ways from which it had previously been barred.[43]

In this aspect of the exercise—persuading the work groups to cooperate or at least not to resist change—the stewards were the key figures. Whether management and union officials liked it or not, they were forced to come to terms with them wherever they enjoyed the backing of their work groups.[44]

In determining their attitudes towards many of the proposed changes in working practices especially, they had to be guided by the senior stewards' views, and even perhaps leave the decision entirely to them. For one thing, the stewards knew far more about the relevant facts and the men's reactions [than did the union officials].[45]

The cutting of overtime and getting rid of restrictive practices meant an increase in supervision. Where productivity agreements are associated with a change from piece-rates to time-rates, the need for tighter control by supervision is emphasised even more. For under piece-rates supervision can be quite loose. Once the rate is fixed the worker acts partly as his own foreman, because if he doesn't work his pay will drop. Under time-rates there is nothing apart from the foreman to make the worker keep working hard.

The abolition of piece-work is supposed to cut the power of the shop stewards, however, because they are the people who negotiate the piece-rates. But because a change to time-rate leads to tightening of supervision, there is increased conflict between workers and foreman which can only lead to a further strengthening of the power of the shop stewards, and even to more frequent spontaneous unofficial workers' action.

At Fawley it is clear that instead of increasing the management's freedom of action, the package deal limited it *still more*, because the stewards refused to allow the management to go one inch beyond what had been formally bargained (despite vain hopes on management's part that the agreements would be read 'in the spirit rather than the letter'). In short, the shift from conventional bargaining to intensive plant-level productivity negotiations had the important effect of *enhancing* the role of the stewards and making them still more central in the politics of the refinery.

The lessons from Fawley are clear: 'Managements that engage in productivity bargaining have to be prepared to devote more, not less, of their time to labour relations and to expect that their tasks will become more onerous and exacting'.[46]

It was after the concluding of the Fawley agreement—the agreement intended to strengthen managerial authority—that the first unofficial strike in the history of the refinery took place.[47]

Productivity agreements or not?

Whether workers are bribed as at Fawley, or blackmailed as at the Fairfields shipyard,[48] into selling their rulebook, experience will prove that they cannot for long sell 'restrictive practices' which are really rank and file job defences, intended to restrict the authority of management. Five years after the signing of the Fawley agreement the employers have become wise to the inherent contradictions in the new set-up. Thus when the Confederation of British Industry gave evidence to the Royal Commission on Trade Unions it stressed 'the dangers of Fawley-type productivity agreements':

> It was…suggested by the CBI that if restrictive practices were bought out it could lead logically to the creation of new practices, which the workers would then want to sell as a saleable commodity. Mr John Davies, director-general of the CBI, said he understood that new restrictive practices had grown up at Fawley since the agreement was signed.[49]

Shop stewards' organisations: weaknesses and strengths

In evaluating the shop stewards' organisations at present, it is important that trade unionists and socialists are very clear about their weaknesses and their points of strength.

The most significant weakness of shop stewards' organisation today is its fragmentation. As the concentration and centralisation of capital have increased, through the processes of merger and takeover, the great combines running a number of plants across the country have become very prominent. Thus for instance ICI employs 110,000 workers in 100 plants in Britain alone, BMC employs 85,000 in 11 plants, and so on. The need to combine and coordinate the activities of shop stewards at least between the plants of a single combine is self-evident. But moves towards such coordination have been quite slow and faltering.

We have only to remember how the workers at British Light Steel Pressings were beaten after a 13-week battle in 1961[50] to see the importance of these weaknesses. BLSP is part of the Rootes combine, but the BLSP workers were defeated because the stewards in the main part of the combine, in Coventry, did not black the goods from their sister plant in London. The fact that there existed a Rootes shop stewards committee consisting of delegates from the various factories that met regularly once a month did not in itself guarantee united action. And a comparison of wages and conditions in the Rootes factory in Linwood with those in Rootes at Coventry shows how far we still are from unity between stewards even within a single combine. Nor are the reasons difficult to understand. Negotiations are done on a local basis, in a particular factory or even a particular shop. Demand for workers varies greatly between different districts. There is a great unevenness in strength of organisation, in traditions of militancy, and so on.

Added to the above difficulties is the sharp opposition of the trade union bureaucracy towards any industry-wide link-up between shop stewards. Thus in 1960 the General Council of the TUC, referring to 'organisations linking a number of joint committees, either from several factories under the same ownership (for example, BMC) or throughout an industry (for example, electricity generating)', stated that their 'effect is often a challenge to established union arrangements'.[51] As for 'attempts to form a national centre or to call national conferences of stewards irrespective of the industry in which they work (for example, the abortive conference in December 1959 convened in the name of the Firth Brown stewards, or the organisation which goes under the name of the Engineering and Allied Trades Shop Stewards National Council)', the TUC officiously warned:

> The aim of the sponsors of this...type is to usurp the policy-making functions of unions or federations of unions. Unions are advised to inform their members that participation in such bodies is contrary to the obligations of membership.[52]

And if this warning was not enough, the TUC went on, 'Unions should be more vigilant, and if, after a warning, a steward repeats actions which are contrary to the rules or agreements, his credentials should be withdrawn'.[53]

In 1959 the shop stewards committees at Firth Brown (Sheffield) and Ford (Dagenham) jointly called a National Shop Stewards Conference. The Communist stewards play a leading role in both factories. The executive of the AEU banned the conference. Bro Caborn, the convenor at Firth Browns, was suspended from holding office for one year.

The Power Workers' Combine was formed some time ago to fight for improved conditions in the power industry. As usual, the reaction of the full time officials was rapid and hostile. The unions (ETU included) declared that following the last settlement the Power Workers' Combine was no longer necessary. On 14 November 1960 Frank Foulkes, president of the ETU and chairman of the Electricity Supply Industry National Joint Council, declared, 'Unofficial bodies are not in the best interests of the industry.' Bro Wake, secretary of the combine, was then disciplined by the AEU.[54]

Since then the threat of expulsion from the ETU of Charles Doyle, the electricity supply shop steward who led the unofficial power workers' combine, and the order to stop publication of the *Power Worker* have been in the same bureaucratic vein.

Nevertheless, despite the many bureaucratic checks that are placed on the activities of the various combine committees that link the stewards in different factories, there is no doubt at all of their importance. One of the most powerful is the BMC combine committee, and its meetings have an impact throughout the engineering industry, as was shown recently by two economists.[55] Their article detailed at some length the way in which this impact was made, and the conclusions are of sufficient interest to be worth spelling out.

BMC employs an individual incentive scheme for its production workers, by which each separate job has a rate attached to it, and the rates are adjusted each time there is a change in design or method. These individual incentive schemes of course provide considerable room for negotiations between stewards and management in each of BMC's 11 factories. Through the constant bargaining over piece-rates, variations are continually developing between the average earnings of piece-workers in the different plants. As the average piece-rate earnings in the different plants go up, the bonus paid to the skilled time-workers goes up too.

All the joint stewards committees in the various BMC plants are affiliated to a completely unofficial combine committee which holds regular formal meetings every two months and coordinates the activities of the stewards in all the main plants.

> The committee is primarily concerned with the rates of pay in the separate plants, particularly with piece-rates. The knowledge of the higher piece-rates or earnings in some plants acts as an inducement to those stewards in the plants with lower piece-rates of earnings to catch up. Thus, although the individual incentive rates in the various plants were not centrally controlled by management and permitted variations in average earnings between plants, the unofficial combine committee created pressure to equalise the earnings upwards in all the plants in all the regions.[56]

Ford stewards are in a weaker position. For one thing, Ford pays all its workers on a time-rate, according to grade. There is an unofficial combine committee that links the factories, but 'it leads a much more furtive existence than the BMC committee and the official unions, and central management have far more control over the level of earnings in each plant in Ford'.[57]

However, weaker though they are, the Ford stewards are in touch with the BMC combine committee, and through these links they are able to compare their earnings with those won by BMC workers. And in negotiation with Ford management, Ford workers are able to raise themselves up by comparing themselves with BMC. This is also true of the other car firms: 'Consequently the combine committees not only create pressures to equalise earnings upwards in the different works of the same firm, but they seek to narrow earnings differentials between firms'.[58]

So gains made by one group of workers in a BMC factory, say in Birmingham, are firstly generalised to the rest of the BMC plants (including the time-workers), then to the rest of the motor industry. But this is very far from being the end of the story:

> Virtually all the specialist car producers—Rolls Royce, Daimler, Armstrong Siddeley, Jaguar, Rover Co, etc—are important manufacturers of other products. Consequently the shop stewards in these firms are interested in earnings in more than just the motor vehicle group. For example, a certain luxury car producer manufactures automobiles and aircraft engines. A strong unofficial shop stewards' combine committee exists in this firm which meets fairly regularly to compare notes about the earnings, incentives and time-rates, and general working conditions in the different works—both the motor vehicle and the aircraft works... As a result of the existence of combine committees such as this one, pressures are engendered to narrow the differentials between the automobile and the aircraft groups.[59]

And so it goes on. Firms in the aircraft industry like Vickers and English Electric are also engaged in other, non-aircraft business, and the stewards in these great combines are interested in earnings in still other sectors of engineering. As a result, workers throughout the whole engineering industry in the end stand to gain over a period of time from a gain made originally in one factory of BMC.

Quite apart from ethical socialist considerations, it is clear that the motto 'Injury to one is injury to all' makes sense in strictly financial terms. The defeat of a strike or other form of action in a factory in the motor industry is a defeat for the workers in the entire engineering industry. And since other, worse organised workers compare themselves with engineers, it is a defeat for the entire working class.

Given the leading position of the BMC workers and their stewards in the motor industry, and the leading position of the motor industry in the engineering industry, it is hardly surprising that, as the table we quoted earlier in the chapter showed, BMC workers have more strikes than other firms in the motor industry. In a very real sense, they act as the vanguard of the wages movement.

As this long example has shown, the principle of 'comparison' is very important for workers. But it is also important for the employers, who try to use it in reverse. Where workers compare themselves with their stronger and better-organised brothers, and use the comparisons to improve their wages and conditions, the employers try to force the stronger workers to accept the conditions of the weaker. This is the significance of the recent strike at Ford (Dagenham) in January 1966.

Paint sprayers at Dagenham work in very bad conditions. A few hours work in the paint booths on the production line is sufficient to saturate a worker's skin and clothes in paint. Because of these bad conditions Dagenham paint sprayers had managed to win for themselves 104 minutes every eight-hour shift in rest periods. On 22 November 1965 the management proposed to the unions at a meeting of the Ford Efficiency Committee (a body set up after the defeat of the Dagenham strike in 1962-63) that bonus rates for paint sprayers should be increased by 2d an hour, but that the rest times would have to be cut. The unions would have none of this. The main argument used by the management, however, was that shorter rest times were in force at their Halewood plant, and what was accepted by Halewood workers would have to be accepted by Dagenham workers too.

The workers at Halewood are in a weaker position than at Dagenham. The Halewood factory was built less than five years ago (with government help) in a special development district, and Ford arrived on the Liverpool scene in the role of saviour (just as Rootes built its Linwood plant in Scotland 'to ease the local unemployment situation'). This saintly posture, by both Ford and Rootes, enable them from the beginning to pay lower bonus and overtime rates, and to enforce stricter working conditions than they could do in their older and better organised plants. The strike in January 1966 at Dagenham has led to an inquiry by the motor industry's 'trouble shooter', Jack Scamp (ex personnel director of GEC), whose findings, when they appear, are likely to support the Ford management's comparisons between Dagenham and Halewood.

The importance of stewards' joint action to raise pay and working conditions to the level of those won in the best organised factories is clear. If the stewards don't do this, the management, faced with a squeeze on their profit margins, will attempt to force the reverse on workers.

The importance of stewards' links is heightened by the fact that the union bureaucracy cannot be relied on to initiate joint, supporting action. Their hostility to unofficial strikes and unofficial combine committees is well known, but even in the case of official strikes their role is often, to put it mildly, dubious. Take, for instance, the case of the recent strike at the Woolf rubber factory in Southall. There some 600 Indian workers went on strike for seven weeks. The strike was declared official by the TGWU, yet not only was no strike pay given to them (because they were coloured?) but also, even worse, no move was made by the union officials to have goods produced by scabs at Woolf's boycotted by workers at Ford or Vauxhall until the last week of the strike. There are 13,000 TGWU members at Ford, and the strike could have been much more successful if joint action of this sort had been initiated sooner. The weaknesses due to the isolation and self-sufficiency of the local stewards revealed themselves in this dispute too, for it was several weeks before the first collections in support of the strike were being taken in even the best organised local factories.

Fragmentation is a problem necessarily faced by any movement based on the workshop. But it is a problem which can be overcome, as was shown by the shop stewards' movement that developed during the First World War and the period immediately following it. Take, for instance, the case of Leonard Hargreaves, a fitter employed at Vickers factory at Brightside, Sheffield. A skilled man, he was called up to fight in the trenches for the glory of Britain while dilutees remained in the factory.[60] This was a contravention of an agreement between the unions and the government of the day.

> The shop stewards' committee of Sheffield demanded that he be released in line with government assurances, and a mass meeting held under its auspices on 13 November threatened to strike unless its demands were complied with. On 15 November Hargreaves was released from the army, and the government agreed to meet the society to devise a scheme which would meet their objections. This news did not reach the Sheffield workers and on 16 November they struck work as planned, and two days later workers from Barrow-in-Furness came out in sympathy. Work was resumed only when Hargreaves appeared on the platform at a mass meeting of the men and confirmed that he had been released unconditionally.[61]

A mass strike in defence of one worker! Actually many of the strikes at that time were massive affairs. Today the majority of strikes are, by comparison, quite small. There are more shop stewards than ever before—many more than there were 50 years ago—but still there is not a *movement*.[62]

This doesn't of course mean that there are no bridges at all between workers at different places of work. In the engineering industry, as we have shown, these bridges exist, and are often very important in spreading gains made in wages and conditions. And joint action in defence of workers who are sacked is far from rare. Take the case of the Turriff dispute in 1965—308 workers were locked out by Turriff, the building contractors, from their Barbican site in London. It was only when stewards from a large number of sites in and around the Barbican area rallied to the aid of the Turiff workers and a meeting of stewards called for a day's stoppage and mass picketing on 24 September that the tide turned. From this to victory was but a short step. Or again in late January 1966 a group of lorry drivers were sacked by British Oxygen in Wembley. There was an immediate strike by all drivers, not only in this depot but in another three depots of the same company, that assured the workers immediate victory.

Even so, with these and all the other examples of solidarity that can be quoted, it is still premature to talk of a shop stewards' *movement*.

Besides fragmentation there is another associated weakness of the shop stewards' organisations of today—on the whole, the horizons of these organisations are quite narrow. They tend to react to events more than they shape them, and they pay more attention to wages than they do to the equally important question of redundancy.

Above all, the problems of people who cannot defend themselves very well—people like old age pensioners, nurses, etc—are not central in workers' activities and thinking. It is true, of course, that thousands of workers—lorry drivers, dockers, engineers —showed a wonderful generosity of spirit in going on sympathy strike in support of the nurses' pay claim in May 1962. But still we must admit that action like this is the exception, not the rule.

Then again the shop stewards' organisations are largely restricted to the narrow horizon of economic, trade union demands. They are, largely speaking, politically apathetic. To limit oneself to economic demands, of course, is to deal with the *results* of the capitalist system as a system, and to miss the *causes*, the roots of the system. As Rosa Luxemburg, that great socialist revolutionary, put it, 'Economic, trade union struggle is a labour of Sisyphus.' Sisyphus was a mythological king who was condemned to spend eternity rolling a huge stone to the top of a hill, from which it kept rolling back, so he had to start over and over again, incessantly heaving the boulder up the hill. As long as the capitalists own the means of production, workers—whether their wages are high or low—will still be oppressed, alienated, exploited. Capitalism cannot be abolished 'step by step'. As Tawney put it, 'You can peel an onion leaf by leaf, but you can't skin a tiger claw by claw.'

This does not mean of course that the economic struggle—that 'labour of Sisyphus'—is useless. After all, Sisyphus did develop strong muscles as a result of all his labours. And in the same way the industrial workers, through the struggles at their places of work, learn self-confidence, self-reliance and strength.

When in the future the capitalist system enters into sharper contradictions, and when the speeds of the different escalators on which workers rise vary less and less, then out of the shop stewards' organisations will rise a new socialist movement, much mightier than ever before. Its roots will be in the class struggle at the point of production, and it will lead the fight against all forms of oppression—economic, national, cultural or political.

To defend and extend the shop stewards' organisation of today is to build the socialist movement of tomorrow. To fight for the socialist movement of tomorrow is to strengthen the shop stewards of today.

Chapter Eight: Anti-union legislation

Incomes policy means curbs on unofficial strikes

Several years ago two Fabians, writing in support of the idea of an incomes policy, pointed out very clearly the meaning of such a policy for the right to strike in Britain:

> Acceptance of an incomes policy will also have implications for the right to strike. Clearly, to be operable, such a policy cannot have hanging over it the threat of a strike by a dissatisfied union.[1]

The *Economist* has made the same point strongly and plainly: 'The price of securing an incomes policy in Britain will be a willingness to stand up to strikes'.[2] 'Another weapon against unofficial strikes is that, quite bluntly, blacklegging must become respectable again'.[3]

And an economist recommended a vote for the Labour Party in the 1964 general election because he felt that Labour was more likely than the Tories to achieve success with an incomes policy. He explained his recommendation in the following way: 'Paradoxically, one of the strongest economic arguments for a Labour government is that, beneath layers of velvet, it might be more prepared to face a showdown in dealing with the unions'.[4]

The same point was made by a number of other commentators.

First steps

Last year the TUC persuaded the unions to submit their wage claims to it voluntarily for 'vetting'. This 'voluntary early warning system' could only be the first step towards the introduction of legislation to provide a compulsory early warning system for pending wage claims. However much the trade union 'leaders' may support the idea of an incomes policy, they cannot entirely ignore the pressure for higher wages from their own members, and under a voluntary system the government can't rely on the union leaders to toe the line all the time. New legislation on trade unions is therefore necessary, first of all to make certain that the union brass play their part properly. Legislation is a must if the incomes policy is going to mean anything at all.

In this chapter we shall examine first of all George Brown's new bill to enforce the early warning system, and then the suggestions for new legislation that have been put forward to the Royal Commission on Trade Unions.

A bill for new teeth

On 24 February 1966 George Brown presented his new Prices and Incomes Bill to parliament. This bill is intended to give new teeth to the incomes policy.

The new law is to apply to all pay claims or any other claims relating to the terms and conditions of employment.[5] Within seven days of making a claim, the claim must be notified to the appropriate minister. If a union does not do this it will become liable to a fine of up to £50. It is made clear in the terms of the bill[6] that not only national wage claims but also all local claims for improved pay or changes in conditions are to be covered by the law.

When an award is made or a settlement reached the minister must be notified within seven days, or the employer will be fined £50.[7] It is difficult to see why any employer should resist this. Every employer will hope, of course, that the government will rule against a pay rise on the grounds that it is too high! We needn't expect to see many prosecutions under this section.

No pay award may be implemented until 30 days after the minister has been notified. The minister has the power to refer all awards to the Prices and Incomes Board to be considered by Aubrey Jones. If he does decide to refer it, the award may not be implemented for up to three months, while the Prices and Incomes Board considers it.[8] Any employer who pays his workers the extra money they have won in the bargaining session before the government's permission has been given can be fined up to £500—a not very likely event! And any trade union or group of trade unionists who try to make their employer pay up immediately by taking any form of action—strike, go-slow, overtime ban, etc—will be liable to be fined £500.[9]

What the press described as a 'concession to the TUC' has been introduced into the bill. No proceedings can be taken by the state without the consent of the Attorney-General. This is supposed to be a safeguard...

There is one other point about this law that is worth noting. Union officials are only liable under the act if it can be proved that they consented to or connived at strike action, or if any 'neglect' on their part can be proved.[10] There is thus an additional legal pressure on union officials to oppose unofficial strikes actively, and to fail to provide support for the members whose interests they are supposed to represent. The new law will therefore increase the separation between the full time officials and the rank and file of the unions. As the *Observer* commented, 'What really matters is that the threat of legal action should be so designed as to press the unions themselves to put their own house in order—to give them a leverage in dealing with their own members which exhortation has so far failed to produce'.[11]

The new bill will give union officials yet another excuse for failing to support their members and refusing to call official strikes.

The bill does not give the Prices and Incomes Board statutory powers to enforce the judgments contained in its report. Not yet. But as the *Economist* put it, 'It does represent a plausible thin end of a wedge to test whether legislation can prevent the more flagrant cases where a policy of expansion without inflation has been made impossible by the unions' high degree of monopoly power'.[12]

The *Economist* urges that the government should apply the act in particular to what we described in Chapter Five as 'keynote settlements', or what they call 'the genuine, annual front-running wage claims in the economy'.[13] And no doubt it is to these national claims that the act will apply first of all. But it can easily be applied to all local negotiations on any matter concerning wages and conditions.

More suggestions for anti-union legislation

The Labour government set up a Royal Commission on Trade Unions and Employers' Associations, which has been receiving evidence from 'interested bodies'. There has been a spate of suggestions to the Royal Commission on the form that new trade union legislation should take. All sorts of ideas have been put forward, from the Ministry of Labour, the Confederation of British Industries, the Engineering Employers Federation, the AEU, the Tories, etc, etc. These suggestions need to be understood.

The Tories' proposals are contained in their election pamphlet, *Putting Britain Right Ahead*:

> Certain types of collective agreements, notably those on procedure, should be enforced...
>
> We also suggest that a new range of industrial courts are required. These would concentrate on the settlement of industrial disputes...
>
> Our suggestion is to establish a new and powerful Registrar of Trade Unions and Employers' Associations.[14]

The *Economist* spelled out, for those who might have any doubts in the matter, what the role of this 'new and powerful Registrar' would be: 'The fact that only registered unions would have rights under the Trades Disputes Act would mean that people who called lightning unofficial strikes, without due notice and in breach of contract, would be liable for suits for damages'.[15]

In other words, the legal immunity for strike action, won after decades of agitation through the 19th and early 20th centuries, would be lost to any group of trade unionists who asserted their rights by taking strike action, etc, in breach of procedure. This would mean that car workers, for instance, because they would have to follow procedure or face heavy damages in the courts, would have to put up with at least three months' speed-up in the factories before their cases were judged by the central negotiating body at York.

The Engineering Employers' Federation also used tough language in its written evidence to the Royal Commission:

> The Engineering Employers' Federation, representing 4,500 firms throughout Britain and Northern Ireland with over 2 million workers, has suggested that unofficial strikers should be fined. They should be subject to a monetary penalty for every day they take part in a strike or other action in breach of procedure, the federation says...
>
> The engineering employers, in their evidence to the commission, supported the

proposals of the Confederation of British Industry for tightening the law so far as trade unions were concerned. They agreed with the appointment of a registrar for the unions to see that the rules were properly applied and in cases of any breach to instruct them to take action. The registrar would have power to strike unions off the register and to impose penalties.

The federation thought that the prohibition of benefits in respect of strikes in breach of agreement might assist unions in resisting pressure from their members for such payments, and it was felt that the unions' hands might be strengthened if they were required to impose penalties on their members in respect of unofficial strikes.[16]

The motor industry employers are equally anxious to have unofficial strikes prohibited. In the autumn of 1965 they asked Ray Gunter to introduce legislation to enable a panel of employers and union officials to impose fines on workers who broke procedural agreements, and to establish a closed shop in the motor industry so that the trade unions would help to discipline the workers. But Ray Gunter told them it would be difficult to apply only to the strike-prone motor industry, and so in February 1966 they told the Royal Commission they wanted labour courts with statutory powers to fine trade unionists (or employers!) who failed to observe agreed procedures. Their written evidence to the Royal Commission asserted baldly that 'legal sanctions will be required if unofficial strikes are to be effectively curbed'.[17]

Unlike the Engineering Employers' Federation, the motor industry employers are in favour of closed shop agreements provided that they lead to the union officials exercising greater discipline over their members.

The motor industry employers were asked, when they presented their evidence, what would happen if unofficial strikers were fined, with deductions from their pay, and the men then went on strike against the deductions:

> 'Then we would be in trouble,' agreed Mr R R Hopkins, the personnel director of Vauxhall. But he and other employer representatives went on to argue that the fines would have a deterrent effect.[18]

Other employers have had doubts about the idea of fines by the courts, and have suggested alternatives. Thus Mr Stanley Raymond, chairman of the British Railways Board, argued in his evidence to the Royal Commission that:

> …it would not be practicable to introduce sanctions enforceable at law against people who took part in unofficial disputes. A method which he would prefer for making a man 'think twice' would be to include provisions in agreements with unions so that a man who went on unofficial strike might suffer a suspension of some of his fringe benefits, such as the withdrawal of travel privileges, sick pay and annual leave. He thought there would have to be some form of industrial court— though it would not be a court of law—to determine what the appropriate penalty should be.

The board's evidence also put forward the view that the unions might accept responsibility for disciplining workers who took part in unofficial actions.[19]

Enter Ray Gunter, minister of labour, with wide experience in the difficulties of being a trade union leader:

> Workers in the car industry who are responsible for unofficial strikes might be
> expelled from the industry, it is suggested in a memorandum sent to trade union
> leaders and employers by Mr Gunter, minister of labour.
>
> The proposal is intended to work with another, which the employers are con-
> sidering, that all workers in the industry should be members of a trade union. The
> suggested 100 percent membership is aimed at enabling unions to discipline men
> who ignore union policy and instigate unofficial action.[20]

Unfortunately Ray Gunter's suggestion of a closed shop in the motor industry, and the expulsion of 'troublemakers' by union officials acting as unpaid
foremen, has met with a number of snags:

> Preliminary reactions from confederation leaders suggest that there is little hope
> of the closed shop scheme being put into effect. With such a conglomeration of
> competing unions in the motor industry, there would probably be open warfare be-
> tween them over the sharing out of 'compulsory' trade unionists, and there is no
> sign of the car unions being ready to take the form of drastic action against their
> members which a closed shop would require.[21]

Ray Gunter did get support, however, from Sir William Carron, director of
the Bank of England and president of the AEU. Indeed, Sir William went even
further than Gunter. He suggested a closed shop, not just for the motor industry, but for the whole of the engineering industry, with the right of unions to
expel troublemakers everywhere. In a memorandum to the Royal Commission,
the AEU executive:

> ...states that if legislation were introduced to enforce the closed shop and the
> check-off (deduction of a man's union contribution from his pay packet by his em-
> ployer), unions 'would probably agree also to outlaw forever unofficial strikes'.
>
> In these circumstances, the unions would have far more power to discipline their
> members, for with expulsion the ultimate sanction leading to the loss of a worker's
> job it would be more than a sufficient deterrent to an individual thinking of ig-
> noring his union's advice.[22]

But again there are snags in this suggestion of Sir William's. With 32 trade
unions in the Confederation of Shipbuilding and Engineering Unions, who is
going to guarantee that all the unions would march in step? Above all, is the
leadership of any union powerful enough to kick out a mass of workers on strike?
As the *Times*, commenting on the AEU executive's offer to act as a special disciplinarian in unofficial strikes, put it:

> A union agreement to outlaw unofficial strikes would represent only good inten-
> tions. Some unofficial strikes are directed as much against the unions as against
> the employers, and it would be hardly less difficult for the unions to expel a ma-
> jority of workers in an undertaking than it would be for the government to put them
> in jail.[23]

Snags

The Ministry of Labour, in its evidence to the Royal Commission, was very much more cautious in its recommendations. Very usefully, it considered the various suggestions that might be put forward, pointing out the absurdities of some of the more extreme proposals for curbing strikes. A first suggestion dealt with is the one that unofficial strikes should be open to criminal prosecution:

> There is one body of opinion which holds that the answer to this problem is in some way or another to make unofficial strikes illegal. In its ultramontane form this view would seem to be self-defeating, on the simple ground that it would be impracticable. Wartime experience would certainly seem to support this conclusion. Quite simply, in the last resort, it is not practicable, nor would it be conducive to good industrial relations, to try and put a large number of people in jail.[24]

Another suggestion, that 'unofficial strikes should be penalised by the loss of entitlement of rights based on continuity of employment' such as pension rights, sickness benefits and so on—Stanley Raymond's suggestion—also has its unfortunate snags:

> Apart from the difficulty of defining an unofficial strike…and the danger of introducing an inflexible element into the situation, the most serious defect of provisions of this kind is that the penalty is not an immediate one. All that happens is that if and when the worker is dismissed or becomes redundant he does not get the benefits of certain rights he would otherwise have had. It is to be doubted if this would be an effective deterrent.[25]

And there are snags too in yet another suggestion, that instead of banning damaging strikes by law, the law should demand a 'cooling-off' period between the date on which the union gives notice of its intention to strike and the actual start of the strike:

> In the United States, when a strike threatens to cause a national emergency, the president has the power to invoke a procedure, involving independent inquiry and a vote by the workers on the employer's last offer, which must be completed before the strike may proceed. Experience of this procedure has not been encouraging. It has been found that the attitudes of the two sides are at least as likely to harden as the reverse during the cooling-off period, and every vote that has been held on the employer's final offer has, in practice, gone against acceptance.[26]

And:

> It would not seem practicable to require a cooling-off period or a secret ballot in the case of unofficial strikes because such requirements could not be enforced. For this reason the suggestions have been considered only in relation to official strikes.[27]

So in the end, as the Ministry of Labour sees it, the only proposal that remains at all viable is that of using the trade unions themselves to discipline their members: 'The most promising may be to attempt to induce the trade unions to take more action than at present against unofficial strikes by making procedure agreements for the settlement of disputes legally enforceable'.[28]

It was in a similar vein that the Devlin report wrote on the Transport and General Workers' Union in the docks:

> When its officers negotiate with the employers on the dockers' behalf, the employers lack reasonable assurance that any agreement which emerges will be accepted by the dockers... To start with, the T&G must re-establish its power and authority in the three major ports... It must fight the dissidents on their own ground. This will entail a great campaign in which the union concentrates all its available resources on the docks.[29]

In order to encourage the union officials to be more active in disciplining the rank and file of the unions whenever they show any independence of activity, labour courts will have to be established to enforce the collective agreements that the officials negotiate with the employers:

> Collective agreements are not, in the United Kingdom, enforceable in the courts. Collective disputes are settled through the voluntary machinery set up by collective agreements, usually known as 'procedure.' A statutorily established arbitration tribunal, the Industrial Court, is available for those who wish to make use of it. If labour courts were to be given jurisdiction over collective agreements, so that disputes could be taken there at the instance of either party, and the court's decisions were legally binding, this would be the same as making such agreements legally enforceable.[30]

And to guarantee that trade union officials wouldn't hesitate in disciplining their members, fines should be imposed on them if they couldn't prove that they did their utmost in this direction:

> The argument would then be that it is desirable in the national interest that pressure should be exerted in trade unions to give more attention to the activities of shop stewards and other subordinate bodies. The proposition to which this argument leads would be that in the case of unofficial strikes (or strikes in breach of procedure which in practice are much the same thing) the trade union concerned should be subject to defined penalties, according to the length of time the unofficial strike lasted, unless they could show to some independent tribunal that they had taken all steps open to them to prevent the unofficial strike taking place, or to bring it to an end as soon as possible.[31]

The pattern of labour legislation that is to be has not yet completely crystallised, although its main characteristics are already very clear—the main enemy is the unofficial strike, and to fight the unofficial strike the courts and the trade union officials must join hands.

Further steps

As the tide of criticism of the unions from the employers, their government and their press has mounted over the last year or so, many union leaders have been hastening to show that they are quite as respectable in their outlooks as the next man, whether the next man is an engineering employer or a press baron.

Thus, for instance, Sir William Carron reacting to an unofficial strike of BEA workers:

> I would like to see a most searching examination of the activities at London airport, whether under the auspices of the Ministry of Labour or some other body.
>
> *For all I know, MI5 might be as appropriate as any other.*
>
> An inquiry is imperative.[32]

In several industries agreements have been signed between unions and employers that lead to penalties for unofficial strikers. Thus in the municipal bus industry, which employs 77,000 people, a provisional agreement has been reached between management and union officials that means that fines will be imposed on unofficial strikers.[33] The unions involved in this were the TGWU, NUGMW, AEU, ETU, NUVB and NUR.

And the NUGMW signed a closed shop agreement with Ilford Limited (a company part-owned by ICI) that guarantees the company freedom from unofficial strikes and unofficial wage demands. The union will police the agreement, expelling any 'troublemakers' from the union and the factory in one blow. The union will act as a foreman for Ilford Limited, helping with a drive for 'greater productivity.' As the *Guardian* commented on this agreement, the result will be:

> ...a much more authoritarian industrial situation with the union wielding greater power over its members... But the benefit to the individual production worker is less obvious.[34]

Laws with a bias

One thing is very clear about all the proposals for changes in the labour laws, including George Brown's new bill—employers and workers are not going to suffer the same sanctions. Thus George Brown makes it clear that only claims by workers for changes in their pay or their conditions are to be referred to the government. There is no suggestion that an employer who wants to introduce speed-up, or who wants to cut a piece-rate, has to ask for the government's permission first.[35] But workers who want to reduce their speed of work, or who want to raise piece-rates, are supposed to inform George Brown first.

If the early warning system is not followed by workers they will break the law, and they will be liable to fines. Of course, any law that doesn't have sanctions is useless. The proposed sanctions are financial, but what if strikers or union officials refused to pay the fines? Then of course their property would be seized and they would suffer imprisonment. But nothing like this faces employers who reject wage demands, who increase speed-up, sack workers or make working conditions so abominable that they provoke workers to go on strike.

Also all the suggestions for making workers stick to procedure are very biased, because the agreements on procedure are biased in favour of the employers, as we showed at the beginning of Chapter Seven.

There can be no doubt that all the proposed legislation is a direct attack on working class organisations. This is necessary if the incomes policy is going to work at all. And it is equally clear that if it is to be effective it must lead inevitably to the further joining together of the forces of the trade union bureaucracies and the state on the side of the employers. They need the help of the law to enforce their will on the workers. If at the beginning the new laws seem to be fairly weak and faltering, it is also certain that they will have to be made tougher and tougher.

Chapter Nine: The way ahead

Before going on to consider the present condition of the British working class movement, it may be useful to summarise briefly our argument so far. We began with an examination of the changing conditions under which the British capitalist class is operating today, and the way in which these conditions make them anxious to introduce an incomes policy.

In particular we pointed to their growing need to plan ahead, the increasing effects of international competition on their profit margins, and the especially acute pressures of the balance of payments problem on the growth rate of the British economy. The employers and the government, we suggested, are seeking to redistribute the wealth of the country away from wages and towards profits, as has happened in a number of other advanced capitalist countries. In the past our rulers escaped from allowing the workers' share of the national income to rise through inflation, but conditions of international competition have made this solution more and more problematic.

We asked whether the government was seeking to introduce an incomes policy that would apply equally to all incomes, or whether their real intention was a form of wage restraint, and we attempted to show that, since profits and prices can not be controlled under capitalism, the incomes policy amounts to nothing more than wage restraint, in the interest of higher profits. It cannot, therefore, be seen as in any way a socialist measure.

Thirdly, we examined the assertion that an incomes policy would lead to economic growth in Britain. A model of the way in which incomes policy might be supposed to achieve this result was examined, and rejected as totally out of touch with reality. The inescapable conclusion was that, because of all the 'leakages' in the economic system in Britain, an incomes policy would contribute almost nothing to economic growth. Nevertheless, we suggested, the economic mode that we examined and rejected lies behind most of the government's attempts to plan, and we pointed out the difference between the sort of planning that the Wilson government is attempting and socialist planning. In the conditions of modern capitalism, it is foolish to assume that planning is necessarily an anti-capitalist measure.

Turning to the way in which workers win their wages, we showed the growing importance of local bargaining in the economy, and of the 'wage drift' resulting from this. At the same time we pointed out that national negotiations have by no means lost their importance—they are still important as one of the two legs on which workers walk. We showed that the idea, still accepted by many trade unionists, that an incomes policy will lead to greater social justice by redistributing wealth from the better-off to the worse-off sections of the working class, is completely phoney—the harder the stronger workers fight for better pay and conditions, the more help they give to their weaker brothers and sisters.

We therefore concluded that there was not one decent argument in favour of an incomes policy under capitalism from a socialist point of view. Incomes policy is a capitalist measure, directed against the working class under the conditions of modern capitalism. It is clear that socialists and trade union militants must reject it, and the assumption on which it is based, without exception. It is a policy designed to weaken the labour movement. We therefore turned to a consideration of the ways in which a fight against the incomes policy could be most successfully developed, while at the same time moves towards strengthening the labour movement could be made. The trade union bureaucracy, we suggested, because of its increasing integration into the machinery of the capitalist state, does not provide a basis for fundamental opposition to the incomes policy. More and more the union leaderships are an impediment to socialist advance. But increasingly they are being superseded as the real leaders of the working class movement by the shop stewards and their organisations, and we attempted to show how important shop stewards committees and similar rank and file organisations have become today, analysing their weaknesses and strengths. Any real opposition to the incomes policy and any policy for socialist advance in Britain must look first and foremost to the shop stewards.

Finally, we looked at the proposals for trade union legislation that go hand in hand with the moves towards an incomes policy. These proposals will present the working class with more and more legal threats to its points of real strength, in particular through attempts to control and punish unofficial strikers.

In this last chapter we conclude with a few comments on the prospects for the socialist movement in Britain.

The reformist tradition

For a very long period in British history the prevailing ideology in the British working class was that of parliamentary reformism. This old-style reformism had one central feature of particular importance to socialists. As an ideology it told workers, 'Leave it to your leaders—your MPs and your trade union chiefs—to win reforms for you.' This was, in other words, 'reformism from above', and its history in the working class movement is a very long one. It decisively influenced the ways in which generations of workers thought and acted.

But, like all beliefs and ways of acting, it was rooted in a particular form of society. And over the last generation a whole number of changes in the situation, of capitalism—and thus in the situation of the working class—have decisively reduced the hold of this kind of reformism. These changes may be summarised as follows—old-style reformism from above rested on a particular sort of ruling class, a particular sort of state, and a particular sort of working class. All these three have changed, and in changing they have altered the prospects for socialist politics in Britain quite fundamentally. We will look at them one at a time.

The ruling class

The position of the owners and controllers of industry and finance has changed considerably, especially as a result of the growth in the size of individual firms. All through the 19th and well into the 20th centuries the typical employer was a great deal smaller than he is today. And the market in which he sold his goods was extremely competitive. Not only were firms much smaller in size than today, but there were far more of them in any particular line of production. Being small, and being in fierce competition among themselves, these firms could not on the whole afford, individually, to pay their workers more or grant them greater concessions than their competitors. An employer who granted his workers very much more than his competitors granted to theirs ran the risk of putting himself out of business.

Also, the economy was subject to a cycle of booms and deep slumps, and the heavy unemployment characteristic of this earlier stage in the capitalist economy provided employers with a reserve army of unemployed workers. In this situation the employers felt no especially strong need to compete with each other for labour by offering their workers a little more to stay with them. And, to a greater extent than today, workers' skills (or lack of skills) were more transferable between factories and industries. This was true of skilled and unskilled workers alike. Thus, when the employers were forced to grant reforms to the workers, they tended to do this all together and all at once, through such agencies as parliament. The 19th century and the early 20th century were the great periods of reforms won for workers through parliament. It was through national agitation and propaganda, focused on the parliamentary centre, that workers made many of their gains, through their representatives—or their misrepresentatives! When they had to, to avoid worse trouble, the employers paid out for these reforms. Reforms applied to all workers equally, and the cost of them was borne by employers equally. In this way no employer was put at a competitive disadvantage with his rivals.

The last great period of this movement of reforms from above, won through parliament, came with the Labour government after the Second World War. Whenever possible, of course, the employers made sure that the reforms that workers were granted were paid for by the workers themselves. All manner of administrative devices were developed for making sure that welfare services, etc, that were granted to the working class were paid for by charges to the workers, not to the employers. If a welfare service involved redistribution of incomes, then as far as possible this was paid for by making the better-off workers support the worse off.

But the important point is that the reforms, which undoubtedly raised the general standard of life of workers in Britain, came from the centre. To win them the working class had to look to its national representatives, in parliament and in the trade union leaderships.

But today the situation has changed, and the employers are very different. The typical employer of today is a great deal bigger, and there are far fewer employers. As firms have grown in size their monopoly control over the market has increased, and competition, in the national market at least, has become much less cut-throat. Because of their size, and because they are less afraid of their competitors than they were, they are more ready to grant reforms to their workers one at a time and on their own.

Also, with some exceptions in backward areas like Northern Ireland, the British economy since the beginning of the Second World War has had almost continuous full employment, and today there is a shortage of workers. With the virtual disappearance of the reserve army of the unemployed, labour has become a scarce commodity, and the employers are very worried about recruiting and keeping their workers. Machinery and technical processes in factories nowadays are a great deal more expensive than in the past, and also far more complicated. Because of technical changes, in many industries—and especially in the new, fast growing and technologically advanced industries—it is becoming increasingly expensive to train workers, and increasingly expensive to lose them. The employers hate labour turnover today almost as much as they hate strikes.

As a result of these changes, employers are increasingly willing to grant reforms and make changes in their own factories regardless of what their competitors are doing. There has been a decline in the reforms won from the centre, and an increase in reforms won in the big firms. This is not only true of wages, but of all kinds of fringe benefits as well. One example will do.

We are constantly being told that we live in a 'welfare state', and it might reasonably be imagined that at the heart of any welfare state provisions we would find pensions. It might be thought that if workers want to retire on decent pensions, then the place to go to ask for these would be to the MPs. In fact, today, if workers want good pensions, the place to look for them is, to a growing extent, not in parliament, not from MPs of left or right, but in the fringe benefit schemes of the large employers. Since the war there has been a phenomenal growth of private pension schemes, actively encouraged by the Tories with offers of large tax reliefs. In the mid-1950s Professor Titmuss estimated that the cost of these private occupational pension schemes to the Exchequer was between two and three times the cost of the state pension schemes, even though the private schemes covered a much smaller proportion of the population.[1] Although the lion's share of these private pensions goes to managerial and, to a lesser extent, white collar staff, by the end of the 1950s about half the non-agricultural working population was covered by these schemes, and the numbers are growing steadily year by year. Since the return of the Conservative government in 1951 the government's contribution to welfare services has been steadily declining.[2] Through the increasing use of flat rate contributions and many other devices, the redistributive aspects of the welfare services have been progressively reduced. The whole balance of welfare provision in Britain has turned decisively against the working class since the war. Before the war, sickness, pension and unemployment benefits were much higher, in real terms, than they are today. On the other hand, those who are better off get increased tax concessions for all the private welfare schemes they arrange for themselves, their children get far more out of the free educational services than do the children of workers, and so on. One critic asked in 1958:

> The middle classes get the lion's share of the public social services, the elephant's share of occupational welfare privileges, and in addition can claim generous allowances to reduce their tax liability. Who has a welfare state?[3]

And Professor Titmuss provides an answer to his question: 'Those who have benefited most are those who have needed it least'.[4]

Slowly but surely the welfare services in Britain have been emasculated in the period since the war. The importance of state-sponsored central reforms has been declining. Today the workers have less to gain and less to hope for from national reforms. And thus the role of their national representatives, the Labour MPs, has been declining too. There is less to be had from them today than perhaps ever before.

This is not to say that there are no reforms to be had any more. Reforms can be and are still being won, but increasingly the place in which they are won is not parliament, but the large corporate enterprise, the great business empire of modern capitalism. The employers prefer it that way.

The state

Another change that has profoundly affected the ideology of reformism from above and its hold over British workers has been the change in the role of the state.

In the last century, and well into the present century, the capitalists' ideal role for the state was no role at all. According to the prevailing economic doctrine of the day, the state was supposed to keep out of economic life as much as possible. All it had to do in the world of business and production was to make sure that the parties to contracts kept their bargains, and no more. The idea of the state intervening directly in the sacred freedom of the market was unthinkable.

And despite all the misery caused by fierce economic competition, and by recurrent heavy unemployment and poverty, the state by and large kept out of economic life. Politics and economics were kept strictly separate, as far as this was possible.

And partly because the state kept out of economic life, and because of the separation of politics and economics, it was not difficult for workers to see the state as being somehow 'neutral', above the conflict between workers and employers, and not taking sides. It was not so difficult either to believe that, if only the representatives of the working class could be elected to parliament in large enough numbers, these representatives would then legislate their way to socialism and a just society. The fact that it was possible to see the state as neutral made it that much easier to believe in reliance on parliamentary representatives to solve workers' problems.

But today the state is very different. The state is responsible today for some 45 percent of all fixed investment in this country, and for 20 percent of output. The state is the country's largest single employer of workers, and by no means the best employer in Britain either, as the miners and railwaymen have found out yet again already this year. And the state is deeply involved in the economic life of the country, in a way that would have been inconceivable even before the Second World War.

As we said in the first chapter, the units of capitalism are now so large and their investments are now so complex that the capitalists have, however reluctantly, had to accept the idea of planning and coordination by the state. As other countries have entered the world market and Britain's share in the world market has continued to decline, international competition has in many ways replaced competition in the local British market, and there has been increasing concern with 'the national interest'—the interests of British capitalism as a whole—an interest that only the state can properly define and push. So the state today, through NEDDY, the Department of Economic Affairs, the Prices and Incomes Board, and the many other state planning and coordinating agencies, seeks to do British capitalism's planning job. This it does, of course, on the capitalists' own terms, and wherever possible it draws in businessmen to help the civil servants. The state and business have thus become much more highly integrated today. Politics and economics can hardly be separated any more. And it is difficult to see the state as 'neutral' outside the conflict between the classes. Tory or Labour, it makes less and less difference—the government of today is much more clearly a government of the employers, for the employers and by the employers. This is only emphasised by the declining power of parliament in relation to the cabinet and the government departments. What good is there in pinning all your hopes on a bunch of Labour MPs who can do nothing anyway, because they are powerless?

And the trade union leaders too are drawn into the state's planning and coordinating processes. They have moved, as George Woodcock said, out of Trafalgar Square and into the committee rooms (where, as we showed, they promptly lost any power to influence the government in any significant way).

Trade union leaders sit on innumerable government committees and agencies, and affect government and business policy hardly at all. For their services to 'the nation', they win knighthoods from the government and suspicion from their members. Of them and the MPs together it is hardly unfair to say, 'Power corrupts, but lack of power corrupts absolutely.'

The working class

Thus the ruling class has changed and the state has changed. So too has the working class, and this is the third and most important point.

The first and most obvious feature of the working class today is that—particularly because of full employment—workers are better off than ever in the past. In the 19th century, and right up to the Great Depression of the 1930s, the lives of workers in this country were dominated by the twin facts of poverty and regular, deep unemployment every five to ten years.

In the past, when the workers acted militantly, they did so generally, as a *class as a whole*. Consider the strikes of the 1920s, great defensive struggles in the engineering industry, on the railways, in the mines and, finally, in the General Strike of 1926. These were general strikes, all of them, strikes that involved workers right across the country. They are a part of the British working class's heritage of militancy. Being general strikes, they were directed from the centre, by the national trade union leaders. Here too attention was focused necessarily on the centre, and reforms depended in part on reformism from above.

It is proper that the achievements of the working class in the 1920s should be remembered with pride, but we should avoid being sentimental about the past. When the workers in the period before the last war were strong, they were often magnificent in their struggles, but a succession of bitter defeats and the return of mass unemployment left them defeated and demoralised, and working class politics went out of the window. The 1930s are often remembered as 'the red 30s' because of the activities of the unemployed workers' movements, but the 1930s were also a period of low strike activity, of the greatest Tory vote this century, of workers fighting one another for jobs or scraping before their foremen to keep their jobs, of declining union membership, of despair and demoralisation. In their poverty workers often generated a marvellous sense of solidarity, it is true, but often too this was not a fighting solidarity but the solidarity of misery and defeat.

To workers dominated by poverty and unemployment, as so many were in the decades before the last war, a solution to their problems through parliament and through their national trade union leaders often seemed the only answer, even though time and again their leaders at the centre let them down, most notably in 1926 and 1931. In the old conditions of capitalism, reforms from the centre, reformism from above, were the only solutions that seemed to make sense.

How different is the picture of the working class today! The first and most obvious thing about workers today, as we said, is that they are better off than they have ever been before. So much so, indeed, that some writers have gone so far as to suggest that many workers have been made 'middle class' by 'afflu-ence'. These writers have suggested that the fact that many workers today drive their own cars, or have television sets or washing machines, has somehow made them 'middle class' in the ways that they think and act, and that therefore there is no future for socialist politics in Britain any more.

This of course is plain nonsense. A rising standard of living doesn't tell you anything about workers' political and trade union activity, for a start. If the fact of owning a television set or a car or earning higher wages is enough to stop a worker acting like a worker, then why didn't the rising standard of living in the second half of the 19th century stop workers joining trade unions? How is it that they joined trade unions more, not less? And why has union member-ship gone up since the last war? Why are there more strikes today than ten years ago? Why are there more, not less, shop stewards in the unions? Why hasn't the number of Labour voters gone down since the 1930s, instead of being consistently higher? And why should the most 'affluent' area in Britain today—the Midlands—also be the area that seems to have most strikes? It's clear that a better explanation of what has been happening to the working class is needed.

The first change that has taken place has been widely misunderstood by the writers who assume that workers are becoming 'middle class'. This is the in-creasing apathy that many workers feel and express about 'politics' (and even, perhaps, 'trade unionism'). But what does this mean? It is certainly true that in-dividual memberships of the Labour Party have declined in number, from 1,005,000 in 1953 to 830,000 in 1963.[5] And the proportion of workers attend-ing trade union branch meetings is also very low, as we showed. It's also prob-ably true that many workers today feel very apathetic about national political issues. But in view of the fact that there's less and less to be won in the national political and trade union arenas, this isn't really very surprising. Nor should socialists or militants feel too worried about this—they'd have more reason to be worried if workers *did* show deep interest in parliament, for instance, for it would mean the workers didn't realise that next to nothing can be had from par-liament these days!

What has happened, in a very important sense, is that workers have turned their attention and their militancy to the areas where real gains can be and are being made. And the most important of these areas, of course, is the shopfloor. It is here that a growing part of their wages is won, and it is here, if anywhere, that any welfare benefits can be won. It's to shopfloor meetings that a worker is likely to go today, not to union branch meetings, and it's in electing his shop steward that he's more likely to be interested, not in electing a branch or a dis-trict or national union official.

Another factor of importance for the working class movement since the war has been the growing unionisation of white collar workers. As manual workers have become stronger and better organised, and have bid up their wages, the differentials between white collar and manual workers have tended to lessen, making it more and more apparent to white collar workers that if they wish to preserve their position they will have to organise. Also, with the growth of large-scale bureaucratic organisation in offices as well as in factories, their conditions of work have become more similar to those of the manual workers. And in some parts of the white collar work world office work has become as mechanised as factory work. It is among white collar workers that trade unions have made their largest membership gains since the war, especially among technical and highly skilled stall personnel in industry:

> During the 11 years 1950-61, the leading non-manual unions affiliated to the Trades Union Congress chalked up these gains: Association of Supervisory Staffs, Executives and Technicians 128.9 percent; Clerical and Administrative Workers Union 92.5 percent; Draughtsmen and Allied Technicians' Association 56.3 percent; National and Local Government Officers 44 percent; Society of Technical Civil Servants 40.7 percent; and National Union of Journalists 35.4 percent. Outside the TUC (although actively discussing the possibility of joining) is the Institution of Professional Civil Servants, which expanded by 65 percent in the same period.[6]

Despite these gains the level of white collar organisation is still quite low, but the trend is of great importance. The most successful of these white collar unions have shown great militancy in pursuing their members' claims, and this appears undoubtedly to have been a condition of their success. Thus DATA, for instance, declares every strike by its members official, and being almost without any strike funds at all relies entirely on levies of its membership to provide *full pay* for DATA members on strike. The prospect of large numbers of white collar workers joining trade unions clearly worries the employers, especially as the white collar unions are becoming much more militant these days. In June 1964 a confidential report was circulated among the employers affiliated to the British Employers' Confederation (now the Confederation of British Industry), in which the following paragraph appeared:

> In spite, however, of the limited extent to which staff unionism appears to have developed up to the present time, some members of the Wages and Conditions Committee reported that there is now a growing tendency for staff workers to join trade unions and that this is making it increasingly difficult for employers to resist pressure from staff unions for the negotiation of agreements. It is recognised that staff unions, because of the type of worker they represent, are generally more articulate, more militant and more effective than the manual workers' unions, and that any developments of staff unionism on a major scale will present serious problems for employers.[7]

Brushes with the government have also had their effect on white collar militancy. The experience of Selwyn Lloyd's pay pause in 1962 was undoubtedly a contributing factor in NALGO's decision to affiliate to the TUC, and in that union's sudden increase in militancy.

With white collar workers—people who always used to look on themselves as 'middle class' and a cut above the manual workers—joining unions and becoming more militant, the only way the changes in Britain can be explained, it seems, is by saying, not that workers are becoming 'middle class', but that a good section of the people who used to call themselves 'middle class' are now beginning to recognise that they are workers too. Many of them come from working class homes anyway, so it's hardly surprising. The more white collar workers organise and become militant, the more this will strengthen the labour movement as a whole.

Looking at the movement as a whole, there are two predominant features of particular importance for socialists. The first is a cause of concern, though not for pessimism, and the second is a definite cause for optimism.

Fragmentation

In the period before the war, as we noted, when the working class acted militantly, then workers felt together as a class and acted together as a class. The 'general strike' was the natural expression of this situation. Today things are different. We have a militant working class, that takes part in more strikes, of shorter duration, and that is more confident of its own strength than ever before. But as the pattern of strikes shows, struggles today are essentially local and fragmented. The whole condition of the class struggle is changing.

Today workers win gains from employers in small groups, and the relatively small, unofficial strike or go-slow is the natural expression of this.

Although in the longer run an improvement for one section becomes an improvement for all, in the short run it appears as if some workers are gaining faster than others. And in the short run the issues facing different groups appear to bear little similarity. Workers today struggle in small groups, and not very often in a general way, as a class as a whole. All the fights against employers on the shopfloor, the struggles which reveal more than anything else the strength of workers today, do not by themselves have the effect of unifying the working class, because they are seen as essentially *private* fights, particular to workers in one shop or one factory. They do not necessarily engage the attention or the sympathy of workers in other shops or factories, let alone other industries, even though, as we attempted to demonstrate, a victory or a defeat for one group of workers means in fact a victory or a defeat for considerably more workers than are actually engaged in that particular struggle.

The fragmentation of action goes hand in hand with the contemporary apathy towards larger political issues that so many have commented upon. Apathy has been well described as the state in which people seek *private* solutions to *public* evils.[8]

Fighting and making gains in relatively isolated groups on separate fronts, workers undoubtedly do tend to lose the sense of cohesion and class meaning that socialists see in their struggles. And because in a very real sense workers see their struggles as for themselves alone rather than for the working class as a whole, those who have neither the ability nor the power to organise on their own behalf tend to get left behind. As we showed in our chapter on the wages front, workers who are well placed to make wage gains prepare the ground for those who are not quite so well placed, and provide them with an incentive to keep up. But there are some people in the working class who have nothing at all with which they can fight, even to keep up, and they get left behind. This more than anything else explains the continuance (and growth) of poverty in post-war Britain:

> In 1953-54 about 8 percent of the population—nearly 4 million people—were living at a standard no higher than the average family on National Assistance. *Preliminary results for 1960 showed that the number had nearly doubled.* Seven and a half million people were in households with incomes at or below the average amount allowed to similar families on National Assistance. As many as 2 million had less than the basic National Assistance scale on which, it has been officially stated, nobody is expected to live.[9]

Who are these people? Typically, the old age pensioners, the sick, the mentally deficient, the unskilled worker with a large family, and others, all of them with little or no bargaining power. These are the people to whom above all class solidarity could mean most in terms of their standard of living, and these are the people who gain least from it. They represent in all 15 percent of the population.

Again, another factor going with the fragmented condition of the struggle at present is the colour prejudice of many workers. Perhaps as many as 95 percent of manual workers are in favour of the Labour government's reactionary white paper on immigration control. It was in a sense apt that it should have been the workers of Smethwick, in the middle of the Midlands engineering belt, who did not stop the unspeakable and very successful campaign of the Tory Peter Griffiths in the 1964 general election. If there were no more to the contemporary class struggle than the workers' offensives against their employers for higher pay and better conditions it is difficult to see what point of unity there could be between workers in their different situations. But it is doubtful whether it is on the offensive that working class unity can be and will be rebuilt. Two things in particular in contemporary capitalism tend to unify the workers.

The first is the continuing tendency towards larger and larger units of industry. Takeovers and mergers continue at a high rate, and provide the conditions for united action in combine committees, linking workers in different factories and different regions, and emphasising their common problems. Indeed, because the typical large firm today spans a group of industries rather than being concentrated on one narrow sector of production, the conditions are created for links across industrial boundaries

The second is the attack upon the workers. However fragmented the workers' offensives against the employers may be, their effect on the bosses is felt as a *general* effect. The employers and the state cannot just single out groups of workers in their counter-attack on the working class. Their incomes policy and their legislation against unofficial strikes, their deflationary budgets and their cutting back of welfare services affect all workers, and not only as Midlands engineers or London railwaymen, but as members of the working class. It is especially at the point where workers are forced to unite by the general attack that is mounted upon them that the real moves towards unity can be made,[10] not at the point where offensives are prepared, but where defences are raised. These are the areas above all that socialists should emphasise in their propaganda, the points where the workers' militancy can be unified.

'Do it yourself' reforms

We began with a discussion of the roots of reformism from above, the long and deadly tradition of reliance upon representatives that has bitten deeply into the consciousness and activity of British workers. Today this tradition is weaker than ever before. When, as today, workers do not win their best wage rises through national bargaining, or their best pension schemes from the state, when workers can gain less and less from their representatives in parliament and in the trade union leadership than once they did, then there is good reason for optimism among socialists.

The decline of reformism from above in Britain means a new possibility in British politics once again, the possibility of the rebirth of a revolutionary working class movement. For wherever workers are fighting for themselves, fighting for better wages, fighting in defence of their shop stewards and fighting for their right to control the conditions of their work, wherever they are doing things for themselves and not leaving it to their leaders, they are growing in self-confidence and growing in their ability to run things for themselves. Wherever they are doing these things, they are destroying the tradition of reformism from above. They are developing a new tradition, of 'do it yourself' reforms, that expresses their growing self-reliance and self-assertiveness.

More than 100 years ago the International Working Men's Association—the First International—was founded in London. The opening sentence of its General Rules, written by Karl Marx, stated, 'The emancipation of the working classes must be conquered by the working classes themselves.'

No one can win socialism for the workers—they must do it themselves, relying on their own strength and their own organisations. Wherever 'do it yourself' reforms are won, the seeds of socialism as the self-emancipation of the working class are being sown.

The working class of Britain is fragmented, it is true, but it is also the most potentially revolutionary working class in the history of Britain. The principal tasks of socialists are to do what we can to unify the working class, and to encourage the movement from below.

In the face of the massive campaign against shop stewards and against unofficial strikes, the natural abilities of the stewards must be developed and deployed to the full. In the past the stewards have shown a multitude of talents for organising their fellow workers, adopting and adapting new and ingenious methods of struggle, despite the solidarity of the employers, the state and the trade union bureaucrats. In the main, however, these struggles have, as we said, been directed only against their individual employers. Now they are faced with the task of organising their fellow stewards in other firms, in other areas and in other industries, to defend themselves against a powerful consortium of the employers, the government, the press, the law, the Tory party and the trade union brass, all of them equally determined that this time the shop stewards will be curbed, and with them, of course, the rest of the organised working class's will to resist.

It is the general nature of the threat facing stewards that allows the opportunity for developing them into a widely based *movement*. And the very fact that the attack is being launched against them by a Labour government indicates the need for a political as well as an industrial response from the rank and file movement in the factories, the docks and elsewhere.

The first essential task for any worker is that of ensuring that his own immediate organisation is in fighting shape, that every factory and place of work has a joint stewards committee (including all stewards regardless of their union membership, and covering white collar workers like draughtsmen too), that every company with different factories is covered by combined stewards committees to coordinate activities and prevent 'splitting' activities by the employers. More broadly, the rank and file must find forms of organisation—area rank and file committees, etc—that can do the job the trades councils used to do. Only the new organisations must be based on the factories rather than on geographical place of residence.

Most of these tendencies are in their infancy, but the threat to the shop stewards is now so acute that the implementation of these basic tasks must be accelerated and largely achieved in a relatively short time, creating the conditions for the formation of a national shop stewards' movement—an idea which, since the First World War, has existed almost solely in the minds of some of those whom Harold Wilson calls 'wreckers', and whom we see as the potential builders of the mightiest socialist movement yet in the history of Britain.

Notes

For reading the typescript and commenting upon it we have to thank Geoff Carlsson, Roger Cox, Paul Derrick, Jim Higgins, James Hinton, Mike Kidron, Geoff Mitchell, Bob Rowthorne, Bill Taylor and Peter Turner. They are of course not responsible for any errors of fact or judgment that may remain. —Tony Cliff and Colin Barker, May 1966.

Chapter One

1   A Shonfield, *Modern Capitalism* (London, 1965), pp95-96.
2   *Guardian*, 31 December 1965.
3   *Sunday Times* Business News, 16 January 1966.
4   A Shonfield, *Modern*, p42.
5   Quoted in S Mallet, 'Continental Capitalism and the Common Market', *New Left Review*, March-April 1963.
6   C Vittorio Foa, 'Incomes Policy: A Crucial Problem for the Unions', *International Socialist Journal*, June 1964.

7   W A H Godley, 'Pricing Behaviour in the Engineering Industry', *Economic Review*, May 1964.

8   R R Neild, *Pricing and Employment in the Trade Cycle* (Cambridge, 1963), p42. Similarly, it was found that the net return on capital (before tax) of the 'big six' car producers changed between the years 1954 and 1963 as follows (A Silberston, 'The Motor Industry 1955-64', *Bulletin*, Oxford University Institute of Economics and Statistics, November 1965):

	1954	1963
BMC	32	15
Ford	44	21
Vauxhall	43	16
Rootes	23	1
Standard–Triumph	23	-
Leyland	16	15
Average	34	16

9   National Institute of Economic and Social Research, *Economic Review* no 16.

10   N Davenport, 'The Split Society,' *Spectator*, 8 November 1963.

11   A Shonfield, *Modern*, p106.

12   A Shonfield, *Modern*, p106.

13   See P Baffi, 'Monetary Stability and Economic Development in Italy, 1946-60', *Quarterly Review*, Banca Nazionale del Lavoro, March 1961.

14   G C Allen, 'The Causes of Japan's Economic Growth', *Three Banks Review*, September 1962.

15   G C Allen, 'Causes'.

16   A Shonfield, *British Economic Policy Since the War* (London, 1959), pp167-168.

17   F W Paish, *Studies in an Inflationary Economy* (London, 1962), p310.

18   F W Paish, *The Limits of Incomes Policies*, Hobart Paper 29 (1964), pp24-25.

19   It is worth noting, by the way, that one of the people expressing views very similar to those of Professor Paish was George Woodcock: 'George Woodcock, replying to Nigel Lawson on the TV programme *Gallery*, gave an answer equally remarkable for its fuzziness of words and its clarity of intent when he was asked what his reactions would be to 600,000 or 700,000 unemployed. Here it is: "Oh well, one would regret it but if this, in the circumstances, that is in the short run, is the only way we can really get ourselves on an event keel, we have to face it"' (*Spectator*, 28 May 1965).

20   The long term investment planning to which capitalism has been tied since the Second World War is a phenomenon intimately associated with the other changes we have pointed out in this chapter—the speed of technological change, the cutting of trade barriers, the existence of more or less full employment. All these developments are rooted in the fact that for a long period now—in fact since the beginning of World War Two—crises of production in capitalism have been more or less eliminated. This in turn is rooted in the war economy and its successor, the permanent arms economy. For further elaboration, see T Cliff, 'Perspectives of the Permanent War Economy', in *A Socialist Review* (London, 1965), pp34-40; M Kidron, 'Rejoinder to Left Reformism', *International Socialism* 7 (Winter 1961-62); and H Magdoff, 'Problems of United States Capitalism', *Socialist Register* 1965, pp62-79.

Chapter Two

1   M Spicer, 'Implementing an Incomes Policy 3—And What About Profits?', *Statist*, 8 January 1965.

2   F W Paish, *Limits*, p20.

3   F W Paish, *Limits*, pp20-21.
4   Fabian Group, *A Plan for Incomes*, April 1965, p3.
5   K Alexander and J Hughes, *A Socialist Wages Plan* (London, 1959), pp60-61.
6   N Davenport, 'The Split Society,' *Spectator*, 29 November 1963.
7   J R Sargent, *Out of Stagnation* (1963), p33.
8   C George, 'Snags for Industry in a Prices Review,' *Statist*, 1 January 1965.
9   Cmnd 2098 (Public Records Office, 1963), p54.
10 *Guardian*, 22 November 1965.
11 R M Titmuss, *Income Distribution and Social Change* (London, 1963), p108.
12 R M Titmuss, *Income*, p110.
13 R M Titmuss, *Income*, p110.
14 *Times*, 14 March 1960, quoted in R M Titmuss, *Income*, pp110-111.
15 *Observer*, 17 September 1961.
16 R M Titmuss, *Income*, p112.
17 'The Indefensible Status Quo', *Economist*, 15 January 1966, p218.
18 Quoted by R M Titmuss, *Income*, pp111-112.
19 *Economist*, 15 January 1966, p217.
20 *Economist*, 15 January 1966, p218.
21 R M Titmuss, *Income*, p136.
22 *Financial Times*, 10 March 1964.
23 *Financial Times*, 7 April 1964.
24 *Financial Times*, 30 June 1964.
25 *Times*, 1 September 1965.
26 *Economist*, 11 April 1959, p105, quoted in R M Titmuss, *Income*, p180.
27 R M Titmuss, *Income*, p178.
28 G Goodman, 'From Consent to Compulsion?', *Statist*, 7 May 1965.

Chapter Three

1   M Barratt Brown and J Hughes, *Britain's Crisis and the Common Market* (London, 1961), p4.
2   M Barratt Brown and J Hughes, *Britain's Crisis*, p4.
3   A Shonfield, *Observer*, 24 April 1960.
4   A Shonfield, *British*, p42.
5   A Shonfield, *British*, p38.
6   A Shonfield, *British*, p46.
7   S R Sargent, *Out of Stagnation*, p3.
8   T Balogh, *Planning for Progress* (1963), p19.
9   NIESR, *Economic Review*, February 1964, p6.
10 TUC, *Productivity, Prices and Incomes* (1965), p7.
11 Table drawn from Nigel Lawson, 'St George and the Incomes Policy', *Financial Times*, 10 March 1965.
12 A R Conan, 'The Unsolved Balance of Payments Problem', *Westminster Bank Review*, November 1963.
13 *UK Balance of Payments 1965* (London, 1965).
14 C McMahon, *Sterling in the Sixties* (London, 1964), p9.
15 *Times*, 25 September 1957.
16 A R Conan, 'The Impact of Post-War Capital Movements', *Westminster Bank Review*, August 1963.
17 V Perlo, *The Empire of High Finance* (New York, 1957), p294.
18 V Perlo, *The Empire*, p295.
19 A Shonfield, *British*, p222.
20 W Davis, 'They Sell Sun And Tax Escapism In The Bahamas', *Guardian*, 24 January 1966.

21 A Shonfield, *British*, p211.
22 Letter of 16 September 1957, printed in 'Minutes of Evidence Taken Before the Bank Rate Tribunal' (December 1957), p101.
23 A Shonfield, *British*, p105.
24 *Economic Trends*, March 1965.
25 M Chichester, 'Imperial Relics or Outpost of the Free World', *Statist*, 4 December 1964.
26 *Times*, 29 October 1965.
27 *Military Expenditure Overseas*, Ninth Report of the Estimates Committee for 1963-64, para 44.
28 *Military Expenditure Overseas*, para 32.
29 *Economist*, 17 July 1965.
30 *The National Plan* (London, 1965), p182.
31 Lombard, *Financial Times*, 18 October 1965.
32 Lombard, *Financial Times*, 12 August 1965.
33 Lombard, *Financial Times*, 12 August 1965.
34 *Times*, 30 July 1965.
35 M Barratt Brown, *After Empire*, pp313-314.
36 *Observer*, 2 April 1961.
37 N Davenport, 'The Split Society', *Spectator*, 22 November 1963.
38 *Guardian*, 20 January 1966.

Chapter Four

1   *The National Plan*, p4.
2   A Shonfield, *Modern*, p134.
3   A Shonfield, *Modern*, p139.
4   A Shonfield, *Modern*, p138.
5   *The National Plan*, p55.
6   *The National Plan*, Part II, p65.
7   *The National Plan*, p72.
8   *The National Plan*, p93.
9   *The National Plan*, p102.
10 *The National Plan*, p107.
11 *The National Plan*, p57.
12 *The National Plan*, p162.
13 *The National Plan*, p165.
14 *The National Plan*, p129.
15 *The National Plan*, Part II, p204.
16 *The National Plan*, p38.
17 *The National Plan*, p57.
18 *The National Plan*, p57.
19 *The National Plan*, p102.
20 *The National Plan*, p204.
21 *The National Plan*, p204.
22 *The National Plan*, p182.
23 *The National Plan*, p7.
24 *The National Plan*, p15.
25 A A Rogow and P Shore, *The Labour Government and British Industry* (Oxford, 1955), p66.
26 R Bailey, 'Neddy and the Planning Process', *Westminster Bank Review*, November 1965.

Chapter Five

1 Even here there is a small amount of wage drift, resulting from the fixing of piece-rates in the situations where they do apply, from more liberal grading of workers, etc.

2 Ministry of Labour, *Statistics on Incomes, Prices and Employment*, December 1964, Table B12.

3 L A Dicks-Mireaux and J R Shepherd, 'The Wage Structure and Some Implications for Incomes Policy', *Economic Review*, November 1962, p42.

4 L A Dicks-Mireaux and J R Shepherd, 'The Wage Structure', p42.

5 That wage drift does push up wage rates is clear from the following table:

WAGE RATES AND EARNINGS, OCTOBER 1958 TO OCTOBER 1963

	Percentage change on a year earlier		
	(1) Average hourly wage earnings, excluding effect of overtime	(2) Average hourly wage rates	(3) 'Wage drift': column (1) minus column (2)
October 1958	+ 3.1	+ 3.7	- 0.6
October 1959	+ 2.7	+ 1.3	+ 1.4
October 1960	+ 7.6	+ 5.5	+ 2.1
October 1961	+ 6.9	+ 6.4	+ 0.5
October 1962	+ 4.4	+ 4.1	+ 0.3
October 1963	+ 3.6	+ 2.3	+ 1.3

HM Treasury, *Economic Report* 1963, March 1964, p15. Whereas the rate of increase of hourly wage rates reached its peak in 1961 and its lowest point in 1959 and 1963, the rise in weekly earnings reached its peak in 1960 with lowest points in 1959 and 1962. Thus changes in weekly earnings (and in wage drift) appear generally a year earlier than changes in wage rates. The drift, therefore, although smaller than the rise in basic rates, accelerates the rise in basic rates. The same causal relationship between wage rate and wage drift was found in a sample of 45 firms in the engineering industry. See S W Lerner and J Marquand, 'Workshop Bargaining, Wage Drift and Productivity in the British Engineering Industry', *Manchester School of Economic and Social Studies*, January 1962.

6 National Board for Prices and Incomes, *Remuneration of Administrative and Clerical Staff in the Electricity Supply Industry*, Cmnd 2801, October 1965, p14.

7 National Board for Prices and Incomes, *Remuneration*.

8 K C J C Knowles, 'Wages and Productivity', in G D N Worswick and P H Ady (eds), *The British Economy in the 1950s* (London, 1962).

9 C Clark, *The Conditions of Economic Progress* (London, 1950), p460.

10 H A Turner, *Wage Policy and Economic Development* (Manchester, 1962), pp9-12. See also T Cliff, 'The Economic Roots of Reformism', in *A Socialist Review*, pp48-58.

11 National Board for Prices and Incomes, *Pay and Conditions of Service of British Railways Staff*, Cmnd 2873, January 1966, pp32-33.

12 K G J C Knowles, 'Wages', pp524-525.

13 L A Dicks-Mireaux and J R Shepherd, 'The Wage Structure', p38.

14 M Stewart and R Winsbury, *An Incomes Policy for Labour*, Fabian Tract 350 (October 1963), p23.

15 *Economist*, 15 January 1966.

16 *Financial Times*, 10 January 1966.

Chapter Six

1   M Stewart and R Winsbury, *An Incomes Policy*, p14.
2   M Stewart and R Winsbury, *An Incomes Policy*, p18.
3   M Stewart and R Winsbury, *An Incomes Policy*, p27.
4   V L Allen, *Trade Unions and the Government* (London, 1961), p32.
5   V L Allen, *Trade Unions*, p12.
6   *TUC Report* 1952, p300; cited V L Allen, *Trade Unions*, p23.
7   H Pelling, *A History of British Trade Unionism* (Harmondsworth, 1963), p235.
8   V L Allen, 'Trade Unions in Contemporary Capitalism', *Socialist Register* 1964, p157.
9   V L Allen, *Trade Unions*, p35.
10 M Harrison, *Trade Unions and the Labour Party since 1945* (London, 1960), p294.
11 M Harrison, *Trade Unions*, pp294-295.
12 W McCarthy, *The Future of the Unions*, Fabian Tract 339 (September 1962), pp23-24.
13 W McCarthy, *The Future*, p25.
14 H A Clegg, A J Killick and R Adams, *Trade Union Officers* (Oxford, 1961), pp21-22.
15 H A Clegg, A J Killick and R Adams, *Trade*, p39.
16 *Abridged Report of the Second Biennial Conference* (London, 1965), pp46-58.
17 *Abridged Report*, pp108-117.
18 *Abridged Report*, pp79-95. In addition, the leadership of the ETU insisted that representation at conference should be on the basis of one delegate per branch, regardless of the size of the branch. The result: 'We find that in branches of one to 30 that 46 delegates represent 1,200 members, whilst at the other end of the scale we find that only 14 delegates represent 30,000 of the membership' (*Abridged Report*, p97). Also, it is up to the executive to decide on the merging or splitting of branches. So, quite simply, if the leadership is in need of a few more delegates to support them, all they have to do is to create a few more tiny branches.
19 *Abridged Report*, p8.
20 *Abridged Report*, pp55-56.
21 *AEU Journal*, July 1965.
22 H A Clegg, A J Killick and R Adams, *Trade*, p79.
23 H A Clegg, A J Killick and R Adams, *Trade*, pp72-73.
24 H A Clegg, A J Killick and R Adams, *Trade*, p90.
25 H A Clegg, A J Killick and R Adams, *Trade*, p85.
26 What we have said should not be taken to imply an indiscriminate personal attack on every individual full time union official. As a body, however, full time officials are becoming further and further removed from their members by a number of separate but related pressures. Many of them undoubtedly act in direct opposition to the men and women they are supposed to represent, and put their association with the employers before their members' interests. Some, we are sure, try to avoid this situation. What matters in this context, however, is that any strategy of opposition to incomes policy that looks to trade union officials, of the left or of the right, to play an important role in this opposition is fundamentally misconceived. No one would in any way wish to exclude left wing union officials from socialist movements, we imagine, but to rely upon them to play an important role, or to focus too much attention on them, is as ridiculous as seeing the fate of the working class movement in this country as dependent upon the activities of a few socialist university professors.

Chapter Seven

1   A I March and R S Jones, 'Engineering Procedure and Central Conference in 1959: A Factual Analysis', *British Journal of Industrial Relations*, vol 11, no 2.
2   A I March and R S Jones, 'Engineering Procedure'.
3   See J B Jefferys, *The Story of the Engineers* (London, 1945), pp231, 236, 234.
4   *Final Report of the Committee of Inquiry under the Rt Hon Lord Devlin Into Certain Matters*

Concerning the Port Transport Industry, Cmnd 2734, August 1965, p4.

5   H A Turner, *The Trend of Strikes* (Leeds, 1963), p2.

6   H A Turner, *The Trend*, p8.

7   *Ministry of Labour Gazette*.

8   J Rescoby and H A Turner, 'An Analysis of Post-War Labour Disputes in the British Car Manufacturing Firms', *Manchester School of Economic and Social Studes*, May 1961.

9   *Times*, 25 April 1960.

10 *Financial Times*, 2 February 1966.

11 *Final Report*, pp4-5.

12 N Dennis, F Henriques and C Slaughter, *Coal is Our Life* (London, 1956), p63.

13 *Financial Times*, 18 October 1965.

14 H A Turner, *The Trend*, p14.

15 Royal Commission on Trade Unions and Employers' Associations, *Written Evidence of the Ministry of Labour* (London, 1965), p52.

16 C Chivers, 'The Pattern of Collective Bargaining', in B C Roberts (ed), *Industrial Relations: Contemporary Problems and Perspectives* (London, 1962), p133.

17 G Turner, *The Car Makers* (Harmondsworth, 1964), p59.

18 *Economist*, 4 September 1965.

19 *Written Evidence*, p68.

20 G Turner, *The Car Makers*, p80.

21 G Turner, *The Car Makers*, p124.

22 J B Jefferys, *The Story*, pp181-192.

23 J B Jefferys, *The Story*, pp241-242.

24 A I Marsh and E E Coker, 'Shop Steward Organisation in Engineering', *British Journal of Industrial Relations*, June 1963.

25 H A Clegg, A J Killick and R Adams, *Trade*, p153.

26 A I Marsh and E E Coker, 'Shop Steward'.

27 *TUC Report* 1960, p128.

28 M Harrison, *Trade Unions*, p110.

29 Data taken from J H Goldthorpe, 'Orientation to Work and Industrial Behaviour Among Assembly-Line Operatives: A Contribution Towards an Action Approach in Industrial Sociology' (Unpublished, Department of Applied Economics, Cambridge University, 1965).

30 A I Marsh and E E Coker, 'Shop Steward'.

31 T Topham, 'Shop Stewards and Workers' Control', *New Left Review*, May-June 1964.

32 M H Spicer, 'The Importance of the Shop Steward', *Statist*, 25 December 1964.

33 Quoted in S Papert, 'Strikes and Socialist Tactics', in *A Socialist Review*, p125.

34 H A Turner, *The Trend*, p18.

35 *TUC Report* 1960, pp125-126.

36 A Gorz, 'Trade Unionism on the Attack', *International Socialist Journal*, April 1964.

37 A W Gouldner, *Wildcat Strike* (London, 1955), p33.

38 For a general official account of the Fawley negotiations, see A Flanders, *The Fawley Productivity Agreements* (London, 1964). For an excellent article on package deals generally, see T Topham, 'The Implications of "Package Deals" in British Collective Bargaining', *International Socialist Journal*, September-December 1964.

39 A Flanders, *The Fawley*, pp13-14.

40 A Flanders, *The Fawley*, p246.

41 A Flanders, *The Fawley*, p102.

42 A Flanders, *The Fawley*, p199.

43 A Flanders, *The Fawley*, p201.

44 A Flanders, *The Fawley*, pp202-203.

45 A Flanders, *The Fawley*, p203.

46 A Flanders, *The Fawley*, p207.

47 A Flanders, *The Fawley*, p102.

48 The method used at Fairfields is quite interesting. Firstly, it must be remembered that shipbuilding and ship repairing is more strikebound than any other industry. A worker in

the industry lost on average 2.3 days on strike annually in 1956-64. The comparable figures for the docks were 1.1 days and in textiles 0.03 days (*Final Report*, p4). Thus the shipbuilders have to be disciplned! Secondly, the use of 'nationalisation', with the state owning half the capital and with union funds brought in to collaborate with private capital, is intended to soften up workers' resistance. Thirdly, once the employers in Fairfields force the workers to give up 'restrictive practices', employers in other shipyards will use this as a lever against their own workers.

49 *Financial Times*, 24 November 1965.
50 There is an excellent account of the BLSP strike in K Weller, *The BLSP Dispute: The Story of the Strike*, Solidarity Pamphlet no 8 (London, no date).
51 *TUC Report* 1960, p129.
52 *TUC Report* 1960, p129.
53 *TUC Report* 1960, p130.
54 K Weller, *What Next for Engineers?* (London, no date).
55 S W Lerner and J Marquand, 'Regional Variations in Earnings, Demand for Labour and Shop Stewards' Combine Committees in the British Engineering Industry', *Manchester School of Economic and Social Studies*, September 1963, pp261-296.
56 S W Lerner and J Marquand, 'Regional Variations', p282.
57 S W Lerner and J Marquand, 'Regional Variations', p283.
58 S W Lerner and J Marquand, 'Regional Variations', p284.
59 S W Lerner and J Marquand, 'Regional Variations', p284.
60 Dilutees were unskilled workers brought in to do skilled workers' jobs during the First World War.
61 J B Jefferys, *The Story*, pp181-182.
62 But the Hargreaves strike was the shop stewards' movement at its best. The problem of fragmentation was, in fact, less acute in Sheffield than elsewhere. Both today, as has been shown, and during the 1914-22 period, shop steward organisation was most powerful and well developed in the more economically dynamic sectors of the engineering industry— then armaments, now motor cars and aircraft. In Sheffield this presented no problem, as over 60 percent of the metal workers were employed in five big armament firms. On the Clyde, for example, where armaments production employed no more than 20 percent of the enginering workers, the problem of expanding the shop stewards movement from the arms firms into the more important shipbuilding and marine engineering firms held back the development of the movement for several years. The Clyde Workers Committee suffered a resounding defeat in the spring of 1916, largely because of its failure to build a bridge to the mass of engineering workers in the shipyards and the marine engineering firms. They failed in this because they had been content to regard themselves as the key section of the workers (which they were), a section sufficiently powerful to be in a position to dispense with the task of drawing other sections of the class into the struggle (which they were not). Shop stewards in the key sections of the engineering industry today, faced with a government offensive under the name of the incomes policy, would do well to learn from this defeat of an earlier shop stewards' movement.

Chapter Eight

1 M Stewart and R Winsbury, *An Incomes Policy*, p18.
2 *Economist*, 5 June 1965.
3 *Economist*, 4 September 1965.
4 S Brittan, *The Treasury Under the Tories, 1951-1964* (Harmondsworth, 1965), p276.
5 Prices and Incomes Bill, 24 February 1966, para 11.
6 See especially Prices and Incomes Bill, para 11, subsection 4.
7 Prices and Incomes Bill, para 12, subsection 2.
8 Prices and Incomes Bill, para 12, subsection 6.

9   Prices and Incomes Bill, para 14.
10 Prices and Incomes Bill, para 20, subsection 3.
11 *Observer*, 27 February 1966.
12 *Economist*, 26 February 1966, p773.
13 *Economist*, 26 February 1966, p773.
14 *Times*, 7 October 1965.
15 *Economist*, 4 September 1965.
16 *Times*, 25 January 1966.
17 *Guardian*, 16 February 1966.
18 *Guardian*, 16 February 1966.
19 *Times*, 5 January 1966.
20 *Times*, 16 September 1965.
21 *Financial Times*, 16 September 1965.
22 *Financial Times*, 9 November 1965. The practice of the check-off and the closed shop is well known in the US, where its main effect has been to remove the shop stewards from direct pressure from their members, since they don't have to go around collecting dues any more. In the US it is also common for the stewards to be paid by management—as Jim Conway of the AEU suggested, they should be paid by the union in Britain. As an American trade unionist commented, 'Freed from their regular jobs and from direct contact with the workers, stewards have become indistinguishable from foremen in their appearance, except that they are much harder to find when needed.' See M Glaberman, 'The American Working Class in the Sixties', *International Socialism* 21 (Summer 1965).
23 *Times*, 9 November 1965.
24 Royal Commission on Trade Unions and Employers' Assocations, *Written Evidence of the Ministry of Labour* (London, 1965), p7.
25 Royal Commission on Trade Unions and Employers' Assocations, *Written Evidence*, p79.
26 Royal Commission on Trade Unions and Employers' Assocations, *Written Evidence*, p79.
27 Royal Commission on Trade Unions and Employers' Assocations, *Written Evidence*, p80.
28 Royal Commission on Trade Unions and Employers' Assocations, *Written Evidence*, p43.
29 *Final Report*, Cmnd 2734, August 1965, p105.
30 Royal Commission on Trade Unions and Employers' Assocations, *Written Evidence*, p93.
31 Royal Commission on Trade Unions and Employers' Assocations, *Written Evidence*, p7.
32 *Sunday Mirror*, 13 June 1965.
33 *Financial Times*, 4 November 1965.
34 *Guardian*, 29 October 1965.
35 Prices and Incomes Bill, para 11, subsection 1.

Chapter Nine

1   R M Titmuss, 'Pension Systems and Population Change', in *Essays on 'The Welfare State'* (London, 2nd edn 1963), p63.
2   See N Harris, 'The Decline of Welfare', *International Socialism* 7 (Winter 1961).
3   B Abel-Smith, 'Whose Welfare State?', *Conviction* (London, 1958).
4   R M Titmuss, 'The Irresponsible Society', in *Essays*, p229.
5   P Anderson, 'Problems of Socialist Strategy', in P Anderson and R Blackburn (eds), *Towards Socialism* (London, 1965), p252.
6   C Jenkins, 'Tiger in a White Collar?', *Penguin Survey of Business and Industry 1965*, (Harmondsworth, 1965), p60. These figures may be a little inflated, particularly in the case of ASSET.
7   Cited in C Jenkins, 'Tiger', pp55-56.
8   The phrase is Edward Thompson's. See E P Thompson, 'At the Point of Decay', in *Out of Apathy* (London, 1960).
9   T Lynes, 'Poverty in the Welfare State', *Aspect*, August 1963, cited in R Blackburn, 'The New

Capitalism,' in *Towards Socialism*, p139.

10 In this respect the present situation is far more favourable to the development of a united shop stewards' movement than the situation in the First World War. In the latter case the government's offensive was over the issues of dilution and conscription. Both of these had an immediately divisive effect upon the working class, setting grade against grade—dilution because, while it threatened the economic defences of the skilled men, it widened the prospects of advance for the less skilled, conscription because for a long time the skilled men were exempt. The threat of incomes policy and anti trade union legislation today affects all grades.

Labour's addiction to the rubber stamp

Labour Worker, January 1967

Ralph Miliband, in his book on the Labour Party, points out:

> Of political parties claiming socialism to be their aim, the Labour Party has always been one of the most dogmatic—not about socialism, but about the parliamentary system. Empirical and flexible about all else, its leaders have always made devotion to that system their fixed point of reference and the conditioning factor of their political behaviour...
>
> The leaders of the Labour Party have always rejected any kind of political action (such as industrial action for political purposes) which fell, or which appeared to them to fall, outside the framework and conventions of the parliamentary system. The Labour Party has not only been a parliamentary party; it has been a party deeply imbued by parliamentarism. And in this respect there is no distinction to be made between Labour's political and industrial leaders. Both have been equally determined that the Labour Party should not stray from the narrow path of parliamentary politics.[1]

A number of historical factors have conditioned the mass of British workers to accept parliamentarism. Above all, parliament, for over a century, has been at the centre of reforms granted to the workers.

Competition

All through the 19th and well into the 20th centuries, the typical employer was a great deal smaller than he is today. And the market in which he sold his goods was extremely competitive. Not only were firms much smaller in size than today, but there were far more of them in any particular line of production. Being small, and being in fierce competition amongst themselves, these firms could not on the whole afford individually to pay their workers more or grant them greater concessions than their competitors. An employer who granted his workers very much more than his competitors ran the risk of putting himself out of business.

The economy was subject to a cycle of booms and deep slumps, and the heavy unemployment characteristic of this earlier stage in the capitalist economy provided employers with a reserve army of unemployed workers. In this situation the employers felt no especially strong need to compete with each other for labour by offering their workers a little more to stay with them. And, to a greater extent than today, workers' skills (or lack of skills) were more transferable between factories and industries. This was true of skilled and unskilled workers alike.

When the employers were forced to grant reforms to the workers, they tended to do this all together and all at once through such agencies as parliament. The 19th century and the early 20th century were the great periods of reforms won for workers through parliament. It was through national agitation and propaganda, focused on the parliamentary centre, that workers made many of their gains through their representatives (or their misrepresentatives). When, to avoid worse trouble, the employers paid out for these reforms, they applied to all workers equally, and the cost of them was borne by employers equally. In this way no employer was put at a competitive disadvantage with his rivals.

So long as sharp competition between workers for scarce jobs and cut-throat competition between capitalists were predominant features of the economy, reforms through parliament were central to workers' lives.

Over the last two decades the situation has changed. The typical employer of today is a great deal bigger and there are far fewer employers. As firms have grown in size their monopoly control over the market has increased and competition, in the national market at least, has become much less cut-throat. Because of their size, and because they are less afraid of their competitors than they were, they are more ready to grant reforms to their workers one at a time and on their own.

Shortage

Also, with some exceptions in backward areas like Northern Ireland, the British economy since the beginning of the Second World War has had almost full employment and today there is a shortage of workers. With the virtual disappearance of the reserve army of the unemployed, labour has become a scarce commodity—and the employers are worried about recruiting and keeping their workers.

Machinery and technical processes in factories nowadays are a great deal more expensive than in the past and far more complicated. Because of technical changes, in many industries—and especially in the new, fast-growing and technologically advanced industries—it is becoming increasingly expensive to train workers and increasingly expensive to lose them. The employers hate labour turnover today almost as much as they hate strikes.

The workers therefore turn their attention and their militancy towards the shop floor, which is the most important area where wage gains and fringe benefits can be won, and away from parliament, which has ceased to be a central locus of reform.

Indifference

The workers have become more and more indifferent towards parliament. A Gallup poll showed that many people do not know who George Brown is—some think he is a band leader, others that he is an escaped train robber! Everyone, of course, knows the Beatles. The explanation is probably quite simple—one gets more pleasure from the Beatles than from Brown.

While parliament has ceased to be a locus of any serious reforms, and hence hardly in the centre of workers' attention, it gets a further knock by showing itself completely impotent in face of the real powers that be. The legend of the sovereignty of the British national parliament has shown itself to be a complete sham.

Today Britain is no longer the capitalist 'workshop of the world', but merely one among a number of advanced capitalist countries. It is by no means the largest, and its share in world trade drops year by year as other nations enter the market as industrial producers.

The British government is not the only, or even the most important, agency deciding what happens in Britain. This is particularly clear with regard to its 'social welfare' policies. Even if the Labour government had wanted, for instance, to give the old age pensioners their increased pensions immediately it came to power in October 1964, the pressure of *international* banking opinion made this impossible. The same is true of its 'incomes policy', the present squeeze, the wage freeze, and so on. International business opinion sets the policies of a British capitalist government within quite narrow limits.

This is true of all capitalist countries, of course, but it is especially true of Britain, which is disproportionately 'open' to the pressures of the world market. The fact that the pound is maintained as an international reserve currency, that Britain is dependent on the world market for its importing and exporting activities, and so on, places severe limits on the freedom of movement of any British government that accepts the existing capitalist rules.

Governmental decisions are not made in parliament. They are made at the points of intersection of industry, finance and the civil service, in the cabinet, the new 'planning' bodies and so on—anywhere, indeed, except in parliament. Parliament largely exists now to rubber-stamp decisions made elsewhere. Questions of central importance are made without reference to parliament at all—the decision to manufacture the atom bomb is a famous example, when even the defence minister, Shinwell, was not informed of the decision by Attlee and the chief of staff.

Even today knowledge about how the government made its decisions about the Suez campaign is kept a closely guarded secret. At no stage was parliament given a chance to vote on the growth patterns for different industries proposed in the National Plan. George Brown's plan was drafted on the basis of discussion with the management side of industry and on information supplied by business. Not even the Labour MPs, let alone the rank and file of the labour movement, were consulted about it. The first time the plan was discussed by the Parliamentary Labour Party was on the morning of 3 November—the eve of parliament's reassembly after the summer holidays, and some six weeks after the plan was published.

The rising role of Royal Commissions, State Boards and government inquiries is further evidence of the decline of parliament. Its complete impotence as a focal citadel of power becomes clear in every financial crisis. Lord Cromer, the governor of the Bank of England, managed to negotiate a $3,000 million loan in one night in November 1964.

The atrophy of parliament radically affects Labour MPs. If power corrupts, lack of power corrupts absolutely. If the 'gnomes of Zurich'—or international capitalism, of which British big business is a part—decide the central policies of Britain, why should we bother to send MPs to parliament, each costing us £3,250 a year? Wouldn't we do better to send a delegate to Zurich?

Independent

With increasing capitalist planning, with the continued merging of big business and the state, and with the growing importance of the state, the executive becomes more and more independent of parliamentary decisions. There is an increasing consensus between the heads of government executives, Tory or Labour, and the needs of planned capitalism, above all with regard to the planning of wages.

It is true that remnants of old, traditional Labourism remain in the present, more modern, party. Just as within and alongside the new planning, old capitalist anarchy can still be found, so inside the Wilsonian Labour Party there are still footholds of the old reformism, particularly in the defensive actions on behalf of workers in depressed areas or declining industries.

Irrelevant

Suspended between state monopoly capitalism above and an indifferent mass of people below, Labour MPs are completely powerless and more and more irrelevant.

Until 1914 Marxists called the parties of the Second International—to which the British Labour Party belonged—socialist parties. It was the traumatic experience of August 1914, when the very same leaders who year in and year out inveighed against imperialism and war, jumped on the nationalist bandwagon and rushed to vote for the military budget, that caused Lenin and Luxemburg and their friends to change their characterisation of these parties.

They were no more called socialist parties but reformist parties, which did not intend to overthrow capitalism but to preserve it while, at the same time, carrying out some reforms within its framework—in other words, tinkering with it. They were called parliamentarian-reformist, as they were attached to the bourgeois parliament as the arena for carrying out reforms.

Discipline

In the present stage of planned state-monopoly capitalism social democracy enters its third state. It is neither socialist nor even authentic parliamentary reformist. It is much less than this. Its main task is to discipline the workers to the needs of state-monopoly capitalism.

The struggle of the left inside the Labour Party, and the attitude of socialists towards the party, will be the subject of our next article. This subject is of particular importance, for the overwhelming majority of organised workers still by tradition see in the Labour Party *their* political organisation.

Notes

1   R Miliband, *Parliamentary Socialism* (London, 1961), p11.

On perspectives

International Socialism (first series) 36, April-May 1969

On 22 May 1968 the French prime minister, Pompidou, told the National Assembly, 'Nothing will ever be exactly the same.' Today such a statement sounds platitudinous. We shall continue to work and struggle in the glow of the French May events. Just as between 1789 and 1848, the imagery—the personnel, the dramatic events of the first French Revolution—were the terms of reference of all revolutionaries, and when one reads Lenin or Plekhanov prior to 1905, the events of 1848 and 1871 are central in evaluating the current events in Russia decades later, so France 1968 will be central to the analysis of the tasks and perspectives of revolutionaries in advanced industrial societies in the years to come.

What is necessary, however, is not a euphoric generalisation about the great days of May and June 1968, but a sober analysis of the lessons of these events.

Two dress rehearsals

The best way of evaluating the specific characteristics of the French events is to juxtapose them with the Russian Revolution of 1905, which was a dress rehearsal for 1917. This comparison is made here in an effort to throw light on the specific characteristics of the period in which we live.

First of all the general strike in France far surpassed in magnitude anything that happened in Russia in 1905. In France at the height of the strike some 10 million workers were involved. In Russia, in the month of October 1905, when the strike was at its peak, a little more than half a million workers participated.[1]

However, the duration of the revolutionary wave in France was incomparably shorter. The Russian Revolution continued over a period of some three years. It started in January 1905 and reached its apex in the December insurrection of the same year. This insurrection ended in defeat and the Tsarist autocracy went onto the offensive. In 1906 workers' strikes and peasants' and soldiers' outbreaks were much weaker than a year earlier, but were still very formidable. In 1907 the workers' struggle grew weaker still. However, only at the end of 1907, after three long years, can one speak of the end of the revolution. The wave declined completely, and the level of struggle returned to the pre-1905 standard. The picture becomes clear when one follows the strike statistics:[2]

		Number of strikers
1903		86,832
1904		24,904
1905	First quarter	810,000
	Second quarter	481,000
	Third quarter	294,000
	Fourth quarter	1,277,000
1906	First quarter	269,000
	Second quarter	479,000
	Third quarter	296,000
	Fourth quarter	63,000
1907	First quarter	146,000
	Second quarter	323,000
	Third quarter	77,000
	Fourth quarter	193,000
1908		64,166
1909		46,623

Qualitatively, as regards the form of revolutionary organisation of the class, Russia in 1905 was far ahead of France in 1968. The year 1905 witnessed the birth of soviets—of workers' councils.

The first soviets arose out of the strike movement even prior to the October general strike. In May 1905 a soviet was formed in Ivanovo-Voznesensk, a month later in Kostroma, while in September soviets of printing, tobacco and other workers were formed in Moscow. In October a soviet was formed in St Petersburg. Shortly before the December insurrection in Moscow, the Moscow Soviet of Workers' Deputies came into being, its example being followed in Kiev, Kharkov, Rostov-on-Don, Odessa, Nikolayev, Ekaterinoslav, Vladikavkaz, Revel, Novorossisk, Saratov, Chita, Irkutsky, Krasnoyarsk, Baku and elsewhere.

In France not one workers' council was formed. In fact in only a very few instances were strike committees democratically elected. In practically every plant the trade union nominated the delegates to the strike committee. In Renault there were a few attempts to get elections by the rank and file, but with the exception of one department they were squashed by the CGT and the CP. In the central Citroën factory the officially appointed strike committee was not challenged, and although it was in one of the subsidiary factories (in Nanterre), the attempt failed. As against this, in the chemical factory Rhône-Poulenc-Vitry, the demand for a rank and file committee was so strong that the official one was overthrown, and a new one was elected by union and non-union workers alike.[3]

It is interesting that even in Citroën, where for 16 years there had not been a strike, and where only 7 percent of the workers were organised in trade unions, the union bureaucrats still managed to prevent the election of a democratic rank and file strike committee, and imposed a nominated one. They hastened to do this even before the strike began, as they were afraid that things might get out of hand with such a weak organisation. This is also the reason why the CGT full time officials took the initiative in calling the strike. The most obvious lack in the strike was a network connecting the different strike committees. It did not exist even for factories belonging to the same firm.

If the CGT could not stop the strike it was able to sabotage it by fragmenting the movement—taking what had been a mass movement of the class as a whole and reducing it to a series of disconnected struggles in different industries. Thus on 27 May the Administrative Commission of the CGT declared, 'What the government and employers have not agreed on a national, inter-trades level, we must obtain from them on other levels by means of negotiations which we must demand immediately in each separate branch of industry and trade, such as are being carried on in the nationalised and public sectors.' Thus negotiations with different employers transformed the strike from being general into a collection of separate strikes.

Not only was there no network of strike committees, but in practice the trade union bureaucracies did their best to isolate one strike committee from another. Thus, for instance, the Renault Billancourt CGT refused on 23 May to receive a delegation from Renault Flins.[4]

In Russia the revolutionary political organisations were incomparably larger, more massive and more influential than the groupuscules in France. In November 1906 there were 150,000 members in the Russian Social Democratic Party— 33,000 Bolsheviks, 43,000 Mensheviks, 13,000 Letts, 28,000 Poles and 33,000 members of the Bund.[5] Since the total number of workers employed in large factories was 800,000,[6] the party constituted quite a high proportion of the industrial proletariat. In Petrograd the party had 6,000 members compared with 81,000 workers in large factories in the St Petersburg Gubernia. In the Central Industrial Region there were 20,000 members, and the number of workers in large factories was 277,000.[7]

The membership of the French revolutionary organisations is still to be counted in hundreds, and this out of a working class far larger than that of Russia in 1905-07. The revolutionary press in France is puny compared to that of Russia in the periods under comparison. In Petrograd alone three Social Democratic daily papers were published, with a circulation ranging from 50,000 to 100,000.[8] Trotsky and Parvus, with no organisation, took over a tiny paper, the *Russian Gazette*, and transformed it into a mass, popular paper: 'Within a few days the circulation rose from 30,000 to 100,000. A month later it reached the half million mark'.[9] In France there was not one revolutionary daily, and the circulation of the weeklies was only a few thousand.

In part the explanation of the difference between the pattern of events in France in 1968 and in Russia in 1905 lies at the organisational and ideological levels. In France there is a strong conservative workers' party, beside which there are small, weak revolutionary groups. The resilience of the French Communist Party, and the difficulties facing the groupuscules in gaining credibility in the eyes of the masses, are important factors.[10] The situation in Russia was completely different.

But this is only part of the explanation of the failure of the French struggle to develop to a higher level. The strength of the reformist organisations and ideas and the 'crisis of leadership' are inherent in the objective situation. The two decades of capitalist expansion since 1948 have profoundly affected the labour movements of Western Europe, resulting in 'the fragmentation of the working class', 'privatisation' or, in conventional terms, 'apathy'. This false consciousness was defined by E P Thompson as the idea that individual and sectional problems which are essentially social can be solved by individual and sectional efforts.

The other side of the coin of apathy—cause and effect thereof—is the increasing bureaucratisation of the traditional workers' organisations, the parties and trade unions, and their increasing collaboration with employers and state.

The alienation of workers from their traditional organisations has gone on over a whole generation. This expresses itself in a number of symptoms. Before the First World War the British labour movement had two daily papers—the *Daily Citizen* and the *Daily Herald*. Today with the Labour vote much larger than 60 years ago, the labour movement has not even managed to maintain its weekly *Reynolds News*, later renamed the *Sunday Citizen*.

The French CP, with some 2 million voters, finds it difficult to maintain *L'Humanité*, whose print order is less than 200,000 (of which a big proportion goes to Russia and Eastern Europe). It is true that the Labour Party has 6 million members, but it is doubtful if 10 percent of these know that they are members. The process of alienation is not a conscious act of rejection—the majority of workers are unconscious agnostics, not real atheists, towards the traditional organisations.

The Russian Revolution of 1905 came after a decade of continuous development of the workers into a more and more united, politically conscious class. The 1968 events in France followed a long period of fragmentation and privatisation. In Russia the revolution followed a decade of increasing politicisation of the working class—in France it followed years of depoliticisation.

Reforms and the revolutionary struggle

The basic difference between the background to the 1905 revolution in Russia and the last couple of decades in Western Europe is summed up clearly in the relation between reforms (wage rises, etc) and the generalised, revolutionary, political struggle in the two periods under comparison.

There has probably never been in the history of capitalism a period of 20 years in which real wages rose as quickly as in Western Europe in this period. In Britain real wages have doubled since the war. In the five years 1959-64 hourly earnings rose in Britain by 35 percent, in France by 50 percent, in West Germany by 54 percent, and in Italy by 74 percent.[11] As against this, in Russia wages were practically stagnant up to the 1905 revolution. The average earnings of a factory worker were:

1901	201 roubles	1906	231 roubles
1902	202 roubles	1907	241 roubles
1903	208 roubles	1908	242 roubles
1904	213 roubles	1909	236 roubles
1905	205 roubles	1910	242 roubles
Average for five years: 206 roubles		**Average for five years:** 238 roubles	

This shows that the year 1905 was a turning point: 'Until 1905 the Russian factory worker's wages averaged 206 roubles. After 1905 they average 238 roubles, ie *32 roubles more per year*—an increase of 15.5 percent… The year 1905 improved the worker's living standard to a degree that normally is attained during several decades'.[12]

While workers in Britain, as well as those in other advanced industrial countries, have won the overwhelming majority of strikes during the last two decades, the Russian workers were beaten in the majority of cases, except for the period of the revolution itself: 'The statistics show that during ten years, 1895-1904, the employers won 51.6 percent of the strikes (according to the number of strikers involved); in 1905, 29.4 percent; in 1906, 33.5 percent; in 1907, 57.6 percent; in 1908, 68.8 percent'.[13]

On the basis of the Russian experience Lenin could repeat hundreds of times that reforms are the by-products of revolutionary struggle: 'Partial improvements can be (and always have been in history) merely a by-product of revolutionary class struggle'.[14] 'The truth that reforms are possible only as a by-product of a movement that is completely free of all narrowness of reformism has been confirmed a hundred times in world history and is *particularly* true for Russia today'.[15]

Yet the stabilisation of Western capitalism on the cone of the H-bomb made it possible for reforms to be achieved over a long period independent of revolutionary politics. This is the basic difference between the background to 1968 France and 1905 Russia. This is the main objective factor making it possible for the PCF and CGT leadership to transmute a revolutionary general strike into a series of wage demands.

The new phenomenon, the May-June mass struggle, has not wiped out the inheritance of 20 years, Actually, it must be explained as an outgrowth from this same background. The new, the revolutionary, grew upon the general period of fragmentation, political lull and apathy. This explains, basically, how the greatest revolutionary struggle was channelled into the struggle for such puny, reformed aims.

For decades Marxists used to infer the state of mass consciousness from a few institutional barometers—membership of organisations, readership of papers, etc. The deep alienation of workers from traditional organisations smashed all such barometers to pieces. This explains why there was no way of detecting the imminence of the upheaval in May 1968. And also, more important, it explains the extreme, explosive nature of the events. If the workers in France had been accustomed to participate in the branch life of the trade unions or the Communist Party, these institutions would have served both as an aid and as ballast preventing the rapid uncontrolled spread of the strike movement. The concept of apathy or privatisation is not a static concept. At a certain stage of development—when the path of individual reforms is being narrowed or closed—apathy can transform into its opposite, swift mass action. However, this new turn comes as an outgrowth of a previous stage— the epilogue and the prologue combine. Workers who have lost their loyalty to the traditional organisations, which have shown themselves to be paralysed over the years, are forced into extreme, explosive struggles on their own.

Traditional barometers missing, the policies of the bosses and the state, as well as those of the trade union bureaucrats, are much less sure, much more vacillating, than before. Their reaction, even to marginal challenges, may be unexpected, brutal and seemingly irrational.

The stability of Western capitalism is beginning to falter. This does not mean that Western capitalism is faced with collapse, as in the 1930s. In the coming years we can expect an unevenness in the rate of economic growth, and intermittent expansions. The contradictions in the permanent arms economy, appearing above all in the international liquidity crisis, will prevent systematic growth of the economies of Western Europe. In this unstable situation the forms by which the ruling class exercises its political and ideological control will become more contradictory. During the period of steady economic expansion the bosses were ready to accept a practically autonomous shop stewards' organisation inside the factory and more or less 'liberal' policies outside. The economic faltering, with traditional barometers broken, means that many of those tolerant attitudes will have to go. The political impact of the contradictions in capitalism under such conditions must far exceed their economic significance. By itself apathy, or a declining interest in the traditional reformist organisations (the Labour Party, Communist Party, trade unions, etc), does not mean the *overcoming* of reformist ideology. For this a long struggle is necessary, in which all sections of society are involved, in which all parties and ideas are put to the test, and in which the victory of revolutionary ideas over reformist ideas takes place.

Beyond the fragment

For some two decades the picture of Western capitalism as expanding, with ups and downs but still in a fairly orderly way, and its concomitant, a fragmented working class, more or less fitted reality. Today the picture is much more complicated.

The fragments have not ceased to exist, but the boundaries between them are not static, but conditional and changing. The pure fragment is non-existent. New generalisations rise as superstructures on the fragments, without completely eradicating their boundaries. The vast subsoil of the old fragmentation still exists, but on top of it a new kind of generalisation rises. The picture is a mosaic, patchy and inelegant. But this is the picture of transitional stage we find ourself in today.

To give a few examples. In the booklet *Incomes Policy, Legislation and Shop Stewards* we wrote, 'The need to combine and coordinate the activities of shop stewards at least between the plants of a single combine is self-evident, but moves towards such coordination have been quite slow and faltering'.[16]

Since then, and especially over the last few months, fantastic strides have been taken in building real combine committees, above all in ICI, BMC, Ford, Rolls Royce and GEC-AEI-EE. Who would have visualised a few months ago a complete ban on overtime in Rolls Royce's many factories employing over 50,000 workers to defend the jobs of some 700 workers, or the national Ford strike—the first ever—on 24 February? Again, the 27 February strike called by the Scottish miners, even if it involved only a few tens of thousands, was the first militant political strike since 1926!

The generalisation, beyond the fragment, takes original, unprecedented, complicated patterns. Workers at Injection Moulders in north London occupy their factory for 18 days and nights, 2,100 workers at Armstrong factory in York do the same for a day, so do a few thousand workers in Dagenham's Body Plant. The inspiration did not come from immediate experience—probably LSE and other student sit-ins provided it. When locked out Ivy Bridge building workers decide to try and install 100 homeless families in the almost-completed flats, this is a new kind of generalisation very different to the traditional one of contacting building and other workers to ask for help in their own struggle.

The Prussian minister of internal affairs Herr von Puttkammer coined the famous phrase, 'In every strike there lurks the hydra of revolution.' Lenin, commenting on this statement, said:

> If you say that every strike conceals the hydra of revolution, and he who fails to understand this is no socialist, you are right. Yes, the socialist revolution looms behind every strike. But if you say that every single strike is an immediate step towards the socialist revolution, you will be uttering empty phrases…undoubtedly, clear as it is that behind every strike there looms the hydra of socialist revolution, it is equally clear that the assertion that every strike can develop into revolution is utter nonsense.[17]

What is necessary, above all, is to understand dialectically the relation between the partial—the strike, the struggle for reforms in the fragment—and the total struggle against the system. It is necessary to understand the richness, the many-sided nature of the way—through contradictions, conflicts and upheavals—the fragments are being bridged in real life.

With the increasing fusion of state and business (incomes policy and labour legislation) the boundaries between fragments have become more and more conditional and dynamic. Something new grows out of the old—different 'stages' appear simultaneously. In such a situation sharp changes, sudden turns, unexpected combinations of different and conflicting elements of struggle, consciousness and organisation in the working class are bound to appear again and again. The whole movement can develop only as the result of very long and numerous struggles.

Young workers and other workers

To add to the complexity of the picture one must not only remember that all the boundaries between 'fragments' of the working class are dynamic, but that cutting across the class is the division between young and not-so-young workers.

The student rebellion had some effect in radicalising at least one section of the French working class—the young workers. They, more than anyone else, are affected by the economic crisis of French society. It is very difficult for them to find a job, and if they do, it is often dead end. From childhood they are roughed up by the police as 'delinquents' or rebels. They are affected by the ideological and moral crisis of society.

When the students proved on 6 May that not only were they ready to fight the police, but they were also able to stand their ground against them, thousands of young workers joined them. The number increased even more on 10 May, the Night of the Barricades. After that thousands of workers started visiting the Sorbonne. The revolutionary elan there caught their imagination. The young workers are very similar in their attitudes to society to the students. They rebel against the whole set-up. The old workers' thinking is basically concrete. It grows from bread and butter issues that are with him all his life, from trade union consciousness. The young workers have usually been in a particular factory only a short time and they have no great interest in the specific work conditions. Socialist consciousness transcends trade union consciousness. The young workers, like the students, are practically free of trade union consciousness.

The young workers can provide much of the enthusiasm necessary for sustaining a revolutionary organisation. When massive working class resistance to the system is lacking, the youth's protest can focus the aspirations of many working class militants, and give confidence to old timers who have been let down time and again by the traditional organisations and feel isolated among the more backward workers. In France the young workers showed much greater self-confidence than the old ones. Unfortunately the cleavage between the age groups caused many of the young workers to leave the factories during the struggle and to move to a milieu more congenial to them—among the students in the Latin Quarter.

For Marx the concept of exploitation transcends that of alienation. The latter describes the situation of the individual in an inimical society; the former explains the cohesion of collective workers in opposition to the ruling class. The young workers cannot sustain a struggle unless they unite with workers of all ages against the ruling class. The young workers cannot sustain a struggle unless they unite with workers of all ages in organisations based on the place of work.

From the general to the particular

The introduction of the incomes policy means that workers in a factory face not only their individual employer but also the state, as the representative of the ruling class. The two, employer and state, do not make a simple, unified, homogeneous front. While Barbara Castle dictates the general norm, the individual employer opens up a second front, offering the workers a rise above the norm at the price of worse conditions and weakened shopfloor organisation.

The response necessary is both general—political; and particular—applicable to specific industries and places of work. Transitional programmes of demands connecting the particular with the general are needed. Such programmes, by definition, must be adapted to the specific conditions of different industries, different plants, etc. The point of reference of every such programme must be a many-sided investigation of the dialectical relation between the state, the employing class and the workers in the particular industry or plant. Some two and a half years ago we wrote:

> Both the rise of the 'shop steward' organisations and the number of unofficial strikes are symptoms (among other things) of the common aspirations of the working class towards workers' control. Under capitalism the worker is a cog in the machine with no say in the running of production, and no part in the creative organisation of his work. The growing number of strikes in Britain express the worker's rebellion against this subordination, this mutilation, limitation and alienation of his own creativity, only too clearly.[18]

> The urge for workers' control is becoming more stridently expressed in strikes, as the decline in the proportion of strikers over purely wage issues shows: 'In the 20 years of high employment from 1940 the proportion of strikes about "wage questions *other than* demands for increase" and (particularly) about "working arrangements, rules and discipline" rose remarkably, from one-third of all stoppages to three quarters... One *could* say that these disputes involve attempts to submit managerial discretion and authority to agreed—or failing that, customary—rules; alternatively, that they reflect an implicit pressure for more democracy and individual rights in industry'.[19]

With productivity agreements beginning to play a central role, all issues of conditions become much more clearly and closely intertwined. The question of workers' control over production and the question of political power will come to the centre of the arena of workers' struggles.

The strategy, if one may grace the chaotic, spontaneous, practically blind reaction of the industrial rank and file militants over two decades with this word, was simple—let the national leadership of the trade unions deal with industry-wide bargaining, fixing the floor of wages, and let the shop stewards deal with local bargaining to raise the ceiling. What the militant cared most about was the latter, wage drift. Bargaining within the individual firm took place over such matters as piecework rates and other forms of payment by results, additions to wage rates such as bonuses and local rules and practices including the manning of machines and demarcation questions.

We cannot follow the syndicalists in idolising fragmented militancy. However militant a body of workers, unless this militancy is generalised into political action, it is bound to increase the gulf between workers in less fortunate positions (old workers, or workers in stagnating or declining industries) and workers in a strong position. Sectional militancy multiplies the fragmentation of the class, substituting local or sectional consciousness for class consciousness. Hence it is possible for Smethwick workers to be quite militant industrially and at the same time racist. The sectional pressure delivers better wages, but it cannot solve problems like housing, which depend on state-wide policies (policies that depend very closely on international factors such as the strength of the pound, the dollar, its effect on the interest rate, etc). The racist trap is the result of the limitations of sectional action and sectional consciousness.

With state intervention in incomes policy, and the drive towards productivity agreements, the helplessness of local militancy that does not tie up with the general experience of the class will become more pronounced. With the move away from piece rates, the sharp cuts in overtime working (and it was control over these two things which made the shopfloor organisation decisive), and negotiation of productivity agreements in individual plants passing into the hands of full time union officials and 'experts', the challenge to the shopfloor organisation is greater than ever before.

The vacillation of the trade union bureaucracy between the state, employers and the workers, with splits in the far from homogeneous bureaucracy will continue, and becomes more accentuated during the coming period. The union bureaucracy is both reformist and cowardly. Hence its ridiculously impotent and wretched position. It dreams of reforms but fears to settle accounts in real earnest with the state (which not only refuses to grant reforms but even withdraws those already granted), and it also fears the rank and file struggle which alone can deliver reforms. The union bureaucrats are afraid of losing what popular support they still maintain but are more afraid of losing their own privileges vis-à-vis the rank and file. Their fear of the mass struggle is much greater than their abhorrence of state control of the unions. At all decisive moments the union bureaucracy is bound to side with the state, but in the meantime it vacillates. It is important to see that this attitude actually introduces confusion and disorganisation into state policies themselves—for instance, the hesitations of James Conway in the Ford dispute must make Barbara Castle's steps less sure.

It is wrong to confuse the employers and the state with the ambivalent union bureaucracy, and to ignore the conflicts between them or to brush them aside. For the very reason of its bureaucratic position, the union bureaucracy is in conflict with the workers, but because of its dependence on its members it is bound to reflect workers' pressures to some extent. Its policy is not consistent. Even the pattern of its retreats in the face of threats from employers or the state is not completely predictable. During a whole historical period the shopfloor organisation existed alongside but relatively independent of the trade union machine. The mutual relations between these two was clearly expressed by the existence of wage drift, determined by local negotiation, and the national consolidation of gains by the union. During the long period of coexistence of shopfloor and trade union machinery, the latter became more and more bureaucratic, and the workers less and less interested in it. Democracy on the factory floor managed to coexist with bureaucracy in the trade union structure. But even in the heyday of shopfloor militancy the syndicalist apathy or indifference towards the official unions was unjustified. The shop stewards' committees always relied on the union machine in lesser issues against management (court cases about accidents, etc) and they quite often found it very important to try to get official recognition for strike action. They often used the union as an important channel of communication with other fragments of the class. Above all, they needed union recognition in order to get support from the more backward workers in their own place of work.

Productivity deals and long term agreements must encourage the intervention of the full time officers in local negotiations. The trend will be to transfer local negotiations away from the hands of the shop stewards and into the hands of experts. The interests of the employers in disciplining the shopfloor militants, and the trade union bureaucracy in integrating the shop stewards into the union structure, converge. But this is only one trend. In the United States it is practically completed because it has had a run of some three decades almost free of deep economic convulsions in the economy. The shop stewards in the United States are often simply the trade union bureaucracy's policeman on the beat.[20] In Britain the trend has begun too late, in a period of much greater convulsions in British capitalism, and it will meet incomparably greater resistance. Even if this trend is bound to win ultimately, in the meanwhile Marxists cannot deal only with ultimates but must participate in the struggles against it. Apathy towards the trade unions will become more and more an impediment even to the immediate economic struggle for the defence of labour conditions. The demand for workers' control of the trade unions will become more and more vital. This demand can take the authentic form of a demand for radical changes in the structure of the unions—election of all union officials, right of recall, paying them wages no higher than those of the members they represent—or the purely reformist, opportunist form of the CP and 'left' labour—'Vote for X.'

The question of workers' control over conditions, over speed-up, staffing of machinery, etc, and the question of workers' control over the trade unions, will become more and more intertwined.

Bankruptcy of the traditional left

The trade union bureaucracy is basically divided in its attitude to the incomes policy into two sections—the right accepts it; the other, the 'left' (Hugh Scanlon, Frank Cousins, Jack Jones, Clive Jenkins, etc), tries to circumvent it by getting extra pennies for the workers in exchange for selling conditions. Both sections of the bureaucracy try to avoid a massive workers' confrontation with the employers and the state. The Parliamentary Labour Party and the CP with its 'British [parliamentary] Road to Socialism' are prisoners of this strategy.

The main industrial strategy of the CP has been for a long time winning official positions in the trade union hierarchy. With the increasing integration of the union bureaucracy with the state, and its ideological justification under 'Labour', the irrelevance of CP policies is bound to increase.

CP policies are being undermined from another direction too. For decades it used to get a new infusion of blood from thousands of industrial militants who in practice cared less for trade union elections than for plant militancy. Many of them were to all intents and purposes less interested in the CP as a *political* organisation, then as a community of industrial militants. The majority of CP members in industry for many years have been really pure syndicalists. With the encroachment of general on local issues—incomes policy, legislation to emasculate the shop stewards, etc—the coexistence of syndicalist tactics and political reformism is undermined. Every time a general issue is raised, the CP members in industry are split from top to bottom. Thus, during the anti-Devlin strike in 1967, CP dockers in Southampton supported Devlin and scabbed; so did Lindley, the CP leader of the lightermen in London; Will Paynter's policy of no resistance to closures and attacks on absenteeism split the CP miners, etc.

The crisis of the international Communist movement increases the impotence of the CP. This has left the members of the party cynical, apathetic and disillusioned. The CP plays more and more a routine bureaucratic role. Its incapacity to mobilise its own members in any campaign is unbelievable.

The traditional organisations, the Labour Party and CP, will prove completely incapable of attracting the youth, students and workers who are in rebellion against the whole capitalist system.

Difficulties for revolutionaries

The old forest of reformism is withering away. The trees are without leaves; the trunks are dying. But in society old ideas are not wiped away unless they are replaced by new ones, and the shoots of revolution are very small indeed in the British labour movement. Reformism can never be defeated by programmes. It can only be defeated by deeds. The education of the masses—not the pedantic SPGB version—can never be separated from the independent political revolutionary struggle. Only struggle discloses to the workers the magnitude of the struggle, widens their horizons, and clarifies their minds.

The point of departure of a revolutionary organisation is the experience—

the action, thinking and organisation—of the workers, and the aim of its operation is raising the historical initiative and drive of the working class.

The weakness of revolutionaries in Britain at present is quite obvious. Small in number, often isolated because of social composition—white collar and student—from the main sections of the working class, split into a number of groupings, and above all lacking experience in leading mass struggles. But these weaknesses can be overcome. Readiness to learn, readiness to experiment systematically, above all readiness to try and translate the general theories into practical activities—this is what is necessary. In a complex and rapidly changing situation, readiness to move from simple tasks to more difficult ones, above all readiness to overcome one's own mistakes, is crucial: 'The fighting party of the advanced class need not fear mistakes. What it should fear is persistence in mistakes, refusal to admit and correct the mistakes'.[21]

The greatest defect of revolutionaries who have been isolated for years from the mass movement is their inclination to make a virtue out of necessity, and concentrate on theories to the exclusion of practice, forgetting that above all the duty of a revolutionary is to raise theory to the level of practice.

To say that we are in a transitional period is not enough. We must be clear what is specific to the transition, and devise forms of propaganda and organisation that will take account of the specific characteristics of the situation. The main features of the immediate period are, to recapitulate: quick changes, fluctuations, economic, social and political, reflecting both the expansion of capitalism and its intermittent, unsystematic nature; reactions on the part of bosses and state that are disproportionate to the economic challenge, and hence appear as irrationally nasty; withering away of loyalties to traditional organisations—the 'vacuum on the left'—and inertia of old reformist ideas, so long as they are not positively replaced by revolutionary ones; fragmentation of the working class and generalisation beyond the fragments, co-existing with the boundaries between the fragments conditional and changing swiftly, and their combination in a many-sided fashion.

Fatalism, that is inimical to Marxism in general, exposes its poisonous nature especially under such dynamic conditions. The initiative and perseverance of revolutionaries are at a special premium.

Postscript

For clarity of direction it will be very important to locate the concept of the new transition period we have entered into, in the context of our previous analysis. What follows will try to do just this.

(1) After the Second World War three options were open to Marxists in the evaluation of the immediate future of capitalism:
(a) To assume that the war changed the features of capitalism very little, ie that massive unemployment, very low wages, etc, will continue. (This, basically, has been the line of the SLL.)

(b) Capitalism has changed completely, is no more irrational and anarchic. (This was the position of Anthony Crosland and John Strachey.)

(c) Capitalism is as irrational as ever but now its irrationality is not so much in non-use of productive capacity, but in misuses—the permanent arms economy.

The theory of the permanent arms economy is both a continuation of the basic position of Lenin, Luxemburg and Trotsky about the completely reactionary nature of modern capitalism and a partial negation of this position. The new stage in the permanent arms economy over the last couple of years—the increase in the element of instability, especially the increasing international competition between national capitalist powers, the liquidity crisis, etc, are nothing but a further development, ie a continuation and negation of the same.

(2) What about workers' consciousness? The numerous defeats of the British workers in the 1920s (Black Friday in 1921, the engineers' lockout in 1922, the defeat of the miners in 1926) shattered the workers' self-confidence. The massive unemployment of the 1930s went further to weaken their resistance. The full employment (or near full employment) of the war and the post-war period gave the workers new confidence, but at the same time fragmented the working class—sectional consciousness largely replaced class consciousness. 'Do it yourself' reformism was a partial advance—to self-reliance and self-activity—but also a partial retreat.

The development of the consciousness of the class was spiral in form. Now, again, the new stage is a partial negation of the stage before: the locus of action breaks the boundaries of the fragment.

(3) The propaganda and agitation of revolutionaries. Before the Second World War the agitation carried on by revolutionaries was putting forward, on the whole, highly generalised slogans. The 1938 Transitional Programme written by Trotsky was very characteristic. Dealing with mass unemployment, with the mass threat of fascism and war, there is no reference to local points of struggle (shop steward committees, unofficial strikes, etc) at all. However, the general political slogans had no impact to speak of in the labour movement. (The effectiveness of a Transitional Programme depends not only on the logical connection between its parts, but above all on the actual class forces which make it possible to carry the transition from one demand to another.)

After the war, because of the general expansion of capitalism and the great improvement in workers' wages, a propaganda that tried to generalise from the fragments again had no impact to speak of.

Now, with the new stage—the increasing similarities between the experiences of workers in the different fragments and the trend to break down the borders of fragments—a revolutionary agitation that is both *general* and *specific* can start having a greater impact than ever before.[22]

International Socialism, up to now at best an ideological trend, now faces the challenge and opportunity to become linked with the mass working class movement.

In summing up, one can say that the third stage the British working class has entered is a 'negation of the negation', synthesising elements of the first stage (the 1920s and 30s)—class identification—and of the second stage (1945-65)—self-confidence. The synthesis is higher than the individual elements joined in it and pregnant with great revolutionary possibilities.

Notes

1 V I Lenin, *Collected Works* (London), vol 23, p247.
2 V I Lenin, *Collected Works*, vol 19, pp534-536.
3 *Action* 6.
4 *Analyses et Documents* 155.
5 V I Lenin, *Collected Works*, vol 11, p265.
6 V I Lenin, *Collected Works*, vol 11, p357.
7 V I Lenin, *Collected Works*, vol 11, p358. Lenin was, of course, not satisfied with the size of the party. He wrote, 'We must learn to recruit five times and ten times as many workers for the party... We suffer from routine, we must fight against it... Our slogan is: for a larger Social-Democratic Labour Party' (V I Lenin, *Collected Works*, vol 11, p359).
8 V I Lenin, *Collected Works*, vol 23, p248.
9 L Trotsky, *My Life* (New York, 1970).
10 T Cliff and I Birchall, *France: The Struggle Continues* (London, 1968), pp45-50.
11 *Financial Times*, 10 March 1965.
12 V I Lenin, *Collected Works*, vol 28, pp258-259.
13 V I Lenin, *Collected Works*, vol 26, p385.
14 V I Lenin, *Collected Works*, vol 26, p170.
15 V I Lenin, *Collected Works*, vol 19, p327.
16 T Cliff and C Barker, *Incomes Policy, Legislation and Shop Stewards* (London, 1966), p97.
17 V I Lenin, *Collected Works*, vol 27, p95.
18 T Cliff and C Barker, *Incomes Policy*, p89.
19 T Cliff and C Barker, *Incomes Policy*, p90.
20 *Sunday Times*, 9 February 1969.
21 V I Lenin, *Collected Works*, vol 26, p58.
22 Only once before in the past generation has Trotskyism had some real links with the mass working class movement—during the Second World War.

The employers' offensive: productivity deals and how to fight them

First published 1970

Preface

Ten years ago productivity bargaining was a new and strange phenomenon to most workers in British industry. Today it is at the very centre of our industrial life. Employers, trade unions and, above all, government ministers have come to champion the cause of 'productivity'. The prices and incomes policy, at first hardly more than 'wage freeze' in disguise, is now aimed at forcing workers to abandon the straight wage claim in favour of a productivity deal. Already more than 30 percent of industrial workers are covered by such deals. Many are coming back for the second or third 'bite at the cherry'. But an increasing number of workers are finding that they got a very bad bargain—that the relatively large wage increases have soon been eaten away by inflation, but the conditions they sold and the changes in work practice they accepted have become a serious threat to job security, earnings and, above all, trade union organisation within the factory.

The central argument of this book is to show that 'productivity' is part of a major offensive by the employing class of this country to shift the balance of forces in industry permanently in their direction. The author has investigated over 100 'deals' in order to discover the underlying trends that go to make up the offensive, to show how techniques such as time and motion study, measured day work and grading schemes are aimed at 'disciplining' the workers and undermining the power of the shop stewards who, more than anything else, have been the instrument by which workers have maintained their standards in the last 20 years.

In addition to investigating almost the entire output of the Prices and Incomes Board, I have drawn directly on the experience of workers who have been involved in productivity deals in a whole range of industries. In the final chapters I attempt to draw up a strategy for fighting productivity deals and conclude that the total nature of the employers' offensive requires a total strategy in reply—that is, a socialist strategy.

There is no doubt that in the field of productivity bargaining employers are at an enormous advantage when it comes to access to information, facts and advice. This book aims to give shop stewards and their members the same advantages, and to play a small part in arming the working class to resist the 'productivity offensive'. As far as possible I back up statements with facts and figures that socialists and militants in the unions will be able to use in discussions with fellow workers.

Not many people will want to read the book right through at one go, so it may be useful to have a short summary of it. In this way it will be easier to look up different parts of the argument as they are needed.

The structure of the book is as follows:

Part I: Reasons for the employers' offensive (Chapter One).
Part II: Nature of the offensive—the nature of productivity bargaining (Chapter Two to Chapter Eight).
Part III: The legal attack on workers' rights (Chapter Nine).
Part IV: The ideological argument (Chapter Ten).
Part V: The role of the unions (Chapter Eleven and Chapter Twelve).
Part VI: How to resist (Chapter Thirteen).

The present book tries to aid militant workers and socialists in understanding the general nature of productivity deals and their various specific features. The book aims to help to develop a working class strategy which fits the current industrial and political objective situation but at the same time uncompromisingly asserts the primacy of rank and file control, both at the place of work and in the union, and over the state.

As productivity bargaining is rooted in government incomes policy, the present book is a continuation of a previous work, for which the present author was responsible—*Incomes Policy, Legislation and Shop Stewards* by Tony Cliff and Colin Barker (London, 1966).

The central theme of this book was:

(1) Changes in the nature of capitalism—increasing size of monopolies, sharpening international competition, radical technological progress, etc—make it necessary for capitalism to 'plan wages', to have an incomes policy.
(2) Incomes policy is nothing but a wages policy, shifting the distribution of the national cake to the advantage of capital.
(3) The main butt of attack of employers and state will be the shopfloor organisation, shop stewards committees and the like.
(4) Anti-strike legislation will be enacted to discipline the rank and file.
(5) The state will strive to incorporate the trade unions into partnership with management, and incorporate the shop stewards into the official union machine.

(6) The general attack on workers' conditions and organisation will lead to general resistance—economic, ideological and political.

(7) A new workers' movement would arise, overcoming the fragmentation of the working class.

Looking back, three and a half years later, it is clear that the above analysis —to be precise, points (1) to (5)—stood the test of time. However, the analysis in points (6) and (7) erred by telescoping the process. Life proved much more complex than the theory put forward. The general incomes policy did not stem the rise of all wages. It affected different sections of the working class differently. Government incomes policy was transmuted via numerous and very varied productivity deals. In addition, the process of general integration of the trade union bureaucracy into the state was uneven and very contradictory—some union leaders moved to the left, while others continued to drift to the right. The generalisation of workers' struggle was impeded also by subjective factors—the lack of a strong militant socialist party to unify the class.

The present book is both a continuation and, I hope, an improvement on the previous one.

I hope the book will prove useful. For workers and socialists today, as always, there are three tasks in the struggle for socialism—studying the changes in capitalism and the working class, making propaganda among other workers, and organising for struggle. If this book can help at all in these three tasks it will have served its purpose.

Chapter One: Why productivity deals?
The avalanche of productivity deals

Few would dispute that productivity agreements are among the most important facts of industrial life in Britain today. Yet it is less than ten years since the first major deal was negotiated at the Esso oil refinery at Fawley in Hampshire. How many workers who read of this strange new phenomenon would have guessed that in such a short time it would come to dominate the lives of so many? The Fawley deal was signed in July 1960. It was not until the spring of 1962 that the details became known to the press. News of the agreement marked the beginning of a movement which was slow in getting off the ground. During 1963 and 1964 negotiations for four similar agreements were taking place at British Hydrocarbon Chemicals Ltd, Shell Chemicals (Petrochemicals) at Carrington, Alcan Industries at Rogerstone, and the Spencer Steelworks at Richard Thomas and Baldwins. Negotiations for a productivity deal also went on for several years in the electricity supply industry, culminating in an agreement on 1 July 1964.

The Esso Milford Haven agreement and the Mobil Oil Coryton agreements followed suit. Roughly at the same time several agreements concerned with the distribution of oil were made, followed by various other road haulage agreements for such bulk products as beer. London busmen were encompassed by a productivity deal in 1964. A year later, in November 1965, municipal busmen were granted a productivity bonus when they operated large capacity standee and one-man buses.

In December 1966 the PIB estimated the spread of productivity deals thus: 'Over the last six years, productivity agreements…have probably affected no more than half a million workers'.[1]

But immediately after the publication of this report there was a landslide towards the adoption of productivity criteria throughout the nation's negotiating machinery. In 1967 the number of productivity deals registered at the Department of Employment and Productivity averaged about 60 per month. Once the rush had started, the pace grew more intense. For the first five months of 1968 the number of deals registered rose to 75 per month, and the number shot up in June of that year to a level of about 200 per month for the remaining seven months of the year. Since the beginning of 1969 the number of productivity deals registered at the DEP was at a lower level, but still double that of the first half of 1968.

> In February 1969 this register recorded some 2,500 cases covering around 41 million workers, or 20 percent of all employed workers…at the end of June 1969 the register recorded some 3,000 cases covering approximately 6 million workers, or 25 percent of all employed workers.[2]

It took about 100 years for the piece-work payments system to spread until it encompassed two fifths of the British working class. Productivity deals engulfed some 25 percent in a few years. What fantastic speed!

With justified satisfaction the *Financial Times* could declare, 'The country's present obsession with productivity probably exceeds the wildest dreams of those who were trying to spread the word five years ago'.[3]

All-embracing

Productivity deals have engulfed all sections of the labour market, from the 350,000 miners and 138,000 workers in the electricity supply industry to the 120 employees involved in the Milford Haven agreement. Altogether around 5 million manual workers are now involved in productivity deals. But that is not all—for increasingly white collar workers are being drawn into the net.

In a research paper on productivity agreements in offices, published by the Engineering Employers' Federation, it is stated:

> The notion that white collar, especially clerical, workers cannot be measured effectively is a myth that must be dispelled. Investigations made during the course of this study have shown that there are few areas indeed which are impractical or non-economic to measure.
>
> Information collected by the writer from many organisations in addition to the one providing case study material bore out the contention that most white collar areas were only 50 percent effective, and that in most clerical areas the effectiveness was less.
>
> Installation of control techniques almost invariably increases total effectiveness by at least 25 percent.[4]

Although slow to start with, productivity bargaining has advanced rapidly into offices since 1967, and by 1970 around 1 million office workers were covered by them.

The 'productivity' offensive

It is the aim of this book to show that the dramatic growth of productivity bargaining is not an accident but part of a determined offensive by the employing class which has as its final aim the shifting of the balance of forces in industry significantly in its favour. The attack is a total one—in other words, it seeks to bring all the weapons into the field against the worker: the state with its Prices and Incomes Board and anti trade union legislation; the trade union bureaucracy, almost unanimous in their backing for 'productivity'; the so-called 'science' of work study; and a massive propaganda campaign through the mass media aimed at convincing workers that they have a common bond with employers in promoting industrial efficiency and the 'national interest'.

The aim of the employers' strategy is to split the workers one from another, to destroy workplace organisation by either muzzling the shop stewards or integrating them into the union machine, and to use the union leadership as a disciplinary agent against those who fight back. In other words, the strategy is aimed at finding a *permanent* solution to employers' problems.

That this strategy has been clearly and carefully thought out is nowhere more dramatically demonstrated than in a secret circular from the headquarters of ICI to the senior management of its local factories, which has come into our hands. This document, sent out during ICI's battle to implement its first productivity deal in 1965, which was known as MUPS (Manpower Utilisation and Payment System), shows very clearly the forces at play—on both sides—in the productivity battlefield. For this reason I have reproduced it in full at this stage:[5]

MUPS progess report

Q: Some considerable time has elapsed since the publication of the company's proposals. Why has so little real progress been made?

A: It appears that resistance to MUPS is mainly due to organised groups of militant stewards in the main centres of production (Teesside, Huddersfield and Manchester).

Q: What action has the company taken to combat this attitude?

A: The policy of the company has been to 'short circuit' this activity by direct appeals to employees via company publications (house magazines, etc) and to enlist the aid of national officers to 'discipline' the most active participants.

Q: Has this resistance any political significance?

A: It is thought that certain 'leftist' groups are active on Teesside, and at Huddersfield there are at least two members of the 'extreme' political 'left'. The position in other areas is more obscure.

Q: Why has the company not used sanctions against the 'offenders'?

A: These militants are active in recognised 'official' trade union bodies (district committee, branch officers, etc) and any attempt to discipline them by the company could result in the hardening of national officer opinions of our objectives within the scheme.

Q: What is the extent of 'unofficial' shop steward activity within the company?

A: There exists an unofficial 'national committee' comprising a number of the most militant shop stewards, which meets regularly, from time to time.

This sort of activity appeals to the more militant of the company's employees and for that reason must be taken seriously.

The policy of the company is to engage these groups in protracted discussions on limited objectives, at the same time attempting to make *real* progress in the more *receptive areas*.

Q: What about factory 'organisation'?

A: Shop stewards 'committees' exist in some factories, but these are by no means general throughout the company. There is conflict of interest between craft and general workers' unions, and the MUPS proposals sharpen the more basic of these.

Q: When can the elimination of this resistance be expected?

A: It is thought that as government pressure is brought upon the unions' national bodies to conclude the MUPS, some of this pressure will be exerted by the national officers on their more recalcitrant members, so that in time the trade union side will itself remove this resistance.

There is evidence that 'outside the company' influences have a bearing on this problem (tutorial staff at further education centres and universities are formulating policy, etc, and providing research for the more organised militant groups).

Q: What steps can be taken locally?

A: Every effort must be made to publicise the successes of the trial sites and to minimise the 'setbacks'. Militant shop stewards should be 'presented' to more reasonable employees as 'troublemakers', etc, and any action, industrial or otherwise, should be accorded the minimum of publicity, if any.

Attempts must be made to isolate the militants from their membership before any sanctions are applied.

Motivation of the Teesside manufacturing complex appears to be egotistical on the part of the main protagonists and some success may be achieved if this is recognised and approaches made accordingly.

'Official' trade union opinion is that a 'hard core' of shop stewards is responsible for the relatively slow progress of the MUPS proposals.

These, then, are the questions we must answer. Why is it that ICI is so desperate to implement the deal? How can it be so certain of the support and backing of the government and trade union officials in this job? What are the weaknesses in the workers' unity that ICI expects to exploit, and why does the management expect the unofficial committees and 'militant groups' to provide the only serious opposition to its plans? Above all, it is clear that ICI sees as its greatest strength the ignorance of the mass of the workers of the real aims of the deal and its results in terms of their wages and conditions. This is where we hope that this book can play a part in developing an effective counter to the 'productivity' offensive.

Reasons for incomes policy

One cannot grasp the massive move towards productivity deals without understanding the role of the government's incomes policy in softening up workers, preparing them to accept the plunge. The motives behind productivity bargaining are the same as those that animated the incomes policy.

Practically all the Western capitalist countries have embarked on an incomes policy course—France, Italy, Sweden, the Netherlands, Belgium and Austria. In Britain it was the Tory government of Macmillan that first started on this road. In July 1961 the then Chancellor of the Exchequer, Selwyn Lloyd, introduced a pay pause as part of a national incomes policy. The pause was to end in March 1962, and be replaced by a more permanent regulation of wage rises. In February 1962 the government issued a white paper called 'Incomes Policy: The Next Step', which set out the notion of the 'guiding light'. The increase in wages and salaries in 1962 was to be kept within the 2.5 percent figure by which it was expected productivity would rise during the year.

When Wilson came to power he continued along the same path.

To understand the motives behind the move towards incomes policy over the past decade in practically all countries of Western Europe, we need to comprehend the changing situation facing those who own and control industry, the capitalist class.

[Editor's note: The next two sections, 'The Changing Pattern of Investment' and 'International Competition', were reproduced from *Incomes Policy, Legislation and Shop Stewards*, and can be found on pp28-32 of this book.]

Chapter Two: The general characteristics of productivity bargaining
Incomes policy fails to stem wage rise

The Labour government's incomes policy has gone through a number of stages. In December 1964 representatives of the government, the Trades Union Congress and the employers' organisations signed a 'Joint Statement of Intent on Productivity, Prices and Incomes'. Following in its wake, the National Board for Prices and Incomes (PIB) was set up, under the chairmanship of former Tory MP Aubrey Jones. Since the board's recommendations were not mandatory, this first stage of the policy was 'voluntary'.

In the second stage, lasting from July 1966 to June 1967, the government imposed a standstill on all wage increases for six months, and then severe restraint accompanied by a harsh deflationary policy for another six months. During this stage wages were allowed to rise only under exceptional circumstances. The freeze was on.

In the third stage, between July 1967 and March 1968, the nil norm for wage increases was replaced by a 3 to $3^1/_2$ percent norm, and the government took the power to delay a proposed pay increase for up to six months.

The fourth stage began in April 1968, with the cancellation of the government's power to postpone wage rises. A ceiling was imposed on all rises of $3^1/_2$ percent, although subject to specific exceptions, namely where there was a marked contribution to productivity. This stage continued (according to the Prices and Incomes Act 1968) until the end of 1969, during which time the government had the power to hold wage rises beyond the $3^1/_2$ percent ceiling for up to 11 months.

On the face of it such a massive legislation should have curbed wage rises. However, its impact was very limited indeed. Up to July 1966, as the incomes policy was merely 'voluntary', it hardly affected wage rises at all. In the period July 1966 to June 1967 the dampening of wage rises was very successful. Between the second quarter of 1966 and the second quarter of 1967 the total wage bill rose by no more than 2 percent, as compared with rises of 4.1 percent and 5 percent respectively in the comparable periods of wage restraint of 1957-58 and 1961-62. However, after June 1967 a thaw set in. In 1967-68 total wages increased by 7 percent, as against 4.9 percent in 1958-59 and 4.5 percent in 1959-60. For the two years together, the 1966-68 rise of 9.2 percent was exactly the same as in 1957-59, and slightly lower than the rise of 9.7 percent in 1961-63.[1]

All in all, in the four years from October 1964 to October 1968 the average hourly earnings (excluding effects of overtime) rose by 27 percent, as against 23 percent in the four preceding years.[2]

Even Aubrey Jones is very cautious regarding the effectiveness of the incomes policy. He believes that the net effect of the policy has been that the 'average annual increase in earnings in recent years may have been just under 1 percent less than otherwise it would have been'.[3]

This was a very tentative conclusion. Of course there is no sure way to tell what the increase in earnings would have been had there been no incomes policy.

Nevertheless a declaration of intent, and even a paper law, could not stop well organised workers in their trade unions from pushing their wages upwards to try and keep pace with rising prices. But the indirect effect of the incomes policy was much greater than its direct effect. For the incomes policy prepared the ground for spreading productivity deals, a far more sophisticated weapon for the employing class.

The 1965 white paper on prices and incomes,[4] as well as the 1967 white paper, stressed that there was one 'legitimate' loophole to the earning norms fixed by the PIB. Pay is allowed above the norm 'where the employees concerned, for example by accepting more exacting work or a major change in working practices, make a direct contribution towards increasing productivity in the particular firm or industry'.[5]

Aubrey Jones crossed the t's and dotted the i's:

[There] is a strong case for encouraging the spread of productivity agreements which conform with the requirements of a prices and incomes policy. We attach great importance to this relationship between the two for, just as we think productivity agreements can further the aims of the policy, so we believe a prices and incomes policy can provide the most favourable environment for successful productivity agreements.

The rate of growth of productivity agreements will depend in our view upon the maintenance of a prices and incomes policy. All that we have heard suggests that the effect of government policy, especially since July 1966, has been to direct the attention of both the employers and trade unionists away from conventional bargaining and towards productivity bargaining. But since productivity agreements require time and effort whereas conventional bargaining is easy, many of them might turn back if the pressure were removed.

The Labour government blocked the path to a direct advance of wages, but left the trapdoor of productivity bargaining wide open.

One should not, however, draw the conclusion that incomes policy has served only as a prelude to the introduction of productivity deals. The failure of incomes policy in itself contributed to the pressure for productivity bargaining. The failure of incomes policy to hold down wages dictated the move towards productivity deals—ie making workers pay, by working harder, under worse conditions, for their wage increases. This is where the employers' offensive springs from. The years of effort to impose the incomes policy located the main obstacle —shopfloor organisation. Hence the determination to eliminate this power, not by direct confrontation, but by structural alterations to the entire fabric of industrial relations, which would seek to isolate and undermine this power.

A long sales talk

Because an authentic productivity deal represents a radical change in work (and life) conditions, its introduction and implementation takes not only months, but often years. In its written evidence to the Royal Commission on Trade Unions and Employers' Associations (the Donovan commission), Esso Petroleum Co sketched the following time schedule:

The time scale at Fawley went as follows:

Mid-1957: Work started at the refinery on identifying areas of inefficiency.

November 1958: Memorandum from the consultant.

November 1958-December 1959: Development period. Discussion at plant and shopfloor level, involving stewards, supervisors, management and men.

February-May 1960: Formal negotiations.

July 1960: Signing.

July 1960-July 1962: Implementation period.

In marketing the time scale is as follows:

1962: Operations department set up. Planning started.

February 1964: Notice to leave employers' panel given.

June 1964: Notice expired.

June-September 1964: Discussions in the field with managers, supervisors and
men to draw together proposals for negotiation.

September 1964: First proposals put before the trade union—'Green Book'.

January 1965: Informal negotiations with trade union.

February-October 1965: Continuous discussion with trade union at national and local
level to find solutions to problems that had been identified nationally and locally.

November 1965: Formal negotiations with trade union.

January 1966: Further session of formal negotiation. Deal signed.

February-August 1966: Implementation period.[6]

Similarly the implementation of the ICI deal is taking a considerable time. Discussions in the company started in 1962. The unions were brought in in 1965, and the first trial agreement was signed in 1967. This agreement, the Manpower Utilisation Payment Structure, provided for a one-year trial period and was operated on only nine sites involving about 5,000 workers. At the end of the trial period a revised agreement, the Weekly Staff Agreement, was drawn up and signed. By January 1970, eight years after the idea was first mooted, only seven sites are actually operating the WSA. About 40,000 workers out of a total of 67,000 manual workers employed by ICI have not yet even been approached.

In the docks the preparations for a productivity deal took many years. In September 1962 the Rochdale committee recommended the decasualisation of dock labour, a key item in any productivity deal. Three years later, in August 1965, the Devlin report went further in the same direction. Between the publication of this report and the implementation of the first phase of the agreement, a further three years elapsed. The first phase has now been going for more than two years, and we still have not arrived at the more decisive second stage of Devlin.

In Rootes factories the implementation of productivity deals 'has been a seven or eight year process'.[7]

In the long time negotiations take, management is very cautious in softening up workers' resistance, with management-steward meetings occurring several times a week, interspersed with weekend conferences in pleasant surroundings. As the task of changing work conditions to a productivity deal's requirements is a slow process, in opening negotiations the management can write into the agreement proposals whose full implications cannot, so early on, be seen on the shopfloor. It is at this stage of the negotiations that quite lavish wage increases are granted to the workers. Thus, while in these first stages the management appear to make quite modest demands, they are banking on the later fruition of these demands and, contrarily, when workers agree to a productivity deal they judge its merits on the present and immediate wage concessions.

The lengthy period of preparation, negotiation and implementation can be extremely advantageous to management. It means that at the end of the process they will have a far better understanding of how their own factory really operates

—of unofficial working practices and of workers' ad hoc methods of under-mining the management authority. Even more important, the length of time makes effective opposition to the productivity agreement very difficult. At first workers' attitudes are likely to be, 'Well, we might as well have a look at it—we don't have to commit ourselves.' However, as the talks drag on attitudes shift very gradually until the deal comes to be accepted as a 'fait accompli' with-out any decision ever being taken. Shop stewards involved in negotiations as-sociated with a productivity deal similarly find that they are being gradually drawn into a discussion of the details instead of the principle of the deal.

What is a productivity deal?

D A C Dewdney, former vice-chairman of Esso and member of the PIB, has this to say:

> What distinguishes what has come to be called productivity bargaining from the daily efforts which any competent management makes to secure the optimum use of its resources is the comprehensive nature of the approach.
>
> A true productivity bargain, to me, is one that looks at the labour force as a whole and the factory operation as a whole, and is as ready to develop new systems of pro-duction control, the deskilling of manufacturing methods, new shop layouts, new storekeeping procedures, new accounting methods, as it is to debate with the shop stewards the lines of demarcation between craftsmen, and between maintenance workers and operatives. The whole package ought to be looked at as a whole.[8]

Every productivity deal has a basic set of components to it, even though in-dividual productivity deals will combine the parts in varying proportions and according to different schedules. According to one expert industrial consul-tant, they were:

> (1) Reduction in non-working time at each end of shifts, at breaks and between jobs.
> (2) Reduction in the amount of overtime worked and the control of this within policy limits, with agreement that it will be worked when necessary.
> (3) Greater flexibility in the deployment of labour.
> (4) Completion of work to schedule even when follow-on work is not available.
> (5) The elimination of mates for craftsmen or their more effective use.
> (6) Reduction in lateness and absenteeism.
> (7) Elimination or reduction in claims for special allowances.
> (8) The maintenance of a specified tempo of working.
> (9) The gradual removal of inter-trade barriers—demarcation.[9]

Actually productivity deals change all conditions of work. As Sir Peter Runge, vice-president of the Confederation of British Industry (CBI) and joint vice-chairman of Tate & Lyle Ltd, put it, 'Productivity deals...genuinely trade a new way of work (and life) for a new wage structure'.[10]

Because productivity agreements aim at a total change in work practices it is not a once and for all bargain. Signing the agreement ends the discussion on pay, but only begins the introduction of work study, flexibility and all the other implications:

> In a conventional agreement the signature marks the end of the process. In productivity bargaining the signature marks the end of the negotiating stage—and the beginning of the implementation stage.[11]

Phase one prepares the ground for phase two, and so on. Phase one can be represented by a loose application of new methods of work and quite a good wage increment. But this is only the beginning. E J Robertson, who is the director of research at the Engineering Employers' Federation, has emphasised that a productivity deal 'is a continuing process demanding constant follow-up'.[12]

This is particularly true of the ICI WSA. The agreement says, 'A continuous programme of examination and change will be required.' There are no limits in development—ICI already has full work study, job assessment and continuous shift working—neither, so far as is known, have the unions asked for any limits or guarantees.

Similarly, George Cattell, director of manpower and productivity at the DEP, wrote in Rootes' house magazine that he prefers to call the Rootes deal 'an enabling agreement'. It prepares the basis for the introduction of work study, etc.[13] By using the term 'enabling agreement' Cattell clearly means that it enables management to introduce such methods and loads of work as it sees fit. Any illusions about being able to 'bend' a productivity deal in line with workers' interests, by selling outdated practices or imaginary conditions for example, are quickly dispelled as the first stages are superseded by subsequent stages. It is these later stages which carry the real weight of a productivity deal's work innovations.

Another general characteristic of productivity deals is the way in which they formalise labour relations in the factory. This is very detrimental to shopfloor bargaining, which relies very much on the informal, matter of fact approach. As one writer put it:

> It may be doubted how many managements who agree to let stewards share in the allocation of overtime, the settlement of workloads, the introduction of work-sharing as an alternative to redundancy, and the settlement of conditions under which new machinery will be introduced, would be prepared to sign formal agreements which revealed the extent to which these matters have now become a matter for joint regulation. Traditionally these are still thought of as areas of 'managerial prerogative', particularly by those who are not actually responsible for the day to day conduct of industrial relations.[14]

Both the Donovan commission and the PIB have recommended highly formal agreements at plant level. Once labour relations are highly formalised, then hurdles can be put in the path of workers who attempt to improve conditions on the factory floor (for further elucidation see Chapter Nine).

In this study we deal only with comprehensive productivity deals. Besides these, there are the traditional, or 'partial', productivity deals. A comprehensive agreement covers a number of related changes in working conditions and affects all the workers of the establishment, whereas a partial agreement affects only one work practice and often only a single group of workers. A director of Joseph Lucas (Batteries) Limited and CAV Limited, A J Nicol, confused the two types of productivity deal when he said to the Donovan commission, 'We are making very small productivity bargains all the time—this is a constant part of our operation, and it is the way in which we give increases, the way we get a higher productivity increase per year'.[15]

The difference between partial and comprehensive productivity bargains is not merely one of size, but also involves qualitative, radical differences. While the former has been a feature of pay settlements in industry for a long time, the latter is a completely new departure for British collective bargaining. Since we are examining what is specific to this new era in the class struggle, then we have to concentrate on comprehensive productivity deals alone.

Chapter Three: The sugar on the pill

When the employers prepare the ground for productivity deals, they are all sugar and honey. The changes they suggest in work conditions may be quite moderate, and the main talk is about the benefits accruing to the workers—above all, about the improvement in wages. The question we have to ask is this: is the sugar on the pill as thick as they pretend?

Uneven amounts of sugar on different pills

The proportion of labour costs to total costs varies widely in British industry. At one extreme are the capital intensive industries such as refineries, chemical works, electricity supply and multiple steel works, where labour costs are between 5 percent and 22 percent of total costs.[1] At the other end of the scale are the labour intensive industries such as buses, railways and coal mining, where the proportion of labour costs to total costs is as high as 60 or 70 percent. Where labour costs make up a small proportion of total costs it is much easier for the employer to pay high prices for the introduction of a productivity deal. Where labour costs are high it is much more difficult although nonetheless compelling for the employers. The sugar coating depends very much on whether the industry is growing or declining. Last, but not least, the thickness of the sugar coating is in direct proportion to the strength and determination of the workers' organisation in the industry. Where workers' resistance is very weak, the employer can make productivity bargaining into a sheer bargain for himself.

So we find the Fawley refinery productivity deal giving the workers a rise of 40 percent in their wage rate, the ICI agreement giving 12 to 22 percent, the first phase of Devlin paying the dockers a large rise of 30 percent, while miners got 5 percent and craftsmen in the railway workshop between 5.8 percent and 7.8 percent.[2]

To appreciate the significance of productivity deals on wage negotiations they must be looked at over a span of time. One must remember that many workers did get a wage rise at the time without accepting the strings of productivity deals. Hence the effect of productivity deals can be gauged by comparing wage rises with other industries not associated with productivity deals. Let us look at a few cases.

Fawley

The first and most celebrated productivity deal was the elaborate agreement concluded in July 1960 between the management of the Esso refinery at Fawley, near Southampton, and the trade unions, the Transport and General Workers' Union and seven craft unions (AEU, ETU, etc). As a result of the agreement the rate of pay was raised by as much as 40 percent. As Alan Flanders, the author of the story of the Fawley agreement, put it:

> Fawley management had declared in its introduction to the Blue Book that one of the aims was 'to place our employees among the highest paid in the country'. *This had been achieved.*
>
> Certainly the success of the Blue Book depended on the spectacular increases in wage rates that it was offering. This meant too much to the unions and, above all, to their members, for the 'package deal' to be disregarded or treated lightly.[3]

But history has belied the promise of Fawley. Wages in Fawley have risen very slowly indeed since 1960. In September 1962 the wages of skilled workers had risen by 4½d an hour, and in March 1963 by a further 3d.[4]

And then for four years a complete standstill in wage rates. No wonder Fawley wages slipped badly compared to wages of workers elsewhere. In the evidence to the Donovan commission, the management of Esso had to admit:

> We did a recent survey in the Southampton area in the oil industry, chemicals, shipbuilding, heavy electrical, light engineering, a nationalised industry and a contracting industry. We found in these eight industries...on hours worked in the week it was lowest; and on total weekly earnings [Fawley] came sixth out of the eight.[5]

It is also probable that Fawley had become one of the lowest paid refineries in the country—evidence of the loss of shopfloor control. As a result Esso was able to negotiate a new deal in 1968 with radical extensions of flexibility and reduction in staffing.

Post Office engineers

There was hardly anyone in this country more enthusiastic for productivity deals than the general secretary of the Post Office Engineering Union, Lord Delacourt (formerly Charles) Smith: 'It is by putting the dynamic thrust of the trade union movement for higher pay and better conditions behind the plans for higher productivity that we can produce more rapid progress in the direction of modernisation'.[6]

Prior to the introduction of the productivity deal, the principle underlining the wages of Post Office engineers was the comparability principle, repeated both by the Tomlin commission (1929-31) and the Priestley commission (1953-55). The 'Priestley Formula' summarised the position: 'The primary principle is that of fair comparisons with the current remuneration of outside staffs employed on broadly comparable work taking account of other conditions of service'.[7]

However, after the introduction of the productivity deal the comparability principle was overthrown and replaced by the productivity principle. The result was that notwithstanding worsening conditions the wages of Post Office engineers have not improved at all compared to those of other engineers. Worse conditions for no extra money—that was what productivity bargaining meant for Post Office engineers.

The rise in wages of Post Office engineers, as compared to other engineers, between January 1966 and January 1969 was as follows (in percentage):[8]

Post Office engineers (national maximum rate of pay)		All engineering industries (earning for standard week, excluding overtime)	
Technical officer	21.4		
Senior technician	20.1	Skilled	22.0
Technician class 1	20.8		
Technician class 2A	21.5	Semi–skilled	18.1
Technician class 2B	20.6		
Labourer	23.3	Labourer	20.9

Thus the Post Office engineers got, in exchange for great productivity concessions, no more than what other engineers got without strings. Not surprisingly it provoked the first national strike of the POEU, some 82 years after the founding of the union!

London busmen

On the face of it London busmen got quite a bargain when they accepted their productivity deal for 1968 and then a new one from October 1969. Each time their basic was raised by £1. However, if we look at these 'gifts' a bit closer, we find that not a penny was actually paid for productivity.

The 1968 productivity deal gave the busmen £1 in return for accepting one-man operated buses throughout the fleet and a few minor concessions such as a small cut in running time in the off-peak periods. This was the first increase for two years, while in the previous period wages rose every year by this same amount:

1963	£1 13s 0d
1964	£1 0s 0d
1965	£1 0s 0d
1966	£1 0s 0d
1967	—
1968	£1 0s 0d
1969	£1 0s 0d

In 1969 the board said that the busmen would get no rise unless they accepted further productivity. After wasting six months talking about productivity the Central Bus Committee finally came out unanimously against further concessions. The board then offered to settle on 17s if they accepted one-man operated double deckers plus a commitment to discuss further productivity. After a threatened overtime ban this figure was increased to £1, the final 3s payable in October.

Electricity supply

Workers in electricity supply agreed to a very onerous productivity deal in July 1964. When it comes to cash, they found in a very short while that their wages were lagging behind those of workers in other industries.

WEEKLY EARNINGS IN ELECTRICITY SUPPLY AND OTHER INDUSTRIES 1964-67 (AVERAGE WEEKLY EARNINGS, MALE MANUAL WORKERS)[9]

	Electricity supply industry		All industries		Manufacturing industries	
	Amount £ s d	Index	Amount £ s d	Index	Amount £ s d	Index
April 1964	16 19 4	100.0	17 12 5	100.0	18 4 3	100.0
April 1964	18 0 3	106.2	18 18 2	107.3	19 8 10	106.7
April 1964	18 18 3	111.5	20 5 0	114.9	20 19 4	115.1
April 1964	18 19 9	111.9	20 11 7	116.8	21 2 7	116.0

To add insult to injury, in September 1967 the PIB, in reply to a request of 5 percent wage rise put forward by the unions, offered 3.7 percent with very heavy new productivity strings attached.[10]

While in practically all productivity deals the amount of lolly delivered in the flush of introducing the agreement is much larger than in the follow-up, there are agreements in which this slope is written in and obvious to all the negotiators.

The agreement for electricians in the contracting industry offered the following: at Stage I (March 1967) 13.3 percent; Stage II (January 1968) 5 percent; Stage III (September 1968) 2.9 percent.[11]

Other wage benefits cut

Even when wage rises are promised by a productivity deal, other wage allowances are frequently sacrificed. A most important case is the cost of living allowance, which has been sacrificed in a number of productivity deals. Workers in the steel industry had to agree 'that future wage negotiations will only take place in the context of productivity bargaining, and this means the abandonment of all outside influences on wage levels, holiday pay, etc, including cost of living adjustments and national awards'.[12]

Then the productivity agreement for the electricians in the contracting industry, referred to above, outlawed bonuses when giving the wage rise:

> The rates negotiated in the NJIC are standard and may not be supplemented by bonus, incentive or site payments. Any firm making such payments is liable to expulsion from the NFEA.[13]

As a result, to use the words of the PIB, a couple of years later in the electrical contracting industry 'over the full course of the 1966-69 agreement, wage drift may well have been negative'.[14] To put it in simpler English, some electricians lost as much as £6 a week bonus.[15] In the case of workers in the railway workshops, they were granted a wage rise of 5.8 to 7.8 percent, but at the same time other measures, it seems, would cut the wage rise:

> The elimination of certain allowances.
> The reduction in overtime in the regions.
> A reduction in overtime working while still maintaining the same level of output.
> Labour costs would remain broadly constant.[16]

The 10,000 workshop workers in Derby, Swindon, Doncaster and Crewe pointed out that earnings would be cut by the switch from piece-work, cut in overtime, etc. No wonder they refused to implement the agreement.

Workers' share in increasing cake

Productivity agreements are on the whole very vague when it comes to sharing out the overall savings. In a general review of productivity deals, the PIB reported, 'In about half the agreements, the workers received about half of the estimated benefits; in the others the share varied, sometimes being more and sometimes less than half'.[17]

Furthermore, it is no coincidence that concrete information on the actual sharing of the savings from productivity agreements is very sparse.

The Green Book, the productivity agreement for the steel industry, states that the workers' share should be $43^1/2$ percent of the savings, while $56^1/2$ percent should go to the employer.[18]

In evidence to the Donovan commission:

> Joseph Lucas gave an interesting example of reorganised arrangements at CAV
> Ltd for work testing and adjustment of pumps, under which the workers engaged
> on testing pumps also carried out certain adjustments to faulty pumps. This bargain
> was very satisfactory to the company. It reduced the labour force by 17 percent—
> one fifth of the savings secured as a result were paid out in the form of extra wages.[19]

The sharing of savings in other industries can only be vaguely guessed. Unfortunately we needn't scrimp for examples where workers sold their conditions for a song.

In the years 1964-66 the trading balance of the electricity supply industry rose by 40 percent, while its wage and salary bill rose by only 11.82 percent.[20]

In the mines, between June 1966—the time of the power loading agreement—and June 1969, the output of coal per man year rose from 380.7 to 453.9 tons, or by some 20 percent.[21] In the same period real wages declined. In June 1966 the daily wage of a miner in Doncaster, paid according to the National Power Loading Agreement, was £4 2s 6d. In November 1967 this was raised to £4 3s 10d, and in November 1968 to £4 5s 2d—altogether a rise of 2s 8d per day, or 3.3 percent over a period of two years.[22] During the same period the rent charged by the National Coal Board to its miner tenants of its houses was raised. Thus in Bentley, near Doncaster, for instance, it rose for old pre-1919 houses from 17s 8d per week to £1 0s 4d, or by 2s 8d (a rise just equal to that of wages!), and for new houses from £1 1s 3d to £1 13s 3d, or by 12s 1d per week. The national average cost of living rose during the same period by 10 percent.

As a consequence of the Post Office engineering agreement, over the last three and a half years the total savings were £89 million, and only £18 million of these were shared among the workers.[23] Getting away with murder, the Post Office dared to offer in July 1969 a wage rise of 4 percent to its engineers, while stipulating that overtime should be cut by one hour. This would have reduced the wage rise offer to 2 percent, and that in exchange for a whole series of new productivity measures. The suggestion was answered by the general strike of the Post Office engineers.

Another interesting case is that of the busmen. When London Transport suggested the wide introduction of one-man operated (OMO) buses into the fleet, the TGWU argued first of all that there should be a substantial increase for all busmen and secondly in addition OMO drivers should get 50 percent of the savings. However, the final settlement was for a flat payment of about £3 5s a week as a bonus. This was then equivalent to about 20 percent of the basic, but as the payment has not been increased with either of the last two wage rises this percentage has declined to about 18 percent. A Bristol busman put it to me this way: 'Of the money saved by cutting out the conductor, the driver gets what was saved in social security and SET contributions, uniform, training and other expenses of the conductor while the employer keeps his wages.' That can't be far off the point and is a long way off the union's original call for a 50-50 split.

OMO drivers, those who do the job of driver and conductor, got the follow-ing bonuses added to their basic rate:[24] 5, 10, 15, 16, 17, 18, 20, 25 percent! How niggardly!

Sector or undertaking	Percentage addition to base rate	Remarks	
Company sector (NCOI)	15	Subject to enhancement, Sundays, rest days and public holidays	
Municipal sector (NJIC)	15 16 17 18	Seat capacity -60 61-70 71-80 81-90	} Flat rate
London Transport Country	10 15	Up to 26 seats } Over 26 seats }	Subject to full enhancement
London Transport Central	15 5	Conventional } 'Red Arrow' }	Subject to full enhancement
Manchester	20 25	Single-deckers } Double-deckers }	On NJIC flat rates
Birmingham	20	Subject to enhancement. Base rates include service pay increments	
Coventry	17	Flat rate on basic of £18	
Reading	15	Plus £1 extra flexibility bonus. Flat on NJIC base rate.	

During the long campaign of 1967-68 the London Transport Board tried hard to persuade the busmen to accept its productivity deal. They issued one glossy news sheet which included this sugary promise: 'The status, pay and conditions of London busmen…would…be improved far beyond that which exists today'.[25]

After finally accepting this deal the busmen found that this was so much eye-wash. Real wages have declined since the deal—a fact underlined by the present shortage of drivers and conductors of over 20 percent—one of the highest ever.

At Ferranti's in Edinburgh the management have introduced automatic design equipment. This equipment does not produce drawings, but tapes which are used on the factory floor directly to operate machines. This process repre-sents the telescoping of three major functions: planning, methods work and draughting together. The DATA (draughtsmen) members at Ferranti, against their union's advice, accepted such a telescoping in a productivity deal which gave them a pathetic 6 percent increase.

The National Graphical Association signed in October 1969 a two-year pro-ductivity deal that granted craftsmen 20s a week on 1 November 1969 and 20s on 1 November 1970, auxiliary workers 17/6 and women 14/6. Since the cost of living is rising annually by something like 14s a week, the NGA sold condi-tions for practically nothing. The printing employers and the NGA leadership

Broadway Melody of 1967

(Dedicated to the belief that 'there's one born every minute', and that most of 'em drive London buses)

Will you walk into my parlour?
Said Old Broadway to its crews,
In the cause of 'Productivity'
We have exciting news,
We know our 'Working Party'
Dropped poor Woodberry in the
    soup,
So we've planned our latest
    carve-up
Through a harmless 'Study
    Group'.

With our 'Technical
    Developments'
We've clobbered you before,
Our 'Package Deals' and 'Bonus
    Schemes'
Have left you feeling sore,
But if you'll give us one more
    chance
Then just for Auld Lang Syne,
We promise you a rich reward
And bags of overtime.

If you will bake a bigger cake
We promise you a share,
The fruit for us—the crumbs for
    you
Now surely that's quite fair?
We're trying hard to help you
And it really isn't greed,
So listen while we tell the tale
Of what we really need.

Just a tiny cut in services
(Say twenty-five percent),
A thousand more 'Red Arrows'
To help to pay the rent,
Five miles-an-hour more on speed
Two thousand more one-
    manners,
With coin-box fares to help us
    turn
All 'fourpennies' into 'tanners'.

Then eighteen-hour spreadovers
Would save us lots of lolly,
While bunks for crews inside the
    bus
Would make the day quite jolly,
It's a piece of 'Productivity'
And that is how it's meant,
We wouldn't charge you for the
    kip
See what you'd save on rent?

And so, dear brother Nobby
    Clarke
They're after you again,
They want to drive you harder yet
With sweat and toil and strain,
If you're prepared to take it on
When all this you've digested,
You really ought to nip off quick
And have that big bonce tested.

Disraeli

This poem was written by George Moore, editor of the *Platform*, the busmen's rank and file paper, during the 1968 productivity talks, as a contribution to the fight against acceptance of that deal. It was first published in a special issue of *Platform* in August 1968.

could get away with this because psychologically workers are inclined to treat payment arising from a productivity deal as being just another addition to the wage packet. The danger then is that having accepted a worsening of conditions it is impossible to revert to the usual run of wage rises with which the productivity negotiated wage rise was confused. One ends up financially no better off.

Then take the case of the dockers. We are informed that the 'entire UK to Australia container trade eventually amounting to some 2,000,000 tons a year could be handled by one berth at Tilbury employing just 15 men'.[26]

In August 1967 the McKinsey survey estimated that with new cargo handling techniques the labour force at the docks would be reduced by 90 percent over the ensuing ten years. Of course this was an exaggeration, but a deliberate one as part of the general plan to make dockers fear for their employment. But even if the labour force would be cut not by 90 percent but by 50 percent, wages, real wages, should double if the share of workers in the product of labour should remain the same as at present. (In money terms because of inflation wages should rise much more than by double—cumulatively by at least another 7 percent per year.) The fortnightly paper the *Port* reports that on Number 43 berth at Tilbury, a multi-user berth handling up to 250 containers a day, the 'dockers turn round 14 ships a week. Up to four vessels are fully discharged and loaded in a day. The berth is claimed to be the busiest berth in the country.' It employs only 26 dockers and 'the average pay packet is in the region of £50 to £55 a week'.[27] That sounds like marvellous pay until one realises that each man is now doing the work previously done by 100.

All these agreements have one thing in common. Not only are the payments relatively small but in almost every case the payments replace the normal wage increases and are not an addition to them. By making productivity bargaining replace normal wage negotiation employers are in fact getting the concessions in the deal for nothing. They can get away with this because workers are psychologically conditioned to an annual wage increase in a particular range—say £1 a week. Also it is here that the previous policies of wage freeze and incomes policy have their value in persuading workers to accept productivity bargains that are particularly advantageous to the employers.

Workers' share—the principle

To justify the small share of wages in savings resulting from productivity deals, one apologist for the system, A J Thompson, director of management services of Tubes Ltd Group, argues in the following manner:

> For the company as a whole…some formula is required for dividing the extra profits derived from efforts of workers and management between shareholders, customers, staff, workers and the company for capital investment. One possible solution depends on the interesting fact discovered by Rucker. He found that in any given firm there was a more or less constant ratio over a long period of time between the total labour cost and the added value. Added value is defined as sales minus all bought-out items such as materials, consumables, services, etc. It includes labour and salary

costs, depreciation, fixed charges, interest and profit. If, for example, in a given firm, the ratio of labour cost to added value for the past six or seven years has been 27 percent, then it is possible to tell the workers that the company will guarantee to pay this ratio in future. If the workers respond to this and increase the added value, they will continue to get 27 percent of it and hence will increase their wages.[28]

The workers' share should be in the future, as in the past. This is the natural law...the natural law of exploitation.

One argument quite often used by advocates of productivity deals is that workers are not entitled to all the benefits of the deal, as a large proportion of the rising productivity results not from labour efficiency, but from that of capital. It is necessary, says the PIB, to carry 'a differentiation between the contribution of labour and the contribution of capital. It is important that this differentiation be maintained, and, difficult though it may sometimes be, clearly drawn'.[29]

But who creates the capital, if not the workers? In the main it is workers employed by the company itself. In 1963, 81.3 percent of the funds of all quoted companies (with net assets of £500,000 or more, or income of £50,000 or more) came from internal resources.[30] Another no less phoney argument runs, or rather limps, like this: workers should get only a portion of the savings resulting from productivity deals, as the general public—the consumers—should also share in the benefit. Thus, for instance, London Transport, when introducing its productivity deal, suggested that the public should get an important share in the savings from the 'reshaping plan'.[31] Since then services have been cut and fares raised by 50 percent. This was the benefit to the public!

Another really fantastic principle regarding the division of the savings resulting from productivity bargaining is incorporated in the agreement between Swan Hunter and the Boilermakers' Union: 'It is a fundamental condition of this collective productivity scheme that the savings made are divided on the basis of *one third to the employees, one third to the company and one third for the acquisition of improved machine tools and equipment*'.[32]

How stupid do management and the union bosses think workers are? A third for the workers, a third for the company and a third for buying machines. Who owns these machines? The workers?

The real insult to workers' intelligence, added to the injury of increased exploitation, is revealed in another paragraph of the same agreement: 'Compensation will be paid to those members of the society whose earnings are adversely affected by this agreement at the rate of *£30 for every £1 difference between their existing average weekly earnings on normal hours since January 1960 and the new minimum rates* for their particular group'.[33]

Imagine a worker loses, say, £1 a week and he gets £30 in compensation—in other words, he is compensated for only 30 weeks. As a matter of fact many welders in Swan Hunter lost more than £10 per week as a result of the productivity deal (for a time the lump sum paid to them kept the welders quiet, but then a bitter strike broke out).

Chapter Four: A new wage pay system, measured day work

One of the main purposes of most productivity agreements is to get rid of piece-work, of payment by results (PBR), and replace it by one kind or another of fixed day wages, if possible by measured day work (MDW). The reason is quite plain—the system of payment prevailing over many decades somehow got out of the control of management. This point needs going into a little deeper.

[Editor's note: The next section, 'National Wage Negotiation and Wage Drift', was reproduced from *Incomes Policy, Legislation and Shop Stewards*, and can be found on pp61-63 of this book.]

For a clear illustration of the impact of 'wage drift' we need only follow the story of the three years of package deal (1964-67) in the engineering industry. The nationally agreed basic wages of skilled workers moved at a nil rate in 1964, nil rate in 1965, 2.4 percent in 1966, and 2.3 percent in 1967. Over the whole period wages should have risen by as little as 4.7 percent. However, between October 1964 and April 1967 wages rose by 17.1 percent—the wage drift was as high as 12.4 percent.[1]

You can see from the graph on the next page how the difference grew while the agreement was in force.[2]

The employers become extremely worried at the 'drift'

In 1956 the Coventry and District Engineering Employers' Association established a working party to analyse the drift. A similar body published an extremely interesting study in 1968 entitled *Working Party Report on Wage Drift, Work Measurement and Systems of Payment* (referred to from now on as the Coventry Blue Book).[3] The main author of this book was George Cattell, a Rootes director, since loaned to the DEP to aid the government in its efforts to introduce productivity deals:

> The problem of wage drift and the fact that Coventry wage levels were well above the national average continued to cause concern. The average hourly earnings nationally in the federation for skilled production workers in September 1955 was 5s 3$\frac{1}{2}$d while the comparable figure in Coventry was 7s 3$\frac{1}{2}$d, a gap of 2s.
>
> In 1948 the average earnings nationally had been 3s 4$\frac{1}{2}$d, while those in Coventry had been 4s 3 $\frac{1}{4}$d, a gap of 10$\frac{3}{4}$d. Thus the gap in hourly increases in seven years had increased by 1s 1$\frac{1}{4}$d.

And the gap went on widening:

> By June 1964 the national average weekly earnings for skilled production workers in the federation was 363s 8d, with the comparable figure in Coventry being 497s,

ie a differential of 133s 4d... In June 1964 the earnings of skilled production workers in Coventry were 11s 10d compared with a national average of 8s 8d, a gap of
3s 2d per hour. However, in June 1965 the earnings of this category in Coventry
was 13s 2¹/₂d compared with a national average of 9s 9d, ie a gap of 3s 5¹/₂d.

In the years since World War Two ended, national increases have only accounted
for about one third of the total increase in wage levels in Coventry. This contrasts
with the national average position where national increases have accounted for
about half of the total increase in wage levels since the war ended.[4]

The above process is illustrated clearly by the graph on the next page.

There is hardly any doubt that the driving force behind wage drift is payment
by results.

Actual earnings of fitters and labourers in EEF firms compared with package deal effects on June 1964 earnings (overtime excluded)

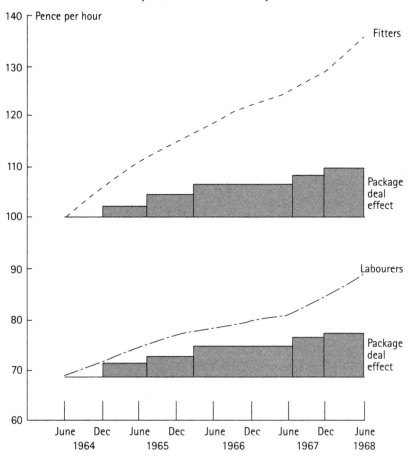

Piece-work systems encourage wage drift—in simple terms because of the apparent impossibility of objectively fixing a piece-rate and management turning a 'blind eye' to such looseness particularly in the early stages to get the job off the ground, which become impossible to adjust later on, while methods remain the same. Furthermore, the looseness so embodied acts as a catalyst to other individuals or groups on older jobs to seek a similar increase in earnings potential, and as the earnings of the piece-workers in general go up in the establishment or district there is also pressure from the time-workers for their rates to be raised to catch up; this pressure will eventually run right through the establishment.[5]

Wage drift—the problem: the rise in hourly earnings of skilled engineering workers 1956 to 1966

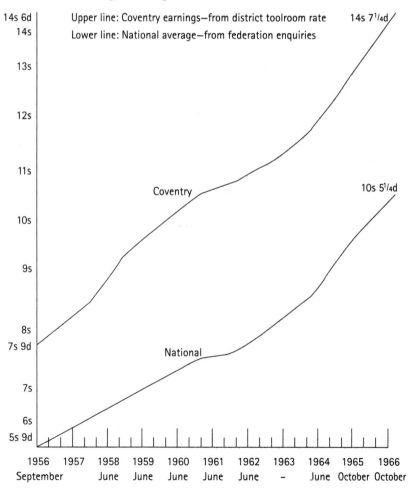

To support the contention that PBR is the fly in the ointment the Coventry Blue Book compares the wages of four Coventry motor firms operating under piece-work systems and a motor company which does not belong to the Engineering Federation and has a time-rate wage structure (probably Ford).

COMPARISON OF SKILLED PRODUCTION WORKERS' EARNINGS 1957–65 AT FOUR MOTOR MANUFACTURING FIRMS IN COVENTRY AND A NON-FEDERATED MOTOR MANUFACTURING FIRM

	Non-federated firm	A	B	C	D
May 1957	6s 6d	8s 4^1/$_4$d	7s 1^1/$_2$d	7s 8^3/$_4$d	8s 8d
December 1965	9s 3^1/$_2$d	13s 2d	13s 4^1/$_4$d	14s 0d	13s 7^3/$_4$d
Total increase 1957–65	2s 9^1/$_2$d	4s 9^3/$_4$d	6s 2^3/$_4$d	6s 3^1/$_4$d	4s 11^3/$_4$d
Due to national increase	2s 9^1/$_2$d	1s 9^3/$_4$d	1s 9^3/$_4$d	1s 9^3/$_4$d	1s 9^3/$_4$d
Wage drift	–	3s 0d	4s 5d	4s 5^1/$_2$d	3s 2d

The same effect of payment by results on wage rises was clear also from other industries besides engineering. Thus while dockers in Liverpool work on average some four hours per week longer than in London, their earnings were about a quarter lower, because payment in London is by piece-rate, while Liverpool is not primarily a piece-rate working port.[6]

Effects of wage drift on wages of white collar workers

The wage drift of workers on piece-rate affects the wages and salaries of other workers in the same establishments, including the white collar employees. As the Coventry Blue Book complains:

> In recent years there has been increasing militancy and activity by the growing staff trade unions with regard to salary levels. It is fair to say that apart from the normal argument of comparability with staff salaries elsewhere in the district, the most recurring argument put forward by the staff trade unions is the adverse relationship between staff salaries and manual workers' wage levels… There can be little doubt that wage drift is a factor tending to cause dissatisfaction about salary levels among staff generally.[7]

Between January 1962 and June 1966 the weekly salary of Coventry draughtsmen rose by £5 15s 0d; in the same period the average of Coventry skilled production workers rose by £5:

> There can be no doubt that the elimination or significant reduction of piece-work wage drift would therefore tend to remove one of the staff unions' traditional arguments based really upon manual workers' wage drift. At the same time it would

probably remove a source of real dissatisfaction amongst staff employees. Tackling the problem of wage drift should therefore be regarded as tending to deal appreciably with the growing problem posed by the staff trade unions seeking to achieve or maintain a certain parity or differential with manual workers' wage levels.[8]

The last but not the least plank in the condemnation of PBR by the employers is that it undermines the prerogatives of management to manage.

It 'slowly and surely wrests from management an area of control that is essentially a management function, until inevitably shopfloor management have little or no control whatsoever and workmen are then able to reach that point where they can achieve their rate of incentive payment by negotiation and work at whatever rate suits them best'.[9]

Piece-work turns on its maker

For generations piece-work has been the employers' most valuable weapon in intensifying exploitation, its aim to make the worker drive himself continuously in order to earn his daily crust. For decades the employers tried their hardest to force it upon an unwilling workforce.

In 1852 members of the Amalgamated Society of Engineers, the main engineering union, were locked out for six months, in the main for their opposition to the introduction of piece-work.[10] Workers' resistance to piece-work was so stubborn that even as late as 1886 only 5 percent of the workers in engineering were paid on a piece-rate system.[11] In 1889 a fierce ten-month struggle against payment by results was defeated by the employers. In 1889, after a 30-week lockout of the Amalgamated Society of Engineers, the employers imposed the Terms of Settlement Agreement which, among other things, stated:

> The right to work piece-work at present exercised by many of the federated employers shall be extended to all members of the federation and to all their union workmen.
>
> The prices to be paid for piece-work shall be fixed by mutual arrangement between the employer and the workman or workmen who perform the work.[12]

Even after the First World War the principle of opposition to piece-work was not conceded.[13] But the employers did not stop their pressure.

However, over the last 30-odd years the situation has changed radically. Before the Second World War a reserve pool of unemployed workers could be used (or threatened to be used) by employers to discipline employed workers. The PBR system rested upon a bargaining relationship between employer and employee, and management knew that they were by far the stronger of the two in the 'bargain'. But under the conditions of full employment which has lasted since the Second World War workers gained the upper hand. They had the bargaining power of a shortage of labour behind them. Coupled with a strong factory floor organisation, workers have been able to more and more encroach on the power of the management—there has been creeping workers' control.

The employers introduced piece-work to bypass the unions. 'Mutuality' meant that prices were agreed between the employer and the individual worker, without union interference, and with the worker in a weak position to bargain. The spread of PBR in itself stimulated shopfloor organisation, finally turning 'mutuality' into a weapon in workers' hands—collectively they can hold out for a good price, while management does not want a long dispute over a price that only involves a handful of workers.

Whereas at its introduction PBR was a very effective method of intensive exploitation, today, in highly organised plants, workers can gain from it higher wages and a degree of control over the organisation of the plant.

In the negotiation of certain piece-rates there will be some discussion on basic engineering problems, such as achieving certain quality standards, but the speed of working is never discussed. The control over speed is the prerogative of the worker.

One management adviser described the way workers controlled output under the piece-rate system like this:

> We all know that some piece-rates are 'loose' whilst others are 'tight'. We also know that, frequently, employees restrict their reported production. They may hold back the job tickets on which payment is made on days when they feel they have produced more than it is wise to turn in. By thus 'banking' the tickets they can build up a 'kitty' to use on days when they may be working on jobs with a 'tight' rate or when, perhaps, they are feeling unwell and unable to produce what is regarded as normal output. In a recent study…97 percent of the employees reported that the 'kitty' was very important to them, in that it evened out wage fluctuations and helped to guarantee a steady take-home pay. More fundamentally, it gave them a measure of control over their own situation; they did not feel they were at the mercy of forces outside their control; to some extent they were 'masters in their own house'.[14]

Now nothing irritates management more than workers' control, even if it is very partial. The employers, having been fervent supporters in the past of the piece-rate system, are now looking for a change to a system that will restore to them the control that they have lost in their establishments and at the same time tackle the problem of wage drift.

Tightening managerial control over piece-work

The ideal alternative to piece-work from the employers' standpoint is measured day work, with which we shall deal presently.

Where industry is neither flow production nor mass production, the cost of the product would not justify the extremely high level of supervision which is the prerequisite of MDW. Where batch production prevails—and this covers the employment of millions of workers—management cannot undertake measured day work. The best option open to management is the tightening of control within the piece-work system, by undermining 'mutuality'.

The argument for such policies was advocated coherently both by the PIB and by the Coventry Blue Book.

The PIB urges management to control the operation of PBR rigidly so that workers can raise their earnings only through greater effort. Systematic work study should be used. Rate-fixing should be insulated from shopfloor bargaining pressures. The worker should be free to bargain only with his foreman, whose own decisions should be closely controlled by higher management. The board suggests that piece-work systems should be so operated that bonus earnings make up only a quarter of the average worker's pay packet, and it prefers 'time saved' systems (which set a maximum limit to earnings, however hard the worker sweats) to straight piece-work. Formal negotiations at factory level should lay down the procedure to be followed when setting rates, together with 'standard' earnings for each grade of worker. The board summarises its basic intention thus—'mutuality' has to be removed from the individual job to the enterprise as a whole.[15]

A PBR system is working successfully where:

(a) The rate of increase of average hourly earnings (excluding overtime and increases paid under industry-wide agreements or their equivalent in non-federated firms, and excluding also increases demonstrably attributable to increased worker effort) is 1.5 percent or less a year.

(b) The proportion of average earnings (excluding overtime) which takes the form of variable output bonus does not exceed one quarter.

(c) Standards of performance are set by work measurement carried out by adequately trained stall whose consistency in rating is regularly checked.

(d) Enterprise or industry agreements establish clear ground rules separating the process of pay negotiation from the setting of work and ensuring uniformity of practice in respect of the latter.

(e) The 'learning curve' of 'improvement effect' is taken into account when establishing work standards for new jobs and new workers, or revising them for old jobs.

(f) The differentials between the pay of different occupational groups are determined in detail by job evaluation, or a systematic and comprehensive agreement (or both), and are specified not merely in terms of basic rates, but of 'standard earnings' or the equivalent.

(g) The suitability and administration of the system has undergone a major investigation within the past three years.[16]

The Coventry Blue Book also suggests the imposition of more rigid managerial control over piece-work. Like the PIB it also sees the solution in abolishing the principle of 'mutual agreement' on piece-rates between management and the individual worker. Instead it recommends that job times should be fixed unilaterally by 'work study engineers', with no opportunity for bargaining. These times would he translated into rates of pay, by means of a 'conversion factor' negotiated for the factory as a whole. Workers would lose the means of raising wages through shopfloor pressure: 'The complete elimination of bargaining about money or payment between the operator and the rate fixer *means that management is in a much better position to control its labour costs than at present.*' Under existing piece-work systems many shopfloor bargains take place every day, and management is usually reluctant to risk a strike which could close the whole factory over the wages of a handful of workers. Under the new system bargaining would take place only when the unions submitted a formal claim for an increase in the 'conversion factor' for the whole factory. With such a claim, 'as higher management will normally be able to anticipate the possibility of a confrontation, it should be able to plan ahead…*and may decide it is worth contemplating a serious strike*'. Employers would be confident that, if the unions were defeated in such a strike, 'they will be unlikely to submit another claim before a reasonable period of time has elapsed'.[17]

Measured day work

However, all suggestions for tighter control of piece-work are only palliatives. The ideal solution, from management's point of view, is MDW. This has been defined thus:

> A fixed hourly rate payment system based upon quantified performance standards which have been established by work measurement techniques. When operators fail to reach standards through their own fault, this becomes a question for discipline or retraining.[18]

Under MDW the worker gets time wages, yet management establishes and enforces production standards. Instead of merely controlling the price for each item produced by the worker, the management controls the worker's production on an hourly basis throughout the day.

MDW is not new. The term was used in the United States in the 1930s, and the consultants who introduced it to Britain installed their first scheme in 1947. However, until the last few years the advance of MDW was very intermittent. In 1956 Vauxhall went over to MDW, sometime later the big engineering enterprise Glacier Metal followed suit, then Pet Food, and a short time later the whole cigarette industry adopted the system.

A variation on the straightforward MDW has been adopted by Philips Industries, the electrical appliance producers employing more than 30,000 workers in Britain. The system Philips adopted was halfway between MDW and an ordinary incentive scheme. Jobs are classified, with a scale of pay for each class. Performance is measured by adopting 70 work-units an hour as the minimum for a trained operator. A worker who thinks he can maintain this rate accepts a 'contract' that he will do so whenever possible, the company pays him at the appropriate rate for all hours, and 'when the next performance step has been attained, the worker is free to accept a new "contract", involving the higher target and improved pay level'.[19]

In the mines the Power Loading Agreement of 1966 meant a change from piece-rate to MDW. Under the agreement 'method study' is used to determine the number of men employed about the coalface. Members of these teams are paid a fixed wage per shift, which is based on the average earnings in each area before the agreement. The spread of earnings between regions is thus being narrowed, and it is intended that all power loading teams shall be on the same rate of pay by 1971.

Strengthening power of management

Upper Clyde Shipbuilders also moved towards MDW, following the pioneering work of the shipyard of Alexander Stephens & Sons, and then Fairfields. So did the Swan Hunter shipyards on the Tyne. MDW was also introduced into the railway workshops.

MDW is also being rapidly adopted in the car industry—first Vauxhall and Ford, and then came the turn of Rootes which, having successfully pushed it into its new Glasgow plants, has more recently got it adopted at the Coventry factory, although in a somewhat modified form. British Leyland has not so far got MDW introduced generally—in, for example, the new Scottish truck plant or in the Pressed Steel Fisher factory at Llanelli. Also, at the new British Leyland factory, Crofton Hackett, Longbridge, a brand new £26 million semi-automatic plant producing the new Maxi engine, workers are on an interim MDW system. It seems, however, as if British Leyland is about to make big efforts to get this system introduced into its main plants.

One of the main aims of productivity deals, in the words of Allan Flanders, publicist of the famous Fawley productivity agreement, is to put an end to the 'abrogation of management by management':

> This is the aspect of productivity bargaining that I particularly want to stress. I find it difficult to see how the accumulated disorder, which is the heritage of two decades of post-war growth in the unofficial system of collective bargaining, can be cleared up without the help of productivity agreements. The re-establishment of order and control is central to my case for productivity bargaining, because in the long run this may be far more important than the immediate gains that can be found in terms of increased labour productivity.[20]

And, with considerable relish, the same author reports:

> More and more managements seem to me to be becoming aware that the labour situation has drifted dangerously far and that they are faced with the need to re-establish control over their workers. And since in the modern world they can't re-establish control unilaterally, the plant productivity bargain seems to them a logical first step towards a modern viable system of managerial control over pay and effort.[21]

The Coventry Blue Book explains how and why MDW will reduce the power of shop stewards: 'The complete elimination of bargaining about money or payment between the operator and the rate-fixer…means that higher management is in a much better position to control its labour costs than at present'.[22]

At the same time MDW will enhance the power of foremen:

> If a company decided that it wished to change from piece-work to a fixed rate

system of payment it would be necessary…to improve the quality and increase the quantity of supervision.

Rootes Group has over the past year been considering the implications in regard to supervision of a move from piece-work to a fixed day rate. They concluded that the supervisor has a more direct responsibility for production in that he must ensure that each operator does, in fact, perform the operations, as specified, at the required rate and for the set period. They concluded that if the foreman were to do this effectively a higher density of supervision would be necessary and they have set out to reduce the ratio of men to supervisors from around 50 to one to 25 or 30 to one.

This should effect the re-establishment of the supervisor as a leader and manager of his section. He will be expected to take more decisions and exercise much closer control over his operators—for example, he would have to assess an operator's capability, skill, reliability and future potential…

He will be required to criticise subordinates when work or conduct fall below set standards. Further, he may be responsible for making an assessment of the subordinate's rates of payment relative to his work level and, if necessary, persuade higher management to change the rate if he, the supervisor, feels that it is inconsistent with the work being carried out by the subordinate.[23]

In fact, in Rootes Stoke engine plant, since the introduction of MDW, the number of foremen has increased considerably. The ratio at present is about one to 20. The final aim is one to ten (because of their new uniforms, workers can see them coming).

Again, in the mines, since the Power Loading Agreement, there has been a rise in the number of supervisors and management officials. The table below gives an example for the North Derbyshire area NCB:

MANPOWER IN NORTH DERBYSHIRE AREA NCB[24]

	Number of underground officials (excluding managers and under-managers	Number of underground workers
June 1967	1,766	21,257
July 1968	1,500	14,141

The ratio of officials to workers was approximately one to 12 in June 1967 and one to 9.5 in July 1968.

A Doncaster miner wrote to me:

Since the National Power Loading Agreement, power certainly has passed from the pit. Previously payment resulted from argument at the point of production, between checker (charge man), leading collier elected by his mates, and the official. Now argument is only possible on the fall back rate. The charge man increasingly is a management man.

The miners' lodge has been impotent, union officials being trusted even less.

If you go in with a union official you have got less chance of a favourable settlement than if you go in yourself.

The one remaining rank and file power lies on the safety question, the authority of the worker-appointed inspectorate being very strong.

Shop stewards in ICI wrote the following to me:

Charge hands on the floor had up to now certain duties other than man management. Foreman was an office job. Now the term charge hand has been abolished —all made up to foremen—but all of them are employed on the floor, and ancillary duties have been removed.

Leslie Blakeman, when he was labour relations officer of Ford, summed it up well, saying, 'A day-rate plant probably requires 25 percent more supervision than one on payment by results, but this is a small price to pay for freedom from disputes and control over costs and methods'.[25]

Undermining the shop steward

All productivity deals aim to undermine the power of the shop steward. The Coventry Rootes 1968 Draft Agreement states:

It is accepted that the present system of shop steward representation will be revised in line with the reorganisation of both the management structure and the changed system for payment. This change will enable a more realistic approach to representation to be adopted, and will ensure more effective union representation with management at all levels. The elimination of piece-work and therefore the elimination of: (a) piece-work negotiations; (b) piece-work booking; and (c) claims for ALC and other compensatory payments will automatically alter the function of the shop steward, making it unnecessary to have representation on a gang basis. The introduction of additional foremen provides a more readily accessible contact with management...

In view of these facts there will be an agreed and reduced ratio of shop stewards to employees which will ensure proper representation on a predominantly geographical basis.[26]

Rootes' purpose was to restrict the stewards' mobility within the factory. As the finishing touch Rootes proposed to turn senior stewards into minor appendages of management.

Following this, on 15 October 1969, Rootes management suggested a new procedure. The union's representatives rejected the management proposals out of hand, but past experience suggests that similar proposals will nevertheless form the basis for subsequent discussion.

Rootes' proposals cover four main areas: negotiating machinery, grievance procedure, shop stewards and union status.

(1) 'Authoritative bodies' will be formed jointly of management and union representatives at local and national level to discuss 'efficiency', and wages and conditions.

The aim is clearly to eliminate traditional shopfloor bargaining and substitute bureaucratic joint bodies remote from shopfloor pressure. The stewards insist that the only authoritative negotiating body is the joint shop stewards committee at each plant.

(2) The new grievance procedure will require the worker himself first to raise any problem with his foreman, who will make a written report if no settlement is reached. Three stages of meetings will follow, which may involve up to three weeks delay. Only then will strike action be allowed—and then only after ten days notice has been given, national union officials called in, and a meeting held of the local negotiating council.

The proposals restrict the right of stewards to raise grievances on behalf of their members. They require formal written grievances which may well deter individual workers from raising problems and, while obliging the unions to exhaust procedure before taking action, place no restriction on management's right to change conditions (and so are even more biased against the workers than is the official Engineering Procedure).

(3) The management intends to decide jointly with the unions the number and 'constituencies' of stewards. Its aim is for geographical constituencies, in some cases with stewards representing members of several unions. Stewards will be allowed to leave their sections or see their convenor only after receiving permission from their supervisor. All stewards will have to attend 'induction courses'. If a steward is moved from his section (mobility is one element in the MDW agreements) a new steward must be elected within two weeks.

The aim is clearly to impose numerous restrictions on the rights of stewards and their ability to exercise their functions. Attempts will be made to brainwash stewards. Where this fails, management has merely to move a militant steward to deprive him of his position.

(4) Management proposes a closed shop for new employees and a checkoff system. Unions will discuss with management their areas of recruitment and representation. Permission will be needed for union meetings in working hours. This will involve notifying the subject of the meeting and the decision reached. Management will even be able to control what goes on union noticeboards.

These proposals reflect the general intention to integrate the unions within the company's authority structure and to limit all rights of independent initiative.

While the union side rejected these proposals, some features of the recent discussion are ominous. The company proposals were apparently sent to national union officials two or three weeks before the meeting; local union officials seem to have seen them only a few days beforehand, while convenors in general seem to have had no advance warning. Copies have not been provided for ordinary stewards, and there are reports of convenors refusing to discuss the proposals with the shopfloor or even with their JSSCs.

Similarly the productivity deal in ICI is going far in undermining the power of the shop steward. As an ICI steward wrote to me:

> Prior to it jobs were assessed according to Work Study Standards, the minutest detail being haggled over by the steward, invariably the steward's point being won. The fight here is for the wage packet.
>
> Under the productivity deal (Weekly Staff Agreement) the intention is that Work Study Standards should be strictly adhered to, especially since they are 'scientifically' appraised. The process of argument will be entirely different. A new process will be issued two weeks in advance of implementation. Time will be given for the stewards to haggle all right, but not in front of the machine and operative as before. Instead, even if there is no agreement, the process will be implemented after the two-week period has ended. Discussions under this arrangement are still allowed to continue.
>
> The danger of management logic becomes obvious. It moves the steward away from the point of production and engages him in prolonged arguments over the minutiae of production.
>
> It ceases to be a direct argument about money and becomes merely a diversion. The two-week rule takes power away from the steward.
>
> Even if discussions continue, it is harder to reverse a process once started, and the changes, taken separately, are so small anyway that the operative is not going to argue.

Productivity deals are seen by employers as a means to curbing the militant shop steward. They hope to do this thus:

(1) Reorganise their payments systems in such a way as to remove from the bargaining table the issues around which stewards have traditionally argued and in doing so gained their strength. These are mainly the wage levels associated with piece-work rates but also include such questions as waiting times, availability of materials, etc.

(2) To deny stewards the right to bargain on details of new work systems such as MDW.

(3) Increase the number of supervisors substantially and to try and channel workers' grievances through these lower rungs of management—thereby by-passing the shop steward.

(4) To introduce highly formalised grievance procedures within the factory which enable the management to exclude shop stewards and replace them by the local union officers.

(5) Under cover of flexibility clauses to establish the right to move militants around the factory whenever they begin to build a base and win support.

(6) Under cover of the deal to step up the indoctrination of stewards by means of joint management/union-sponsored courses.

The extent to which the employers are successful in these objectives depends very largely on the strength of the factory organisation. What the productivity deal does is to open the way for the acceptance of such changes which, under normal circumstances, would not even be countenanced.

Chapter Five: Greater flexibility in the deployment of labour

A central feature in practically all productivity deals is the increasing flexibility in the use of labour.

The original ICI productivity deal (Manpower Utilisation and Payment Structure) states:

(a) Production operators with suitable training can use tools to carry out the less skilled craft tasks which form only a subsidiary part of their work.

(b) In appropriate circumstances tradesmen will be expected to operate plant.

(c) Tradesmen and general workers can be given general supervision by men of any background.

(d) Tradesmen can do work of other trades which forms a subsidiary part of the main job of their own trade, according to their availability at the time.

(e) Support work for tradesmen can be done by tradesmen, semi-skilled or general workers as is appropriate in the circumstances.[1]

This labour flexibility boils down to one worker having to do the job of two! Similarly the draft productivity deal at Rootes, Coventry, says:

(a) All employees will, as far as is practicable, be interchangeable and mobile between jobs in the same or different departments at Coventry. Mobility of this type will not he restricted by demarcation issues.

(b) Employees will carry out as far as is practicable associated or ancillary work at present carried out by men of other trades, and/or by mates.

(c) Employees operating machines will carry out their own simple maintenance work, eg tool changing.

(d) Where necessary and practicable, in a limited number of production operations, work normally carried out by males will be reclassified as female occupations, so long as this does not adversely affect the security of employment of existing employees.[2]

In the docks labour flexibility has been the main ingredient of the productivity agreement:

(b) At any time during an operation men may be transferred temporarily to meet more urgent requirements or when work on the initial operation cannot be continued (shiphands transferring to other ship work and quayhands to other quay work).

(c) Men working on non-continuity work shall be regarded as fully mobile between job and job, and may be transferred to continuity work during a working period.[3]

Up to now, however, these articles have been largely dead letters. Since the eight-week continuity strike in October and November 1967 the employers have rarely, if ever, tried to impose the above clauses.

The idea of flexibility is also to be seen in the steel industry's Green Book[4]— where it is announced in a much more brutal and extreme fashion. The language here is not that of negotiation between two parties who are at least formally equal—employer and employee—but is the language of a master to his servant:

Mobility and interchangeability

(i) Maintenance of plant and equipment will be undertaken by all employees according to the skills required and the competence of the individual.

(ii) There will be complete mobility and interchangeability between all craftsmen throughout the division. There will also be complete interchangeability and mobility between all non-craft maintenance employees throughout the division.

(iii) Craftsmen and non-craft maintenance employees can be called upon to work in any department within Margam & Abbey works to meet any eventuality as required...

(iv) It is the intention of the division to set up mobile task forces. These mobile task forces will work on either day or shifts on or off the division's premises as required. Their deployment will be decided by the management both as to numbers and grades of craftsmen and maintenance employees...

(vi) Craftsmen and maintenance employees will work as required, either on their own, in pairs, or groups and will be responsible for their own slinging and rigging, the operation of jib and pendant control cranes, and the erection of scaffolding.

Skills

(i) The management can make the fullest use of the skills of all craftsmen and maintenance employees anywhere on or off the division's premises. Management will be free to decide which type of skilled, semi-skilled or unskilled employee will carry out a task in part or whole. This may be varied as conditions require from day to day.

Working with or without assistance

(i) All craftsmen will work with or without assistance as required. This means that craftsmen will do without assistance as long as it is within his physical capacity to do so.

(ii) Assistance will be given by any other employee as required.

Movement and use of employees

(i) There will be no restriction on the movement and use of employees either by department, section or works. All employees will be available for work anywhere on or off the division's premises. The division would be able to deploy employees to meet any need of service to the other works in the division.

(ii) All employees will be requested to mutually assist each other as required in order to ensure efficient operation, safety and maintenance of plant and equipment and to cooperate fully in any emergency that may arise.

(iii) Members of production and maintenance groups can be moved from unit to unit for a whole or part shift as directed to meet prevailing circumstances.

(iv) Management will deploy individual employees in any manner they consider will be efficient. Existing arrangements or agreements whereby employees may claim specific jobs or type of jobs under rota or such systems will be cancelled. Agreements and rotas giving any automatic movement from one department to another will cease.

Mobility and flexibility
All employees to be freely available to undertake any work within their existing or lower job grade and within a higher job grade subject to the limitations of their competence, ie disregarding all existing demarcations.

The term 'freely available' means capable of being deployed with full mobility anywhere on or off the division's premises.

Skilled workers must do any job they are told to, not only in their own trade, but in any trade. They even have to do the job of sweeping and cleaning—and all this in exchange for the wages of only *one* person:

Cleaning up
(i) Keeping the work area clean and tidy shall be the responsibility of the employees normally working there. They will use what means are necessary to do this. There shall be no division of cleaning and cleaning responsibilities, and anyone required to do this will do so.[5]

And where do we have to go to get fitted with the ball and chain?
Although the worker has to accept the most complete flexibility he gets no guarantee against loss of earning when transferred from one job to another:

Redeployment
(i) If, for any reason, a worker is required to move from his normal occupation to another which is not in the same promotion line, he shall be deemed to have been redeployed and, subject to payment for the period specified in 4(c)(ii) below, he shall be paid the rate of the job to which he has been redeployed.[6]

After a year he gets nothing. The result of these clauses is to remove from the worker all security as regards both his job and his earnings.

In the case of the railway workshops the worker is not even entitled to a higher rate when moved to a higher trade: 'When staff are employed for up to 25 percent of their time on higher category work, the lower rate will apply throughout'.[7]

This means management can man one job by a roster of four men, each doing 25 percent of the job, and only pay the cheap rate for it.

The proposed productivity deal of Pressed Steel Fisher Ltd, Common Lane, includes the following:

Supervision will decide upon those employees to be retained within the group/section/department and those to be released to the labour pool—a basis for selection will be attendance and general disciplinary record.

Labour pool employees, who will be supervised as a separate section, will be expected to fulfil tasks as directed by management. Selection of employees from the pool for specific tasks will be at the discretion of the supervisor.

During the first four weeks [workers at the pool] will receive the rate for the job from which they were released to the pool.

The skilled pool will receive not less than the grade rate for Grade V [lowest skilled grade]. The other pool [of semi-skilled and unskilled workers] will receive Grade I rate [lowest, unskilled rate].[8]

One advantage that flexibility of labour deployment gives to the employer is, of course, the complete elimination of some jobs. Flexibility makes it much easier for an employer to intensify work by using 'natural wastage' to run down the integrated labour force. However, in the long run there is an even more important gain for the boss. Such flexibility enables him to split up shop organisation by constantly moving workers from one shop to another. This measure can be wielded particularly against militants specially, and can thus strengthen managerial control. As Jim Nichol, an AEF steward in Linwood, put it:

I'll tell you what flexibility means… If you work with a group of men for some time, then maybe you'll form a militant block—begin to make demands which are taken up by other groups and so on.

'Flexibility' means that on the advice of a so-called expert, the management can move men all over the shop and the factory. Very quickly the most militant sections get broken up. It's happening already, every day.[9]

A steward in Ryton's Rootes factory wrote to me:

It is six months since the productivity deal has been signed. As a result of arbitrary transfers, shop organisation is being undermined. Three weeks after a steward has been removed from the shop he automatically loses his credentials.

The change to shift work (new rostering patterns, seven day working, etc)

One element common to many productivity deals is the introduction or expansion of shift working and the development of more onerous rostering systems. The last few years have seen a tremendous expansion of shift working.

In 1967 the then minister of labour, Ray Gunter, stated, 'The number of manual workers engaged on shift work has grown by more than half during the last decade'.[10]

Since then shift working has very much expanded again. Not only does shift work spread hand in hand with productivity deals, but the shifts become burdened with a far more onerous rostering system.

This is written into the agreement for the railway workshops:

Revision of rostering arrangements in order to produce a more effective balance between the availability of labour and the demand for it.

Under present arrangements rosters can be agreed locally in which Saturday forms part of the guaranteed week. It is now agreed, in principle, that Sunday can also, in certain circumstances, be rostered within the guaranteed week subject to local agreement.[11]

When it comes to steel workers, the management does not bother about niceties:

Day and shift working
All employees will work on days or shifts for short or long periods as required. It is the intention of management to work with a minimum of day and shift manning and also to work light on days or shifts as circumstances warrant. Any day employee asked to cover a shift vacancy or work with a shift employee during part of his day will do so as part of his normal day hours. Any loss in earnings resulting from moving from shifts to days is dealt with in Appendix B.

Changing of work rota
(i) Management will decide the number of shifts to be manned on any unit of plant in the light of prevailing circumstances.[12]

Probably the worst conditions were dictated to the power supply workers:

Four main types of stagger pattern were provided: staggered days, staggered hours, winter/summer stagger and workload stagger. Each had its advantages to the boards in different conditions.[13]

Maintenance men in power stations would work what we call a seven-day stagger; they would work five days in seven, but the five days in the first week would be different from the five days in the second week, and so on, so that you go five days round and a man is hitting a Saturday and hitting a Sunday on a regular rota, but these become a normal part of his duty in his service with us. He is not there on a Saturday or Sunday doing voluntary overtime, he is there doing part of his normal job.[14]

The hours of work were also staggered. In the area boards:

...the commonest patterns here are those involving staggered hours, which allow for the day to start as early as 6am or, with a much later start, finish as late as 8pm and, though usually involving five working days, permit four days of ten hours each to be worked. But patterns spreading five working days over five and a half or six days are also used quite frequently. In the power stations staggered hours are also used to some extent, but the vast majority of power station day-workers now work a five-day week spread over seven days, which closely corresponds with the demands of modern plant that must be continuously manned, and as far as possible serviced and overhauled at off-peak periods.[15]

The most fantastic stagger is the winter/summer one. This allows management to cut the working week by as much as five hours a week in winter and 'transfer' the time to the summer period, without paying a penny for overtime.

How to play 'Productopoly'

Rule 1—Any number of people can play and are divided up into trade unions, employers, stock and/or share holders, press, and Prices and Incomes Board (PIB). Trade unions play as an independent group but the rest play as a team.

Rule 2—Play is commenced by throwing dice which are loaded in favour of the PIB.

Rule 3—Trade unions must make the first move by applying for an increase in wages and/or salaries. All claims must contain an offer to increase productivity by working harder, working longer hours or abolishing protective practices.

Note: Claims based on higher rents, rates, mortgages, fares, food, clothing or the increased cost of producing the next generation of workers are forbidden, and players will be disqualified.

Rule 4—Any offer by the unions to really increase productivity by having a say in what amount of goods or services shall be produced by representation on the board of directors is not allowed as too much might be produced and the selling price would go down.

Note: Persistent offenders will be stamped on until they resume their rightful position as workers, on hands and knees.

Rule 5—The PIB retains the right to change the rules at any time, eg disallowing past savings to employers by increased productivity on the part of the workers.

Rule 6—The press must condemn any claim and/or action in support of a claim as greedy and irresponsible on the grounds that the 'country' (employers) can't afford it or that the 'public' (other trade unionists) will be alienated.

Rule 7—Any attempt to further a claim by action or talk of action will result in trade unions going to jail or being fined.

Rule 8—Stock and/or share holders must support all demands for increased productivity by shouting, 'Hear, hear!' or displaying 'I'm Backing Britain' badges and flags, etc.

Note: In the event of the trade unions asking the stock and/or share holders how they are increasing productivity, there will be a deathly silence and the press will not report it.

Rule 9—The winner must always be the employers, and the PIB, press and shareholders will be awarded joint second place for their loyal support. Acquiescent trade unions will be declared losers and return to square one.

Rule 10—Any trade unions that refuse to back down or to be intimidated, and win, will not be declared the winners because they did not play the game fairly according to the rules and the press will report the event as un-British, a red plot, anarchistic, or blackmail, as the mood suits them.

In any event, the PIB etc are bad losers.

Reprinted from *Playfayre*, the magazine of the PLA branch of the National Association of Local Government Officers.

The fire service scandal

In some cases the term productivity effort is being used simply to cover up for a long—very long—work period. MDW, flexibility, work study, etc could not be applied to the fire service—so what alternative is there for productivity-mongering but to press for a very extended duty period? The ultimate form of this is day manning. This is the system many fire authorities are pressing to introduce wherever possible. The idea is that men live in tied houses adjacent to the fire stations, usually at a cheap rent. While the basic working week of a fireman is 46 hours. with another ten hours, usually of overtime, the fireman on day manning is on call 120 hours a week. If there is a temporary shortage of men, a fireman on day manning is expected to cover the whole 168 hours of a week. He is paid the same rate as all firemen for 56 hours, which are apportioned to that part of the day when most fire calls are received. For the other 64 to 112 hours a week, during which the day-man is on 'retained obligation', he gets an annual sum of £65, plus extra every time he attends a fire call.

If they are needed for a fire they are called in from home by a siren before 11pm, or between 11pm and 7am by bells in the house—one in the bedroom and one downstairs The firemen have the absolute right to two periods of 24 hours off per week. Apart from that 48 hours they are *obliged* to go into the fire station every time the fire bell or siren sounds.

The system makes numerous encroachments into both the independence and privacy of the 'victim' and his family. For instance, the entire household may be woken when the bell sounds in the small hours—not a pleasant situation and particularly annoying when there is sickness in the home. Should a man want to take his family out at the weekend he would not be able to—he must wait at home in case the siren sounds. A member cannot venture more than a few minutes from the fire station, except on rota days, and even rota days can be in jeopardy on some occasions.

A militant fireman wrote to me:

> A good example of the all-embracing nature of the system occurred in Hertfordshire. Shortly after a fireman moved into his house at the day manning station, a social evening was arranged at the fire station. Our member chose not to go. The next day the officer in charge of the station called the man into his office and demanded to know why he had not attended the social the night before. The fireman explained that he had decided not to go, and that was all there was to it. The officer, however, had other ideas, and informed our member that since the social had taken place during his period of 'close availability' he had no option but to attend. Our member was also told that he was expected to join in the social life of the station… It is a good illustration of the attitude adopted by the employers once they get as much of the system as they want.

To the fire authorities day manning is a financial windfall. The savings to the employers arising can be illustrated by comparing costs at Clacton fire station, where at this time Essex County Council is trying to change over to day manning from the two-shift system.

The two-shift system requires 45 men, working a 56-hour week. In wages alone this would cost £61,195 approximately. On day manning 21 men would be needed to cover the week. They are paid the same as the two-shift men for the 56 hours per week. For the hours over that they would be 'retained' and receive an annual retaining fee of £65 plus hourly rates for each fire they attend—for the first hour of every fire they get 23s, and 9s per hour thereafter. This would bring the wage bill to approximately £30,615. In addition to this there is the initial expenditure of building the houses around the fire station, and then letting them to the fireman occupants at a 'cheap' rent—£90 per annum in Essex.

If one examines the situation more closely, the county council would save National Insurance, superannuating, uniforms and training. The station would be unoccupied for most of the time, and this would save heating, etc. The county council estimated, in 1969, a net saving of £27,000 if the system were introduced at Clacton. No wonder the PIB is in favour of day manning, stating, 'We recommend that the Fire Brigades Union should discuss with the employers the conditions under which an extension of the day manning system on a voluntary basis could be made more generally acceptable'.[16]

The fire authorities achieving a 24-hour day, five to seven day week work period must surely serve as a shining example to other employers!

The impact of shift work

There has always been some night work in society. Some groups of workers, specially in the service industries, are forced by the very nature of the job to work awkward hours—firemen, transport workers, postmen, etc. However, most industries that have adopted shift working have not done it in order to provide a public service but simply to increase profits. Factory owners, quite early on, recognised that by keeping machinery working round the clock their profits would rise. Today the pressure for continuous shift working comes strongest from those employers who operate the most expensive machinery. It is these employers who see a productivity deal as the simplest way of introducing shift working and are quite often willing to pay relatively high sums for the privilege. Whether these improved wages can ever compensate workers for the disadvantages of shift working we must see.

All the evidence points to the fact that shift work has a debilitating effect on man—physically, psychologically and socially. A number of studies have been made on the question. One of these:

> ...found that day workers get an average of seven and a half hours sleep per night, which is an hour more than the overall average of rotating shift workers. But when they are working the night segment of their shift, rotating workers average only five and a half hours of sleep. The biggest problem for rotating shift workers occurs when they move from their turn on the day shift to the night shift.

The same study:

> ...reports that only 37 percent of the workers adjust to the new sleeping times

immediately, while 28 percent of the workers said that they took four days or more to adjust to the night shift... Another study of operators in two different power plants in the United States found that only 31 percent of the men working under an extended seven-day week rotation reported that they adjusted to their hardest shift change within a day or less. Even fewer, just 5 percent of the men working a monthly rotation schedule, stated they could adjust to their hardest shift change in one day. Under the latter schedule, 70 percent reported that their adjustment to the new schedule took four days or more.[17]

The *quality* of sleep is also affected. The study:

...reported that even the sleep that these workers get is not so refreshing as sleeping at the normal time. Eighty three percent of the rotators said that they felt most fatigued on the night shift, and only 9 percent felt fatigued most frequently on the day shift.[18]

Other physical processes besides sleep are adversely affected. For a start there is appetite. Thus the study:

...found that 20 percent of the shift workers interviewed complained that shift work affected their eating habits adversely. Wyatt and Marriott (1953) report that 74 percent of their respondents enjoyed eating most on the day shift. Only 3 percent of their sample said that they enjoyed their food most on the night shift.[19]

A higher proportion of night and rotating shift workers reported that they were fatigued much of the time, that their appetites were dulled, and that they were constipated much of the time.[20]

We also found that the prevalence of ulcers and rheumatoid arthritis was higher among workers who had relatively more difficulty adjusting their rhythmic functions.[21]

All studies into the subject agree that the weekly rotating shift system was even worse for the wellbeing of workers than the fixed-shift system:

It was found that the higher the level of complaints, the more frequent and severe were upper respiratory infections and headaches. The prevalence of soaking sweats while sleeping, asthma and rectal diseases were also found to be higher among the high complaint group and among the rotators who adjust their time-oriented body functions less readily. Thus the higher the level of complaints about rhythmic functioning or the slower rate of adjustment of these functions, the poorer the health of the worker.[22]

Another study 'done among German workers showed that the ulcer rate was eight times as high for the rotating shift workers as for the fixed shift group'.[23]

The psychological impact of shift working is probably more serious than the physical effects. One of the most common spontaneous complaints about shift work is that it interferes with family life. A study on German workers, for instance, showed that '74 percent of the married men and 45 percent of the single men who followed a shift schedule which included night work complained of disturbances in family life'.[24]

> The most frequently mentioned difficulties in husband-wife relationships concern the absence of the worker from the home in the evening, sexual relations, and difficulties encountered by the wife in carrying out her household duties....
>
> Another area of family life that seems to be adversely affected by certain kinds of shift work is the father-child relationship.[25]

As one shift worker put it to me, 'The only thing that has saved my marriage is an electric blanket!'

Many workers expected that after a time they will become adjusted to shift work. But research has shown this not to be the case:

> We had expected that, with the passage of time, the worker would become accustomed to his shift. It was most interesting to us that this was not the case. Regardless of his age or length of service on his shift he could still have difficulty adjusting his time-oriented body functions to his shift.[26]

From the employers' point of view 'shift working' is not a difficult question. If it increases profits then it is to be welcomed. After all, very few company directors work a night shift—at least not one they get paid for. For us as trade unionists and socialists the question is far more difficult. It is difficult to oppose all shift working in principle as we would have to do without buses, telephones, electricity, etc. In a socialist society we would probably decide whether to work shifts on the merits of the case—by balancing the disadvantages to the worker against the benefits to the community of the article being produced. If it's houses to solve a serious housing problem then we might say yes. If it were colour TV sets the answer should be no. In industry today we can use no such yardstick, for the simple reason that the product belongs to the employer and not to the community. A better bet is to say that we will resist the extension of shift working wherever we can. We don't consider that our health, our families and our sanity can be sold for any price.

A favourite argument to justify shift working is that 'our competitors abroad operate their plant round the clock and so we can't possibly keep in the market if we don't follow suit', the inference being that you have a choice—shift work or the sack. Of course, we can turn that argument on its head: 'If we don't accept shift working then there will be no reason why our fellow workers in other countries should have to go on putting up with it.'

Basically the spread of shift work clearly shows up capitalist priorities: property versus man. One writer makes a remarkable assessment of the priorities:

> A rapid shift is taking place from the human being to the machine... No longer is the producer a man serviced by machines but a machine serviced by men. For the possibilities of this new situation to be realised a change is required in the work culture from a man-centred to a machine-centred attitude—*a machine culture.*[27]

Reduction of tea breaks, relief time, etc

This is very crucial to productivity deals. The Green Book for the steel industry states, 'Set tea breaks will not be allowed anywhere on the plant, but tea may be drunk provided the programme of work is not interrupted'.[28]

On meal breaks, the Green Book says:

The division is seriously concerned with the amount of time lost as a result of meal breaks being extended beyond the time laid down in agreements. It wants the 30-minute maximum time, including reaching the mess, washing, eating, cleaning utensils and returning to the place of work, strictly observed.

In Ford's no tea break is allowed to manual workers, and the same goes in a recent productivity agreement for the white collar workers.[29]

At the Rootes factory in Linwood workers are entitled to two ten-minute tea breaks, and 15 minutes daily relief. But as one Linwood worker writes:

Even these 15 minutes are not assured. If the relief man on your section is away, or has to stand in for someone else who's off work, or for someone who has an accident, you just don't get a relief that day. Theoretically, each section is supposed to have permanent 'stand in' men attached to them as well as 'relief' men, but I've not come across any as yet.

Prior to the productivity deal of 1968, the line used to stop seven minutes before 4.30pm for 'cleaning up'. Since the agreement, workers have to work until the bell rings. The principle is 'bell to bell working'. If a worker were found leaving his place of work before normal stopping time, the following action would be taken:

On the first occasion, a final warning. On the second occasion, three days suspension. On the third occasion, immediate dismissal.[30]

Some 100 years ago Marx wrote:

These 'small thefts' of capital from the labourer's meal and recreation time, the factory inspectors also designate as 'petty pilfering of minutes', 'snatching a few minutes', or, as the labourers technically called them, 'nibbling and cribbing at mealtimes'.

'If you allow me', said a highly respectable master to me, 'to work only ten minutes in the day overtime, you put a thousand a year in my pocket. Moments are the elements of profit'.[31]

The vital importance of this issue of tea breaks was very well put by one engineering militant:

Tea breaks are necessary, not just as a physical break from work but as a constant demonstration to the bosses that the workers cannot be completely dominated by the production line and the bosses' god of productivity. If you can stop the production line for a cup of tea you can equally well stop it to support your steward.

You can't have effective shop stewards if the workers are unable to escape the complete domination of the production line and to realise that they are a collective, even if it is only round a tea trolley for ten minutes.[32]

Tea breaks allow informal shopfloor meetings, contacts with stewards, etc. Tea breaks are the foundation of shopfloor democracy.

If any confirmation was needed that the 'small' issue of tea break or meal times can have a central and crucial place in workers' feelings, the recent mass miners' strike provided it. Some 160,000 miners went on strike—in the biggest strike since the General Strike of 1926, and the biggest unofficial strike ever—on the question of 20 minutes meal time for surface workers, a question that directly affected only about 10 percent of all miners.

However, whatever the paper agreement regarding tea breaks and relief time, it is very much up to shop stewards and the workers themselves to bend the agreement. Thus a shop steward in one ICI factory writes:

> Official dinner break is half an hour; actually anything up to two hours and certainly averaging 50 minutes we spend at dinner time… stewards' control over output is such that 'the daily stint' can be easily finished an hour before knock-off.[33]

Again, a worker in the Dagenham Ford foundry writes to me:

> Officially relief time in the foundry is 4 percent. In any top level argument one is told 20 minutes in the morning and 15 minutes in the afternoon. In practice it varies from department to department, and in the department from job to job. The foundry management is much more complaisant as regards relief than any other plant. On jobs that are either very noisy or very hot and smoky, men work half an hour on, half an hour off, or 50 percent relief. This is to try to ameliorate bad working conditions. On certain other jobs, for instance, instead of two men each loading three cores, one man loads six and they work half an hour about. Most men get one and a quarter out of nine anyway. These are moulding and hot metal conditions. In the core shop and fettling shop men usually get two half-hours and a quarter of an hour. This is usual but unofficial.

Getting rid of 'restrictive practices'

One item that appears time and again in productivity deals is the elimination of restrictive practices.

The provincial and municipal bus employers in their evidence to the PIB list the following as restrictive practices:

Restriction on the length of duties.
Restrictions on the number of split duties.
Refusal to accept flexibility of drivers working as conductors.
Resistance to the employment of part time and seasonal staff.
Refusal to accept standing passengers.
Restrictions on the size of one-man buses…etc.[34]

In its evidence to the court of inquiry chaired by Lord Cameron, the building contractor Bernard Sunley and Sons Limited:

...listed a large number of activities which it described as restrictive practices and which it claimed had taken place on the site. These included refusal by the stewards to accept non-unionists on the site, despite appropriate provision in the Site Procedure Agreement, or to permit the unloading of lorries driven by non-unionists, refusal to accept that management had to discharge operatives from time to time because of poor timekeeping or absenteeism, and attempts to undermine the authority of site supervision by demanding the removal of members of the site staff.[35]

Refusal to work with non-unionists is a 'restrictive practice'!

A book written for managers goes so far as to give the following long list of possible restrictive practices:

(1) Timekeeping—late starting and early finishing.
(2) Carry-over of time booking.
(3) Unofficial stoppages for meeting purposes and meetings extended.
(4) Extension of official tea breaks.
(5) Stewards leaving shop without permission of foreman.
(6) Union restrictions resulting in lower labour intake than would otherwise be possible.
(7) Shop stewards required to approve overtime.
(8) Claim by employees that 'one in, all in' on overtime.
(9) Reluctance to accept double and treble shift working.
(10) Resistance to changes in production methods that can reduce operational times.
(11) Resistance to changes to grade of labour for job, eg skilled to semi-skilled.
(12) Some unions demanding exclusive right to certain work in opposition to other unions.
(13) Resistance to transfer of labour from one type of machine to another which may have been necessitated by absenteeism.
(14) Objection by electricians to relatively simple connections being made by fitters, etc.
(15) Absenteeism after weekend working.
(16) Refusal to accept stopwatch in all departments.
(17) Interchange of labour between departments where there are related trades.
(18) Demand that certain jobs are the prerogative of certain shops in spite of inconvenience and change in technology.
(19) Refusal by certain shops to allow recruitment when they have a wage claim in.
(20) Refusal of employees to work with outside employees who are not union members.
(21) Refusal to cooperate with outside contractors unless they are in appropriate unions.
(22) Refusal to modify jigs and equipment that have been manufactured outside.
(23) Limitation on recruitment of apprentices.

Reluctance to accept double and treble shift working, refusal to work with non-unionists, refusal to change grades etc, are restrictive practices.[36]

There are various kinds of what are called 'restrictive practices'. Many practices are an essential defence of jobs and conditions. Others are time-honoured but no longer of much relevance, and workers do not much mind selling them for a price. Yet others, eg many craft rules, erect barriers within the working class which are difficult for socialists to defend in any principled way.

When workers sell restrictive practices in one productivity deal they immediately try to create a new one. The bosses are not unaware of this. Take, for example, the following interchange between Lord Donovan and Sir Maurice Laing of the Confederation of British Industries:

> Chairman: Let us suppose you buy off your restrictive practices either by national agreement or by plant agreement. I take it that the categories of restrictive practices are not closed, particularly with new processes coming along. Even if you buy some off, is there not a possibility of others taking their place? And if that is so, where do we end?
>
> Sir Maurice Laing: The great difficulty I foresee is the one you foresee. This encourages the very extension of restrictive practices so that at a later date they can be bought off.[37]

The same question was referred to in a research paper of the Engineering Employers' Federation:

> Will the negotiation of a deal to buy out restrictive practices not lead to the creation of new ones?
>
> It would be contrary to human nature to say that such a possibility is inconceivable. *However, one of the major points of productivity bargaining is that it gives management a chance to regain control in a rational way.* If management relaxes this new found control to permit the building up of new restrictive practices then it has certainly thrown away the opportunity which a successful bargain can confer.[38]

The key point is contained in the sentence emphasised. If management approaches the deal, as Flanders suggests, not with a shopping list of practices to buy, but with the aim of re-exerting positive control—and if it is successful—then it is very difficult to create new restrictions. Either the workers must obtain new strength or management relax its control.

Socialist attitude to 'restrictive practices'

For the capitalist, every custom or method of work which affects his profits in any way is a restrictive practice. Workers, of course, recognise that such 'restrictive practices' are often essential defences of their wages and conditions, and even of their security in their jobs. Socialists have long pointed out the hypocrisy of such gentlemen as lawyers or company directors who criticise the 'restrictive practices' of ordinary workers, when their own demarcation rules and time-wasting practices would put any trade unionist to shame. It is very important for militants to expose the ruling class ideology, which attacks workers' protective practices as unjustified restrictions. At the same time, they must show the serious dangers often present when such practices are 'sold' in a productivity deal.

It would be wrong, however, to make a fetish of *every* traditional practice employed by workers. Tradition is not in itself a guarantee of strategic importance. For this reason, a management invitation to 'sell the rulebook' should not be opposed in the abstract—no rulebook is sacrosanct—but because the rules involved have some concrete value which workers can readily understand. There are rules and practices—though far fewer than the bosses and press lords would have us believe—which, though time-honoured, no longer serve any obvious purpose. When the productivity-mongers turn up practices which fall into this category, then there is no reason why they should not be regarded as saleable. Indeed, there is a lot to be said for keeping top management happy by inventing a few such practices specially for sale. On the other hand, the practices which companies are most anxious to buy out are usually those which are genuine defences. Restrictions on machine staffing or pace of work are physical safeguards for workers, and in addition often protect employment in trades or areas where this is particularly insecure. Output and earnings ceilings protect against rate-cutting, and also prevent jealousy and competition between workers. Restrictions on mobility prevent management from constantly moving and isolating militants, or breaking up sections with a reputation for collective action. Tea breaks, washing time, etc are times when workers can meet collectively to discuss problems with their stewards and with each other. They also represent an erosion of management *control* over the use of working hours.

Probably the most delicate type of practice on which to take a principled stand concerns so-called 'craft restrictions'. One of the central elements of the Fawley deals was the reduction of intercraft demarcations, and the elimination of craftsmen's mates. And the aim of greater 'flexibility' of skilled labour is equally central in many other productivity packages. Socialists have long recognised the difficulty of formulating a policy towards craft practices in general. In essence, the institution of the craft sets a section of workers apart from all others, as an 'aristocracy' with exclusive right to a narrowly-defined area of work, which must be jealously defended against the rest of the class. It cuts across the principle of class unity, sanctifying within the trade union movement the capitalist principle of division of labour. Clearly the objective for socialists should be the elimination of artificial barriers between different crafts and between craftsman and labourer, so that workers' energies can be directed towards their common interests as a class.

But, equally clearly, this principle cannot be mechanically applied when the attempt to remove 'craft restrictions' is made *by employers* as part of a productivity deal. Here the aim of management is to exploit sectional divisions among the labour force in order to *intensify* the pressure of work for one section, the craftsmen, and usually also to *eliminate* a substantial number of employees—as with the redundant labourers at Fawley. Here opposition to the employers' attack on workers' conditions must be unqualified. But such opposition must not take the form of unprincipled opportunism. Socialists must base their opposition firmly on class rather than craft arguments.[39] Workers' resistance to management's attack may be fatally weakened by a failure to transcend sectional jealousies and divisions. (Indeed, it should be an urgent priority for militants to combat such divisions *before* management attacks.)

To summarise, the following test should be applied whenever a company attempts to 'buy out' what it considers a restrictive practice. Workers must ask themselves, does this practice help make conditions more bearable? Does it help maintain our earnings or make our employment more secure? Does it increase our strength of our organisation and add to our control on the shopfloor? If the answer to any of these questions is yes, then naturally any concession would be dangerous, and the aim must be to see that every worker understands why. But if the practice serves no important defensive purpose, then there is no reason of principle to fight to retain it—though clearly workers will want to get the highest possible price for abandoning it.

Such a strategy naturally means that there can be no 'blanket' sale of all workers' traditional practices. Flanders, the PIB, etc advise managements that a productivity deal should eliminate *all* workers' practices which are not specifically listed to be retained. This can well mean that workers recognise only afterwards that essential practices have been sold in the package—and it makes the invention of *new* restrictions far harder to get away with. Workers must clearly insist that the reverse principle should apply in any deal—nothing is sold unless specifically listed and paid for. Unless this basis is accepted, workers have a cast iron case for refusing to have anything to do with management's 'bargain'.

Penalties

All productivity deals tighten labour discipline. Hence many of them include penalty clauses.

In the municipal bus industry which employs 77,000 people, an agreement has been reached between management and union officials that fines will be imposed on unofficial strikers. The penalty clause was this—a bonus of about £12 10s paid twice a year would be withheld from any busman involved in an unofficial action. The unions involved in this agreement were the TGWU, NUGMW, AEU, ETU, NUVB and NUR.[40]

And the NUGMW signed a closed shop agreement with Ilford Limited (at the time part-owned by ICI) that guarantees the company freedom from unofficial strikes and unofficial wage demands. The union will police the agreement, expelling any 'troublemakers' from the union and the factory in one blow. The union will act as a foreman for Ilford Limited, helping with a drive for 'greater productivity'. As the *Guardian* commented on this agreement, the result will be:

...a much more authoritarian industrial situation with the union wielding greater power over its members... But the benefit to the individual production worker is less obvious.[41]

Similarly, the National Joint Council of the Building Industry, in a ten-point productivity deal, included the following:

(7) 'Making entitlement to annual holiday credits dependent on completion of a

normal week's work.' So any time lost through lateness, sickness, wet time, etc will lose that week's annual holiday stamp.

(8) Introducing realistic penalties for operatives leaving service in breach of the Working Rule Agreement. Fines for throwing in your job.

(10) 'Providing for the suspension of the weekly guarantee in the event of dislocation of production through industrial action on the site.' If anyone dares to oppose this slaves' charter by a strike, go-slow or work to rule they will be subject to still more severe penalties.[42]

The suggested productivity deal for the exhibition workers, an agreement which was vetoed by the PIB, included an item that stated that for selling certain conditions every worker would get 10s a day wage rise. There was, however, a sting in the tail—for coming late or missing a day or for industrial misdemeanour the 10s bonus would be taken off.[43]

The productivity deal between Upper Clyde Shipbuilders Ltd and the trade unions guaranteed that there would be no redundancies before August 1970 for all workers with nine months' continuous service. However, 'any employee taking part in an unofficial strike would lose his guarantee until he had completed nine months' continuous service following return to normal working, ie working under the conditions of this agreement'.[44]

Similarly the productivity deal between Swan Hunter and Tyne Shipbuilders Ltd and the Boilermakers' Union states:

> The company guarantees security of employment for two years to all employees covered by this agreement who, at the date of its implementation, have completed at least one year's service with the company. This guarantee of employment will become invalid in the case of proven industrial misconduct by an individual or individuals or by *unofficial industrial action* against the company.[45]

The agreement goes on to state, 'This guarantee does not in any way restrict the right of the company, after consultation with the society, to lay off employees *in the event of shortage of materials or service resulting from causes outside the company.*

Productivity agreements for electricians in the building industry went furthest of all:

> (a) Any employer, participant or employee participant who, in the opinion of the National Board, has behaved in any manner contrary to Rules 13 or 14 or prejudicial to the interest of the Joint Industry Board, shall be liable, at the absolute discretion of the National Board, to the following penalties:
>   (i) A censure.
>   (ii) The forfeiture of all or any of the welfare benefits accrued or other benefits which such participation would or might otherwise be or become entitled to receive from the Joint Industry Board.
>   (iii) The suspension of such participant, for such period not exceeding three months for each separate offence, from all or any of the rights and privileges of membership of the Joint Industry Board, including the right to receive all or any of the welfare or other benefits which such participant might otherwise become entitled to receive from the Joint Industry Board during such period.

(iv) The payment to the Joint Industry Board of a fine, which shall not for any single offence exceed £1,000 in the case of an employer participant or £100 in the case of an employee participant.

(v) Expulsion from membership of the Joint Industry Board.[46]

In this case at least there is no doubt at all that the disciplinary measures of the ETU leadership, who supported the above agreement, were quite effective in cutting drastically strike actions.[47]

	Number of strikes	Man–days lost
1961	50	31,836
1962	55	36,801
1963	49	9,365
1964	35	5,477
1965	54	11,981
1966	48	9,904
1967	No record kept	—
1968	31	5,350

Probably the most famous of the penalty clauses associated with productivity deals, and which led to an extremely important strike, was that at Ford.

For layoff benefit the company would pay 4s per employee per week into a fund, but if there was an unconstitutional action in any plant all the workers would lose all the payment for six months. For the holiday fund the firm would pay 10s per worker per week—with a similar suspension, this time for 12 months, if any unconstitutional action took place in the plant.

Unconstitutional action was defined by the agreement in a very wide and encompassing way:

(1) Withdrawal of labour.

(2) Overtime bans.

(3) Concerted restrictions of work output, whether by quantity of work produced, quality of work produced or the range of work undertaken.[48]

However, as a result of a very militant and massive strike Ford management's penalty clauses were smashed to pieces. The above clauses were changed radically.

The agreement was as follows. For layoff benefit the company would pay 4s per employee per week into a fund, but if there was unconstitutional action in any plant it would make no payments *for that week*.

For the holiday fund the firm would pay 10s per worker per week, with a similar suspension for weeks of unconstitutional action in any plant. A minimum payment of £15 would be made to *all* qualified workers. With no suspensions, the full payment would be nearly £25 (more if there was a surplus in the layoff fund), but above the £15 minimum any worker who indulged in unconstitutional action would have his bonus reduced (ie by $^2/_{49}$ if he had been on strike in two weeks). This is a far cry indeed from disqualification for six or 12 months for any action. The penalties have been radically weakened.[49]

Following in Ford's wake, Vauxhall tried in its productivity deal offer of April 1969 to get an almost completely free hand to discipline the workers:

> The unions will not cause or permit their members to cause, nor will any member of the unions take part in any unauthorised work stoppage, slowdown or curtailment, restriction of or interference with production at Vauxhall plants.
>
> The union will not cause or permit their members to cause, nor will any member of the unions take part in any strike or work stoppage until all the procedure as established by agreement has been exhausted.
>
> The company reserves the right to discipline any employee taking part in any violation of this undertaking and will expect the union to review the conduct of any member in violation within rules and constitution and to support such action as may be necessary and appropriate.[50]

The port employers are also trying to tighten discipline. Up to now disciplining has been in the hands of the Dock Labour Board, made up of five employers and five union members.

In the absence of a majority decision it is difficult for the employers to impose penalties on the dockers. This became very clear early in 1969 when the employers attempted to suspend for up to five days several thousand dockers who went on unofficial strikes over a pay demand. The attempt failed. After this employers drew up proposals for changes in dock legislation which they intend to put to the government through their National Association of Port Employers. It could therefore apply to all ports in the country. In addition to the three-day unilateral suspension (which might be operated every time action was taken, or only once a year on each offender), the employers also want the appeal body for other disciplinary measures to be reconstituted—with one employer member, one from the unions and an 'independent' chairman. They also want their agreement with the unions changed so that when a man takes unconstitutional action he loses his right to fallback pay for a whole week instead of just for the few hours in which he actually took the action. As a matter of fact, outside London most ports already penalise dockers for the whole week rather than for the length of the action.

One of the more general, even if less open, disciplinary measures is the power, written into most productivity deals, of transferring a worker from one grade to another—the deployment of labour. This is an especially serious weapon where the differences between the pay of different grades is very great indeed (as in the steel industry). In the mines the use of disciplinary power by management is set out in the following statement: 'If any team member is found to be unsatisfactory, the management, after consultation with the union, may transfer him to other work in keeping with his capabilities'.[51]

When other work may mean a wage cut of 50 percent, this is really a punishment! Grading, together with great wage differentials, is a sword of Damocles hanging over workers' heads.

One crude weapon for disciplining workers is the tachograph or the 'spy in the box'. When the Transport Bill becomes law it will be compulsory for all commercial vehicles to have one of these instruments fitted. The advocates of the tachograph claim that its purpose is to increase road safety, by ensuring that the vehicle is driven correctly, that the driver does not drive for a period longer than is stipulated and become overtired. The lorry driver regards the 'spy box' as a sophisticated stopwatch in the hands of his employer.

The principle of the tachograph is not new. A cruder version of the instrument appeared in Britain before the last war when a dairy gave secret instructions to its fitters to install a box underneath its trucks. The drivers got to hear of it. The box became accident prone, and was quickly withdrawn.

An inspection of the tachograph at the end of the run will reveal the following:

When the vehicle was started.
When it returned.
How many miles were travelled.
How fast it was driven.
Whether it was delayed by customer or supplier.
When and where it stopped.
Whether or not the engine was left idling during stops.
Whether or not the rush order got rush treatment.
Which driver was at the wheel (driver and co-driver have their own keys).[52]

The idea of snooping on workers appeals to other employers besides those in haulage. Thus, following the widespread absenteeism on New Year's Day, the Confederation of British Industry issued a report suggesting five courses open to management to combat absenteeism:

(1) To arrange a visit to the employee's home by a member of the company's welfare department.

(2) To arrange for workers with records of persistent absence to be examined by the company medical adviser on their return to work...considering whether a change of job would be appropriate.

(3) To refer workers with particularly bad records of sickness absence to a joint works committee which would require such persons to explain their high level of sickness absence.

(4) To issue direct warnings to persistent absentees and finally to effect dismissal on the grounds that they are impeding the efficiency of the company.

Before this they may be offered alternative employment where their absence is less harmful.

(5) An employer may also be able to safeguard himself against employing people of this type either by asking for references that cover the point or by asking to see workers' insurance cards before signing them on.

If the stamps are conspicuous by their absence the applicant for employment should be closely questioned as to the reasons.[53]

So a company representative is going to snoop on you, even if you are at home in bed!

One of the problems with the more direct kind of penalty clauses—ie where you lose bonus payments for going on unofficial strike—is that they tend to make strikes longer as workers will demand an undertaking that the clauses will not be enforced before returning to work. This, of course, destroys the whole object of the penalty clause. It seems likely that in future employers will favour alternative methods of tightening labour discipline, specially those such as the agreement in the electrical contracting industry which allows sanctions to be taken against individual militants rather than whole groups of strikers.

'Phoney' productivity deals?

Quite often in the first round of a productivity deal workers are convinced that they have sold the bosses a dud for a good price—that they have given up nothing, or at most very little, and that they will be able in future to control the situation.

Thus a convenor of a large engineering factory in Essex wrote to me:

> In one shop we agreed with management to cut the number of workers doing a certain job from 21 to 16, when in fact there had been all along only 16 men on the job. As a compensation the workers were paid 1s 6d an hour extra...this was a very worthwhile productivity bargain.

A shop steward in another engineering factory in north London tells a similar story:

> We got an increase after a survey of £1 plus a bonus scheme which gives an actual increase of 45s (totalling £3 5s). The concessions for this £3 5s were some equipment altered—eg stores moved two floors down to same level—quite sensible, made work easier, gantry fixed full length of shop (but in the wrong place). They wanted to introduce vending machines and stop fixed tea breaks. But this was successfully resisted. They wanted partial integration of work between pump fitters and engine testers —ie, each could be asked to do the work of the other. Also rejected. But the integration of maintenance under exceptional circumstances has been accepted in principle, although this has not so far been implemented.
>
> It has turned out to be a ridiculous bonus scheme and anti-productive from a management standpoint because it is possible to turn out loads of results which mean nothing where it is really better to turn out fewer but effective results. Strong shop organisation has made it possible to keep real output stable because it is so easy to confuse the lower management who don't really understand the work done by the testers.

A third example comes from a more recently signed productivity deal:

> We are confident of our ability to resist...organisation is strong and the management weak...since the productivity deal, output has gone down 25 percent. Workers have stopped all the dodges they used to maintain high production under piece-work...whenever the work study engineers come in we are able to end up with a job easier than before.

Many workers, especially experienced militants, agree to productivity deals often because they think they can control them. If the agreement says that this or that should be measured by the stopwatch man, the workers are so well organised and militant that they can 'bend' the agreement. But if the leadership in the factory or the shop ever changes, and this is natural and happens again and again, or if at any stage the management decides that they are going to transplant this agreement into another section of the group where they have a weak shopfloor organisation, the dam is broken and the light chains of the productivity deal turn into very heavy ones.

Even an 'innocuous' deal can be very dangerous to the workers. It may well be the thin end of a wedge. Workers may become accustomed to the idea of productivity bargaining, while the employer may have learned that he has been conned, and in next round he will drive a much harder bargain.

Chapter Six: Job evaluation, grading and rating

The introduction of measured day work usually goes through the following stages: (1) job evaluation; (2) grading; (3) rating; (4) determination of the 'production standard'.

Job evaluation is done by listing the main features of the particular job (especially skill, effort, responsibility and working conditions), allocating points to them and then adding them together. Once this has been done for all the jobs they are placed in one of a number of grades, which cover a range of job content points. Then a scale of wage rates is allocated to each grade. We shall deal with these three steps in the present chapter. The last step determining production standards is usually achieved by timing the job to be done. This will be the subject of the next chapter.

Grading is a prerequisite for the flexible redeployment of labour. In practically all productivity deals workers are being grouped into a small number of grades. Thus, for instance, in Alcan over 40 grades were reduced to seven. Esso Distribution has reduced the number of pay grades among tanker drivers and plant operators from 15 to six. ICI is dividing all its labour force into eight grades. At Ford, where 'merit bonus' as a negotiable item increased the differences between wage packets of workers in one and the same grade, a new agreement in September 1967 completely abolished merit rating and substituted five grades (with a variable service increment). In the mines 6,500 jobs were classified, in 1955, into 13 separate grades—three for craftsmen, five for underground and five for surface workers. In the building industry Professor Phelps Brown found that there are hundreds of actual job descriptions, and suggested that these should be divided into about eight or nine grades covering the variety of building skills.[1]

To determine to which grade a job should belong, management resorts to job evaluation—ie comparing jobs in a systematic way so as to determine their relative position in a job hierarchy. A PIB survey in September 1968 showed that a rapid expansion of job evaluation in recent years encompassed some 25 percent of workers in manufacturing industry and certain services. (Since this survey the extent of job evaluation spread even further.)

> The advance of job evaluation has not been uniform throughout industry, and it seems significant that the leaders are coal mining, virtually a single-employer industry, and tobacco manufacture, a trade dominated by a few large companies. In both these industries more than 70 percent of their employees are covered. Next are two process industries, characterised again by large concerns—oil refining and chemicals—with over 50 percent of their employees covered. Air transport, also dominated by large corporations, follows with a 40 percent coverage.[2]

Job evaluation is spreading rapidly. Britain today is not lagging far behind the United States, where probably some 50 million workers, or about two thirds of the labour force, are graded under job evaluation schemes.[3]

A number of methods of job evaluation are being used. They range from the single ranking schemes based on consideration of the relative importance of each job as a whole to more sophisticated, analytical methods, which break down and evaluate each job in terms of its basic components. Only 20 percent of the schemes surveyed by the PIB were of the single-ranking method. The most common is that based on 'points rating'. Under this method points are allocated to a range of factors selected to cover the most important requirements of the job which is being evaluated.

As it is extremely important for workers, and for socialists, to understand the phoney nature of the 'science' of job evaluation, we shall enlarge on this. We will deal with job evaluation as practised in ICI and in Ford.

ICI JOB ASSESSMENT MAINHEADS

Mental requirements	Personality requirements	Physical requirements	Skill and knowledge requirements
Memory	Even temperament	Muscular strength	Education and
Reasoning	Cooperativeness	Stamina	training
Visualisation	Perseverance	Agility	Experience
Planning	Initiative	Sensory accuracy	Special skills
Control of the work of others	Sense of responsibility		
Original thinking	Leadership		
Speed of reaction	Decisiveness		
Clerical sense			
Mechanical sense			
Disparate attention			

The ICI workers were not allowed into the secret of the methods of weighing all the points from 'cooperativeness' to 'sense of responsibility' or 'leadership' or 'even temperament'. If a great weight is given to these attributes, no militant would get high marking. It is true the job and not the men is assessed, but possibly management would say, 'So and so is not capable of doing such and such a job.' A management bias in job assessment becomes obvious when we know who will be casting judgement:

> The job will be assessed by a team of management and will normally include chemists and engineers, depending upon the job to be assessed. There will never be less than four assessors.

Once all the points are added, the rating of the workers takes place:[4]

Total marks	Salary grade
185 and above	Specialist and technical
155–184	7
125–154	6
95–124	5
65–94	4
35–64	3
5–34	2
0–4	Standard basic rate

Ford

When the women machinists went on strike in Ford the management was compelled for the first time to raise the curtain of secrecy a little over the method by which job evaluation has been carried out.

> The company and the consultants selected 28 characteristics (under the four main headings of responsibility, working conditions and physical and mental demands) which were considered to be the principal requirements of the hourly-paid jobs in the company. The company and the consultants selected 56 'benchmark' jobs, representative of the whole range of hourly-paid work throughout the company's plants, which would serve as reference points in the study of all the other jobs. The benchmark jobs provided examples of each level of rating in all 28 characteristics and included examples of jobs affecting each of the 20 unions.[5]

Then different characteristics were weighted—that is, a number of points were given to each factor. Ford management refused to reveal to the unions the weighting applied to profile characteristics and the points value assigned to each job.

Let us take an example to explain the working of this complex grading system. Below is a summary of the marking of a job.[6]

| Characteristic | Rating | | | |
	Low	Moderate	High	Exceptional
Responsibility Effect of poor work on subsequent operations			X	
Working conditions Noise and/or vibration		X		
Physical demands Manual dexterity				X
Manual demands Knowledge of machinery, tools and processes		X		

The above table dealt with only four out of 28 characteristics for each job. If all of them were included the table would have been seven times longer. At the second stage of calculation the weighting factors have to be included. The weighting factors comprised two elements: (1) a factor for each of the four levels of rating—low, moderate, etc—which would apply throughout the 28 characteristics; (2) a weighting factor for each individual characteristic. These weightings were not necessarily the same from characteristic to characteristic.

The way these weighting factors were used to convert the markings on a profile into points values is illustrated in the following table, which is based on the example above. The figures quoted are hypothetical:

| Characteristic | Factor | Level of marking by assessors | | | |
		Low Factor 0.6	Moderate Factor 1.0	High Factor 1.9	Exceptional Factor 2.8
Responsibility Effect of poor work on subsequent operations	7.0			13.3	
Working conditions Noise and/or vibration	2.0		2.0		
Physical demands Manual dexterity	5.0				14.0
Manual demands Knowledge of machinery, tools and processes	5.0		5.0		

The points values so obtained for each of the 28 characteristics were then totalled to give the total points value for the profile.[7]

Now all this looks terribly scientific. But what determines the weights given to different characteristics? This is kept secret. Years after the grading system was introduced, the management still refused to divulge the weighting of the different characteristics of jobs to the trade unions. The reason is obvious. As these weightings are the result of individual men's assessment, they can always be challenged by another man if they become known by a worker or his steward.

To add to the farce at Ford, the grievance procedure was described by a Ford steward:

> At the start of grading grievances there were four assessors so, if one asked for a reassessment, one had a 25 percent chance of getting the same assessor as one had in the first place. When the number of grievances lessened there was one, so a man was asked to say he was wrong in the first place. Was this likely?

The completely unscientific, biased nature of job evaluation, as exposed in the weighting method, is admitted by a book written specially for management:

> As the factors vary according to the particular job population and according to the views of those responsible for the evaluation exercise, so do the total number of points (the weighting) given to each factor. The allocation of points under the factor plan system encourages one of the major fallacies about job evaluation— that it is a scientific, or at the very least an objective, technique which introduces definitive criteria into the emotive and subjective matter of determining levels of remuneration.
>
> Perhaps unfortunately, job evaluation does not become an objective technique merely through the attribution of numerical values to certain selected factors. The measurement is spurious, as any examination of the way factors and their weightings are determined will reveal...
>
> However much care is taken, the fact remains that the factor plan system of job evaluation is not only time consuming but gives a spurious air of objectivity to an intensely subjective matter.[8]

How unscientific job evaluation is can be seen from the fact that there are hardly any research studies on it. The only piece of research on the subject in hand is by the US army. Fortunately, the US has no problems about wages or making its workers (soldiers) do what they are told, and the top brass want to know which of them are *really* efficient. The only really scientific study was done in 1951 by the US army.[9]

There are two questions to ask. First, how many raters are there and do they agree with each other (reliability), and second, even if they agree, are they correct *objectively*—ie as measured by some accurate means (valid)? For example, five colourblind people could agree 100 percent that a green apple was red. Their reliability would be 100 percent, but their validity would be nil! Several studies show that with five or less raters the judges disagree about half the time as to which of the categories a job should go in. To agree with each other, there would have to be something between ten and 100 raters for each job.[10]

Further, the number of raters is more important than the particular method used in determining *validity*.[11]

In spite of this evidence, most companies can only afford one rater, and as the intention is *not* to measure accurately but is part of their strategy to con the workers, they don't care. In fact one of the world's leading consultants in job evaluation, with branches in the US and Britain, only uses one rater! The important point, however, whatever the disagreement amongst the raters is, is are they measuring something objectively? In this connection it is worth quoting the best study at some length.[12]

A *simple* job was selected—filing production records—to test how *valid* the ratings were. This job is much more simple than most unskilled production work, and thus the technique should work at its best. Production clerks were responsible for filing several documents and locating information. A complex analysis of the movement of records allowed an objective measure that showed how effectively each clerk did his job. This was compared with supervisors rating the clerks' efficiency, using categories like 'Excellent', 'Very good', 'Good', 'Fair' and 'Unsatisfactory'.

The following correlations were obtained when comparing the objective results with the supervisor's ratings. (A correlation score of 0.99 means that both the raters and the objective measure agree, if they say that the same operators are efficient or inefficient, etc. A score of 0.00 to 0.25 means little agreement, and 0.50 only about half agree. Social scientists are generally only satisfied with scores of 0.75 or higher.)

Job element	Correlation between ratings and production records
(1) Filing information	0.43
(2) Filing folders	0.24
(3) Leaning folders	0.44
(4) Locating information	0.26
(5) Filing cards	0.46
(6) Transfer of records	0.38

Thus there is little agreement between supervisors' ratings and the objective measure. The authors say:

> The evidence is that the relationship between production records and ratings is not high enough to justify substituting one for the other. This conclusion is even further substantiated by the fact that the raters had the production records available to them.[13]

Two conclusions stand out for those faced with job evaluation. (1) Insist that the management use between ten and 90 raters for each job. (2) Advise the management that as there is little relation between their results and reality that they might just as well throw a dice to decide the issues. If they still insist that the technique is to be used, demand that an independent social scientist, selected by the stewards, examine their data and records!

In practice, the relative wages of different grades of workers depend more on the organisation and militancy of the workers than on any other factor. To quote again from this same book:

> No practical job evaluation system can in itself give a financial value to a job or group of jobs —that is, it cannot 'evaluate' in the strict sense of the term. Company norms vary enormously. Compare the pay of welders in various industries, for example, in relation to other skilled and semi-skilled trades. Market rates also vary enormously across the country. Compare the earnings of an electrician in a steel works in the north east with those of the same trade in Coventry or Slough.[14]

The report of the court of inquiry into the sewing machinists' dispute at Ford had to admit, ' "Job evaluation must by its nature contain subjective elements," or as the ILO manual *Wages* well put it, points rating "uses system but not science in the grading of jobs".'

How scientific can a method be which confirms the most extreme forms of discrimination against women?

> The discrimination against the machinists was symptomatic of the company's more general discrimination against women. Of 38,000 male production workers, 9,000 were in Grade C—roughly one in four. The 850 female production workers included only two in Grade C—one in 400. Even with technical and clerical work included, there were only 12 women in C. There were no women at all in the two top grades D and E.[15]

For a number of reasons job evaluation is central to productivity dealing strategy. First of all it encourages flexibility of labour deployment. By grouping the workers into large groups, job evaluation tends to eliminate all present craft and job titles, and facilitates the squeezing of more labour from the workers. (This does not mean to say that, in reaction to grading, quite often workers do not become even more conscious of skill demarcation—this raises their resentment and determination to defend craft titles.) Secondly, it serves as a weapon to 'divide and rule' the workers. Thirdly, by dividing workers into a small number of wage grades, it makes it more difficult for them to push wages upwards by climbing from one rung of the ladder to another close above it: 'A job evaluated structure also reduces leapfrogging claims by small groups at the workplace or enterprise level, and imposes a discipline upon ad hoc decisions on pay by managers and supervisors'.[16]

We can see how far grading can be used as a weapon of 'divide and rule' from the following two examples. First, Ford. A steward in Ford's Dagenham foundry writes:

> The productivity deal with its classifying of a thousand or so jobs wrecked the class solidarity at Ford for about a year and a half. Instead of the workers pushing for a general rise as they have always done, you got the position of 33 plumbers

pushing for an upgrading of plumbers, a couple of dozen welders doing the same, etc. This also applied on production, with small groups of workers pushing for upgradings of their individual jobs. It was noticeable amongst Foundry trade stewards that various trades were prepared to do each other's work to get an upgrading. It was not until nearly all appeals against grading were out of the way that militants could work up some solidarity for the 1969 stoppage. Had the 1967 agreement been a straight wage increase there would not have been the 15-month free for all and damn the hindmost, and our solidarity would have gone on from there.

Secondly, the case of the Rolls Royce electricians' dispute. At Rolls Royce, Hillington, Glasgow, a new grading system was recently introduced. As a result of job evaluation the number of grades was cut from over 90 to 14. It was in the six skilled grades where the trouble arose. The AEF and works committee accepted the management's assessment of grades, giving all-round increases of around 30s, making the three top grades'—four, five and six—rates of pay £24 5s, £24 16s and £25 10s respectively. The electricians were unsatisfied, and claimed that ordinary maintenance electricians should be on grade six, the top skilled grade, and that a new grade, seven, should be brought in for those sparks with special skills, eg electronics. This claim was taken through procedure to Central Conference with no settlement, and on 11 August 1969 the 70 electricians walked out and were given official support. The strikers have been paid double strike pay, £8 per week, by the EETU/PTU executive, a procedure that is unusual to say the least. Is Les Cannon suddenly a fighter for workers' interests? This official strike continued for some three months.[17]

At the time of writing a strike on the issue of grading is taking place at International Harvesters (Doncaster). Skilled men belonging to the AEF and ETU are striking to force a new grade—to maintain differentials as the present top grade has been attained by semi-skilled and even unskilled workers. One study estimates the advantages of job evaluation and grading as follows:

> ...facilitates job flexibility. The greater the number of grades in a structure, the more difficult it may be to move employees to other types of work, without arguments about payment. It makes managerial control of the wages structure easier, as the distinctions between the grades are clear-cut. Managements are likely to experience pressures from employees for upgrading with any grade structure. 'Escalation' is difficult to prevent if there are a large number of grades and the differences between them are blurred as a result.[18]

One carrot the management dangles in front of workers is that job evaluation opens the career path to workers. While one worker is being pushed against another in fixing the point system, it is assumed by many that there are wide opportunities to rise up the grade ladder. But this is not so. The number of places at the top of the pyramid is very small indeed. This was how the workers were divided up at Ford (in round figures):[19]

Grade A	1,800 workers (lowest grade)
Grade B	30,000 workers
Grade C	8,400 workers
Grade D	4,800 workers
Grade E	2,300 workers (top grade)

Above all, job evaluation represents an effort to smash rank and file control over working conditions by substituting for it a so to say 'neutral science'. As Jim Conway, general secretary of the AEF, put it before a conference of the Engineering Employers' Federation:

If we can get a simplified wages structure, to a very large degree we get rid of the power of the unauthorised shop stewards and the militants inside our factories, because their power rests in their ability to bargain at local level on piece-work prices. So, in looking at the grading system of breaking down the wages structure and simplifying it, we are going a long way towards getting rid of and solving some of the problems that face us.[20]

No wonder the Engineering Employers' Federation is in a very expansive mood when speaking on job evaluation:

We would submit, however, that what is needed is a nation, not industry, wide definition of job titles and descriptions, and this operation could be handled more properly by the appropriate ministry in collaboration with all industries and academic institutions. Such a document could be beneficial to industry and governmental bodies in many ways.[21]

The example of the United States beckons to the EEF:

This is a daunting exercise—and a lengthy one—but it can be done. Reference the activities of the United States in their Department of Labour Dictionary of Occupational Titles (third edition, 1965). This dictionary is in two volumes. Volume I contains alphabetic arrangement of job titles with a corresponding job definition. Volume II places titles into occupational categories, divisions and groups. Each occupation is classified and codified. The dictionary covers occupations over the entire US economy and encompasses some 40,000 titles. The value of this is to help the user discern relationships among occupations, and as a standard approach to classifying the abilities, vocational experiences and potentials of workers. It must be stressed that this dictionary is not an infallible document and is used primarily as a guide by many American companies.[22]

One should not come to the conclusion that job evaluation, like any other scheme initiated by management, cannot be turned by the workers to their own advantage. Where the workers have built a strong trade union and shop steward organisation they can turn job evaluation against the bosses. They can use it for 'comparability' purposes—thus using it as a weapon to try and catch up and even overtake sections of better paid workers.

However, in order to be able to turn this weapon against its creators, the workers, first of all, must be clear that job evaluation has no scientific base at all. They have to avoid the trap of seeing themselves set in a grade hierarchy, which sets their status and wages, and thus play the bosses' game of 'divide and rule'. Workers must be conscious that working conditions depend above all on their own activity, unity and determination. Despite what management say, workers should attempt to treat all results derived from job evaluation as negotiable.

Chapter Seven: Time and motion study and speed-up

For half a century the piece-rates system was associated with the rate-fixer and his stopwatch. The rate-fixer was probably the most detested man in the factory. Time study has now become part of the wider, allegedly scientific approach of work study. Work study aims to make a rational study of the whole work process. This has become central to modern management, whatever the method of payment. In Britain the pioneering role was played by ICI, whose handbooks have become standard works for all employers.

With the move to MDW, work study has come to play an absolutely central role indeed. Once job evaluation, grading and rating have been settled, what remains to be settled is the determination of the 'production standard'. For this, work study is necessary. With the spread of productivity deals, work study has mushroomed. One cannot but agree with *British Industry Week*, the paper of the CBI, when it states:

> For one profession the measures introduced by Mr Wilson have done more good in three years than anything else since the war.
>
> The profession in question is work study. Manufacturers, service industries, local authorities—virtually every sector of the economy—are now realising the need for it. In many respects they have little choice… The recent government edict that only general productivity deals will be passed call for better and more accurate work measurement control.[1]

During the years 1965-68 the number of members of the Institute of Work Study Practitioners has increased threefold—to 15,000!

By the way, how far the 'profession' tag can be applied to work study 'engineers' is debatable since, for example, ICI trains its own 'Productivity Service Officers' over a very shallow course. In the words of one of ICI's stewards, 'The last batch was made up of redundant charge hands in not more than three months.'

The trade unions have uneven attitudes to work study. Many are lukewarm, while a few are highly enthusiastic. Among the latter, special place is taken by the ETU. In its evidence to the Donovan commission, the ETU reported proudly about 'joint trade union/management study courses' for ICI:

The ETU chose the shop stewards while ICI central management arranged for plant release. About two dozen top ICI management representatives, covering personnel in the production departments including works managers, took part in the course, together with a full time officer of the ETU.

Then the ETU organised other courses—for the GLC, BOAC and Fairfields shipyard:

The course for ETU shop stewards employed by the Greater London Council was quite different. This was a straightforward work study course including an examination of how work study could be employed in the GLC.

As examples of good industrial communications these were most rewarding exercises. So it was with British Railways' main workshops, with BEA, with BOAC and with several others.

Probably the most exciting and rewarding courses were those run in conjunction with the new management of Fairfields shipyard. Management in this case brought down to the college all their shop stewards and deputies, boilermakers, engineers, electricians, carpenters, painters—all 13 unions with the shop stewards in the plant were brought to the college in three courses. Top management, including most members of the board, technical management at key levels, PA (management consultants), trade union officials, all applied themselves to looking at the problems facing the new company. They determined how work study and critical path analysis could help to solve the production problems of their enterprise and how, if successfully applied, they could guarantee all their employees a high level of earnings.[2]

And the ETU leadership goes on to wax poetic about future prospects:

In the field of joint union/management courses great benefits are waiting to be reaped. An increasing number of firms are now realising that the training of their workpeople in the application of work study, for instance, should be viewed with as great an importance as the training of technical skills. New bridges require to be built—they are indeed being built, but too slowly.

At boardroom level the tendency is to ask what the catch is. At trade union local level there is still the fear of the past and of being brainwashed for the future. But the need is a real one and it must be satisfied.

The ETU is eager and able to satisfy that need. What it requires is cooperation from a much wider range of employers than has yet been willing to give cooperation. Also, since the benefits to be gained from such courses will accrue not only to the members of the ETU but also to the firm, it would seem not unreasonable if they were to bear some of the costs. In the cases so far cited the firms concerned have been cooperative in this respect, as in so many others.[3]

What is work study?

Work study is a combination of method study and work measure merit. Method study is the systematic recording and critical examination of existing and proposed ways of doing work, as a means for reducing costs. Work measurement is a technique designed to establish the time spent by a qualified worker in carrying out a specified job at a defined level of performance. The actual working out of time and motion study is as follows:

First stage: The most effective method of working is determined by a work study engineer.
Second stage: The conditions under which the time study takes place are observed and recorded.
Third stage: The *actual time* taken by the worker is observed and recorded.
Fourth stage: The actual time is adjusted to a *basic time* by means of the work study engineer effort-rating the worker's performance.
Fifth stage: The basic time is converted to a *standard time* by applying a fatigue rate and personal allowance rate.

The standard time constitutes the *allowed time* for the work to be performed. Let us examine the process more closely. One writer described the problem thus:

> The object of modern time-study is to determine the work content of a job in terms of the time it should take a fully trained and experienced operative to perform the job when working at a normal rate—a rate which he could maintain for the whole of the work period without undue fatigue... At present there is no uniformity of definition as to what constitutes normal rate.[4]

This definition is useful, not only in that it states the aim of time study, but also because from it we can infer the method's major deficiencies.

How is the selection of 'average workers' to take place? What are the conditions under which the experiment takes place? How should the job be divided into its elements? For how long will the experiment go on? How would you rate the skill, effort and consistency of the worker? What is a 'normal' pace? How do you measure effort? How do you measure fatigue? What allowances should be made for personal needs, for relaxation, etc?

What is an 'average' worker? Statistical experiments have shown that the difference between the fastest and slowest worker can be as much as five to one.[5]

The time allowed to workers for personal needs is, of course, completely subjective. One survey of time study literature showed a range of personal allowances from a maximum of 4 percent under one system to a maximum of 50 percent under another.[6]

The problem of allowances for fatigue is even more difficult:

> All writers on this subject are agreed that there are no direct physiological measures of fatigue. They are still in the laboratory stage and are not sufficiently advanced for use in the workshop.[7]

Because of the vagueness of the concept of 'average', 'normal', etc, the results of time and motion studies are not scientific at all:

> The most striking feature of time study rationale is the contradiction between the claims which the practitioners make of scientific accuracy and their general admission of the extent to which their practice requires intuitive judgments... Everything, we are told, depends on the objective measurement of the exact time required by a given worker for a given operation. And yet it is always admitted, though often reluctantly, that there are certain difficulties. The most serious one stems from the fact that the 'required time' cannot be defined without intuitive guesses as to what is in fact a normal, reasonable, fair, average or right degree of effort for any particular task.[8]

The upshot is that time study boils down to being sheer guesswork. The inconsistency of the individual time study engineer and the variation between engineers is fantastic. To take a few examples.

In one American study:

> Five operators each did four different jobs at five different paces (90, 100, 110, 120 and 130 percent of normal). These rates of work were set on the average judgement of six time study engineers. The 100 situations were filmed and the pace of work was rated twice by six other time study men, with a month's interval between the two ratings. Results showed that:
>
> (1) The smallest variation in their own ratings by individual observers was a 'standard error' of 10.1 percent, 'which is quite large'.
>
> (2) Different observers showed variations as high as 28 percent.
>
> (3) Different workers on the same job were rated differently by as much as 15 percent.[9]

Even a controlled experiment under laboratory conditions showed extreme unevenness. A brief outline of the methods used may be helpful in assessing the value of the results.

> Three tasks were devised...the preparation of a solution...a simple assembly operation, and...a machining operation... In the planning of them special care was taken to ensure the minimisation of chance errors occurring through variations in the materials or equipment used or in the physical working conditions. In short, the aim was to investigate consistency under favourable circumstances, not to contrive tasks or conditions to prove that experienced practitioners could be inconsistent.

Three operators were carefully trained in these tasks, and invitations were sent to 13 firms or organisations which between them provided 24 time study engineers. There were ten pairs from the same organisation, of whom seven pairs normally worked together in the same factory.

After excluding the 5 percent of:

> ...observers who gave extreme standard times, the main conclusions can be stated as follows:
>
> (1) The range of variation within the pairs of studies made by the same observer

was 12 percent...

(2) Similarly trained observers showed variations among themselves of up to 32 percent...

(3) Observers from different organisations or with different training showed variations of up to 76 percent...

(4) The variation in the final figures between observers in general was as much as 84 percent.

The writer reporting this experiment drew the following telling conclusion:

One commonly hears time study spoken of as being a procedure accurate to about 3 percent... The inference is then that this experiment has shown that time study is 14 times as inaccurate as it is commonly supposed to be.[10]

Time and motion study is based on the simple assumption that the worker is a machine, without human emotions, without group solidarity, a machine that can be measured and manipulated to carry out a certain task. In 1911 the father of 'scientific management', Frederick Winslow Taylor, expressed his view very clearly: 'Now one of the very first requirements for a man who is fit to handle pig iron as a regular occupation is that he shall be so stupid and so phlegmatic that he more nearly resembles in his mental make-up the ox than any other type'.[11] No more need be said.

Once the 'scientific' veil of the time and motion study is torn off, its effectiveness in controlling and manipulating workers is completely blunted. This is admitted by one American expert, who advised management:

The only situation in which it is advantageous to management to retain the claim that its ratings and specifications are scientific occurs when [management] knows but labour *does not know* that they are unscientific... [this] may be sufficiently persuasive so that the rating results are accepted without challenge. In that case, consistent biases in applying the process would in the long run favour management. However, it should be noted that this strategy is an extremely risky one, since it becomes ineffective as soon as labour becomes *aware of the true nature of the process*.[12]

If the scientific pretentions of time and motion study are exposed, and workers' organisation is militant, then workers can manipulate TMS in their own interest. In fact, it is astonishing what employers can do with allowances for relaxation, fatigue, etc under workers' pressure!

On the other hand, one should not underestimate the danger inherent in the work study engineer, even if the immediate impact on work conditions of the stopwatch are minimal. This is described very well in a letter to the author from a militant in a large north London engineering factory, after the work study engineer studied his shop:

It's hard to say whether the work study really achieved anything for the management. In terms of the agreement probably little or nothing has been lost—because of high level militant organisation, experienced stewards, justified suspicion of management and work study men—but the work study is dangerous because individual workers were watched closely for long periods and the job is so varied, and so are their attitudes to it, that even while consciously trying to fool the work study man they could unconsciously betray the organisation of work from the workers' point of view.

Even given safeguards which the management concede quite readily, like only allowing the work study man to talk to a worker if the steward is there, time limits, etc, *if* the management know what to look for they can find out such things as: who the militants are and how they communicate, which workers are biased towards management, what annoys the workers about the management, what annoys the workers about other workers, and where the divisions are among the workers.

Speed-up

The aim of work study is to squeeze more labour from the workers. There is hardly a document making this more crystal clear than the Green Book of the steel industry. As we have already said, this is not written in the language of negotiations, but in that of brutal command:

Manning
(i) Manning levels for each operation to be at the discretion of management, who would be free to assign to a job only that number of employees of any grade considered necessary, and to amalgamate or combine various jobs or groups of jobs where this is advantageous. There will be provision for work measurement at the request of either the management or the trade unions, with the result freely available to both.
(ii) The management will decide the manning of each job and this can be varied from day to day, consistent with variations in the workload, to provide for the right number of employees to be economically employed on each job.
(iii) Management will decide what class or grade of employee will be used on any job including where there is a change in work method or type of material adopted.

Working at a reasonable pace
(i) All work will be performed at a reasonable pace as required by the management, who will determine the reasonable pace and performance they require.
(ii) Industrial engineering techniques will be used at management's discretion to determine the pace of work on a rational basis, with the results freely available to all.
(iii) If the results are not acceptable to the unions, independent engineers can be brought in. The cost of this will be borne by the division.[13]

At Rootes, Linwood, the speed of the line has been recently increased so that instead of 26 cars an hour 46 are being produced, a rise of 80 percent, while the Car Assembly Block labour force has increased by only 60 percent.

In Ford, Halewood, before the productivity agreement of 1967 was introduced, production was at the rate of 1,000 cars a day. Now it is 1,170. What is more, the management has carried through an aggressive programme of sackings so that the workforce has been reduced considerably. The result of this is that a smaller number of men are being forced to do 20 percent more work.

In Ford, Dagenham, especially after the workers' defeat in 1962, a great speed-up has taken place. In the foundry, for instance, the line went at 12 feet per minute before the strike and 15 feet per minute after it.

Ford management increased the workload on the track by the following methods:

(1) Gradually increasing the line speed with more cars going down per hour without any increase in the labour force.

(2) Breaking up an operation previously done by one man into five or six parts and giving each part as additional work to another man on the line, thus eliminating a man.

(3) Using the fluctuation of car sales to force men to do more work. For instance, if 100 men were producing 100 cars and the number required dropped to 90, then ten men would be taken off. But when the schedule went up to 100 jobs again only seven men would be put back. Thus 97 men would be doing work previously performed by 100. With the schedule of vehicles fluctuating daily this device had led to many clashes.[14]

The management was especially arrogant and brutal in pushing speed-up after the terrible defeat of the shop stewards organisation at the end of 1962. Ford always insisted that the determination of manning, speed and workload was the prerogative of management alone. However, with a return of strength to the factory organisation over the last couple of years, the workers have in practice if not in theory had quite a say in determining speed, manning and so on. Whatever the formal arrangement, in practice, the strength and militancy of the shopfloor organisation determines what actually takes place. Thus a steward at the Dagenham foundry writes to me:

In spite of the joint works council and stewards' meetings the determination of speed, manning, workloads, etc, is very much in the hands of the individual stewards and will depend on their capabilities and the support they can command. It also depends on their political education. A capable and determined shop steward can demand and will get consultation on speed, manning, workload, etc, and every change in his department will be discussed with him, and normally management will bend over backwards to avoid trouble. In another department a steward will be informed bluntly, 'We are doing this,' or, 'We are doing that,' and he accepts it if he is told at all. If he argues, he is told that what is good for Ford is good for the national economy and a number of stewards are still naive enough to believe this. There have been cases where changes of stewards have, in months, got departments from one condition to the other.

A shop steward in one of the biggest glass factories in the country described to me the effort of workers to control speed:

I stand over the conveyor belt with a stopwatch in my hand. Whenever management dares to speed it up beyond what is reasonable, I, being responsible for quality control, do the following. I pick up a bottle, newly produced, raise it up towards the light, turn it this way, turn it the other way, for a time, until I'm sure that it is up to the required standard...in the meantime, the conveyor belt goes on…and tens of bottles are smashed to pieces. Then slowly I put the bottle down and pick another one for a check of quality. In no time at all the supervisor rushes up to me and asks for an explanation, and then the speed of the conveyor belt is reduced.

One good example of the way workers' pressure shifts management on the question of manning and speed-up is the case of the Rootes factory at Ryton, Coventry. On 2 June 1966 the senior shop stewards were informed of management intentions to cut the number of workers on the track from 86 down to 67 on the pre-mount track and 70 on the final assembly track. The stewards refused, and on 13 July the management had to retreat and suggest that 72 workers were on the track. Again the workers refused. In October management retreated again to 76 workers per track. A year later the track was still manned by 86 men. At the end of a period of very stubborn resistance by the workers, the management was compelled to deviate from standard measured day work practice to the extent that the final productivity agreement provides for mutuality on work standards. The implication is that workloads are not unconditionally set by work measurement but are subject to negotiations. (How this will work in practice cannot yet be predicted but the workers at least partially won the first round.)

The damaging effects of speed-up spread also into the offices. To give one example, in one electronics factory in west London, where they did not even get a productivity agreement, the draughtsmen accepted that there would be a productivity increase. They now have 17 members doing the work of 35 in the main mechanical design area, and the work tempo is so frantic in that department that there have been four nervous breakdowns in the last 18 months.[15]

One by-product of the speed-up has been the increase in work accidents.

In those industries covered by the Factories Act, the total number of accidents, measured by the criterion of three days or more off work, has increased by an annual average of 9.1 percent every year since 1962. In 1962 there were 190,158 reported accidents in factories, docks and warehouses, and on all kinds of building sites. The 1968 total stands at 312,430, of which 625 were fatal. In factories alone the number of *reported* accidents rose from 157,500 in 1962 to 254,500 in 1968 (between 20 and 30 percent of reportable accidents are not reported). And the accident frequency rate, which measures the number of accidents against the number of man-hours worked in some 5,000 of the most safety conscious factories, shows a rough 47 percent increase from 1962 to 1967:

> Total accidents in 1968 were 312,430 against 304,016 in 1967 and 296,610 in 1966. Total deaths for the same three years were 625, 564 and 700. Once again, the highest number of deaths and accidents were in the building and construction industries.[16]

After taking a 5 percent sample of accidents in 1968 the chief inspector of factories reported that 'in 50.3 percent of the cases no reasonably practicable precautions could have been taken by anyone in the factory to prevent the accident or mitigate the injury'.

Investigations of the 359 factory fatalities 'suggest that there were breaches of the law by the employer in 128 cases and by the deceased in two cases'.

And in the construction industry, reports 'suggest breaches of the law in 134 cases by the employer, in four by the deceased and in five by a fellow workman' out of 238 deaths. More than a third of factory deaths and 56 percent of construction fatalities were due to criminal breaches of the Factories Act and regulations by employers.

If these proportions are applied to all accidents, 60,000 factory accidents and 25,000 construction accidents were due to criminal breaches of the act and regulations by the employers. But the inspector blandly reports that only in 1,597 cases were complaints filed against employers for breaches of safety regulations.

In the mines the number of accidents continued to rise over the years.

MINE ACCIDENTS PER 100,000 MAN-SHIFTS[17]	
1955	126.95
1960	143.70
1964–65	185.96
1965–66	210.33
1967–68	212.06

The psychological effect—the actual nightmarish effect of speed-up—cannot be expressed in figures, but it is extremely serious in damaging the whole quality of life of millions of workers. One worker on a car assembly line described it to me in a letter this way:

I work on an overhead section of the track. For the first few weeks you go home and dream about these monsters always coming at you over your head. Then you accept it so much that you can't even dream about it any more. While you're working, if you look away, at something that isn't moving, you feel giddy, like when the train at the other platform moves away and you adjust yourself as if your train was going.

Most of the day you just hope that the line will stop—that there'll be a breakdown. And you'll always find the men on the track ready to walk out on strike when the men working on sub-assembly would rather stay in.

The car gets to you and you've so many minutes or seconds of work to do on it. So you walk along—underneath it, by the side of it, in front of it or behind it (depending on where you are on the track)—pacing it. If you drop a screw or a hammer you have to go back to pick it up and then run forward to catch up the car again. Some jobs can be done quickly, so a man will only walk a few feet by each car. Others take a longer time, so a man can walk several yards by it. The faster the speed of the line, the faster you walk—or, if anything gets dropped, run.

You hate the moving line so much that if you could you'd try and keep it stopped all the time. In the 'body and white' (build line), and trim and final lines, the official way of stopping the track is to press a button, spaced evenly all down the line. But you have to hold on to it to keep it stopped. Only the foremen have got keys to lock the stop mechanism. In the 'body and white' the cars are moved on floats hitched to a line at floor level. There men often put bits of metal into the works to get the line to jam, or when a 'natural' breakdown occurs they cover up the point where the trouble is. In the trim there's no such chance. The cars are moved on trolleys attached to an overhead line—which you can't get at.

To close every loophole to the workers so that they will not shirk their work-load, the management in the steel industry even makes use of the medical service. Actually this section of the Green Book is probably the one most hated by steel workers:

Medical examinations
(i) If the management request it, no employee shall refuse to be medically examined by the division doctor. The management will make such requests for the doctor's opinion when a matter of doubt arises as to an employee's fitness to continue in his trade, to take promotion, or to his ability to continue driving a crane, machine, loco, etc.
(ii) The management would prescribe certain jobs where safety is involved as requiring annual eyesight tests.
(iii) In cases of return to work after illness, even when the employee's own doctor has certified a man as fit to return to his normal occupation, the management may, if they so wish, defer the employee's restart pending further consultation with the division doctor and a discussion with him of the type of work normally performed. To facilitate such discussions the management shall have the right to refer an employee to the division doctor for examination.
(iv) There will be full consultation between the division doctor and the employee's own doctor, but the results will not be published.
(v) The division will protect the employee's earnings for a period of six weeks and will set up a procedure for determining whether an employee is capable of performing his normal job.
(vi) Should it be necessary to transfer an employee from his normal job for medical reasons, the division would attempt to find alternative work in the same grading, but this would not be guaranteed and must be subject to medical reports.[18]

These paragraphs regarding medical examinations are resented bitterly by steel workers. After a number of years of work under the very hard and unhealthy conditions of the industry, a steel worker's health is, of course, damaged, and a medical check can serve, in the hands of the management, as means of downgrading workers. Thus one blast furnaceman told the author how, after such a medical examination, he was downgraded because his eyesight was found not to be perfect, and lost nearly £15 per week in his wages! One is well reminded of similar medical checks in the gold mines of South Africa. Every year the miners are checked meticulously. The motive is not the welfare of the miners but the profit of the companies. When the X-ray shows a sign of pneumoconiosis the miner is quickly packed off to the African Reserves. Otherwise, after a time, when the sickness becomes obvious, management will be bound to pay compensation. The above-quoted blast furnaceman argued that 'if a man's health has deteriorated because of his job then he is entitled to protection of his previous earnings'.

Even safety precautions are not permitted to impede the increase in labour load:

Safety
It is the responsibility of the management to decide what are safe working practices and conditions. No delay in carrying out a task shall be caused by interference by individual employees, except that the individual employee has the right to say that he thinks the job is unsafe.[19]

The Green Book for the steel industry is more brutal and frank than any other productivity agreement the present author has seen. However, increasing the workload, through speed-up, etc, is central to every productivity deal.

By the way, one can ask, why is the steel Green Book so brutal? Why is it in state-owned industries—BR, electricity, mines—that management dictates the grimmest productivity deals? Is it that the state capitalist enterprise is ready to take a greater strike risk in a showdown with the workers? The state acts as the main buttress to the big corporations, making an example of real productivity bargains.

Chapter Eight: Productivity deals and the threat of redundancy

Productivity deals are associated with redundancy, both as a cause and as an effect. On the one hand, the introduction of productivity deals, quite obviously, is helped if workers' determination is weakened by unemployment, or the threat of unemployment. On the other hand, productivity deals bring about unemployment by 'rationalising' and streamlining production.

Unemployment softens workers' resistance to productivity deals

When Ian Stewart, chairman of Fairfields, was striving hard to get a productivity deal into his shipyard, it was obvious to him that the threat of redundancy was his main weapon. Stewart is not afraid to confess:

The men were over a barrel, and I intended to keep them there until they understood our new techniques and trusted them, and until the yard was running as I wanted it to run. It was a case of, 'Follow me, be prepared to listen and learn and share in the profitable future, or go and work somewhere else.' That is how I put it to them.[1]

Commenting on the above, the authors of the story of Fairfields say:

In order to maintain this pressure or discipline, Stewart omitted one thing which all sophisticated industries would consider the main essential. He had no marketing or sales organisation in the whole new company. He expressly made no attempt to obtain orders until the yard had been totally and tightly reorganised, for he wanted to use the precipice of unemployment to keep the men on the narrow path he needed them to follow.

Throughout all the preliminaries of the Fairfields experiment, Stewart had avoided filling the order book too full, so that the threat of unemployment loomed during the 'educational' period as a real possibility.[2]

For some months before the introduction of Phase I of Devlin the port employers diverted shipping away from the militant ports. This resulted in large-scale unemployment which, of course, undermined the men's resistance. In fact, at present, the port employers are again using the same tactics in London in order to make the men amenable to Phase II of the Devlin plan.

Similarly, British Leyland is preparing the ground for productivity dealing at Morris Radiators, Oxford, by softening the workers up through redundancy. At Radiators the management have demanded that the piece-work operatives agree to a cut in their hourly earnings. The present rates are between 16s and 25s an hour. The management said that unless these are reduced to a normal 15s an hour no more work will be tendered for by the firm. The toolroom at Radiators has been starved of work for months. This, of course, is a straight piece of intimidation.

A large part of Radiators is now on short time. Work that should normally come to Radiators is being deliberately sent to other factories. For instance, the contract for the new Mini grill has gone to Pianoforte Supplies, a non-union firm. Work on a new petrol tank has gone to Fisher & Ludlow. And the new exhaust system which is being shared with the Llanelli plant may be lost altogether if Llanelli gets a paint shop. The Mini grill would have meant 16,000 hours work for the toolroom alone, and far more for the rest of the plant, but it has been sent to a scab firm while men in Radiators are on a three-day week. This situation has been deliberately created by the bosses, who are carrying out their threat of refusing to tender for any more work until the men agree to let them cut the piece-rate to 15s an hour. The whole of British Leyland has been advised to send no more work to Radiators— in other words, British Leyland is putting pressure on the Radiators management to run down the factory and put hundreds of men out of work.

And the rot won't stop at Radiators. The reason British Leyand has picked on Radiators first is that until 1966 Radiators was one of the best organised and, as a result, best paid factories in the whole BMC combine, and the men at other plants looked to Radiators as an example of what could be achieved by militancy and organisation. This is why Radiators was chosen as one of the first British Leyland plants to try on the introduction of MDW.

Again there is no doubt that the relative case by which the National Coal Board got away with murder as regards the miners was largely thanks to the threat of closure of collieries. Look simply at the two graphs on the next page:[3]

With such a swift rise in output per manshift the traditional militancy of the miners could have seen to it that their wages would have been pushed up. As we have seen elsewhere,[4] miners' real wages have been practically at a standstill over a number of years. Instead miners' resistance has been sapped by the sack and the threat of the sack.

a) Average manpower

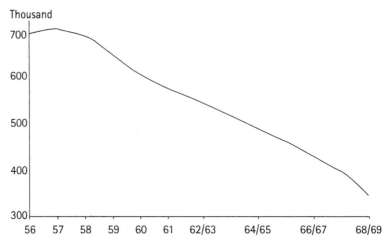

b) Output per manshift

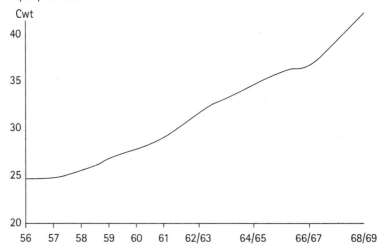

AVERAGE ANNUAL NUMBER OF DAYS LOST IN STRIKES PER 1,000 WORKERS[5]	
1930–38	1,034
1947–55	778
1956–64	627
1967	225
1968	125

Again the British Steel Corporation used the terrible threat of the sack to impose the draconian Green Book on its workers. As Sir Roy Harrod said in a radio broadcast on 15 December 1966, 'Some industrialists have told me that the squeeze, involving a certain increase in unemployment, has been having a good effect on discipline in the factories'.[6]

Government deflationary policies

While in opposition, Wilson was very scathing in his attack on the Tory policy of 'stop-go'. He said in the House of Commons on 18 June 1961:

> Surely the government have learnt by now that when one restricts production, whether by hire purchase restrictions, interest rate policy or any of the other techniques which they have used over the years, the result is not a fall in prices but an increase in unit costs—and that means higher prices... When the call has been for expansion, more production, more investment and more exports the government has met every crisis with panic measures and restrictions which hold down production and hold back investment so that when the next crisis came the nation's economic base was too narrow and thin to sustain the burdens and strains that were put on it.[7]

And eight days later he declared of Selwyn Lloyd:

> He had to satisfy the international banking community by masochistic and irrelevant cuts in our standard of living, harmful restrictions on our production, and needless increases in our costs and price structure, because he believes that international speculators are impressed only by actions which in the long term harm the economy. The government's policies are so bankrupt that all we can do, 16 years after the war, is to go for international aid and to buttress the economy with costly, unnecessary short term borrowing at 7 percent, which is a magnet for 'hot' money from all over the world to come here again.[8]

But once in power, Wilson continued the Tory policies, in even harsher form. While Selwyn Lloyd's budget of 1961 cut spending by £210 million, Wilson's 1966 budget had reduced domestic purchasing power by more than twice the amount—by £516 million. The 1968 budget went even further— more than £900 million was taken out of the economy. The 1969 budget squeezed another £340 million. The only difference from the practice of his Tory predecessor is that the 'stop' phase of Wilson's 'stop-go' policy has become much longer.

The most important effect of deflationary policies is unemployment. Unemployment has, just recently, been the scourge of the working class for a greater number of years than at any time since the Second World War.

Government encouragement of mergers

To 'rationalise' and streamline British capitalism Harold Wilson used another weapon, besides deflation, to cause unemployment. He has encouraged takeovers and mergers in industry.

Before coming to power the Labour leadership was quite clear about the danger to the people inherent in the great concentration of economic power. Indeed, in its *Signpost for the Sixties*, published in 1961, it said:

> In private industry the directors of a few hundred giant combines determine between them what Britain should produce. As their power increases these men, together with the directors of the leading insurance companies, are usurping the functions of government, which is theoretically responsible to the whole people. Takeover follows takeover in a bewildering fashion. British firms swallow each other and are then swallowed by Americans. No enterprise, however successful, is safe from its big brother, however inefficient. The free enterprise system provides no check to this dangerous trend.

In December 1966 the Industrial Reorganisation Corporation (IRC) was set up by an act of parliament. It was charged with the task of 'promoting industrial efficiency and profitability and assisting the earning of the UK or any part of the UK'.

The corporation is able to promote rationalisation schemes by making loans itself—up to £150 million can be drawn from the government, consisting of £100 million in the form of loans and £50 million on which a dividend is payable. Since its establishment the IRC has invested over £60 million in mergers, re-groupings and development projects.[9]

Its purpose was well put by the under-secretary to the Department of Economic Affairs as 'not to encourage socialism to creep, but to encourage private enterprise to gallop'.

It will become clear quite how effective the IRC has been in promoting mergers if we list its activities for a period of one year—April 1968 to March 1969:[10]

April 1968	Broom & Wade/ Holman	IRC encouraged merger to form International Compressed Air Corporation
May 1968	British Oxygen	IRC made £2.5 million loan to BOC to help develop Edwards High Vacuum. Rate of interest: $7\frac{1}{2}$ percent
June 1968	George Kent/ Cambridge Instruments	IRC spent £6.5 million supporting Kent's bid for Cambridge in face of a rival offer from Rank Organisation
August 1968	Davy Ashmore/ Armstrong Whitworth	IRC supported merger as an important step in the rationalisation of the steel and non-ferrous equipment industry
September 1968	General Electric/ English Electric	IRC supported the merger, given certain assurances by the companies. £5 million of an earlier loan of £15 million to English Electric was repaid to the IRC and

		the terms for the remainder renegotiated
November 1968	Sigmund Pulsometer/ Plenty and Son	IRC backed merger as a further rationalisation of the pump makers
December 1968	British Rollmakers/ Johnson's Rolls	IRC backed merger
January 1969	Racal Electronics/ Controls & Communications	IRC backed this communications merger
January 1969	British Leyland Motor	IRC supported the merger of Leyland and British Motor Holdings with a £25 million loan at 71 percent interest
January 1969	Donside Paper Mill	IRC lent Bowater Paper and Reed Paper £1 million each to buy the mill jointly. Rate of interest: 81 percent
February 1969	Clarke Chapman	Clarke Chapman bought two crane makers. IRC lent it £2 million at 9 percent to assist in the rationalisation
March 1969	GKN acquisition	IRC supported the purchase of RH Windsor as a step which would strengthen the plastics machinery industry
March 1969	Dobson Hardwick/ William Park and Co	IRC supported this merger of two mine equipment suppliers
March 1969	Reyrolle Parsons/ Bruce Peebles	These two electrical companies merged with the IRC's approval. IRC offered standby credit of up to £4 million

The jewel in the crown of the IRC is, no doubt, the takeover of AEI by GEC and the merger of the latter with English Electric. The creation of British Leyland also owes a lot to its activities.

Government effort has lubricated the trend of centralisation of capital, resulting from the concentration of capital and the increasing international competition of the amassed capitals. The rate of mergers and takeovers has accelerated very much over the last few years. In 1958 the total value of companies taken over was £121 million. In 1966 the expenditure on mergers was £447 million, in 1967 £781 million, and in 1968 £2,313 million.[11]

The figures underestimate the true extent of the merger movement, as only takeovers by large companies are counted. Bank takeovers are excluded and agreed mergers such as that between GEC and English Electric are only included at the price GEC paid for English Electric, £277 million, and not the £900 million value of the newly merged company. The *Times*, listing mergers and takeovers of over £10 million, had a total for 1968 of £3,455 million. It is difficult to say what a realistic figure would be for 1968, but it is certainly well over three times that for 1967:[12]

> The trend has not diminished in any way in 1969. In fact, according to the *Sunday Times* of 12 January, in the first eight working days of 1969 no fewer than 14 public company bids were made involving about £461 million, very considerably more than the figure for the whole of the year a decade ago.[13]

The result of the mergers aided and abetted by the government is the creation of giants employing mass armies of workers: GEC employs 230,000 workers; ICI 187,000; British Leyland 176,000; Courtauld 110,000; GKN 108,700; Hawker Siddeley 106,000; Unilever 80,000 (in Britain and 220,000 abroad); Plessey 65,000; Ford 64,000; Tube Investments 61,000; and Vauxhall 33,000.

Takeover and merger are motivated by the search for maximum profitability. And if this demands a shake-up of the labour force and cutting it down, then so be it. The GEC-AEI-EE merger has already led to the sacking of 12,000 workers and the immediate threat of sacking of another 5,300.

Productivity deals causing unemployment

If unemployment strengthens the hands of the bosses in their effort to initiate productivity deals, the latter, in turn, stimulate unemployment.

Some of the productivity agreements have been in expanding industries. In a number of them there is a no-redundancy guarantee written in. Thus, for instance, the Fawley agreement. Similarly the Alcan Industries and BEA agreements stated that the proposals would not result in any forced redundancy. In both cases the process of trimming the labour force was to be carried out through 'natural wastage'.

However, even in these cases of a written-in promise of 'no-redundancy', management quite often went back on its guarantee. At Fawley the agreement coincided with a period of rapid expansion, but a few years later it became clear to the management that it would pay to prune the labour force. Consequently a redundancy agreement involving a not very mean severance pay was introduced.

When it came to the Milford Haven agreement, Esso, having learned from its experience at Fawley, refused to include a 'no redundancy' pledge. Instead it gave a general 'statement of intent' regarding redundancy:

> We do not envisage that the implementation of this agreement would give rise to anyone being made redundant. However, should any redundancy arise we believe that the necessary reduction in manpower would, in the first instance, be covered by natural wastage. If this were not so the company would be prepared to assist in placing any redundant personnel and would be prepared, if necessary, to give active consideration to retraining anyone redundant, so that he would be equipped to find alternative employment. We should also be prepared to give anyone affected at least three months notice of redundancy, the last month of which would count as the month's notice required under the Contracts of Employment Act, 1963. We should also be prepared in this situation to make severance payments at a more

favourable rate than is called for under the proposed 'Redundancy Payments Bill' printed on the order of the House of Commons on 31 March 1965.[14]

Many productivity deals do not worry about giving the no-redundancy pledge and rely on natural wastage to cut down the labour force. The worse the labour conditions, the greater is the natural waste. The worse the productivity deal as a whole, the less management has to worry about its need to use the sack. On the railways 40 percent of a grade like porters may change in a year. There has been less unrest there over redundancy than at the docks, where the run-down was much slower.

In some cases management uses dodges to avoid defraying redundancy pay, while sticking to the letter of the agreement on 'no redundancy'. Railwaymen at Central and Exchange stations in Manchester, two stations closed in May 1969, were guaranteed against sacking:

No one will be made redundant. Therefore no redundancy pay will be given.

'Suitable alternative employment' will be offered to all the men. Lists of vacancies at a third city station, Victoria, have been published.

The jobs offered at Victoria are not being filled. Railwaymen find that there are no jobs in their existing grades, or the vacancies are for 'rest day relief men'.

A 'rest day' man fills in another for worker on his day off. He can be sent anywhere, told to do anything. It's a job British Rail can't usually fill. No one wants it.

If men from Exchange and Central don't take up the jobs offered, then they can be 'offered' work anywhere in the north west region. And there is no pay for travelling time.

The result will be that many railwaymen will leave in disgust, 'voluntarily'. That way, BR will save redundancy pay.[15]

Similar policies make it possible for the National Coal Board to dodge the payment of redundancy pay:

NCB and government strategy on closures has been clever. Once a redundancy is announced the NCB industrial relations men move in, offering 'secure jobs for all in the Midlands'.

They foster the idea that the government and the NCB have the miners' welfare at heart. The truth is that the offer is based on a calculation that not more than 15 percent of the men will take it up. If more men opted to move, the NCB would have to delay and refuse jobs.

For the majority who remain, the jobs policy is more clever. Men are transferred to other pits in the area. This seems reasonable, except that the NCB is carrying out a deliberate policy of overmanning, turning marginal pits into 'uneconomic' ones and then closing them.

The results suit the employers. The men get fed up with being pushed from pit to pit (in the last two years many miners have worked in as many as five pits) and finally leave voluntarily, which is interpreted by the NCB as 'natural wastage'. Financially the NCB saves in redundancy payments and early payment of pensions.[16]

William Brown

(Tune: 'So Early in the Morning')

A nice young man was William Brown,
He worked for a wage in a Yorkshire town,
He turned a wheel from left to right,
From eight in the morning till six at night.

Chorus
Keep that wheel a-turning,
Keep that wheel a-turning,
Keep that wheel a-turning,
And do a little more each day.

The boss one day to William came,
And said, 'Look here, young what's-your-name,
'We're far from pleased with what you do,
'So hurry the wheel or out you go.'

So William turned and made her run,
Three times round in the place of one.
He turned so hard he was quickly made
The Lord High Turner of his trade.

The nation thrilled to the wondrous tale,
The news appeared in the Sketch and Mail,
The railways ran excursions down,
And all to look on William Brown.

He turned all day with a saintly smile,
The goods he made grew such a pile,
They filled the room and the room next door,
And overflowed to the basement floor.

But sad the sequel to our tale,
He turned out more than his boss could sell,
The market fell and the price came down,
Seven days more and they sacked young Brown.

Traditional song (written before 'productivity')

Again Upper Clyde Shipbuilders gave a 'no-redundancy' pledge in return for mobility, flexibility, relaxation of working practices, job evaluation and measured day work. However, ways were found to dodge the pledge. On 24 November 1968, a couple of days before the *QE2* began its trials, the 600 men—joiners, electricians and labourers—who had sweated to finish the boat on schedule were sacked by John Brown's. The timing was important. On the very same day all the shipyard unions except the boilermakers signed the agreement which will give workers on the Clyde a two-year guarantee of employment.

A few months later the management of Upper Clyde Shipbuilders showed they could use other dodges to violate the 'no-redundancy' pledge. On 27 February 1969 some 11,000 shipyard workers on the Clyde took part in the one-day strike against anti-union legislation. In retaliation, their two-year jobs guarantee was withdrawn by Upper Clyde Shipbuilders:

> Every worker with nine months continuous service received the employment guarantee. But any men who took part in an unofficial action—strikes, over-time bans or working to rule—automatically broke the continuity and lost the safeguard.[17]

Quite often management fraudulently appeals to workers' needs for job security to soften them up for a productivity deal.

The need for security is uppermost in workers' minds, and in introducing MDW management often cheats, offering stable pay without saying whether it is stable per day or per week or per month. Thus three of the senior shop stewards who negotiated the Ryton Rootes agreement said:

> We have been greatly irritated by press reports of '£2,000 a year' for Coventry workers, and 'Ryton workers get £35 per week'...
>
> We would like it to be understood as widely as possible that this can only be obtained when the working people have been employed for 40 hours a week.
>
> Since last November production workers at Ryton have [had] only three full working weeks. For the moment, anyway, with short time working and layoffs, due to shortages of materials, £35 is very much a pie in the sky.[18]

In some cases the 'no redundancy' pledge is quite clearly hedged. ICI's productivity deal aims at cutting the labour force by 15 percent without sacking. But ICI explains:

> The annual labour turnover for men on payroll in the Huddersfield works in 1965 was 25.54 percent... With this turnover of labour the general problem of dealing with surplus should not be insurmountable.

But then the management goes on and adds as an afterthought, 'although there will almost inevitably be some difficult individual cases'.[19]

However, with all the guarantees in the world, productivity deals are bound to be pregnant with two consequences for redundancy. Firstly, if the successful implementation of the new methods of work weakens the workers' organisations then the employers are bound to ignore their previous 'guarantees'.

Secondly, and of much greater consequence in the long run, even if the 'no-sacking' guarantee is adhered to, and there is merely a rundown of the labour force relying on natural waste, the effect on job opportunities can be very serious indeed. The full impact of this will be felt, after a timelag, by the school leavers. Workers who sign productivity deals pledging 'no redundancy', side by side with a decline in the labour force through natural waste, are really asked to collaborate with management in denying job opportunities to their own children when they leave school.

British industrial output and productivity (1963 = 100)

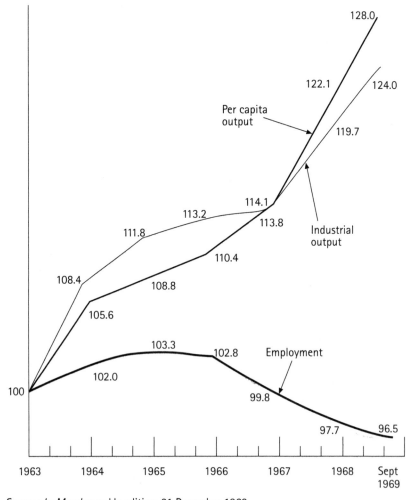

Source: *Le Monde* weekly edition, 31 December 1969

Chapter Nine: Legal shackles on workers
Curbs on unofficial strikes

Several years ago two Fabians, writing in support of the idea of an incomes policy, pointed out very clearly the meaning of such a policy for the right to strike in Britain:

> Acceptance of an incomes policy will also have implications for the right to strike. Clearly, to be operable, such a policy cannot have hanging over it the threat of a strike by a dissatisfied union.[1]

The *Economist* has made the same point strongly and plainly: 'The price of securing an incomes policy in Britain will be a willingness to stand up to strikes'.[2] 'Another weapon against unofficial strikes is that, quite bluntly, blacklegging must become respectable again'.[3]

And an economist recommended a vote for the Labour Party in the 1964 general election because he felt that Labour was more likely than the Tories to achieve success with an incomes policy. He explained his recommendation in the following way: 'Paradoxically, one of the strongest economic arguments for a Labour government is that, beneath layers of velvet, it might be more prepared to face a showdown in dealing with the unions'.[4]

The same point was made by a number of other commentators. Sir Patrick Hennesy, Ford chief, stated, 'It is my conviction, following the latest moves— the cooperative action between the industry, the trade unions and the Labour government—that it may not be long before we see action to prevent unofficial stoppages'.[5]

Harold Wilson did not disappoint Sir Patrick Hennessy. One of the first acts of the Labour government was the appointment of the Donovan commission.

The Donovan commission

In June 1968, after three years deliberations, the Royal Commission on Trade Unions and Employers' Associations, chaired by Lord Donovan, delivered its report.

The main target was clear—factory floor organisation:

> The central defect in British industrial relations is the disorder in factory and workshop relations and pay structures promoted by the conflict between the formal and the informal systems. To remedy this, effective and orderly collective bargaining is required over such issues as the control of incentive schemes, the regulation of hours actually worked, the use of job evaluation, work practices and the linking of changes in pay to changes in performance, facilities for shop stewards and disciplinary rules and appeals.[6]

The aim of the Donovan report was the integration of the shop stewards into a streamlined union machine, into a plant consensus. This process of integration could be helped by greater legal and managerial discipline. Order has also to be brought into the working of the unions: 'Certain features of trade union structure and government have helped to inflate the power of work groups and shop stewards'.[7]

The rules of the unions should contain 'unspecified' requirements relating to discipline, expulsion, the role of shop stewards, etc.

The bugbear of the Donovan commission was the unofficial strikes. The commission recommended that the definition of trade unions should be altered to exclude 'temporary combinations' of workers and that only registered trade unions should come under the scope of laws which protect combination, including the strike law. Section III of the 1906 Trade Disputes Act, which protects workers on strike against civil action for damages, should apply in future only to registered trade unions. The effect of this would be to place all workers on unofficial strikes at the mercy of the litigating employers. To soften the blow, and in contradiction to the above, the commission recommended that no legal sanctions should be introduced against unofficial strikes as such. The commission expressed the hope that the institutional reforms which they proposed would effectively reduce the incidence of strikes. The commission argued against the wisdom of penal sanctions.

Among the institutional changes proposed by the Donovan commission was, first of all, the substitution of factory agreements for industry-wide agreements. These agreements should be registered with a suggested new body, the Industrial Relations Commission:

> The act should provide for the establishment of an Industrial Relations Commission, with a full time chairman and other full time and part time members and its own staff. The commission would, on a reference from the Department of Employment and Productivity, investigate and report on cases and problems arising out of the registration of agreements.
>
> These proposals will assist an incomes policy to work effectively by exposing the whole process of pay settlement to the influence of policy. The functions of the Industrial Relations Commission and the Prices and Incomes Board are different but the work of each will assist the other.[8]

Further, the Donovan commission suggested that the power of the Industrial Court should be very much strengthened: 'Compulsory unilateral arbitration by the Industrial Court should be made available in industries, sections of industry or undertakings in which the Secretary of State for Employment and Productivity has certified, on the advice of the Industrial Relations Commission following an inquiry, that it can contribute to the growth or maintenance of sound collective bargaining machinery'.[9]

The Donovan commission did not go so far as to propose making collective agreements into binding legal contracts. Hence it did not suggest to impose legal sanctions on individuals who strike in breach of procedural agreements.[10]

The Heath-Wilson consensus

The Tory press expressed great dissatisfaction with the Donovan report because, in their eyes, it was too 'soft' on the unions—it failed to recommend anti-strike legislation. Shortly before the publication of this report Tory central office came out with a report of its own making clear what it would like to see included in any anti-union legislation. The report, amusingly, was entitled 'Fair Deal at Work' (April 1968).

Some seven months after Donovan, Barbara Castle came out with her own variation on the same theme, 'In Place of Strife'. This went far beyond the Donovan report and approached the proposals in 'Fair Deal at Work' quite closely. It is very instructive to compare 'In Place of Strife' with 'Fair Deal at Work'.

Firstly, regarding trade union legislation:

> There would be a new Registrar of Trade Unions and Employers' Associations with powers to ensure that their rules are just, secure fair democratic control, and are not contrary to the public interest. Registration would be a compulsory condition for any organisation wanting to have the full legal status of a 'trade union'.[11]

> To require trade unions and employers' associations to have rules on certain subjects and to register; to create a new Registrar of Trade Unions and Employers' Associations.[12]

The Tory report suggested that a registrar should impose his will, depriving all unregistered unions of their legal status. Barbara Castle's report wanted to enforce the same thing by imposing fines on unions whose rules are in conflict with the registrar's regulations.

On the legal status of trade unions, the two reports state the following:

> Trade unions would have corporate legal status—subject only to immunity against civil proceedings when acting in furtherance of a lawful trade dispute which is not in breach of agreement.[13]

> To enable a union to be sued in tort, except in the circumstances of trade dispute.[14]

New kinds of industrial courts were suggested by both:

> There would be special industrial courts comprising legally qualified chairman sitting with 'lay' members from both sides of industry.[15]

> To establish an industrial board to hear certain types of case against employers, trade unions and individual employees.[16]

The Tories proposed that the state should have new powers to intervene in strikes:

> (1) Where all other methods have failed, the Minister of Labour should have power to apply to the Industrial Court for an injunction to delay or stop a strike or lockout if, in his view, such action would seriously endanger the national interest.

However, he could only exercise this power after receiving the report of an independent board of inquiry.

(2) The maximum period for such an injunction should be stipulated in the act. In our view, it should not be less than 60 days.

(3) Where an injunction was granted, the minister—acting on the advice of the board of inquiry—should have power to order that a secret ballot be held at any appropriate time while it was in force.[17]

Labour's plan would:

...enable the secretary of state by order to require those involved to desist for up to 28 days from a strike or lockout which is unconstitutional, or in which for other reasons adequate joint discussions have not taken place, and to require the employer meanwhile to observe specified terms or conditions...

To empower the secretary of state, where an official strike is threatened, by order, to require a ballot.[18]

The main difference between the government and the Tories is that, where the former would make the compulsory return to work last for 28 days, the latter would extend it to 60 days.

The Tory report, like Labour's one, favoured fining workers going on strike in breach of procedure:

The recovery of such damages, in the event of inability or failure to pay, should be by attachment of wages—as already applies to maintenance orders.[19]

The [Industrial] Board will have power to impose financial penalties on an employer, union or individual striker as it found appropriate. These penalties would be recoverable in England and Wales only in the appropriate county court by attachment of earnings and other civil remedies for the collection of debts, and procedures with similar effect will apply in Scotland.[20]

Snags in enforcing anti-strike laws

However, there is all the difference in the world between the enactment of laws against strikes and their effective implementation.

This was made clear by the Ministry of Labour in its evidence to the Donovan commission:

There is one body of opinion which holds that the answer to this problem [of unofficial strikes] is in some way or another to make unofficial strikes illegal. In its ultramontaine form this view would seem to be self-defeating, on the single ground that it would be impracticable... Quite simply, in the last resort, it is not practicable, nor would it be conducive to good industrial relations, to try and put a large number of people in jail.[21]

There is more than a touch of humour in the answers given by representatives of the Motor Industry Employers to the Donovan commission:

Mr Woodcock: What would you do if the shop struck against deductions from pay?
Sir George Harriman: If we had a strike as a result of deducting a fine from pay?
Woodcock: Yes, what would you do?
Harriman: That would be the next problem, sir, would it not?
Woodcock: What would you do?
Lord Rootes: We are in trouble.[22]

More forthright in declaring the impotence of anti-strike legislation was A J Nicol, personnel director of Joseph Lucas Ltd:

> I am personally convinced anyway that legislation against strikes cannot be made to work. It is not a question of it being desirable or not. I do not think it can be made to work. The proponents of legislation against strikes have, I think, failed to realise that power has moved away in trade unions from the top, from the permanent officials, particularly from the national officials, and in fact power now is concentrated on the shopfloor, and it is concentrated in the shop steward, and it is concentrated in the local leader, and is not concentrated at the top.[23]

If strikes were made illegal, 'it will only make people turn to all sorts of other things that are more difficult to deal with'.[24]

Even if the law could enforce a reduction of strikes, this could be offset by a corresponding rise in overtime bans, working to rule and go-slows. Workers always find ways of getting round all kinds of rules and procedures.

Similarly the representative of the Shipbuilding Employers' Federation said in his evidence:

> I do not see how you are going to make a sanction work. You just cannot put 5,000 strikers in jail, and if you fine them and they do not pay the fine, what are you going to do? I do not see how this would work out in practice, unless everyone observed the law voluntarily. If people kick over the traces in large numbers, the law is helpless...
>
> *Question:* Could you not deduct the fine from wages, or do you not think that would be practicable?
>
> I think if you did that you would find the employees would just go elsewhere, and you would get an administrative machine which would get so gummed up you would not be able to trace all the people.[25]

As a proof beyond doubt that the law by itself cannot curb unofficial strikes, Sir Harold Emmerson, former permanent secretary of the Ministry of Labour, brought before the Donovan commission the story of the Kent miners' strike of 1941:

The Betteshanger colliery

Doubts about the practicability of prosecuting large numbers of men for going on strike illegally were put to the test at the Betteshanger colliery, in Kent, in December 1941. There had been trouble at this colliery about allowances for work in a difficult seam where working conditions changed almost weekly. After all else had failed the company and the men agreed to go to arbitration and to abide by the award. An experienced arbitrator decided that the allowances offered by the management were reasonable and erred, if at all, in being excessive. The men rejected the award and work stopped. About 4,000 men were idle.

Under the National Arbitration Order the strike was illegal, and to make matters worse it was backed by local union officials...

The magistrates met in Canterbury. The news had spread to other coalfields, and colliery bands decided to accompany the culprits. Local colliery workers made it an outing for their families, and chartered coaches to take wives and children. The Mines Department authorised the Regional Petroleum Officer to allow petrol for the journeys.

Everything on the day was orderly and even festive. Bands played, and women and children cheered the procession on its way to the court. The proceedings in court went smoothly. Everyone pleaded guilty. The three union officials were sent to prison. The branch secretary was sentenced to two months with hard labour. The local president and a member of the local executive each received one month with hard labour. Thirty five men were fined £3 or one month's imprisonment, and nearly 1,000 were fined £1 or 14 days.

Protests came against the severity of the sentences, particularly against the imprisonment of three union officials. Many of the miners in the area were in the Home Guard, and Kent was in the front line. 'Was this the way to treat good citizens?' There was talk of sympathetic strikes. But the real trouble was that the only men who could call off the strike were now in jail. The secretary for mines went down to Kent to see them accompanied by Mr Ebby Edwards, then the national president of the Miners' Union. Negotiations were reopened, and five days after the hearing an agreement was signed, in prison, between the colliery management and the Kent Miners' Union. Apart from some face-saving words, it gave the men what they wanted. Then the secretary for mines took a deputation to the home secretary asking for the immediate release of the three local officials. The men would not start work until their leaders were free. After 11 days in prison they were released. The mine reopened—and in the first week the normal output of coal was nearly trebled.

In the Ministry of Labour there was gloom and apprehension. Certainly we had shown that it was possible to prosecute on a large scale if everyone cooperated. But even if the remissions were necessary for work to start, they were bound to weaken the authority of the order. Also what would be the effect on the men who had been fined? We were soon to know, for the clerk to the justices reported that of the men who had been fined only nine had paid. Before he went to the trouble of preparing nearly 1,000 commitment warrants the clerk asked whether it was proposed to recommend remission. The county jail could only accommodate a few at a time, and it would take several years to work through the list. He understood that the men had been at work for some weeks, they had made good the lost output, and he believed the country needed coal. There might be an outcry if men were sent to prison for not paying the fines, when the original sentences of imprisonment on the leaders had been remitted. He asked for guidance.

The company also wanted to avoid further trouble. They asked if they could pay the fines on behalf of the men—the cost to them would be so much less profits tax!

They were told on no account to do this. The court was advised not to enforce the unpaid fines.

Of course, someone asked, 'What about the nine men who paid their fines? Should they have their money back?' But it was not until 1950—eight years later—that the National Union of Mineworkers asked formally that the paid fines should be returned. The union was told, in appropriate official language, to forget it.[26]

More recent lesson from Australia

In Australia in 1948 the Labour government gave penal powers to the Federal Industrial Court. At the time the Chifley government was faced with a national emergency arising from a prolonged miners' strike, and introduced a bill which enabled it to break the strike. The enactment of the bill was also motivated by a desire to gain electoral advantage. However, the Labour Party lost the elections, and the incoming administration of Robert Menzies had a ready-made tool of anti-union legislation.

Looking back, however, it is clear that the law did not prevent Australia having more days lost in strikes than, for instance, Britain. In the years 1964-66 the number of days lost in strikes per 1,000 employees was 190 in Britain and 400 in Australia.[27]

Finally, in May 1968, the anti-strike law was knocked completely into a cocked hat.

On 15 May Clarrie O'Shea, leader of the tiny Victoria Tramways Union, was jailed for contempt of court after refusing to disclose to the Federal Industrial Court the union's books when so ordered. The court had endeavoured for three long years to lay its hands on the books. O'Shea had not paid fines, by now totalling $8,000, for unauthorised strikes by his union, or paid the penalties for non-compliance with the court order:

> Since the jailing of Clarrie O'Shea it is not only the relatively small Tramways Union which has adopted a policy of refusal to pay any further fines under the penal powers. It has been joined by the 2,000-strong Boilermakers' and Blacksmiths' Society, which has said it will not pay the $16,000 fines outstanding against itself.
>
> And then the 83,000-strong Amalgamated Engineering Union, second biggest union in the country, at its first autonomous Australian national conference, has declared that it too will refuse to pay the fines.[28]

In the week following the arrest of O'Shea Australia faced the biggest strike struggle in its history. One million workers took strike action from Sydney to Perth, from the far north of Queensland to Tasmania.

To get the government off the hook an anonymous donor appeared and paid O'Shea's fine. (A similar thing happened in Western Australia the year before when boilermakers refused to pay fines and a state-wide general strike was only averted at the last moment by an 'anonymous' donor paying the fines.)[29]

Australia won't do—what about Sweden?

Again and again Labour and Tory leaders alike have pointed to Sweden's anti-strike laws as an example to follow. And on the face of it the law in Sweden seems to have been very effective. The number of days lost in strikes per 1,000 employees in 1964-66 was only 40, as against 190 in Britain.[30]

But, unfortunately for the myth-makers, Sweden is very unlike Britain. Swedish capitalism has had extremely favourable conditions for development, for a start. Industrialisation took place very late, most of it during the Second World War. That means a high average quality of plant and equipment. Sweden has not been involved directly in any war for some 140 years, while its industries reaped fat profits from the war efforts of other countries. Sweden's standard of living is the highest in the world (comparable, probably, to that of the US), while there are not the same cleavages between sections of the working populations that exist, say, between blacks and whites in the US, or between south and north in Italy. Industrial workers are over 95 percent organised, and white collar workers about 50 percent. The trade unions are very small in number and highly centralised. The power of the Swedish TUC (LO) is great. Every trade unionist pays the LO 48s a year, against the 1s 3d paid to the TUC in Britain:[31]

> Virtually no strike may be called without top LO approval. This is not forthcoming unless central LO and other efforts have failed to secure a peaceful settlement. While constitutional restrictions of this kind are important, the moral influence of the central authority remains dominant.[32]

The unions sign collective agreements usually for a period of two years. During the period of the agreement workers are not allowed to go on strike. If a worker does go on strike he is liable to a fine of up to 200 crowns (about £14).

> Workers cannot resort to strike action as long as there is a valid collective contract existing at the workplace. If, however, an unofficial strike occurs, the local trade union as well as the national union have to react as rapidly as possible to get their members back to work. To begin with the local trade union has to call for a meeting where the union informs its members of the legal rules. It is also considered a duty for the national union to threaten the strikers with expulsion if they do not go back to work within a reasonably short time. The general experience is that illegal strikes in Sweden are finished within a few days or, in many cases, hours.[33]

Unofficial strikes are very rare indeed. The main curb is not the law but the unions. If a worker goes on an unofficial strike he risks being expelled from the union. Since the doling out of unemployment benefit is in the hands of the union, the penalty is very serious indeed.

The continuous and quite regular expansion of Swedish capitalism made it possible for such a corporatist integration of big business, the state and the unions to work.[34]

British capitalism, with its great unevenness between the different sectors of industry, with its 'stop-go' policies, etc, could hardly emulate Sweden, with its class conflicts and social tensions kept below the surface.

By the way, even Sweden cannot suppress capitalism's inherent contradiction, as the current widespread unofficial strikes show. The *Financial Times*, which for many years put Sweden's labour relations on a pedestal, has this to say:

> Sweden's gilded image of a strike-free community whose labour-management relations are held up to the world as a modern industrial miracle is beginning to look a little tarnished. For once the system has failed to cope. Five thousand employees of the state-owned LKAB mining concern in Lapland have gone on a wildcat strike, now in its third week and considered the worst in 35 years. In addition, about 1,000 dock workers have been on strike this year and, to make sure that 1969 goes out with a bang, most of the doctors employed in hospitals are threatening a go-slow and limited strike action at selected points.

The *Financial Times* ends its report with the following conclusion:

> If the LKAB strikers have all their demands met—at present it is not precisely clear how far these go—it could signal the start of a free for all wages scramble and a breakdown of central negotiations. If this does happen its impact on the Swedish economy and political situation could be of the same relative magnitude as that of the French disturbances of May 1968.[35]

An anti-strike law certainly would not do the trick in Britain.

The TUC to the rescue of Donovan

The corporatist ideal of the merging together of the unions, the state and business both attracts and repels the union leaders. To some—on the right, like Les Cannon of the ETU, Lord Cooper of the GMWU and Dai Davies of the ISTC—it is quite an alluring prospect. To others—like Jack Jones and Hugh Scanlon—the idea of becoming messenger boys in the corridors of power is quite appalling.

As a result of this double pressure—from the state on the one side and the workers on the other—the TUC came to a position that did not go as far as 'In Place of Strife' towards full-scale corporatism but nevertheless tended in the same direction. Actually the TUC's 'Programme for Action' is very similar to the Donovan report. The TUC accepts the basic assumption of Donovan (and 'In Place of Strife') that industrial relations ought to be reorganised so as to impose a centralised system of control over the workers. Strikes, especially unofficial ones, have to be curbed.[36]

The TUC accepts the assumption that workers have to make sacrifices and discipline at work in order to cure the economic ills of the country. The TUC, however, disagrees with Barbara Castle that the government should take the power of discipline into its own hands. Instead the TUC should do it.

Should a union refuse to abide by a decision, the General Council proposed that it could take action under Rule 13, with the result that the union would be suspended, reported to Congress and possibly expelled. The General Council would also 'require unions to satisfy them that they had done all they could reasonably be expected to do to secure compliance with a recommendation (or an award)' by its members, 'including taking action within their own rules if necessary'. This, of course, could involve fines by unions on their members, or expulsion from the union. The latter would in many instances mean the loss of a job where a closed shop operates. The TUC's Rule 11 is concerned to keep the General Council informed about disputes arising between unions, men and employers. The General Council is empowered, in certain conditions, to use its influence to bring about a settlement. The proposed revision to Rule 11 would extend both this obligation to inform and the right of the General Council to intervene in unconstitutional stoppages of work where the dispute affects a large number of workers, either directly or indirectly, or seems likely to be protracted or have serious repercussions.

On the question of arbitration, the General Council said it 'fully recognises …the valuable work of conciliation carried out by the DEP', but believes that in many industries 'there would be great advantage in making provision once again for abjuration at the request of one party, through the reintroduction of Order 1376', and suggests the setting up of new machinery to provide for cases to be dealt with on a regional basis so that disputes could be dealt with more rapidly.

The TUC repeats its welcome for the CIR and 'the very important job' it will have. It asked for the closest cooperation by trade unions with the DEP in its job of registering procedure agreements of large companies.[37]

As *Socialist Worker* summed up at the time, the difference between the TUC and the government:

> …is a Battle of the Bureaucracies. It has little to do with the workers' fight against the attacks being launched and everything to do with sorting out the details of how the control of workers and their organisations is to be institutionalised.[38]

The Swedish example appeals very much to the TUC—the agent of change in labour relations is to be a strong, tightly-disciplined trade union movement working in close partnership with government and management.

'Programme for Action', like 'In Place of Strife', has mainly ideological motivations. Legal restraint by itself can hardly change the balance of class forces. It can, however, provide cover for right wing or weak-kneed 'left' leadership of the unions when they make concessions to both management and government. It can sap the ideological defences of the militants and isolate them from the mass of backward workers. This could shift the balance of forces in the long term battle for control over the factory floor. And it could prepare the ground for mass, determined, frontal attacks on the working class in the future. On the ideological level 'Programme for Action' is no less insidious than 'In Place of Strife'.[39]

For 'partnership' of employers and unions

The real aim of Donovan, 'In Place of Strife', etc is basically not to smash the unions, or even to weaken them as organisations, but to integrate them with management. This 'partnership' is to be embodied in productivity deals and formalised procedures in the plants.

The introduction of comprehensive formal agreements at factory level is the normal result of productivity bargaining and the central proposal of the Donovan report. The reasoning behind this proposal is most clearly expressed by Allan Flanders—the historian of the Fawley productivity deals, whose theoretical arguments strongly influenced Donovan, and who has been rewarded by a £6,500 job on the Commission of Industrial Relations.

Flanders diagnoses the central problem, for management and the government, as 'a progressive loss of managerial control over pay and work, and therefore over labour costs, at plant level'.[40]

To say that management has lost control is to say that workers have *won* an area of control—over piece-rate bargaining, overtime, manning, allocation of work, pace of production. All these areas of control which workers have been able to wrest from management—and which productivity deals are intended to restore to management—have arisen, Flanders argues, because collective bargaining at factory level is 'largely informal, largely fragmented and largely autonomous'.[41]

Bargaining takes place *at the point of production*, where workers' power is most effectively organised and where management is weakest. Lower level supervision—whose overriding concern is to get production out, and whose own reputation in the eyes of their superiors can be damaged by a strike—can be pressured into making concessions, informally, which top management would never sanction. And stewards can press hard, knowing precisely what the feelings of their members are, and largely free of the restraining influences to which full time officials are subject.

Flanders identifies management's attitude to shopfloor bargaining as the heart of the problem. Workers' power in the workshop cannot be ignored—concessions have to be made—but because workshop bargaining is informal, top management may not know, and is certainly not willing to admit, that its 'managerial prerogatives' have been undermined in this way.

'This mixture of realism and pretence, of being forced to yield to bargaining power on the shopfloor while denying it any legitimacy,' Flanders insists, 'is the most fundamental cause of the weakening of managerial control.' But this analysis itself suggests the 'remedy': 'The paradox, whose truth managements have found so difficult to accept, is that they can only regain control by sharing it'.[42]

'Sharing control' is, for Flanders, a process in which management formally admits the right of unions to negotiate on all aspects of their members' employment, but within a framework which is dictated by management. Productivity deals fit this pattern: 'The distinguishing, common feature of all the major, genuine productivity agreements is that they are attempts to strengthen managerial control over pay and work through joint regulation.'

The *formal* nature of the agreements is essential for this purpose: 'The object is to create a more controlled situation, and specification in agreement is one important means of control'.[43]

There are four obvious ways in which greater formality *will* normally mean greater control for management. First, we have seen that the first-line foreman, bargaining with a small group of workers, often makes concessions which top management would strongly resist. Most stewards in well organised factories can cite concessions which they know the works manager would never accept in a written agreement—indeed he would probably have a heart attack if he knew about them! One common reason for proposing a formal productivity deal is precisely to get rid of the unwritten rights and customs which have accumulated informally. Once the deal is signed, management will be instructed at *all* levels to ignore any old rights or practices which are not in the formal agreement. This is a particularly attractive way for management to attack the workers' shopfloor *organisation*. The formal national engineering agreement concedes shop stewards only the bare minimum of recognition and facilities, and ties them rigidly to the York procedure, but in any well organised factory stewards have tacitly won the right to exercise far wider powers. Their rights—to hold meetings, move round the factory, raise grievances directly with senior management, be consulted (with an effective veto) before all work changes—have often been won informally. The negotiation of a new formal agreement is a means for management to attempt—as at Rootes—to abolish all these unwritten rights.

The second advantage for management is the inflexibility of a formal agreement. As the Royal Commission's research director put it, 'Stewards have an interest in informal bargaining because it helps them to slide forward the frontier of their influence'.[44]

Rights can be gradually accumulated by pressure for small concessions in strongly organised sections, which are then extended throughout the factory. The process can be so slow and piecemeal that management does not recognise the erosion of its control, and sees no need to develop a coherent strategy of resistance. But where formal plant agreements govern the organisation of work and the rights of stewards, any change must be formally demanded and formally negotiated—coming under the scrutiny of management at every level. Determined resistance is far more likely.

The third implication has been emphasised by Flanders: 'One thing is certain—the formalisation of plant bargaining will call for a much greater involvement of full time officials in plant affairs'.[45]

The elaboration of formal rules governing the negotiations, the fact that any bargaining affects the factory as a whole, and the likelihood that a written agreement at one plant may be cited as a precedent in another—all entail that the union official will be expected to supervise and direct plant bargaining. And because—as we will see—of the pressures to which the officials in turn are subject, this is likely, as the Coventry Blue Book recognised, to be 'advantageous to the employers'.

Finally we should note the ideological importance of the formalisation that Flanders recommends. Informal plant bargaining, based on strong shop steward organisation, is an open expression of a relationship of conflict. Workers use their collective power to win concrete concessions in pay and working conditions, and to *carve out an area of control*. Because the inherent conflict is so obvious, the principal limit to workers' demands is their own consciousness of their strength. And it is their increasing awareness of this strength which is so frightening the ruling class. But formal plant bargaining necessarily means that the relationship is *apparently* transformed. Management meets union representatives as 'equal partners' in discussing the organisation of work. Their negotiations aim at 'joint regulation' of managerial questions. And the procedure under which these negotiations take place is mutually agreed. In place of conflict there is cooperation. Of course, such 'cooperation' is one-sided—as Flanders cynically puts it, management 'regain control by sharing it'. Management can allow union participation in 'joint regulation' only if the rules are stacked in its favour, and if the basic economic aims of the company are unquestioned. There must be, Flanders makes it clear, 'a common system of joint control based on agreed objectives'.[46]

There is a very real danger that the less politically sophisticated workers (and even stewards) will swallow this eyewash—that they will accept that formal plant bargaining has replaced the old relationship of conflict by a 'fair' system of joint control. Believing this, they will feel it wrong to act 'unconstitutionally', outside the formally agreed procedure, and in this way they emasculate themselves, destroying the basis of their existing strength. This is the basic hope of Flanders, Donovan and all who propose more formal agreements. The hopes of workers and stewards alike must lie in preventing this.

In conclusion

There are two strands among the advocates of anti-strike laws. First, those who support a hard line, following the Australian pattern (or Betteshanger). Second, those who support a soft line—the Donovan report, 'In Place of Strife' and 'Programme for Action'. This calls for formal plant bargaining, 'integration' and 'education' of stewards, 'reformed' procedures, the basic strategy to bring the majority of stewards under official control and bash the minority who resist. Closed shop and check-off are part of the strategy.

The prototypes are Sweden and the United States. The aim is to turn the trade unions into management policemen.

There is a reciprocal relationship between the 'hard line' and the 'soft line'. The former is used to blackmail union leaders to submit to the latter. The 'soft line' is much more in tune with the objective situation, is most insidious and dangerous.

Perhaps the most likely way they'll introduce anti-strike laws in future is to back 'freely negotiated' (by the trade union officials) agreements by law.

Chapter Ten: The ideological offensive: production for what?

A central theme in the whole productivity bargaining campaign is the need for 'efficiency' and 'modernisation' in the interests of the nation. By raising the issue of productivity the government and the employers are forcing politics onto the shopfloor. Socialists must take up the challenge.

When the government and the employers talk of efficiency, socialists have plenty to say on that score. About the anarchy and waste of capitalist production, the fact that more is spent on advertising than on basic research, that millions are wasted on armaments, that constant retooling of car plants takes place not because the tools are worn out but because competition demands accelerated obsolescence and never ending 'new models'.

The very purpose of production becomes an industrial issue. Should production be aimed at benefiting the workers, the old age pensioners, etc or serve only to raise the profits of the rich?

The ideological offensive is in full swing. From government ministers, industrial tycoons and the political pundits of TV and the press we hear the same tune: 'Forget about inequalities of wealth—that's all old hat—if we all pull together and increase productivity then everyone will benefit.' It all sounds so plausible. If industry produces more then there will be more goods and services to go round! In a socialist society this would be true. By raising the productivity of labour we would give ourselves a choice—either a higher standard of living or shorter working hours. Today there is no such choice, because industrialists see higher productivity as a means to higher profit, and in fact often have no wish to *increase output at all*. We see this contradiction most clearly in the motor industry. Although they are unable to sell all the cars they make at present, the manufacturers are desperate to push up productivity and make their workers work even faster. It is desperately important that we expose the employers' pious talk about 'efficiency' and 'production in the national interest'. If BLMH lay off 20 percent of their workers and still maintain the same level of output then there is a very obvious gain for BLMH. For the 20 percent who get the sack, and for the community as a whole, there is nothing gained at all. In the economy as a whole 'productivity' can go up and is going up while production stays still—and 'structural' unemployment grows.

The demands for increased productivity in the interest of greater profit should be countered by the socialist idea of production for use.

By talking in terms of the 'national interest' the ruling class is attempting to divert attention from the really important question of the *distribution* of income and wealth between the classes. Of course the wealthy want to treat this question of distribution as being of minor importance—after all, their portion of the cake is in fact growing from year to year. For us, however, these *are* the important questions, and it is here that our challenge must be made.

'Wages are too high'

One of the main arguments for a national effort to increase production is that without it Britain could not withstand the international competition in the world market. The story that British wages are much too high compared to those paid in other countries, competing countries, is so assiduously spread that many workers really believe in it.

Even if they don't go so far as to believe that their *own* wages are too high, they are very likely to consider *other* sections of workers as overpaid, particularly when they hear extravagant tales about earnings in print, motors, etc. This, of course, is a major factor in isolating groups of workers when they are in conflict over pay.

This story is not new. As long ago as 1897, we are informed by a historian of the engineers, the employers pleaded that competition from cheaper labour in Germany prevented them from shortening hours. They claimed that financially the firms could not stand the increased cost which an eight-hour day would involve. And this despite the fat profits at the time![1]

Are British wages really high by comparison with wages in other industrial countries? The graph on the next page gives a clear answer.[2] The actual trend is for wages in other European countries to rise much faster than in Britain. Thus between 1958 and 1967 gross wages rose by 51 percent in Britain, 70 percent in Belgium, 83 percent in France, 99 percent in Germany, 103 percent in the Netherlands and 106 percent in Italy.[3] In the 12 months ending June 1969 wages have gone up by 18.7 percent in Japan, 8.1 percent in France, 8.8 percent in Germany, 8.6 percent in Italy, 7.9 percent in Holland and only 7.7 percent in Britain.[4]

When it comes to sharing out financial benefits other than direct wages, the British worker fares much worse than his European or North American counterpart: 'Compared to the average European worker, the Briton gets much less from his employer in the shape of social security, holidays, pensions, sickness aid and bonus'.[5]

The following table shows clearly to what extent Britain lags behind a number of West European countries when it comes to social security, family allowances and so on:[6]

	Total expenditure on social welfare and security as a percentage of GNP, 1966	Monthly family allowance for family with three children (in dollars), July 1968
Belgium	14.8	18.75
France	14.0	57.30
Germany	15.1	55.60
Italy	15.1	27.45
Luxembourg	15.6	44.30
Netherlands	16.3	32.10
UK	12.8	16.64

Wage costs per working hour 1965

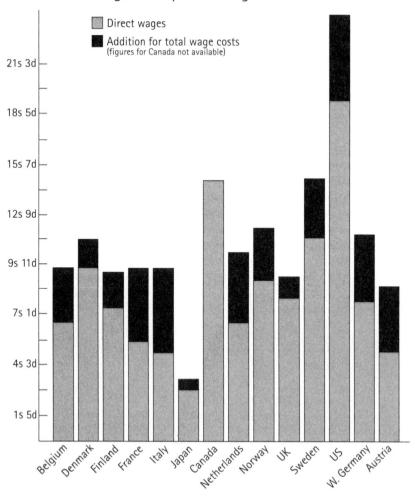

■ Direct wages

■ Addition for total wage costs
(figures for Canada not available)

The British worker fares no better when it comes to paid holidays:

HOLIDAYS WITH PAY—INTERNATIONAL COMPARISON, BEGINNING OF 1966 (TERMS GENERALLY APPLICABLE IN METAL INDUSTRY)[7]

After service of	Holidays with pay (days)		Paid statutory holiday (days)
	1 year	5 years	1 year
Great Britain	12	12	6
Belgium	18	18	10
France	21-24	21-24	7-10
Germany	18-24	18-24	9
Italy	12	14	17
Luxembourg	18	18	10
Netherlands	15	15	5-7
Austria	18	18 (24 after 15 years service)	12
Denmark	18	18	9
Norway	18	18	8-10
Sweden	4 weeks	4 weeks	9-10
Switzerland	12-18	12-18	8

It is clearly arrant nonsense to talk of British industry being priced out of the market because of high wages. Labour costs in British industry are in fact lower than for most of its competitors. Every national ruling class attempts to use the fear of international competition as a brake on wages, and a spur to greater output. To play according to the rules of this game can only lead to an international depression of workers' standards.

A very interesting summing up of the situation of British workers regarding fringe benefits compared to their West European brothers can be seen in the diagram on the next page. It shows the share of industrial fringe benefits in the real wages of engineering workers.[8]

Waste

Appealing to workers to make greater efforts while allowing the worst cases of waste and mismanagement is quite criminal. And the waste and mismanagement under capitalism are really terrifying. A library of volumes will not suffice to describe these cases. For lack of space, we will have to suffice with very few examples.

The investiture of Prince Charles in 1969 cost half a million pounds, not counting the cost of police, soldiers, civil servants and flunkies. It is thought that

Hourly paid employees

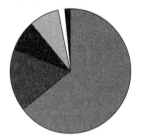

Luxembourg

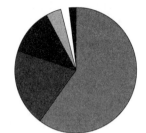

Belgium

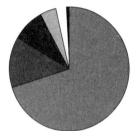

Holland

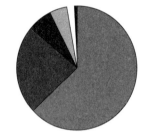

France

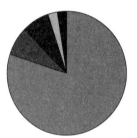

United Kingdom

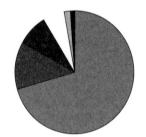

Germany

- ● Direct pay
- ● Statutory benefits
- ● Holidays and vacations
- ● Other cash (bonuses, etc)
- ○ Voluntary or contractual benefits
- ● Others

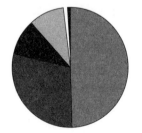

Italy

the final total for one day's royal fun and games was close on £1 million. That sort of money could have been put to better use in Wales, which has 40,000 unemployed, and where 31 percent of the houses are more than 80 years old. Some £30,000 was spent on temporary toilets for the day. In Wales 37,000 houses have no water closets and 1,840 have no bathrooms.

Another example readers will remember is the Ronan Point disaster in May 1968, when 22 storeys of the high block of flats in east London tumbled to the ground through an explosion and five people were killed. An inquiry revealed:

> The outer walls of the Ronan Point flats, which bear most of the weight of the 22 storeys, are six inches thick (compared with the 18 inches recommended by the Kaiser report). The four-ton floor slabs are fitted into slots into the walls. One and a quarter inches of the slab rests on the wall on each side, and the gap in the rest of the slot is filled with concrete on the site, thus making a 'joint'. There is no other tie between the wall and the floor, so that if the wall is pushed by a quarter of an inch or more, the new concrete almost certainly splits from the prefabricated concrete and the floor falls in. The fall will almost certainly release the floors above and below from the grip of the wall panels, leading to what is known in the trade as 'progressive collapse'...
>
> There seems little doubt that the chief advantage of the Larsen-Nielsen system is in cost. Fixing steel joints into the concrete panels is more expensive, clearly, than not doing so.
>
> The extra cost of fixing in proper steel joints or of building a load-bearing frame (as in all major office buildings) would not be much more than 5 percent of the total, but that 5 percent is crucial in the competitive world of building tenders.
>
> A recent report says that there are ten major construction firms involved in system-built buildings, but 'so far their shares have not shown any weakness that could be ascribed to new fears in the wake of Ronan Point' (*Construction News*, 22 August 1968).
>
> The tenants of Ronan Point, and of Abraham Point next door, who, unlike every other interested party, were not collectively represented at the public inquiry, are not reported to hold any major shareholding in any of the ten firms.[9]

Then there is the case of the criminal waste on the Concorde airliner. In 1962, when Concorde was first mooted, the cost of research was estimated at £150 million. The current estimate is £700 million—before one plane flies with passengers.

According to Mr Christopher Edwards, an economics lecturer at East Anglia University who has written a paper on Concorde costs:

> Even on the very favourable assumptions set out in this report, Concorde will make a loss, even after writing off the £380 million already spent... The loss to the UK economy from going ahead with the project could be as much as £150 million... That does not include £380 million already spent. The total loss to the two countries (France and Britain) could be £650 million.

This can be measured against the fact that an investment in Britain of some

£350 million over the past seven years would have been enough to completely re-house the city of Glasgow in the best modern housing available, replace every slum school in London with the best possible school building, or wholly refurbish the health service with an array of new hospitals with the most modern equipment.

And all this waste on Concorde—what for?

> For the privilege of crossing the Atlantic some two hours quicker than before…
> Stockbrokers and executives from British boardrooms will be able to get to Madison Avenue in time for lunch.[10]

The following table compares the cost of certain items of government and local authority spending:[11]

Military research and development (1968-69)	£25.4m	Medical Research Council (1966-67)	£14.2m
Provisions and victualling allowances for the navy	£58.6m	Food for patients and staff in hospitals	£44.6m
One Polaris submarine with base	£87m	Crawley New Town	£38m
Refit of Ark Royal	£30m	New Royal Free Hospital, Hampstead	£15.6m
Guided missile destroyer Glamorgan	£14.1m	New Lister Hospital, Stevenage	£6.2m
One Phantom aircraft One Polaris missile	£1.3m £400,000	One new comprehensive school	£400,000
One Bloodhound missile	£100,000	110 new tractors	£90,000
One Chieftain battle tank	£90,000	30 council houses	£90,000

When the government and the press tell us that we have to produce more, they forget to tell us what the priorities are—capitalist priorities are different to socialist ones.

Anarchy

The appeal to workers to increase efficiency turns out to be really just a cynical farce when one takes a look at the criminal anarchy of the capitalist economy.

Over the four years 1964 to 1968 gross domestic product rose by an average of 1.78 percent per year. If the rate of growth had instead been, let's say, 6 percent, a minimum of £1,400 million of extra resources a year would have been available. The cumulative impact of such an addition over a number of years would have been fantastic.

Under Wilson the old stop-go policies continued. The only change has been that the 'stop' was longer and the 'go' shorter.

That the 'stop' is becoming larger and deeper with time—and this is the nature of the contradictions of British capitalism—becomes even clearer from the following graph:[12]

Unemployment and vacancies in Britain (thousands)

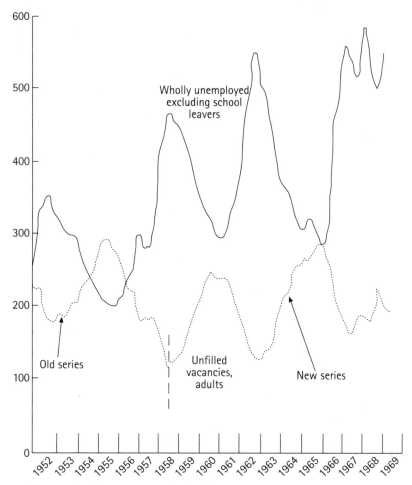

Three-month moving average: seasonally adjusted

COMPARISON OF CYCLICAL MOVEMENTS AND LEVELS[13]

Annual percentage growth rates

GDP and components at constant prices:	Upswings			Downswings	
	1958 IV–1961 I	1962 IV–1964 IV	1967 III–1969 II	1961 I–1962 IV	1964 IV–1967 III
GDP (compromise index)	5.2	5.8	2.7 *	1.2	1.8
Consumers' expenditure	4.0	4.4	0.7 *	2.3	2.1

	Peaks			Troughs	
	1961 I	1964 IV	1969 II	1962 IV	1967 III
Unemployment (thousands, average of quarter)	288	322	525	477	534

* partially estimated

How irrational capitalism is can be seen clearly when the government tries to overcome unemployment. For instance, look at the case of unemployment in the depressed regions. A capitalist investing in a 'development area'—north, north west, Scotland, Northern Ireland, etc—gets an investment grant of 45 percent. Thus if he invests £1 million he has to fork out from his own pocket only £550,000 while the rest is given to him as a gift by the taxpayer. The rate of 45 percent is 20 percent above the standard rate of investment grant. These extra amounts at present cost some £80 million a year. In addition, the industrialist investing in the development areas gets a wage bill subsidy of 37s 6d a week for every man he employs (30s of that is guaranteed for seven years). However, the impact on employment is minimal. As Dr Jeremy Bray, MP for Middlesbrough West, put it in the House of Commons:

In many cases the effect of this indiscriminate handout, given without any test of the number of jobs created, is actually to reduce employment in the development areas. ICI, probably the biggest single recipient, has received £106 million in investment grants in the last three years, of which perhaps £40 million represents the development area differential. Yet employment in ICI, net of acquisitions, has remained steady at around 127,000 for the past four years. In effect, ICI has been given £40 million for making no contribution to development area policy.

Of the £285 million paid in investment grants in 1967-68, £110 million went to the chemical, oil and steel industries. Easily the greater part of the £55 million paid in the northern region must have gone to these industries where the final effect will be actually to reduce employment in these industries in the region.

Recently, when Mr David Barran, the chairman of Shell, spoke at an open day at this refinery, he confirmed that Shell was not influenced by the subsidy in coming to Teesside and that it did not want capital subsidies. Furthermore, as a result of the capital subsidies, the refinery was so designed as to have a higher degree of automation and to employ fewer men than any other comparable Shell refinery, including other refineries being built at the same time outside development areas.

Jeremy Bray's conclusion:

The government development area subsidy to create one job at one particular plant often runs at well over £20,000 per job created. And even then this often calls for the closure of other plants, actually destroying jobs. It would be cheaper to invest the money and pension off the workers to live in the south of France, taking into account foreign exchange costs.

In the north we have seen too much money which is meant to be going into social development and raising employment levels going straight into the pockets of absentee shareholders and subsidising customers as a bribe to do what they were going to do anyway.[14]

£20,000 of the taxpayers' money to create a job for one worker! The waste becomes especially clear if we remember that even in highly modern car factories the total capital investment per worker is somewhere between £2,000 and £5,000. The figures are British Leyland £1,900, Rootes £2,630, Ford £3,720, and Vauxhall £4,870.[15]

Another example of the waste inherent in the anarchy of the capitalist system is labour turnover. Because of bad conditions, low wages, etc, labour turnover in industry is very great indeed. Although it is very difficult to put a figure on the cost of training workers for jobs which they leave shortly afterwards, one estimate will do: 'The British Institute of Management estimate that the cost to British industry of labour turnover is of the order of £700,000,000 per year'.[16]

The same wastefulness, accompanied by brutal callousness towards the needs of the poor, was exposed clearly in the following incident:

[In] answer to an oral question (House of Commons, Hansard, 14 April 1969, vol 781, cols 773-774) Mr Crossman informed the house that for the half year from September 1968, £1,900 was spent in clerks' wages alone in checking fraudulent claims for free prescriptions in Manchester. 6,600 forms were checked, 43 cases were found to not be in any of the exemption categories, and £8 was recovered for the taxpayer.[17]

Besides the large-scale wastage, every worker knows from his own experience the fantastic waste that results from capitalist mismanagement in his own place of work. To quote a few examples, one docker wrote to me:

There are many occasions when gangs are allocated to jobs when the ship doesn't even arrive. There have been occasions when gangs have been allocated to a hatch on the ship, opened the hatch and found no cargo. There are more stoppages due to the employers not having barges ready for the discharging operations than all the strikes combined in dockland. Many disputes are caused by sending 11 men to a job which by custom and practice has always been a 12-handed operation, while at the same time the employer has sent home men unemployed on full back-pay.

On the same theme an employers' paper wrote:

Very often it is the user, particularly the exporter, who causes a port to work inefficiently. With general cargo, especially, thousands of single items might converge on a port from various parts of the country all within a few days, thus causing a high concentration of labour effort both in time and place.

Bunching of cargo at the end of a ship's loading time is another problem. Many exporters fail to send their goods until the last two days of a seven to ten day loading period, although labour has to be there for the full period.

On occasions it suits a ship owner to have his ship discharge its cargo slowly to fit in with the ship's schedule. The result is poor performance in terms of cargo passing over the quay, while other ships are kept waiting. The obvious remedy here is the imposition of discipline by the port management. But this might not be so easy, when the governing board of the port authority is largely composed of ship owners and shipper interests.

One report has analysed the delays in the loading of 3,000 tons of cargo to one ship. The operation took seven days and 185 hours were lost for several reasons. More than 30 hours of work, for instance, was lost through rain, 20 through quayside congestion, 12$\frac{1}{2}$ while waiting for labour, and almost 20 through unofficial stoppages.[18]

A London busman wrote to me:

It's crazy. The more desperately they try to save money, the greater the waste and chaos they create. Due to their failure to pay enough wages there is a desperate shortage of conductors—and as a result in this shed there are drivers who haven't turned a wheel for weeks and buses that haven't carried a passenger for as long. As a result the bus queues grow longer and the loss in wasted time must be fantastic. Why can't they make the only really worthwhile economy by cutting out fares altogether and run the buses as a service—save millions on fare collection, security, accounting, checking and banking—and at the same time provide a quicker, better and more reliable service to the public? I'd call that real productivity.

Similar examples of waste resulting from capitalist mismanagement were quoted by a worker in a large engineering factory in north London in a letter to me:

We found, in the scrapyard, several hundred expensive electrical components for cars. They were checked and found to be in order. So we helped ourselves. We later found that it was cheaper for management to scrap these parts than to store them in the warehouse.

It is said that if you walk around the factory all day you will be quite safe as long as you have a piece of paper in your hand. I worked it out—to requisition 12 nuts and bolts of six different sizes with normal washers requires 18 requisition cards. Each card carries the same information except the different sizes required. The same with time sheets—the number of times you have forgotten the job number, so you invent one—nothing seems to happen.

The 'national interest'

The appeal to the 'national interest' is used as a spur to raise productivity. In a class-divided society such an appeal obscures those divisions and thereby helps the rich and powerful to become richer and more powerful.

It is not necessary to quote many facts to show how deeply divided Britain is into a handful of mighty rich and millions of relatively poor and often very poor people: 'According to estimates published in the *Economist* the richest 7 percent of the population owned 84 percent of all private wealth, while the richest 2 percent accounted for 55 percent of the total'.[19]

Share ownership is, in fact, much more concentrated than the ownership of other types of property. Only 4 percent of the adult population hold any shares in commercial or industrial companies, according to a recent stock exchange survey. An earlier investigation found that the top 1 percent of the adult population owned 81 percent of privately owned company shares.[20]

To get an idea of the dimension of the wealth concentrated in the hands of the few we call take the case of the three top directors of GEC—D Lewis, K R Bond and A Weinstock. The following table deals with the shares they own in the company (they probably also own shares in other companies):

KEY DIRECTORS' SHAREHOLDINGS[21]

Director's name	Ordinary shares held (including 'B' shares) (at 5s per share)	Approximate market value (at 25s per share)	Approximate gross dividends received (1968–69)	
	£	£	£	
D Lewis	20,956,124	26,195,155	752,664	} including joint holdings
K R Bond	19,018,972	23,773,715	684,864	
A Weinstock	4,613,148	5,766,435	161,460	
Total	44,588,244	55,735,305	1,598,988	

In 1969 the stock exchange price of GEC's ordinary shares fluctuated between 22s 1½d and 34s 10½d. Every time that the share price rises by 1s, the value of Mr Lewis's shares goes up by £1,047,806, those of Mr Bond by £950,948, and Mr Weinstock's by £230,607. In addition to their dividends, and the potential capital gain on their shareholdings, the directors are paid a wage! Arnold Weinstock, as managing director, receives £23,000, and the chairman, Lord Nelson of Stafford, receives £19,000. Six other directors receive over £10,000 each, and a further five are paid between £5,000 and £10,000.

The Wilson regime has not damaged the shareholders at all. As a matter of fact, John Hughes estimated that between 1966 and 1968 the market value of stock exchange equities rose by well over £10,000,000,000.[22]

No wonder there are now more millionaires in Britain than ever before.

The *Times* reported, 'Britain's millionaires appear to have flourished under the Labour government.' One indicator of increasing inequality in Britain is the extent to which unearned income derived from ownership of capital is rising faster than earnings from paid employment. Between 1963 and 1967 the money value of all earned income rose by 28 percent, but unearned income rose by 32 percent—and the latter figure does not include capital gains. Payments of dividends and interest alone in this period went up by 42 percent.[23]

The state pampers the rich

The government, through its taxation policy, is doing its best to put a greater and greater burden on the poor and to lighten the burden on the rich. This can be seen clearly from the following table:

TOTAL TAXES PAID AS A PERCENTAGE OF ORIGINAL INCOME *
(ALL HOUSEHOLDS)[24]

| Pre-tax income per week £ | Percentage of income paid in tax | |
	1964 %	1967 %
5	22	25
7	31	28
11	29	32
19	30	35
28	31	35
40	32	36
60	38	39
All incomes	31	35

* Original income refers to the gross income of all members of the household, and includes any cash benefits received—pension, family allowances, etc.

The burden of taxes rose by 1 percent on households with incomes of £60 per week and by 5 percent on households with incomes of £16 per week.

The total revenue raised from all taxes on wealth and profits (surtax, death duties, capital gains tax, profits and excess profits tax) amounted to £661.7 million in the fiscal year 1968-69; this was less than the revenue raised mainly from working people by the tax on tobacco alone (£1,105.2 million) or on alcohol (£777.6 million).

At the same time the Labour government has been pouring a fantastic amount of money into private industry. State aid to private industry increased from £325 million in 1964-65 to £1,192 million in 1968-69.[25]

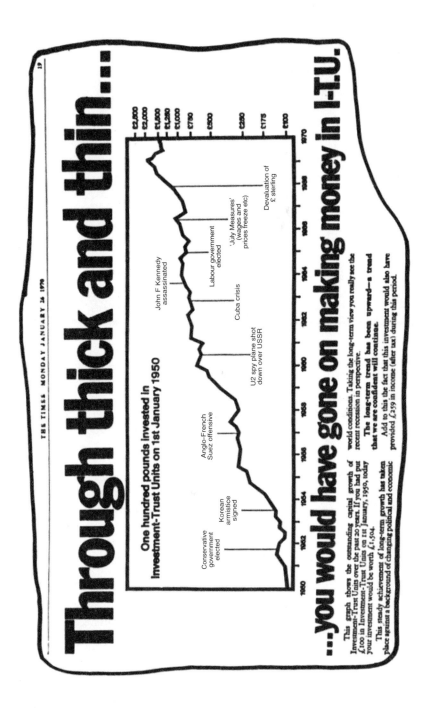

An advert for Investment-Trust Units in the *Times*, 26 January 1970

Public assistance to private industry (£ millions)

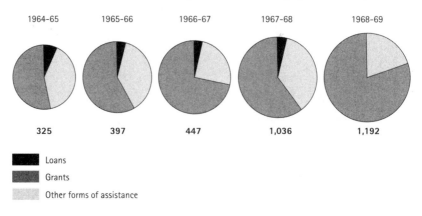

1964-65	1965-66	1966-67	1967-68	1968-69
325	397	447	1,036	1,192

■ Loans
■ Grants
▨ Other forms of assistance

The poor continue in their poverty

For reasons of space we shall have to restrict ourselves to quote only a few examples proving that while the rich become richer, the poor continue in their poverty.

There are 3 million houses in Britain without a bath, hot water or an inside WC. One family in five has to live in one of these houses—10 million men, women and children.[26]

The sample census taken in Scotland in 1966 shows that of one-person households (overwhelmingly old people), 67.2 percent have no hot water taps and 76.7 percent have no fixed bath.[27]

Take the health of the poor.

In the early post-war years very few cases of rickets were reported in Britain. Welfare milk, fortified with vitamin D, had made this one of the diseases of poverty from which British children seemed immune. An article in the *Lancet* reports the reappearance of rickets in Scotland, with Glasgow contributing 114 of the 150 in-patient cases recorded in 1964-66. The *Lancet* article suggests that this may be 'only the tip of the iceberg' of vitamin D deficiency among young children in Glasgow, as well as elsewhere in Britain. Complacent assumptions that severe poverty and malnutrition have been abolished in the affluent society seem to be hiding the real incidence of such diseases of poverty as rickets. Only 10 percent of the Glasgow cases had been diagnosed before attending hospital.[28]

G W Lynch, head of the Social Nutrition Research Unit at London University, reports that a survey of children in the East End of London showed 25 percent of children going short of nourishment. Dr Lynch argues that the main cause is the withdrawal of free school milk for secondary school children as part of the January 1968 measures.[29]

The Labour Party screamed blue murder when Tories put charges on welfare foods in 1961—but have not reduced charges. In fact, as part of the July 1967 economy package, welfare milk for children under five was put up from 4d to 6d a pint. (Each child is entitled to one pint a week, thus the total extra weekly cost 1s 2d per child.) Low income families are supposed to get this milk free, but government figures for 1967 show that (apart from families on Supplementary Benefit) 96 percent of families entitled by low income to get free milk were not getting it.[30] This particularly leads to vitamin D deficiency, the cause of rickets.

To show how mean the government can be towards the poor one need only quote the following: 'Total expenditure by local authorities on mental health and mental deficiency services is £3.5 million per annum—ie substantially less than the £4.9 million paid out in compensation and expenses in dealing with fowl pest'.[31]

'A fair day's pay for a fair day's work'

One of the main ideological planks used in support of productivity deals is that they are fair. The slogan of 'a fair day's work for a fair day's wage' or 'a just wage' quite naturally has an appeal for workers who believe in justice and fairness. But is there really such a thing as a fair wage? A landlord's understanding of a fair rent is different from the tenant's. To a socialist, who opposes the private ownership of houses, all rent is unfair. The same applies to wages. As Marx wrote, 'Instead of the conservative motto "A fair day's wages for a fair day's work," trade unions ought to inscribe on their banner the revolutionary watchword, "Abolition of the wage system".'

So long as the worker is forced by circumstances to sell his labour power to the owners of property, he is bound to produce a surplus appropriated by the owners of the means of production. This is the meaning of exploitation.

One of the most important things workers should know is what the rate of exploitation is at present in Britain, and what the trend of this rate is. Is it rising, declining or remaining constant? It is no easy task, however, to calculate the rate of exploitation. It is not difficult, of course, to calculate the *declared* profits of a company and compare these with the wages bill paid by the company, but unfortunately even the simple question of determining the real profit of one company is studded with difficulties. It is quite easy for a company to hide its real profits. Remember the case of Ferranti? Or look at the wrangles over the real profits of Robert Maxwell:

> According to Professor Edward Stamp, head of the department of accounting and business methods at Edinburgh, there are over 1 million different possible combinations of setting out the items in a balance sheet.[32]

> The result of all this is that the profits you see described as 'true and fair' in an auditor's report could in many cases be doubled, halved or pitched anywhere in between and still be 'true and fair' using a different but equally respectable set of accounting principles.[33]

A booklet, *Published Accounts: Your Yardstick of Performance*, published as an aid to management:

...shows how one company calculated its return on capital employed in nine different but all legally possible ways. The range of returns went from 8 percent to 39.8 percent.

The company calculated its returns over a four-year period. This showed that using Method A showed a more than doubling of return on capital employed from 17.5 percent to 39.8 percent—a splendid record of growing efficiency, you might think. However, using Method I, the return improves only by one third from 6 percent to 8 percent. In addition, three of the methods used show a rise in return between the third and fourth years, whereas the other six show a fall in return.[34]

Even when we have calculated the total profits and compared them with the total wages in Britain we still do not know the real rate of exploitation. After all, a proportion of the worker's wages is taken away from him in taxation (direct and indirect). Then again, the cost of all unproductive expenditures in society—advertising, merchandising, armaments, etc—is also carried by the productive workers.

A very careful and useful analysis of the rate of exploitation in Britain was carried out by Lionel Sims.[35] His conclusions are that, whereas Marx, in the middle of the 19th century, argued that the rate of exploitation stood at about 100 percent, today, in the latter half of the 20th century, the rate of exploitation has increased to about 200 percent. For every hour the 19th century proletarian spent on creating his own subsistence, another hour went on creating the capitalist's surplus. Now for every hour the 20th century productive worker spends on creating his subsistence wage, two hours are spent on creating the capitalist's profit. Not only has the rate of exploitation doubled, but the rate of increase in the rate of exploitation has increased during the last decade.

One of the main reasons why workers are prepared to accept the arguments in favour of productivity deals and wages control is because the inequalities of wealth are either taken for granted or more often not really appreciated. The low paid worker sees the printer or docker apparently getting £35 a week. He does not ever see the man who gets £500 a week for doing nothing. Therefore it is very important to get across the meaning of inequalities in wealth with plenty of facts and figures. Under such conditions no worker should be feeling guilty about hammering the employers for every penny they can.

Under such conditions anything that raises wages at a *cost to profits* is fair to the workers; anything that raises profits at a cost to wages is unfair.

Productivity bargaining raises the question of the distribution of the product between labour and capital in an entirely new way. In traditional wage negotiations a demand for 10s is put forward without any gloss of 'mutual interest' between labour and capital: 'We want 10s, and that's that.' When the wage demand is formulated as a demand for a 3 percent rise, especially if it is demanded as a rise to accompany rising productivity, the terms of reference are different. It is then formulated as if there were a community of interests between labour and capital, a partnership between them. Hence it is now more vital than ever for socialists to expose the exploitation of labour by capital, the class antagonism that tears capitalist society asunder.

In conclusion

The struggle for the hearts and minds of workers is now more important than ever before. By raising the question of productivity, the government and employers have raised the question of the purpose of production, the question of the way the product is divided among the people, the question of who controls the means of production, distribution and exchange.

Productivity bargaining with its underlying ideology is forcing politics onto the shopfloor. Socialists should take up the challenge. Their slogan should be not production for profits, but production for use.

Chapter Eleven: The role of the trade unions

In the immediate post-war years the leaders of Britain's major unions were, almost without exception, a group of reactionary yet uninspiring 'yes men', happy to go along with whatever policy the government chose to follow— whether it was wage freeze at home or support for America abroad. Today the situation is different. In the two largest unions we have general secretaries who are themselves left wingers and opponents of the government on central issues such as Vietnam and wage freeze, Hugh Scanlon of the AEF and Jack Jones of the TGWU. These changes *are* important for workers who are fighting for better wages and conditions, but there are severe limits to the degree that such changes in leadership can alter the situation. In Scanlon's case at least the very fact of his victory over an entrenched right wing group in the AEU gives hope and encouragement to the rank and file activists who did the groundwork for his win. More important, the fact that their union is officially opposed to government policies of wage freeze greatly strengthens the hand of the militant within his own place of work.

In the past the weakest elements, the gov'ner's men, the potential scabs, could always oppose any action in the name of Carron or Deakin. Now they can be told, 'This is official policy—as the union is opposed to wage freeze we are only putting the policy into practice by fighting for higher wages.' Left union leaders make rank and file action far easier but they cannot be a substitute for it.

The union leader, left or right, is part of the professional apparatus, of the union—he comes to power largely by means of the apparatus, by cashing in on the complex system of patronage that has become part of all large unions, the TGWU probably most of all. Their whole background restricts their concept of trade union action to the official channels of negotiation. Along with the lower echelon of union officers they owe their whole position to the existence of agreed procedures. It is these loyalties that prevent left officials from giving a real lead to their members and throwing procedures overboard where they act as an impediment to progress.

TGWU members may have got a great deal of satisfaction from Cousins's orations against the wage freeze, but as far as actually getting more money they did no better than AEF members, led by the redoubtable Bill Carron. The demand for a £15 minimum wage has been kept carefully for conferences and debates. On the factory floor, where it could have provided fuel for a real fight on the issue, it has been kept well out of sight. The dustmen, who have been struggling along on a low basic wage for years, didn't find Jack Jones ready and willing to lead them into battle, but had to use their own initiative to do battle on their claim for £5 a week. Put through the procedure such a claim would never have got to the negotiating table—it would have been turned down by the officials as being 'unrealistic'!

The left union leaders are always very militant when the issue is raised in the general form but less so when the issue comes down to a conflict between *actual* workers and management. It is when workers are really up against the wall that they find out the real character of their leaders. Ask a London bus worker after the 1958 strike his opinion of Cousins and the answer was likely to be unprintable. The same goes in the docks over Jack Jones's role with Devlin.

When it comes to productivity deals the limitations of the left union leaders become very clear. Productivity deals pose the dilemma in the most acute form —either go through the procedure, and according to the rules laid down by the government this must mean 'productivity' concessions, or take direct action to win increases. Tied to procedure, union officials are also tied to productivity.

Trade union support for productivity deals

Because productivity bargaining is a soft option in wage negotiations, both right wing as well as left wing trade union leaders are inclined to accept this willingly. The right wing leaders' commitment to an incomes policy does not exclude getting extra money for his workers by selling conditions. The left wing top brass is happy to oppose the incomes policy without defending workers' conditions. The only one who suffers is the worker.

On 1 May 1967 the Central Bus Committee considered the advisability of tabling a wage claim with the London Transport Board. The official minutes of this meeting state:

> The chairman (Bill Jones—chairman of the London Busmen Negotiating Committee, vice-president of the TGWU) expounded the views of the London Transport negotiating committee...he spoke of the difficulties of making a straightforward wage application at this moment of time and he believed that the only way to overcome this problem would be to put forward a productivity scheme that would prove acceptable to London Transport and within the terms of the government's present wage policy.

The late George Moore (veteran militant, editor of the busmen's rank and file paper the *Platform*) commented on this:

> And there we have official TGWU policy revealed in all its nauseating, twofaced hypocrisy.

The TGWU will *fight to the death* against the government's policy of *wage restraint*—providing the London busmen restrict their claims *within the terms of the government's policy of wage restraint.*[1]

With the notable exception of DATA, all trade unions have shown no opposition at all to productivity deals, although of course opposition to particular strings in particular deals is quite common.

Long, long ago Les Cannon argued against productivity deals. Thus in 1955 he said, 'The idea of productivity and the means of achieving it, however beneficial they might at first seem, will have the effect of considerably speeding up the worker, without a proportionate increase in earnings.'

On work study, Les Cannon had this to say:

Work study is an instrument being used by the monopolies in the drive for maximum profit. It does not give increases in earnings proportionate to increases in productivity.[2]

Dealing with an agreement very similar to that which set up the JIB—the JIB that was blessed, if not conceived, by Les Cannon—he was no less antagonistic.

Les Cannon, speaking on behalf of the executive at the 1951 ETU policy conference at Hastings to a motion calling for 'the compulsory registration of electrical operatives and the granting of powers to the Electricity Authority to enforce a higher standard of workmanship', declared:

I think the danger here is of taking the prerogative away from our union and passing it *on to some composite body*, many of the representatives of which have attitudes towards the working class which are open to suspicion. It must also be borne in mind that the registration of electrical operatives must imply that the operatives can be deregistered, and it may well be that on the bodies who authorise all kinds of circumstances other than the skill of the operative will be taken into consideration to deregister him.

However, Les Cannon has changed radically since then.

The ETU has held conferences and courses for shop stewards involved in particular productivity agreements. The journal of the CBI reported:

A major innovation recently introduced is joint management/shop steward courses unlike any other trade union colleges.

Ford, ICI, British Rail, British European Airways, the Greater London Council and BOAC have taken part in courses analysing and dissecting pay deals.

Now some 1,000 trade unionists attend the courses given by Jock Haston and his staff. They include shop stewards, branch secretaries, and other full time officials.[3]

The General and Municipal Workers' Union and the TGWU also hold regular courses for trade union full time officials and shop stewards on productivity deals.

The AEF general secretary, Jim Conway, reported:

To deal with the many aspects of productivity bargaining, method study and time study our production department was set up, which not only advises and assists our officials in day to day negotiations but has also designed and now operates an agreement analysis service.

This is the only service of its kind in Europe. It is being used most frequently, and is highly praised by our divisional organisers and district secretaries.[4]

On another occassion Conway made the philosophy behind his enthusiasm for productivity deals abundantly clear:

We sometimes miss the loyalty of workpeople to the company who employs them, and we have got to utilise that loyalty to the company, because what is good for the company is good for the industry and, in the outcome, what is good for the industry is good for the standard of the country in which we live.

The problems we are in at the present moment in time mean that there are not two sides. There is managed and management, management and workers, but the thing that draws us together, of course, is the question of our standard of living, and this is not a very wide gap. We have got to start from the right premises, with the knowledge that we are all workers now, that we are all accountable in the eyes of the accountant…

For the life of me, I still cannot understand why we look upon profit as a dirty word. It is in our own interests, and we have got a vested interest in the profitability of a company. This is the lesson we have tried to get across and this is why we come to accept productivity bargains.[5]

The enthusiasm of the TGWU for productivity deals is practically unlimited. Thus, for instance, in the introduction of Devlin into the docks, the TGWU was more active than the employers in undermining any attempt to resist Phase I. For the first time in the history of the docks the TGWU employed what was known as 'flying squads' to travel from dock to dock to explain the more attractive parts of the scheme—ie the security of permanent employment, increased unemployment pay, and the (minimal) improvement in pensions. The TGWU did, in fact, on two occasions discipline the docks militant Terry Barrett because of his publication of some of the clauses of the scheme. Due to the following he had in the West India Dock Liaison Committee these attempts failed. At the same time the unions collaborated with the port employers in the publication of a new newspaper (the *Port*) which was used to propagate the advantages of Devlin on a grand scale.

Trapped as they are in the logic of their own position and reacting to mass pressure more than they initiate it, it is no wonder that the soft option of wage rises through productivity deals appeals to the top union officials—even the most 'left' of them. Scanlon and Jones support productivity deals everywhere. The CP-controlled ETU was central in carrying through the Fawley agreement.[6] As a general rule, full time officials are not averse to productivity deals as these are bound to increase the power of the officials vis-à-vis the shop stewards.

It is not only the top officials who are attracted to the 'soft option' of productivity bargaining. Many local officers and lay members—branch officials, stewards' representatives, etc—who are all too well aware of the deficiencies of their own organisation at grassroots level, are attracted to them as an alternative to an all-out battle for a straight wage increase against the combined forces of employers and the state. However, generally the closer the official is to the shopfloor the more responsive he will be to the pressure of his members who have so much to lose in a productivity deal.

Failure of unions to grapple with redundancy

It is particularly sad that the unions have failed to face up to the problems of redundancy, so intimately connected with productivity deals.

One of the saddest accompaniments to the threat of unemployment in declining industries is the horrible squabbles between the trade unions about who should get the sack first.

Look, for instance, at the printing industry. Print is an extreme example as regards redundancy—along with rationalisation and mergers, affecting all industries, goes tremendous technological change. This makes the redundancy problem a fundamental structural one, not just a matter of trimming.

There is no doubt that thanks to the strength of union organisation in the printing industry, especially in the large companies publishing national newspapers, resistance to cutting down the labour force managed to continue successfully for a very long time indeed. Even without changes in the methods of printing, without new equipment, it would have been possible to cut down the labour force radically without affecting output. The inquiry into the newspaper industry carried out in 1966 by the Economist Intelligence Unit gave the following potential savings (in percentages):[7]

	Process	Foundry	Machine room
Daily Telegraph	50	18.5	46.0
Daily Express	50	20.6	51.6
Daily Mail	50	13.0	50.0
Daily Mirror	50	12.0	47.5

With the swift technological changes in printing, demarcation lines between different skills have been eroded while at the same time job opportunities in the print have shrunk very much.

How did the unions face up to the challenge?

In 1963 the International Publishing Corporation declared that Odhams press at Long Acre would be closed down, and that a new factory using the web offset process would be established at Southwark to print a number of periodicals published by the corporation, and also to undertake general printing work for others. The International Publishing Corporation suggested cutting down the labour force, while a double-shift system was introduced along with other productivity measures. In return for this, it undertook to improve wages, sickness benefit, etc. In 1965 the machines were installed in the Southwark factory. Straight away an inter-union conflict broke out, a conflict between the skilled unions (NGA and ALSP) on the one hand, and the so-called unskilled union (SOGAT) on the other:

> Broadly, the ASLP and NGA took the view that the machine should be operated under the arrangements agreed nationally for sheet-fed lithographic machines, on which their members perform the more skilled, and the assistants drawn from SOGAT 1 certain of the less skilled, duties. SOGAT 1, on the other hand, took the view that web-fed lithographic printing was a completely new process and that arrangements for sheet-fed lithographic machines were irrelevant.[8]

The management had to admit:

> That experience had shown that a man with knowledge of the industry could be trained in about six months to perform adequately the skills called for to operate the presses at Southwark Offset to the standard required for the production of periodicals. It also asserted that it would be possible to train somebody entirely new to the industry to the same level of ability, within the same period.
>
> The company emphasised, however, that such a person would be competent to handle only the particular kind of work carried out at Southwark Offset on the machines installed there. It did not claim that a man capable of producing work of higher quality, still less a fully qualified lithographic printer, could be trained in so short a time.[9]

SOGAT 1 had put forward the proposal that web offset presses should be operated on a basis of integrated manning under which each operator on the press, regardless of the union to which he belonged, would carry out the full range of duties on one unit. SOGAT 1 believed that the traditional division of responsibility on presses between its members and those of the craft unions was artificial, and that it was particularly undesirable, in view of the technical and operating requirements of these machines, that this division of responsibility should be applied in manning web offset presses:

> SOGAT 1 stated that it could no longer tolerate the traditional situation in which its members were unable to advance to the most responsible positions on presses, no matter how great their experience might be, because these were held by members of the craft unions. It did not believe it to be right that the demarcation of duties between unions should prevent a man filling the highest positions on a press commensurate with his ability. SOGAT 1 accepted that there were a variety of facilities available for the upgrading of machine assistants by adult apprenticeship to the status of craftsmen, but it asserted that these were not substantial enough. It also alleged that in London its members were prevented by the NGA from benefiting from the facilities it provided for adult apprenticeship.[10]

However, the NGA and ASLP did not agree, and so, after a very sharp conflict between the unions, a government court of inquiry was established.

Another more recent case revealed the blindness of union leaders in the face of the threat of redundancy. All those who worked in Manchester printing the *Sun* newspaper, 200 NGA men, were sacked. In London 300 NGA members were affected. Rupert Murdoch now prints the *Sun* on the machines which print the *News of the World*. At present these machines are manned 100 percent by SOGAT members, while the *Sun* was formerly printed by members of SOGAT and the NGA. SOGAT suggested that about 24 NGA members from the *Sun* should be transferred to the *News of the World* machine room, but when they leave or retire they should be replaced by SOGAT members. They would keep their NGA cards but their union would make a token payment of 6d a man to SOGAT. As against this, the NGA wants to establish that any jobs which fall vacant later in the *News of the World* machine room should be filled by any NGA members still unemployed as a result of the *Sun* changes. What a tragic farce.[11]

While unemployment is growing among printers, the unions signed agreements that really threaten to cut job opportunities very seriously. The Thomson Night Publishing Chapel, Manchester, signed an agreement in October 1968 that cuts manning as follows:

Daily Mirror—a standard of 104 men instead of 107, 129 or 140 (according to the number of pages per issue).
Daily Telegraph—56 men instead of a maximum (dependent on the number of pages per issue) of 92.
Sporting Chronicle—nine men instead of ten to 23.
News of the World—Saturday, 127 instead of 154 to 182.
Sunday Mirror—Saturday, 121 instead of 148 to 168.

The record of the steel unions in the face of redundancy is even worse than that of the printing unions.

In his evidence to the Donovan commission, Sir Harry Douglass, general secretary of the Iron and Steel Trades Confederation, by far the biggest union in the steel industry, proudly claimed that his union had never fought sackings:

We have not introduced one machine in steel that has waited one day to go into operation but it has gone into operation the day it has been put in, completed. We have had to agree there is going to be a certain amount of redundancy in the steel industry... What nearly always happens to the men is that they get a worse job than the ones they have had... They have simply got to recognise the inevitability of it and the number of men who suffer reductions in wages because new machines are coming in is legion, believe you me... I can tell you of men who have been reduced from £30 a week to £12 a week overnight...

The problem I have is hundreds of men, all highly paid, who would be suddenly thrown out of work because new machines have come in, and taking on labouring jobs and in some cases no jobs at all. There has not been one machine that has not come into operation in the steel industry the minute it has been put inside. Furthermore, we have run this machine for seven days a week and for 24 hours a day, putting a lot of men out of work.[12]

Parallel to this supine attitude towards management on the issue of sacking, the same ISTC shows a really fighting spirit in protecting the jobs of its members against the competition of other unions.

At Port Talbot the ISTC is refusing, at the time of writing, to operate a new £18 million basic oxygen steel making plant until the Steel Corporation agrees that 32 middle management staff should be in the ISTC. But much less fuss is made of the fact that the new plant will mean the loss of 1,100 jobs for members of ISTC elsewhere.[13]

At the Spencer works, at Newport, where out of 450 middle management personnel 60 are members of the ISTC, the union threatened a strike if their recognition demand was not satisfied—and the union won:

> The ISTC has been told that in view of the 'special circumstances' at the Spencer works the management was prepared to negotiate a recognition agreement for its middle management members there. However, BSC spokesmen refused yesterday to divulge what these special circumstances were.[14]

At the same time the ISTC was very adamant indeed in insisting that the Steel Corporation should not grant recognition to the Clerical and Administrative Workers Union (CAWU) or the Association of Scientific, Technical and Managerial Staffs. In this move the ISTC is being supported by the AEF, TGWU, Boilermakers, ETU, GMWU, Blast Furnacemen and others. After a dispute in 1968 the CAWU reached agreement with the corporation that the union would be granted recognition where it could show that it had at least 50 percent membership in the works. This would have to be achieved by the end of January 1969.

In the three plants at Scunthorpe in Lincolnshire the CAWU claimed it had reached the required 50 percent membership in the clerical grade to qualify for recognition. But this was rejected by the management—under pressure of the other unions—which said that membership audits by chartered accountants showed that the CAWU has recruited only 47.2 percent of the people in this grade. (By the way, recognition usually follows a much lower percentage than this.) The result? A strike by CAWU members, unsupported by the other steel unions.[15]

The ambivalent nature of union officialdom

How can one explain the feebleness of union leadership in the face of the employers' and state offensive? How can one explain the fact that leaders of millions of workers did not resist the introduction of productivity deals?

The root cause lies in the contradictions dominating the position of the full time union officials.

The trade unions are organisations for the defence of workers against their employers, but the social conditions of the full time officials separate them as a caste from the workers.

More than 50 years ago in his excellent pamphlet *The Workers' Committee:*

An *Outline of its Principles and Structure,* J T Murphy, a leading industrial militant and Communist, had this to say about trade union officials: 'Everyone is aware that usually a man gets into office on the strength of revolutionary speeches, which strangely contrast with those of a later date after a period in office'.[16]

How are we to explain this change of heart?

Now compare the outlook of the man in the workshop and the man as a full time official. As a man in the workshop he feels every change: the workshop atmosphere is his atmosphere; the conditions under which he labours are primary; his trade union constitution is secondary, and sometimes even more remote. But let the same man get into office. He is removed out of the workshop, he meets a fresh class of people, and breathes a different atmosphere Those things which were once primary are now secondary. He becomes buried in the constitution, and of necessity looks from a new point of view on those things which he has ceased to feel acutely. Not that he has ceased to feel interested, not that he has become dishonest, not that he has not the interests of labour at heart, but because human nature is what it is, he feels the influence of new factors, and the result is a change of outlook.[17]

Even the most left of the top union officials is trapped by his social environment. And worse, he has to work through an official machine whose personnel are very much prisoners of this same social environment.

The official's white collar and his briefcase, together with the fact that in most cases he does not have to face election, give him quite often a feeling that he is a member not of the working class but of the middle class. As one study based on interviews with hundreds of officials stated:

We attempted to measure the feelings of trade union officials towards the social standing of the jobs by asking them to place their own jobs and the posts of the general secretaries in a list of 30 occupations according to what they thought would be 'the generally accepted view' of their social standing.

The question was answered by 79 percent of the sample, and of these 64 percent placed their general secretary's post as equivalent or superior to that of a medical officer of health or a company director, and 36 percent put it somewhere between a county solicitor and an elementary schoolteacher; 10 percent rated their own posts as equal to or above that of a civil servant (executive grade), 69 percent put themselves between a nonconformist minister and an elementary schoolteacher, and 21 percent somewhere below the schoolteacher.[18]

Most full time officers rate themselves among the holders of middle class posts (and rate their general secretaries close to the top of a scale of social standing).[19]

Not surprisingly, very few trade union officials went back to the ranks after giving up their jobs, for whatever reason:

FULL TIME OFFICERS: SUBSEQUENT POST OF RESIGNED OFFICERS[20]

Post in nationalised industry	48
Government post	25
Managerial post in private industry	14
Post in another union	11
Back to 'shopfloor'	13
Own shop or business	7
Labour Party post	4
Elected Member of Parliament	4
Post with other organisations	9
Other	9
Unknown	122
Total	266

Thus the trade union bureaucracy, rising above the rank and file membership of the unions, and feeling that it belongs to a group with a higher social status, hardly ever thinks of going back to the rank and file. To this degree it is alienated from those it supposedly represents.[21]

The alienation of top trade union officials from the actual life of the lay members is clear from the salaries they are getting. The last NUR conference, for example, raised the salary of its general secretary, Sidney Green, from £3,706 to £5,000: 'The salaries of the NUR's two assistant general secretaries, George Brassington and Sidney Weighell, go up from £2,800 to £3,700; that of Russell Tuck, senior organiser, from £2,357 to £2,800; and those of the 21 district organisers from £2,104 to £2,500.'

Jack Jones, general secretary of the TGWU, receives £3,750, and Harry Urwin, the assistant general secretary, £3,250.

> Large pay rises are being sought by leaders of the Amalgamated Union of Engineering and Foundry Workers. The increases would raise the annual salary of Hugh Scanlon, the union's president, from £2,150 to £3,500—a rise of about 62 percent.
>
> This claim was decided by the union's national executive whose seven members—apart from Mr Scanlon—would receive proportionate rises, from £1,800 to about £2,900.[22]

Lord Cooper, general secretary of the General and Municipal Workers' Union, gets an annual salary of £4,000. The ten NUGMWU district general secretaries receive £2,756 per year and the nine national industrial officers receive £2,520. NUT general secretary Sir Ronald Gould gets over £6,000. Walter Anderson, general secretary of NALGO, also gets £6,000.

It is quite interesting to note that the employers' spokesmen, who begrudge rises of shillings to the workers, not only don't complain at the good salaries union officials get, but want them raised even further. The Economist Intelligence Unit, for example, commented on the newspaper industry:

> The trade union official should be generally equal to the managers with whom he negotiates in ability, training, status and salary. It is not unreasonable to equate the responsibilities of the general secretary of a major union with those of the managing director of a large industrial concern...
>
> The general members must be made to realise that if they want high quality representation they must be prepared to pay for it and not rely only, or mainly, on the dedication of the officials concerned.[23]

Decline of the union branch

An added factor contributing to the alienation of the officials from the rank and file membership is the fact that the trade union branch, once the cell that connected the rank and file to the union machine, has radically declined in importance over the past few decades. This decline of the union branches has been brought about by a whole number of irreversible forces. Firstly, as a great deal of collective bargaining has become more centralised, the local union branch has come to have little or nothing to do with the fixing of wages and general conditions. Secondly, the detailed working out of the way in which general national agreements are to be applied is being done more and more in particular establishments by shop stewards and works committees rather than by the branch. The only exceptions are those few places, outside the mining and steel industries, where the works and the branch do coincide. Thirdly, the function of the branch as a friendly society has largely disappeared as the state has come to play a more important role with regard to health, insurance, and so on. Fourthly, the union branch used to be a social centre for talk and drink, but here too there has been a decline as more and more workers have come to work far away from home.

As the branch has declined, so organisations built on the basis of the branches like district committees and trades councils have declined too. In many big unions individual branches no longer send delegates to national union conferences or district committees, but are grouped together for the purpose of selecting a delegate. This weakens the branch, and the delegate representing several branches necessarily has less direct contact with those he is supposed to represent.

The union branch is the basic unit on which the higher levels of the trade union administration rise. The weakening of the branch is a further element—both as cause and as result—in the increasing centralisation of the unions, their bureaucratisation. If the decline of the branch is the result of the centralisation of capital and the centralisation of collective bargaining on a national level, this decline of the branch also accentuates the tendency towards centralisation. A study of Luton workers showed that only 7 percent attended branch meetings regularly. Excluding skilled workers, the proportion was only 2 percent. Only 26 percent of the sample regularly voted in branch elections. This contrasts sharply with the participation in shopfloor affairs—83 percent voted regularly in shop steward elections.[24] Much earlier one writer dealing with the TGWU came to the conclusion that 'the shop steward is for most rank and file members their first and only contact with the union. To them the shop steward rather than the branch is the union'.[25] Similarly a study of workers in the car industry also suggests that 'the shop stewards organisation has become the real union'.[26] Lack of power and function for the branches breeds apathy among the membership at branch level, and apathy is the reverse of the coin of centralisation.

Check-off agreements and the closed shop

Faced with withering union branches, the leadership has in recent years resorted more and more to check-off agreements.

This is the practice whereby employers deduct trade union dues from the wages of members in their employment and pay them over to the unions. In 1968 a study of this problem stated:

> It is estimated that about 21 percent of the members of these unions were covered by the check-off—ie roughly $1^{3}/_{4}$ million workers. On the basis of their survey the authors estimate that the check-off probably affects at least 2 million trade unionists—ie about one union member in five.[27]

It covered the seafarers, miners, rail workers, National Health Service workers and workers in electricity supply, and about 1,200 private firms:

> Among trade unions the check-off has made a good many converts in the past few years. Among these are the Transport and General Workers, the General and Municipal Workers, the National Union of Dyers, Bleachers and Textile Workers, the United Rubber Workers of Great Britain, the Clerical and Administrative Workers' Union, the National Union of Public Employees, the National Union of Lock and Metal Workers, and the Electrical Trades Union, as well as those trade unions concerned with railways and the Treasury's offer to civil service staff associations of 1965.[28]

The check-off system is very detrimental to members' participation in union affairs. Thus an American study found out that 'the dues check-off system is negatively related to participation. Higher attendance ratios are found in locals that collect dues through stewards in the plant or at meetings'.[29]

The check-off system has tended to make relations between union members and the union officials even more tenuous than before. The closed shop has in recent years been clearly associated with this system. For generations militants in industry fought for '100 percent trade unionism'. In the recent past it has been modern management that has inscribed the closed shop on its banner. It is true that there are still many antidiluvian managements who resist trade unionism (Kodak, Roberts Arundel and BSR have been the most infamous in most recent times). But on the whole management has changed its view on this issue. Modern management sees in the closed shop a way for employers and union officials to work hand in glove to discipline the rank and file. For instance, Mark

Young, national officer of the EPTU, writes, 'We have suggested to management of the Standard Telephone Company that it is in their interests as well as our own that there should be a high level of union organisation'.[30]

In the electricity supply industry an agreement on 100 percent trade union membership was reached on 19 July 1969. Mr Bob Roberts, chairman of the management side of the National Joint Industrial Council, said that the purpose of the agreement was to lessen disruptive elements and stabilise good industrial relations:

> It will become increasingly difficult for unofficial bodies like the breakaway Electricity Supply Union—which is a registered union but in no way recognised —to survive. It will also be harder for militants to defy officially negotiated agreements, because they will risk losing their jobs if they are expelled from their union.
>
> This particularly applies to militant electricians, because the EPTU takes a tough line against unofficial activity.[31]

The four unions that signed the Electricity Supply Agreement are the EPTU, the General and Municipal Workers, the AEF and the TGWU.

A similar agreement was reached on the railways by management on the one hand and the NUR and the TSSA on the other. These two unions cover the overwhelming majority of railwaymen. Talks are going on with the Associated Society of Locomotive Engineers and Firemen (ASLEF) and the unions affiliated to the Confederation of Shipbuilding and Engineering Unions which represent nearly half the manual employees in the railway workshops. But no doubt these unions will want compulsory membership also. The *Times*, certainly no socialist newspaper, explained why British Rail loves the idea of the closed shop:

> The closed shop principle greatly strengthens the union... If all the unions concerned in the railway negotiating machinery agree, they will be in a position to threaten recalcitrant members with expulsion not only from their union but also from their jobs. Signalmen or drivers who disrupted train services by sudden unofficial strikes could thus be quickly brought to heel.[32]

The check-off system on the railways produces the incredible situation that the LDC representative (railway shop steward) does not know who the paid-up union members are, but the station master does! As one militant rail worker from Manchester remarked, 'This is the kind of closed shop we don't want'.[33]

Lack of real democracy in the unions

That many unions are extremely undemocratic is well known. The ETU, for instance, clearly demonstrates this.

A few months ago Les Cannon, president of the Electrical and Plumbing Trades Union, ended the election of full time officials: 'As from 22 September

1969 all full time officials shall be appointed by the executive council from the members of the union.'

Then the final appeal committee that had hitherto been composed of 16 rank and file members was to be revised. Instead:

> The executive council shall appoint five of its members to constitute the disciplinary committee. The general president and general secretary shall not be members of the disciplinary committee... The remaining members of the executive council shall constitute the appeals committee.

Thus the executive wish to act as prosecutor, judge and jury.

Thirdly, the rule allowing for the election of rank and file trustees was cancelled. Instead:

> The property and funds of the unions shall rest in a sole corporate trustee... Such trustee shall be appointed by the executive council.[34]

These measures prepared the ground for the merger of the ETU-PTU with the NUGMW. In the latter, bureaucratic control is complete. As far as the nomination and election to national office are concerned the rules provide that 'only candidates who have satisfied the national executive committee as to their fitness and qualifications shall be submitted to election'. All appeals go to the general council...but the general council may well have been the original disciplinary body (and under Rule 43 it may well refuse to state any reason for its action).[35]

The extreme authoritarianism in the ETU can hardly be better illustrated than by an incident in August 1968 when union members demonstrating at union headquarters wore masks to cover their faces for fear of victimisation.

The set-up in the Iron and Steel Trades Confederation is hardly better. It is a quite common occurrence for the Iron and Steel Trades Confederation to suspend and even expel local branch officers. On 8 July 1969 14 branch officials and official work representatives at the Corby steel works were suspended by the executive for leading an unofficial strike.

Things are different in the TGWU and AEF, not to speak of DATA and a number of other unions. (Of course, there are also big differences in the behaviour of different officials of one and the same union. In the TGWU, Moss Evans is not Kealey. In the AEF, Reg Birch is certainly not John Boyd.)

However, even in unions like the TGWU, things are far from satisfactory in respect of democracy.

The bureaucratic set-up in the TGWU was exposed clearly by Tony Corfield (national secretary—political, educational, and international) in a pamphlet he published on the eve of the last election for general secretary of the union (1968). Corfield wrote:

> In my submission the power vested in the man who becomes general secretary in this union has increased, is increasing and ought to be diminished.[36]

The more all the important decisions tend to be concentrated in the hands of one man, the less the various governing bodies can feel genuine responsibility for the proposals they suggest. Instead of exercising their own initiative, they are likely to have to wait to be told what to do.[37]

The present set-up:

...tends to insulate the general secretary, however well intentioned he might be, from the feelings of his members. Because he is there for life, he has less need to take a close day to day account of the wishes and needs of the rank and file.[38]

Corfield's conclusion was forthright:

In the forthcoming election for general secretary of the Transport and General Workers' Union the members now have the right to make a decision on this critically important issue. They may vote for a candidate for the position of general secretary who aspires to take the job for life. Alternatively, they may decide to support the man who stands for collective leadership. If elected, this man would use the mandate to call for a rules revision conference to make the office of general secretary tenable for a period of four years, each incumbent holding the office once only.[39]

No wonder Corfield was removed from his union post. How dare he suggest that the term of office of the general secretary should be only four years instead of a life term?

(Of course, for good reasons Corfield's intervention was resented by militant members of the TGWU. They objected, quite rightly, to a full time officer using his authority to intervene in union elections, especially as the man Corfield supported—Larry Smith—is not a great shake of a militant.)

The extent to which many officials in the unions are completely free of control from the members is clear from the fact that only a very small number of them have been removed by standing for re-election. Over a period of some three decades only 3 percent of them suffered this unhappy fate.[40]

Increasing collaboration with the state

While quite alienated from the rank and file, the caste of union officials finds itself more and more closely associated with the state. This association has a long history. In 1931-32 there was only one government committee on which the General Council of the TUC was represented according to the TUC directory of committees. By 1934-35 the directory listed six such committees,[41] and the number has been increasing steadily ever since. The Second World War in particular saw a change in the relationship between the unions and the state:

No established right of access to the government was conceded to unions...until the Second World War... The long duration of the war and the much longer duration of post-war economic problems encouraged its establishment. Indeed, communications often moved in the opposite direction. Frequently it was the prime minister or one of his ministers who wanted to meet the trade union leaders.[42]

After the Tories came to power in 1951 the union leaders showed no desire to diminish their rights of access to the government or their policy of collaboration with it. Thus the General Council of the TUC stated:

> It is our longstanding practice to seek to work amicably with whatever government is in power and through consultation with ministers and with the other side of industry to find practical solutions to the social and economic problems facing this country. There need be no doubt, therefore, of the attitude of the TUC towards the new government.[43]

Often, indeed, the policies of the union leaders expressed this relationship very well. Often their views were considerably closer to those of the Tory government than they were to those of many of the union rank and file, as a far from unfriendly commentator noted:

> The TUC leaders, led by Deakin of the Transport and General, Tom Williamson of the General and Municipal, and Will Lawther of the Mineworkers, saw to it that the cautious and moderate policy which they had pursued under the Labour government was maintained under the Conservatives. Among other things, they ensured that resolutions denouncing all forms of wage restraint—such as were regularly submitted to Congress by the Communist-dominated unions—were voted down by adequate majorities.[44]

Despite the fact that the Conservative government had no 'emotional bonds' with the unions, the number of governmental committees on which the unions were represented rose from 60 in 1949 to 81 in 1954, and these covered a wide range of subjects. The most prominent of these committees have been the two general advisory committees, the National Joint Advisory Council to the Minister of Labour and the National Production Advisory Council on Industry.[45]

Whatever the colour of the government, the trade unions have direct access to government departments. In 1946 Arthur Deakin could say, 'We have an open door in relation to all state departments and are thus able to get our difficulties examined in such a way as would not have been possible with any other party in government'.[46]

But the situation did not change once the Tories came to power:

> The Conservatives preserved the system almost intact after 1951, although there was not the same familiarity of contacts with Conservative ministers as under the Labour government. While the TUC might not convince the government on any major economic issues, there was less difference on the everyday technical level. But the unions' views were heard. 'If I want to talk to the minister,' said a leading trade unionist in 1957, 'I just pick up that telephone'.[47]

The convergence of union leaders and the state was impelled further by Labour coming to power in 1964. The tie-up of union leaders and the state has been strengthened by the ideological commitment of these leaders to the parliamentary system and to Labour Party politics. As one writer put it:

> Union leaders not only reject industrial action for political ends, but show their enthusiasm for the system by involving themselves in parliamentary politics in

opposition and as members of governments without reservation. They enjoy the trappings of political power, the traditions and ceremonies and the social distinctions which participation confers on them. Their involvement stems from the pressures of political conformity but it reacts as a consolidating influence.[48]

The shackles of procedure

One of the worst features of trade union leaderships is their attachment to 'procedure', in other words to formal agreements negotiated with the employers. Procedure dictates that when workers are in dispute with employers they should use all the constitutional rungs before they declare a strike.

Procedure is usually an extremely tortuous process, involving a number of stages: negotiation between local union officials and management; then negotiation between more senior union representatives and the district employers' association; and finally negotiations between national union officials and national employers' associations. In industries with joint industrial councils the final stage of negotiation may be at the council itself or else a committee of the council.

In engineering the process of procedure takes, on average, about three months. Quite often, if no agreement has been reached at the end of all the stages of negotiation, the entire process is begun all over again.

Not only is the process very slow indeed, but the number of cases that are resolved is tiny.[49]

One of the worst features of procedure is that it is very discriminatory. Workers are not allowed to bring about a change in wages or conditions until procedure has been exhausted, but employers are free to introduce changes in conditions, in speed-up, piece-rates, etc, and only after the change has been made can workers take them through procedure. Workers are not allowed to withdraw their labour until they have gone right through procedure—employers are free to sack workers without going through procedure first.

For nearly 50 years the union leaders stuck to the York memorandum! Now practically everybody—Donovan, Barbara Castle, Hugh Scanlon, Jack Jones and probably even Les Cannon—accepts that the York memorandum is obsolete and unfair. Under pressure the procedure will quite possibly be changed fairly soon.

Scanlon and company will then insist that workers observe procedure, many workers will accept their arguments, and it will be far easier to discipline those who don't. It's essential to remember that *all* procedures which restrict the right to strike are 'unfair' and objectionable—any new procedure in engineering will be 'better' only in detail, not in principle.[50]

Full time officials' urge to control shop stewards

Employers and many top trade union officials have a common complaint—that workers breach procedure. Thus in his evidence to the Donovan commission Harry Nicholas, then acting general secretary of the TGWU, said, 'If a group of our members strike because they have not got the employers' agreement on a modification of a particular bonus scheme or something of that order, then we require them to go through the procedure.'

However, often the workers get their demands after breaking procedure, and this is wrong:

> Having said that, we know of cases where employers have given way. One of the arguments I have long used against employers, and I blame them for this, is there are certain trade unions who have the label militant applied to them who in the past have taken this sort of action and have secured adjustments because of it, and we have had to say to the employers, why do you do this, because those of us who wish to implement the procedure find ourselves at a tremendous disadvantace when you do it? Why do you not say to these people, 'Go through the procedure and we will deal with it'? Do not necessarily give way if you think your case is strong enough. Let us test it through the procedure. We have always tried to take that stand but it is exceedingly difficult at times.[51]

A similar whine came from Lord Carron in his evidence for the AEU to the Donovan commission.

> What I do grumble at is if, in the first place, these representations are made and they are rejected by the employers and they go to the further stage in our procedure, and at the finality of that procedure or somewhere in between the suggestion of a threat or some other circumstance happens, and the employers then concede what they refused to us all the way through the procedure, conceding it at the final pressure point—then this is making nonsense of the procedure. This, I might say, does a considerable amount towards removing the control from where it should be and demonstrating that the best way to concede anything is to make an application, turn the heat on, and it will have success, but that if you go through the procedure then nothing will ensue.
>
> What you are saying, I gather, is that the employers themselves have not observed the procedure, or halfway through it they have conceded under threat what they would not concede for reason. Exactly, and this has been done for many reasons.[52]

Similarly, the ETU in its written evidence to the Donovan commission stated, 'Management could help by ceasing to concede more to those who take unofficial action than they concede to those who carry out the procedure laid down'.[53]

The same tune was sung by Vic Feather:

> There should be an element of reality on the part of the employers, and try to negotiate nationally on a rate of 10s when they know in fact that they are going to walk out of the boardroom and pay 1s, 2s, 3s above the rate—which is the real rate they have to pay...
>
> Mr Lowthian: Without any bargaining, they pay this.
>
> Mr Feather: It is referred to as wage drift, and this is wrong.[54]

To reciprocate, many an employer expressed sympathy with the plight of the union full time official who faces rebellious shop stewards. Lord Rootes had this to say:

> We would like to make it clear that in our view there is considerable identity of interest between employers in industry and responsible trade unionism, and we prefer to see all improvement brought about by means of strengthening the position of the trade unions and enabling them to control their members more effectively than hitherto, so that agreements which are freely entered into on both sides are honoured.[55]

And John Davies, director-general of the CBI, had this to say:

> We believe that trade unions genuinely do not want this unconstitutional, irresponsible behaviour by their members in breaking agreements which the union has gone into. We all know many prominent trade union figures who, in the past and today, have expressed themselves in most forthright terms on this subject— you would think perhaps their greatest enemies were not employers but those of their rebel members who were bringing the unions into disrepute.[56]

In the same vein, when Lord Cameron dealt with the long drawn-out dispute at the Barbican and Horseferry Road building sites, he recommended '(i) more effective union control over works committees, and (ii) closer and more effective contact between unions and stewards'.[57]

To strengthen trade union control over shop stewards Lord Cameron recommended that the unions impose penalties on unruly stewards:

> The range of penalty must necessarily be sufficiently wide to cover a variety of failures or breaches of varying degrees of gravity so that it would be appropriate that the penalty should vary from reprimand, suspension from office or disqualification from future office, to monetary fine or even in appropriate cases the extreme penalty of expulsion—subject in all cases to such right of appeal as the union procedure permits. We would also *recommend*, however, that in case of appeal against suspension or disqualification the sentence should be effective unless or until withdrawn or modified by successful appeal.[58]

Particular animosity has been shown by union officials towards any industry-wide link-up between shop stewards. Thus in 1960 the General Council of the TUC, referring to 'organisations linking a number of joint committees, either from several factories under the same ownership (eg BMC) or throughout an industry (eg electricity generating)', stated that their 'effect is often a challenge to established union arrangements'.[59] As for 'attempts to form a national centre or to call national conferences of stewards irrespective of the industry in which they work (eg the abortive conference in December 1959 convened in the name of the Firth Brown stewards, or the organisation which goes under the name of the Engineering and Allied Trades Shop Stewards National Council)', the TUC officiously warned:

> The aim of the sponsors of this...type is to usurp the policy-making functions of unions or federations of unions. Unions are advised to inform their members that participation in such bodies is contrary to the obligations of membership.[60]

And if this warning was not enough, the TUC went on, 'Unions should be more vigilant, and if, after a warning, a steward repeats actions which are contrary to the rules or agreements, his credentials should be withdrawn'.[61]

In 1959 the shop stewards committees at Firth Brown (Sheffield) and Ford (Dagenham) jointly called a National Shop Stewards Conference. The Communist stewards play a leading role in both factories. The executive of the AEU banned the conference. Bro Caborn, the convenor at Firth Brown, was suspended from holding office for one year.

The Power Workers' Combine was formed some time ago to fight for improved conditions in the power industry. As usual, the reaction of the full time officials was rapid and hostile. The unions (ETU included) declared that following the last settlement the Power Workers' Combine was no longer necessary. On 14 November 1960 Frank Foulkes, president of the ETU and chairman of the Electricity Supply Industry National Joint Council, declared, 'Unofficial bodies are not in the best interests of the industry.' George Wake, secretary of the combine, was then disciplined by the AEU.[62] (Both Foulkes and Wake were members of the Communist Party!)

Similarly, the TGWU condemned the London Building Workers' Joint Sites Committee. It:

...deprecated the activities of the Joint Sites Committee, feeling that it had not a proper role to fulfil. The unofficial activities that had taken place had done only harm to the trade union movement, weakening the authority of national executives and officials.[63]

So also did the AUBTW: 'The union deprecated the activities of the Joint Sites Committee and on proper evidence were prepared to discipline any members participating in unofficial activities of that kind'.[64]

Impotence of trade union leadership

Vacillating between the contradictory forces of workers on the one hand and employers and state on the other, the union leaderships on the whole prove themselves quite impotent. The TUC undoubtedly seeks to be 'reasonable' in its dealings with civil servants and ministers but the power of its voice is remarkably small, for all the reasonableness and sweetness of its tones:

The growing frustration experienced by the council can be seen from a study of the reports which its specialist committees make to Congress. Here one can read of the failure of the economic committee to influence budgetary policy; the production committee records its criticisms of government plans for high unemployment areas; and the education committee reports its unsuccessful attempts to secure the implementation of the Crowther report. But the decline in influence can be seen at its most tragic in the field of social insurance and industrial welfare, topics of great concern to the unions, where the General Council's past achievements have been considerable.[65]

Thus the TUC has failed to get the number of factory inspectors increased to a satisfactory level (in spite of a continuing high rate of industrial accidents), has failed to get concessions for the industrially injured, has failed to get compensation benefits standardised for those injured before 1948, etc. Many of these failures are nothing short of pathetic:

> Labour's National Health Act gave the minister power to provide appliances for the disabled. Consequently motor-tricycles were provided for those whose disability involved a loss of both legs. During the last few years specially adapted small cars have been designed for the use of the disabled, and they have been supplied, under the National Health Service, to the war disabled. Yet successive Tory ministers have refused to extend this provision to the industrially disabled. The TUC has pointed out that tricycles are less reliable than cars, and in cases of breakdown disabled men have been stranded for long periods... Despite the injustice and hardship caused...and the trifling cost involved, the representations of the TUC have had no effect.

At the 1963 Congress, George Woodcock claimed proudly that the TUC had moved from Trafalgar Square to the committee rooms. The abject failure to gain any real influence in those committee rooms is only too clear. Organised force could have won cars for the industrially disabled in five minutes. There can be no doubt of the generous and sympathetic reaction that a call for industrial support for this claim would have produced from many groups of workers. But the TUC has long been cut off from the working class, and such a call to action today would be unthinkable.

The impotence of the trade union leaders was summed up by Hugh Scanlon when he declared that shop stewards could get more money from local management in half an hour than the employers would give after 12 months of national negotiations.[66]

The cavalier treatment of union leaders by the Wilson government was another indication of their real powerlessness. Even the glorious 'surrender' of Wilson on the penal clauses occurred only after rank and file mobilisation and mass strikes on 27 February and 1 May 1969 and the February-March 1969 Ford strike.

Acting for the workers

Central to the position of the top union full time official is the feeling that to do his best he has to act *for* the workers, instead of them acting for themselves. Moss Evans, the TGWU representative on Ford's NJNC, gave a brilliant exposition—full of statistics and very cutting logic—of the case for wage parity with the Midlands. However, Evans did not find it necessary to issue leaflets, regularly, explaining the problems to the Ford workers, or hold mass meetings, etc. Acting *for* the workers at best is the characteristic of many a left top union leader.

This explains the sad (really it is tragic) position of people like Lawrence Daly. He was elected general secretary of the National Union of Mineworkers on a militant programme of guerrilla strikes, but now he did not come out in support of the biggest miners' strike since 1926, in October 1969.[67]

The left leaders quite honestly believe that they do their best for their members, the majority of whom are apathetic and backward. Hugh Scanlon, for instance, could in all honesty argue that he can't possibly pose a confrontation with employers and the government when only a small minority of his members are prepared to back a genuinely militant line, and when he can't even count on a majority for such a policy in the national committee. He therefore has to compromise, and if, for example, endorsing the TUC 'Programme for Action' is the only way to stop a far more damaging attack by the government, it is a price worth paying.

The answer to this of course is, granted that a union leader can't be expected to march ten miles ahead of his membership, what is Scanlon actually doing to use his influence as president to enlarge the consciousness, the aspirations, the capacity for self-activity of his members? What is he doing to weaken their stultifying dependence on the union hierarchy to substitute itself for their own activity? In fact, his support for productivity deals, his willingness to adhere to a reformed procedure, his acceptance of stronger union disciplinary powers, all tend in the reverse direction.

It is necessary for militants to both recognise and expose this inconsistency in his position, *and* to work to enlarge rank and file consciousness and militancy, so as to remove any possible excuse for right wing policies.

Of course, there are real differences between the attitudes of right and left union leaders. However, the role of the union leaders as such sets rigid limits to their field of action. Left leaders are subject to the same pressures as the others, to cooperate with management and the government. They have to sign agreements, and the terms obtained reflect the level of militancy and consciousness of the membership as a whole, not the most advanced sections. Once agreements have been signed, they feel obliged to stand by them, refuse to support 'unconstitutional' strikes and even discipline militants. Whatever their personal feelings, the position of left leaders is bound to set them at times in opposition to militants. Again the desire to 'influence' governments and industrialists leads left leaders, just as much as right, to take a 'moderate' stand and reject militant strategies.

The vacillation of the left union leaders is plain for all to see. On the one hand, we find Jack Jones, as a district secretary of the TGWU in Coventry, militantly organising engineering workers, and later making the Ford strike official. On the other hand, we find the same Jack Jones doing his utmost to break the last three Liverpool dock strikes and the September 1967 national dock strike against Devlin.

Then take Hugh Scanlon. He made the Ford strike official. But at the same time he overruled the Paisley district committee of the AEF in its opposition to the productivity agreement at Linwood (in 1968) that led to a very long and bitter strike. He (as well as Jones) supported the TUC taking disciplinary measures against unofficial strikes.

Top left wing union officials, having come to their position of power through the apparatus and continuing to be dependent on it, cannot avoid continuing to work within the limits imposed by it. They are ready to use it to commandeer the workers in the struggle for reforms, but they are averse to self-activity and independence of the rank and file. In the final analysis, the full time union officials are like the proverbial wheelbarrow—they move only as far as they are pushed. They are a rusty wheelbarrow at that.

The basic programme of rank and file independence must be the same as that of the shop stewards in the First World War: 'We will support the officials just so long as they rightly represent the workers, but we will act independently immediately they misrepresent them.'

American model

Productivity bargaining suits union leaders—both right and left—as a soft option. It makes wage rises possible, at least for a time, without resorting to 'irresponsible' militancy.

By transferring negotiations to the hands of full time union officials, productivity deals also fit the urge of the officials to control the shop stewards.

In the final analysis the perfect mould for productivity bargaining is American unionism.

The bureaucratisation of trade unions in general has gone much further in the United States than in Britain. It was found that 28 percent of all delegates to the United Auto Workers' Convention were full time officials.[68] In general, the number of full time officials is much greater in the United States than in this country. In the US there are 60,000 full time union officials, or one for every 300 members.[69] In Britain the number of full time union officials is about 3,000, or one official for 3,800 members.[70]

The pacifying, disciplinary role of the American unions was described thus:

It is difficult for a manager, faced with an aggressive group of union leaders across a bargaining table, to realise that the trade union performs a vital function *for him*. All he can think of is that, because of the union, he has lost some of his power. And to a great extent this is true—he cannot fire a man at whim, promotions are on the basis of seniority, a foreman cannot make job transfers, these are performed by the union. But in taking over these powers the union also takes over the difficult function of specifying priorities of demands, and in so doing, it not only relieves management of many political headaches, but becomes a buffer between management and rank and file resentments.

In the evolution of the labour contract, the union becomes part of the 'control system of management'. He becomes, as C Wright Mills has put it, a 'manager of discontent'.

The union often takes over the task of disciplining the men when management cannot. This is particularly true during 'wildcat strikes', when the men refuse to acknowledge the authority of management but are forced back to work by the union leaders who, by the logic of a bargain, have to enforce a contract.[71]

In the United States the shop steward has been so well integrated into the official union machine that he is—in the words of a UAW leader—the 'policeman on the beat'.[72] This does not mean, of course, a complete identification of union and management.

In effect then, the logic of market unionism leads to a limited, uneasy partnership of union and company, or union and industry, uneasy because in many cases employers would still prefer to exercise sole power, although the more sophisticated employers know the value of such powerful allies as the unions in safeguarding their interests—uneasy, too, because there is an historic tendency of labour, acting as a social movement, to oppose the employers as a class.[73]

In conclusion, workers' struggles against productivity deals will not be helped by trade union officialdom. Hence the fight for workers' control over the unions will become a central, vital part of the struggle against productivity bargaining, and all the associated weapons in the armoury of the bosses and the state.

Chapter Twelve: Rank and file response
Strikes

The response from below to the employers' offensive, aided and abetted by the state and not faced up to by their leadership, will be increasing militancy of the rank and file, who will try to push the unions ahead and often bypass the official union machine. This is taking place—and will increasingly do so—against the background of decades of strong shopfloor organisation, expressing themselves in outbursts of unofficial strikes.

Outside the declining industries (coal mining and textiles) and to some extent the docks there has been an uninterrupted growth of strike movements over the past three decades, as the following table shows:

MAN-DAYS LOST IN SEVEN MAJOR INDUSTRIES[1]

	Annual average number of man-days lost through disputes (thousands)				Average number of man-days lost yearly in disputes per thousand insured persons			
	1930-38	1947-55	1956-64	1965-68	1930-38	1947-55	1956-64	1965-68
Docks	39.8	344.4	169.1	238.7	285	3,134	1,091	2,325
Shipbuilding and ship repairing	54.2	194.2	514.6	176.2	328	890	2,349	869
Coal mining	1,002.6	616.1	444.0	173.7	1,034	778	627	298
Engineering and vehicles	88.0	441.7	1,290.3	1,206.7	80	162	411	402
Construction	71.6	87.9	172.0	203.0	60	69	110	130
Textiles	1,504.0	21.0	27.1	33.7	1,311	22	30	41
Food, drink and tobacco	5.4	12.0	22.4	29.7	10	15	27	35

As one expert, Professor Turner, has noted:

If one takes...that five-year period up to 1961, one finds that the number of *workers* reported to have been involved in strikes is comparable with that in the five years of unrest up to and including 1926—the year of the General Strike itself—and that the number of separate *strikes* reported is very much higher than for any comparable period since figures first began to be systematically collected in the 1890s.[2]

And furthermore:

For ten years up to 1956 the reported annual number of stoppages fluctuated around 500 (which was also pretty similar to the rate for the immediate pre-war years). In 1956 itself it was 570, but the number then rose: in 1957 to 640; in 1958 to 670; in 1959 to 780; in 1960 to 1,180; and in 1961 to 1,220.[3]

Continuing the figures from the point at which Turner left off, we find: in 1962, 1,244; in 1963, 1,082; in 1964, 1,456; in 1965, 1,496; in 1966, 1,937; in 1967, 2,116; and in 1968, 2,350.[4] In other words, between 1956 and 1968 the number of strikes recorded by the Ministry of Labour nearly quadrupled. Actually many strikes escaped the net of official statistics. Firstly, go-slows, overtime bans and cases of working to rule are not recorded in official statistics. Secondly, the number of actual strikes which have not been reported to the Ministry of Labour and thus have escaped being tabulated is very large, especially nowadays when strikes tend to be shorter in duration.

Especially impressive was the rise of the strike movement in the motor industry, as illustrated clearly in the two graphs on the next page.[5]

The overwhelming majority of strikes are unofficial—as many as 95 percent.[6]

Of all the strikes in the car industry in 1967, only 1 percent were made official through the endorsement of the union concerned.[7] 'Since 1926 there has been no nationwide strike sanctioned by the National Union of Mineworkers, and since 1939 every single dispute has been unofficial, unsupported by the National Union of Mineworkers'.[8]

There has been only one official strike involving NUR members in the railway industry since the 1926 General Strike, and that was on 3 October 1962 when a one-day strike was called.[9]

Why the hue and cry about strikes?

The employers and their organisations, the Tory leaders and the right wing Labour leaders, and above all the capitalist press, have for years tried to put the blame for all the country's woes onto workers going on strike, and especially on unofficial strike. To reject this nonsense it is enough to remember that in Britain nearly four times more days are lost through unemployment and seven times more days are lost through sickness and injury, as the following figures demonstrate:

Strikes—4,700,000 days lost in 1968.
Unemployment—146,000,000 days lost in 1968.
Sickness, injuries and prescribed diseases—324,000,000 days lost in 1967.

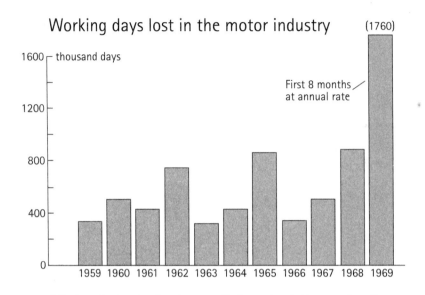

Working days lost in the motor industry

(1760)

1600 ┌ thousand days

First 8 months
at annual rate

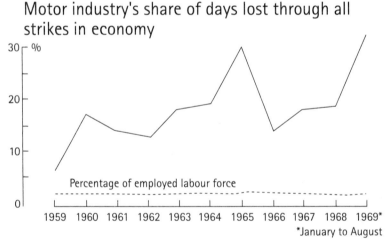

Motor industry's share of days lost through all strikes in economy

Percentage of employed labour force

1959 1960 1961 1962 1963 1964 1965 1966 1967 1968 1969*

*January to August

To place strikes in true perspective one need but look at the graph on the next page.[10]

The lower, broken line shows the number of working days lost through strikes each year since 1948. The line at the top shows the far heavier wastage that can be ascribed to industrial accidents. If the figure for the number of working days lost through illness were to be plotted on the same graph on the same scale, the resulting line would lie some 18 inches above the top of the page.

The middle line is the index of industrial production on a 1958 = 100 base. And the *Financial Times* drew the conclusion from the graph:

There is quite clearly no relationship at all between this index and the loss of working days through strikes.

To put it in yet another way, if one eighth of the working population has been forced to take two days off as a result of the Mao flu epidemic this Christmas, then the little germs will have done more damage, in terms of working days lost, than all the strikes of 1969.

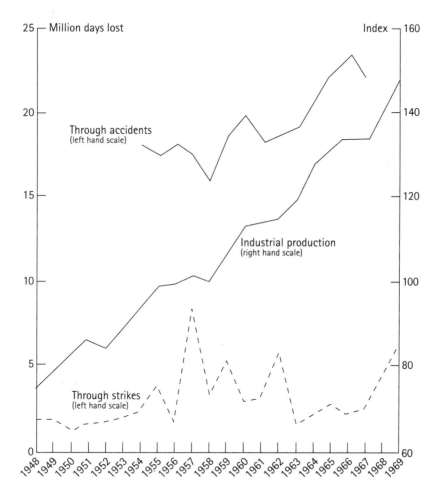

The truth is the employers and their spokesmen are not bothered so much by the effect of strikes on production as their effect on profits and on the bosses' prerogative to manage. No doubt the CBI showed a good class instinct when in its evidence to the Donovan commission it stated:

> Some of the evidence showed that their effect [the strikes] on production, although serious, is not as serious as all that. Why then, are we so bothered? It is not primarily because of their effect on production but because of their effect on

earnings and work practices. They create inflationary wage drift and perpetuate restrictive practices and inefficient manning scales.[11]

One important aspect of unofficial strikes was pinpointed by Sir George Pollock:

There are the unofficial strikes that do not take place, if I may use that phrase. The threat of unofficial action is one of the main causes in any settlement of concessions which are very difficult to reconcile with the national incomes policy.[12]

Of course, the number of days lost through strikes is much smaller than that lost through sickness. But sick people do not raise wage levels, while strikers do—and that's what matters to the bosses and their supporters.

Shop stewards

And who leads the struggle at plant level for improved pay and conditions? Who spearheads the wage drift (or wage drive) movement? Who acts as the main organiser of the unofficial strike? Who really worries the management? Above all, the shop stewards committees and similar rank and file committees. Some very interesting statistics relating to shop stewards in the engineering industry show clearly the acceleration in shopfloor representation over the past few years. In the eight years from May 1947 to June 1955 the number of AEU shop stewards in federated establishments rose by 24 percent, or about 2.8 percent a year. As against this, in the period from June 1955 to December 1966 the number rose by 65 percent, or some 4.5 percent a year.[13] The total number of shop stewards in Britain is estimated at 175,000.[14]

Shop stewards are characteristically to be found in large firms especially. In small firms they are much more rare. About half of all British trade unionists are covered by shop stewards authorisations, and this half is typically the best organised section of the trade union movement, and also often the most militant.

The urge to control

Both the rise of the shop stewards organisations and the number of unofficial strikes are symptoms (among other things) of the common aspirations of the working class—towards workers' control. Under capitalism the worker is a cog in the machine, with no say in the running of production, and no part in the creative organisation of his work. The growing number of strikes in Britain express only too clearly the workers' rebellion against this subordination, this mutilation, limitation and alienation of their own creativity.

The urge for workers' control is becoming more stridently expressed in strikes, as the decline in the proportion of strikes over purely wage issues shows:

In the 20 years of high employment from 1940 the proportion of strikes about 'wage questions *other than* demands for increases', and (particularly) about 'working arrangements, rules and discipline', rose remarkably—from one third of all stoppages to three quarters... One *could* say that these disputes all involve attempts to submit managerial discretion and authority to agreed—or, failing that, customary—rules, alternatively, that they reflect an implicit pressure for more democracy and individual rights in industry.[15]

It is only if one understands the deep urge to control, and to overcome the basic alienation of workers in capitalist production, that one can understand the 'folly' of workers who lose more money in waging a strike than they could possibly gain even if they won it completely. How else, too, can one explain the non-monetary causes of so many strikes?

A determination not to have the conditions of their work entirely dictated to them, a refusal to recognise what the capitalist press sometimes refers to as 'management's inalienable right to manage', and a simple assertion of their quality as human beings rather than as the dumb animals that capitalist production requires them to be much of the time, constantly expresses itself in the struggles of workers on the shopfloor, whether they refuse the foreman the right to swear at them, resist speed-up, or deny that management has the right to decide how long a girl may spend in the lavatory.

Even in strikes for monetary causes, the rebellion against the basic alienation is never far from the surface. One writer put this very well:

> Wage claims are motivated much more frequently by *rebellion against working conditions* than by rebellion against the economic *burden of exploitation* borne by the labour force. They express an insistence *to be paid as highly as highly as possible for the time lost, the life wasted and the freedom alienated* as a result of working in such conditions. The workers insist on being paid as much as possible, *not because they put wages* (money and what it can buy) *above everything else*, but because, *as trade unions stand at the moment*, they can dispute the price of labour power with the employers, but not control over conditions and the character of the work.[16]

And in one of the very few detailed studies of a single strike, an American sociologist showed how a group of relatively backward semi-rural workers expressed their resentment at increased supervision and tighter discipline by striking for a wage rise:

> To the extent that workers viewed the changing social situation in the plant as 'increased strictness', and most did, their reaction was influenced by their notion of what was causing these changes. In large measure, workers perceived these changes as economically motivated. As one worker said bitterly, 'They'll do anything to save a nickel.' In other words, 'strictness' was held to be due to the company's effort to save money at the worker's expense. In such a setting, a wage demand became a punitive retaliation—it was an effort, as one worker put it, to 'hit the company where it hurt—in the pocketbook'.[17]

The shop stewards organisation as such is nothing but the expression of workers' urge to control their own destinies. In setting rules for the manning of machines, in insisting on safety standards, in demanding a say in the pace of work, in seeking control over overtime and shift work, the workers announce clearly that they are no passive cogs that management can push about as it will. Similarly the demand to control 'hiring and firing' (or at least to veto managerial decisions on this question), a demand that has led to innumerable strikes since the war, represents a challenge to the employers' authority at its most vital point.

In one and the same plant two opposed and quite contradictory powers—management with their foremen and workers with their stewards—face one another. The two camps put forward two opposing principles and sets of demands—the prerogative of authoritarian management versus the democratic self-expression of the workers.

It is true of course that this demand for workers' control is only partial; it is essentially *defensive*, it is fragmentary, and it is bound by the limits of the shop or the factory. But this demand for workers' control, a demand that is voiced in a thousand different ways every day that workers go to work, is the embryo of full working class control at every level of society, political and economic alike. For socialists it is the most important fact about modern industrial capitalism—for the 'bloody-mindedness' of workers, and the thousand and one ways in which they express their demand, implicitly and explicitly, for control over their own lives, is the embryo of workers' power, of socialism.

Shop stewards organisations: weaknesses and strengths

In evaluating the shop stewards organisations at present, it is important that trade unionists and socialists are very clear about their weaknesses and their points of strength.

The most significant weakness of shop stewards organisation today is its fragmentation. As the concentration and centralisation of capital have increased, through the processes of merger and takeover, the great combines running a number of plants across the country have become very prominent. The need to combine and coordinate the activities of shop stewards at least between the plants of a single combine is self-evident. But moves towards such coordination have been quite slow and faltering. Nor are the reasons difficult to understand. Negotiations have been done on a local basis, in a particular factory or even a particular shop. Demand for workers varies greatly between different districts. There is a great unevenness in strength of organisation, in traditions of militancy, and so on.

Even where there are shop stewards combine committees, they are usually very weak indeed and their weakness is revealed clearly during industrial disputes.

Take the role of the Guest, Keen and Nettlefold combine committee in the 1966 Shardlows strike. Then a strike of three weeks duration against the sacking of a steward did not get real help from the combine committee, although the convenor of Shardlows was the secretary of the combine committee.

Similar weaknesses plagued combine committees in other industries. Take the case of the docks liaison committee. These unofficial committees never had the backing or the organisation which the trade union enjoys. One must realise that, although there has been solidarity among dockers on day to day issues in each port, it has always been very difficult to get the ports united nationally. The docks, like the engineering industry, differ from factory to factory in terms of the various types of work practices, local attitudes and literally hundreds of local agreements. Also dockers in all ports tend to behave in an insular fashion due to the nature of their industry. One of the major weaknesses was that the London liaison committee, which was the only unofficial committee and had a continuous history of activity, was sometimes unwilling and often unable to engage in activity with other ports. Only one member of the liaison committee, over a period of two years prior to Devlin, had been actively engaged in travelling round the ports for the purpose of building national resistance.

The need for combine committees becomes especially urgent with the increasing mergers of companies and the rise of the giant corporations—often international in nature. The heads of the giant corporations can weaken workers' organisations and worsen conditions by shifting or threatening to shift output from one subsidiary of the firm to another where wages are lower and organisation weaker:

> Although difficulties such as distance between plants, differentials in wage rates and the local employment situation seem to be major obstacles, it is not very different from the problems that workers faced when they first started to organise single factories. There were numerous wage differentials then, the management played one department against another, and there was often a pool of unemployed outside the gate. But difficulties of a past period were faced up to and largely overcome.[18]

Besides fragmentation, there is another associated weakness of the shop stewards organisations of today—on the whole, the horizons of these organisations are quite narrow. They tend to react to events more than they shape them, and they pay more attention to wages than they do to the equally important question of redundancy.

Above all, the problems of people who cannot defend themselves very well—people like old age pensioners, nurses, etc—are not central in workers' activities and thinking. It is true, of course, that thousands of workers—lorry drivers, dockers, engineers—showed a wonderful generosity of spirit in going on sympathy strike in support of the nurses' pay claim in May 1962. But still we must admit that action like this is the exception, not the rule.

The shop stewards reflect their base, and while this is their strength it is also their weakness. When the majority of workers are not really socialist or even militant, the shop stewards they elect cannot be either. A survey carried out among shop stewards came to the following conclusions:

> There is little evidence that shop stewards are more militant than their members, or more likely to favour unconstitutional action. For the most part stewards are viewed by others, and view themselves, as accepted, reasonable and even moderating influences, more of a lubricant than an irritant.[19]

A most insidious trend appearing in recent years is the increase in the number of full time convenors, shop representatives, deputy convenors, works committee members, etc who spend an increasingly long period away from their increasingly nominal jobs. In many factories the ordinary worker who is elected shop steward very rapidly finds himself (if he's good at representing his men) taken away from the shopfloor more and more often. Then he gets put on a 'soft' job, to allow management to take him away without disrupting production. It's no wonder that many get completely divorced from their base. With factory convenors this is particularly strongly felt. Often the only contact they have with the workers is when they appear to try and persuade the men not to walk out over a grievance. The only answer to this process of incorporation is to insist on regular shopfloor meetings.

In many cases workers became alienated not only from the union officials but even from the shop stewards. They see them as a buffer between themselves and management. Hence the growing phenomenon, in the motor car industry especially, of *unofficial* unofficial strikes in which the workers act on their own without even the endorsement of their shop steward. Sir Jack Scamp reports, 'At Morris Motors Limited, Cowley, for instance, the council found that in 1965 256 out of 297 stoppages of work had occurred before the senior shop steward had even had a chance to put the grievance into procedure'.[20]

Quite often the shop stewards do not keep in close touch with their constituents. Thus, for instance, one shop steward in Ford Dagenham body works wrote to me:

There is a mistrust between the workers and the shop stewards committee in the Body Group. This has come about because of the lack of consultation between stewards and workers. Many stewards do not go to meetings.

Again, a shop steward from the foundry of the same factory:

There is a complete lack of written propaganda in the plant. During the strike (March 1968) an issue of the *Voice of the Ford Worker* was discussed. It still (October 1969) has not been issued, and there have been no plant mass meetings to my knowledge. When in the foundry 15 percent of the shop stewards attend a shop stewards meeting and in the Body Group about 30 percent, there must be an obvious lack of communication.

On the whole, however, shop stewards are somewhat more advanced than their constituents. They are the backbone of most union branches.

Their attendances are much higher than members', and 44 percent said that they are present at nearly all branch meetings. Only 13 percent of stewards in the sample, as against 44 percent of members, claimed that they were quite out of touch with branch life. Three stewards in ten have held an office in their union, and two of these were in the branch. Two out of ten said they would like to become branch officer in the future.[21]

Also, politically, shop stewards on the whole are somewhat more aware than their constituents: '70 percent of stewards paid the political levy, compared with 41 percent of union members, but a further 18 percent of the latter did not know if they paid it'.[22]

Then again, the shop stewards organisations are largely restricted to the narrow horizon of economic, trade union demands. They are, largely speaking, politically apathetic. To limit oneself to economic demands, of course, is to deal with the *results* of the capitalist system as a system, and to miss the *causes*, the roots of the system. As Rosa Luxemburg, that great socialist revolutionary, put it, 'Economic, trade union struggle is a labour of Sisyphus.' Sisyphus was a mythological king who was condemned to spend eternity rolling a huge stone to the top of a hill, from which it kept rolling back, so he had to start over and over again, incessantly heaving the boulder up the hill. As long as the capitalists own the means of production, workers—whether their wages are high or low—will still be oppressed, alienated, exploited. Capitalism cannot be abolished 'step by step'. As Tawney put it, 'You can peel an onion leaf by leaf, but you can't skin a tiger claw by claw.'

This does not mean of course that the economic struggle—that 'labour of Sisyphus'—is useless. After all, Sisyphus did develop strong muscles as a result of all his labours. And in the same way industrial workers, through the struggles at their places of work, learn self-confidence, self-reliance and strength.

One magnificent experience in the history of the shop steward movement in Britain made it quite clear that it is not beyond the potentialities of the working class to create a really unified shop steward *movement*. This took place during the First World War and the period immediately following it. Take, for instance, the case of Leonard Hargreaves, a fitter employed at the Vickers factory at Brightside, Sheffield. A skilled man, he was called up to fight in the trenches for the glory of Britain while dilutees remained in the factory. This was a contravention of an agreement between the unions and the government of the day:

> The shop stewards committee of Sheffield demanded that he be released in line with government assurances, and a mass meeting held under its auspices on 13 November threatened to strike unless its demands were complied with. On 15 November Hargreaves was released from the army, and the government agreed to meet the society to devise a scheme which would meet their objections. This news did not reach the Sheffield workers and on 16 November they struck work as planned, and two days later workers from Barrow-in-Furness came out in sympathy. Work was resumed only when Hargreaves appeared on the platform at a mass meeting of the men and confirmed that he had been released unconditionally.[23]

A mass strike in defence of one worker! Actually many of the strikes at that time were massive affairs. Today the majority of strikes are, by comparison, quite small. There are more shop stewards than ever before—many more than there were 50 years ago—but still there is not a *movement*.[24]

The widening of the front

With a replacement of piece-work by MDW, with the abolition of tens of hundreds of wage levels in a plant and their substitution by few grades, with a plant negotiation instead of piecemeal negotiations, the ground is being prepared for a wider unity of workers in struggle. Whatever the intentions of management, workers' solidarity could be strengthened by these changes.

This becomes obvious by comparing the pattern of strikes in Ford, based on MDW, grading, etc, and British Leyland, where PBR is prevailing. The strikes in the former have been on the whole on a much greater scale and continuing for a longer period.[25] Also the issues in the strikes, in the case of Ford, have been on the whole more fundamental, dealing with managerial prerogatives, production matters on the one hand and victimisation of workers on the other.[26]

As a matter of fact, productivity deals in themselves incline to provoke workers into greater militancy. At least after the ginger on the cake starts peeling off, it becomes clear that it means a much greater effort for the workers for relatively little or no extra lolly.

Just look at the case of the POEU. In a fanfare of publicity it signed a productivity deal in January 1966. Three years later the first national strike in the 82-year history of the union took place. Similarly with the dustmen. In March 1967 the PIB suggested productivity bargaining for manual workers in local authorities, involving time and motion study, etc, for the magnificent wage rise of 5 percent, or some 14s.[27] During the whole of the summer of 1969 the unions were negotiating for the dustmen a wage increase of 18s, and then at the beginning of October the dustmen went on strike. Their demands were not dampened at all by the past experience of productivity bargaining. On the contrary, they were demanding an additional £4 11s, which would have brought their basic wage up to £20 a week. In the event, they were practically straight away offered a 50s a week rise in London (or 16 percent), and 30s (10 percent) in the provinces.

The miners followed suit and under the threat of a national strike (which actually broke out on a different issue and was the biggest miners' strike since 1926 and the biggest unofficial strike ever) got 27s 6d for the surface workers—the largest wage rise in the history of the mines! The firemen followed suit. Under threat of a strike on the eve of Guy Fawkes night, London firemen got £4 10s and the provincial firemen a £3 10s wage rise.

Electrical power supply workers were next in line. Way back in September 1967 the PIB, in reply to a request for a 5 percent wage rise put forward by the unions, offered 3.7 percent with very heavy new productivity strings attached.[28] Instead electrical power supply workers followed the example of the firemen and threatened strike (in a few stations it even came to actual strike), so getting a wage rise of 10 percent.

The teachers followed suit. The employers offered them a £50 interim rise on the annual basic wage (under 4 percent). The union leaders declared this 'derisory'. Quite rightly, the *Times* explained:

> An offer of £50 would have satisfied most teachers six weeks ago, but since then there have been awards of 16 percent to dustmen, 9 percent to miners and 12 percent to firemen. Now even the right wing of the NUT will not be prepared to accept an offer of less than £70.[29]

It is very possible that productivity bargaining contributed indirectly to the size and height of the strike waves. Workers' expectations have risen when they hear from state and employers about the benefits of productivity deals, while the reality was so much poorer. After a time all productivity deals become tarnished.[30]

The incomes policy propaganda and the big rumpus about productivity bargaining concentrated the attention of workers towards comparing wages. Hence the phenomena of the, so to say, epidemic of wage demands—the dustmen inspired the miners, the firemen, the teachers. Similarly a couple of years ago, the figure of £17 a week became a magic formula in Merseyside. Once the dockers at the end of 1967 got £17 basic, the Liverpool bus workers fought for the same, then the lorry drivers and then the tugmen.

The factor of comparability—and the struggle for parity—increases also as a result of mergers. It is not an accident that with the rise of British Leyland the struggle for parity has raised its head inside the corporation (hence the long strike at the five Preston factories). The same is true in the car industry in general. Similarly, and prior to the rise of British Leyland, it was the joining of Morris and Austin into BMC that pushed the Morris Oxford factories, which used to be very peaceful, onto a much stormier course.

Total offensive of employers

The implementation of productivity deals is associated with a total attack on workers, total meaning that it tries to use all weapons—the state (incomes policy and anti trade union legislation), the trade union bureaucracy, 'science' (time and motion study alike) and ideology (the ideology of 'national interest', of 'partnership of labour and capital'). The aim of the employers' strategy is to split the workers, to subdue the shop stewards and integrate them into the union machine, and incorporate the unions into the state. The workers need a total, a general, class strategy to replace the employers' offensive, to move from defence to attack.

Chapter Thirteen: How to fight productivity deals

Probably the greatest mistake made by those who have not directly experienced a productivity deal, and specially by those outside of industry, is to think of these deals coming in a fully prepared 'oven-ready' condition so that all workers have to do is to say yes or no. But of course this is *not* the way it works. If management were to turn up one fine day with a finished deal, clauses A to Z, it would be ten to one that they would have it thrown back in their faces, and they know it. In most cases the aim of management is to start discussions with workers and their representatives around the 'general principles' of a 'proposed' productivity deal and to lead on from this in such a way that the 'yes or no' question is never actually put but taken for granted. Thus they hope to develop productivity talks in such a way that their workers move from a consideration of 'whether there should be a deal' to one of 'what should be in the deal' without really realising that this crucial change has happened. We have already seen how many employers are ready to give really large wage increases in return for a seemingly worthless piece of paper that commits shop stewards to no more than future talks on 'productivity'. They are willing to do this because they understand the value of getting their foot in the door. In productivity bargaining the traditional form of negotiations—workers making demands on their employer for better wages and conditions—is reversed. Now it is the employers who are demanding changes, and in doing so try to force the workers into taking a purely passive role and simply responding to these demands. Naturally the employers want to conduct the negotiations for a productivity deal in the manner that gives them the upper hand, one which enables them to take advantage of the traditional divisions between workers, and one that keeps workers' organisation permanently on the defensive.

First we must decide what the weaknesses and divisions are that can attract individual workers to a productivity deal, and then try and develop policies and demands that will overcome these sectional pressures and create a common interest. For a whole generation workers have compensated for low basic rates with overtime, shift working and racing after bonuses, etc. The man who drives a five-ton lorry on a basic wage in December 1968 of £11 3s 6d[1] has little alternative than to work 55 or 60 hours a week in order to bring home a living wage. Is it any wonder that he is ready—even eager—to accept a productivity deal that brings him a five-day, 40-hour working week but also speeded-up schedules, round the clock shift working and greatly increased supervision?

Dockers who work under really obnoxious conditions, with a pool system not much different from a cattle market, dealing with filthy merchandise, etc, found it impossible to resist at least Phase I of Devlin. The daily lot of the docker was humiliating, degrading and insecure. The competition for work brought sharp divisions and bitterness among the men, and this was to the employers' benefit, as was the favoured treatment of a minority of permanently employed men. The Devlin proposals, offering as they did to end the 'pool' system of casual labour and to end with it the terrible insecurity felt by the docker, were inevitably quite attractive to the ordinary docker. The employers were not averse to increasing the pressure by forcing as many men as possible onto the 'fall-back' pay while the talks were taking place.

Although under piece-work systems many workers have been able to push their earnings up very considerably, there is no doubt that as a whole PBR systems are a divisive and weakening influence on workers.

Throughout industry the payment by results system produced an incredibly complex earnings structure that seemed far from fair to workers, thus preparing the ground for the introduction of measured day work. In 1967 one economist, Derek Robinson, carried out a survey of the pay of 12 identifiable occupations in a locality. He found that the difference in pay between workers doing comparable work in neighbouring plants was sometimes as much as 100 percent. Robinson could not even find a pattern in the payment of wage increases. Different amounts were paid, sometimes tending to widen them. Indeed, the only hypothesis he could sustain was that 'individual firms have a great deal of freedom in determining what wages to pay their workers'. He concluded that the state of the local labour market was 'bloody chaotic'.[2]

One factory worker expressed the prevailing dissatisfaction thus:

> I am so disgusted with the system I cannot be bothered with it. We do not get what we earn…we sometimes feel we have worked a lot harder and are getting less money…it is run like a football pool. They pay us what they think they will and the harder you work the less you get.[3]

The feeling of insecurity was among the main motives conditioning workers, especially in the car industry, to accept MDW. Thus the normal earnings of the average car worker:

> …during 1962-63 were about £23 or £24 a week, but only on a minority of occasions did his actual earnings come within these figures, and in particular weeks in that period his gross wage rose above £31 and fell as low as £13. But a worker in the trim shop had a different pattern of earnings fluctuation. For him, a 'normal' weekly wage would be between £25 and £27. However, and though this amount again represented the lesser part of his total experience, his actual wage never rose above the last figure but very frequently fell to as low as £11 in one week. In such a context 'normality' has little meaning.[4]

No wonder that in the face of such fluctuations MDW should appeal to workers' urges for security. In general, workers' desire for stability and what they think is fairness in the method of payment is very important. In most conventional piece-work systems, waiting time and fall-back rates—guarantees against interruptions in output caused by factors outside the workers' control—are significantly below average earnings. Thus when management fail to maintain a steady flow of work it is the workers who suffer an immediate loss.

Obviously the more interruptions there are, the more earnings will fluctuate. It is this instability, rather than simply a drive for higher earnings, which often prompts workers to try to win control over the piece-rates. However, quite often this urge for control is not successful and the door is wide open for the productivity bargaining merchants. Wherever the differences between the conditions of different workers in the same place of work are large it is quite easy for management to sell a productivity deal which will play one section of workers against another. Thus, for instance, the recent deal offered by the building employers of a wage rise of 26 percent over 19 months to building workers[5] will seem quite an attractive proposition to many low paid building workes, while to those who earn a high bonus it may mean a really savage cut in earnings, as the agreement will probably have strings attached, like restrictions on bonus earnings. If the higher paid workers refused the deal, employers and trade union officials will be able to turn to the lower-paid workers and say, 'We are on your side—it is the high paid workers that prevent you from getting the extra money you so need!'

One cannot but agree with the excellent pamphlet *Know Your Enemy*, which says:

> In attempts to introduce changes within the factory, employers are quick to exploit any differences which exist between sections of the workers. They will try to turn day workers against piece-workers, lower paid against higher paid. If they can convince a few sections that change is in their interest, the resistance of the whole factory may be undermined. This is the old policy of 'divide and rule'. To prevent this it is essential to show that all sections will suffer if the strength of shopfloor organisation is broken...
>
> At the time when management attacks it may well be too late to overcome the legacy of past jealousies and build a united resistance. The time to create real solidarity is now. Strong links must be forged both within and between factories, so that adequate organisation exists before the attack comes.[6]

In addition to this very reasonable desire for a more ordered and 'rational' earnings structure there is the traditional socialist opposition to piece-working. For over a century it has been condemned as being at the root of increased exploitation, bad working conditions and a low level of safety at work.

One South Wales miner wrote to me:

> Certain face workers had a wage average of above £22 10s per week, and to some extent they did oppose the abolition of piece-working, but the vote in favour of the agreement was solid. It was an acceptance of a principle adopted by the old Miners' Federation of Great Britain 60 years ago—the abolition of piece-work in the interests of health and safety. Under piece-work many a miner was in such a hurry to earn a living that life was quite a risk. There were those in far off days, as there are today, who considered abolition of piece-work as necessary in the interests of the working class—remove distinctions and wage differentials—equality of wages.

And a docker writes to me regarding piece-work, 'Never again. To anybody who had to to deal with hoof and horn, fish meal, chillies or cement, the thought of going back to piece-work is simply appalling.'

These anomalies of low basic wage, great differences between the payments going to different workers doing the same or similar jobs, etc were reflections of the basic characteristics of the British labour movement over a very long period—since the Second World War. Instead of a class effort, sectional effort. Instead of generalised strategy, a patchy, hand to mouth reaction to the situation. It is much easier to get an extra ten hours a week overtime than to get a higher consolidated basic wage. It is much easier to get concessions from employers in an expanding profitable industry where there is scarcity of labour than to get a general advance in all workers' wages. The whole past approach and philosophy of the labour movement—its fragmented nature, its tendency to take the line of least resistance, its lack of an overall working class strategy—are now bearing fruit. The workers have been softened up to accept the soft sell and the blandishments of the productivity deal merchants.

For a whole generation there has been almost complete apathy among workers regarding the trade unions. It seemed good enough to know who the shop steward was—who the hell cared about who controlled the union as a whole? Now with plant negotiations, the foundations of all productivity bargaining, this apathy emerges as the source of a very dangerous weakness—the workers are unarmed.

Apathy towards politics was natural when reforms could be achieved on the factory floor, and while the only politics visible were those of Tweedledum and Tweedledee, of parliamentary Toryism and parliamentary Labourism. However, now with productivity deals thrusting politics onto the factory floor, political backwardness can be clearly seen as the Achilles' heel of the working class.

The fragmented industrial struggle has been accompanied *at many levels* by a narrow, fragmented, contradictory consciousness. *Support for organised political opposition to the system dwindled* while the path of improving one's own conditions seemed to be open. (That this path was not a real solution to workers' problems was beside the point.) *Productivity bargaining, by its direct attack on working conditions and the remaining workers' organisations, changes all this—it generalises workers' experiences and resentments.* Parochialism and shortsightedness become impossible impediments.

Taking the offensive

Now comes the $64,000 question—how do we fight a productivity deal? I hope that no one who has read this book so far will be in any doubt where I stand on the question of productivity deals—bitterly and unalterably opposed to them. But this does not in itself solve the problem of developing a strategy for fighting them. Any fool can denounce a productivity deal and say we should have nothing to do with it. It is an entirely different matter to lead a group of workers in successfully resisting such a deal. The exact strategy to be adopted will depend a great deal on particular circumstances in the factory or industry concerned.

What is the bargaining strength of the workers involved? How desperate are the employers for changes in working practices? Does technology force them to adopt round the clock working? What is the attitude of the unions—is it DATA (Draughtsmens' Union), who are against productivity deals, or Les Cannon's Electrical and Plumbing Trades Union, who will buy them at any price? What are the traditions of militancy or how strong are the divisions between workers? These are the factors that will determine the final outcome. In some cases, particularly where employers have only offered derisory increases, a productivity deal has been thrown out of the window with little difficulty. In other cases even the most experienced and militant leadership has only been able to draw the worst teeth in the deal.

Yet whether the final outcome is complete victory or, as is far more likely, partial success, the actual strategy to be adopted is the same. We must always start by opposing the productivity deal completely and then later, if necessary, retreat to a position where we try and get the best out of the deal we can. It is far too easy to decide from the start that we don't have the strength to force the employer to abandon the deal. Not only is this writing off one's own membership before the start but it plays right into the employer's hands. He is only too ready to come forward with 101 changes that he wants in the cause of productivity, and then 'with great reluctance' and under 'pressure from the union' to reduce this to the five concessions that he really wanted in the first place.

When management comes to workers and offers them a relatively large wage rise as part of a productivity deal, if the rank and file leaders simply say no they run the risk of becoming isolated. They provide the most backward workers with a very dangerous weapon: 'We would have been £5 a week better off if only those shop stewards had accepted the deal.' One Linwood worker put it clearly in a letter to me:

> From the signing of the productivity deal last year (in 1968) all semi-skilled workers at Linwood got 11s 3d an hour, and in January 1970 there is 1s an hour rise due making it 13s 5d (we got the first 1s in January this year). Labourers at the moment get 11s 10d an hour. These wages are the highest for semi-skilled workers in the West of Scotland, and this is a very important factor to be understood in analysing why measured day work was accepted initially. If you compare these rates with those of Singers, Clydebank—also approximately 7,000-8,000 workers, also ten miles from the centre of Glasgow—this point comes out. At Singers piece-work allows most semi-skilled men between 8-10s an hour—the fall-back rate is 7s 6d.

In rejecting an empty, negative approach one should not fall into the trap of the compromisers and opportunists. Recognition of the danger that the militants may isolate themselves from the rank and file has to be balanced by two other considerations. First, the duty of the militant is to enlarge the consciousness of the mass by offering a principled lead—he has to find a middle way between mindless militancy and tail-ending. Second, any steward has to remember the first rule of negotiation—the girl who starts by saying no gets a higher price for her virtue than the girl who talks money at the outset.

The first and most important part of any strategy against productivity deals is that it must be an active and offensive strategy. It must carry the fight to the employers by making demands that will force the employers to go beyond their sugary promises and expose the real objectives of the deal. It must be an active strategy in that it must seek to inform and educate the rank and file at all times. The leading rank and file organisations, the combine committee, the joint shop stewards committee, branch committee or whatever must get over to the membership a general view of the situation arising from an imminent productivity deal. Through the media of factory meetings, shop meetings, newsletters and bulletins they must give a comprehensive alternative to the employers' propaganda. They must reject the notion that workers have any responsibility for the competitive position of the employer—as socialists we oppose competition in industry, either nationally or internationally. They must announce for all to hear their conviction that workers have a *right* to drastically improved wages without any productivity concessions. They should make clear that they consider conditions won in struggle over the years to be *non-negotiable* and certainly not to be sold for a few miserable shillings. They should make clear that in the long term the standards of workers will be determined far more by the extent to which they defend and strengthen their basic organisation than by the size of the next increase. It is not only propaganda but practical experience that teaches workers that the different elements of the economy are interdependent. It is impossible to concentrate on wages alone while not paying attention to government employment policies, to government and monopoly pricing policies, inflation, etc. Questions of the balance of payments, the total activities and priorities of the national economy, government anti-union legislation, etc have to be faced up to, not avoided. What any rank and file leadership needs to establish for its members is that all these problems have alternative, socialist, solutions that do not involve the evils of productivity deals.

As part of what we might call the 'counter-propaganda offensive' there needs to be a careful assessment of the role of the union officers. Many workers seeing that both management *and* unions are in favour of productivity deals believe that here is something that *is* for the common good. The aim must be to put forward a series of demands within the union which demonstrate to the members that we consider it to be *our* union which must be brought under *our* control. The independent power of full time officers within the union should be curbed and power transferred in practice to the rank and file. Such demands could include the following:

(1) All trade union officials should be elected and subject to recall by the membership.
(2) Union officials should get the same rate of pay as the average of the members.[7]
(3) All strikes should be considered as official.

(4) No member of the union should be banned from holding office for political reasons.

(5) Shop stewards' credentials should be the property of the shop members and not subject to withdrawal by the executive.

(6) Combine committees and joint shop steward committees should be a recognised part of the trade unions and supported by them.

(7) Industrial conferences and regular local shop stewards' meetings should have a constitutional position in all unions.

Under capitalism, of course, man's welfare depends largely on the money he gets, so it is quite natural that on the whole workers will put money before conditions, and will put conditions before organisation. The employers, in fact, encourage this scale of priorities. A drop in pay is felt much more immediately than is a weakening of shopfloor organisation. So socialists have to carry on a very strenuous and difficult propaganda, to explain the long term effects, to show workers why they must shift their priorities.

In negotiations with management as much consideration should be given to the effect on one's own members as on the employer. One of the aims of the shop steward training courses is to convince the steward that he has the capacity to argue with management—that his sheer negotiating skill will win the day. In this way they want him to forget that the strength he brings to the negotiating table is not the brilliance of his rhetoric but the industrial strength of his members.

Alongside the efforts taken to win the minds of the workers, attention should be paid to exactly those points which divide workers and make total opposition difficult: raising the earnings of low paid workers to reduce excessive differentials; establishing a tradition of mutual assistance between day workers and piece-workers, and between different piece-working sections; developing a *factory-wide strategy* through the joint shop stewards committee; negotiating a bonus system for day workers linked to piece-work earnings; bridging the gap which often exists between stewards and their members by instituting regular section meetings, etc; stimulating regular shopfloor meetings to discuss JSSC policy, etc, etc.

Obviously not all these can be achieved in the short period prior to productivity negotiation, but the mere fact that they are in the pipeline, that they are being demanded, will be a unifying factor in the situation.

First stage demands

One of the aims of employers is to make productivity bargaining *replace* wage bargaining. Thus if the workers concerned could normally expect to get a £2 increase and are instead persuaded to accept a settlement of £4 as part of a productivity deal then the employers have in fact paid only £2 for the deal. In some cases, for instance the London busmen, workers have got no more in a productivity deal than they had previously won in straight wage talks. The first demand of all, then, should be for a substantial 'across the board' wage increase before any talks on productivity. Not only does this make it certain that in any deal that does emerge the workers are in fact getting paid for the concessions made in the deal rather than falling for the three-card trick, but it also means that it is a great deal easier to convince workers that they should tell management what they can do with their productivity deal. This may sound very obvious, but it is surprising in how many cases the major reason why a deal was accepted was that the men hadn't had a rise for an extended period.

As for the amount of such a claim, this must obviously be decided in the light of circumstance, but the method adopted by the dustmen during the 1969 strike—£1 for every finger on your left hand—has its merits!

Wherever management propose productivity bargaining they should be *immediately* faced with a series of demands as a precondition for any talks. They should be told openly (so that the shopfloor gets the message as well) that the shop stewards (convenors, representatives, etc) are extremely suspicious of any productivity deal, and in order to judge the good faith of management require the following demands to be satisfied before talks can commence:

(1) Guarantees against redundancy, rundown of labour force, short time working or plant closures during the full period of the agreement and for a period of five years after it is terminated.
(2) A cost of living bonus, to be treated as separate in the sense that, no matter what rises in pay result from it, management undertakes not to use it when considering any pay claims other than claims based on the cost of living.
(3) Rights of the union within the factory to be consolidated. Where not already guaranteed, shop stewards must have full freedom of movement throughout plant at all time. Right to hold meetings in company's time and at its expense.
(4) There is to be no change in working conditions without prior agreement with shop stewards. No transfer of labour on an individual or group basis without the agreement of stewards.
(5) That any new agreement cannot come into effect unless voted on section by section by all workers in the plant. This means no package voting.
(6) Shop stewards should have the right to invite in any 'experts' they want at any time to consult with them, etc. The 'experts' might be local militants from other factories, local 'intellectuals' or union officials (not necessarily their own). If management has the right to bring *its* consultants in, why not the stewards?
(7) Where the shift system is used widely, management must put aside a day every month, on full pay, for general factory meetings, for meetings of the stewards from all the shifts, etc.
(8) Shop stewards should have the right to inspect all company stocks, and management should supply a written report on stocks every fortnight (management can prepare for a strike by stockpiling in advance).

In the unlikely event of these 'first stage' demands being accepted they will have drawn most of the teeth from any possible productivity deal. If they are rejected then the position of a shop stewards committee in fighting the proposed deal will have been enormously strengthened. They can turn to their members and say, 'There you are, they won't give the assurance so you know what to expect from the productivity deal—redundancy, an attack on the shop stewards, and an attack on working conditions.'

Fighting the deal from within

We have to remember that employers view a productivity deal as a long term investment. They have the reserves that allow them to wait for the return on this investment. Workers, on the other hand, living in a far more hand to mouth manner, are not able to put off the next wage increase in a similar way. All this builds up pressure on stewards to at least 'have a look at' a proposed productivity deal and this pressure will probably be strong enough in the majority of cases to force the rank and file leadership away from out and out rejection of the deal and to a situation where they have to consider the details of the productivity bargain. It is far better for such a leadership to choose their own time for making such a change so that the offensive strategy can be maintained and demands put forward that will undermine and expose the deal from within. The alternative of maintaining an inflexible rejection of *any* productivity deal can lead to a catastrophic division between the stewards and their membership which will be eagerly exploited by the employer and may lead in the end to the acceptance of a far worse deal than was necessary. To agree to talks on a proposed productivity deal *does not mean* that we have abandoned our policy of opposition to the basic principle of productivity bargaining, and this has to be made very clear.

Once we are forced to consider the details of a proposed deal the question arises of how to maintain the offensive, and how to destroy the worst aspects of the deal in the process. The only way to do this is to put forward detailed demands as a counter to the concessions demanded in the productivity deal.

We shall deal, first of all, with the specific strategies needed for the different aspects of productivity deals—MDW, grading, time and motion study, shift working, etc. The guidelines described below are the result of long discussions with many militants from various industries who have faced numerous productivity deals. Workers in struggle show an amazing amount of initiative and imagination. However, the experience of different workers in different factories and industries is hardly ever integrated. The following guidelines are not to be taken as simple recipes for different situations but as a summing-up of some experiences, and as an aid, we hope, to the further development of working class tactics.

Although solutions in the form of demands that must be advanced at all times are out of the question, since situations are so varied, there must be a common denominator to all tactics put forward. In every situation the central question should be, how far can we improve our control over the situation, maintain and advance the level of organisation inside the factory, and limit the management's power to dictate to the workers? How far can we advance trade union and political understanding in our handling of the specific situation and bring out the best response from the workers?

Again and again in the following programme of demands we will find the question of 'mutuality'—or 'the right to bargain'—coming to the fore. Whether it be mobility of labour, job evaluation, overtime or safety, the demand for 'mutuality' strikes a dagger at the heart of a productivity deal. By establishing the right to bargain on these questions we gain a limited degree of workers' control over the productive process—and this is exactly what productivity deals are aimed at eliminating. As we saw earlier, the employers' aim in replacing piece-working with measured day work is to reassert 'managerial authority' in the factory. They cannot do this and at the same time agree to mutuality. In the case of measured day work this is particularly important. By raising the demand for mutuality—of speeds, work standards, manning scales, etc—we expose the employer's motives in introducing MDW. In fact, MDW with mutuality is of no value to the boss and he would almost certainly rather have the piece-work methods than this.

The relevance of a revolutionary socialist programme must be judged by three criteria:

(1) Does it fit the current objective industrial and political situation?
(2) Does it assert the primacy of rank and file control at the workplace, in the union and towards the state?
(3) Does it raise the awareness of the nature of power in the system and encourage the workers to grapple for it?

Of course such a programme cannot offer more than the general contours. The real flesh and blood of a programme can be given only by the struggle of the workers themselves.

This programme of demands is certainly not complete and its order in many situations will certainly prove incorrect. It is put forward as a necessary reaction to ruling class strategy with the hope that it may provide a number of points which workers can use in fighting back against the offensive of the employers and the state (and if successful must lead on to the next stage of struggle). Obviously this gives only a rough idea of the demands that can be made—these will vary from industry to industry and from plant to plant. The important thing is that the rank and file should take the initiative and not just react to the employers' proposals.

For reasons of convenience, the different aspects of productivity deals are dealt with separately, even though we realise that they overlap and interlock considerably. For this reason, the demands overlap and interlock, and there is some degree of repetition in their presentation.

The list of demands put forward has to be judged by this criterion—do they fit the objectives of the productivity deal in each particular case, and are they a positive response to the management's attack? The reader may find it useful to compare each list of demands with the section of the book that analyses that particular aspect of productivity deals. In this way, the unity between these demands and the overall revolutionary socialist perspective should be clear.

Measured day work

In introducing MDW management's main aim is to remove or reduce all the elements of workers' control over wages and conditions—in other words, to abolish what is termed the principle of 'mutuality'. In a militant workers' programme, therefore, the emphasis must fall precisely on the protection and extension of mutuality.

When management proposes the introduction of measured day work this should be opposed to the hilt. While MDW is being opposed, and/or after this resistance is broken, the following demands should be put forward:

(1) The principle of mutuality should be applied to:
    (a) The speed of the track.
    (b) Work standards.
    (c) Any movement of labour.
    (d) Allocation of workers to and size of the labour pool.
    (e) Staffing.
    (f) Any changes in working practice.
(2) A guarantee that there will be no redundancy or cut in the size of the labour force for the full period of the agreement.
(3) A 35-hour week without loss of pay.
(4) Payment of a bonus tied to increases in production, to be paid on a shop or plant basis and to be calculated by shop stewards and management.
(5) A guaranteed wage to be paid for the period of the agreement. This guaranteed wage should cover holidays, sickness, short time, waiting time, labour pool, etc. All special payments like merit awards should be consolidated.
(6) A cost of living bonus, to be treated as separate in the sense that, no matter what rises in pay result from it, management undertakes not to use them when considering any pay claims other than claims based on the cost of living.
(7) Total support for all claims for parity and for equal pay for women.[8]
(8) A guarantee of 26 weeks full pay and 26 weeks half pay for sickness. Full pay for the first three days of sickness, without a doctor's note.
(9) Four weeks holiday with full pay, plus six statutory days, with no qualification clauses (eg based on length of service).
(10) In any dispute arising over a given job, the status quo to be maintained until the dispute is settled.
(11) As much time to be given as workers feel they need to consider all management proposals, with advance guarantees of back pay.

Mobility of labour

(1) There should be no mobility without mutual agreement.
(2) No workers should be transferred without the agreement of all shop stewards concerned—in other words, the stewards from both the old section and the new.

(3) There should be no reduction in the size of the total labour force of the factory.

(4) Any transferred worker should be guaranteed average earnings. These earnings should be either those in his old section or in his new one, whichever is the higher.

(5) All retraining must be at the company's expense, with no loss of earnings for any workers involved.

(6) There should be no mobility of shop stewards, etc without agreement.

Work study

We have seen that the claim that work study is an accurate science is nothing but a fraud. It is an attempt to use a phoney science to bring about an intensification of work. For these reasons the traditional opposition to the stopwatch should be maintained wherever possible. When it is introduced we must be absolutely clear that the final timings will be largely determined by the strength of the union and shop stewards organisation. Never bother to argue with a work study man—just fight him. Where work study is carried out workers should demand:

(1) Shop stewards have the right to negotiate on all timings.

(2) Work study engineer to be a member of the same union as the men he is studying.

(3) All job records to be available for inspection.

(4) No timings to take place without the shop steward being present.

(5) All times to be mutually agreed.

(6) All job descriptions to be mutually agreed and available for inspection.

(7) Shop stewards to make sure that allowances for fatigue, relief, delays, etc have been provided in proper amounts.

(8) The 'status quo' to be maintained on all disputed timings and speeds until mutual agreement is reached.

(9) Shop stewards to 'select' average workers whom the management wish to time.

Job evaluation and grading

As we have seen, job evaluation and grading are used by managements to reduce workers still further to the status of interchangeable cogs in a machine and at the same time to foster divisions among workers. Therefore we have to stress demands which increasingly help workers to realise the possibilities inherent in the larger collectivities that management forces them into. In this way management's weapons can be turned on their creators.

(1) The creation of numerous grades should be opposed.

(2) All weightings should be fully explained, and there should be mutual

agreement on the allocation of points, etc.

(3) All gradings should be mutually agreed.

(4) Any managerial dominance on evaluation committees should be strongly opposed.

(5) There should be no loss of procedural rights.

(6) Differentials between grades must not be increased.

(7) A clear link between the different ranges of pay must be built into the structure. In order that the existing differentials should not increase and in order to strengthen the common interest and unity of all workers, flat rate rather than percentage increases should be demanded.

(8) In all grading disputes the emphasis should be placed on raising wage levels rather than maintaining or raising wage differentials.

(9) There should be a phased agreement for narrowing the differentials between unskilled, semi-skilled and skilled workers by bringing up the wages of the lower paid workers.

(10) No worker should be downgraded through the introduction of new techniques.

Redundancy

The capitalist class regards the right to hire and fire whoever it likes, as and when it pleases, as one of its most important rights. The fight against redundancy denies the boss this important privilege. Obviously, therefore, the amount of control and the degree of organisation that are obtained *before* the redundancy question intrudes are decisive. If, during a period of booming trade, there has been some degree of control over hiring and firing, then it will clearly be easier to resist sackings. The right to work is a central socialist demand.

(1) A 35-hour week and increased holidays with pay should continually be fought for. They will provide immediate benefits for existing workers, but will also increase the job opportunities for others, including the youth who have yet to reach working age.

(2) There should be no plant redundancy as a result of productivity deals.

(3) Guarantees that there will be no redundancy or cuts in the size of the total labour force should be demanded from management. Without such guarantees there should be no cooperation with any rationalisation plans.

(4) A guaranteed weekly wage should be demanded—full pay for any hours not worked through layoffs, short-time working or work sharing. Management must be forced to accept full responsibility for those it employs. Five days work or five days pay.[9]

(5) Overtime should be allowed only by agreement with the shop stewards and the appropriate district committees, etc, and its contribution should be under the control of the stewards.

(6) No work should be transferred from one factory to another without the full agreement of the shop stewards committees involved.

(7) *Prior to* the introduction of productivity deals, and *prior to* company mergers which threaten sackings, the following demands should be fought for:

(a) Written guarantees of continuous employment for as long as can be obtained.

(b) The establishment of guaranteed wages for layoffs.

(c) The establishment of funds to pay benefits in excess of those laid down under the Redundancy Payments Act.

Shift work

Shift work is, firstly, the means by which modern management seeks to increase the use of its capital and, secondly, the point at which wage slavery most blatantly dominates over workers' private lives.

Shift work production brings enormous savings for employers and with them a big boost in profits. Therefore they should be made to pay dearly for the privilege of destroying workers' social lives—that is, where they can't be denied the privilege altogether.

A number of demands arise in connection with shift work:

(1) Double pay for night shifts.

(2) Opposition to three shifts, rotating shifts, continental shift systems, etc.[10]

(3) The normal working week to be Monday to Friday.

(4) Guaranteed provision for weekly meetings of all shop stewards, irrespective of shifts.

(5) A four-night week of eight-hour shifts, without loss of pay.

(6) All shift working to be voluntary.

(7) Opposition to women working night shifts.

(8) Provision for factory meetings of all shifts to discuss all important issues.

(9) All facilities in the factory to be available during night shift, eg medical services, canteen facilities.

Safety

Despite 100 years of factory legislation the number of accidents in British industry goes up year by year. In 1968 there were 597 fatal accidents in factories and on building sites. Out of these the factory inspectors found that there had been 262 breaches of the regulations by employers and only six by the workers. When faced with productivity bargaining shop stewards should treat the question of safety as of utmost importance. If management are so keen to raise productivity, why don't they tackle first of all the problem of lost production due to industrial accidents? In 1968 there were 21.9 million working days lost through accidents as opposed to just 4.6 million lost through disputes.[11] The employers' priorities are predictable. They find it far more important to prevent workers going on strike than to prevent them getting killed. 'Productivity through safety' is a slogan that can be very effective in fighting a productivity deal. A number of crucial demands come to mind:

(1) Safety officers to be elected from the workers concerned and fully trained at management's cost.
(2) Monthly meetings of safety officers with doctors to consider safety matters. All complaints on safety to be minuted.
(3) Safety officers to have rights as shop stewards to inspect plant at any time.
(4) Shop stewards in consultation with safety officers to have the right to stop production processes considered dangerous pending investigation.
(5) Specified amount of working time of maintenance workers to be spent on safety problems each week. All work done to be recorded.
(6) Full medical services to be provided (to include clinics, ambulances, etc).

Overtime

Overtime should be treated as being only acceptable when it is used to meet very special occurrences—breakdown of plant, etc. Systematic overtime should be refused as management have the alternative of employing extra labour. If they cannot recruit such labour then they must improve wages in order to attract it. On the other hand, workers should be discouraged from working overtime regularly as a means to higher earnings. We should therefore make overtime expensive for the employer but not attractive to the worker. Overtime can be used as a weapon by a management in order to force a productivity deal through. If workers rely on it to maintain a reasonable take-home pay then they will be in great difficulties if it is withheld over a period. Such workers are far more likely to be attracted to the sugar coating on a productivity deal.
We should demand:

(1) Time and a half for normal overtime, double time for weekend working, *plus* time off in lieu for all overtime to be taken at the worker's convenience.
(2) All overtime should be mutually agreed by shop stewards, district committees, etc, and management.
(3) All workers should have equal opportunities to work overtime.
(4) No management should be permitted to select the employees to work overtime.
(5) All overtime should be voluntary.

Tea breaks, relief time, etc

(1) All cuts in tea breaks should be opposed. A minimum of two ten-minute breaks per shift should be secured.
(2) All meal breaks should be paid.
(3) A minimum of 40 minutes per shift personal relief time should be guaranteed,

in addition to the two tea breaks.

(4) The right to sit down or leave the machine during a tea break should be ensured.

(5) Sufficient relief men should be employed to guarantee full relief periods, and to allow for lateness and other emergencies. The number of relief men needed should be decided by agreement between shop stewards and management.

(6) There should be sufficient standby workers in every section or gang to cover up to 20 percent absenteeism.

Procedure

(1) An agreed and speedy time limit should be set for the exhaustion of procedure.

(2) The 'status quo' should be maintained until procedure is exhausted.

(3) There should be no penalty clauses or restrictions on the right to strike, to ban overtime, to work to rule, etc.

(4) All restrictions on the right of apprentices, youths, etc to participate in dispute action should be removed.

(5) All clauses requiring trade unions to give written notice before dispute actions should be strongly opposed.

(6) There should be powerful opposition to trade unions being involved in managerial disciplinary action, etc.

Discipline

(1) Total opposition to all penalty clauses.

(2) Demand written disciplinary procedure within factory with right of appeal against decisions with workers' right to representation by shop stewards at all disciplinary hearings.

(3) Oppose right of foremen to take action against workers—suspension, dismissal, etc.

(4) No action to be taken against a worker as a result of past record unless the specific circumstances are recorded and witnessed by the worker concerned.

Conditions or money

So far we have dealt with the demands that can frustrate the employers' objectives in introducing a productivity deal. Unless we are completely successful in our fight to have the deal thrown out we will sooner or later face the question of the rewards being offered as an inducement to accept the deal. The changes encompassed in a productivity deal are very valuable to the employer and so he is often willing to pay a high price.

The prospect of a considerable rise in earnings—perhaps as much as £8 or £10 a week—is likely to be very attractive to workers, who may at first discount the less obvious deterioration in their conditions that will result from the deal. However, when conditions are sold they are gone for ever, while money gains lose their value through inflation, so it is necessary for socialists to place more emphasis on conditions than on money, improved holiday pay, sick pay, shorter hours, longer holidays—all these are improvements that can be maintained, while a few shillings in the form of a productivity bonus can soon be eaten away by rising prices.

By insisting that any concessions are paid for not with cash but with improved conditions and benefits we also leave the way open for an immediate wage claim when the productivity talks have finished. If we don't do this then the increases arising from the productivity deal are almost certain to be seen as replacing our normal wage increase. These are the kind of demands that should be put:

(1) 35-hour week with clause that this will be reduced according with any national settlement on hours.[12]
(2) Sick pay to be 100 percent of average earnings.
(3) Holiday pay to be 100 percent of average earnings plus holiday bonus.
(4) An additional week's holiday.
(5) Free life insurance for two years average earnings.

Permanent productivity

A productivity deal is not a once and for all phenomenon. In fact, as far as employers and government ministers are concerned it would make a very attractive permanent feature of industrial life, replacing completely traditional wage negotiations. The signing of a deal is not the end of the fight—it is almost just a beginning. From now on the employer will be trying to get talks going on phase two of the deal. Workers, if they have any sense, will be trying to reverse the existing deal wherever possible. This can be attempted in a number of ways:

(1) Outright refusal to accept parts of a deal that has been signed. The refusal of Ford workers to accept the penalty clauses in the 1969 agreement are an illustration of how successful this can be.
(2) Repudiation of the deal. In the initial stages of many productivity deals workers are promised 'substantial improvements in earnings'. After the deal has been signed these promises are found by many to be just what they were intended to be—promises. Under such circumstances workers can—with considerable justification—tell the boss, 'As you haven't honoured your part of the deal we will accept no more flexibility, mobility, single manning, etc.'
(3) Demand the renegotiation of sections of an agreement under threat of industrial action. This becomes possible when workers begin to feel the full effect of the changes involved in the deal: 'We never expected that this would happen when we agreed to the deal.'
(4) Misinterpret sections of the deal. Under this heading it should be possible to maintain tea breaks, washing-up time, etc.

All these actions require considerable militancy to be effective, and obviously it is far better not to get involved in the productivity deal in the first place. Yet, with over 6 million workers already involved, the question of developing a strategy to fight back against existing deals and above all to prevent further inroads into workers' conditions is of prime importance. With so little experience to call on it is not possible to formulate a detailed programme for this fight. What we can say is that no deal should be considered as irrevocable. It is becoming increasingly obvious that productivity deals, by enormously raising workers' expectations but not producing the goods, are contributing to a rising tide of militancy in British industry. In this atmosphere it is not impossible to turn back the pages of any productivity deal.

Politics

The ideological offensive of employers and state, of press and television, plays a crucial role in the introduction and implementation of productivity deals. The struggle against the propaganda of 'national interest', of 'partnership of labour and capital', must therefore be central in the fight against productivity deals. Class confrontation is the only answer to those who preach collaboration of workers with employers.

The role of the state was and is central in the introduction of productivity deals. If not for Barbara Castle's blackmail of the $3^1/2$ percent or thereabouts, the employers would not have been able to entice 30 percent of the working class into accepting productivity deals over the short period of a few years. As one main aim of the productivity campaign is to incorporate unions into 'partnership' with management and the state, the Donovan report, the CIR, etc are vital elements in the campaign. Hence a struggle against productivity deals demands a constant fight against government policies of incomes policy and anti trade union legislation. A socialist political struggle is crucial for resistance to productivity deals and to their overthrow.

The ideological and political offensive of the ruling class pushes politics onto the factory floor. The total offensive of the employers and the state, aided and abetted by trade union officialdom, will raise the question, which class is to control industry and society? At the centre of the arena will be the fight for workers' control, both partial and general.

A defensive, conservative position will not do on the ideological/political front. It is not only the insidious capitalist propaganda, but also practical experience that teaches workers that the different elements of the economy are interdependent. It is impossible to concentrate on wages alone while not paying attention to government employment policies, to government and monopoly pricing policies, inflation, etc. Questions of the balance of payments, the total activities and priorities of the national economy, the government anti-union legislation, etc have to be faced up to, not avoided. Also demanding an answer is the question of the general role of the trade unions—should they be integrated into the state and serve as policemen to keep the rank and file in order, or should they be controlled by the rank and file to fight the employers and the capitalist state? The question of bureaucracy versus democracy inside the union cannot be separated from the struggle around the question of productivity deals.

The fundamental system of wage slavery which imprisons us, the threat of war that hangs as a terrible question mark over the future of our children, the problems of poverty, ill health and the frustration of creativity, the crazy destruction of the environment, city and countryside alike—all these problems are rooted in the structure of capitalist society. All of them have to be tackled.

We need politics. We need socialist politics. We need a revolutionary socialist movement, which will counterpose, to the arbitrary and destructive rule of the tiny minority who own and control industry, finance and the mass media, the control by the working class of industry and society.[13]

Notes

The knowledge of many militant workers contributed to the writing of this book. If not for them this work could not have been written. The greatest help in contributions, advice, criticism and information was given by Chris Davison, Bernard Ross and Steve Jefferys. Also helpful were Terry Barrett, John Charlton, Roger Cox, Laurie Flynn, Vaughan Harrington, Bob Harrison, Fred Higgins, Jim Higgins, Nick Howard, George Kelly, Jim Kincaid, Jim Lamborn, Dave Peers, Roger Rosewell, Sabby Sagall, Fred Silberman, Bryan Simmons and John Southgate.

Special help in research was given by Nick Richmond. Thanks are due to Lionel Sims and Colin Barker for correcting the book—Tony Cliff, 15 February 1970

Chapter One

1   Prices and Incomes Board report no 23, *Productivity and Pay During the Period of Severe Restraint*, Cmnd 3167, p8.
2   Prices and Incomes Board report no 123, *Productivity Agreements*, Cmnd 4136, p3. Among the number included in the DEP register are some which were regarded by the department as not authentic productivity agreements. In August 1968 the number of such agreements was considered to be some 130, covering about 48,000 workers.
3   *Financial Times*, 29 September 1969.
4   J E Bayhylle, *Productivity Improvements in the Office* (Engineering Employers' Federation, 1968), pp6-7.
5   ICI, CLD 6/68, Senior Management, Div MUPS CO/RD.

Chapter Two

1   F W Paish, *Rise and Fall of Incomes Policy* (London, 1969), p49.
2   *Statistics on Incomes, Prices, Employment and Production*, March 1969.
3   Prices and Incomes Board report no 77, p12.
4   Cmnd 2639.
5   Prices and Incomes Board report no 36, *Productivity Agreements*, Cmnd 3311, p1.
6   'Written Memorandum of Evidence Submitted by the Esso Petroleum Company in Advance of the Oral Hearing', Donovan commission reference WE/143.

7   Pathfinder, *Arrow* (Rootes journal), July 1969.
8   Engineering Employers' Federation, *A Productivity Bargaining Symposium*, 1969, p23.
9   Engineering Employers' Federation, *A Productivity Bargaining Symposium*, pp39-40.
10 P Runge, *The Relations of Productivity to Price and Wage Control* (London, 1966), p14.
11 Donovan commission report no 39, *Evidence of Esso Petroleum Co Ltd*, p1672.
12 E J Robertson, *Productivity Bargaining and the Engineering Industry* (London, 1968), p29.
13 *Arrow*, July 1969.
14 Donovan commission, research paper no 1, p29.
15 Donovan commission, 'Minutes of Evidence' no 47, p2038.

Chapter Three

1   C Prattern, R M Dean and A Silberston, *The Economics of Large-Scale Production in British Industry* (Department of Applied Economics, Cambridge, Occasional Papers 3, 1965).
2   For Fawley: A Flanders, *The Fawley Productivity Agreement* (London 1964), p187; docks: B Nicholson, 'The First Year of Devlin: A Review of the Docks', in K Coates, T Topham and M Barrett-Brown (eds), *Trade Union Register*, 1968, pp213-214; ICI: 'Weekly Staff Agreement', July 1969; railway workshops: NUR, *Pay and Efficiency (Workshop Staff)*, March 1969, p9; miners: National Coal Board, *Report and Accounts 1968-69*, House of Commons paper 447, p85.
3   A Flanders, *Fawley*, p197 (my emphasis).
4   A Flanders, *Fawley*, p183.
5   Donovan commission report no 39, *Evidence of Esso Petroleum Co Ltd*, p1676.
6   Charles Smith at POEU conference, 1965.
7   Donovan commission report WE/288, *Written Evidence of the POEU*, p22.
8   J Higgins, 'Even Handed Justice,' *Live Wire*, POEU Met West Branch, June 1969.
9   Prices and Incomes Board report no 42, *Pay of Electricity Supply Workers*, Cmnd 3405, p29.
10 Prices and Incomes Board report no 42, *Pay of Electricity Supply Workers*, p22.
11 Prices and Incomes Board report no 120, *Pay and Conditions in the Electrical Contracting Industry*, Cmnd 4097, p15.
12 Steel industry Green Book: *The Manpower Productivity Agreement Between the British Steel Corporation SCW Division (Margam & Abbey Works) and the Amalgamated Engineering Union, the Electrical Trades Union, the United Society of Boilermakers, the Amalgamated Society of Woodworkers, the Amalgamated Society of Painters and Decorators, the Plumbing Trades Union, the British Roll Turner Trade Society*, 8 March 1968, p3. Hereafter referred to as the Margam & Abbey Green Book.
13 Prices and Incomes Board report no 24, *Wages and Conditions in the Electrical Contracting Industry*, Cmnd 3172, p7.
14 Prices and Incomes Board report no 120, *Pay and Conditions in the Electrical Contracting Industry*, p15.
15 T Berwick, *Labour Worker*, February 1968.
16 NUR, *Pay and Efficiency (Workshop Staff)*, pp6, 7, 23, 24.
17 Prices and Incomes Board report no 123, *Productivity Agreements*, Cmnd 4136, p29.
18 Margam & Abbey Green Book, p2.
19 Donovan commission research paper no 4, *Productivity Bargaining*, p20.
20 Prices and Incomes Board report no 42, p8.
21 National Coal Board, *Report and Accounts 1968-69*, p84.
22 Prior to the National Power Loading Agreement, when piece-rates were negotiated locally, in Bentley colliery, near Doncaster, miners working under the Meco-Moore set-up were paid in 1964 £3 5s 4d, and in 1966 £4 1s 10d, a rise of 16s 6d over two years, or 26 percent.
23 *Financial Times*, 9 July 1969.
24 Prices and Incomes Board report no 50, *Productivity Agreements in the Bus Industry*, 3498, p16.
25 *Busman*, September 1967.

26 *Sunday Times*, 23 November 1969.

27 *Port*, 6 November 1969.

28 Engineering Employers' Federation, A *Productivity Bargaining Symposium*, p100

29 Prices and Incomes Board report no 123, p35.

30 *Economic Trends*, February 1966.

31 *Busman*, September 1967.

32 *Summary of Agreement between Swan Hungar and Tyne Shipbuilders Limited and the Amalgamated Society of Boilermakers, Shipwrights and Structural Workers*, 25 October 1968 (my emphasis).

33 *Summary of Agreement* (my emphasis).

Chapter Four

1 *Proceedings of a Special Conference between Engineering Employers Federation and Confederation of Shipbuilding and Engineering Unions*, 31 October 1967, p5.

2 National Board for Prices and Incomes report no 104, *Pay and Conditions of Service of Engineering Workers*, Cmnd 3931, p37.

3 Coventry and District Engineers' Employers' Association.

4 Coventry Blue Book, pp2-3.

5 Coventry Blue Book, p7.

6 *Final Report of the Committee of Inquiry under the Rt Hon Lord Devlin into Certain Matters Concerning the Port Transport Industry* (London, 1965), Cmnd 2734, pp16-17. Hereafter referred to as the Devlin report.

7 *Final Report*, p33.

8 *Final Report*, pp4-5.

9 Coventry Blue Book, p9.

10 J B Jeffreys, *The Story of the Engineers* (London, 1945), pp34-42.

11 J B Jeffreys, *Story*, p139.

12 Coventry Blue Book, p9.

13 Coventry Blue Book, p189.

14 N C Hunt, 'Second Thoughts on Management Education', *Manager* no 28, 1960, quoted in R Marriott, *Payment Systems* (London 1960), p25. A description of a really beautiful system of shopfloor control of PBR is to be found in S Lerner and others, *Workshop Wage Determination* (Oxford, 1969), pp87-94. Each department elects a piece-rate committee subject to the control of the JSSC. Each committee maintains a fund by levies on workers in the department. An annual works meeting decides a 'minimax' earnings level for the whole factory. This minimum figure becomes the target for all piece-rate negotiations—no worker can accept a price which the piece-rate committee thinks inadequate. Where the price offered is inadequate, the worker goes slow and his loss of earnings is made up by the committee from its fund. The 'minimax' is also an earnings ceiling—any earnings above the figure must be paid over to the committee, and deliberate rate-busting can attract serious penalties. When the rates on most jobs allow the majority of workers to reach their ceiling without much trouble a decision can be taken to raise the 'minimax'.

This is an extreme and very effective form of collective control over PBR, which prevents the conflicts between individuals or sections which are often generated.

15 Prices and Incomes Board report no 65, *Payment by Results Systems*, Cmnd 3627, pp49-54.

16 Prices and Incomes Board report no 65, *Payment by Results Systems*, pp64-65.

17 Coventry Blue Book, pp17-18 (my emphasis).

18 Coventry Blue Book.

19 *Metalworking Production*, 19 February 1964.

20 A Flanders, in Engineering Employers' Federation, A *Productivity Bargaining Symposium*, p14.

21 *Steel Review*, July 1966, p6.

22 Coventry Blue Book, p18
23 Coventry Blue Book, pp34-35.
24 R H Heath, 'The National Power-Loading Agreement in the Coal Industry and some Aspects of Workers' Control', *Trade Union Register* 1969, p190.
25 *Financial Times*, 19 November 1968.
26 Rootes Motors Limited, Coventry, *Proposed Agreement*, May 1968.

Chapter Five

1 *Agreement for Trials of Proposals on Manpower Utilisation and Payment Structures Between Imperial Chemical Industries Limited and the Trades Unions Concerned*, pp1-2.
2 Rootes Motor Limited, Coventry, *Proposed Agreement*, p8.
3 *Agreement Concluded with the Enclosed Docks Employers with the Transport and General Workers Union and the National Amalgamated Stevedores and Dockers to provide for the Introduction of Permanent Employment of Labour*, 9 June 1967.
4 Margam & Abbey Green Book.
5 British Steel Corporation, *Proposals for Heavy Steel Agreement*, 10 May 1969: '4(b)(ii) For two successive periods of 13 weeks following demotion he shall receive payment according to the following schedule:

Period	Earnings of new job plus the undernoted percentage of any loss in shift earnings exclusive of all premium payments
First period of 13 weeks	80 percent
Second period of 13 weeks	60 percent

6 British Steel Corporation, *Proposals for Heavy Steel Agreement*, 10 May 1969, p9: '4(c)(ii) For four successive periods of 13 weeks following redeployment, he shall receive payment according to the following schedule:

Period	Earnings of new job plus the undernoted percentage of any loss in shift earnings exclusive of all premium payments
First period of 13 weeks	80 percent
Second period of 13 weeks	60 percent
Third period of 13 weeks	40 percent
Fourth period of 13 weeks	20 percent

7 NUR, *Pay and Efficiency (Workshop Staff)*, p16.
8 *Productivity Development Agreement between Pressed Steel Fisher Limited, Common Lane, and Amalgamated Engineering and Foundry Workers' Union, Birmingham and Midland Sheet Metal Workers' Union, Electrical and Plumbers Trade Union, National Union of Vehicle Builders, Transport and General Workers Union*, July 1969.
9 *Socialist Worker*, 23 November 1968.
10 Ministry of Labour, *Introduction to Shift Working* (London, 1967), Preface.
11 NUR, *Pay and Efficiency (Workshop Staff)*, pp6, 23-24. This last item has been rejected in the main railway workshops.
12 Margam & Abbey Green Book, Appendix A.
13 Donovan commission report no 21, *Evidence of the Electricity Council*, p771.
14 Donovan commission report no 21, *Evidence of the Electricity Council*, p788.
15 Prices and Incomes Board report no 42, *Pay of Electricity Supply Workers*, Cmnd 3405, p4.
16 Prices and Incomes Board report no 32, *Fire Service Pay*, Cmnd 3287, p13.
17 P E Mott and others, *Shift Work: The Social, Psychological and Physical Consequences* (Ann Arbor, 1965), p235.
18 P E Mott and others, *Shift Work*, p236.
19 P E Mott and others, *Shift Work*. p236.
20 P E Mott and others, *Shift Work*, p301.

21   P E Mott and others, *Shift Work*, p281.

22   P E Mott and others, *Shift Work*, p280.

23   P E Mott and others, *Shift Work*, p15.

24   P E Mott and others, *Shift Work*, p18.

25   P E Mott and others, *Shift Work*, p18.

26   P E Mott and others, *Shift Work*, p303.

27   E L Trist and others, *Organisational Choice* (London, 1963), p259.

28   Margam & Abbey Green Book, Appendix A.

29   *Financial Times*, 29 March 1969.

30   J W Cameron, personnel manager, circular of 9 October 1969.

31   K Marx, *Capital*, vol 1 (Moscow, 1962).

32   R Cox, *Socialist Worker*, 15 March 1969.

33   He added, 'Cricket, dominoes, darts, sunbathing on the roof...internal discount trading schemes all in the boss's time...and increasingly in front of him. Card schools have come out of the locker room onto the floor.'

34   *Taking London for a Ride* (London, 1967), p9.

35   *Report of a Court of Inquiry into Trade Dispute at the Barbican and Horsferry Road Construction Sites in London*, September 1967, Cmnd 3396, p35.

36   D T B North and G L Buckingham, *Productivity Agreements and Wage Systems* (London, 1969), pp197-199.

37   CBI evidence to the Donovan commission, nos 6 and 9, p256.

38   E J Robertson, *Productivity Bargaining and the Engineering Industry*, p25 (my emphasis).

39   The failure to make a firm stand by this principled distinction was an important reason for the eventual failure of the 1914-18 shop stewards movement—the development of a genuine *class* movement was prevented.

40   *Financial Times*, 4 November 1965.

41   *Guardian*, 29 October 1965.

42   *Socialist Worker*, June 1968.

43   Prices and Incomes Board report no 117, *Pay and Conditions of Workers in the Exhibition Contracting Industry*, Cmnd 4088.

44   *An Interim Productivity Agreement between the Amalgamated Society of Boilermakers, Shipwrights, Blacksmiths and Structural Workers and Upper Clyde Shipbuilders Ltd*, November 1968, p3.

45   *Summary of Agreement between Swan Hunter and Tyne Shipbuilders Limited and the Amalgamated Society of Boilermakers, Shipwrights, Blacksmiths and Structural Workers*, 25 October 1968 (my emphasis).

46   *Explanatory Notes and the Rules of the Joint Industry Board for the Electrical and Contracting Industry*, July 1967, pp25-26.

47   Prices and Incomes Board report no 120, p8.

48   *Memorandum on the Definition of 'Unconstitutional Action' Which Determines the Six-Month Period of Disqualification for the Benefits of the Company's Income Security Plan*, 23 January 1969.

49   In the footsteps of Ford workers, municipal bus workers have also achieved a similar softening of the penalty clauses in their agreement. The penalty clause which until now has meant a loss of bonus for six months for those who stop work was changed so that the bonus is only lost for the week in which the stoppage occurs. *Financial Times*, 31 May 1969.

50   Vauxhall, *1969 Wage Negotiation*, Productivity Considerations, Article 5.

51   *National Power Loading Agreement*.

52   P Hobday, 'Tachograph', *DATA Journal*, November 1968.

53   *Morning Star*, 2 January 1970.

Chapter Six

1 *Financial Times*, 10 November 1969.
2 Prices and Incomes Board report no 83, *Job Evaluation*, Cmnd 3772, p10.
3 Prices and Incomes Board report no 83, *Job Evaluation*, p28.
4 ICI, *Weekly Staff Job Assessment Scheme*, July 1969.
5 *Report of a Court of Inquiry Under Sir Jack Scamp Into a Dispute Concerning Sewing Machinists Employed by the Ford Motor Company Limited*, Cmnd 3749, August 1968, pp9-10.
6 *Report of a Court of Inquiry Under Sir Jack Scamp*, p33.
7 *Report of a Court of Inquiry Under Sir Jack Scamp*, p34.
8 D T B North and G L Buckingham, *Productivity Agreements and Wage Systems*, pp97-98.
9 R H Gayland and others, 'The Relation of Ratings to Production Records: An Empirical Study', *Personnel Psychology*, vol 4, no 1, 1951.
10 J T Hazel and D K Cohen, 'Evaluation of Airmen', Lackland Airforce Base, Texas, Ref R.PRL TH 66/ 3, Study 640567, 1966.
11 A G Bayroff and others, 'Validity of Ratings as Related to Rating Technique and Conditions', *Personnel Psychology*, vol 7, 1954.
12 J T Hazel and D K Cohen, 'Evaluation of Airmen'.
13 J T Hazel and D K Cohen, 'Evaluation of Airmen', p363.
14 J T Hazel and D K Cohen, 'Evaluation of Airmen', p99. One study analysed average standard hourly earnings (excluding overtime) for various occupations in 40 firms and calculated the earnings for each occupation. This showed that, out of the 77 manual occupations for which data were available, 49 had a spread of 50 percent and 12 a spread of over 100 percent. In only two occupations was the spread less than 30 percent. This means that in 12 occupations men were earning more than double what others in the same industry and locality were earning. D Robinson, 'The Myths of the Local Labour Market', *Personnel*, December 1967, pp36-39, quoted in Prices and Incomes Board report no 83, *Job Evaluation*, p22.
15 J T Hazel and D K Cohen, 'Evaluation of Airmen', p16.
16 Prices and Incomes Board report no 83, *Job Evaluation*, p37.
17 A similar strike was called by the ETU and the United Patternmakers' Association at Pressed Steel Fisher, Cowley, in April 1968. See *Report of a Court of Inquiry Under Sir Jack Scamp*.
18 D T B North and G L Buckingham, *Productivity Agreements*, p117.
19 *Ford Bulletin: Wage Structure Special Edition*, 11 April 1967.
20 Engineering Employers' Federation, *A Productivity Bargaining Symposium*, p70.
21 J E Bayhylle, *Productivity Improvements*, p53.
22 J E Bayhylle, *Productivity Improvements*, p54.

Chapter Seven

1 *British Industry Week*, 3 May 1968.
2 Donovan commission report no 57, *Written Evidence of the ETU*, pp2465-2466.
3 Donovan commission report no 57, *Written Evidence of the ETU*, p2466.
4 D J Desmond, 'The Statistical Approach to Time-Study', *Statistical Method in Industrial Production*, 1951, p37.
5 W Gomberg, *A Trade Union Analysis of Time Study* (2nd edn, London), p193.
6 R Marriott, *Payment Systems*, p111. There is no scientific basis for the statement in a book on work study in the building industry that '6 percent covers normal needs such as tea breaks, visits to the lavatory, etc' ie, 28 minutes in an eight-hour day (R Geary, *Work Study, Applied to Building* (London, 1965), p33).
7 R Marriott, *Payment Systems*, pp111-112.
8 W Baldamus quoted in R Marriott, *Payment Systems*, p98.

9   R Marriott, *Payment Systems*, p114.

10 R Marriott, *Payment Systems*, pp115-116.

11 F W Taylor, *Principles of Scientific Management* (New York, 1911), p59.

12 A Abruzzi, 'A Realistic Model for Rating Procedures', *Proceedings of the 17th Annual Time and Motion Study Clinic*, 1953.

13 Margam & Abbey Green Book.

14 Joint Ford Shop Stewards Committee, *What's Wrong at Ford* (1963), p6.

15 *DATA News*, 25 April 1969.

16 *Annual Report of HM Chief Inspector of Factories, 1968*, September 1969, Cmnd 4146.

17 From the annual report of the National Coal Board for the years 1955, 1960, 1965-66 and 1968-69.

18 Margam & Abbey Green Book.

19 Margam & Abbey Green Book.

Chapter Eight

1   S Paulden and B Hawkins, *Whatever Happened at Fairfields?* (London, 1969), p95.

2   S Paulden and B Hawkins, *Whatever Happened*, pp95, 188.

3   National Coal Board, *Report and Accounts, 1968-69*, charts 2 and 3.

4   This chapter, p162.

5   If unemployment and union passivity led to a decline in strikes, the general malaise in the mining industry led to increasing individual 'solutions' of workers' problems by rising absenteeism. The rate of absenteeism in the mines was: in 1954, 12.21 percent; 1960, 14.75 percent; 1965-66, 18.01 percent; 1968-69, 18.1 percent.

6   *Listener*, 15 December 1966.

7   *Guardian*. 19 July 1961.

8   *Guardian*, 27 July 1961.

9   *Barclays Bank Review*, August 1969, p50.

10 *Financial Times*, 21 July 1969.

11 *Board of Trade Journal*, 14 March 1969.

12 *Labour Research*, May 1969.

13 S Newens in the House of Commons, *Hansard*, 7 March 1969.

14 K Jones and J Golding, *Productivity Bargaining* (London, 1966), pp19-20.

15 *Socialist Worker*, 12 April 1969.

16 J Nichol, 'Hardship And Danger Increase For Durham Miners', *Socialist Worker*, June 1968.

17 *Socialist Worker*, 15 March 1969.

18 *Arrow*, July 1969.

19 ICI, *Explanatory Notes on the Manpower Utilisation and Payment Structure Agreement for Trial Sites*, p4.

Chapter Nine

1   M Stewart and R Winsbury, *An Incomes Policy for Labour*, Fabian Tract 350, October 1963, p18.

2   *Economist*, 5 June 1965.

3   *Economist*, 4 September 1965.

4   S Brittan, *The Treasury Under the Tories, 1951-1964* (Harmondsworth, 1965), p276.

5   *Evening Standard*, 12 October 1965.

6   Donovan report, p262.

7   Donovan report, p262.

8   Donovan report, pp263-264.

9   Donovan report, pp264-265.

10 Donovan report, p268.

11 'Fair Deal at Work', p63.
12 'In Place of Strife', p37.
13 'Fair Deal at Work', p63.
14 'In Place of Strife', p37.
15 'Fair Deal at Work', p63.
16 'In Place of Strife', p36.
17 'Fair Deal at Work', p40.
18 'In Place of Strife', p37.
19 'Fair Deal at Work', p33.
20 'In Place of Strife', p21.
21 Donovan commission report no WE/75, *Written Evidence of the Ministry of Labour*, p7.
22 Donovan commission report no 23, *Evidence of Motor Industry Employers*, p899.
23 Donovan commission report no 47, *Evidence of Richard O'Brien and A J Nicol*, p2020.
24 Donovan commission report no 47, *Evidence of Richard O'Brien and A J Nicol*, p2021.
25 Donovan commission report no 48, *Evidence of the Shipbuilding Employers' Federation*, p2106.
26 Donovan report, pp340-341.
27 H A Turner, *Is Britain Really Strike-Prone?* (London, 1969), p7.
28 *Morning Star*, 29 May 1969.
29 Similarly in 1968 the electricity supply employers were forced to pay the fines of their workers jailed for striking before a peace settlement could be concluded. The employers rushed to pay the fines, release the strike leaders and take them by taxi to work.
30 H A Turner, *Is Britain*, p7.
31 Donovan commission report no 34, *Evidence of Swedish Employers Confederation*, p1455.
32 A Kornhauser and others (eds), *Industrial Conflict* (New York, 1954), p494.
33 Donovan commission report no 34, *Evidence of Swedish Employers Confederation*, p1448.
34 The general rosy prospects for Swedish capitalism explain why Sweden could remain practically strike-free while wages have escalated—much more than in Britain. Over the years 1956-66 the Swedish average hourly wage rate rose from Kr6.5 to Kr11. Swedish capitalism found such a rise not intolerable, while British capitalism, with a much smaller rise in its average hourly wage from Kr4.71 to Kr6.83, found it almost back-breaking. *Financial Times*, 2 May 1968.
35 *Financial Times*, 31 December 1969.
36 By the way this is not a very new notion. Already in 1903 Sydney Webb, the founder of Fabianism, the theory of right wing Labour, argued that strikes were an outmoded way of settling disputes. Donovan commission report no 3, *Ministry of Labour Evidence*, p123.
37 Similarly the CIR was welcomed by *Tribune*. On the occasion when Will Paynter, ex general secretary of the National Union of Mineworkers and longstanding member of the executive of the Communist Party, joined the CIR, the editor of *Tribune*, Richard Clements, wrote, 'The function of the CIR is not to weaken trade union power but to enhance it. Much of its job will be to put into effect demands which have been the subject of resolutions at countless TUCs. Who would find fault in that? The CIR has nothing to do with the offensive parts of the government white paper—the strike ballot and the "cooling-off period". I have no doubt that Will Paynter did his homework very carefully before he decided to get himself involved in the body. What a splendid thought that he can continue to help the trade union movement even after he has retired from an active part in it.' *Tribune*, 7 February 1969.
38 P Osborne, 'Nasty Medicine', *Socialist Worker*, 29 May 1969.
39 At the TUC conference at Croydon in June 1969 only the following unions voted against 'Programme for Action': DATA, ASTMS, AUBTW, Sheet Metal Workers, Metal Mechanics, Lightermen (and, for extreme right wing reasons, the ETU-PTU). Both the TGWU and AEF voted for. As a matter of fact, although the national committee of the AEF rejected 'Programme for Action' first, Scanlon declared his open support for it. And at the end, in the teeth of opposition by Reg Birch, Scanlon managed to pull the national committee behind him.
40 *Collective Bargaining: Prescription for Change* (London, 1967), p25.

41 *Collective Bargaining: Prescription for Change*, p28.
42 *Collective Bargaining: Prescription for Change*, p32.
43 *Collective Bargaining: Prescription for Change*, p72.
44 Donovan commission research paper no 1, W E J McCarthy, *The Role of Shop Stewards in British Industrial Relations*, p73.
45 Donovan commission research paper no 1, W E J McCarthy, *The Role of Shop Stewards*, p74.
46 A Flanders, *Fawley*, p32.

Chapter Ten

1   J B Jeffreys, *Story*, p145.
2   *DATA Journal*, June 1967.
3   *Guardian*, 22 September 1969.
4   *Financial Times*, 23 October 1969.
5   *Management Today*, March 1968.
6   EC Press and Information Service, *The Common Market and the Common Man* (Brussels, 1969).
7   *Proceedings at a Special Conference between Engineering Employers' Federation and Confederation of Shipbuilding and Engineering Unions*, 31 October 1967, p42.
8   *Management Today*, March 1968.
9   P Foot, *Private Eye*, 30 August 1968.
10 P Foot, 'The Criminal Waste Of Concorde', *Socialist Worker*, 23 October 69.
11 *Labour Research*, April 1968.
12 *Employment and Productivity Gazette*, August 1969.
13 R C O Matthews, 'An Upswing Of A Sort', *Times*, 13 October 1969.
14 House of Commons, *Hansard*, 3 November 1969, vol 790, cols 721-723.
15 *Labour Research*, August 1969.
16 *DATA Journal*, November 1968.
17 *Poverty* no 11, 1969, p15.
18 *Financial Times*, 11 June 1969.
19 'Still No Property Owning Democracy', *Economist*, 15 January 1966, quoted in R Blackburn, 'The Unequal Society', in A Cockburn and R Blackburn (eds), *The Incompatibles* (London, 1967), p17.
20 R Blackburn, 'The Unequal Society', pp18-19.
21 Institute for Workers' Control, *GEC-EE: Workers' Takeover* (Nottingham, 1969), p12.
22 J Hughes, 'The Increase in Inequality', *New Statesman*, 8 November 1968.
23 J Kincaid , 'Incomes', *International Socialism* no 37.
24 *Economic Trends*, HSMO, February 1969. Original income refers to gross income of all members of the household, and includes any cash benefits that may be received, pensions, family allowances, etc.
25 'Public Money and Private Industry', *Barclays Bank Review*, August 1969.
26 *Census of England and Wales*, 1961, housing tables, table 14.
27 Calculated from *Sample Census of Scotland*, 1966, housing tables.
28 *Lancet*, 13 April 1968.
29 *Medical Officer*, 24 January 1969.
30 *Poverty* no 4, 1967, p17.
31 R N Litmuss, *Commitment to Welfare* (1968), p107.
32 *Times*, 11 September 1969.
33 G Searjeant, *Sunday Times*, 7 September 1969.
34 *Times*, 22 September 1969. It is obvious that under such conditions of business intricacies the demand of the TGWU for workers' representatives to be allowed to inspect companies' books when negotiations for productivity deals take place is really quite innocuous.
35 *International Socialism* no 42.

Chapter Eleven

1   G Moore, 'An Each-Way Double', *Platform* special issue.

2   Quoted in *Electricians' Voice*, December 1968.

3   *British Industry Week*, October 1967.

4   *DATA Journal*, September 1969.

5   Jim Conway, 'A Trade Union View', in Engineering Employers' Federation, *A Productivity Bargaining Symposium*, pp 68-69.

6   'The ETU's attitude...was particularly interesting. Not only did this union have a Communist leadership nationally at the time [of the signing of the Fawley Agreement] but the [full time official] and the senior steward were also avowed and longstanding members of the Communist Party. Anyone naive enough to conclude that the union must therefore he hostile to such union-management cooperation as the Blue Book implied would be mistaken. Throughout the negotiations the ETU [full time official] who was chairman of the CUC [Croft Union Committee] adopted a very constructive attitude, and in this was strangely supported by his senior steward.' A Flanders, *Fawley*, p112.

7   Economist Intelligence Unit, *The National Newspaper Industry* (London, 1966), part 1, p92.

8   *Report of a Court of Inquiry Into the Problems Caused by the Introduction of Web-Offset Machines in the Printing Industry and the Problems Arising from the Introduction of Other Modern Printing Techniques and the Arrangements Which Should be Adopted Within the Industry for Dealing With Them*, Cmnd 3184, 1967, p29.

9   *Report of a Court of Inquiry Into the Problems Caused by the Introduction of Web-Offset Machines*, p36.

10 *Report of a Court of Inquiry Into the Problems Caused by the Introduction of Web-Offset Machines*, p46.

11 In sharp contrast to the inter-union squables is the success of the liaison committee at Odhams, where the *Sun* and the *People* were printed. It showed how much can be achieved by worker cooperation. S Geraghty and P Foot, 'Press Barons' Quest For Profits Threatens Jobs In Fleet Street', *Socialist Worker*, 5 June 1969.

12 Donovan commission report nos 61 and 65, TUC Evidence, p2751.

13 *Financial Times*, 25 August 1969.

14 *Financial Times*, 30 August 1969.

15 It is interesting to note that the steel unions did not raise objections to the corporation's recognition of the Steel Industry Management Association, which was largely the creation of management, which formed a potential blackleg force. See the speech by H Smith of DATA at TUC conference, *Morning Star*, 4 September 1969. It seems that the ISTC is thinking of a merger with the Steel Industry Management Association (*Guardian*, 5 January 1970).

16 J T Murphy, *The Workers' Committee: An Outline of its Principles and Structure* (London, 1918), p3.

17 J T Murphy, *The Workers' Committee*, pp3-4.

18 H A Clegg, A J Killick and R Adams, *Trade Union Officers* (Oxford, 1961), pp72-73.

19 H A Clegg, A J Killick and R Adams, *Trade Union Officers*, p90.

20 H A Clegg, A J Killick and R Adams, *Trade Union Officers*, p85.

21 What we have said should not he taken to imply an indiscriminate personal attack on every individual full time union official. As a body, however, full time officials are becoming further and further removed from their members by a number of separate but related pressures. Many of them undoubtedly act in direct opposition to the men and women they are supposed to represent, and put their association with the employers before their members' interests. Some, we are sure, try to avoid this situation. What matters in this context, however, is that any strategy of opposition to incomes policy and productivity deals that looks to trade union officials, of the left or of the right, to play an important role in this opposition is fundamentally misconceived. No one would in any way wish to exclude left wing union officials from socialist movements, we imagine, but to rely upon them to play an all

important role, or to focus too much attention on them, is as ridiculous as seeing the fate of the working class movement in this country as dependent upon the activities of a few socialist university professors.

22 *Financial Times*, 4 August 1969.

23 Economist Intelligence Unit, *The National Newspaper Industry*, part 1, p231.

24 J Goldthorpe and D Lockwood, *The Affluent Worker: Industrial Attitudes and Behaviour* (London 1968), pp98-103.

25 J Goldstein, *The Government of British Trade Unions* (London 1952), p24.

26 H A Turner, G Clack and B Roberts, *Labour Relations in the Motor Industry* (London, 1967), p222.

27 A I Marsh and J W Staples, 'Check-off Agreements in Britain: A Study of Their Growth and Function', Donovan commission, *Research Papers* no 8, p45.

28 A I Marsh and J W Staples, 'Check-off Agreements', p50.

29 A S Tammenbaum, 'Unions', in J G March (ed), *Handbook of Chicago*, 1965, p749.

30 *Contact*, July 1969.

31 *Financial Times*, 20 July 1969.

32 *Times*, 26 August 1969.

33 *Socialist Worker*, 12 April 1969.

34 ETU ballot papers, September 1969.

35 It is interesting to note that during the period in which Communists controlled the ETU no attempt was made to strengthen the position of the union's conference whose policy, determination constituted no more than a 'recommendation' to the executive council. ETU 1958 rules, rule 19.

36 T Corfield, *Collective Leadership for the Transport and General Workers Union* (London, 1968), p2.

37 T Corfield, *Collective Leadership*, p2.

38 T Corfield, *Collective Leadership*, p3.

39 T Corfield, *Collective Leadership*, p3.

40 H A Clegg, A J Killick and R Adams, *Trade Union Officers*, p79.

41 V L Allen, *Trade Unions and the Government* (London, 1961), p32.

42 V L Allen, *Trade Unions and the Government*, p12.

43 *TUC Report*, 1952, p301, cited in V L Allen, *Trade Unions and the Government*, p23.

44 H Pelling, *A History of British Trade Unionism* (Harmondsworth, 1963), p235.

45 V L Allen, *Trade Unions and the Government*, p35.

46 M Harrison, *Trade Unions and the Labour Party Since 1945* (London, 1960), p294.

47 M Harrison, *Trade Unions and the Labour Party*, pp294-295.

48 V L Allen, *Militant Trade Unionism* (London, 1966), p34.

49 Thus in 1966, for instance, of 519 cases involving the 1,300,000 manual workers in federated firms in the engineering industry that were sent to the Central Conference in York, only 55 were settled (85 were referred back, 127 more were retained in the hands of the central authorities, in 239 cases a 'failure to agree' was recorded, and so on). A I Marsh and W E J McCarthy, *Disputes Procedures in Britain*, Donovan commission research papers no 2, part 2, p21.

50 How far union officials are trapped completely by procedure can be seen from the fact that, while Jack Jones 'opposes' incomes policy, 'Mr Jones wanted Mr Feather to state publicly that 280 of the 686 pay claims notified to the TUC during the past year came from the TGWU, although the TGWU opposed the government's prices and incomes policy at the Trades Union Congress at Brighton last September.' *Financial Times*, 8 September 1966.

51 Donovan commission report no 30, TGWU evidence, pp1228-1229.

52 Donovan commission report no 24, AEU evidence, p969.

53 ETU evidence to the Donovan commission, no 57, p2461.

54 Donovan commission report nos 61 and 65, TUC evidence, p2713.

55 Donovan commission report no 23, evidence of the Motor Industry Employers, p889.

56 Donovan commission report no 69, evidence of the CBI, p2988.

57 *Report of a Court of Inquiry into Trade Disputes at the Barbican*, p67.

58 *Report of a Court of Inquiry into Trade Disputes at the Barbican*, p68.
59 *TUC Report*, 1960, p129.
60 *TUC Report*, 1960, p129.
61 *TUC Report*, 1960, p130.
62 K Weller, *What Next for Engineers?* (London).
63 *Report of a Court of Inquiry into Trade Disputes at the Barbican*, p30.
64 *Report of a Court of Inquiry into Trade Disputes at the Barbican*, p38.
65 William McCarthy, *The Future of the Unions*, Fabian Tract 339, September 1962, pp23-24.
66 *Financial Times*, 22 October 1968. Scanlon himself proved the point when he signed the agreement with the engineering employers in October 1968. Instead of the original demand for £2 a week the agreement gained two general increases of 6s 4d each spread over three years. In addition the consolidated rate of £19 looks like a pretty impressive jump from the previous £12 17s 8d. However, most skilled men have already been paid much more than £19 so it won't make much difference. The cost of the employers' concessions worked out at between 3¼ and 4 percent a year. Not a grand achievement after 16 months of negotiations from June 1967!
67 That the roots of Daly's behaviour during the recent strike were not purely personal is emphasised by the behaviour of his predecessor as general secretary of the miners' union, Will Paynter. During the nine years (1959-68) he held the post the number of pits declined from 793 to 376 (46 a year) and the number of miners declined from 692,700 to 391,000 (33,400 a year). To crown his career, in February 1968 Paynter joined the government's Commission on Industrial Relations, which seeks to crack down on militant rank and file action in industry. He sits alongside Leslie Blakeman, the former personnel director of Ford, who dreamed up the famous penalty clauses to outlaw unofficial strikes. And for this service Paynter earns, not the £15 of the surface worker, but a nice £6,500 a year. Paynter was a member of the CP for 39 years, and for more than 20 years a member of its national executive. On the day he retired CP general secretary John Gollan spoke of Paynter's 'brilliant service to the miners and the Communist Party'. *Morning Star*, 5 December 1968.
68 W A Faunce, 'Delegate Attitudes Towards the Convention in the UAW', *Industrial Labour Relations Review* 15, 1962.
69 R A Lester, *As Unions Mature* (Princeton, 1958), p116.
70 Donovan report, p188.
71 D Bell, *The End of Ideology* (New York, 1961), p215.
72 *Sunday Times*, 9 February 1969.
73 D Bell, *The End*, p216.

Chapter Twelve

1 *Final Report of the Committee of Inquiry under the Rt Hon Lord Devlin into Certain Matters Concerning the Port Transport Industry*, Cmnd 2734, August 1965, p4. Also calculated from *Employment and Productivity Gazette*.
2 H A Turner, *The Trend of Strikes* (Leeds, 1963), p2.
3 H A Turner, *The Trend*, p8.
4 *Employment and Productivity Gazette*.
5 *Economist*, 18 October 1969.
6 Donovan report, p19.
7 *Report of a Court of Inquiry Under Sir Jack Scamp*, p8.
8 N D Fernando and C Slaughter, *Coal is Our Life* (London, 1956), p63.
9 Evidence of the NUR to the Donovan commission, no 17, p607.
10 *Financial Times*, 6 January 1970.
11 Donovan commission reports no 6 and 9, CBI evidence, p286.
12 Donovan commission report no 2, evidence of the Ministry of Labour, p62.
13 A I Marsh and W E J McCarthy, *Disputes Procedures in Britain*, p29.

14 Donovan commission report, p190.

15 H A Turner, *The Trend*, p19.

16 A Gorz, 'Trade Unionism on the Attack', *International Socialist Journal*, April 1964.

17 A W Gouldner, *Wildcat Strike* (London, 1955), p33.

18 G Carlsson, 'Combine Committees—Key To The Fight Against Bosses' Offensive', *Socialist Worker*, 16 October 1969.

19 Donovan commission research papers no 10, quoted in W E J McCarthy and S R Parker, *Shop Stewards and Workshop Relations*, p5.

20 *Report of a Court of Inquiry Under Sir Jack Scamp*, p10.

21 Donovan commission research papers no 10, quoted in W E J McCarthy and S R Parker, *Shop Stewards*, p37.

22 Donovan commission research papers no 10, quoted in W E J McCarthy and S R Parker, *Shop Stewards*, p14.

23 J B Jeffreys, *Story*, pp181-2.

24 But the Hargreaves strike was the shop stewards movement at its best. The problem of fragmentation was, in fact, less acute in Sheffield than elsewhere. Both today, as has been shown, and during the 1914-22 period, shop steward organisation was most powerful and well developed in the more economically dynamic sectors of the engineering industry—then armaments, now motor cars and aircraft. In Sheffield this presented no problem, as over 60 percent of the metal workers were employed in five big armament firms. On the Clyde, for example, where armaments production employed no more than 20 percent of the engineering workers, the problem of expanding the shop stewards movement from the arms firms into the more important shipbuilding and marine engineering firms held back the development of the movement for several years. The Clyde Workers' Committee suffered a resounding defeat in the spring of 1916, largely because of their failure to build a bridge to the mass of engineering workers in the shipyards and the marine engineering firms. They failed in this because they had been content to regard themselves as the key section of the workers (which they were), a section sufficiently powerful to be in a position to dispense with the task of drawing other sections of the class into the struggle (which they were not). Shop stewards in the key sections of the engineering industry today, faced with a government offensive under the name of the incomes policy, would do well to learn from this defeat of an earlier shop steward movement.

25 See H A Turner, G Clack and B Roberts, *Labour Relations*, ch IX.

26 See H A Turner, G Clack and B Roberts, *Labour Relations*, p263.

27 Prices and Incomes Board report no 29, *The Pay and Conditions of Manual Workers in Local Authorities, the National Health Service, Gas and Water Supply*, Cmnd 3230.

28 Prices and Incomes Board report no 42, *Pay of Electricity Supply Workers*, Cmnd 3405, p22.

29 *Times*, 7 November 1969.

30 Other elements that caused the recent burst of wage levels are the failure of low paid workers, and workers not paid by piece-rate, to keep up with the rising cost of living, and the worsening of their earnings relative to the earnings of other workers.

Chapter Thirteen

1 Prices and Incomes Board report no 86, p26.

2 J Edmonds and P Radice, *Low Pay* (London, 1968), p15.

3 G Jones and M Barnes, *Britain on Borrowed Time* (Harmondsworth, 1967), p122.

4 H A Turner, G Clack and B Roberts, *Labour Relations*, p162.

5 *Times*, 22 November 1969.

6 Bernard Ross, *Know Your Enemy* (Coventry, 1968), p14.

7 To this could be added a demand that the official gets the same conditions of work as his members. He might then be less willing to sell important items like tea breaks and shift work for a few pence!

8   The comparability factor—what workers will call class solidarity—is one of the greatest impediments to the introduction of productivity bargaining and has to be used to stop productivity bargains becoming sheer bargains for management.

9   The fight against redundancy must, however, be not only industrial but also political. The state should be forced to guarantee five days work or five days pay, if necessary by establishing state enterprises.

10 Where possible (as in the docks) even the two-shift system should he opposed, since management's aim in introducing this is to provide a bridge leading to a three-shift system and seven-day working.

11 Figures from *Sunday Times*, 8 February 1970.

12 It is often worthwhile to convert demands for better conditions into money values so that we have an idea how much they would cost the employer. Thus an extra week's holiday is equivalent to about 10s a week for each worker if he is getting the average industrial wage of about £25 a week.

13 This book on productivity bargaining was produced by the International Socialists as a response to the widespread feeling in industry that on the question of productivity the militant trade unionist has found that there is nowhere to turn for advice and assistance. With few exceptions the traditional organisations in the trade union movement have either come out in favour of productivity deals or have maintained an embarrassed silence on this important issue. We hope that the reader has found this book of some value in redressing the balance.

There are, however, many facts and figures, particularly relating to individual factories and combines, that it has not been possible to include due to lack of space. If any reader has any need for this kind of information or requires assistance on any problems associated with the fight against productivity deals which they think we might be able to help with, please write to the IS Industrial Committee. Our resources, although limited, are always at the disposal of workers in struggle.

After Pentonville: the battle is won but the war goes on

Socialist Worker, 5 August 1972

This has been the greatest victory for the British working class for more than half a century. The battle has been won, but the war against capitalism is still going on.

After such a great victory it is important to take stock, view the battlefield as a whole and, while full of enthusiasm and the will to struggle, keep a cool head and think out the strategy, tactics and organisational measures necessary to lead the struggle forward.

The motive behind the Tories' attack on the working class is not the nastiness of the rulers, nasty though they be, but the deepening crisis of world capitalism.

The weapons the ruling class uses are determined largely by the immense strength of workers' organisation and workers' resistance. In fact, as Lenin put it, there is no crisis of capitalism the capitalists cannot find a way out of if the workers are ready to pay the price.

The workers' resistance makes it more and more difficult for the bosses to get their way. Let us look at the weapons bosses have been using for the last few years.

Incomes policy: The aim of this is to shift the distribution of the national income from wages to profits.

In the 1920s and 30s, with massive unemployment and a weak shop organisation, the employers never dreamed of offering a wage rise of $3^1/2$ percent or 5 percent. Instead they cut wages all round.

Productivity deals pay homage to working class strength. Basically, a productivity deal is a bitter pill in terms of worse conditions, speed-up, etc, but it is covered with sugar.

In the 1920s and 30s management didn't dream of saying, 'We will give you an extra £3 a week on condition you accept deterioration in working conditions.' They simply dictated, 'If you want a job, have it. If you don't, out you get.'

Key wage settlements: The idea of taking on the post workers and keeping down their wages, plus setting an example to other sections of the working class, is again homage to working class strength.

In the 1920s and 30s the employers reduced all workers' wages. There wasn't one weak section to become an example to the strong sections—all sections of the working class were weak.

Anti trade union legislation: Again homage to our strength. When shop organisation was weak and unemployment massive, the philosophy of capitalism was non-intervention of the state in labour relations.

Let there be a free for all and the best man win. And you can guess who won.

But, because of the present strength of workers' resistance, the capitalist machine does not work the way the bosses want. The driver steers and the machine doesn't turn. He presses the accelerator and it doesn't speed up. He puts on the brake and it doesn't stop.

What, in heaven's name, is affecting the engine? The answer is the workers' will and ability to resist.

For example, the question of key wage settlements. It is true that the government managed to beat the post workers at the beginning of 1971. They got only a 9 percent rise. This meant a cut in real wages of some 5 or 6 percent.

When the cost of living is rising by 10 percent the workers must get 15 percent—as a third of any wage rise goes in deductions—just to stay in the same place. But the defeat of the post workers did not prevent Chrysler workers getting a rise of £6 a week in the same month.

Ted Heath and before him Harold Wilson believed that unemployment would introduce discipline on the wages front. (Remember Wilson's 'shake-out of the labour market'?)

For nearly two decades Paish's Law was accepted as a holy truth. Professor F W Paish of the London School of Economics had been economic adviser to the Tory government. His theory was that a certain level of unemployment—anything between 2 and 2½ percent—would break workers' resistance and put them in their place, so that wages would be contained. However, even with unemployment running at a million, Paish's Law did not work at all.

Workers' organisation is too strong for unemployment of the present magnitude to break their will to fight. Actually, unemployment in many cases spurs workers on to further claims. A Dundee building worker told me about a year ago, 'Because of the heavy unemployment among builders in my town we decided not to work for less than £1 an hour.'

The Paish logic, on the other hand, is that, if under conditions of more or less full employment a building worker is ready to work for 75p, he will come cap in hand to the boss and be ready to accept a wage of 60p if there is unemployment.

But the workers argue exactly the opposite: 'If I am sure of 40 hours a week, then I can manage on 75p. But if there is unemployment I must demand at least £1.'

Finally, the Industrial Relations Act didn't work the way the Tories expected or hoped. Now we don't have to waste too much space to prove this, emerging as we are from five days that shook Tory rule.

It is true that if a ship loses its rudder the captain may use the left engine and stop the right, and then use the right and stop the left.

But this is a costly and ineffective way of moving a ship. If the five rank and file docks militants had to be freed from prison perhaps pliable Jack Jones can serve now as the disciplinarian of the rank and file.

The threat of £55,000 over his head may serve to soften him up. We always knew that we have the best trade union leaders money can buy!

Workers' memories, however, aren't as short as all that. Perhaps two months ago a £55,000 fine would have terrified the rank and file, at least for a time, into submission. But why should workers stop picketing Midland Cold Storage even if Jack Jones has to pay the £55,000?

There is no compulsion on him to pay. He can fight back. If a strike can free the five, it can also prevent the imposition of a fine. If the TUC declared in advance that they would bring the country out on a one-day strike every time a fine was imposed, the ruling class would find the gain not worthwhile.

Every day workers in this country produce goods and services to the value of £150 million, so let's say to our rulers, 'You fine us £55,000 and we will take it back not in thousands but in millions.' That is only fair. It is not an equal exchange, but then we do not live in an equal society. So again this weapon of the ruling class somehow doesn't hit the target.

Partial struggles: The other side of the coin to the ineffectiveness of Tory oppression is the fragmentation and volatility of the workers' struggle. If we juxtapose the great victory of the dockers and workers who came to their aid over the five days, against the fight of the Fine Tubes workers for more than two years, we see how fragmented the struggle is.

The management of Fine Tubes are far smaller in calibre, in weight, in resources than the executive committee of the capitalist class as represented by the state. On the other hand, the workers of Fine Tubes are members of two of the biggest trade unions in the country—the TGWU with 1,700,000 members and the AUEW with 1,400,000.

How is it that unions with more than 3 million members cannot crack a peanut the size of the Fine Tubes management? The answer is that the trade union bureaucracy was much more effective in paralysing aid to the Fine Tube workers than in paralysing the dockers and the workers who came to their aid.

But the struggle is fragmented also in another way. Take the miners. They won a magnificent victory. They smashed the Tory wage norm. They wiped the smile off Ted Heath's face.

But they could not prevent the rise in the cost of living, or the loss of Family Income Supplement, free milk, etc. What they held in their hand largely slipped through their fingers.

Again, the dockers five weeks ago saved three of their members from going to prison. But the very same weekend the giants of the City of London went on strike and they and other big businessmen transferred hundreds of millions of pounds out of this country.

The result? The floating pound and rising prices. The docker can prevent his mates being arrested but he cannot prevent his children losing school milk or the rise in prices now or after Britain joins the Common Market.

Every partial struggle under capitalism means that no victory is really complete.

Volatility: The working class movement has been suffering the last few years not only from fragmentation, from the partial nature of the struggle, but also from extreme volatility.

If one looks back to the 1920s or 30s the struggle was largely systematic in its development. One event followed another in practically a straight line.

If one looks at the 1940s and 50s until the mid-1960s, again, for a whole generation we face a systematic development in the class struggle. Year by year workers' real wages improved practically everywhere. Strikes were small in size, short in duration and practically always victorious.

Of course to all these steady developments there were important exceptions. After all, capitalism is an anarchic system and there cannot but be many exceptions to any rules governing the way it works.

As against this long period from the First World War to the mid-60s, the last few years have seen great volatility in the movement. Take only a couple of examples.

The defeat of the post workers led to the same or lower wage settlements involving millions of workers. 1971 was a year of declining wages all round, with important exceptions. Then came the miners' victory and following it the railwaymen's. A fantastic zigzag!

The volatility is even clearer in the case of the struggle against the Industrial Relations Bill. On 8 December 1970 half a million workers came out on strike against the Industrial Relations Bill. The struggle rose.

On 21 February 1971, 140,000 workers demonstrated against the bill. There must have been many hundreds of thousands, if not millions, who identified themselves with these demonstrations in Liverpool, Manchester, Birmingham, Glasgow, and so on.

On 1 March 1½ million workers came out on official strike against the bill. On 18 March a similar number came out again. On that day the TUC made it clear they were not ready to give a lead in the general struggle against the bill. The result? There was an immediate 180-degree turn.

The militants' slogan now was 'Stop the retreat'. From an offensive posture they turned to a defensive one. This volatility affects largely the advanced sections of the working class. It is rooted in: (1) the feeling of the militant that quite often he cannot carry the majority of his own workmates with him; and (2) his isolation from militants in other places of work and, even more, in other industries.

Three cog wheels: The trade union movement, with 11 million members and 250,000 shop stewards, is a powerful cog, with by far the strongest shop organisation of the working class anywhere in the world.

Let's assume that we had in this country a revolutionary socialist party, a combat organisation, steeled in struggle and schooled in the art of strategy and tactics for the overthrow of capitalism. Let's assume that we, the International Socialists, who are building such an organisation, had 50,000 members.

There is no question that this would indeed be a powerful cog wheel. However, one cog wheel of this size could not have moved the cog wheel of 11 million. If it tried it would only break its cogs. A connecting cog wheel is necessary between the two.

This is the organisation of militants in different unions and industries who work together round specific issues, issues wider than those affecting a small group of workers in one place of work and not going as far as to aim at a complete emancipation of the working class by the overthrow of the capitalist system.

IS members participate in building such a cog wheel in the form of rank and file organisations round papers like the *Carworker,* the *Collier* and *Rank and File Teacher.* The aim of these is to influence the policies of the trade unions.

The rising conflict will disclose to workers the magnitude of the struggle, will widen their horizons and will help to clarify their ideas. It is very important for members of IS to do their best to recruit militants into our political organisation as well as to strengthen all existing rank and file industrial and trade union organisations.

Generalise the struggle: One of the main strengths of the dockers' five-day struggle was the clear unity between the particular life and death interest of the docker protecting his livelihood and the general interest of the working class to break the yoke of the Industrial Relations Act.

In the coming stage of the dockers' struggle this unity has to be preserved. There is no doubt that the media, television and the press, that serve big business, will do their best to show the dockers' struggle as a struggle of one group of workers in their own selfish interests against other workers.

It is extremely important that the dockers make it absolutely clear that their struggle is a struggle for the right to work. Now more than ever it is important to have leaflets and posters by the thousands putting this case.

It is important that dockers themselves should go around factories, power stations, mines and so on and put this case clearly forward. One live docker can make more propaganda for the truth than 1,000 copies of the *Daily Express.*

In the new stage the question of generalisation rises in another way. During the five-day struggle the rank and file showed itself in all its glory while the trade union bureaucracy, including Jack Jones, showed their complete bankruptcy. Now that the dockers' strike is official, the danger is that those bankrupt full-time officials will take over the running of the strike.

It is even more important now that the joint Port Shop Stewards' Committee is central in actively running the strike, in publicising the issues and in developing the strategy and tactics of the struggle.

The question of generalisation arises also in yet another way. The Tory press is arguing that a docks strike can go on for a long time without damaging the economy, that is, big business. To some extent it is whistling in the dark.

However, the experience of 1970 with a $2^1/_2$-week docks strike makes it clear that to spread the struggle is important. A docks strike affects exports but it also affects imports.

When the miners' strike started, the Tory press was confident that the government would win because it assumed that the miners would simply picket the mines. But the rank and file miners were 100 percent right when they showed their initiative in picketing the power stations. This is a lesson that the dockers should not overlook.

The question of generalisation of the struggle also raises a question of new institutions created in struggle. In the short five-day struggle very close relations were created between the dockers and the printers in Fleet Street. It is important that those close relations continue.

It won't be amiss if the printers refuse to print particularly obnoxious attacks on the dockers. After all, we are told we live in a free, democratic country, and if six owners of the press have a right to dictate what is being published in their papers, why shouldn't the printers also have some say?

In the five days of struggle the embryo of a 'Council of Action' connecting dockers and printers and other workers was in the making. In new, more prolonged, wider struggles the question of a Council of Action will really come to the fore.

The last point in terms of generalisation—episodic struggles are very prone to accidents. Their outcome depends on the relation of forces in every specific situation.

Because the ruling class is highly centralised, its ability to manoeuvre is much greater than any individual section of the working class.

Therefore the need for a revolutionary party, to repeat, as a school of strategy and tactics, and at the same time an active combat organisation, will become more vital than ever.

1972: a tremendous year for the workers

Socialist Worker, 6 January 1973

1972 was a tremendous year for Britain's working class. The struggle rose to new heights, both in terms of the number of workers involved, the size of strikes and their length, and above all in the quality of the struggle.

There have been far more large-scale and prolonged strikes this year than in the previous ten years, as the table below shows.

November and December figures have not yet been published, but there is no doubt that the total number of strike days has reached or exceeded 30 million this year. If one excludes miners' strikes, only once in British history has the number of strike days been greater—that was in 1919.

The 1972 figure is more than four times 1969, and some nine times the yearly average for the previous 20 years.

	Number of workers involved (thousands)	Number of working days lost (thousands)	Average number of days per worker on strike
1953–64 (average)	1,081	3,712	3.3
1965	876	2,925	3.3
1966	544	2,398	4.4
1967	734	2,787	4.0
1968	2,258	4,680	2.1
1969	1,665	6,876	4.1
1970	1,801	10,980	6.1
1971	1,171	13,551	12.1
Jan–Oct 1972	1,353	22,202	17.1

The year 1972 saw the first national miners' strike since 1926—and this time the miners won—and the biggest building strike ever, with 300,000 out over 12 weeks. The last similar confrontation was in 1923, when the employers locked the builders out.

The quality of the struggle has also been very advanced. There has been a purely political strike, to free the Pentonville Five. There has been a solidarity strike of 50,000 Birmingham engineers in support of the miners, 10,000 of them marching to Saltley Coke Depot. For the first time we have had strikes in support of old age pensioners, with 6,000 construction workers in Anchor, near Scunthorpe, coming out.

The workers have shown great initiative. But the trade union bureaucracy has been treacherous. Look at the miners' strike. The government offered the miners only £2. The official claim of the miners' union was £9, £6 and £5. Joe Gormley declared on the eve of the strike that if the government had raised the offer just a little the strike would not have taken place—he would probably have signed for £3.

The Tory press was absolutely convinced the government would win this round as they won against the post workers. They were looking for a confrontation. It was the initiative of the miners' rank and file, in picketing power stations instead of wasting effort on picketing the pits, that led the way. Helped by railwaymen, lorry drivers and workers in the power industry, they won a magnificent victory.

While 60 percent of the miners of Barnsley went on picket duty outside Yorkshire, the Labour MP for Barnsley contributed to victory by standing for a whole ten minutes on the picket line at Battersea power station. By sheer accident the television cameras were there at the same time.

We shouldn't criticise. It was cold, and he had to rush back to the House of Commons for some important vote, probably on dog licensing.

The shadow minister for fuel and power, Harold Lever, attacked the Tories for mismanaging the dispute, declaring that if Labour had been in power they would have settled the miners' wage claim for less than the Tories.

While the leaders did not manage to prevent the miners' victory, they did manage to sign an agreement sabotaging future battles, by allowing the date of the agreement to be shifted from November to February. Until now the annual agreement has run from November to November. The present one runs until February 1973.

If at the end of February the Coal Board rejects the NUM claim, the executive will have to organise a ballot and prepare miners for action, which will take a month or two. For miners to go on strike in summer is not the best of tactics. The 1926 General Strike, remember, started in May.

Ice cream workers should have agreements from May to May, miners from November to November. Although the rank and file miners won the battle in spite of the bureaucrats, the latter managed to sabotage the next round.

Again, look at the dockers' struggle. It was a magnificent victory over the government when the five dockers were freed. The strike was unofficial. Jack Jones kept his mouth shut, and did nothing at all to help the dockers. Reg Prentice, the shadow minister of labour, attacked the five dockers for breaking the law, and seeking self-advertisement.

Barbara Castle was more hypocritical. The Pentonville Five were arrested on the anniversary of the Tolpuddle Martyrs. 'In Place of Strife' Babs put a wreath on the grave of one of them. If he were not dead, and if she were in power, she would surely have put him in Pentonville instead.

After the Pentonville Five were freed Jack Jones threw his weight and that of the union on the side of the dockers and job security, declaring an official strike, which lasted three weeks. If 41,000 dockers could win an unofficial strike, the support of a union of 1,700,000 should surely have won them the official one.

But the result was the Aldington-Jones sell-out. Lord Aldington, former Tory MP, former vice-chairman of the Tory party who gave £30,000 to buy *Morning Cloud* for Ted Heath, the vice-chairman of GEC that sacked more than 50,000 workers over four years, was sold to the dockers by Jack Jones with promises of job security.

After the Pentonville Five affair the Tory government was reeling. In July and August the Tory press spoke of Ted Heath's government being bankrupt.

But in September the TUC snatched victory out of the jaws of defeat for this government. It was Vic Feather and the TUC who suggested the idea of an incomes policy at the September conference in Brighton. Ted Heath spelt it out by suggesting an all-round price of £2, and so the ground was prepared for the 90-day freeze.

The fantastic potential power of the rank and file and the treason of the trade union bureaucracy make it necessary now, more than ever, to build rank and file organisations in the unions to fight for democratic control, and to create combat organisations connecting workers from different places of work so that they can discuss questions of strategy and tactics.

The struggle over the past year has also shown that it is important to bridge the gulf that exists in many factories and other places of work between the militants and the rest of the workers. For a long time battles were won in individual shops by mobilising a small number of workers, or by threatening to do so. With today's mass confrontations the key problem is how to involve a massive number of workers in the struggle.

Often militants in one factory are without any contact with workers in the factory next door, or with the workers in another factory of the same empire. No less serious, however, is that militant shop stewards do not always involve their own workers in discussing the strategy and tactics needed to raise their fighting strength and understanding of the issues facing them.

During 1972 members of the International Socialists participated in launching a number of rank and file papers—the *Collier*, the *Steelworker*, the *Dockworker*, among others. We decided also to build *Socialist Worker* groups in factories.

The aim is to discuss with workers the general question of socialist politics facing the working class. Such groups should be active and intervening at all stages of the struggle. They should dig deeper roots for *Socialist Worker* inside the factory, by increasing its sale, getting reports for it, criticising it, and collecting donations.

The paper is more and more a workers' paper—not a paper just for workers.

It is written to a large extent by workers in struggle. But however good the paper, improvements and criticism are always necessary.

When Lenin said the paper is an organiser, he meant not only, say, the car workers' paper, but also separate factory bulletins in different car factories, written by militants in the factory itself, read by the whole workforce in the factory, not only the minority of militant socialists.

If decisive proof were needed that cabbage-patch militancy is not enough, the case of James Goad and the Lucas Birmingham factories has given it.

The Sudbury Lucas workers, where Goad used to work, went on strike against the Industrial Relations Court's £50,000 fine on the Engineering Union and called on their Birmingham colleagues to come to their aid. But under the influence of the right wing officials the Birmingham Lucas shop stewards decided not to take any action.

If they had decided differently and the 20,000 Lucas workers had come out in solidarity with Sudbury, the impact would have been tremendous. The snowball effect could have been as big as the Pentonville Five.

Things could have turned out very differently if the left in Lucas Birmingham were better organised. Many of the militant stewards did not know about the stewards' meeting. Not one of the stewards knew that a request from the Sudbury strikers to send a delegation to the Birmingham meeting had been turned down by the district secretary.

For lack of space I cannot deal adequately with the bankruptcy of the AUEW leadership in the Goad affair—a subject I will return to in the next few weeks.

Members of the International Socialists and other militant workers in Lucas Birmingham factories started a monthly bulletin called *Lucas Worker* about a month ago. Had they started it, say, a year earlier...if...if... A different initiative from the local Lucas leadership could have brought a totally different outcome.

The struggle in one field—in Birmingham Lucas—can become decisive for the whole labour movement. In the great chain of events, even an individual link can be decisive at a particular point in time. Socialists, organising in their place of work, should see their work as relevant not only to the workers directly involved, but also, potentially, to the whole of the working class.

In the second issue of the *Dockworker*, published a few days ago, a docker's wife wrote a marvellous letter. I shall quote just the final paragraph: 'After trying for ten years "officially" to get these [thalidomide] kids some money, without success, it's about time that something was done "unofficially". I am surprised that dockers have not done something about blacking Distillers' products, which I am sure are exported through some docks in the country.'

She is absolutely right. The dockers who could free the Pentonville Five have the industrial power to force Distillers to cough up money for those unfortunate children.

The workers have the power to force the Tory government to give a £16 pension to the old age pensioners. They have the power to smash the Tory government. They have the power to blow capitalism to kingdom come.

1972 has gone. Welcome to 1973.

Factory branches

First published as a pamphlet in 1973

Introduction

Factory branches are an innovation for revolutionary socialists in this country. For over a generation the revolutionary movement has had too tiny a foothold in the working class to contemplate building party branches in places of work. Our own experience is very limited. The factory branches we have—some 32 at the time of writing—have existed for a few weeks or days only. This pamphlet, which is the fruit of the collective effort of a number of comrades, tentatively aims to make some general observations and point out some immediate practical steps that will hopefully be of some help to comrades organised in factory branches or engaged in building them. After a few more months of experience we will no doubt be able to revise the pamphlet and sharpen its conclusions. The pamphlet intentionally does not try to present the material in elegant form, nor generalise further than our shallow, patchy and uneven experience would allow us to do satisfactorily. We need to face up to the problems as realistically as possible, without flannelling and without evasion. Criticism, suggestions for additions and amendments, will be welcomed. And life itself will of course be the best teacher.

The main tasks of factory branches

Workers' power lies mainly in the factories, docks and other places of work. A revolutionary socialist organisation must be built not as a collection of local branches, but as a union of factory branches. It can lead the decisive sections of the working class if it has strong party branches in the factories, especially the big ones.

The factory branch will be responsible for carrying the party's policy to the workers in the factory, on all current questions, as well as on the party's long term programme, thus ensuring the unity in action of its immediate and final aims. The factory branch should be the driving force in raising the class consciousness of the workers round it, developing their political education, their organisation, their initiative, enthusiasm and fighting ability, so that from the factory they are drawn into the struggle of the working class as a whole.

Factory branches should organise the vanguard of the working class at the point of production. The factory is the best centre of the organisation of the working class in struggle, not only in the factory itself, but around it.

The factory branch should consist of the party members employed at the same place, in which they represent the party as a whole. The branch is not simply a collection of individuals who hold the same views, who merely meet to discuss points that especially interest them. The members have a collective responsibility to win the workers in their place of work to the party policy as a whole.

In many places of work we have an individual member or couple of members. In practically all factories that are not too small, pits, depots or workshops, it is possible and necessary to build IS branches. To overcome many existing obstacles, a correct political appraisal is necessary, and persevering collective effort by individual members, the local branch and the district organisation.

What are the tasks of a factory branch?

First of all, a factory branch has to unite the socialists, the militants in the factory. In every place of work the real socialists are few in number. They are isolated, often feel depressed and suffer from a volatility of mood. Frequently one socialist militant does not even know the others in the same factory. The IS branch aims to bring them together. Though one finger may be weak, five fingers make a fist.

Second, the factory branch will relate the advanced socialists to the majority of the workers. If there are 1,000 workers in a factory, in all probability there will be a tiny minority of scabs at one extreme and a tiny group of militant socialists at the other. Between them stands the big majority—not right wing but simply an uninformed conservative mass. The IS branch, with the help of leaflets, bulletins and the rank and file papers relevant to the industry, will try to influence the mass of workers in the factory.

Third, the factory branch has to hold regular meetings to plan the fight for resolutions and policies that are laid down by the national organisation. This could mean, for example, a pledge of solidarity strikes with any worker arrested under the Industrial Relations Act or campaigns against the Tory Housing Finance Act.

Fourth, the branch has to hold regular meetings to discuss how IS members should fight for shop stewardships and other important positions and delegations in and from the factory.

Fifth, the branch has to hold regular political meetings to discuss a basic education programme and current events, features in *Socialist Worker*, *International Socialism* journal or any other publications of the International Socialists.

Winning leadership in the factory

A central theme of the work of the factory branch must be the attempt to win the leadership of the workers in the factory.

For this it is necessary for the branch to get to know the facts about the factory, its links with other plants in the same empire or other empires, its profits, its directors and their fees, donations to the Tory party, etc, how many workers (skilled and unskilled), women, youth, etc, are employed, to what trade unions they belong, the wages structure prevailing, etc, etc.

After acquiring this basic knowledge the branch can begin to work out a policy for the factory which will take into account the immediate problems facing the workers there, and relate them to the general industrial and political policies of IS. Such a policy should become a guide to the branch in the development of its work.

Every factory branch should produce a programme for the factory, to be reproduced in every issue of the factory bulletin.

There is fantastic unevenness between our factory branches in terms of their possibilities of taking over the leadership of the factory in the foreseeable future, or even in their ability to seriously influence the actions of many workers.

To give a few examples. On the one hand, out of the 8,000 workers in Rowntree's factory in York we have a factory branch consisting entirely of young, as yet inexperienced workers. The workforce is organised mainly in the GMWU, a union that holds very infrequent branch meetings. Just under half are part time women workers who work either mornings, afternoons or evenings. The factory has no militant tradition at all; it has had only one strike that lasted more than a few days—a five-week strike of fitters in 1972. Shopfloor meetings called by shop stewards are rare and not every shift has a shop steward. In the last series of elections, all the shifts did not even get a chance to vote.

There are a number of other IS factory branches of a similar nature.

On the other hand, we have the CA Parsons factory branch in Newcastle where we have the majority on the 13-man negotiating committee. Individual members of the branch have impressive records of leading successful disputes, some of which have been very long and difficult—eg 15 weeks struggle for increased holidays, 13 weeks for 100 percent union membership, six weeks of occupation during several months of fighting off massive redundancies.

While our comrades in Rowntree's, York, however vivid their imaginations, could not think of taking the lead in their factory in the foreseeable future, others, like our comrades in Standard Triumph, Merseyside, could write in their report, 'We believe that within 18 months we should be in a position of strength on the shop stewards committee, and be able to take a decisive lead.'

It is obvious that in order to become the leadership of the factory IS members must fight for shop stewardships. However, in doing so, big differences between the situations in the different factories need to be recognised. It is not only that our comrades in CA Parsons will find the going much easier than in Rowntree's, but there are also many varieties of interrelation between shop stewards and the active militancy of the rank and file. To take an example—Chrysler Ryton factory.

Ryton employs about 4,000 workers. None of the shop stewards work on the job. This is not, by and large, for the best of reasons—that they are all too busy taking up union business. It is generally because the management has encouraged them to stay off the job. The shop stewards act like their counterparts in American car factories. In the United States the shop steward has been so well integrated into the official union machine and into management that he is, in the words of a UAW leader, 'the policeman on the beat' (*Sunday Times*, 9 February 1969).

The combination of 'measured day work' (MDW), which helps integrate many of the stewards into the company, and the fact that the basis of the factory is a track sensitive to minor disputes, means there is rank and file activity which takes place independently of the stewards. In the body shop in particular, stoppages occur without any lead from the stewards. This means that when we say we have no stewards amongst our 11 members this is not so disastrous as may apply elsewhere. During the most recent strike it was the initiative of our members that created the Ryton Action Group, that initiated the flying pickets, picketing the engine factory at Stoke instead of Ryton, thus making a much more crippling impact on the Chrysler empire as a whole.

The shop stewards were dragged behind the men. Of course this should not be interpreted to mean that IS members should not fight for stewardship in Ryton. On the contrary. If our members were stewards they would prove in practice that they could use the office for leading a militant struggle.

Again, in Albion Motors, which employs some 3,500 workers, our members have no stewardships, but this did not prevent them from playing a considerable role in what happened in the factory recently. The report on the Albion factory branch says, 'Just before the holiday two weeks ago the shop stewards finally recommended specific MDW proposals to the workers at a mass meeting. Four of our members spoke (one of them was denounced as being IS) and were instrumental in securing a 60-40 rejection of the proposals—in which rejections they were considerably aided by the production of a bulletin just prior to the decision.

The variety of problems is practically as great as the number of factory branches. Sometimes even winning the major influence in the shop stewards committee poses new, much greater difficulties. What use can we make of control of the shop stewards committee in a small factory which is part of a large combine? Having a very strong position in a small, but—in terms of the car industry—quite important, coil spring factory—Woodheads, Ossett—is a cul-de-sac. Hence our comrades initiated the Combine Committee for the five factories in the Woodhead empire, started a monthly Combine bulletin, and have a major influence in editing this organ.

Whether our members have control over the shop stewards committee, a foothold in it, or no influence at all, and whatever the short term prospects, the principle dominating their work in the factory should be the same: to increase the participation of workers in determining their activities—for mass meetings and shop meetings to decide policy, and to mandate shop stewards and delegates. Obviously we would prefer to be in a minority getting, say, 100 votes among 500 workers at a meeting, to an IS majority of seven among ten workers coming to a meeting.

(The IS factory branch's role of raising the consciousness, the self-activity and organisation of workers at their place of work distinguishes it from the Communist Party factory branches. Those that exist—a remnant of a much broader movement decades ago—are reformist; they exist to manipulate workers either in support of the 'left' trade union bureaucrats during elections, or as a reserve army for the parliamentary electoral activity of the party. For lack of space we cannot elaborate; a single instance will have to serve to show the difference between IS factory branches and the CP's branches: the former will try to involve workers in the anti-racist campaign against the recent House of Lords decision on black immigrants; the CP branches will see in this only a diversion from the *real* important job of winning votes in the elections of full time officials in the unions.)

Industrial branch versus factory branch

We now have a number of industrial branches not based on a single place of work, which present a number of difficult problems. In a factory branch we have a clear perspective of work; this is not the case in an industrial branch. As a matter of fact the variation between industrial branches is so great as to make it necessary to describe at least a few of them.

The Merseyside building workers' branch has 12 members. The report from the branch describes the situation thus:

> As the branch is only newly established, it is still trying to mould the branch to suit all the members, and as one glance at our membership will show, this is going to be a difficult task.
>
> At the present our work falls into two fairly distinct areas—the building trades (UCATT and TGWU) and the subcontracting specialists (EETPU, H&D, etc). Although these two areas are related in some ways, their separateness leads to a drastic stretching of our slender resources. Other problems which we face also tend to weaken our overall effect. Such problems as short term periods of unemployment which are endemic in the industry, added to the acute regional problem of unemployment in some trades (mainly in the direct building trades, UCATT and TGWU), mean that inevitably some of our members are unemployed. Also the multiplicity of union branches (there are up to 50 building trade union branches on Merseyside alone, and probably 20 UCATT branches and a dozen TGWU branches) only exaggerates our own fragmentation inside the unions and the trades as a whole. Often our members are forced to fight alone in their branches, but confronted by a considerable number of CPers.

The Merseyside district organiser commented on the subject:

We *tried* to overcome this by recommending that as many of the members as possible try and get work on the same site, but unemployment in the industry as a whole is making this nigh on impossible to implement. Of course we keep on trying but with so many branch members unrelated to struggle it also means that trade union work is not a satisfactory substitute. They can't really lead in their union, not only because of CP dominance but above all because they never lead on site.

The branch has a large percentage of its members unemployed. Those that are at work are, with one exception, all on small sites or in situations (new jobs, etc) where they have to be extremely careful about their politics and views. These problems are exaggerated by the fact that a number of the branch members are labourers and therefore without any special skills. Because of heavy unemployment in the Merseyside area among this category, and some hints of victimisation and blacklisting for a couple, it all means that their chance to take the lead on the sites is very flimsy indeed.

Then we have the London hospital workers' branch, described in the following terms: 'The main problem of the branch is that it is an anomaly. It differs from the other functional branches in the area in that it covers such an immense geographical area. For example, it could cost some comrades up to 50p to attend a branch meeting.' In addition there is no concentration in one particular place of work. The most members in any one hospital is two (St Leonard's):

> The geographical problem has meant several things. The older, in terms of length of membership, members tend to dominate the branch. They have got into the habit of attending meetings, long boring ones at that. They are the ones prepared to go to any meeting. The newer members can fit in a few meetings but not all of them. Because it is the more conservative, petty bourgeois members who like meetings, several decisions have been taken regarding the branch. They agreed to have a host of meetings. In each month there could be a business meeting, a public meeting, two education meetings, and two meetings of the All London Health Workers' Alliance to go to. Some of the older members tend to think that because some comrades can't make all these meetings they aren't proper members. At one stage one of the hospital workers complained that all the branch did was meet—it didn't do anything. The problem of geography and meetings has meant that it is difficult to get all the subs in and also to distribute the paper.

The Leeds hospital workers' branch has many similarities, but also important differences, to the London hospital workers' branch. In Leeds we have 16 members (14 hospital workers and two non-hospital workers, helping in the work of the branch). Of the 14, nine are in one hospital, St James's, of whom two are NUPE shop stewards. The concentration of the majority of members in one hospital makes the Leeds branch much more of a factory branch than the London branch.

Again, in the Oxford hospital workers' branch we have six members, all members of the same NUPE branch, all working for the same management group, and five working in the same hospital.

(By the way, one issue connected specifically with hospital branches is: should the branch include only ancillary workers, or also nurses and doctors? If the decision is to include all who work in hospitals, we must make sure that: (1) ancillary workers become the big majority in the branch; (2) the leaders and spokesmen of the branch should be the ancillary workers.)

Then we have the Leyland workers' branch in Coventry, another kind of hybrid. Here our members, half white collar, half shopfloor workers, are spread among six of the 11 Leyland factories in the city. Up to now the common activity of our members has been around the Leyland Action Group, which is described in a report from Coventry:

> It is a white collar group with a considerable base—taken into eight of 11 factories, with branches, convenors and one JSSC supporting it and giving cash. For the first bulletin four times the cost was collected. More recruits are coming through this—also a couple of shopfloor members are on the way. The main problem is going to be holding together a ramshackle empire. It holds no public meetings but regular business meetings.

The industrial branch is a compromise forced on us—what we want is separate branches for every place of work.

In Coventry Leyland the branch is clearly a halfway house. As Leyland employs over 20,000 workers in the town we aim within the not too distant future to produce separate factory bulletins associated with the building of separate factory branches.

In Leeds hospital workers' branch the aim should be to build a separate St James's Hospital branch and see if any similar branches can be built elsewhere (although the going will undoubtedly be rough, and the time probably long). The same applies to our Oxford hospital workers' branch.

In the London hospital workers' branch, after a number of trials and tribulations, the following were the conclusions reached in the report on the branch:

> It has been stressed that the main responsibility of members is to concentrate on their own and neighbouring hospitals with the aim of calling four local public meetings quite soon. This has enthused the new comrades again—the fact that they can have a meeting to which they can bring their mates. When a few people have been recruited at these meetings, it will then be possible to split the branch into two or three.
>
> A further point is that with a branch of this sort it is difficult to talk specifically about the different workplaces and different problems in the branch as such. You need to spend a lot of time talking to the comrades individually. Should the venture have been started? Despite the problems I think yes. We have been able to orient the comrades on the workplace more than in a geographical branch. We have also been able to keep a few comrades in the group who might have left. But if we have to do this again we must watch certain points more closely. It needs to be emphasised to the comrades much more from the start that the branch is only temporary and that their task is to split up into several branches as quickly as possible. The danger is that it's easy to say that we've got our own branch, now the problems are over, all we have to do is consolidate. Again it was a mistake to try to hold

central branch public meetings. People will just not come unless they already know a lot about the organisation (ie should have been recruited long ago).

Edinburgh building workers' branch faced the same danger of an industrial branch turning in on itself. Their report says:

> One of our first mistakes was either collectively or individually to use the branch as a buffer. The feeling was, 'Well, we have our own building workers' branch, so there!' This was raised at our last meeting from which came the decision that everyone bring along a close contact. We have realised the danger of not growing fast enough. Also we realised that we are a transitional branch. Because of the nature of the building industry it is difficult to set up site branches.

The difficulties of building real workplace branches require a major effort in many directions:
(1) In recruitment, because most of the problems follow from our present numerical weakness.
(2) In strengthening national industrial fractions. To quote the report of the Merseyside building workers' branch:

> The building workers' fraction needs a regular bulletin (or the IS Internal Bulletin needs to be transformed into something more beneficial to its *industrial* members). Many more pamphlets relevant to specific fractions need to be published— *Socialist Worker* and the rank and file papers are the best stuff we have and are responsible for the development of our work. If we had more of this sort of stuff, our growth would be that much quicker and better.
>
> Because of the lack of any real fraction organisation, the branch is now taking upon itself the task of writing and producing some basic pamphlets that we feel are necessary. Already we have made a start on one dealing with the proposed restructuring of the industry. Others being contemplated are on the Lump, and the need for a rank and file building workers' movement. However, our ability to bridge the credibility gap is restricted.

(3) The industrial branch can be prevented from turning in on itself, above all in participating in all trade union activities open to the members: sending delegates to trades councils, to trade union conferences, moving resolutions at different trade union bodies, collecting money for workers on strike, etc.
(4) In participating in IS district campaigns and demonstrations, in holding common meetings with area branches.
(5) In using every opportunity to increase the sale of *Socialist Worker* at the place of work, getting reports for the paper and collecting money for its fighting fund.

Let us sum up. *Factory branches* is a misnomer for many of the branches we have formed. For many the term *industrial branch* would be better. This distinction is important for a variety of reasons, and isn't purely a question of semantics. A factory branch, however weak it might be, is a clear declaration of strength. Even if we only have youngsters at the moment, it still is the embryo of a future alternative leadership. Without underestimating the real difficulties which lie in our path, at least here the perspective is clear. The industrial branches, although they may subjectively, in terms of our past, represent a newly acquired strength, are in fact an admission of objective weakness—our inability to form workplace branches in these instances, and our need to group our militants together. They will be much more problematic institutions in the long run than the former.

Again we have in some way an in between institution, say the GKN branch or the Coventry Leyland branch, based on workplaces but not a single work-place. Here the perspective must be to a number of branches based on individual workplaces. *We must guard against the mechanical application of this rule to some industrial branches.* To push the London hospitals' branch, for example, along the same perspective might well prove disastrous, in terms of the disillusionment created by the objective difficulties.

Again we must not be blinded by apparent similarities. There is in reality a world of difference between a York bus workers' branch and a north London one. The geographical scale of operations, total workforce, etc, are all elements to be taken into account.

Industrial branches pose very intractable problems. One cannot be sure that they can survive for any length of time. The matter needs to be more deeply con-sidered. The rank and file papers, the unions, etc can provide a focus in the ab-sence of the place of work. However, the branches should be interventionist—factory ones will almost inevitably be. Industrial ones can sustain themselves on growth for a period, but if they do not become based on workplaces, and in the absence of a generalised struggle (national strike or whatever) their outlook is grim.

To the extent that the members of industrial branches work in the trade union structure, they have many ties connecting them with members of factory branches, as well as working members of area branches.

Work in the unions

Due to the correct emphasis on rank and file work, in some cases IS members tend to neglect the work in the trade union branch. To overcome this the fol-lowing measures are vital:

(1) Regular attendance at trade union branches—make sure every member is in a branch, that the district knows where every member is, and that what we do there is discussed. For example, in a factory where we have no stewards it may be useful to have a TGWU subs collector so a comrade can move about the fac-tory. Every member must have a copy of the union constitution, must be provided with resolutions (and arguments) to move, and shown how to move them.

(2) Push for positions—especially branch secretary, obviously, but also trades council (fairly easy), district committee, as well as minor branch posts, eg subs collector, etc. Try to transform the branch, eg by having outside speakers or a branch bulletin.

(3) All industrial members (and others) should push for trades council positions

even though the trades council is often a paper organisation. The trades council can be a valuable basis for other work.

(4) It will prove generally *impossible* to have regular meetings of members of union fractions due to pressure of work so there must be a local union fraction secretary to coordinate things. As far as resolutions are concerned, one branch has started a regular discussion on district committee of basic resolutions, etc once a month plus a report-back—about three weeks before each meeting.

To give some examples of what can be done with influence in trade union branches, trades councils, etc:

(1) Control of a few trade union branches can mean a reliable springboard for any campaigns, eg adoption of internees in Northern Ireland, strike collections. (2) A large number of trades council delegates (especially with at least one comrade on the trades council executive) means another place for establishing credibility.

The Coventry district organiser writes:

> The trades council has 22 IS delegates which on many issues gives us control.
> Thus it has organised a public meeting on the Birmingham building workers and
> conspiracy laws, and is organising a large one on the House of Lords' immigration
> decision. We can normally make sure one of the speakers is an IS member.

Factory branch organisation

One of the main problems facing the coordination and work of the factory branch is the prevalence of the shift system.

The report of Scottish and Newcastle Breweries (Tyne Brewery) describes the difficulty: 'The five members we have are on three different shifts, and the only feasible time for meetings is at the weekend.'

From Linwood we get the following: 'The biggest problem will be the meeting time of the branch because of four or five different shift patterns being worked. We hope to resolve this by having Saturday morning branch meetings —although here again we have to try to avoid clashing with Saturday stewards' meetings (monthly), to ensure the branch is serviced and helped with the education programme.'

The report from Monkbridge, Leeds, says:

> It has taken us three weeks to get a satisfactory meeting at which we laid down
> the bones upon which we are to develop the muscles of a very strong organisation.
> We are drawing up a roster of all the shifts we will be working over the next two
> months. This will be continued over the following two months, and so on. This
> will assist us in organising the sale of *Socialist Worker*, develop the habit of getting
> to work early to have a chat to the members going home, and pick up any news
> of what is going on in the factory.
>
> It will also enable us to see clearly when it is most convenient to call meetings
> and at what time of day. We are organising a locked drawer in which messages,

money for subs, *Socialist Worker* sales, etc can be left. The *Socialist Worker* organiser will leave lists of readers for each shift and it will be the responsibility of the members on that shift to make the sale.

The frequency of branch meetings is very different in the different branches. Thus from Coventry we get the following report: 'Chrysler meetings are monthly (except emergencies) on Saturday mornings. Leyland meetings are fortnightly on Sunday evenings. Ford's meetings are at 7.30pm on Tuesdays.'

Another way of dealing with the question of shift work was taken by the Teesside steel branch. It may be of some use to other IS factory branches if we recount the story, as told in its report:

Up to now we have kept a record of each member's shift rota and called meetings at the time when least members were at work. This meant meeting on different days of the week and at different times of day. We have now decided to meet on alternate Thursdays. We meet formally for $1^1/2$-2 hours and most members stay for a drink and a chat afterwards unless they have to go to work. We have to do this because members may come in from work very late and are likely to be put off if everyone else has gone home.

Where the shift system makes coordination difficult, the help of IS members from outside the factory may be vital. Thus the report on Linwood and Albion Motors says, 'Both branches have been allocated one or two other comrades to attend branch meetings in a non-voting capacity to coordinate servicing and to provide any needed "external" political initiative.'

Similarly, the Monkbridge branch decided to elect as its secretary a housewife, who is available by phone most of the time. (Of course in the long run the best solution for factory branches where the Continental shift system or other complicated shift system prevails is to build shift branches—but that is the music of the future!)

Meticulous care is necessary in the organisation of meetings. It is very important that they should be short and businesslike with a definite time of closure. The main purpose of every meeting should be political education, not only on the general situation, but the application of party policy to the branch's factory. Part of the meeting can be given over to formal political education based on a definite syllabus. Sympathetic workers should be invited to the meetings.

There is need for a proper agenda for factory branch meetings. A suggestion is:

(1) Current business (national IS circulars, distribution of work, reports on recruiting, finance, literature, district committee, decisions, etc).

(2) Factory report (workers' grievances, events on shop stewards committee, at trade union branch, etc).

(3) Factory paper or bulletin (discussion on material for the paper. This should be based on the previous discussion).

(4) Political discussion (this should include the discussion of questions put to members by non-IS workers, and wherever possible a political discussion on

the most important events based on *Socialist Worker*, *International Socialism*, and political circulars from the centre).

Detailed business, such as subs payment, literature distribution and money, etc, should not take place at a branch meeting, but should be done at other times, through subs collectors, literature organisers, etc.

The branch secretary should prepare the agenda beforehand, should draw the conclusions from the discussion, and record decisions, including the names of those responsible for carrying them out.

In planning, care must be taken to avoid overloading members with meetings —*which is disastrous*. Even after severe pruning of the number of public meetings (only monthly branch meetings), one finds that 'a typical Chrysler member may have the following in a month: two trade union branch meetings, one IS branch meeting, one IS industrial aggregate, two Action Group meetings, two education meetings, plus any district committee, branch committee, *Carworker*, extra meetings. And all this is really the minimum.'

In a factory branch, even more than in a territorial one, the role of leadership, of clear political and organisational guidance, is central to the effectiveness of the work. In a territorial branch, because of the multiplicity of jobs to do, the failure of one comrade or one activity will have a less damaging effect than a similar failure in a factory branch, whose cohesion is potentially much greater, but where the different activities are much more intimately integrated. The technical difficulties of organisation—the shift system, above all—will require the strictest punctuality, the clearest division of labour, the utmost sense of responsibility and regular checking that decisions have been carried out.

It is important that every member has a job to do: *Socialist Worker* or pamphlets to sell, meetings to attend, his own contacts to see. In a revolutionary party there is no rank and file. Every member must be a leader. Hence every member must get on top of the job.

To facilitate this they must get day to day instructions from the branch regarding their activities—not merely general instruction—and their actual work has to be supervised by the branch. Every activity must be tested by its results. Results mean the demonstrable increase of IS influence in the working class, whether by increase of membership, increase of *Socialist Worker* readership, or the securing of control of working class organisations.

The branch officers should include the maximum number of members. Thus in the Chrysler branch, Coventry, the following officers were elected—chairman, secretary, treasurer, *Socialist Worker* organiser, *Carworker* organiser, *Socialist Worker* sellers, subs collectors and *Carworker* sellers on each shift at each factory. All these officerships are coordinated through the branch committee.

IS branches in factories differ in size and face different shift systems, hence one should not be dogmatic about the desirable structure and working of the branch. Our experience is also much too limited. Even within a few days structures and emphasis of work will change. The one thing that simply cannot be afforded is a situation in which for fear of 'losing face' comrades will not be prepared to reverse a decision made at a previous meeting.

One office that every factory branch should have is that of membership secretary. This is to see that each member reports the names of those he is seeking to win for the organisation, and these names should be frequently reviewed. Every member must be on the lookout for those workers who argue for our politics or are active for them.

While the main job of the members of the factory branch is to recruit in their own place of work, they should not lose opportunities for winning new members for IS in their trade union branch or among workers in other factories whom they can meet. The factory branch should list such factories, and allot responsibility for making contacts and members among the workers there. Such responsibility may be given to an existing factory branch if suitably situated, or to the local branch, or to an individual member of IS, or to a team of factory workers from existing factory branches.

Methods of establishing personal contacts include striking up an acquaintance with workers in the factory during the meal break or when leaving work, or in the buses, the pubs and clubs, or in the trade union branch or trades council. The important thing is to get one IS branch or one comrade to make the connections—then a way will be found.

One of the main weapons in the hands of the factory branch to spread IS policies, and attract workers towards the organisation and recruit them, is *Socialist Worker*. Selling the paper and writing reports for it, being interviewed by the paper's journalists, will make the paper more and more central to the life of the advanced section of the working class, and will attract advanced workers into IS.

Workers' letters to *Socialist Worker* can play a particularly important role. Letters telling of grievances or relating incidents as they occur, taken together, constitute a picture of workers' lives and can be of great agitational value. The factory branch should see to it that articles and letters are sent to the paper regularly.

A way of creating a bridge to workers in the factory to facilitate their recruitment to IS is the regular collection of donations to *Socialist Worker*. A fighting fund for the paper can play an important role in building IS.

In these ways *Socialist Worker* can become not only the best agitator for IS but also the best organiser.

How and when to form a factory branch

(1) Every industrial member should have the perspective of forming a factory branch.

(2) But, when there are two members, regular but probably informal discussions should take place round the problems: (a) to whom can we sell *Socialist Worker* next? (It is important to think of a sale in ones and twos, not a mass sale which may be counter-productive. This builds the confidence of the shy or inexperienced. (b) is there one fellow worker we can spot as a potential recruit?

(3) When we have three we are in business. This can be the nucleus of a new branch. Regular and more formal chats should take place—once a week at dinner time, for instance—with the two basic questions from (2), plus, who

can we invite to a regular *Socialist Worker* discussion group? It is important to stress—think 'small', don't overreach and risk demoralisation.

(4) At this stage, and up to the actual formation of a factory branch, it is important to stress the need for integration into some wider 'grouping' of the organisation—eg geographical branch, a local industrial fraction, education group, etc, because:

(i) The two, three or four aren't going to get their political education from each other.

(ii) They aren't going to enjoy the full rights of membership.

(iii) They need to see something a bit more exciting than their own tiny group.

(iv) The formation process in all cases will not be the days, weeks, or even month it took for the first 32 branches. There will be local problems of personal qualities and specific work situations which can make growth slow.

(5) The timing of the move from nucleus to branch is of crucial importance. If the move is made too quickly the risk of a setback is high. But we must recognise that to put it firmly on the agenda can bring a qualitative change in the approach and enthusiasm of the members. For all the reasons of vulnerability and instability underlined in the section 'Factory Branch Organisation', we should perhaps aim at eight members (even ten) before recognition. We can be flexible. In a very small workplace—say a small drawing office—perhaps necessity dictates a smaller number, but in most places of 500-plus why not eight or ten?

(6) All of this throws special responsibilities onto geographical branches and district committees to take full responsibility for assisting comrades in these situations. Perhaps districts should look at nuclei of branches in a very similar way to established branches.

Relations with the district

Often the large factory can be a centre for rallying the working people in a whole area. The party branch in the factory must not only be directly responsible for mobilising that factory round the party policy, but also play its part in moving the workers of the whole town or district round it.

There is no Chinese wall separating the factory from the world outside it—factory workers do not live in a world cut off from life in the surrounding area. Local issues such as rents, fares, social services, etc affect them, being in fact disguised wage cuts. Hence the factory branch has to relate to all these and similar issues. Above all, racism as a weapon in the hands of the employers must be combated inside the factory and in its neighbourhood.

Where one large enterprise dominates a whole district the connection between what happens inside and outside the factory is particularly vital.

One field in which the factory branch should play an integral role in the district is in the local campaigns. Thus we read in a report on work against racism in the Coventry area, in addition to a district industrial meeting to be addressed by George Peake, to be held this month, the following measures have been taken: resolutions through trade union branches, getting people to meetings, selling *Chingari*, selling the Foot pamphlet on racism (1,000 ordered), inviting speakers to trade union branches and the trades council.

Tickets should be sold inside the factory for all the big public meetings and events organised by IS on a district or local scale. This is particularly so for rallies and demonstrations, and should be an important means of strengthening IS in the factory on the one hand, and in contributing to the effectiveness of the rally on the other.

There is a need also to develop new forms of meetings, perhaps combined with social activities, in order to get over the problem of workers living in widely separated places, and enable the comrades to bring their wives along.

The initiative should be taken in organising factory gate meetings, lunchtime discussions, public meetings and collections for strikes. In this connection it is encouraging to read in the report of the CAV Acton factory branch:

> We organised a meeting with stewards from Perkins Engines. This was an open-air meeting at dinnertime which attracted 100-150 workers (organised officially by *Carworker*). £10 was collected for Perkins. At a further meeting in the evening a steward from the toolroom appeared with a further £11 collected in his shop that afternoon. The meeting embarrassed the factory leadership and gave a big boost to us. This is the type of activity we want to repeat.

As the organisational interrelationship between the IS factory branch and the district organisation is at the moment in flux everywhere, and as the area in which the structure evolving has gone furthest is Coventry, it will perhaps help the comrades in other factory branches and districts to look at the structure built there as described in the report of the district organiser:

District aggregate (once in two months).

District committee (all or almost all workers, meets fortnightly).

Secretariat (branch secretaries—all or most—plus district organiser and unemployed members. To cover routine, implement decisions, pass on to branches where needed. Meets weekly).

Branch committees (meeting weekly, after district). Discusses branch work and district committee decisions.

Branch meetings (monthly in established factory branch with more frequent work groups).

District fractions (women, Ireland, race, trade union fractions).

In addition, we have industrial meetings (invitation only—at present monthly, less frequently as soon as district improves), public meetings (none till October), district fraction public meetings/invitation meetings (eg Ireland, women, race, teachers).

Once this structure is set up—by the end of September—we will definitely have an efficient machine. Then we will be able to initiate activity, not simply react. It means also that faced with a dispute, other events, initiatives from the centre, we will be able to immediately discuss and act on it.

A less developed form of district organisation—but perhaps suitable for the local situation—has been evolved in York. In a report from the York district organisation we are informed:

> The district committee is composed of two delegates from the town branch, two from the buses and two from the Rowntree branch. The district secretary is elected by all three branches. The committee meets fortnightly at present, or more often if needed. The committee decides on all joint activity from public meetings to estate work. The buses branch decided a few weeks ago to devote some time to contact work on the estates, etc. We are in the process of setting up a propaganda committee to run public meetings in the town. This will be made up of one member from each branch. We intend also to set up an education committee to deal with the education in all three branches. Both these committees will be directly responsible to the district committee. The district committee also has powers to co-opt further members. It is clear, even at this early stage, that the district committee is developing into the leadership in the town.

It is necessary for comrades from factory branches to take the lion's share in the district committee. This will strengthen the district leadership, and at the same time will strengthen the factory branches through broadening their outlook, seeing the struggle of the working class in wider terms, and helping to prevent a narrow industrial outlook.

One of the dangers that will probably arise in future will be the lack of contact between local and factory branches working in the same area. Close contact between them could assist both the local and the factory branch. It would direct the factory branch away from any tendency to concentrate only on economic issues, and should encourage political discussion and action on the general line of IS. In the local branch it will improve the understanding of industrial questions, and of the way in which it is necessary to work in order to build closer relations with the organisations of the labour movement in the localities.

There will be a need to develop organised methods of interchanging information between factory and local branches. Thus local branches should be informed of factory comrades living within their area, so that they can invite them, and their wives and families, to branch events. Similarly, factory comrades joining a local branch should be encouraged to join the factory branch if one exists, or to build one. The question of increasing regular close contact between factory branches and local branches will come into greater prominence with the increase in the number of factory branches, and the improvement in the social composition of local branches, eg when workers become predominant in them.

An important area of work in which the factory branch can dovetail with the work of the district is around the trades council.

We aim to re-establish the trades council's role of uniting centres of local activity. The trades council can become an invaluable channel for IS propaganda, providing opportunities for bringing under our influence local trade union branches, as well as local shop stewards committees. For this purpose our comrades should be encouraged to become delegates to the local trades council. If we have a number of members on the trades council, they should elect a fraction secretary who should arrange a meeting of the fraction before the trades council meeting to go through the agenda, propose resolutions, arrange movers and seconders, etc.

The factory branch must be central in the working of our trade union fractions locally and nationally. It must see to it that every member sells the appropriate rank and file paper, goes regularly to his trade union branch meetings, tries to become a delegate to the district committee, trade union conference, etc. In carrying out such activities, again the factory branch may dovetail with the work of the district.

The decisive role the factory branch can play in the development of the whole district is being realised in fact by the Chrysler IS branch, which sent this encouraging report:

> On the more general front, many of our members have involved themselves in work in other areas. It was the Chrysler branch's initiative which began our first ever work around Massey-Ferguson. It was the Chrysler branch that put a new lease of life into a stagnating and dormant *Carworker* organisation. It was the Chrysler branch which enabled IS to start work in the Hinckley area. It was the Chrysler branch into which militant housewives have come and are launching off into completely new ventures. It was the Chrysler branch which led IS to a position of serious influence on a working class community newspaper. It was the Chrysler branch which has given a push in the setting up of the new Ford's Leamington branch. *But above all, it was the Chrysler branch which gave a huge boost to the existing membership in the area and stimulated them to further recruitment.* Our members are directly responsible for the recruitment of many new workers in the Coventry branch, who have come to IS because of what our branch is achieving, or because our own new members (and it has been new members in particular) have felt able to say that they belonged to an organisation of which they were proud and which they felt was going places.
>
> To sum up: we believe that the setting up of factory branches has been a huge step forward in the work of the organisation. Far from stifling the so called 'politicisation' of the workers in the organisation, it has led to increasing enthusiasm, increasing demands for general education, increasing 'looking outwards' of the industrial membership. It has meant that we can once again start talking, not in an ultra-leftist way, about activities which we have always considered to be very peripheral—women's work, tenants' work, community work: all these are beginning to slot into place and to fit in neatly with our industrial activity.

While the factory branch can have an important effect on the development of the whole district, a bad district organisation can seriously damage factory branches.

Because the factory branch is by nature so close-knit, the loss of one key member can have a serious impact—at least at the beginning of such a branch. If a territorial branch loses an engineer through him turning foreman, the branch can compensate itself by recruiting another member, but the same event can have a deeply damaging effect on the factory branch. Hence the factory branch needs to be nurtured very carefully for quite a long time, and a bad district organisation can therefore be very harmful for a factory branch. If a factory branch makes a serious mistake, the impact is much more damaging both in the short term and the long term than if an area branch makes one. In the factory, with a much more closed community, memories linger longer. Leadership is much more put to the test, is much more carefully scrutinised by workers in the situation of struggle in the factory. Mistakes and deviations of revolutionaries are punished more severely under such conditions.

On victimisation

One of the worst mistakes a militant socialist can commit is to carelessly expose himself to avoidable victimisation unnecessarily.

Of late some of our members in factories have suffered attempted or successful victimisation. It is a problem which will increase as we become more of a threat to the employers, and as the economic crisis deepens. It is therefore something which each factory branch has to concern itself with, both in terms of prevention, and by preparing now for a struggle, in the eventuality that it should happen.

It is really impossible to give general rules and advice on the best way to operate, since conditions can vary so much. Obviously a badly organised tinpot of a place is totally different from a place where the management lives in constant fear of the shop stewards. At one extreme, comrades may be totally unable to operate openly in the plant without being immediately sacked. At the other extreme, paper and bulletin distribution is done quite openly, internally and without fear of any retaliation. Quite clearly our comrades have to choose the best way of working in each case, taking care both not to expose themselves unnecessarily, but also without being so secretive that their existence in the factory becomes a closely guarded secret and they reduce themselves to total ineffectiveness.

Comrades must thus remember that, while being a revolutionary requires daring and initiative, we are not looking for unnecessary martyrdom. This is not just an individual problem—the victimisation of a member weakens our general effectiveness in the factory.

A few rules of thumb are perhaps useful.

(1) The rule that revolutionaries should always be the best workers is quite right. It is important first of all because no member of IS must appear a skiver to his workmates, but it is also important since the management will be looking for opportunities to victimise a dangerous employee. In most workplaces lots of breaches of discipline are normally committed. Workers clock each other on and off, take turns to absent themselves from work, play cards in work time, return late from the sports field or the nearby pub. Pilfering is a normal feature of factory life. All these things are well known to management—their ability to do something about it depends on their analysis of the cost involved in attempting to control it. In most cases they will decide that it is not worth taking risks, and they will make allowances for all these things in their accounting.

But no trouble might be too much to get rid of a powerful militant. Then the various 'instant dismissal' clauses, which are never used, are all of a sudden brought into operation. No member of IS should put himself or herself into such a position.

(2) Losing one's temper to supervisors is an excellent way to keep them in their place. But again care must be taken not to place oneself out on a limb.

(3) Secrecy may at times be necessary. As a rule, however, one should attempt to operate as openly as possible. The greater risk for our members is the possible suspicion on the part of their workmates that we have not been honest. The 'reds under the bed' scare can be devastatingly effective if one has kept one's politics carefully hidden. The best defence is honesty, and being able to say it was all above board. In the last analysis the best defence is the support one gets from one's mates. This will not be forthcoming if they can be convinced that they have been taken for a ride.

(4) Positions in the official movement strengthen our hand against victimisation, especially in case the unions decide to give the employers a helping hand. Thus while the shopfloor organisation is the most important one, our comrades must take positions in the union. Even a place on a branch committee might be of help. Being branch secretary, chairman, or on the district committee is of course even better. Being a delegate to the trades council may be of use. There is to all these positions a treble importance. It is important for our work in the unions. It may discourage the employers and union bureaucracy from moving against us. Lastly, in case of victimisation, these positions will be invaluable in organising support against it.

(5) One last point. It is always important to maintain relations of some friendliness with left elements on the works committee or the union structure. Their aid may well be the crucial extra bit which we need to defend our members in any given situation.

The factory branch and rank and file paper and organisation

An important part of our national work is rank and file papers, and our members are expected to involve themselves in their distribution, sale and production. Such papers are the logical extension of the internal bulletins on a national scale. Through them we attempt to break down the isolation of plant from plant, combine from combine, within the same industry. Some rank and file papers are produced for specific unions and groups of workers. Their sale in a factory might be a very useful way of making contacts in other unions and to break down the traditional inter-union diffidence.

A factory branch can find such papers a great aid in reaching militants who may not yet be ready to accept our politics, but who may well be prepared to agree to our specific militant programme for the industry. As our printshop expands we are increasingly able to help in producing special issues of the papers to cater for a specific strike. The special issue of the *Carworker* which was produced during the Ryton dispute greatly enhanced our standing. But as in the case of *Socialist Worker* the need is not only to sell such papers but also to use them to organise. Often a meeting called under the auspices of the appropriate rank and file paper may be more useful than one called directly as IS. A number of well known militants who might not be prepared to speak from our platform can then be involved, and a larger audience might well result. Often it will be the nature of the meeting which will determine the sponsorship. An important national event may better suit an IS meeting—one to discuss the latest wage claim may well be best suited to the rank and file organisation.

Through the supporters cards and supporters groups we can also establish a semi-permanent periphery of sympathisers, who will in time be won over to our politics.

The factory branch must try to promote the rank and file paper appropriate in the industry (or union). We have to try to develop the influence of our ideas *beyond* the ranks of those who can be persuaded to join us at a particular time. A Greek philosopher said, 'Give me a lever and I will move the world.' We need our lever. The rank and file movement is our lever. Even when we are ten or 100 times bigger than we are now we will *still* need that lever.

A rank and file movement tries to bring together workers who agree about the need to fight for a limited number of demands in an industry or union but who are *not yet* agreed about the need for a revolutionary party. For example, they may be agreed about the need for the election and periodic re-election of all officials in the union but *not* about whether or not there is a parliamentary road to socialism. Or again, they may be agreed about the need to fight particular cases of racial discrimination (and this is basic) *without* being entirely clear about the question of rejecting all immigration controls. The revolutionary party has to operate through (and build) such movements but without its members making *any* compromise about what they believe themselves. We have to agree to *differ* from many militants on some important questions in order to *unite* with these same militants for some immediate aims.

There are real difficulties in this work of building a rank and file paper and organisation. Comrades sometimes see a contradiction between pushing, for example, the *Carworker* or the *Dockworker*, and pushing *Socialist Worker*, or between pulling people into supporting a rank and file organisation and pulling people into IS. The contradiction does exist. *Sometimes the rank and file movement can be a substitute for building the party. Sometimes building the party can be used as an excuse for not developing the rank and file movement. But both are needed.*

There is a simple test of the effectiveness of a rank and file paper (and movement). Does it draw in people who are not, at the moment, willing to support the full line of our organisation? If it does, it is a genuine rank and file movement. If it does not, it is a fake and we need to look again at what we are doing. (Of course when we say draw in people we are speaking of genuine militants, serious trade unionists, who may support the Labour Party or the Communist Party. We are not speaking of isolated individuals from the various 'revolutionary' sectlets whose stock in trade is the continual carping criticism of IS, because they are *parasites* on our organisation who are merely a nuisance.)

The workplace-based branches have an *indispensable* role in guiding the whole organisation in its work in developing rank and file organisations. They are in a position, as nobody else is, to check the effectiveness of this work, to correct the errors that could otherwise be made, to make their experience available to the organisation. There is a condition—that they themselves take the work seriously as part and parcel of their day to day activity.

Comrades should, however, beware of a number of problems. It would be nonsensical and counter-productive for our members to be constantly 'switching hats', one day an IS member, the next a rank and file paper supporter. The rank and file organisation is made meaningful and worthwhile only if it is larger than IS and if it involves militants we cannot recruit yet. Our constant goal must be to make it a semi-independent group, broadly influenced by our politics but not manned or run only by ourselves.

This is very important. Confusion will result in one of two situations:
(1) The rank and file organisation is seen as identical to IS by the workers (and possibly more meaningful because more directly related to their immediate concerns). The rank and file group then becomes a hindrance to growth for IS rather than an aid.
(2) The rank and file organisation is seen as identical to IS by our members. The factory branch is not necessarily hindered, but no effort is made to organise a true rank and file group. A number of opportunities of reaching a broader layer are missed, with very negative consequences at the time of a mass struggle.

When we speak of rank and file movements we are not talking of an *alternative* to the existing trade union movement. We are talking about unofficial movements that base themselves on the rank and file but, amongst other things, seek to influence and, in the end, control the official movement. We have to learn from the long experience of breakaway unions and unofficial movements that turned their backs on the existing unions. They all ended up by isolating militants from the mass of their fellow workers. Of course we are a very long way from dominating the official movement and we have to guard against becoming too much concerned with getting positions in that movement rather than developing the shopfloor base. But the opposite error is also dangerous.

It is essential that every workplace-based branch takes very seriously *union* work as well as direct political and industrial activity on the shopfloor. Sometimes the workplace and the union branch will coincide. More commonly the union branch will be geographically based. In either case the union branch needs to be taken seriously even if, as is often the case, it seems to be something of a shell. And above the branch, the district committee or council ought to be an important area for our work. So ought the trades council, if it has any vigour at all. It will not always be possible to aim so high in the first instance, but there are certain things that *every* workplace branch ought to do. First, the union journal (or journals) needs to be read and discussed. Our comrades need to be better informed than their fellow workers. Second, the state of the union branch (or branches) in the locality, how our influence can be increased, what resolutions our members should put, and so on, needs to be a regular agenda item. So, where possible, does the district committee. In unions like the AUEW, indeed in the longer term in all unions, our comrades need to be aware of national union affairs. This involves regular contact with the national fractions. The rank and file papers are important in this field as well.

Factory branches and IS trade union and industrial fractions

IS factory and workplace branches focus our members' activity on their particular place of work or, in the case of industrial branches, on the same kind of job. Inside many workplaces, however, workers belong to different unions or different union branches, and many union branches include workers from different factories. So even the job of winning official union support for a dispute involving the factory can often involve IS members who work in other factories.

The differences in rules and ways of working between, for example, the EETPU and the AUEW can also mean that the factory branch is not a very useful place to discuss in depth how to move a particular resolution at the branch. A local meeting of IS members in the same trade union can be much more important.

The organisation of IS members in the same union is also vital at a national level because in Britain unions usually decide (or pretend to decide) national policy at conferences of delegates elected at branch (or chapel) meetings without any reference to their jobs or factory shop stewards' organisation. So IS, because we believe in fighting to influence and change the unions, must also have a national presence inside the unions.

Where we have more than 20 or so members in a trade union we set up a *trade union fraction*. This will have a secretary or convenor whose responsibility is to keep an up to date list of IS members in the union, to exchange information through a bulletin if possible, and to call meetings and organise schools for the IS members as frequently as is useful.

Where we have a reasonable number of members in the same industry, it becomes possible for us to set up an *industrial fraction*, like the IS automotive industry fraction. These fractions are based even more closely than the trade union fractions on the factory branches, and in effect represent the factory branches that we have in the particular industry together with the individuals in factories where we have not yet set up a branch. It is likely in the future that some of the industrial fractions will set up subdivisions based on all our members who work within the same combine.

The IS trade union and industrial fractions are the organisations through which we decide specific IS national industrial and trade union policies, and whether or not to involve our members in rank and file papers and organisations covering the union elections, whether or not to put up candidates, and if for example we decide against an IS candidate, who else we should support instead. Local fraction meetings decide these matters for the local areas, and the national meetings decide on national union and industry issues.

The fractions are therefore very important indeed in bringing together in activity IS members from different factories and different parts of the country. They are the means by which confidence and trust between IS members will be cemented at the shopfloor level right across the country.

Members of factory branches should play as active a part as possible in their appropriate fractions. This will mean giving the lead to the industrial fractions and working in conjunction with the local IS district committee on building the trade union fractions.

Factory bulletins

Practically all our factory branches are involved in producing, or intend to produce, factory bulletins. They clearly serve a valuable purpose. The main danger to be avoided is that they should not substitute for direct political work and recruitment to IS, even where they may be doing useful propaganda work. One wonders if that is not the case when we read *Dockworker* no 36, issued by our comrades in Southampton, knowing that they have not recruited one docker, although the bulletin and its editor are highly esteemed by many Southampton dockers.

One must distinguish between factory bulletins published from outside the plant, and internal factory bulletins.

External factory bulletins

The factory bulletin was the means by which IS attempted to gain footholds in the factories *from the outside*. It was normally written by non-workers and distributed on the factory gate by non-workers. The frequency of these bulletins was not dictated by events inside the factory but by the need to provide activity for the IS branch, and the contacts who supplied us with the information tended to remain as contacts rather than become members. After all, if we were doing all this for them, why did they need to join? This approach was inspired by the belief that working class recruits were hard to make, and that we had to 'prove' our seriousness by a hard stint on the factory gate. Indeed, one remembers the virtuous glow one used to get after standing in the rain outside the factory handing out sodden sheets of paper or failing to sell *Socialist Worker* to tolerant but indifferent workers.

This was a stage of our development. One cannot be sure if it was right at the time—it certainly does not fit today. Where circumstances compel us to approach a factory entirely from the outside we should be more direct and more bold. If there is a dispute, *Socialist Worker* remains the best entry—a sale on the gate for two to three weeks, a leaflet which explains IS's policies and stresses our factory branch organisation, plus a direct approach to the convenor to take a *Socialist Worker* order for the factory. It may not work, but such an approach is more likely to bring recruits than our becoming part of the scenery at the gate.

Internal factory bulletins

These are the voice of IS *inside* the works. The objectives they are designed to achieve can vary enormously. Where we have the leadership of the factory or of a significant section of it they can be a weapon in the struggle with the management. The bulletin prepares workers for battles that are coming up, communicates what has been achieved to more backward sections and thereby raises their expectations, and answers the propaganda of the management and local press.

The factory bulletin, like *Socialist Worker*, is a means to an end. The goal is to win as many workers as we can to our revolutionary socialist politics and to convince all the rest of the need to fight against the ruling class. *Socialist Worker* does this at a general level, talking to workers across all industries and all skills, and to those who don't even work in factories at all, like housewives. The factory bulletin is a mini-socialist newspaper with a much narrower audience. There are wide political differences amongst its readers, but all are to a greater or lesser extent 'experts' in one area—the factory, its wages, conditions, its scandals and its politics.

Among the best examples of this combative type of bulletin are the ones our comrades produced at BSC Consett. The bulletins are written by the IS members in the works. They are produced for a specific issue and prepared with care. They have to speak in the language of the works, and be absolutely accurate not only in the facts but in the tone. For example, in the discussion on a particular bulletin on a bricklayers' dispute in the works the word 'shopfloor' was vetoed by the members present as this was not a phrase used by brickies at Consett. They called it the 'pitside'. A little thing, but symptomatic of the care required if the weapon of the bulletin is to be correctly used. We have no shortage of enemies waiting to pounce on the lads who distribute the bulletins in the works to accuse them of spreading lies or of being used by sinister outside forces.

At Consett we produce about 500 copies of each bulletin—paid for by a whip-round of the members—which is distributed in the canteens, tea rooms and workshops. There are 7,000 workers in the plant but the bulletins get passed on from hand to hand. A couple of working men's clubs—with the approval of the committee—place a stack of bulletins on the bar for lads to read and pass around.

The bulletins have become enormously popular with the rank and file, because we not only attack the management and trade union officials, we also take the piss out of them too, and the audacity of the bulletins strikes a responsive chord. Humour is important if it can be done. We're proud of the following example—it followed a full page advertisement in the local paper by BSC in which they apologised for the enormous amounts of red dust the works were pouring over the town, but promised that new improvements would soon bring relief:

> That Red Dust—A BSC Statement. Many of you who live in the Consett area will have noticed a considerable increase in the clouds of red dust billowing from the steel plant recently. This is caused by the men who work in the appalling conditions in the plant shaking out their overalls at the end of their shift. We are,

however, now replacing the older mild-steelworkers who crumbled easily (but were much cheaper) with a new tougher version, more able to resist the conditions imposed upon them by the industry.

These bulletins are really hated by the foremen, management, and the right wing union convenors and officials. The AUEW district organiser convened a meeting of AUEW stewards in the plant to inform them of what was happening over a condition money dispute because otherwise they would only learn about it from the IS bulletins. Also foremen have been asking management to take legal action against us for the rude things we have been saying about them. (We have to be careful about victimisation in these circumstances—hence all the bulletins carry an address of a person not working in Consett rather than that of any of our Consett members.)

IS factory bulletins try to win over workers, sometimes with considerable industrial experience and sometimes brand new to the factory and trade union scene, on the day to day issues that come up in the place of work—things that are discussed in the teabreak as well as decisions taken by the shop stewards. We have to be very specific to show our fellow workers how our politics, IS, and joining us in the fight, is the way forward for them.

In the 6 June 1973 issue of the Glasgow *Albion Worker*, for example, one side dealt with 'The Yoker Situation', referring in four paragraphs to the closure of a section of the factory, and putting demands: 'No contraction terms at Yoker, no redundancies, and no cooperation on the closure or transfer of materials or manpower from Yoker.'

'Junior Workers' Committee' had one paragraph urging support for trade union organisation of the apprentices in the factory.

'Films—Will They Benefit The Workers?' had two paragraphs attacking the shop stewards who had agreed to allow a British Leyland publicity team in to film workers, and urging a down-tools if they came into any section before the workers had been consulted.

The other side of the bulletin dealt with a more general subject, the question of rising prices, but in a very specific way. Called 'Figures Don't Lie…But Liars Can Figure!' it drew up an 'Albion workers' cost of living index' that compared wages with the rise in prices, rents, bus fares, etc. 'But what of our mince and totty man?' it asks. 'At the price of meat today, he's just a totty man.' It then goes on to give exact prices.

One side of the bulletin, then, deals with factory politics—what's happening or not happening, and what socialists say about it. (All the while we stress the need for shopfloor democracy, report-back meetings, shop stewards' bulletins, etc, for opposition to management attempts to 'pay off' our representatives, on the need for action independent of what the full time trade union officials and bosses say, and on the need for working class solidarity, between sections within the factory and with other workers elsewhere.) And the other side deals with those week-by-week national political subjects that are talked about in the factory, such as prices, Lord Lambton or racism.

Sometimes this 'formula' has to be bent because so much is going on in the factory that one side of a piece of paper isn't enough. There's no virtue in inflexibility, and so when factory politics is jumping, so should our bulletin.

The *Chrysler Bulletin*, put out by the Chrysler Scotland IS comrades at Linwood on 25 May 1973, at the beginning of the dispute that led to the strike at Ryton, had articles on 'The Press Shop Lockout', 'The Layoff Claim' and 'A Lesson For Us All' on one side. These were all about how the shop stewards and workers should show more solidarity between different sections of the 8,500 workers at Linwood. On the other side there was a piss-taking reply to a 'message' from the Chrysler UK managing director, which started, 'The past ten years at Linwood have at times been rather like the career of an erratic but brilliant football team.' The IS reply went, 'The past ten years at Linwood rather remind me of the position of Clyde, who, although promoted to the First Division, wants to keep on paying Second Division wages.' And below that an article, 'Our Wage Claim: Does It Exist?' On both sides there were adverts for *Socialist Worker* and a local IS meeting.

The Glasgow district organiser writes:

> There are no hard and fast rules about distributing factory bulletins. At the Chrysler and Albion factories in Glasgow the different shift patterns, the fact that we don't have members in every section of the factory, and that sometimes there is the danger of victimisation if an IS member openly hands out the bulletin, means that some bulletins are distributed inside, sometimes openly for example being left on tea tables and sometimes secretly being left inside cars that then go down the line, but the majority are distributed outside by IS members from other workplaces or from college. On the danger of victimisation resulting from the bulletins, we have found that it is one thing the workers round you knowing that you're involved in the bulletin—we try and collect money to pay for them from other workers—but it can be another thing to be seen by two supervisors actually handing out the thing to workers clocking in. So we don't take any foolish risks.

The bulletins should always be written as much as possible by the IS members and our sympathisers in the factory, because this is what gives them the concrete feeling that really convinces other workers. Sometimes a non-worker comrade can be got to write a good piece of analysis on some development (eg the latest profit figures) that our factory members haven't got the material or time to do. And sometimes a really good article from *Socialist Worker*, or from another factory bulletin, can be used as well.

Regular appearance and continuity of the bulletins are important if they are to play a significant part in the life of the factory. This usually means they should come out fortnightly, or at the very least monthly. But when things are bubbling—a new wage deal, sackings—we should not be trapped by routine into not producing bulletins more often than that.

The issue of a bulletin must be seen as a weapon of the organisation to increase its influence among workers, and to recruit the best of them to IS. With clear cost efficiency calculation, and fighting hard against dead routinism, the factory branch can avoid a rut. It has above all constantly to check what are the tangible results of prolonged activity in producing factory bulletins.

To summarise: factory branches in this period are the voice of the IS organ-isation *inside* the workplace. They should therefore be written by the workers involved, distributed internally, and be produced for a specific purpose. This ob-jective will also dictate how often they appear, eg an interventionist bulletin of an IS factory branch in struggle could appear daily or even every shift if events were moving swiftly enough.

A good bulletin is short, clearly typed, has at least one item relating directly to the factory based on obvious inside information. If a regular one publishes accounts on the front page, it must 'click'—that is to say, it must connect with the real feelings, frustrations, etc of the best militants who are not yet in IS, but who could be. Each bulletin must have a focus—a topic, a stewards' meeting, a dispute, an exposure. There is nothing worse than a bulletin produced for the sake of a bulletin.

On bulletins the following advice may be useful:

(1) Try to get non-IS workers to write letters for it.

(2) Regular appeals for letters, contributions, etc should always be made.

(3) All letters should be commented on by the editor.

(4) Articles should be short. Long articles will not be read.

(5) Long and windy phrases must be avoided. Simple and plain language is much more effective.

(6) Avoid preaching and talking down to workers. Avoid the 'we told you so' kind of attitude.

(7) The layout should be neat and all articles should be clearly headed.

(8) Cartoons are always useful.

(9) Be careful about addresses on bulletins.

Education

An anguished cry coming out of practically all the reports from the factory branches regards education material. To quote a few examples.

The Reyrolles report speaks about the 'lack of guide to and supply of pamphlets and constructive political literature'. The Copper Pass (Hull) report underlines this: 'We need schools along the lines of last year's AUEW fraction schools, if possible held in Hull. We need basic education material on trade unionism and our work in it. We badly need copies of *The Struggle for Socialism* and other long-promised pamphlets.' The report from Chrysler branch, Coventry, says:

> We have encountered problems. The main one that comes to mind is education. Until recently, there was a distinct lack of material which was usable on a wide scale. Even short pamphlets, like [Chris] Harman's on Russia, are too complex to serve as an introduction to the topic. *The Struggle for Socialism* is the most useful. Unfortunately, it is out of date in many respects. We are still anxiously awaiting the reprinting of it. The Merseyside notes will also be useful—it has been suggested by one or two comrades that the notes be expanded into a series of short pamphlets.

There are problems with the education of new members—discussion groups turn into activity groups, new members are coming in all the time, and we are constantly having to be as flexible as possible in the way we set up these groups and branches. Really the problem is with the older membership and the centre: can they keep pace with the demands of new people? If we fail in this task, we could lose these people again very quickly, and lose them for a good long time as well.

The report of the Merseyside building workers' branch says:

One problem which in part already exists, but will become more acute, is the need for *industrial* cadres. It is not enough to have cadre schools as at present, as they mainly appeal to the more intellectual comrades in the organisation. We would like to see specific cadre schools for industrial members both at national level (comparable with the intermediate cadre schools at present) and regional cadre schools (comparable to the basic school). The challenge of workers successfully building and leading the organisation is one that the whole organisation must face up to. Also these cadre schools will have to change in content. There must be an emphasis on organising in industry.

Radical changes in educational and publication policies of IS at the centre, at district level and at factory branch level are necessary. Because of the neglect hitherto in this field we can at best point out only the main guidelines for such a policy:

(1) In a revolutionary party there is no rank and file—all must learn and train to lead.

(2) Systematic and universal training is the backbone of an effective revolutionary organisation.

(3) All members must be trained in an understanding of the principles and policy of IS, the history and tactics of the revolutionary working class movement, and our own work—tactics and strategy and methods of organisation.

One cannot be sure that education can be run totally by the branches, but certainly some education should take place there, perhaps integrated regularly with larger meetings with speakers, organised by the industrial aggregate. Some topics should be:

Stalinism: but seen in relation to what Stalinism is today. Thus: Is there a parliamentary road to socialism? Can the Labour Party with the help of the CP establish socialism? Is the left bureaucracy socialist? Can one leave it to the left bureaucracy? Is there a socialist camp?

Labour history: but again related to today's struggles. Picketing, and the history of the struggle to establish the right to picket. Occupations, and the history of the American sit-ins. A rank and file movement, and the Minority Movement.

The unions: a detailed analysis of the structure, problems and perspectives in the unions involved. Sessions on the coming trade union conferences, etc.

Industrial struggle: How to organise strikes; industrial accidents; productivity deals and how to fight them.

IS itself: Factory branches and the experience of the CP; building the party and the experience of the CP; our work in the unions; what rank and file papers are for, etc.

A few general items: racism, imperialism, etc.

Practical training: in public speaking, chairmanship, writing leaflets, reporting for *Socialist Worker* and for the rank and file papers, how to intervene in trade union meetings, how to conduct an election campaign in the union, etc. Mock bargaining could be quite educational—especially for young, inexperienced comrades.

In addition it will probably be worthwhile to have a crash course for new members, to include the following titles: Politics of IS; Reform or revolution; Party and class; Work in unions; Workers' control; Racism; Ireland; Russia.

The 'mechanics' of this education work in factory branches can take many forms: at branch meetings, or at combined meetings of factory workers and others in the same neighbourhood. Perhaps the Coventry experience is of some value for other IS branches. Chrysler factory branch reports:

> We have set up weekly and fortnightly discussion groups in various areas of the district around Chrysler workers. The first one of these, in the Stoke Heath area of Coventry last Friday, which was set up by two new members of the Chrysler branch, started as a discussion about what was wrong with capitalism, and finished in the recruitment of seven new members (four to Chrysler and three to the town)! This group plans to do some tenants' work. (Again, this will give us a minor problem. We feel it is best to keep all these seven together, as they are all mates, for the time being, until they have found their feet in the organisation. This may involve, in the near future, the setting up of a Stoke Heath geographical branch, with some members of the Chrysler branch having dual membership.)

For all this the leading bodies of IS need to prepare material. *International Socialism* journal should change its character so as to fill an important gap.

The excellent recently published pamphlet *The Struggle for Workers' Power* can play a particularly important role in education work in factory branches as well as in the individual self-education of members. Syllabuses round the different chapters of the pamphlet would be useful.

Because of the shift system, etc, many workers will miss a number of the education meetings, hence the written word needs to be emphasised. Simple, clearly written pamphlets on the various subjects mentioned above and on many others should have a high priority.

Above all, workers' education and cadre training depend on a qualitative rise in the role of workers in IS branches, districts and national leadership. Workers who had a tough and nasty relation with school authorities in childhood certainly don't enjoy the word 'education'. Only when workers take the centre of the arena in IS do they feel the need for more knowledge. When industrial members in every branch and district are brought into the leadership, when they stamp their image on the organisation, the hunger for Marxist education will be strongly expressed. The industrial members must of course stamp their *needs and aspirations* on the educational programme of the branch and the district and national organisation.

Ten years on: 1969 to 1979

Socialist Worker, 26 May 1979

The first five years was a period when the class struggle achieved a level unprecedented in British working class history for generations.

We had two national miners' strikes. One of them smashed to pieces the incomes policy of the Tory government. The other forced the government to introduce a three-day week and then to lose power.

The last general strike of miners before this was in 1926, and this was a very different experience. The miners were beaten, driven to their knees.

In 1970 we had the first national dustmen's strike in British working class history and this one ended in victory. We had a national unofficial docks strike challenging the government's Industrial Relations Act. It led to the imprisonment of five dockers. The government capitulated to the strike and the Pentonville prisoners were set free.

The same period saw the first ever national building workers' strike, the first national teachers' strike and the first national hospital workers' strike. We had a national strike by the engineers against the Industrial Relations Act which forced the government to lift the court fine on the AUEW. Workers facing sackings and factory closure in over 200 factories occupied them, a tactic completely new to the British working class.

If one compares the years 1969-74 with even the best period of militancy in Britain of 1900-14 there is no question that this time the struggle was on a much higher level, much more generalised, and the hatred of the government was all prevailing, all encompassing. This chapter ended abruptly with the electoral victory of Labour in February 1974. The next five years were radically different.

We did not have one national strike in any key section of the class, although we had the national strikes of bakers, of lorry drivers and of provincial journalists.

The struggle was incomparably more fragmented; the level was far lower. One has only to remember that the number of days on strike in 1976 was the lowest for ten years. One reason given for this change is that it was simple loyalty to Labour that cut the level of struggle.

This wouldn't wash in 1969. The strikes of the dustmen and the teachers *did* smash through Wilson's incomes policy. Loyalty to Labour by itself would not have held the dam.

A second reason put forward is the fact that there was an incomes policy. Perhaps this dampened down the struggle. However, all the historical experience, from Selwyn Lloyd's incomes policy to Harold Wilson's, showed that incomes policy by itself only stemmed the battle for a year or, at best, two years.

The third reason given is that militancy was dampened by unemployment and the threat of the sack.

Again, historical experience shows that well organised workers can be whipped into *greater* militancy by the threat of the sack. This is exactly what happened under Ted Heath's government when unemployment rose by half.

To understand the downturn in the class struggle in 1974-79 one must look to the cause in the weaknesses of the labour movement—general causes that were very much in evidence in the first five years.

I gave a list of workers' struggles that ended victoriously in the years 1969-74. Alas, a whole number of important battles in the same period ended in defeat.

In 1970 the national strike of the gas workers was defeated. In 1971 the seven week long and bitter strike of the postmen ended in a complete victory for the employers. In 1972 the wage claim of 2 million engineering workers ended in the dust. In 1973 the building workers' strike, with all its militancy and flying pickets, was accompanied by the arrest and imprisonment of the Shrewsbury pickets. They were *not* freed.

In other words, sectionalism was still rampant in the labour movement.

There were only a few miners, the best organised and the most militant and powerful section of the working class, who came to the aid of the hospital workers in 1973.

The generalising and unifying element in all those strikes was deep anti-Tory feeling. The alternative to the Tories meant the Labour Party. Once Labour was in power that general opposition collapsed.

In all the struggles of 1969-74 the union officials kept complete control over the national strikes. The spearhead of union bureaucracy at that time was the left leaders, Scanlon and Jones. With Labour in power all the union leaders moved towards the 'Social Contract'—this time spearheaded by the same 'terrible twins'.

In the strikes of 1900-14 (which were on the whole on a lower level in terms of size than in 1969-74) independent rank and file socialists played a far greater role and were far more cohesive, far more influential than in the 1970-74 strikes.

In 1969 there were probably something like 500 full time convenors.

Ten years later the number rose to about 6,000. This gave a much wider base to union bureaucracy than existed before (the total number of full time union officials is 3,000).

Because of the massive productivity deals of the late 1960s, and because of incomes policy and unemployment, the power of the individual shop steward, which was largely based on his ability to set piece rates and bonus rates, declined quite seriously.

Wage drift, the difference between national wage rates and the 'going rate' on the shop floor, ten years ago was one of the most important expressions of the power of individual shop stewards. That has now practically disappeared from industry.

Therefore we are in a period in which the struggle must become much wider than the individual shop.

But the organisation inside the factory relating the individual shop stewards to each other *still* goes through the convenor. And many of them are collaborating with management through participation schemes. Faced with participation and the new wave of productivity deals, the shop stewards feel less and less able to act collectively.

In describing a period in our history there is always a danger of a one-sidedness. It was clear that 1969-74 was not only a period of successes for the working class but also a time in which important sections of workers were badly beaten.

Similarly, the period 1974-79 should not be seen simply as a time of decline in the struggle. The picture was far more mosaic. Hundreds upon hundreds of factories entered the struggle, involving workers who never knew strike action. Women and black workers entered the battle.

While the traditional key sections of the working class—miners, engineers and dockers—were by and large acquiescent, other sections came to the fore, especially at the end of the Callaghan government, during last winter. These were hospital workers, local government workers and white collar workers.

Alas, this section, in terms of even the statistics of strike records, didn't fill the gap left by the others.

In the years 1966-76 hospital workers struck for only 8 percent of the number of days that workers in manufacturing industry did.

Similarly, amongst white collar workers, the number of strikes was only 10 percent compared with a similar number of workers in manufacturing industry.

The worst inheritance of the trade union bureaucracy during the Social Contract was that scabbing became respectable. Ten years ago hardly any union official would have dreamt of instructing members to cross picket lines of workers in other unions. But this happened in Port Talbot when the electricians went on strike. The AUEW, the ISTC and other unions instructed their members to cross the lines.

In Leyland when the toolroom workers went on strike, other workers were instructed to cross the picket line. When maintenance engineers in Heathrow went on strike, other workers were told to cross.

Blacklegging not only remained the domain of the top union officials now. We must remember how Jimmy Airlie, the convenor of Govan shipyard, scabbed on the yard workers of Swan Hunter in Newcastle, accepting the blacked Polish ships. This is remarkable when one remembers that Govan shipyard in 1971 was the centre of a national mobilisation of workers in defence of their jobs— Upper Clyde Shipbuilders.

To cap the respectability of scabbing came the Concordat between the Labour government and the TUC. It aimed at castrating the picket line, at weakening solidarity between workers.

Labour laid the foundations and the Tories will now build the structure by using the law.

The role of the SWP

In the first five-year period the International Socialists (at present the Socialist Workers Party) expanded from a group of a few hundred—mainly students and white collar—to an organisation of 3,000 to 4,000 members.

Something like a third of these were manual workers. We managed to implant ourselves in a number of factories, in a whole number of trade unions, both manual and white collar. We were involved in the establishment of a whole number of rank and file groups, with rank and file papers in different unions.

In the second five years the SWP found the going much tougher. With the Social Contract, not only the trade union leaders, but also the Communist Party—the main organisation of the left in industry—veered strongly to the right.

The SWP decided quite rightly to steer left. The organisation was kept intact, but quite a heavy price was paid. Its members found themselves very often isolated and they had to hold on by their fingertips to their positions in the movement.

The organisation has been steeled. The period was not only a period of marking time. We managed to carry out quite important initiatives like the Right To Work Campaign and the ANL, which established our credibility widely in the movement.

To some extent the two periods we are dealing with are similar to two periods in the history of the Bolshevik Party. At the time of the 1905 revolution the Bolshevik Party expanded massively, reaching a membership of 30,000 in 1907. However, in the period of reaction following, demoralisation in the class and police persecution smashed the party.

Of course the years of 1969-74 in Britain didn't see a revolution but saw a massive rise in the class struggle.

The years 1974-79 did not see the victory of reaction and counter-revolution, but did see a serious shift to the right.

The Socialist Workers Party is much better poised at present to take a part in the new advance of the class struggle than it has ever been before.

No individual, and certainly not the movement, can be completely free from the past. Our experience of 1969-74 as well as 1974-79 will affect our movement in the coming days, months and years.

Now, when the Tories are back in power, even if their policies are not harsher than those of Callaghan, they will raise incomparably more anger than he has done.

The government, as the enemy, will help generalise the struggle. With the increasing and deepening crisis of world capitalism, the attack on workers is bound to come.

The possibility of once more building a rank and file movement, far more independent of the union bureaucracy than in 1969-74, is with us. The prize of victory will be much greater, but also the penalty of defeat will be much more severe.

Loyalty to the Labour Party, reliance on the trade union leaders, and sectionalism are the main impediments that workers have to overcome.

The balance of class forces in recent years

International Socialism (second series) 6, Autumn 1979

There have been dynamic changes in the balance of class forces in Britain over the last few years. We need to find out in what direction the balance has been tilted, and what the causes were.

Workers' fight

'In Place of Strife' argued that shipyards, mining, docks and motor vehicle manufacturing, employing some 4 percent of the labour force in Britain, were the industries most prone, by far, to strikes. In 1965 these industries were responsible for 53 percent of all strike days in the country.[1] The specific weight of these industries in the general workers' front is much greater even than the figures show, because of the high level of concentration of workers' power in them. As they are at the heart of the class war, let us follow the history of disputes in these industries in recent years.

The shipyards

It was the struggle in Upper Clyde Shipbuilders that radically turned the tide of the Tory attack. After the defeat of the power workers in December 1970 and the postmen after a seven-week strike, and the sell-out of the Ford workers by Jones and Scanlon after a nine-week strike, the UCS workers took over the yards—one week after the Industrial Relations Act came into being.

Already in June 1971 there were strong rumours of mass sackings threatening workers in UCS. On the afternoon of 24 June over 100,000 workers in Glasgow stopped work and half of them marched in a demonstration through the town. The demonstration included representatives from every factory in the west of Scotland, as well as delegations from over the border. This was the largest Clydeside protest demonstration since the General Strike. On 29 July John Davies, the secretary of state for industry, got up in the House of Commons to announce that employment in UCS would be cut from 8,500 to 2,500. Next day the workers of UCS took control over the four yards.

On 10 August a meeting in Glasgow attended by over 1,200 shop stewards from all over Scotland and the north of England unanimously endorsed the plan for a work-in, and appealed to all workers to give financial support to the workers of UCS.

On 18 August some 200,000 Scottish workers downed tools, and about 8,000 of them went on a demonstration in support of the UCS workers.

Millions of workers from all over Britain contributed financially to the long drawn-out battle. UCS workers were the first to breach the Industrial Relations Act, and even Harold Wilson had to admit in an introduction he wrote to a book by Alasdair Buchan, *The Right to Work: The Story of the Upper Clyde Confrontation*:

> But for the men who work on the Upper Clyde, this story would have followed its conventional course: meetings between management and men would have resulted in failure to agree; the inevitable sackings would have been accompanied by forlorn protest; the dole would have been started and the story would have ended... What the men of the Clyde proclaimed...was 'the right to work'.[2]

In trade union terms the shipyard industry has long been one of the most highly organised industries in the country. Skilled tradesmen have remained dominant in a way which is true of few other industries. In 1963 just over 60 percent of all manual workers in shipbuilding were skilled,[3] and their role in production is central. As a consequence the division of labour and the demarcation between skills was more extreme than in any other industry. The workers had a deep attachment to the industry. Thus a study of one shipyard on the Tyne carried out between 1968 and 1970 reported:

> ...86 percent of the Boilermakers interviewed, 79 percent of the outfitting workers and 61 percent of the semi-skilled had spent more than half of their working life in the industry, and as few as 7 percent of them had preferred a past job outside shipbuilding and marine engineering. (In contrast only 38 percent of the unskilled men had spent more than half their working lives in the industry and one in five of them preferred a previous job outside the industry.)[4]

Shipyard workers have for a long time been tough fighters. Already in 1888 the proportion of trade unionists among them was higher than in any other industry— 36 percent of shipyard workers were members of trade unions, while among general engineers the proportion of trade unionists was 15 percent, among miners 19 percent, textile workers 8 percent, railwaymen 9 percent, and print workers 21 percent. In 1901 the proportion of shipyard workers was as high as 60 percent.[5]

And they were accustomed to long and bitter struggles. Thus, for instance, Shipsmiths in the north east went on strike from November 1904 to June 1905, resisting wage cuts.[6] In April 1908 some 13,000 shipyard workers in Scotland and north England were locked out and held grimly on for a very long time.[7]

Since 1974 the struggle has declined drastically, as shown in the following graph:[8]

British shipbuilders' strike record

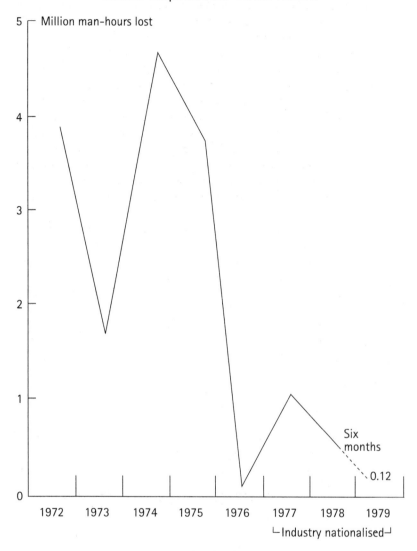

Actually the strike statistics do not tell us the whole story. Shipyard workers have been so depressed and demoralised that they accepted very poor terms. Thus, for instance, 3,500 workers of the Tyne Group of Shiprepairers, in exchange for the 10 percent allowed by government guidelines, accepted the abolition of demarcation restrictions, complete flexibility, and gave a year's no-strike guarantee.[9]

The 168 different bargaining units, which gave power to shipyard workers to push wages up through drift, leapfrogging, etc, were completely given up, and a national wage agreement substituted for them which gave a same day settlement for the whole industry.[10]

In fact Govan, the new name for three of the four former UCS yards (the fourth being Marathon), had been pioneers in the working of a joint union-management monitoring committee for a harsh productivity deal.

They signed a 31-point agreement containing elaborate no-strike pledges, massive concessions on work practices giving management the right to impose compulsory overtime. The agreement at Govan's has since been used as the model of what British Shipbuilders hope to achieve throughout the industry. In addition to the main points, the agreement also states quite clearly, 'Any changes required that will help make the company more efficient will be introduced at any time subject only to the normal process of consultation and mutual agreement.' Govan expects to get the number of man hours to build a ship down from 850,000 five years ago to 400,000 next year. Naturally, in a declining market such productivity increases can mean one thing only—massive redundancies.

Govan reached the lowest depths when they scabbed on their Tyneside Swan Hunter brothers.

Management tried to impose a declaration of intent on the Swan Hunter workers as a precondition for giving them a big proportion of the Polish order. The Swan Hunter workers rejected it. Dave Hanson, chairman of the outfitters' shop stewards committee, said, 'There is a major principle at stake. If we give in, every time the government wants a contract it will try and impose conditions'.[11]

When Swan Hunter workers blacked the Polish ships Jim Airlie rushed to take the job—the same Jim Airlie, one of the workers' leaders at UCS in 1971, who asked at that time, 'Are the other shipyards going to accept our orders and let my men starve?'

But by 1979, during the Swan Hunter dispute, he sang a new tune: 'If Newcastle are losing six ships through disputes, we will build them. If not us, then the Japs will.'

To prove their loyalty to management Govan shop stewards agreed in July 1979 to give up their holidays in order to complete Polish ships in time—ie, as Willie Lee, the Chrysler AUEW shop steward, put it, 'in order to close the shipyard on time'.

This abysmal betrayal of every trade union principle is taking place in an area where unemployment is overwhelming.

The miners

In February 1972 the miners broke the incomes policy of the Heath government. Using the flying picket that culminated in the mass picketing of Saltley depot, they brought the government to its knees. In 1974 the miners managed to bring down the Tory government.

But since then the NUM has accepted Phase I, Phase II, Phase III and Phase IV of the government guidelines. To add insult to injury, they accepted a most divisive and injurious productivity deal.

For some idea of how divisive it is let us look at a few facts. In South

Nottinghamshire the area average bonus for face workers was £27 in the week ending 11 March 1978. At Gedling pit in Nottinghamshire the miners are on a face-by-face deal, and payments vary from £6 to £28. Annesley is also on a face-by-face scheme, and bonuses vary from £17.50 to £45.[12]

Compare the above bonuses with those earned in Maltby pit, South Yorkshire. In a typical ten-week period in the winter and spring of 1978 they varied from precisely 28p per week to £4.14—an average of less than £2 per week.[13]

The division is not only between miners of different pits, or even different faces in one and the same pit, but also between surface workers, usually injured and older men, and face workers, with pay differentials of £50-£60 compared to £20 four years ago.

And the reaction of the miners to the government guidelines? One militant miner from Armthorpe Colliery near Doncaster says, 'The national executive… decided to accept the 10 percent deal and not allow a ballot of miners in case we rejected it.

'What happened in the rank and file? Nothing! We sat at home and watched *Crossroads* as though it was happening to someone else'.[14] The high wave of miners' battles of 1972 and 1974 gave way to a very low level of activity (with one very important exception to which we shall refer below—the spontaneous strike in support of the rescue men in May 1978).

The number of strike days lost—over 10 million in 1972 and over 5 million in 1974—declined to 52,000 in 1975, 70,000 in 1976, 88,000 in 1977, and 176,000 in 1978.[15]

What about the dockers?

Lord Devlin, in his report on the docks in 1965, complained that the dockers had 'an exaggerated sense of solidarity or loyalty'—men accepted without question a policy of 'one out, all out', adopting the 'principle that the man who wants to strike is always right'.[16]

In July 1972 the dockers were unquestionably the heroes of the whole working class. Throughout the first few months of 1972, fighting to defend their jobs, they courageously faced up to the government, the police and the National Industrial Relations Court.

The rank and file showed fantastic initiative. They decided on their own to take action in defence of jobs threatened by employers using non-registered dockers and cheap labour. As Mickey Fenn, one of the most active rank and file leaders in this campaign, put it:

> It was obvious we had to do something about the containers so we began picketing at the same time the Tories were introducing their Industrial Relations Act, but we didn't think it would be a danger to us; but just in case, we made over our houses and cars, etc, to our wives and arranged that if the top four stewards were lifted there would be another four to take their place, and then another four.
>
> When we heard they were planning to arrest three of us outside Chobham Farm there were 3,000 of us and about as many police. The SPG didn't exist in those days,

but there are only 250 of them and 3,000 of us would have given them a hard time. Anyway, later on some bailiff came down but all he got was a rolled umbrella in the ribs, two of them cracked—some dockers do carry rolled umbrellas.

At the same time we began to spread our picketing to more container ports. We would tell any lorry that threatened to cross the picket that they would he blacked in every port in the country. Then we began following the lorries and we followed them all, up to 200 miles we went, and every time a lorry went into a place we would follow.

Well, one day the port shop stewards were having a meeting and we heard four or five of us were to he arrested. Well, anyway, we had decided that it was better for some of us to be arrested than fight the police in the streets, because we could build up a campaign round this. When it happened we immediately decided to shift the centre of our picketing to Pentonville prison and make that the organising centre for our operations. The docks had come out immediately they heard about the warrants, and this went for all the docks all over the country. The problem was that the Tories had planned it so that we would be fighting when every car plant, mine and engineering factory would be closed for the summer. The big problem was how to get around all the different places arguing with each one why they should be out: it took a long long time to argue with each one.

At this time the press was going on about how we had vast financial and organisational resources, but I can tell you, because I was treasurer of the port shop stewards' funds, that we began with £4—but this gradually built up. We had collections among our own lads and donations from outside.

One thing we found out was that if you give people a chance they really can have great imaginations. When we had the posters people asked me, 'Where should we put the posters?' but I said, 'Wherever you think there should be posters put them up,' so posters appeared all over the place—on Buckingham Palace, Lambeth Palace. The NF HQ in Croydon was plastered. We tried the Tory headquarters but policemen were outside so we left it. Transport House was already done when we got there. One bloke managed to get right up the outside of the Bank of England, and I'll never work out how he did it without ropes.

It wasn't easy bringing out Fleet Street, I can tell you, but we went right up there and said to the FOCs, 'Look, your unions were always the ones at the front of the anti Industrial Relations Act demos, and you know that if you were in the same position the docks would be out for you.' And they hung their heads low and had to agree. Soon the papers, I think the Mirror was first, came out and by Sunday all the major papers had stopped. The secondary picketing and the big campaigns to win support were vital. That is why the Tories had to find this Official Solicitor, who was last used about 900 years ago, to pull their rabbit out of the hat.

Anyway, it was seen as a victory, but it wasn't really a dockers' victory, but a victory for the trade union movement.

Now, this glorious chapter in the history of the dockers' struggle was part of a long and fine history.

Let us quote just a few cases of dockers' mass spontaneous unofficial strikes in solidarity even with one or two victimised mates.

May-June 1948. Zinc oxide strike. A gang of 11 men in the Regents Canal Dock, London, rejected a piecework price for discharging 100 tons of zinc oxide. The men were harshly disciplined—one week's suspension and three months disentitlement to attendance money and guarantee. The strike spread over this punishment (later reduced to two weeks disentitlement)—19,000 were on strike by mid-June, then 9,000 walked out in sympathy in Liverpool; 1,000 troops were sent into London; 205,000 days were lost.

April 1949. On national instruction, the London Dock Labour Board ordered 33 men who were old and ineffective to be struck off the register; 15,000 walked out for a week.

April-May 1950. The TGWU executive, after examining the conduct of eight leaders of the London Central Lock-Out Committee during a previous strike, expelled three from membership and debarred four others from holding office. The new Port Workers' Defence Committee called a strike until the three were reinstated; a maximum of 19,000 men responded; 3,000 troops were sent in; the London Dock Labour Board threatened to withdraw registration from strikers on 1 May; the strike folded; 103,000 days were lost.[17]

With all the militant tradition of the docks, however, there has never been any strike that approaches the achievement of the Pentonville stoppage.

Alas, since then there has been a terrible downturn in struggle. Immediately after the Pentonville strike an *official* strike took place following the rejection of the Aldington-Jones Committee report, which recommended rationalisation.

The official strike went on from 28 July till 18 August, and the dockers got sweet Fanny Adams out of it. On 15 August the TGWU Dock Delegates' Conference voted 53 to 30 to end the strike and accept the Aldington-Jones recommendations. Most ports voted to resume normal working. However, there was resistance in Hull, and London dockers continued to black depots which had not agreed to take on registered dock workers. Jack Jones reacted by saying, 'Unauthorised picketing and blacking is unofficial and must not take place... Conference decision was binding'.[18]

In the next few months the labour force dropped catastrophically. By 5 February 1973 it was reported that more than 8,000 out of the 10,000 eligible to get redundancy pay, according to the Aldington-Jones agreement, had done so. The size of the dock labour force was cut from 42,000 to 34,000.[19]

The dockers did not give up the defence of their jobs. But the struggle was intermittent. In February-March 1975 a five week long strike took place on this issue in the Port of London. The strike was defeated, and a sense of demoralisation spread all around.

The demoralisation increased, says Bob Light, a docker in the Royal Docks, because the dockers were cheated:

They were assured that the issue would be solved by other means. First of all there was the Jones-Aldington Committee, which took nearly two years to produce its utterly worthless report. Perhaps had the National Port Shop Stewards Committee been in a fit state at the moment they might have been able to rekindle the campaign of 1972. Secondly, the TGWU were going through the motions of promising to come to grips with the problem on a local basis, which was what eventually led to the 1975 strike in London.

The failure of the 1975 strike, particularly the failure to spread it outside London, is one reason why there has been little or no action on the issue since. It left bitterness and demoralisation in its wake. (In fact to this day I am convinced that the strike was masterminded by Transport House to have just that effect!) Another contributory reason why there has been no action since 1972 was the sheer size of the defeat we suffered that year. It not only deflated the movement, it created a lot of bitterness between ports, and it had the effect of collapsing the National Port Shop Stewards for effectively three or four years.

Another spark of activity was the one-day national unofficial strike on 20 March 1977 in support of Preston dockers against the closure of their port. Mickey Fenn writes:

> About 23,500 dockers stopped work. Bearing in mind that this represents nearly 85 percent of the total registered labour force, and that the strike was organised by an unofficial committee in the teeth of frantic attempts by the TGWU to undermine it, the strike was an impressive show of solidarity.

In addition small acts of solidarity have occurred again and again. Thus it is the custom to black ships that have been diverted from ports in dispute. But with all said and done, the struggle in the docks in the last few years has been at a very low ebb, and this not only in comparison with the Pentonville days, but even with the general picture of struggles in the 1940s, 50s and 60s.

How far the struggle has declined can be seen from the graph on the next page on strike days per worker in the previously militant Liverpool dock.

The engineering industry

Engineering employs more than a third of all workers in manufacturing, and traditionally has been one of the strongest bastions of the working class. It has played a pioneering and absolutely central role in shop stewards' organisation. Let us see if there has been a change in the balance of class forces in the engineering industry in recent years and, if so, in which direction.

The best measuring rod for shop stewards' strength in engineering has always been the wage drift.

Engineering workers' earnings depend on two main factors: firstly, industry-wide bargaining between the national trade union or group of unions and the corresponding employers' organisation; and, secondly, bargaining within the individual firm. National minimum rates are bargained on the national level; while at the local level negotiation takes place over such matters as piece-work rates and other forms of payment by results, additions to wage rates such as bonuses, and the local rules and practices including manning of machines and demarcation questions.[20]

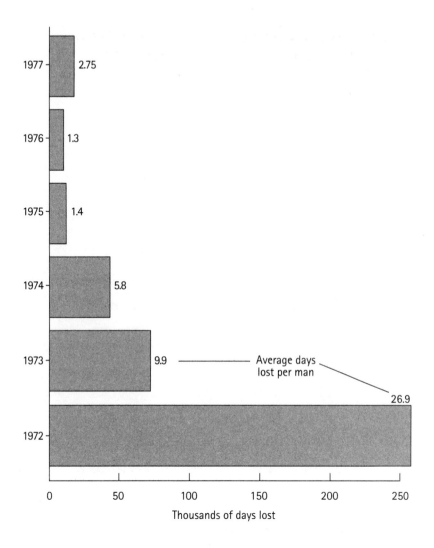

The difference between the two—the floor and the ceiling earnings—is what wage drift is. Actually the term 'wage drift' is a little misleading. It would be better called wage *drive*, since it is the result of pressure from workers in the better organised industries and firms.

Thus in 1964 the national wage rate was 70.3 percent of a fitter's actual average earnings (excluding overtime). The national time rate in June 1968 was only some 56 percent of his national average earnings.

Since then, however, more particularly in recent years, wage drift has been considerably squeezed.[22]

Actual earnings of fitters and labourers in EEF firms compared with nationally agreed rates[21]

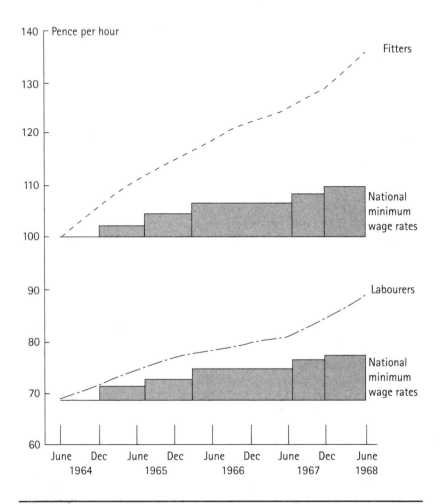

NATIONAL MINIMUM RATE AS PERCENTAGE OF AVERAGE 40-HOUR EARNINGS

	Skilled	Unskilled
December 1970	63.6	72.9
November 1975	71.4	76.2
February 1976	73.0	77.6
April 1978	78.7	77.9

The clearest expression of the decline of the wage drift can be seen by looking at the situation in Coventry. A study of some 10,000 skilled workers in 24 engineering firms in the Coventry district showed that between 1953 and 1970 'only one fifth of all increases in...average piece-work earnings came from national negotiations, while the rest resulted from wage drift'.[23]

Now we find that in this same district there are engineering workers who earn less than the *national minimum*. Thus a report in May 1979 says that 'the Central Arbitration Committee has recently had to award payment of the national minimum rates at firms in the heart of the engineering industry...it is...something of a shock to find medium-sized companies with basic wages lower than the national engineering minimum in an area commonly supposed to be very highly paid'.[24]

Other sections of the working class: hospital workers

Under the anarchic capitalist system all sections of the working class do not move in any synchronised way in one direction or another. But with due reservations, we find the general retreat taking place of the last few years affecting practically all sections of the class.

We have no place in this article to give more than a short resumé of one such group of workers—in the hospitals. Many parallels can be drawn with others—particularly white collar public sector workers in the NUT, NALGO and CPSA.

Bill Geddes describes as follows the changes that have taken place since the hospital workers' strike of 1973:

> The ancillaries took action for the first time in 1973. Looking back I think there will never again be an atmosphere in the NHS when circumstances were so favourable for a victory. The sheer enthusiasm of the strikers was fantastic. The picket lines were a riot of fun and laughter, good at the time but a tradition which we paid for later.
>
> The management were panicking like hens when a cat gets into the yard. They had no idea how to handle strikes; their industrial relations experience was zero. The union leaders' decision to use selective action in 1973 not only lost us the battle on that occasion; they throttled the new-born militancy of hospital workers to such an extent that the effect is still obvious today.
>
> One example of how weak the management were at that time. During the dispute, myself and a few others were handing out leaflets in the canteen, an event unheard of in the hospital before. (We had only set the NUPE branch up a few months previously.) The management saw me handing out the leaflets and the next day I was called into the office and told that I had broken hospital rules. I demanded to see a copy of the rules (I knew there was no such thing). I pretended to be very angry at this attack on my behaviour and walked out, slamming the door behind me.
>
> The next day I got a letter *apologising* for the accusation over the leaflet incident. I fell off my chair laughing!

In the aftermath of the strike—up to 1975—the hospital workers still went forward and gained some significant concessions:

During this period, despite the defeat on wages, many hospital branches achieved a great deal in terms of improved working conditions, union facilities, etc. I drew up a shopping list in 1973 and my branch submitted it to the management. Two years later we had won *everything* on the list.

The victories during this period were often achieved by the *threat* of action (but at the Hammersmith we used to deliberately involve the members in action even when we knew that talking would be enough). This was a time of great confidence in the better organised hospitals.

[But] after 1975 the tide began to flow the other way. The NHS was reorganised; the most obvious manifestation of this to ancillary workers was a massive influx of bureaucrats...

The whole atmosphere changed when the cuts loomed up. Management began to feel the whip on their backs and started to go on the offensive.

For the first time shop stewards met resistance when applying for time off, etc. A number of (unsuccessful) attempts were made to discipline myself and other stewards... Now the crackdown started.

In the years 1977-79:

...the battle of the cuts was lost. All the perks and fiddles which were an unspoken part of the wages in 1973 were taken away whenever possible.

The combination of relatively high manning levels, perks from the past and benefits won in 1973-77 meant that the management had a lot of slack to take up and the workers had a lot to lose.

Management have now become confident enough to take on the rank and file leaders; my own sacking together with a number of other militants in London has been the latest development in this tendency. The fight to stop the cuts has taken place in the same piecemeal way as the wages campaigns of 1973 and 1979, and the result has been defeat after defeat, resulting in a great deal of demoralisation. Very few of the rank and file leaders from 1973 are still around. This means that in an industry with a very high turnover of staff the experience of the past is being lost for ever.

This may seem very pessimistic but I think the recent Low Pay Campaign reflected this tendency. Despite the hysterics in the press very few hospitals (in London) were involved in real tough action other than the nationally sanctioned days of action. The only action which had the anger to fight to a victory were the ambulancemen and they are badly represented in terms of committees and votes in the unions.

The strikes of 1973 and 1979 were very similar in terms of tactics. The vital ingredient which was missing in 1979 was confidence, despite the fact that council workers were also out. In the hospitals there was an air of pessimism which was not there in 1973.

Against the trend

While the strong battalions of the working class—dockers, miners, shipyard workers and engineers—have been on a low level of struggle in recent years, other groups of workers went into battle: BOC workers, Ford workers, tanker drivers, lorry drivers, firemen, bakers, local journalists, BBC and ITV workers, etc.

BOC workers broke the government guidelines in Phase III, as did Ford workers in Phase IV. Added to these two groups, the lorry drivers have emerged as one of the most powerful groups of organised workers. Their use of the flying picket and 'secondary picketing' was fantastic. By and large they got very widespread support from other trade unionists. For example, stewards' committees in Yorkshire, Lancashire and Scotland organised their own internal checks to turn back goods by hauliers. In Nottingham the NUM agreed to provide full facilities for one picket per pit to turn away non-union drivers.[25]

Even more exciting was the victory of the workers at Perkins Diesel, who won after one week of a very militant occupation—evicting the management and blockading the factory.

The firemen, the bakers and the local journalists entered into battle, fought with great perseverance, but alas, they were either defeated, or at best won very partial victories.

Even amongst Ford workers the feeling at the end of the nine-week strike was far from elation. After all, they could have got 9 percent without a strike, and they were still under penalty clauses, however loose.

It would be a grave mistake to put the success of the workers of Ford, BOC and lorry drivers in the same league as the victory of the miners in 1972 or 1974. The victory of the miners changed the balance of class forces in the country as a whole *radically* in favour of the working class. The victories of Ford, BOC and the lorry drivers did not. For a Marxist a sense of proportion is central in grasping reality. The heart of the dialectics—this very important if abused concept— is the relations between quantity and quality.

The victory of Ford, lorry drivers, etc, did not overcome the generally great lack of workers' confidence about their ability to take on the employers and the government.

The wages front

Never since the Second World War had the real wage of workers declined as much as under the Labour government of 1974-79.

Under the Labour government of 1964-70, notwithstanding the incomes policy, real wages continued to rise, even if slowly:[26]

	Average real wage rise (%)
October 1964–October 1965	3.5
October 1965–October 1966	0.7
October 1966–October 1967	3.7
October 1967–October 1968	2.4
October 1968–October 1969	3.0
October 1969–April 1970	1.7

The incomes policy of the Wilson government of 1964-70 only very marginally affected the rise in real wages. Aubrey Jones, chairman of the Prices and Incomes Board, was quite modest in estimating the effect of the policy. He believed that the net effect of the policy had been that the 'average annual increase in earnings in recent years may have been just under 1 percent less than otherwise it would have been'.[27]

Under Heath the annual percent change in real income of a male manual worker (married with two children) rose as follows: 1970-71, 2 percent; 1971-72, 7.4 percent; 1972-73, 1. 1 percent—or an average 3.5 percent per year.[28]

Under the 1974-79 Labour government for the first time real wages went down. In the first year (March 1974 to March 1975) they went down by 2 percent; in the second year (March 1975 to March 1976) by 4 percent; in the third (March 1976 to March 1977) by a further 5 percent.

Of course the slashing of wages could not go on. Workers' resistance had to rise. In the fourth year of the Labour government (March 1977 to March 1978) real wages went up by 5 percent, and in its last year by a further 7 percent.[29]

In March 1979 the real wage of an employed worker was only 1 percent higher than in March 1974. Of course the losses in between were never recovered. Worse than that, the social wage (the quality of the health service, education, etc) was far worse at the end of the Labour government than at its beginning.

If one takes into account the fact that the number of unemployed doubled, it is clear that the real standard of living of the working class as a whole was drastically slashed.

The figures of real wages do not tell the whole story even about the wage changes themselves, as the conditions attached to them are very important. In the last couple of years quite diabolical productivity deals have been dictated by the employers, far nastier than those concluded before, especially those of the first great rush in the years 1966-69.

According to the Department of Employment, at least 1,500 productivity deals were signed between August 1977 and August 1978.

Previously when workers exchanged payment by results for 'measured day work' (MDW) they always got a significant wage rise. Not so now. Thus the 2,000 workers of Westland Aircraft were forced to accept MDW accompanied by a wage cut.[30]

In the Renold Power Transmission factory in Coventry the basic wage was raised by only 3¹/₂ percent—less than the government guideline of 5 percent at the time—but extra money was offered in exchange for a self-financing productivity deal.[31]

5,500 workers at the British Sugar Corporation received a 5 percent rise on their basic wage plus 6 percent on a self-financing productivity deal.[32]

8,600 Michelin workers got a wage rise of 6.5 percent on the basic plus an extra 3 percent for adjustments and consolidation, equalling altogether some 9.5 percent.[33]

Rockwell Kingspeed Engineering received a rise of 5 percent on their basic wage plus a productivity bonus based on acceptance and operation of new productivity techniques and machinery equal to 7 percent. And the 8,000 Kodak workers got a rise of 5 percent on the basic rate plus a maximum bonus with targets achieved of 3 percent.[34]

27,000 Vauxhall manual workers got a rise on the basic wage of between 4.7 percent and 6.3 percent plus new productivity deal measures.[35]

Barroughs Machines, Cumbernauld, near Glasgow, got a 6 percent rise on their basic wage plus 7.7 percent on a self-financing productivity deal.[36]

At Rolls Royce, Derby, 10,545 manual workers got 5 percent for skilled, 4 percent for semi-skilled and 3 percent for unskilled workers.[37]

The 6,000 Rolls Royce workers in Bristol were offered a 10 percent wage rise. In return management demanded greater flexibility and mobility, aimed at achieving manpower savings by taking 'every advantage' of natural wastage, non-replacement of leavers, redeployment, retraining and voluntary early retirement.[38]

The 2,800 manual workers of Hoover's Scottish factories were given a total wage rise of 10 percent, partly in exchange for flexibility and a self-financing productivity deal.[39]

We can go on for pages with lists of similar agreements. What is more, in practically all the productivity deals mentioned the rise in wages does not keep up with even the prevailing, let alone the expected, rise in the cost of living.

One has only to compare the Clegg Commission report in 1979 with the 1971 Scamp Commission, on which Clegg served, to see how far back the low paid workers have been pushed. In 1970 local authority manual workers were given a rise of 17.7 percent.[40] Following this award, hospital ancillary workers were awarded 18.2 percent for men and 19.9 percent for women by the Whitley Council.[41] At that time the annual rate of inflation was about 5 to 6 percent.

In 1979 Clegg added rises ranging from 1.7 to 25.8 percent to the original 9 percent given in March. Half the 1.1 million council workers received increases of 4.9 percent or less, and three quarters of the 270,000 ancillary workers 6.5 percent or less.[42] With an annual rate of inflation expected to reach 20 percent it is clear that to the overwhelming majority of local government and hospital ancillaries this meant a wage cut. (No doubt the disgusting attack by Donnett of the GMWU on NUPE did great damage: NUPE, by and large, covers the lowest paid workers, and they came off much worse out of the Clegg report.)

In 1974-75 the low paid public employees' basic rate was about two thirds of average male earnings. The Clegg report reduces this proportion, so that the conditions of the low paid are far, far worse than in 1974-75 (although they are of course better off than the unemployed).

Heath sacked Clegg (together with Scamp) for his 'generosity' to the low paid. It is very doubtful whether Thatcher will do the same. Probably she agrees with the *Observer* article of 7 August entitled 'Long Life To The Clegg Quango'.

Clegg at the same time meticulously carried out the Tory policy of divide and rule. To a tiny minority of workers (power workers, tanker drivers, ambulance-men, etc) the Tories are ready to give concessions; to the majority of the workers, a kick in the teeth (thus following the secret policy document of Nicholas Ridley, Thatcher's confidante).

The wages dam has not been broken at all. At best the sluices have been opened for a short time so that some of the water can go through and weaken the pressure.

The pattern of industrial disputes

Naturally the best measure of the balance of class forces and changes in this balance is to be gleaned from the pattern of industrial disputes.

In analysing this pattern some preliminary remarks need to he made. First, the method used by the Department of Employment to publish its statistics of industrial disputes is not helpful. Political strikes are not recorded. Thus the fact that we had more than two dozen political strikes under the Heath government and only a couple since is not registered.

Secondly factory occupations are not registered. Thus the fact that over 200 occupations occurred between 1972 and 1974, and that since then the number declined to less than a dozen, and practically all of these fizzled out after a day or two, is not to be found in government statistics. Even the UCS work-in is not mentioned anywhere in the Department of Employment *Gazette*!

Thirdly, government statistics speak of 'disputes', thus not distinguishing between strikes and lockouts. Until a couple of years ago it did not matter, as there were hardly any lockouts. But over the last couple of years things changed. And finally, we are not told whether the strikes were offensive or defensive, or whether the workers won or lost.

Without information about all the above facets of the disputes the use of the statistics may easily lead to shallow and unfounded conclusions. Comparing strike days of different disputes as a measurement of the balance of class forces is like gauging the strength of a person solely from their height.

To give an illustration, let us compare the number of strike days in the following national miners' strikes: 1921, 1926, 1972, 1974. In 1921 72.7 million days were lost, in 1926 146.4 million, in 1972 10.8 million and in 1974 5.6 million.[43]

Even if we take into account that the number of miners in 1972 and 1974 was about a quarter of what it was in 1921 and 1926, still the sheer number of strike days would lead one to the conclusion that the 1921 strike was twice as effective as that of 1972, and four times that of 1974; and the 1926 strike was four times more effective than the 1972 strike, and eight times the 1974 strike. We know of course that it was exactly the opposite.

The categories used by the Department of Employment to define strikes are arbitrary (and subject to change). The system of reporting is haphazard and the DoE's monitoring depends very largely on the press, and certain key employers filling in forms. These factors alone make the official figures very inadequate for revolutionaries.

The analysis that follows tries to overcome these problems. If it is patchy, it is largely for lack of time to sift the massive amount of material collected and collated by Dave Beecham, to whom we are very grateful. (We shall no doubt find another opportunity to develop it.) He studied just over 1,000 disputes in the two-year period from February 1977 to January 1979.

By and large the disputes were much longer than during the previous period. Of the disputes examined, there were 437 lasting more than two weeks. In many cases they were much longer; not just at Grunwick, Garners or Sandersons, but at Massey-Ferguson (11 weeks), Yardleys (seven weeks), East Midlands Allied Press (24 weeks), Chloride (nine weeks), Lucas, Cammell-Laird, Beechams, Birds Eye, Jones Cranes, etc.

The general picture which emerges is fairly uniform—of greater and greater efforts demanded of workers to maintain the status quo, much more aggression from the employers, small victories won at high prices.

To quote four examples. First, the 11-week strike at Massey-Ferguson in Coventry—won after sit-ins, injunctions and a press witch-hunt—was about management taking 130 men off the clock for 'lack of effort' during piece-work negotiations. It was a key dispute for the company, which was trying to bring in a new line of tractor cabs. Subsequently there were three more stoppages on the same issue...to resolve a question that might have involved a two-hour walkout in the heady days of the late 60s.

Then the case of the Lucas dispute later in the same year. This involved two months on the streets, massive layoffs and a bitter press campaign—at the end of which the toolroom returned having defended the status quo on their bonus and with a bit more money—£3 a week plus a small lump sum.

The third is the case of David Brown. There were three serious disputes there during 1977—the first an aggressive but lengthy strike in support of combine-wide bargaining, the second also seeing the shopfloor on the offensive, and the third an important staffing dispute which was very quickly lost.

Lastly the case of Marshall Cavendish. There the journalists had a 4^1/$_2$ month long campaign of sanctions to win a rise outside pay policy and then had to go on strike for nine weeks a year later to enforce the commitment they'd won. They got the money and the company got 30 redundancies (out of 120 staff).

Over and over again similar examples crop up. The problems of protracted disputes, or of management picking further quarrels or of exhaustion among the workforce at having to defend an agreement, run right through the period.

To set against this picture are the examples of magnificent solidarity—well known, like the Cricklewood postmen and Grunwick, or very obscure, like the half-day strike call in Swindon in support of the sit-in at Jones Cranes.

A big proportion of the industrial disputes were clearly defensive. There was a large number of disputes about victimisation and/or union recognition. The results do not make happy reading—out of 74 such disputes, 32 were won, 35 were lost and seven were 'uncertain'. There were disputes concerned with arguments over staffing, work organisation, operation of new processes, etc—a very large cause of strikes in the period, as management has in some cases systematically tried to encroach on areas 'traditionally' left to stewards to sort out. Altogether 316, or nearly a third of the disputes, belonged to this category.

There were in addition 151 token actions, ie one-day or two-day stoppages, usually against pay offers in line with government policy.

This is quite a significant total. When added to the number of cases of work-to rule, overtime bans, etc—157—it presents a picture of a third of disputes being conducted in a very cautious manner: trying to avoid losing money, fear of the rank and file's lack of support, employers' aggression... These were all factors inhibiting clear and determined displays of militancy in the period.

Of all the disputes 80 were lockouts, a massive rise compared to previous years when the number of lockouts a year could be counted on the fingers of one hand. In many cases, even when the workers did win a victory, it was not unmixed. For example, the long Lucas toolroom strike in mid-1977 was a partial victory, but involved some elements of shopfloor defeat as well. Similarly, the provincial journalists' strike last winter saw some people getting 25 percent, others $13^{1}/_{2}$ percent—and the dispute ended with serious victimisation, lockouts and rank and file demoralisation.

Throughout the period there are three turning points: one, the firemens' strike; two, the Ford and lorry drivers' strikes; and three, the industrial action of $1^{1}/_{2}$ million manual workers in local government and the hospitals.

Following the defeat of the firemen, there was a sharp swing to the defensive over the following months, March, April and May. In the week that Callaghan stood firm and the TUC ditched the firemen there were three lockouts. It was Christmas week. Subsequently the press shop at Ford Halewood lost a decisive five-week battle for shopfloor control. The tanker drivers gave up the ghost on an overtime ban (they lost out again the following year). Workers at Raleigh in Nottingham fought a costly dispute for almost no benefit—a $4^{1}/_{2}$ percent productivity deal.

Then came Ford's and the lorry drivers' strikes, and hopes rose for a breakthrough on the wages front. Instead, after the sluices were opened a little they closed sharply on the $1^{1}/_{2}$ million low paid workers in local government and the hospitals.

Throughout the period the picture was much more of a mosaic than in the years before. By and large we find a very contradictory situation. Well organised forces were able to hold out against the odds with unprecedented tactics in some cases. (For instance, the South Wales lorry drivers blockaded railway lines and steel works to win 15 percent without strings. On the other hand, many 'traditional' strong groups fell apart rather than take on the employer.)

In conclusion, in recent years: (1) disputes have been far more bitter and lengthy; (2) the employers were far more aggressive and quite often unready to concede anything except after a long battle; (3) lockouts were back with a vengeance; (4) the proportion of disputes ending with workers' defeats or partial defeats was much greater than in previous years.

What about the growth of union membership?

Does the growth of union membership over the last few years in any way disprove our conclusions about the change in the balance of class forces in favour of the capitalist class?

Let us first sum up the growth in union membership.

TRADE UNION MEMBERSHIP 1970–77 (MILLIONS)[44]

	End of year figures
1970	11.187
1971	11.135
1972	11.359
1973	11.456
1974	11.764
1975	12.026
1976	12.386
1977	12.707

On the face of it, if growth in trade union membership by itself showed growth in workers' power vis-à-vis the employer, that power must have grown much faster in 1975-77 than in 1971-74. In the years 1975-77 membership grew by 943,000, or by 314,000 a year, while in the years 1971-74 union membership grew by only 577,000 or 144,000 a year. The shallow conclusion should be: the real years of working class advance were 1975-77, while those of 1971-74 were relatively unimpressive.

As a matter of fact there is quite often an inverse relation between growth of union membership and the strength of shop organisation, as many a management prefers a closed shop as a way of disciplining its workers. Thus a survey of manufacturing companies conducted in 1978 showed that three quarters of the managers preferred the closed shop.[45] Union membership by itself, however much we prefer members to nons, does not immediately and necessarily represent an increase in the strength of the working class.

T Nichols and H Benyon emphasised this point in their study of ICI: 'The closed shop was enforced…by an agreement between the company and the union… Those who were shop stewards at the time welcomed the agreement because it established the union…and saved them a lot of work. But it also ensured that no widespread, active, recruiting campaign ever took place on site.' As one foreman commented, 'After the closed shop was introduced I would say the union collapsed completely'.[46]

Also, the main addition of members to the unions was in white collar areas which lacked a tradition of struggle.

THE GROWTH OF WHITE COLLAR AND MANUAL UNIONS, 1948-74[47]

| | Union membership in millions | | | % increase | |
	1948	1970	1974	1948-74	1970-74
White collar	1.964	3.592	4.263	+ 117.1	+ 18.7
Manual	7.398	7.587	7.491	+ 0.1	- 1.3

White collar workers are traditionally far less strike prone than manual workers.

NUMBER OF STRIKE DAYS PER 1,000 EMPLOYEES MANUAL AND NON-MANUAL GROUPS 1966-73 (THREE-YEAR MOVING AVERAGES)[48]

	1966 to 1968	1967 to 1969	1968 to 1970	1969 to 1971	1970 to 1972	1971 to 1973
Manual	194	249	380	386	452	419
Non-manual	16	21	46	55	69	49

Therefore, it would be very mechanical, not to say banal, to conclude from the growth of union membership that the balance of class forces shifted in favour of the working class.

Lesson from Grunwick

To understand how far the labour movement has moved to the right, and how far the shop stewards' organisation has been weakened in recent years, nothing could serve better than to look closely at the campaign round Grunwick.

The stamina, courage and valour of the strikers was outstanding. But what kind of aid did they get from the trade union movement? In terms of size of strike and length of dispute, two previous strikes come to mind: Roberts-Arundel in Stockport (1966-67) and Fine Tubes in Plymouth (1970-73). Both, like Grunwick, were about the refusal of management to recognise the union; both started with the sacking of the strikers and the use of scab labour.

The number of strikers in Grunwick was 137, in Roberts-Arundel 145, and in Fine Tubes 169. Grunwick's strike went on for nearly two years, Roberts-Arundel for 18 months and Fine Tubes for three years.

It would not be immensely useful to make an analogy between Grunwick and Fine Tubes. Grunwick's took place in an area with a very high level of trade union organisation existing over many decades. Fine Tubes' strike took place in Plymouth, probably the area with the weakest trade union organisation in the country. 'In the past there has been no tradition of workers' organisation in the Plymouth area,' writes the historian of the Fine Tubes strike. Even during the General Strike of 1926, the Plymouth dockyards, which employed some 20,000 workers, the great majority local people, went on working.[49]

Stockport, on the other hand, like north London, is an area of strong trade union organisation with a very good tradition.

Roberts-Arundel strikers got aid from fellow trade unionists in the district compared to which the aid given to Grunwick's strikers—and equally to Desoutters in the same period—by their own district paled into absolute insignificance. As Roberts-Arundel strikers were members of the AUEW, the Stockport district of the union imposed a weekly levy of 6d. In addition, collections were taken repeatedly around the factories in Stockport and Manchester. Many workers from all over Stockport came day and night to man the picket line. A number of all-Stockport strikes took place. Thus on Wednesday 22 February 1967 a half-day token strike took place in Stockport and surrounding areas—30,000 workers clocked off at lunchtime and many of them went to the Roberts-Arundel factory for a demonstration.

On 1 September, 'Some 40 factories and building sites in Stockport and surrounding areas stopped work. The police had banned any demonstrations outside the factory, but a meeting was planned to take place behind the factory on some waste ground. About 3,000 workers turned up for this, something like one tenth of those who were on strike for the day.'

On 1 October another all-Stockport strike took place. Once more some 30,000 workers stopped work and a huge demonstration marched through Stockport. A number of very militant and violent demonstrations took place around the factory.

Added to this, very widespread blacking took place. The products of the factory were 'subjected to the most painstaking process of blacklisting that surely was ever experienced by any employer in dispute with the unions... The blacklist began with the names of 245 companies... By mid-June 1967 there were only 45 names left. The others had been taken off the blacklist.'

The strength of the workers' organisation was such that even the police had to bend to it. After using violence against pickets both at the factory gates and, worse, at the police station, they were forced to accept that they had acted wrongly. When six pickets were arrested on 22 November 1967 and three of them beaten very badly at the police station the police authorities were forced to apologise, and *pay* compensation to the injured: '...the three victims of police assault were paid agreed damages by the police. Allen got £1,322 for a spinal injury and a broken nose, Heywood £583 for a broken nose and a battered face, Cook £375 for a broken nose, body injuries and subsequent mental anxiety.'

The strike ended in victory. The owner of Roberts-Arundel recognised the AEU after admitting 'that the strike cost him £1 million'. (The manager went into bankruptcy and the factory was closed. At least there was no non-union factory in Stockport and the principle of trade unionism had won.)

Now what about Grunwick? All honour to the Cricklewood post workers who blacked Grunwick and only lifted the boycott under the gravest duress from the union leaders. But what did the other workers who live in north London do to help Grunwick strikers?

Ken Montague was one representative of the Grunwick Strike Committee to go round the factories in the Park Royal area:

We were touring factories where in the years 1971-73 I visited many times and was received with great enthusiasm for action, whether for solidarity strikes or collection of money for workers… We were visiting people we had built up a close relationship with over the intervening years, and this was at the height of the mass picketing, when miners were coming down from Yorkshire to join the picket line. This time we didn't even try to ask for strike action—all that we hoped for was that mass meetings would be held during work time with invited Grunwick speakers and possibly that the workforce might march down to the picket line *perhaps* during work time. The only shop stewards committee to comply was at Racal BBC, Wembley, where the convenor was a close contact of the IS, an excellent convenor anyway, who had recently organised the factory and won recognition with a very young and mainly Asian stewards' committee.

Other than that, the response was one of consternation and timidity. In the established AUEW factories there was a lot of formal sympathy but the argument generally ran that they had 'so many problems' of their own at the moment that they didn't feel they could do very much. This wasn't just an excuse—many of these stewards and convenors do seem to be exhausted and worn down by problems. Even in some of the more recently organised factories there was a fear of putting too many demands on the membership. Associated Automation was a classic example of this. This was a factory which we had helped to organise, where we had effectively led a strike against redundancies that was 80 percent successful, and which was right between the two Grunwick factories. The convenor, assistant convenor and senior steward are all very friendly (genuinely so) and for a time were intimately involved in the Grunwick strike. Yet here the committee really did not feel it was strong enough to call a factory meeting over the issue. They were ashamed of the fact.

In reality these fears, genuine as they were, seemed to be exaggerated. The mass meeting at Racal, for example, went beyond the convenor's expectations— there was a half-day strike and 200 workers marched to the Grunwick picket. On the morning of the 2 or 3 July mass picket I talked to workers at the Associated Automation gate opposite the Chapter Road picket. About 40 workers had gathered there and had refused to go into work. Most of them were resentful that a mass meeting had not been called, and in the end about 30 to 40 Associated Automation workers spontaneously walked out to join the picket line—or so I was told. Perhaps this is more of an extreme example than a classic case but it sums up what seems to be a common condition among many local stewards—extreme reluctance to bring 'outside' issues into the factory, and an increasing unwillingness to expose themselves to mass meetings. I can remember when mass meetings were called at the drop of a hat—but today it's like asking for an all-out strike.

Financial support for strikes

One effect of weakening the role of the stewards has been to produce a marked decline in solidarity action, as demonstrated in the readiness or ability to give financial support to workers involved in disputes.

Let us compare two strikes of workers in one and the same union, and one and the same district—the Acton Works, London Transport, strike of 24 September to 20 December 1969, and the Desoutter strike of 13 May to 30 September 1978. The LT strike was about a relatively unimportant issue, a question of grading. Desoutter was on a very important question of principle—recognition.

In both cases the amount of money collected was about the same—just over £13,000. But between 1969 and 1978 wages had risen about three times, so that the amount collected for Desoutter's was only about a third of the amount collected in real terms in 1969.

More important were the sources of the money. LT Acton got £3,198 from a levy imposed by the North London district of the AEF and £500 from a levy in South London district. Desoutter did not get a penny from a district levy, as the district committee refused to impose one.

In addition LT Acton received regular weekly amounts of money based on factory levies from at least seven big workplaces in addition to the district levy, while only four places collected regularly for Desoutter and none were on a weekly levy.

Roger Cox had the following comment to make on the above facts:

> The question of levies is central. The real difference between 1969 and the summer of 1978, I believe, is not the amounts of money but the inability of stewards in the factories to call a mass meeting and win support for a levy. I think it is here that we face a real problem, because it shows the distance between the shopfloor and the leading stewards. It also shows the total lack of confidence in the rank and file by the leaders. Also I suspect that the stewards no longer want to disturb the members in case they lose.

The level of financial support for Desoutter is poor compared to that of Acton Works. It would pale even more if compared with, let us say, the Marriott strike of 1963. This, like Desoutter, consisted mostly of black workers and was also on the question of recognition. Marriott workers collected £9,500. At that time wages were a fifth of those in 1978. So if we use the same measure of money in real terms, the collection for Desoutter was only a quarter of that for Marriott.

If one looks at a star factory like ENV, that was always ready to raise money in support of workers in struggle, it is clear how far we have been pushed back. The 1,100 workers at ENV collected £ 1,500 during the 13-week strike at British Light Steel Pressings in Acton in 1961. For the Marriott strike ENV collected £1,717.[51] Basically the decline in the levies for strikes reflects the erosion of traditional solidarity, and the decline of a basic socialist attitude that was the inheritance of our movement. To rebuild this tradition again one has to persevere, and one must put the politics of class solidarity to the fore.

The employers' hardened stance

Analysis of the industrial disputes over the last few years shows the employers in a much more belligerent mood. As an expression of their stance a document published on 19 March 1979 by the Engineering Employers' Federation, entitled *Guidelines on Collective Bargaining and Response to*

Industrial Action, is most illuminating.[52]

The origins of the guidelines go back some months. Several major firms, and GKN in particular, threatened to quit the EEF if it did not produce a policy which would enable management to fight stewards' organisation and involve right wing AUEW officials in stamping out militancy. GKN was not alone. Hardline companies, like Westland Aircraft, Serck, Birmid Qualcast, Johnson Matthey, Powell Duffryn, Edgar Allen, Low and Bonar, have all been exerting their influence to get a tough line agreed in the EEF. Not surprisingly, these are the same companies that always impose lockouts (five in March-April 1979 in South Wales alone). They are the same companies that fund blacklisting organisations like the Economic League, and many of them supply members of the Economic League Central Council.[53]

The law

The change in the actual balance of class forces between the working class and the capitalist class, between the heyday of the struggles of 1969-74 and the last couple of years, shows itself in the paradoxical situation that while the Tory Industrial Relations Act existed the employers resorted to the courts against workers far less than they have done in the last couple of years.

A book dealing specifically with the actual working of the Industrial Relations Act has this to say:

> Managers...combined effectively with unions to draw the sting from the law's attack on the closed shops...they believe the use of the law could only make disputes more intractable. Managers were aware that legally enforceable agreements, attempts to end the closed shop, and restriction on the right to take industrial action were strongly opposed by unions and their members.[54]

Thus throughout the two and a half years of the Industrial Relations Act there were only four applications to the National Industrial Relations Court against the closed shop.[55]

In one case, when a worker named Joseph Langston insisted on his right to work in Chrysler Ryton factory, Coventry, and by law he had the right not to belong to the union, he won his case at the Birmingham tribunal (28 December 1972).

> The next day Langston went to Ryton and was met by 'shouting, jeering and swearing workers who had staged a lightning walkout in protest'. Langston was sent home, still on full pay, and arrangements were made to send his wages to him to avoid further confrontation.[56]

Later Chrysler dismissed Langston. Managements connived at getting round the law by including in collective agreements they signed with the unions a disclaimer of any legal binding of the agreements. And the reasons were obvious. Management were frightened of shopfloor reaction: 'Managers recognised that legally binding agreements would not necessarily have been easier to enforce than those binding in honour only'.[57]

Altogether:

There were 33 applications by firms to the NIRC seeking relief from industrial action (there were also four applications by employee organisations against unions seeking similar relief). Obviously these represent only a very small minority of all disputes. For example, in 1971 there were 2,228 stoppages, in 1972 2,497 and in 1973 2,854 stoppages. (These figures also show that despite the Industrial Relations Act the number of strikes continued to increase.) They no doubt underestimate the actual number of stoppages and in addition to those recorded there are various forms of industrial action which are not notified for statistical purposes. The direct use of the Industrial Relations Act in situations of industrial action was extremely rare.[58]

The companies that applied to the NIRC were untypical in their industrial composition: 'The pattern presented is of a use of the act by a small number of firms in private sector service industries'.[59]

The NIRC itself was quite careful not to come too often and openly on the side of the employers: 'Less than half the employers who sought orders of the NIRC got them'.[60]

The government itself quite early got cold feet about the law: 'Some managers told us that the DoE had actively discouraged any use of the act's collective bargaining provisions'.[61]

Where the law did intervene with a heavy hand—the docks and Shrewsbury—in the first case it had to beat a hasty retreat; in the second, because of the betrayal of the union leaders and the weakness of workplace organisation, it was as vicious as it could be. Building workers in North Wales are not in big well organised units, as were the five dockers who landed in Pentonville jail. Hence Des Warren served three years in prison, Ricky Tomlinson two, and Ken Jones nine months. The law used against the Shrewsbury workers was not the Industrial Relations Act but the criminal law regarding 'conspiracy'.

The government tried to use the law against the railwaymen (May-June 1972), but they were very inept. A cooling-off period was imposed, and then a ballot of the workers involved. The results of the ballot showed a better than six to one majority in favour of the union rejection of BR's last offer, and the *Sunday Times*'s comment on this was typical of press reaction: 'It would seem that the ballot which was intended to cool off the crisis has only served to do the opposite'.[62]

All the above shows clearly the actual strength of workers' organisation at the time.

Now let us look at the activities of the court, and police, in industrial disputes over the last couple of years. We need only give a few examples from the courts, and these especially from the Court of Appeal presided over by Lord Denning.

On 29 July 1977 the Court of Appeal sided with George Ward of Grunwick by overruling a High Court decision in favour of ACAS.

On 20 May 1977 the Court of Appeal decided that the Association of Broadcasting Staffs had no right to refuse to transmit the 1977 BBC Cup Final to South Africa. The court ruled that this was not a trades dispute, but 'coercive interference'.

In the same year Lord Denning came down heavily on SOGAT. The journalists of the *Daily Mirror* went on strike and so stopped the production of the paper. The *Daily Express* decided to take advantage of the situation and increased its output by 750,000 copies. The general secretary of SOGAT, Bill Keys, whose members handle the distribution of newsprint, instructed them not to handle the extra copies. The *Express* applied for an injunction to restrain SOGAT. The *Express* lost in the High Court, but then won in the Court of Appeal, which found that there was no dispute between SOGAT and the *Express*.

The case of Star Sea Transport of Monrovia versus Slater, secretary of the National Union of Seamen, had even more serious implications. The International Transport Federation tried to secure that the wage rates paid to Greek and Indian sailors on a Liberian-registered vessel—the *Cammilla M*—were in line with recognised ITF minima, but the employers won an injunction when the unions tried to prevent the ship sailing from Glasgow. The judges said it was an open question whether the action was a trade dispute.

Then just before Christmas 1978 came the case of Express Newspapers versus McShane and Ashton. This arose out of a strike called by the National Union of Journalists against provincial newspapers. Because the local papers also get news copy from the Press Association, the union called upon its members employed in the Press Association to come out on strike as well. About half of the PA did not obey the union instruction. The NUJ then ordered its members employed by the national newspapers to black PA copy. The *Express* sought an injunction against the NUJ officials McShane and Ashton. The High Court granted the appeal, and when the NUJ appealed to the Court of Appeal, their case was dismissed. Lord Denning held that the blacking of PA was not in furtherance of a trade dispute. It seems no act of solidarity is in furtherance of a trade dispute.

Then again the case of United Biscuits versus Fell. This case arose out of the lorry drivers' dispute. Fell, a lorry driver, was running the picket line at Loders and Nucoline, one of the sources of supply of edible oil for United Biscuits. The High Court declared that, as the lorry drivers' strike was not against United Biscuits, to allow this 'secondary picketing' would be tantamount to 'writing a recipe for anarchy'.[63]

When the *Nottingham Evening Post* refused to recognise the NUJ and NGA, the NGA wrote to all concerns regularly advertising in the paper asking them to stop advertising. Sixteen organisations continued to advertise, and at the end of February 1979 they were informed in a joint letter from NGA and SLADE that all members of these two unions on any newspapers or periodicals would be instructed not to handle any advertising submitted by the relevant organisations. Some 26 organisations sought an injunction against Wade, the NGA general secretary, and others. The High Court granted an interim injunction, and when the NGA appealed against this the Court of Appeal dismissed the appeal. Lord Denning made it clear that this was a case of secondary industrial action.[64]

The legal costs to the NGA were as high as £84,000—higher than the fines imposed on the TGWU by the NIRC in 1972 which (like those imposed on the AEU) had been reimbursed to the TGWU.

On 19 July 1979 Lord Denning and the Appeal Court decided that the strike by the 8,000 low paid provincial journalists last winter was unconstitutional. This interpretation of the NUJ Rule Book means that members who scabbed through the strike and then benefited from hard won gains could not be disciplined.

Leicester Mercury journalists were banned from blacking a news agency which supplied copy to the *Nottingham Evening Post.*

NUJ members at the *Stratford Express* on strike in defence of their closed shop were sued for libel over a leaflet they produced. More writs have been threatened to stop the NGA from blacking the *Express.*

In north London two NUJ members at the *Camden and Hornsey Journal* were taken to court by a sub-editor who resigned from the union.[65]

At the time of writing there are a few further cases of courts persecuting trade unionists—for instance, the High Court injunction secured by Wandsworth council against UCATT official Lou Lewis, preventing him picketing in defence of direct labour.

In recent years the courts have been joined with great vigour by the police in cutting down the power of pickets. Besides Grunwick, there are many other cases. The most recent is the case of Andy Darby. He is a GMWU senior steward arrested on 5 February on an unofficial picket line outside the GLC refuse tip in Factory Lane, Croydon. That morning the police had repeatedly tried to stop pickets talking to the lorry drivers coming into the tip. When the police waved on a 32-ton crane lorry Andy stood in front of it and threw a door down in its path. For this he got three months imprisonment for 'threatening behaviour'.[66]

In *practical,* technical terms, present laws and their application are tough enough to satisfy the needs of the employers. The new proposed Tory industrial relations act has mainly ideological importance, to justify the policy, to win the battle of people's minds, to give succour to the police in their breaking of strikes.

Why the retreat?

The change in the balance of class forces in Britain has been caused by a whole number of inter-related factors: incomes policy; the massive establishment of productivity deals which has been associated with the weakening of the independence of convenors and shop stewards; the wide spread of workers' participation in industry; the move to the right of 'left' trade union leaders like Jones and Scanlon; the integration of convenors into the trade union structure; the role of the Communist Party as the main organiser of rank and file activists in industry, both in supporting workers' participation and in supporting the left union officials; the ideological trap of the concept of 'profitability', 'viability', etc, combined with a loyalty to Labour even when Labour attacked workers' living standards; the impact of the economic crisis—cuts, sackings, etc, etc, on all the above factors.

The impact of incomes policy on shop stewards' power

The single most important factor in the deterioration of shopfloor organisation has been the weakening of stewards' bargaining position and role during the period of freeze and incomes policy. In fact it does not make much difference to the power of the shop steward whether incomes policy is of nil growth, $3^1/_2$ percent, £1 plus 4 percent, £6, 10 percent, or 5 percent. As a matter of fact only three of the last 13 years have had no incomes policy.

A more insidious and in the long term damaging effect on shopfloor organisation has been the move towards productivity deals. Our organisation was far ahead of everybody else in recognising this trend. Ten years ago the book *The Employers' Offensive*, subtitled *Productivity Deals and How to Fight Them*, highlighted the ruling class determination to stop wage drift and transform shopfloor relations by removing stewards from effective direct influence on take-home pay, thus weakening the support they had from their constituents.

The Donovan Report on trade unions argued that the abolition of piece-work would undermine the autonomy of shop stewards and would help the unions to integrate the stewards into the union machine, so that they might better control their activities in the interests of managerial order. The main target was clear—the factory floor organisation.

The aim of the Donovan Report was the integration of the shop stewards into a streamlined union machine, into a plant consensus. This process of integration could be helped by greater legal and managerial discipline. Order had also to be brought into the working of the unions: 'Certain features of trade union structure and government have helped to inflate the power of work-groups and shop stewards.'

Among the institutional changes proposed by the Donovan Commission was, first of all, the substitution of factory agreements for industry-wide agreements.[67] The negotiation of piece-rates makes for *permanent* activity in the shop and hence for very close relations between the shop steward and the workers he or she represents.

The elimination of piece-working, especially if it is connected with the transference of bargaining to a company-wide level, necessarily takes away the power of shop stewards to seriously affect the wage packets of the workers they represent. This applies to all industries from engineering to the docks to the mines. The shop stewards become integrated into the union machine and incorporated into management.

Example from the mines

A study of actual working of the union at shopfloor level in the mining industry has this to say: 'At one time the pay structure and methods of domestic bargaining in coalmining had much in common with those in engineering—industry agreements on pay settled minimum rates, leaving ample scope for domestic bargaining in the collieries.'

Things changed radically in 1966, however, when a national agreement on wages—NPLA—was introduced:

> The delegate continued to agree work terms with management, but this became something of a routine. He argued the case of men who wanted to be regraded to a higher rate of pay, or moved to another job or shift; dealt with disciplinary cases; investigated accidents; checked on safety, dust and lighting; advised the injured and the sick on their entitlements; and helped his members with domestic problems —housing, debts, divorce and so on... The delegate's job had thus become largely administrative.

In an interview, Pete Exley, surface fitter at Grimethorpe Colliery near Barnsley, described the work of the four full timers in his colliery—the president, treasurer, secretary and delegate: 'The treasurer's main job is on a Friday, like today, to dish out money for bereavements, old age pensioners. We still have that thing in Yorkshire that we pay so much a fortnight out of the branch funds and you have the old retired miners coming for this money.' The president does 'the same. He is just there for any disputes and negotiates and hangs round in the union box. You see them coming in at 9 o'clock every day. They are gone by about 1.30 or 2 and are in the union box for most of the rest of the time. If there is a dispute down the pit or safety checks or something like that they will go down the pit and do that.'

The dockers

To blunt the edge of shop steward organisation, Devlin Phase II introduced a clever design to divide one port from another. Eddie Prevost writes:

> In different ports there are differences in hours of work, manning, pay. Now negotiations take place at a local level. The national agreement covers only a small proportion of workers' wages and conditions... The main weakness for us was the differences between the ports over the time they negotiate their separate agreements.

'Today the TGWU strategy', writes Bob Light, 'is to *absorb* militancy through the safer channels of officially-recognised shop stewards':

> As far as the employers are concerned, they too now try more to contain militants into official channels rather than victimise them... The shop steward's job can be very easy. There is no supervision by management at all, so there are no hassles about things like timekeeping, etc. A steward could almost come in when he liked and go home when he liked. And some do! We are provided with an office by the employer, and if you liked you could sit in there all day just talking, reading, playing cards, drinking tea—whatever you liked. So there's no doubt at all that shop stewards can have it very easy if they like, and the truth is that many of them do like it.

And Eddie Prevost adds, 'Shop stewards in the Royal work two weeks as a steward and two weeks on the job (in theory). Sickness and holidays mean in practice they don't work that much. In other docks stewards are full time.'

One result of the weakening of dockers' shopfloor organisation has been the practical disappearance of the famous mass meetings. Eddie Prevost writes, 'Since the 1975 strike in London dock gate meetings have been very poorly attended. No doubt the government's pay policy has effectively stifled the shop stewards committees in all docks.'

Manufacturing

The power of the shop stewards to negotiate wage rates has been undermined by productivity deals, and especially by transferring bargaining to plant, or worse, company level.

When collective bargaining takes place at a level above the shop, or above the individual plant, the actions of the negotiators which are of primary concern to the lay members are remote from their control. Hence apathy is quite natural. Now with productivity deal negotiations concluded far away from the shopfloor, the shop steward finds himself more and more isolated in practice from his mates, the convenor even more so.

Lord Acton coined the aphorism, 'Power corrupts, and absolute power corrupts absolutely.' In fact, it would be even more apt to say, 'Power corrupts, but lack of power corrupts absolutely.' The decline of the power of the shop stewards in gaining significant wage rises in recent years again and again led to their alienation from their base, to a loss of confidence of the rank and file in the shop stewards, and to a loss of self-confidence by the shop steward.

As against the tradition of shop stewards' organisation, there is another tradition in the labour movement—that of passive democracy, at best a periodic opportunity to elect the officials. Such a democracy, like bourgeois parliamentary democracy, must lead to general alienation of the officials from the base, and the general apathy of the latter.

Ken Montague describes very well the impact on shop stewards and convenors in engineering factories in north London—the weakening of the ability of shop stewards to affect wages makes them:

> ...feel that they have no control of their situation any more. In almost every case they are reacting to situations rather than setting the pace for the management. The whole struggle has become a defensive battle and I doubt very much if any but one or two committees in the area have any kind of perspective for actually *gaining* anything. There is no real sense of there being a purpose or a future in what they are doing. They are distinctly not building very much up, but hanging on. Perhaps the only exceptions to this are where there is the possibility of building something on a combine or network basis (Racal, British Rail, Smiths Computer workers).
>
> This is true even where organisation is relatively new. Among the old established committees there is a feeling of being overburdened with problems and of resentment towards the membership. In many of the newer organisations there is a tremendous sense of weakness, lack of self-confidence and a feeling that they haven't got a complete organisation or the respect of management. The fact is that

many of these newer committees *are* in a weak position, tend to be in less skilled industries, have had very little support or even contact from the established committees or the district committee. Many of them are in factories and workplaces that are close to the verge of closure.

If the individual shop steward and convenor feel that they cannot rely on their mates, or that they cannot in practice lead their mates into action, it is no wonder that solidarity in different workplaces, which depends crucially on the authority of the shopfloor organisation, withers away.

To quote Ken Montague again:

> There is a strong feeling that every shop stewards organisation is on its own, can't look for more than formal, token support from outside the particular workplace, and therefore only formal support is given in return. All sense of enthusiasm about other people's struggles, the tradition of seeing yourself as part of an *area*, where what happens down the road matters to you, has been drained away.

The impotence of the shop stewards:

> ...explains their reluctance to put things to their members and their virtual fear of the membership. Distrust of the membership, combined with fatalism about the closures, has produced the lack of perspective about the future, the anxiety of keeping the old organisation together, the unwillingness to build up new personnel on the committee. The most striking thing about many of the established committees is the absence of young cadre. There are the politicos who can fight to get on the committee and to whom the older stewards do eventually turn, but there is no tradition left of personal training of voting members and developing successors. My feeling is that the defensiveness of many stewards has reached the point where any up and coming young member is not regarded as an asset but a possible threat.
>
> All this is reflected by (or reflects) the district organisation of the AUEW...the district committee today seems to function on the assumption that it can't do very much. On the whole it is a fairly realistic assumption.

The fear of the district committee of taking initiatives, reflected in the fear of the shopfloor committees to stick their necks out, has also contributed to an attitude of looking to other people to put up token fights. This mainly explains the rise of Brent Trades Council which for about the last five years has been the Communist Party's, and therefore at times the AUEW's mechanism for looking as though they are doing something. In the absence of organising for a real fight, in the context of the weakness and lack of credibility of the Local Area Organising Committee and the Shop Stewards Quarterly, it has always been possible for the trades council to call a conference with MPs and star officials.

However, Ken Montague points out that there were spasmodic local exceptions to the general picture. But these emphasise even more the general drift of things. These exceptions happened:

> ...mainly in 'peripheral' industries and unions. There was the occupation by dustmen and caretakers in Barnet, the strike and occupation by computer workers at Smith's, quite a good turnout at Central Middlesex Hospital from other unions

during a public sector day of action two or three years ago. There have also been two strikes and a sit-in, mainly by women, in the Smith's main factory (MA 1)—in fact the women have pretty consistently kept up the pressure to change the moribund organisation at Smith's. But there are two things about most of the actions that have taken place: they have been extremely dynamic, at times (the Smith's ASTMS occupation/strike 1976, and the recent 'internal picketing' at Frigidaire's) almost anarchic. Secondly they have remained peripheral in their impact on the area as a whole. You can't help feeling that something will have to be pretty explosive to change the prevailing climate in the main industries in the area—and this of course has a deadening effect on the actions that do take place, or it encourages desperation.

The decline of shop organisation reflects itself in the terrible deterioration of the shop stewards' quarterly meetings. Roger Cox writes the following about the north London district quarterly meetings:

> I can remember that in the mid-1960s you could expect to have at least 100 stewards and at most 250. Now you are lucky if you get 100 at the December quarterly when elections to the district committee take place. Mostly it is 30 to 40... The central item discussed was wages—who was earning what... Now it is dreadfully boring and pointless. It could be improved if the district committee campaigned to make the four meetings important. But a district committee that refuses to raise a levy in support of Desoutter workers on strike for recognition is a district committee not of a union but a cemetery.

Full time factory convenors

The institution of shop stewards is profoundly democratic. They are the direct representatives of the workers. They have no privileges. One writer contrasts them with MPs:

> The shop steward...did not, once elected, pack his bags and move to carry out his representational duties in an institution alien to the experiences of his constituents. Neither was his constituency so large that he could remain personally anonymous to the overwhelming majority of his electors... The steward spent the bulk of his time at work alongside those who had elected him... He was highly visible, subject to the same experiences at work as his comrades.[68]

Dave Lyddon, a former worker in Leyland, Oxford, commenting on this description of the steward, argues that it does not apply to the increasing number of convenors who spend their working week on union business, quite a lot of it away from the factory. He writes:

> In larger factories there are probably now half a dozen senior stewards and convenors who don't even have a nominal job but who are provided by management with an office and telephone, and are paid to be full time union representatives in the factory...
>
> Those senior stewards and convenors based in an office cease to be the direct

representatives of the workers on the spot… Senior stewards don't share the work experience of their members… And they don't suffer the car workers' constant insecurity of a fluctuating wage packet. Is it any wonder they get out of touch?[69]

A similar description of the role of the convenor is given by Gerry Jones, a shop steward in Chrysler, Stoke. The convenors 'spend much more time away from the plant than they used to. They're given expenses-paid trips to the motor show, they have visited the National Exhibition Centre on behalf of the company, and they've been taken on trips to Sinica in France and Chrysler in Iran'.[70]

The estrangement of the convenors from the rank and file is not mainly the result of their having a cushy number, but mainly a result of their *function* under plant or, even worse, company-wide bargaining with the 'participation' policy prevailing. The rank and file become apathetic towards the convenor as the other side of the coin of the key decisions being taken away from them.

Over the last few years the number of full time convenors increased dramatically. A study published in 1978 shows this clearly. It was based on a survey of 453 workplaces employing 330,000 GMWU manual workers across a wide range of manufacturing and service industries. Of the total number of workers in the sample, 73 percent were in manufacturing industry and 23 percent in public service (principally gas, water, electricity, NHS, national and local government).

The study showed that in manufacturing 62 percent of all plants employing more than 500 workers had full time convenors, while the corresponding figure for engineers was 69 percent, and for the public sector 21 percent. The study reckoned that there are now four times more full time convenors than there were in 1966—about 5,000 in manufacturing establishments. (In addition, there are another couple of thousand in other places of employment.) Thus the number of full time convenors is about $2^1/_2$ times the number of full time officials.

The shop stewards interviewed were asked whether management had generally resisted shop steward activities at their workplace. The answers were summed up with this very revealing conclusion: 'For manufacturing, only 33 percent of the larger workplaces that experienced current resistance had full time shop stewards compared with 64 percent…where the management accepted the stewards, the implication that management had a strong influence upon the existence of a full time steward deserves special emphasis'.[71]

Of course the position of full time convenors is not *identical* with that of full time union officials. But quite often there is a greater similarity between these two categories than between either of them and the rank and file workers. Some full time convenors get wages plus perks that far surpass the pay of the lower ranks of the trade union bureaucracy. Some have a more permanent job than elected officials. One need but think of Bert Brennan, who served as convenor of Metro-Vicks in Trafford Park until the age of 79, or Dick Etheridge who served for donkey's years as convenor of Longbridge, or the convenor of Rolls Royce, Derby, etc, etc. Derek Robinson's constituency is nearly 100,000. Of course there are no absolutes. In terms of relations with the rank and file, by and large convenors are far more malleable. But this is not always so. One need only compare, let us say, Bert Brennan, Jim Airlie or Derek Robinson, on the one hand, with Lou Lewis, the UCATT full time official in London, or John Tocher, Laurie Smith and Bill Taylor of the AUEW, on the other, to see this.

Workers' participation

Donovan argued for co-partnership of management and unions through the integration of the shop stewards into the structure of the union and their participation with management. Such participation has been introduced into a whole number of key companies in the country.

The result is increasing alienation of the rank and file from the convenors. Dave Lyddon of Leyland writes:

> There are no facilities for report-back meetings to the constituencies, so there are no report-backs. Notes of meetings aren't always put up on noticeboards, and when they are, they don't contain anything considered 'confidential'. The lack of participation by the overwhelming majority is built into the whole set-up. Even the discussions that led to the signing of the participation agreement completely denied the rank and file worker any say. The union meetings that discussed and accepted the Ryder report consisted only of senior shop stewards and senior staff reps.[72]

Similarly Gerry Jones speaks about the secrecy surrounding senior stewards on committees and sub-committees of workers' participation:

> The convenors endorsed the planning agreement but had no mandate. They hadn't reported back in any detail at all. Everything had been done at convenor level. At steward and shopfloor level the feeling is that it is a complete and utter waste of time. The result so far has been that convenors are better armed with managerial arguments—detailed economic arguments. Already they see the exercise as separate from the shopfloor.

An AUEW senior steward at Linwood, Willie Lee, said:

> We used to have a bad time with the full time convenors, who had a very bad attitude towards the shopfloor. When they came into a section with a problem they were very antagonistic, because they were having a job to do. They didn't ally themselves with the people on the shopfloor the way they used to do when they were just straightforward shop stewards, and I think that with worker participation the division will be even worse, because these people will then be in a position—maybe at the moment are in a position in some factories—where they are actually sitting down agreeing with management that there are things that have to be done on the shopfloor. They're talking about increased productivity, finance and production, and manpower. And that obviously puts them in a position where they are going back to try and make sure that what they agreed is carried out on the shopfloor.

The result is the incorporation of senior stewards into management structure.

As Rob Reid, an AUEW steward from Linwood, put it, 'It wasn't so much us participating in management—it was management participating in unions'.[73]

One result of the alienation of the rank and file from the top table was the complete fiasco of the 20 April 1977 national strike against incomes policy, the call for which came from the Leyland convenors and on which not one Leyland factory came on strike on the day.

The same alienation of the rank and file explained the collapse of the struggle for higher wages in Leyland in August 1977:

> The shop stewards at Longbridge put to the membership a call for strike action in support of their 47 percent wage claim. Derek Robinson went on TV to announce that the vote was going to be 50 to one in favour of striking—even though the night shift had not *begun* to vote!
>
> The result was an anti-strike demonstration by several hundred workers. Robinson refused to give a positive lead to the two thirds of those voting who had supported strike action. Instead, the strike was called off.[74]

A year later, again after a lot of huffing and puffing by Derek Robinson and Co, Leyland workers were forced to swallow the 5 percent:

> Stewards and convenors can pose as shopfloor leaders. They can attend combine committee meetings, make speeches, sit on official union committees for years on end. It is only if they try to do something that their bluff will be called, because to *do* anything they need the lads.[75]

An added factor undermining participatory, active, direct democracy on the shopfloor has been the widespread introduction of the checkoff system, the practice whereby the employers deduct union dues from the wages of members in their employ and pay them over to the union—much like a government tax.

Role of 'left' union leaders

For a long time between the two wars and after the Second World War the major unions were headed by right wing leaders. They in principle opposed the activities of shop stewards and all unofficial strikes.

However, the fact that they collaborated with the employers and the state *did not* in the majority of cases bring them into actual conflict with the rank and file. The bureaucracy's bark was worse than its bite. In a number of cases it managed to smash the rank and file organisation—for instance at British Light Steel Pressings (1961) and Ford Dagenham (1962). But usually management retreated under the duress of a short-lived strike—ie before the trade union bureaucracy managed to intervene effectively and discipline the workers. Capitalism was quite prosperous and the employers were ready to give in without prolonged and widespread battles. If a strike went on for only a couple of days, the question of whether headquarters supported it or not was not of overriding importance. In many cases, a central element in the tactics of the militant was to win the strike *before* trade union headquarters heard about it!

In 1967 the left won the presidency of the AEU, in the person of Hugh Scanlon. A year later Jack Jones became the general secretary of the largest union in the country, the TGWU.

The shift from small localised disputes to national confrontations with the government thrust these leaders into the centre of the stage. They were forced, under rank and file pressure, to lead their members in confrontations. So Scanlon and Jones led the opposition to Wilson's incomes policy and 'In Place of Strife' in the late 1960s. Where these leaders acted thus they did so to direct the militancy into official channels and to prevent it escaping their control.

Thus in the first national strike in Ford, the 1969 Penalty Clauses strike, it was Jones and Scanlon who gave support to the rank and file and led them to victory.[76] At that time the National Joint Negotiating Committee (NJNC) of Ford was entirely composed of full time national officers of the various unions. In the aftermath of the strike Ford convenors were brought onto the NJNC to sit with the full time union officers.

Two years later, in 1971, during the national official strike for parity of Ford's wages with BMC, Scanlon and Jones played a completely different role, putting the brakes down hard on the rank and file. After a nine-week strike they came to a secret agreement with Stanley Gillen, chairman of Ford Europe, behind the back of the NJNC and, breaking all traditions, they did not allow a mass meeting to decide whether to go back to work, but instead insisted on a secret ballot, exactly as the Tory Industrial Relations Act demanded. In addition the agreement included two penalty clauses

Whenever Scanlon, Jones and other leaders moved in front of the workers in struggle it was in order to keep control over the strike, keep control over their members. Only under mass unofficial pressure does the official machine move, and that was the case also in the struggle against Heath's Industrial Relations Act. The 1969 strike against the penalty clauses was deprecated by practically all union leaders. The first 'Kill the bill' strikes of 1970-71 were also unofficial, although they were not condemned by the left leaders, while the second wave had some official support. By 1972, after the unofficial strike of dockers spread to print and engineering and threatened to get completely out of hand, the TUC itself proposed to call a general strike against the jailing of the five dockers. However, throughout the campaigns against the Industrial Relations Act both Scanlon and Jones did their utmost to restrict the struggle.

The engineers' opposition to the Industrial Relations Act—the most forthright of any union—had been largely passive and abstentionist. The two-day strikes called by it—on 1 and 18 March 1971—were token actions, a futile gesture previously used by Lord Carron, the right wing president of the AEU, in 1961. Such token strikes serve the purpose of the union leaders by allowing the members to let off steam in a relatively harmless fashion.

The TGWU was even more concerned to avoid confrontation with the act; and it is interesting that its own guidance to shop stewards was altered after the NIRC insisted that the union was responsible for the actions of its shop stewards.[77]

Following the fright they got in the summer of 1972 from the actions of the dockers and their friends round Pentonville, the TUC, including Jones and Scanlon, veered sharply rightwards, and throughout 1973 did their best to come to an accommodation with Heath. Between July and November 1972, again and again, the TUC leadership engaged itself at Chequers and Downing Street in talks with the government and CBI on economic strategy and incomes policy:

> The immediate effect was to help salvage the government's reputation and deflate the political crisis. In the slightly longer term, the talks gave ideological strength to the government's incomes policy proposals.
>
> In the end, of course, the TUC withheld its agreement; but by then this was of minor importance. For in participating in the talks the TUC helped bolster the argument, assiduously fostered by the government and the media, that 'irresponsible' pay claims were a major threat to 'the economy', and that some form of restraint would benefit both the low paid and the 'national interest'.[78]

By the end of 1973 Heath was able to impose the most rigorous and comprehensive pay control ever experienced in Britain, and this was met by no more than token opposition by the trade union leaders.

The treachery of trade union bureaucrats—'left' as well as, of course, right—is not new. The tactics of the left, however, are quite different to those of the right. Arthur Deakin never allowed, let alone encouraged, shop stewards in the docks. It was Jack Jones who introduced them, and this gave him a weapon to control dockers, accompanying their introduction with the introduction of Devlin's productivity deal.

An excellent example of how left wing leaders rise to power in the unions on a wave of militant action by the rank and file, and then take control to prevent the rank and file from doing their own thing, can be gleaned from the case of the Yorkshire NUM leadership.

In September 1969 the miners at Cadeby Colliery near Doncaster came out on unofficial strike over wages. They were instructed to return to work by the Yorkshire Area Executive of the NUM, but they stayed out and tried to spread the strike. Before the issue could be resolved, 70,000 Yorkshire miners were on strike in support of a demand for shorter hours for surfacemen. The strike was spreading to pits in South Wales, the Midlands and Scotland. Altogether 140 collieries were involved.[79]

These mass unofficial strikes demonstrated to the NEC of the NUM the pent-up pressure of the rank and file. At the 1970 conference of the union a resolution for a wages structure of £20 a week for surface workers, £22 for underground workers and £30 for face workers was passed unanimously. An amendment from the South Wales area calling for strike action if the claim was not met was carried by 169 votes to 160.

In September the NCB offered half the amount claimed. The NEC of the union recommended a national strike. A ballot was held and produced a 55$\frac{1}{2}$ percent vote for strike action. At that time, however, the rules demanded a two thirds majority before strike action could be taken. The 'left' leadership hummed and hahed, but the rank and file acted. Within three weeks all but a handful of miners in Yorkshire were out, all the pits in South Wales were out, all but eight in Scotland, and stoppages were also occurring in Kent and Durham.

It was in 1972 that the rank and file showed its magnificent prowess, the culmination of years of unofficial rank and file action.

The flying pickets came into their own. All power stations were picketed. But of all the picketing that occurred in this strike, the one at Saltley Coke Works, Birmingham, will be most remembered. Pickets from the Barnsley area had been there for about ten days. They were routed several times by the West Midlands police. Many were deliberately injured. On 9 February the Birmingham East District of the Engineers' Union passed a resolution calling for an all-out strike and demonstration on the following day.

So far as is known, no unionised lorry driver crossed a picket line; no docker moved an ounce of coal. Seamen offered and gave full cooperation, as did the railwaymen. Thousands of shop stewards in factories laid off due to coal shortages collected thousands of pounds for the strike fund.

By mid-February the power stations were flickering to a halt, many factories were completely closed and most were on short time. A state of emergency had been declared on 9 February. The government was desperate, the miners jubilant.[80]

In the 1974 miners' strike things were different. The leadership kept complete control over the struggle and kept the participation of the membership very low. It is true that only a few days before the strike began Scargill and McGahey had been proclaiming that there would be 'a hundred Saltleys'. The opposite was the case. Unlike in 1972, this time all rank and file initiatives were squashed. Pickets dwindled from six to four to two, and finally in many cases to none at all.

At Saltley Coke Depot queues of 150 to 200 lorries waited unperturbed by pickets and then moved freely through the gates. Included among the lorries were those owned by haulage companies blacked during the 1972 miners' strike.[81]

The fact that Jones and Scanlon and the rest of the trade union leadership supported the Social Contract, while having in their hand new weapons—those of productivity deals—made them much more formidable opponents of rank and file action than Bill Carron or Arthur Deakin were in their time.

The role of the CP and the Broad Left

Another important element in determining workers' struggle is the Communist Party and its Broad Left.

For decades the Communist Party has been the only organisation able to offer a national framework to industrial militants. For a long, long time it represented largely a community of industrial activists. The CP played a big role in strengthening shopfloor organisation and gained very much from the increased power of the shop stewards during the boom years following the Second World War.

Although *The British Road to Socialism,* the first draft of which was published in 1951, spoke about taking the parliamentary road, for the rank and file of the party the main thing was still the activity in industry. They could not but agree with Harry Pollitt's statement to the executive committee of the CP in February 1949: 'There can be no substitute for factory organisation. To underestimate the key role of the factory branch is a social democratic attitude'.[82]

At the 27th congress of the party, 1961, the leadership made a shift towards unity with the Labour lefts. 'We now have the most important situation in the labour movement for a generation,' said John Gollan, general secretary of the CP, at that Easter 1961 congress. He continued:

> The 1960 Scarborough decisions on peace, Clause Four, and the sovereignty of the Labour Party conference are a big step towards real independent working class politics... The present position, however, is a new and much more important stage in the left struggle in the Labour Party. The previously automatic trade union voting majority for right wing policies has been shaken.

The logic of the policy of influencing the leadership of the unions in order to push the Labour Party to the left also meant that the CP's traditional method of building in the workplace was to suffer. A rank and file organisation in the engineering industry, under CP leadership, had existed since 1935. From 1946 it had produced a paper called the *Metalworker* which was associated with an unofficial body known as the Engineering and Allied Trades' Shop Stewards' National Council. This was disbanded in 1962.

There was disagreement within the CP on this change in line until 1967. Part of the resistance to the change in policy may have come from districts or unions and industries where the Communist Party base was strong and still felt able to act and build independently—areas like Clydeside, Sheffield or north London. In the engineering industry these areas were certainly capable of organising within the shop stewards committees, and the branches and district committees of the union without much help from others on the left.

The result was the building of a very effective electoral machine in the unions that involved the shopfloor organisation. Murray Armstrong writes:

> Although the Broad Left was from the beginning an electoral machine designed to shift the balance inside the union, one of the ingredients of its success was its relationship to the shopfloor union organisation. The leadership of the union, under Carron and Conway, was very much opposed to the 'unofficial' activities of shop stewards. The success of shopfloor organisation depended on the ability of stewards to negotiate directly and immediately on piece-work prices and to be able to respond to any changes in work organisation or practices.
>
> But the involvement of those shopfloor activists was *only* at election times. The Broad Left did not play an active part in the day to day problems of the workshops —in formulating a common policy for the struggles in the factories, in raising support or generating solidarity for disputes taking place.

The result was that, 'after the national leadership of the Broad Left achieved their first goal of representation in the national union structure, the links to the shopfloor began to weaken and Broad Left policy became indistinguishable from the official National Committee policy of the union'.[83]

The result was clearly demonstrated in the quarterly meetings of the AEU shop stewards. Jack Robertson, present editor of *Engineering Charter*, was a shop steward in Manchester in the early 1970s. He describes the nature of those quarterly meetings:

> They would always begin with a general attack on the evils of the system (probably by the Manchester district president, Stan Cole) followed by the divisional organiser, John Tocher, or Panther, the district secretary, with a long report of what was happening nationally and locally. Then Betty Crawford (convenor at Ferranti in Oldham), *always* as the token woman. There would be a resolution at the end of the meeting about repression in Greece (whatever the *Morning Star* was pushing at the time) which would be passed unanimously even though nobody had a clue what was happening there. And the next day the *Morning Star* would report, 'Last night at a meeting of shop stewards representing 40,000 workers…'
>
> There were *never* any honest debates about what was happening in the local factories. For a start there was no time. There would only be half an hour at most for discussion, usually ten minutes. Even then, the speakers from the floor would be CP members of the district committee like Stan Brazil (convenor at GEC Openshaw) or Alan Spinks (convenor at Francis Shaws) to emphasise one of the points made earlier from the platform.
>
> These meetings were stifling because they were treated as a chore rather than an infrequent opportunity to bring the leading members in the district together and have a good discussion.
>
> It was obvious from the quarterlies, and the talk in the bar afterwards, that very, very few young people were being drawn into activity by the CP. The old guard ruled the roost. Only a fanatic would have been prepared to even sit through quarterly meetings which were CP propaganda sessions from beginning to end.

Already at that time the Broad Left used more left rhetoric than real action. The organisation in many Manchester factories, Jack Robertson goes on to say, was diabolical. He gives an insight into one of the most important factories in the area, Metro Vicks (whose labour force went down from 30,000 in 1945 to 5,000 in 1972):

> One thing that stuck in my mind was the Victorian control which the company exerted through use of arriving on time. There was a stampede through the huge gates every morning in order to clock on before 7.44. One morning a man collapsed in the scramble ten yards in front of me. His haversack opened on the road beside him, an apple rolled out and his face turned green. Nobody stopped. The tide kept on moving.
>
> The factory was so big it had its own ambulance service. But if any injuries ever occurred (which happened frequently) the victim would be expected to clock off before receiving attention.

In summing up the nature of the Broad Left, Jack Robertson writes:

The extraordinary electoral successes of the Broad Left are not explained by saying that they built a rank and file organisation. But, as the strongest organised group within the official union structure, they were able to control and direct the rank and file by placing the most minimal demand (the vote) on the stewards and branch committees.

Even if at the roots, at the shopfloor and district level in industry, the Broad Left was withering, it still had strength so long as it was led by Scanlon in a very popular struggle—against the last stage of Wilson's wages policy, against 'In Place of Strife', and later against the Tory Industrial Relations Act. Then the CP was quite effective in mobilising rank and file support. It was for the above purposes that the Communist Party built the Liaison Committee for the Defence of Trade Unions.

The Liaison Committee started as a 'lobby organising committee' under the secretaryship of Jim Hiles. It organised its first lobby of parliament on 1 March 1966. Some 4,000 trade unionists participated. A second lobby was organised in June. It was sponsored by a number of rank and file organisations in London: the London Docks Liaison Committee, the Building Workers' Joint Sites Committee, EMI and ENV Engineering Joint Shop Stewards' Committee, Exhibition Workers' Committee, London Sheet Metal Workers' Organisation and the Shop Stewards' Defence Committee. In February 1967 the Liaison Committee for the Defence of Trade Unions, as it had begun to call itself, organised a sizeable lobby of parliament against the Labour wage freeze.

From 1968 onwards the LCDTU turned its attention to the impending threat of industrial relations legislation. As soon as 'In Place of Strife' came out, it managed to organise significant stoppages. In February 1969, 150,000 stopped work mainly on Clydeside and Merseyside, followed by a May Day strike of 250,000, with a 20,000-strong demonstration in London and demonstrations in other parts of Britain. With Labour's retreat over 'In Place of Strife', the committee became relatively dormant.

Not until the Tories came to power in the summer of 1970 did the LCDTU gather fresh momentum, which culminated in the massive unofficial stoppage of 600,000 on 8 December 1970, despite TUC attempts at sabotage. This strike helped lead the way for other stoppages in 1971 against the Industrial Relations Bill. These took place on 1 January (mainly in the Midlands) and 12 January.[84]

The CP at that time already faced a dilemma—whether to be critical of the sell-out of the Ford workers by Scanlon and Jones in 1971 and the disastrous leadership of the national engineering claim in 1972.

The ability of 'left' union leaders to come to the top of the union machine with the help of an aroused rank and file, and when arriving there becoming a shackle on the very people who raised them, is not peculiar to the engineers or to the CP.

Let us look at the Yorkshire miners. At the time of the 1969 and 1970 unofficial strikes, the Yorkshire area executive of the NUM was right wing controlled. 'Hence the panels (assemblies of delegates from each pit corresponding to the

NCB areas) organised in a sort of rank and file committee basis,' writes Bill Message:

> They did more or less represent the aspirations of the militants in the coalfields, whereas today the leadership is 'left' wing in Yorkshire. The panel is used by the Yorkshire leadership in order to try and keep everybody in line with the position that the Yorkshire leadership take—in other words, if the Yorkshire leadership want to move then they'll use the panels as the instrument to get them moving. If they don't want to move then they'll use them to stop them.

What about the caucus around Scargill? Bill Message says:

> The Broad Left in Yorkshire, say eight years ago, was very very strong, well organised. They held their own secret meetings but they held Scargill's—what did he call it?—the Forum, which used to hold public meetings as well, with good speakers, and they used to attract a good audience, but since he's got the position he is in the secret meetings continue but they are more for Scargill's benefit than for the benefit of the militants taking part in them.

The Forum was dominated largely by full time lodge officials, whose workstyle, as described above, is quite different to that of the rank and file. They are paid top wages, while they don't have to work in the horrible conditions down the pit, with the danger of injury or pneumoconiosis. The Forum shaded very much into the Yorkshire area NUM executive, which is completely composed of the area full time office officials plus the NUM agent for each of the NCB areas, plus four members from each NCB area, plus one from all the different NCB workshops—ie some 17-plus full time officials.

Made up largely of officials or aspiring officials, no wonder the Broad Left in the Yorkshire NUM cannot keep its unity. In the last elections for the job of vice-president of the Yorkshire area, there are 14 candidates, at least nine of them Broad Left.

Crisis of ideas

The crisis of the working class at the present is not only a crisis of organisation and leadership that goes from top to bottom of the movement, but also a crisis of ideas.

It is a fact that trade unionists will tolerate from a Labour government what they would not tolerate from the Tories. However, this alone could not explain the massive retreat of the working class over the years of low wages, unemployment, cuts.

Workers' consciousness is usually full of contradictions. In a famous passage in *The German Ideology*, Marx and Engels wrote:

> The ideas of the ruling class are in every epoch the ruling ideas, ie the class which is the ruling *material* force of society is at the same time its ruling *intellectual* force. The class which has the means of material production at its disposal has control at the same time over the means of mental production, so that thereby, generally speaking, the ideas of those who lack the means of mental production are subject to it. The ruling ideas are nothing more than the ideal expression of the dominant

material relationships, the dominant material relationships grasped as ideas; hence of the relationships which make the one class the ruling one, therefore, the ideas of its dominance.[85]

Hence the overwhelming majority of workers have always believed in the 'national interest'. They always believed that profit was necessary—if the employers cannot make profits the workers cannot have jobs. They have always accepted that an inegalitarian distribution of wealth and income was just and inevitable.

These ideas have in no way been able to prevent the class struggle. A worker can accept that profits are inevitable and at the same time complain bitterly that the profits of his own employer are far too big compared with his wages.

Workers' loyalty to Labour has in no way prevented them going on strike while Labour was in power. One has only to remember the fantastic enthusiasm of the miners for the nationalisation of their industry in 1947 and the massive support they gave Labour at the time while at the same time they chose to go on with strikes at a very high level.

Then look at the Second World War. There was no time in which the idea of national unity, especially in face of fascism, was as popular as then. But this did not prevent numerous strikes in the milling industry. Of course the Yorkshire miners supported the war. But this did not prevent them from detesting the owners of the mines, grumbling about the level of wages, complaining about their leaders, and acting accordingly. So the number of strikes rose rapidly in the last five years of the war.

In general the number of strikes and strike days rose during the war compared with the years before. In the years 1934-39 there were 5,700 strikes involving 10,846,000 strike days, while in the years 1940-45 the number of strikes rose to 8,247 and the number of strike days to 11,904,000.[87]

The overwhelming majority of workers accepted the arguments of the Wilson and Callaghan governments about pay, inflation and unemployment. They fell for the argument that wage rises are the cause of inflation and would lead to unemployment if there was no wage restraint. But accepting the argument *in general* would not in itself prevent workers from demanding wage improvements. After all, in all periods of rising prices these arguments have always been used.

Where the argument becomes more convincing is where it is clear that the company the worker works for is facing the danger of closure, or at least of redundancies. And the rising dole queues in recent years strengthens the argument.

Of course if one accepts without question that the rights of private property should apply to the means of production, the rules of capitalism must also be accepted. Once one accepts the right of owners of industry to dispose of their capital then the view that the workers are fundamentally dependent on their employers follows with inescapable logic. If capitalist ownership is sacrosanct then of course 'there must be profit', and if there is no profit there cannot be jobs. The concepts of 'profitability', 'efficiency', 'viability' appear as immutable, natural, commonsense rules.

The fact that the profit system is natural and necessarily beneficial to workers seems in contradiction to the fact that this same system brings mass unemployment and suffering. But the majority of workers have never seen the causal relation between the capitalist system on the one hand and slumps and mass unemployment on the other, and of course the capitalist press and the television do not enlighten the workers on this point.

However, the lack of a coherent answer to the crisis could not by itself paralyse workers' struggle. After all, the irritants in the wages paid, of one group of workers compared to another, has for a long time been the mainspring of industrial action by workers. With rising inflation, workers' focus on comparability increases. It is always in the area of contradictions in consciousness that the spring of struggle for higher wages rises. If not for this contradiction the workers would not fight for 'fair' wages, but for the abolition of the wages system as such.

It would therefore be ahistorical, banal, to attribute the right turn in the working class in recent years to the acceptance by workers of the ideas of 'national interest'. The idea is as old as the working class. Again the ideas of class collaboration are as old as the British trade union movement. After all, the talks between Ben Turner representing the TUC, and Sir Alfred Mond, the ICI chief, in 1927, calling for a joint council of workers and employers, affected the ideological stance of the whole trade union movement for decades afterwards. The question therefore remains, why have those always treasonable trade union officials managed to sell the "Contrick" in recent years much more effectively than they did in the five years before, 1969-74?

Lack of confidence to break, or at least loosen, the vice of government and employers is the key impediment to raising class consciousness. Class consciousness cannot exist independent of class confidence. The decline in the cohesion of the shop organisation under incomes policy, under productivity deals, with workers' participation, makes the ideology of national interest and of Labourism a much stronger straitjacket and impediment to action.

As one element in an equation, the ideological impasse is both a cause and an effect of the crisis of the movement. *Labourism, loyalty to the Labour Party, whether in government or in opposition, is the arc uniting all the elements of ideological confusion and subservience to capitalism dominating workers' thinking.*

In the years 1970-74 the balance of class forces expressed itself in workers' offensive on the economic front—however sectional it may have been—and retaliation and employers' offensive on the political front, above all the Industrial Relations Act, however ineffective that also may have been.

Alas, there is no automatic transition from economic to political struggle. When Lenin said that politics is concentrated economics, he did not in any way identify the one with the other, or assume a fatalistic transformation from the one to the other.

The unstable balance between the political generalisation on the employers' side and the industrial militancy on the workers' side could lead to one of two extremes—to political generalisation of the industrial militancy, or to the decline of sectional militancy. The latter took place as a result of the misleadership of the trade union bureaucracy, the Labour left and the CP.

Hard slog ahead

The present recession, while at the moment less intense, is a much more general and permanent phenomenon than that experienced in the 1930s. Attacks on living standards, cuts, redundancies, plant closures, are going to affect working people in a harsher and harsher way.

This harsh reality, while exposing the crisis of leadership of the labour movement from the top of the TUC to the shopfloor, is a challenge that cannot be met with the weapons of yesteryear. Such fragmented reaction will not do now, on the wages front, not to say on the front of cuts, closures and unemployment. The muddled thinking of workers in the years of the boom did not prevent them from still improving their material conditions. Now what happens in the grey matter of workers' heads is decisive for their material wellbeing. Politics, socialist politics, has therefore to be brought to the shopfloor.

The rank and file organisations must play a central role in fighting the employers and the government while keeping themselves independent from the treacherous union bureaucracies. Within such organisations, revolutionaries can organise together with those workers who want to fight, want to go further than the bureaucrats even though they have not broken fully with reformism.

The fact that the commitment called by Rank and File's 'Defend Our Unions' conference the 'Code of Practice' is so elementary—solidarity, respect for picket lines, collecting money, organising blacking—should not disguise the point that to get such a code accepted and *acted upon* by branches, district committees, stewards committees and the union membership will be a very hard task to achieve.

Many of the defects—and much of the detail of shopfloor weakness—were spelled out at the conference again and again by the delegates who spoke. But, throughout, this sense of realism was combined with hard determination to organise, educate and fight back.

To give but a few quotes: Dick North, executive committee member of the NUT and chairman of the conference, defined the subject of the conference as 'how we can rebuild the trade union organisation at the rank and file level to prepare the fightback against the Tory government... We have to re-establish the rank and file tradition at the shopfloor level, about which we've been talking but which—it's been implicit in many of the contributions—has declined in recent years.'

Phil Gilliatt, chairman of Sanderson's strike committee, spoke about the 'bad state of the movement':

> One of the main problems at the moment is us, the people here and this massive trade union movement we've got—about 12 million. And yet we fail consistently; we fail to win recognition disputes, one by one, longer and longer they go on, everyone failing. It is very easy to turn round and say, 'Why are we losing?' and say, 'Oh well, it's them. It's the officials—they're not doing the job right. They're putting the block on it.' OK, but there is another reason—and that's us; our failure to organise. It's all very well you telling me, 'Oh yes, we've got it, the movement's as strong as ever.' No way. The movement has never been in such a situation as it is now, with attacks coming from all over.

Joe Carberry, TGWU Birds Eye Shop Stewards Committee, said:

What we need to do at this conference is to get back to the basics of trade unionism. The basics of trade unionism are that we do not cross picket lines; we will support other workers in struggle… If you look at the reality of the situation, there
are more workers than ever before, I'd suggest, actually crossing picket lines… If
we're going to win any sort of organisation, what we must do is to say, 'Yes, we will
start to control our strikes; we won't leave it to the union bureaucracy, because
we've been sold down the river too many times by them.'

Gordon Vassall, FBU, said:

It is no good beating about the bush. Our strike was beaten. The Labour government was busy putting out the ardour of the firemen. Demoralisation hasn't just happened to the firemen. It's happened right across the spectrum of the trade union
movement. Over the past few years they've been beaten back, and beaten back
again. The trade unionism that we had, years and years ago, the links that we
had—we've got to build them again. The employers are organised; they know exactly what they are doing. We have got to be organised; we need to take up the fight.

Tommy Douras, chairman, Hackney Joint Works Committee, said:

What the Social Contract did wasn't just to restrain your wages. It did what 'In Place
of Strife' couldn't do in 1969. It did what the Industrial Relations Act couldn't do
under the Tory government. It won the battle of the mind. It won the argument in
trade union branches. It filtered right down to the very shop stewards' movement.
We had shop stewards taking part in workers' participation and coming back like
errand boys and telling workers on the shopfloor to do what the bosses told them to
do. It's not happened all of a sudden, but over the last four years, bit by bit, that the
ideology that we cross picket lines, that we don't put on blackings for other workers,
has crept in.

Tommy Douras was followed by Ann Robertson (ASTMS, North Manchester
Hospital):

As Tommy said, the thing about the Code of Practice is that it really concerns
very basic trade union principles, trade union principles that seem to have been undermined fantastically in the last few years. It might take a long time for the offensive
against the Tories, against Margaret Thatcher. We've got to be prepared for that,
and the only way we can be prepared is building groups of rank and file militants
around us. And that for me is what this conference is supposed to be about.

The aspiration for self-activity of the rank and file must be infused with clear
socialist ideas. Socialism is the only answer to a deepening and permanent capitalist crisis. For all the different battles—in industry, in the hospitals, in the
schools, against the cuts, against racism, against women's oppression—a unifying organisation is necessary, a mass revolutionary workers party. The task of
building it cannot be shirked for a minute.

So long as capitalism was expanding and by and large prosperous, industrial militancy in itself could achieve quite significant results. Today, when world capitalism is in deep general crisis, industrial militancy alone is quite ineffective. General social and political questions have to be faced. The battle of ideas becomes crucial. To build a bridge between industrial militancy, rank and file activity and socialism, we must relate the immediate struggles to the final struggle —the struggles inside capitalism to the struggle against capitalism.

The Tories are going to test out our working class organisations. Hence it is necessary to see every attack in the context of the general offensive. This means it is crucial to rally the greatest possible support for every group of workers in struggle and to relate their struggle to the government's attack. The whole battle has to be given a clear, political—ie, general *class*, socialist—anti-government edge.

The working class has paid and is continuing to pay a very high price for its crisis of leadership. The Labour Party and its CP hangers-on have weakened the workers' movement. However, the dialectics of history, the general crisis of capitalism, are far more powerful than all the bureaucrats. If the crisis accelerates the death of the reformist forest, it will—if revolutionary socialists adopt a correct strategy and tactics—accelerate the growth of the green shoots of rank and file confidence, action and organisation.

Notes

1 C T B Smith, R Clifton, P Makenham, S W Craigh and R B Burn, *Strikes in Britain* (London, 1979), p112.
2 A Buchan, *The Right to Work: The Story of the Upper Clyde Confrontation* (London, 1972), pp9-10.
3 Ministry of Labour, *The Metal Industries*, Manpower Studies no 2, HMSO (London, 1965), p98.
4 R K Brown, P Brannen, J M Cousins and M L Samphier, 'The Contours of Solidarity: Social Stratification and Industrial Relations in Shipbuilding', *British Journal of Industrial Relations*, March 1972.
5 H A Clegg, A Fox and A F Thompson, *A History of British Trade Unions Since 1889* (London, 1964), p468.
6 Footnote missing in original.
7 H A Clegg and others, *History*, p436.
8 *Financial Times*, 25 July 1979.
9 *Financial Times*, 8 September 1978.
10 *Incomes Data Report* 302, April 1979.
11 *Crisis in the Shipyards* (Socialist Worker Pamphlet, 1978).
12 *Collier*, March-April 1978.
13 *Collier*, June-July 1978.
14 *Collier*, March-April 1978.
15 C T B Smith and others, *Strikes*, p93; and Department of Employment *Gazettes*.
16 Committee of Inquiry, Port Transport Industry, *Final Report*, HMSO (London), p8.
17 D F Wilson, *Dockers* (London, 1972), pp314-315.
18 *Financial Times*, 27 August 1972.
19 *Financial Times*, 28 April 1978.
20 T Cliff, *The Employers' Offensive: Productivity Deals and How to Fight Them* (London, 1970), p39.
21 T Cliff, *Employers' Offensive*, p42.
22 *Incomes Data Report* 302, April 1979; and *Incomes Data Report* 304, May 1979.

23 W Brown, *Piecework Bargaining* (London, 1973), p34.

24 *Incomes Data Report* 304, May 1979.

25 D Beecham in *Socialist Review*, March 1979.

26 L Panitch, *Social Democracy and Industrial Militancy* (Cambridge, 1976), p264.

27 Prices and Incomes Board, *Report* no 77, p12.

28 D Jackson, H A Turner and F Wilkinson, *Do Trade Unions Cause Inflation?* (2nd edition, London, 1974), pxv.

29 *Labour Research*, August 1979.

30 *Financial Times*, 20 July, 1978.

31 *Financial Times*, 21 October 1978.

32 *Financial Times*, 30 September 1978.

33 *Incomes Data Report* 292. November 1978.

34 *Incomes Data Report* 295, December 1978.

35 *Incomes Data Report* 299, February 1979.

36 *Incomes Data Report* 302. April 1979.

37 *Incomes Data Report* 304, May 1979.

38 *Incomes Data Report* 286, August 1978.

39 *Incomes Data Report* 284. July 1978.

40 *Incomes Data Report* 103, November 1970.

41 *Incomes Data Report* 105, December 1970.

42 *Guardian*, 2 August 1979.

43 C T B Smith and others, *Strikes*, p129.

44 Department of Employment *Gazettes*.

45 M Hart, 'Why Bosses Love the Closed Shop', *New Society*, 15 February 1979.

46. T Nichols and H Benyon, *Living With Capitalism: Class Relations and the Modern Factory* (London, 1977), p114.

47 R Price and G S Bain, 'The Union Growth Revisited: 1948-74 in Perspective', *British Journal of Industrial Relations*, November 1976.

48 C T B Smith and others, *Strikes*, p31.

49 T Beck, *The Fine Tubes Strike* (London, 1974), pp7, 11.

50 J Arinson, *The Million Pound Strike* (London, 1970).

51 J Rosser and C Barker, 'A Working Class Defeat: The ENV Story', *International Socialism* (first series), Winter 1967-68.

52 *Socialist Review* 11, April 1979, said:
'The EEF document doesn't just invite its 6,000 member companies to take a hard line. It virtually orders them to. It says:
●"These guidelines aim to help employers achieve greater confidence and coherence in the practice of collective bargaining, and in responding to the threat or fact of industrial action."
●The guidelines aim to ensure "any employer following them will not feel isolated".
●"Where an employer has rights under a national, local or domestic agreement, he must be vigilant to exercise and maintain them."
●Employers "should press the need for appointment of stewards with proper qualifications who are competent for office".
●"Abuse of the position and power of stewards should not be accepted."
●"Employees should be made aware that their employer is willing to provide facilities for secret ballots."
●"To maintain the authority of procedure, of union officials and management, companies should refuse to negotiate where procedure has been breached."
●"Layoff pay should not he offered for those affected by disputes in the same plant or wider bargaining unit."
●"Industrial action such as go-slows, refusal to work normally, and blacking of employees, products or machines should not be tolerated for more than a few days. After a warning, with a sufficient period allowed for reflection, suspension without pay should be the normal response."
●"Lump sum payments should not normally be offered by way of settlement as an inducement to return to work...as regards income tax refunds, companies can limit their

obligation to pay them during the course of a strike by giving notice, and passing the obligation back, to the Inland Revenue."

●"A company's striking employee should not be recruited by other companies while the strike lasts: nor should its work be carried out by other companies, unless by agreement. A customer company should not pressurise a supplying company whose employees are on strike to make an unsatisfactory compromise settlement. Any company subjected to such pressures should feel free to invoke the influence of its Association or of the Federation".'

53 R Holt, 'The Employers' Offensive', *Socialist Review* 11, April 1979.
54 B Weekes, M Mellish, L Dickens and J Lloyd, *Industrial Relations and the Limits of Law: The Industrial Effects of the Industrial Relations Act 1971* (Oxford, 1975), p223.
55 B Weekes and others, *Industrial Relations*, p203.
56 B Weekes and others, *Industrial Relations*, p59.
57 B Weekes and others, *Industrial Relations*, p160.
58 B Weekes and others, *Industrial Relations*, p201.
59 B Weekes and others, *Industrial Relations*, p202.
60 B Weekes and others, *Industrial Relations*, p218.
61 B Weekes and others, *Industrial Relations*, p228.
62 *Sunday Times*, 4 June 1972.
63 *Industrial Relations Review and Report* 194, February 1979.
64 *Industrial Relations Review and Report* 200, May 1979.
65 *Socialist Worker*, 1979.
66 *Socialist Worker*, 14 July 1979.
67 T Cliff, *Employers' Offensive*, pp39-53, 126-127.
68 T Lane, *The Union Makes Us Strong* (London, 1974), p198.
69 D Lyddon, 'Leyland, Shop Stewards and Participation', *International Socialism* (first series), October 1977.
70 T Cliff, *Chrysler Workers: The Fight for a Future* (London, 1978), p20.
71 W Brown, R Ebsworth and M Terry, 'Factors Shaping Shop Steward Organisation in Britain', *British Journal of Industrial Relations*, July 1978.
72 D Lyddon, 'Leyland'.
73 T Cliff, *Chrysler*, pp20-21.
74 *Socialist Worker*, 3 September 1977.
75 H Benyon, *Working for Ford* (London, 1977), p216.
76 See H Benyon, *Working*, ch 10.
77 R Hyman, 'Industrial Conflict and Political Economy: Trends of the Sixties and Prospects for the Seventies', *Socialist Register 1973* (London, 1974), p124.
78 R Hyman, 'Industrial', p123.
79 See J MacFarlane, 'The Changing Pattern of Industrial Conflict in the British Coal Industry' (duplicated, Sheffield); B Message, 'The Miners and the Labour Government', *International Socialism* (first series), September 1976.
80 J Charlton, 'The Miners: The Triumph of 1972 and the Way Ahead', *International Socialism* (first series), April 1973.
81 *Socialist Worker*, 2 March 1974.
82 Quoted in M Armstrong, 'The History and Organisation of the Broad Left in the AUEW' (MA thesis, Warwick University, 1978).
83 M Armstrong, 'History'.
84 J Townsend, 'The LCDTU', *International Socialism* (first series), March 1973.
85 K Marx and F Engels, *The German Ideology* (London, 1970), p64.
86 N A Clark, 'Unofficial Strikes on the South Yorkshire Coalfield in the Second World War' (MA thesis, Sheffield University, 1978).
87 C T B Smith and others, *Strikes*, p129.
88 *Socialist Worker*, 9 December 1978.

The state of the struggle today

Interview in *Socialist Review*, April 1986

The Tories are in more trouble than they have been since Thatcher became prime minister. How significant are their problems?

In any war you have to start with the strength and weakness of our army, the strength and weakness of the enemy army, and the balance between the two. There is always a danger that we see only our side, and so we only see our weaknesses.

The splits in the Tories have to do with the extent to which the government managed to smash the working class. Westland is a relatively small company. Two million jobs have gone in manufacturing. Do they care if another 10,000 jobs go? You can't explain it by looking at the thing by itself. It is a symptom of the failure of the Tory government to win the battles against the working class.

They won a lot of individual battles—they didn't win the war. Far from it. When Margaret Thatcher came to office in 1979 she promised to create a lean and strong economy. Now she has a lean economy—it is suffering from anorexia nervosa.

When she came to office, Britain exported £5,000 million more manufacturing goods than it imported. Now Britain imports £4,000 million more than it exports. For the first time since the industrial revolution Britain is a net importer of manufactured goods. Britain was the workshop of the world. There is nothing to show for North Sea oil. Worse, they thought the money for the oil would go down slowly till the mid-1990s. It didn't go slowly—it's gone down by 40 percent in the last few months.

They are very unhappy because the key problem for them was to shift radically the balance between wages and profits. That was the aim of the operation in 1979. Real wages have risen since 1979.

Even the victories of the Tory government were not followed by a cut in real wages. In reality they didn't win on the wage front, which was the key to solving all their other problems. The split in the Tories is about that—she didn't deliver. They are not in good shape.

The Tories are in a mess. But the working class side is also in disarray, with the weakening in shopfloor organisation, the defeat of the miners, and now Wapping, where Murdoch has achieved more already than Ian MacGregor did in a year. How would you assess the balance of class forces today?

In the end any war is lost to the side that loses all the battles. But the cost of victory in every single battle can affect the total results.

If one side loses and the other side wins all the fights, but wins them with fantastic losses, then they can lose the war even if they won individual battles.

Up to now the workers have lost individual battles. Steel in 1980, hospitals and ASLEF in 1982, the NGA in 1983, the miners in 1984-85, now, even worse, Wapping in 1986. But it doesn't mean that the Tories are winning. By and large the unions are still there. There are still 10 million trade unionists. There are still 300,000 shop stewards. So at the end of the day the ruling class are not sure that they are going to win the war.

Again, it is not simply a question of whether they use confrontation or collaboration, but what the proportion is between the two. If confrontation doesn't pay in the long run, then they will switch to cooperation. They can't wait 20 years because the British economy would disappear practically down the plughole. So then different policies would be put forward—wet Tory or right wing social democratic.

It is too simplistic to say that because they lose the individual battles they are going to lose the war. On the other hand, it is also far too simplistic to say that individual battles are not important.

What is necessary under such conditions? It is very important for socialists in general principle to despise the enemy—we are the many; they are the few. But in terms of the specific we have to show great respect to them—because we can be the few and they are the many. So fighting for individual shop organisation, collecting money—all the small things—are terribly important. Unless you tactically respect the enemy you are lost.

The main danger for socialists is that they go from the manic to the depressive because there's very little fight.

You talk about respecting the enemy. But in recent years many people have made fantastic concessions to the enemy. They accept the ideas of those like Hobsbawm that all you can do is move into the terrain of the right. Look at the examples round the TUC—the acceptance of the EETPU scabbing operation at Wapping, the single-union deals. How do you think these ideas will develop in the next few years?

The defeat of 1984-85 was nothing compared to the defeat of the General Strike in 1926, because the number of miners was much bigger then. And in 1926 everybody participated. Today, because of sectionalism, the impact of the defeat is much less. Shop organisation is also much stronger at present.

Still, there is some similarity. If it was complete repetition you don't need theory, you need memory, but there is some repetition. There has been a massive move to the right. At that time it was towards the Mond-Turner agreement—towards no-strike deals and arbitration. This time it is towards the 'new realism' or pragmatism. This will continue for the coming 18 months or two years. I don't see anything radically changing before the next election.

When it comes to a perspective there are two things a Marxist can do well—look at the very long term or the short term. If you come to the medium term—ten years—it is much more difficult to guess.

In the long term the crisis of capitalism is deeper and more fundamental than any crisis of consciousness in the class, or crisis of leadership. The crisis of leadership is important, but secondary.

What's happening in the Philippines is fantastically important for us. If the regime is too disgusting there is a massive rebellion at the end of the day. The Philippines and Egypt show us much more than any place in the world. They are on the periphery of capitalism and so the contradictions are much deeper.

In the final analysis we know there will be a rebellion of the working class. All the talk from Eric Hobsbawm that the working class is finished is stupidity. The working class today is ten times bigger in Britain than it was in 1848. Then only textile workers were in factories of over 100.

The working class today is much bigger even than it was in the 1920s and 30s. The South Korean working class is bigger than the whole working class at the time of Karl Marx.

So in the long term we know the picture. In the short term we also know. In the mid-term I never like to speculate because there are too many unknowns.

For example, will a Labour victory raise the class struggle? It will not be a repetition of 1974 because it doesn't come on the crest of the miners' strike and dockers' strike. But if they repeal some of the union laws—like secondary picketing and the right of blacking, the financial liability of the unions—will workers be more confident now they are not being fined?

And although there is a division of labour between Neil Kinnock and Ron Todd, the division is not perfect. Ernie Bevin led strikes against Ramsay MacDonald and the 1924 Labour government. The TUC opposed MacDonald's cuts in 1931. The unions didn't agree with Labour in 1969 over 'In Place of Strife'.

Under such conditions, will there be more strikes? The answer is probably yes. If there are then the present circumstances can change. I don't think we should speculate about it. What we can say is that there is a move to the right, but not everybody moves to the right. Our slogan should be much more 'Stop the retreat—organise the resistance.' We have to speak much more in resistant terms—not even stopping the retreat, slowing the retreat.

The manic depressive people terrify me. Instead of accepting from Gramsci optimism of the will and pessimism of the intellect, they accept optimism of the intellect and pessimism of the will. So everything's marvellous in the garden, but there's nothing we can do about it. Instead we say, 'Everything in the garden's terrible, but there are things we can do.'

Why? Because there are minorities willing to fight. It's not true the picture of the last six years is one big Tory walkover. If there was no resistance, Thatcher wouldn't have trouble with Heseltine.

We should not be pessimistic about the potential of workers in the immediacy. They are *slowing* down the process of the attack.

The analogy of the war of attrition is very useful. The war of attrition means that every little skirmish is very important.

You talk about pessimism and optimism. We've been denounced as pessimists now for some years. A lot of that was based on the fact that most socialists saw changing the Labour Party as the way forward. The Labour left is now on the retreat. What would you say to those people who stay inside the Labour Party, and what do you think is the future of the Labour left?

We should always speak about the past. We've had nine Labour governments and we're not one step nearer to socialism. But the danger always is that people say, 'Alright, it didn't happen last time but it will happen next time. It is not proof that something happens nine times so it must happen a tenth time.' There have only been nine Labour governments. People say they were exceptions.

It is a question of understanding the nature of the Labour Party. The key to that is understanding the role of the trade union bureaucracy as the backbone of the Labour Party.

William McLean, at the second congress of the Communist International in 1920, said the Labour Party is the political expression of the trade unions. Lenin said no, it is the political expression of the trade union bureaucracy. Can you get rid of the bureaucracy this side of the socialist revolution? Can workers take over the block vote? This is what it boils down to.

Assume the SWP joined the Labour Party tomorrow. We took over all the 630 constituencies because Larry Whitty was asleep and Neil Kinnock forgot the word witch-hunt. The truth is we would have 630,000 votes—Rodney Bickerstaffe and Ron Todd have more than that. Gavin Laird has more than that. Can you break the trade union bureaucracy? Not this side of the socialist revolution.

The base of the bureaucracy is mobilising the passive majority against the active minority. And by and large, in the majority of cases, the majority of the time this side of the revolution, the majority of workers are passive. Revolution means workers are active and come into the arena of history, but otherwise they are passive.

In Russia, where the unions were very young—the printers' union was established in 1903—the Bolsheviks controlled the soviets in Petrograd and Moscow, the majority of factory committees. But when it came to the union machine the Mensheviks controlled it until after the revolution.

The Russian unions were very young. SOGAT is 203 years old. The NGA is two and a half centuries old. The AUEW is 134 years old. They are very old unions.

In Russia many of the bureaucrats finished in Siberia—here they finish in the House of Lords. In Russia they had to make the revolution to smash them.

Here there is no way this side of the socialist revolution we'll smash them.

The left in the Labour Party are dreamers, utopians, completely unrealistic, because they say they can use the block vote if they take it under their control.

Revolutionaries can take control over a district of a union or individual workplace organisation. They cannot take over the whole union machine. To do that you need the majority of workers to be activists and you can't expect it in a non-revolutionary situation.

The Labour Party cannot be changed. People say Neil Kinnock is the problem. He's not the problem. The problem is, why does he get the support of Tom Sawyer, Rodney Bickerstaffe or Ron Todd?

The bureaucracy is like a rusty wheelbarrow—it moves if it is pushed. And there is not massive pressure on Ron Todd to move to the left. In these conditions he'll support Neil Kinnock.

The tragedy of Liverpool is that the comrades there didn't understand it. They thought that controlling the shop stewards' committee in Liverpool was very good. It would be as long as you use the minority base to fight. They waited for the majority. John Edmondson intervened and broke the minority.

You mentioned earlier a return to consensus politics as an alternative to confrontation. But a lot of people, especially those new to socialist ideas, see the increase in policing, the way in which the unions are much more shackled by the law now than, say, ten years ago, and argue there is a much more repressive state. They say that the only way that can be changed is through the election of a Labour government to change the laws, impose democratic controls on the police, and so on. What do you think about that?

The ruling class never rules by persuasion alone. But the ruling class under bourgeois democracy doesn't rule by violence alone. It's a question of the proportion between the two. With the Battle of Warrington in 1983, what was the key problem? Was it the police in Warrington or the fact that Fleet Street was called back to work? No question about it—the key problem was the union bureaucracy.

The police are important as an alibi to the union bureaucracy. It is not true that because the union bureaucracy and the police both serve the same master they are friendly to one another. On the contrary, two servants can hate one another. The NGA is not happy when it is fined hundreds of thousands of pounds or when the police kick the hell out of print workers in Wapping. There is a contradiction between them.

But we have to understand what the relative relation is between the different factors. There are situations where the police are the most important thing in the world—in Franco's Spain or in Chile. There are situations where the trade union bureaucracy is most central—for example, under the Social Contract. Today the police play a bigger role than, say, in 1974-79, but still it is very secondary.

Why was Sean Geraghty only fined £350 during the hospitals dispute? If they'd sent him to prison there would have been a national strike and the implications would have been very big. In reality they are quite pragmatic when it comes to the specific.

They talk about strong states. But when NACODS threatened to come out on strike during the miners' strike, Margaret Thatcher was much more worried about that than confident in the power of the police to give hell to the miners on the picket line.

The most important thing is the policeman in the brain, the one that controls the workers' thinking. And that is not the men in blue, but the Neil Kinnocks and Norman Willises.

What does all this mean in terms of building a revolutionary party? We are often described as unrealistic. We try to build an organisation, and now have 4,000 members, but have been at that figure for some years. People say, 'You don't get any bigger—what do you think you are trying to achieve?'

The argument that we are unrealistic had much more echo three or four years ago in terms of our members and periphery, because the Bennites were on the march. The last few years have proved that basically we are right.

Three or four years ago between us and the right wing were Neil Kinnock, the soft left, then the hard left. A whole number of those have moved to the right.

Remember the 'dream ticket' of 1983—Neil Kinnock and Roy Hattersley. The argument then was, 'Kinnock is alright—it's Hattersley who is the problem.' Now both of them are in the same camp. More important, the people in between are practically all in a terrible crisis. You have to ask yourself why the CP split, the WRP split, *Labour Herald* split, *Socialist Action* split.

Because of the wrong perspective about the miners' strike, expectations rose, and when those expectations were not realised then they started tearing one another to pieces. That's why they are all splitting.

So not only is there very little between us and the right wing. What there is is split and weak. To some extent people don't see it because they are in the Labour Party, which is structured in such a way that people can exaggerate how much they have.

If there are five people in the room you can pass a resolution in the name of 5,000 or 10,000. Therefore they don't know the truth about themselves. But if you know, for example, that the print order of *Labour Herald* is only 2,000 then it's clear that they represent very, very little.

So despite all the ups and downs—the up of the Bennites and the down after the miners' strike—the rest were smashed. We were not smashed.

There were only two organisations that have kept intact—us and the *Militant*. The *Militant* are going to suffer much fraying at the edges because of the bankruptcy of their policy in Liverpool. They went from a demonstration of tens of thousands in Liverpool last year to only 400 after the surcharges last month. Because of that they will suffer as well.

Our prospect is the following. We are going to mark time to a large extent. What do we mean? We can increase our membership marginally. We can't increase it very much because to the extent that people say we are on the margins of the class they are right.

A revolutionary party is not an exact reflector of the class struggle, but it cannot be independent from the level of class struggle. In 1972 I spoke to 6,000 or 7,000 steel workers in Scunthorpe. During the 1980 strike the biggest meeting of steel workers I spoke to was 100.

The level of struggle in terms of solidarity with the miners was much higher in 1972 than in 1984-85. The Fleet Street of July 1972 during Pentonville is not the Fleet Street of 1986 during Wapping. We cannot be independent of the base we relate to.

So can we grow to 6,000 instead of 4,000? Yes, but 50,000 doesn't fit the level of struggle.

I think the organisation is in good shape because while our vision is never too low, we never make concessions on our assumption about the centrality of the working class. That remains central.

When it comes to the tactics, of course we fit ourselves to the level. We don't say, 'Unless there are 6,000 steel workers, we won't speak.' We'll speak to 100, we'll speak to 50.

When people say we are unrealistic, I say on the contrary that we are realistic —the rest are unrealistic because the rest offer a whole number of conceptions that lead to nothing, that lead to catastrophe. That's why they disintegrate.

When conditions are tough, people who don't fit disintegrate. The fact that we didn't shows that we were right. It's nothing to do with psychological toughness— in terms of toughness the WRP are the toughest in the world, but they disintegrated completely because they issued statements which didn't fit the situation at all.

So what is going to happen? In Russia the Bolsheviks were shaped during the period of reaction after 1905. Things were very tough. There were ten members in Ivanovo Voznesensk in March 1917—in July 5,440. Now, there is no guarantee that the ten will turn into 5,440, because you don't know in advance there will be a revolution. But without the ten you won't get anything. Therefore you always have to judge yourself on whether you relate to the struggle that takes place.

The main danger for us is that we can become abstract propagandists. We don't simply say, 'Capitalism is bad, socialism is good.' Our statements on Wapping have been brilliant. Every issue of the paper talks about what is to be done—always very practical. The fact is we couldn't deliver—but we still told the minority the only way to win was by getting mass picketing.

Let's assume the print unions come to a compromise at Wapping. Of course Brenda Dean will benefit from a compromise like that. And of course the majority of printers will say, 'We struck there for months—it's better to save 1,000 jobs than none.' But a minority will say, 'No, we could have done it—the SWP was right.'

I think many people will agree with everything you've said, except they'll say it's such a long way off that it isn't possible. You have already said things are going to be very tough for revolutionaries. How do people hold themselves together?

It will be tough. We are not a mass party like the Bolsheviks in 1905. They went from 40,000 in 1907 to 200 in 1910. Because the upturn was so massive—they organised an insurrection in 1905—the demoralisation after the defeat was incomparably worse than the demoralisation after the defeat of the miners' strike.

Secondly, because they had mass roots in the working class, when the periphery disappeared it pulled the members down. Our organisation is so much smaller that the events in the outside world don't help us in the way that they helped the Bolsheviks. But they also don't damage us in the same way.

You cannot build a mass party on questions. You build mass parties on action. But when it comes to small organisations, questions are very important. Why is this happening? Why is Kinnock moving to the right? Why wasn't the miners' strike victorious? The periphery of people asking questions is incomparably bigger than a year ago.

During the miners' strike, when we said, 'There is not enough picketing or blacking—the strike is going badly,' people didn't really want to hear us. There were other people—also left wingers, supporting the miners—who said, 'Things are not so bad—they are going well.'

Because of that people didn't ask questions. Now they are asking more questions. We can build the organisation on the number of people asking questions. The trouble is, asking questions will recruit people—it's not enough to keep them.

To do that you need to give them action. What do we mean by action? All the time there are strikes and activities. We have to relate to all of those. What is important is that we mustn't be sectional. Today it can be miners, then Wapping, then South Africa.

We can build the organisation. Can it become a mass party? The answer is no, not at present. Say that in 1987 or 1988 there is a Labour government with very right wing policies. There will be disgruntlement in the Labour Party about it, and in the unions. But in terms of polarisation inside the Labour Party it is not on straight away.

If there is activity in the Labour Party we can be a bigger pole of attraction. We'll be saying, 'We are the alternative to Kinnock.' By that we don't mean we're in the same league—not at all. But our level of struggle is an alternative to the level of struggle of Kinnock. And if it comes to the specific, we are even in the same league.

When it comes to getting people to Wapping, the Labour Party mobilises hundreds, we mobilise hundreds. We're not so separate in terms of leagues. Even during the miners' strike perhaps they were ten times bigger than us. They were not 100 times bigger. When it comes to elections, on the other hand, they are far more than 100 times bigger.

It depends on the specific issue where we choose the battle. We are the alternative because on these issues we are not insignificant. Why? Because an organisation of 4,000 is not as small as all that if it intervenes correctly in the specific struggles.

In the balance

Socialist Review, February 1995

In the industrial struggle we have had three stages over the past 25 years: the period of upturn, the period of downturn, and now the third stage—a period of transition. Elements of the first and second stages are combined together in the present situation.

What did the upturn mean? There were massive workers' victories punctuated by a few defeats. In 1971, for example, Upper Clyde Shipbuilders decided to sack 2,500 out of an 8,500 workforce. The workers occupied the shipyard, 200,000 Scottish workers struck in solidarity and 80,000 went on a demonstration. The Strathclyde police were so shocked by the situation that the chief constable phoned the prime minister and told him he could not be responsible for civil order on the Clyde unless the government changed its policy on UCS. So the government did a U-turn and UCS was saved. Following this, 200 other factories were occupied.

Again in 1972 five dockers were arrested for breaking the Tory anti-union laws. This led to a national dock strike, Fleet Street came out, the engineers came out, the TUC called for a national strike and the government capitulated. Then there were the miners' strikes of 1972 and 1974. There was no question of miners picketing miners—there were hardly any pickets at all. Miners were known to put banners on railway bridges saying 'NUM official picket', and the ASLEF driver would stop the train because he would not cross the picket line. There was fantastic solidarity at that time.

These were the big events, the big waves if you like. But the pressure that made those big waves was the strength of shop stewards' organisation, which was highly independent of the bureaucracy. To see how this worked in practice we can look at what was called 'wage drift'. The national union would negotiate a national agreement for wages but the shop stewards in individual workplaces would press for extra money. Between 1964 and 1967 the national agreed wage in engineering rose by 4.7 percent while actual wages rose by 17.1 percent. The wage drift was 12.4 percent, nearly three times greater than the nationally agreed rise. In June 1968 the standard wage of an engineering fitter was £13 per week while the actual average was £23 per week.

Between 1965 and 1968 a full 95 percent of all strikes were unofficial, and in the car industry it was 99 percent. In the docks, between 1960 and 1965, 410 out of 421 strikes—accounting for 94 percent of days lost—were unofficial.

It was commonly said that if you wanted to win a strike it was important to win before the union office heard about it.

Shop stewards were highly confident and aware of their own power. In one north London factory, ENV, the shop stewards were always competing with one another about who could be the first to cause the foreman to have a nervous breakdown. A new American manager came to ENV. He spoke to the shop stewards and told them that they were all one happy family at the factory. The manager left his office for a while and when he came back he found Geoff Carlsson, the convenor, sitting in the manager's chair with his feet on the table. The manager said, 'Mr Carlsson, what are you doing?' to which Geoff replied, 'You said we are one happy family. In my family I always put my feet on the table,' adding, 'I have broken more managers than you've had hot dinners.' This is what confidence of the rank and file really meant.

The more the workers are confident against the bosses, the less dependent they are on union officials. The less dependent on union officials, the more confident they are against the bosses. At the heart of the shop stewards' movement, the cement which held it together, was the Communist Party. The CP, with a few tens of thousands of members, was crucial because around it collected not only CP sympathisers but the Labour left. So, for example, in December 1970 the Liaison Committee for the Defence of Trade Unions called an unofficial one-day strike against the Tory Industrial Relations Bill and 600,000 workers came out on strike. Besides the Liaison Committee there was the London Docks Liaison Committee, the Building Workers Joint Strike Committee, the Exhibition Workers Committee, the London Sheet Metal Workers Organisation, and so on.

Then came the downturn. After the miners' strike of 1974 the Tories lost office. The *Economist*, the bosses' magazine, said what is necessary now is to get Labour to make scabbing respectable. That is exactly what happened.

Workers were clear when it came to a fight against the Tories. The simple slogan was 'Tories out'. But when it came to the alternative, for 99 percent of workers it was simply 'Labour in'. There was no level of generalisation or clarity of consciousness about what to say when Labour came to power introducing anti working class policies. When the Social Contract was introduced by agreement between the Labour Party and the trade union leaders (led crucially by the left), the result was that scabbing became respectable.

In February 1977, 2,000 toolroom workers went on strike throughout British Leyland. The government threatened to sack them. The left engineering leader Hugh Scanlon supported the government. Derek Robinson, convenor of Longbridge with 28,000 workers, himself a former toolroom worker and a leading member of the CP, stood at the gate of Longbridge and instructed the rest of the workers to cross the picket line. The next month, when electricians in Port Talbot went on strike, the rest of the workers were told to cross the picket line, breaking the strike. In April that year 5,000 AEU members went on strike in Heathrow, but 54,000 other workers were told to cross picket lines and the strike went down.

In the long run, though, the decisive breaking of solidarity had most impact in the mining industry. It didn't take the form of miners crossing other miners' picket lines, but the ground for the scabbing of 1984-85 was prepared in another way. The Labour government introduced an incentive scheme. Until then any miner in Britain got the same wages if he did the same job. So a face worker in Scotland or Kent or Nottinghamshire earned exactly the same. Under such conditions solidarity was much easier to obtain.

In 1977 the Secretary of State for Energy at the time, Tony Benn, tried to introduce an incentive scheme so that different areas would get paid according to how much coal they produced per shift. The NUM conference rejected it, then the government insisted on balloting the members, and the members threw it out overwhelmingly.

Then the National Coal Board, together with the right wing leader of the NUM, Joe Gormley, said those areas that want it should take it and those areas that don't should have the freedom not to take it. As a result the wages difference which built up over the next period was absolutely massive. Nottinghamshire miners earned much more than the other areas because the coal seams in Notts, by and large, are much wider than the other areas, so they could produce more coal more easily. This led to the scabbing in Nottinghamshire of 1984-85.

The political difficulty of workers at the time is summed up by the banner of Kent NUM. On the banner there is a miner outlined against a pithead looking towards the House of Commons. The logic of separating economics from politics meant that in conflict with the Tory government there was clarity, but in conflict with Labour there was no clarity at all. This helped the union leaders carry their policies forward. And of course the CP and the Labour left supported those leaders, even if they were critical of the 'Social Contrick', as it was called.

Another thing which fundamentally affected union power was changing the method of negotiating. Instead of national negotiation for basic wages and then negotiation factory by factory or even shop by shop for extras—piece rates, bonuses, and so on—Measured Day Work was introduced. The whole of Leyland would get the same wage rates and there was now no way of getting extras in individual factories, even less in individual shops. This change necessarily affected the structure of rank and file representatives in the workplace. The number of full time convenors rose massively. In Longbridge in the late 1970s the number of full time senior stewards rose from seven to over 50. By 1977 there were over 5,000 full time senior stewards in manufacturing industry alone, three times greater than the number of full time union officials at the time.

The result of all this was the collapse of unofficial strikes, which dwindled massively. In Ford Halewood in Liverpool in 1976 there were 310 unofficial strikes; in 1981, 52; in 1984, 31; in 1987, 12. This was typical.

What of the present, the transition? The defeats of the 1980s were brought about by a very strong government with a very clear policy of divide and rule. They had the Ridley Plan. Nicholas Ridley was a Tory right winger and a friend of Thatcher who wrote a document in 1977 which argued that Heath had made a mistake in 1970-74 because he took the whole trade union movement on in one go. Instead the Tories should take on one union at a time. Ridley made a list of the order of the unions starting with the steel workers because they had a relatively non-militant record. The list finished with the mines, the docks and Fleet Street. And that's exactly what they did.

Throughout the 1980s they stuck to this plan. Even in 1984 when they attacked the miners they made significant concessions to the rail workers. Because of the lack of solidarity after a year the miners were smashed. Once the miners were smashed the government took on the dockers, the seafarers, Fleet Street, and so on. In the 1990s, though, the picture is very different.

Firstly the government is very, very weak. Because of the depth of the crisis of the system the government's attacks are much more generalised. The poll tax attacked every worker. The wage freeze attacks all the 5 million workers in the public sector and affects other workers. Under such conditions the reaction from workers is necessarily different.

Incomes policy, we know from experience, can hold for a time—Harold Wilson's incomes policy of 1966 held for two years, the 1972 policy of Heath held for something like two years, the Callaghan policy of 1976 held for two years and ended in the Winter of Discontent. We face, in a way, a similar situation. But the past still lives with us. It is not the case that the working class can throw off the past and move from victory to victory.

The signal workers' strike was very impressive. Everything was thrown against them. British Rail lost £200 million during the strike, the members of the Institute of Directors lost £180 million, and we don't know how many tens or maybe hundreds of millions of pounds members of the CBI lost. Probably the whole thing cost over £800 million. It is true that there was some scabbing—70 members of the RMT did scab—but 400 signal workers joined the union during the course of the strike. Also the workers won 8 percent. It is not fantastic but it certainly is not a defeat—they won a cut in the working week. It was clearly a defeat for the bosses.

Following that, Rover workers were offered something like 10 percent over two years. The union argued for it strongly and eventually the workers accepted it but with a very close vote, 51 percent in favour and 49 percent against. Then came Jaguar, where workers were offered around 8 percent over two years and initially rejected it (although they later accepted). These three represent significant advances for our side.

Then we had Jack Dromey, a top official in the TGWU, who talked about the agreement the union had reached with local government over wages. He claimed, 'The Tories will choke on their cornflakes' when they hear about the agreement, initially raising hopes of a 5 or maybe 8 percent wage rise. But the rise actually comes to 1.5 percent plus £100 in the first year (around 2.5 percent in total); the next year is 1.4 percent plus £100 (which amounts to 2.4 percent), with no negotiations of any change until the middle of 1996.

So workers' recovery takes place by two steps forward, one step back. It is not simply up and up. After a long period of sickness of the movement you don't get recuperation easily. If you have been in bed for six months because of illness you don't get out of bed and run the marathon. You get up, walk around and come back to bed half an hour later. Getting out of bed is extremely important but the periods of relapse are also inevitable. This is the period of transition we live in.

Unofficial strikes are undoubtedly reappearing, but 95 percent of strikes are *not* unofficial. There is a split in workers' consciousness, between 'new realism' and the anger that leads to a readiness to fight. If this division was one between the rank and file and the union bureaucracy, we could simply push them aside. Even if the split were between workers and workers, let's say 7 million trade unionists are ready to fight and 1 million are new realists, we would push the others aside. Even if it was the other way around, and 1 million were ready to fight and 7 million were new realists, the 1 million would fight and pull others with them. But the split expresses itself in the individual workers themselves. Over the last couple of years the number of resolutions for strikes is astonishing. The number of strikes is much less. There are a number of examples which show the return of the unofficial strike. In Milton Keynes a few hundred UCW workers went on strike. The result was massive support from other Post Office workers, and altogether 30,000 UCW workers went on strike. When a Liverpool Post Office worker hit a foreman who had insulted him because he stammered, he was sacked, resulting in an instant strike in solidarity by 2,000 workers. They struck—it was unconstitutional, it was unofficial, it was illegal, yet they struck for six days and they won. In January 15,000 London postal workers struck illegally in support of victimised workers at one office.

Sefton UNISON is another good example. A group of workers in Sefton went on strike, unofficially and illegally, against privatisation of services. Leading members of the union branch were brought to court and the national union denounced the strikers. Because of the support the Sefton workers got from other workers, hundreds of whom gathered outside the court on the day of their hearing, the court decided not to imprison them but to fine them.

There is a relationship between quantity and quality, and at present the quantity is still too small. The hold of the union bureaucracy is still absolutely massive. It is not that workers admire the bureaucracy. I can't think of a time that the phrase 'sell-out' has been used more often than now. People are angry but at the same time they feel impotent. So most often the anger does not burst through into real action.

Now we come to a problem. The level of generalisation is on the one hand quite low, but at the same time it is quite high. This sounds like a contradiction, but the contradiction is reality. Workers are ready to support other workers in struggle, but only to a low level. At University College Hospital in 1993 60 workers tried to stop a ward closure. They didn't manage to get a strike of nearly 2,000 other workers in the rest of the hospital but they did get 4,000 people demonstrating, including local teachers, post workers and students, in support of the nurses. Those workers demonstrating made all the difference to the UCH workers. Likewise with the signal workers, while it is true that no other section of workers came on strike, those 4,600 signal workers would not have survived if they hadn't got support from other workers. Hundreds of thousands gave money and moral support. So the level of generalisation is in one way low but in another way quite high.

We have to relate to the section, relate to the specific. At the same time we have to raise other issues, get solidarity for other workers. This is even more important at present because the anger is so generalised—the Tories are hated over every issue. In a situation where workers lack confidence because of the experience of the last ten years, to bring the ANL in, for example, over the fight against racism, gives them a fantastic lift. They feel that there are not only 50 of them against the Tories but hundreds of thousands of people angry. All these issues—the Criminal Justice Act, the protests against racism, against the Child Support Agency—need to be connected to the industrial struggle.

Above all, we have to create a network of rank and file socialists in the workplace. Any individual who plays a small role now will play a massive role when the struggle picks up. In the early 1970s the SWP had absolutely nothing in terms of roots in industry, but when the Pentonville dockers went to prison we decided to launch a paper for the docks. We had no dockers. We launched the *Dockworker* and amassed a circulation of 5,000. When the Pentonville Five came out of prison, three of them came and addressed a meeting we had called. We had three miners. In June 1972 I spoke in Barnsley to a meeting of over 100 miners, including a member of the national executive of the NUM, Tate, and a member of the Yorkshire executive, Arthur Scargill. We launched the *Collier* newspaper. We built over 50 factory branches, and big factory branches because the struggle was rising.

Now we are potentially at a much higher level. Capitalism is in a much deeper crisis than it was in the 1970s so the struggle will be much sharper and more political. We are also in a much better strategic position, because in the 1970s the rank and file was organised by the CP, which hardly exists today. Therefore we will be in a much better position when the upturn comes.

It is impossible to tell when that will come. It is absolutely correct to build on the assumption that the slow recuperation will continue. To exaggerate militancy now would be demoralising. But neither should we forget that history sometimes moves in jumps.

In 1933 I was totally depressed. Hitler had come to power in January 1933 and for 13 months life looked absolutely unbearable. Every day newspapers carried some horror story or other. Then in February 1934 the fascists overplayed their hand. It changed the whole situation in Paris and they were beaten by workers.

In 1968 around 10 million French workers went on strike. It was totally unexpected because the strike did not follow on from a growing wave. It was not like 1905 in Russia where you can see how the strikes rose, or Britain in 1972 and 1974. No, 1968 was a break in the continuity—there were right wing governments for many years, workers were on the retreat, the unions were very weak and, then, enough was enough. Because one student was murdered by police in Paris the whole thing burst.

So we have to work on the assumption that there is a slow cumulative recuperation, but if the thing bursts open then we will have to move fast.

Change is going to come: but how?

Socialist Review, June 1997

Many comparisons have been made between the Labour landslide in 1997 and the Labour landslide of 1945. There is a lot in common between the two, but there are also radical differences. Today there are massive illusions in the Tony Blair government among millions of people in Britain, but illusions are double-edged. They can paralyse activity and make people complacent, but they can also raise expectations that can, in the longer run, lead to much greater demands being made on the government. So it would be a mistake to assume that the illusions people have in Blair have only a negative impact.

In 1945 millions of workers voted Labour because they rejected completely the experience of Tory rule and mass unemployment of the 1930s. This resulted in a massive Labour majority of 146 seats. Spin doctors like Peter Mandelson did not exist at the time, and the fact that Clem Attlee was a small man, bald, with a croaky voice, did not affect the vote at all! Attlee's opponent was Winston Churchill, who was very popular as a hero of the war, but at the same time was identified in the eyes of millions with the unemployment of the 1930s. Therefore 1945 was a complete rejection of 30 years of Tory rule.

In 1997, again, the landslide was a result of the rejection by millions of 18 years of Tory rule. There is no question that it was overwhelmingly a class vote—a working class vote.

Both in 1945 and 1997 Labour voters voted for a radical change, and Attlee's government did carry out radical reforms. In the six years 1945-51 unemployment in Britain never passed a quarter of a million. Even as late as the 1987 election the Labour leadership promised to cut unemployment to 1 million. In 1992 they changed the formula, saying they would cut unemployment by 1 million as unemployment at the time was between 3 and 4 million. But now the only promise on unemployment is to cut youth unemployment by a quarter of a million.

The Attlee government also established the welfare state. In those years, despite the economic difficulties after the war, they built 200,000 council houses. In 1996 the total number of council houses built in Britain was only 6,000.

The National Health Service was established and was completely free. In 1950 the government imposed two shillings on prescriptions. Such was the commitment to a free health service that Nye Bevan, the secretary of state for health, Harold Wilson, the president of the board of trade, and John Freeman promptly resigned from the cabinet in protest.

Also in 1945 Labour promised a mixed economy, and Nye Bevan talked about the nationalisation of the commanding heights of the economy. In reality 20 percent of industry was nationalised—the railways, mines, gas and electricity. But this was still a capitalist government.

The Blair government hardly promises any reforms. He speaks a lot about 'new, new, new', although everything that characterises Blair is old, very old. For example, he says that Marxism is old and irrelevant while the market and the worship of the market is apparently something new. But in 1772 Adam Smith in the *Wealth of Nations* expressed the same ideas as Tony Blair, only much better. Blair's politics come from Hobbes—100 years ago. As for Blair's morality, it comes from 2,000 years back—so there is nothing new about him.

Compare Tony Blair's policies with John Smith's. Smith was on the right of the Labour Party. Smith promised that a coming Labour government would repeal all the Tory anti trade union laws, yet Blair is against amending any of these laws. In an article on 31 March in the *Times* he explained that the changes that 'we do propose would leave British law the most restrictive on trade unions in the Western world'.

Smith was for restoring those industries privatised under the Tories to public ownership. Blair is against any of that—in fact, he is even looking for new privatisations. On the question of taxing the rich, Smith was for the rich paying higher taxes—after all, the top rich people in Britain made £70,000 million extra as a result of changes in the tax rate under Thatcher and Major. In contrast, Tony Blair simply says, 'I want more people to become millionaires.'

Smith promised to restore the link between pensions and earnings. In 1981 Thatcher broke this link and instead linked pensions to the cost of living. If the system that existed in 1981 had continued today a single pensioner would get £24 a week more and a couple would get £38 more. Instead of this Tony Blair and Gordon Brown promise only one thing—to cut the VAT on fuel from 8 percent to 5 percent. This is good, but gives a pensioner only 35p a week extra.

One usual explanation given by Blair's apologists for his massive move to the right is that it was the way to win the vote. On the face of it this looks as if it worked. But when you start checking you find that the mass of the people in Britain are far to the left of Blair and his programme. For example, polls show that over 70 percent of people believe that the trade unions are too weak rather than too strong. Between 70 and 80 percent of people believe that the privatised public utilities should be renationalised. Only 11 percent are in favour of the privatisation of the railways. As many as 76 percent think there is a class struggle in this country. And 43 percent of the population and 61 percent of Labour voters believe there should be more socialist planning. Yet there is not one mass circulation paper that argues the case for socialist planning, or one radio station or television programme that refers to it, and still people have those thoughts in their heads.

Why is there a difference between the reformist zeal of Attlee and the conservative complacency of Blair? It is to do with the state of British capitalism. The Labour government of 1945-51 took place when capitalism was expanding more quickly than ever before. There was the long boom, with full employment, that started in 1939 with the outbreak of the war and continued for over 30 years. Tony Blair comes to office after 20 years and three recessions.

Over the last 20 years the total output of manufacturing industry in Britain rose by 1.66 percent (although the number of workers in manufacturing went down by a third). Twenty years ago manufacturing output in Britain rose by 86 percent—this level of growth leaves space both for the profit of the capitalist and reforms for the workers. The path to reform is open when capitalism is expanding, but when capitalism is stagnating the path to reform can only be opened by revolutionary struggle that challenges the whole capitalist system—this is certainly not what Tony Blair and the Labour Party stand for.

What will the fate of the Blair government be? The Attlee government, because it delivered reforms on a big scale, was very popular.

When Labour came to office in 1964, after 13 years of a Tory government, there was a period of honeymoon. First of all people did not expect very much from the new government because the Tory government of 1961-64 had been by and large part of the consensus between Labour and the Tories.

In 1964 Labour won the election by a majority of only four. Two years later, in 1966, Wilson went to the country and won a majority of around 100. Wilson went on the offensive only after the second election. He decided wages were rising too quickly and that there was a danger of inflation. He decided to have a showdown with a group of workers and picked on the seafarers. At the same time Wilson came out in open support of the US in the Vietnam War. This really marked the end of the honeymoon.

The Labour government of 1974-79 came in on the wave of the massive strikes that got rid of the Tories—the two miners' strikes of 1972 and 1974, the national dockers' strike, the freeing of the five dockers from Pentonville prison, the occupation of Upper Clyde Shipbuilders, and another 200 factory occupations. All this gave workers fantastic confidence that things really could not become worse, and Wilson and Callaghan would not dare to attack them. For a couple of years they didn't dare, but in 1977 there was a showdown. This time the government took on the firefighters and brought in the army to break the firefighters' strike. Then there were cuts in hospitals and cuts in real wages. When people talk about the Winter of Discontent of 1978-79 many don't remember what it was about. Denis Healey was chancellor at the time and decreed that no worker was allowed a wage rise of more than 5 percent, when prices were rising by 12-14 percent a year. So there was a massive confrontation with the government, but it took a number of years until the honeymoon ended.

What about today? Firstly, the expectations of the new government are much higher. At the same time there is a lot of goodwill towards Tony Blair. After all, we are at last out of the nightmare of 18 years of Tory rule. But it would be a mistake to speak simply about a honeymoon—this will be a honeymoon racked or intertwined with conflicts. There will be sharp contradictions right from the start. For example, Tony Blair has a majority of 179 in parliament, and the government is the biggest single shareowner of the Liverpool docks, owning 40 percent of the shares. Why doesn't Labour now restore the jobs to the 500 sacked Liverpool dockers?

Again, why is the government so mean when it comes to the National Health Service? Labour has adopted Major's spending plans for the NHS, providing real increases of 1.2 percent this year, 0.2 percent in 1998-99, and 0.1 percent the year after. The King's Fund health policy think-tank says the service probably needs more than 4 percent a year real increase in spending to show any benefit. Those figures don't mean very much to millions of people, but when it comes to the closure of a specific hospital the question will arise—why?

Tony Blair says 'education, education, education'. So why are teachers being sacked in further education colleges, and why is the management at Southwark College trying to get rid of lecturers? Why are Ofsted and Chris Woodhead still attacking teachers, and why are teachers being sacked in Ellen Wilkinson School in Manchester?

There are three levels of consciousness among workers at present—those workers who say they trust Blair, those who are worried about what Blair will deliver, and those who say they don't trust Blair. But the three categories overlap. The same workers who one day belong to the first category will, when it comes to a specific issue like the Liverpool dockers, move to the second category, and so on. The job of socialists is to relate to people who are in agreement with us 60 percent and who can, through activity and argument, come to agree with us 70 percent. The fact that people's consciousness can be split, that people can believe and disbelieve in Blair at the same time, is very important. We have to find common argument and action.

The Blair phenomenon opens the door to both common action and argument. Of course we don't know in advance when the tension between workers and the Blair government will arise—there are too many unknowns in the equation. We don't know what will happen in advance, but what we do know is that conflict will take place. This is because the ideological crisis in Britain is rooted in the fact that millions of workers want big change and Tony Blair refuses to fight for a change. This must create tensions although the form they will take cannot be predicted.

A number of factors will cause the end of the honeymoon, even if it is a tarnished honeymoon. The explosions will be much sharper than in the past. In the 1964-70 Labour government one of the strongest roles was played by Frank Cousins, leader of the Transport and General Workers' Union (TGWU), and a member of Wilson's cabinet. In the 1974-79 Labour government the most important leaders of the unions were Jack Jones, the general secretary of the TGWU, and Hugh Scanlon, the president of the AEU. Both were very much on the left of the trade union movement and both gave strong support to the government, playing a very important role at the time. In addition the Communist Party (CP) existed with something like 30,000 members, and with a big influence among the working class. They controlled the engineering shop stewards, the docks and the mining industry. They were very influential, and both led and contained struggle, which gave stability to the government.

Today there are no Frank Cousins, Jack Jones or Hugh Scanlons around. Union officials like Rodney Bickerstaffe have none of the weight or influence of the leaders of the 1960s and 1970s. The Communist Party has completely disappeared, with the events in Eastern Europe having damaged it massively.

In 1964 our predecessors, the IS, had something like 400 members. In 1974 we had 3,000 to 4,000 members, but we were 10 percent of the size of the CP and much weaker. Today we are in a much stronger position. This means there is a greater responsibility on us and much greater obligations.

Engels wrote that the class struggle takes place in three spheres—the economic, the political and the ideological. Of course between those three spheres there is a relationship, and they are not completely isolated from one another. But there is no mechanical relationship between them either. You may find that the economic and the class struggles can be at a very low level, but the ideological struggle can be very high.

If you look at the example of the Bolshevik Party in Russia, they led hundreds of thousands of workers in the insurrection in Moscow in December 1905, but the party was much smaller than it was in 1906 or 1907. The party grew more after the end of the revolution than in the revolution itself. The reason is simple. Tens of thousands joined the Bolshevik Party in 1906 because they learned the lessons of 1905. Of course this growth couldn't go on for ever. The party grew to 40,000 members, but then when the struggle continued to be at a very low level, when the counter-revolution was victorious, when thousands of workers were thrown into prison and sent to Siberia, the demoralisation spread among the party members, so by 1910 the membership had fallen to only 200.

So ideas cannot be completely separated from the economic base, but the ideas can develop in advance of the economic base for a time. This means that there can be growth in the size and influence of the revolutionary party even if the level of struggle is quite low. Of course at the end of the day there will be either levelling up or levelling down. Either industrial struggle will rise to the level of the ideas or the ideas will go down to the level of the struggle.

In workers' heads at present there are lots of contradictions. The hatred of the Tories means that workers will give Blair the benefit of the doubt. People can both support and feel unease about the leadership. For example, before the general election the NUJ conference met, with 100 delegates. We had four comrades there and they moved a document condemning Blair over his attitude to the unions. Out of 100 delegates, 90 signed the document, although no doubt all of these delegates voted Labour and were, like us, over the moon at the Labour victory.

But the contradictions that exist in the grey matter are less fundamental than those in the material world. To put it simply, because capitalism is in a deep economic crisis, in the final analysis this crisis will demonstrate the bankruptcy of reformism and show the need for a socialist alternative. What Labour does, even if it does not spark massive discontent immediately, can still produce an ideological questioning—as happened over the issue of denationalisation of the Bank of England. Questions about alternatives to the market, such as Marx versus the market, are ones we'll have to deal with again and again.

The period ahead is very promising for socialists and very challenging for the whole working class. People not only want change, they want a vision of a better society. As workers begin to question what Labour is doing in office it will raise an ideological debate inside the working class and inside the colleges. In that situation we can successfully build.

Index

Absenteeism: 199
AEU (AUEW): 70, 98, 99, 195, 369, 399
Airlie, (James) Jimmy (UCS, AUEW leader): 371
Aldermaston marches: 1, 17, 18
Alexander, Ken: 37
Algeria: 9
Alienation: 81, 132, 134, 137, 289
Anarchy of capitalist economy: 250
Anchor site (British Steel, Scunthorpe): 336
Anti Nazi League (ANL): 372
Anti trade union laws: 25, 27, 92-100, 110, 112, 121, 136, 140, 146, 149, 231-243, 281, 295, 301, 313, 340, 371, 396-397, 408, 418, 425, 427, 431, 438
   Australian experience: 237
   difficulty of enforcing: 234-237
   fines on unions: 98, 100, 234
   hard/soft strands of: 243
   officials jailed under: 237
   strikes against: 332, 413, 432
   Swedish experience: 238-239
Argentina: 49
Attlee, Clement (Labour prime minister): xix, 437
Australia
   dock strike (1968): 237
   Labour Party: 237
   mass strike: 237

Bakers: 369, 385
Balance of payments: 31, 44, 47-48, 51-53, 100, 301, 313
Bargaining
   formalisation of: 242
   informal: 242
   local: 138-139, 241, 271, 400, 411, 433

   national: 61-63, 65, 73, 79, 100, 111, 116, 138, 167-168, 192, 271, 277, 375, 431, 433
Benn, Tony: xxv
Bevin, Ernest (Labour cabinet minister): 5, 425
Betteshanger colliery strike (Kent, 1941): 235-237
Bickerstaffe, Rodney (NUPE leader): 441
Birch, Reg (AEU official): 23
Black Friday (1921): 6, 142
Blacklists: 393
Black workers: 371
Blair, Tony (Labour prime minister): xix, 437
Block vote: 426
BMC (British Leyland): 29, 77, 89, 135, 221, 432
Boilermakers Union: 166
Bonus rates: 89
Bray, Jeremy (Labour MP): 252
British capitalism, changes in: 28, 31, 423, 439
British Road to Socialism, The: 411
Broad Left: 410, 412-414
   declining: 413
   electoral machine: 411, 413
   relationship to shopfloor organisation: 411, 413
Brown, George (Labour deputy leader): 19, 23, 26, 35, 38, 42, 53-54, 63, 92
Building workers: 75, 196, 330, 336, 343, 346, 366, 369-370, 397
   shop stewards: 91, 280
   factory branch: 346
Bus
   industry: 99, 157, 195-196
   strikes: 66
   productivity deal: 163

workers: 14, 147, 159-160, 162, 164, 191, 262, 318n, 347-348, 354

Cadeby colliery (South Yorkshire): 409
Callaghan, James (Labour chancellor and prime minister): 40, 371, 390, 415, 435
Campaign for Nuclear Disarmament (CND): xix, 18, 20
Cannon, Les (ETU leader): 70, 263, 273, 300
Capital
  appreciation: 39-41
  concentration/centralisation of: 86, 102-103, 105, 110, 123, 146, 224-225, 298, 334
  gains tax: 40-41
  integration into state: 105, 126
Capitalist
  competition: 123
  crisis (boom/slump): 12, 124, 134, 410, 417, 419, 425, 436, 439, 441
  ideology: 6, 414-415
  planning: 26, 28-29, 32, 35, 42, 54, 105, 113, 125-127
Car
  industry: 37, 95-96, 113, 170, 234, 253, 295, 297, 431
  productivity deal: 175, 180, 183
  shop stewards: 88
  strikes: 76-77, 89, 95, 197, 285-286, 462
  workers: 79, 88, 94, 190-191, 198, 360, 373, 405, 432
  factory branch: 345
Carberry, Joe (TGWU): 418
Carron, Lord (AEU leader): 99, 99, 278
Car Worker: 333
Castle, Barbara: xxiii, 139, 233, 240, 337
Catherwood, Fred (employers' leader): 61
Check-off system (see also closed shop): 272
Chemical industry: 55, 60, 83, 157, 252
  productivity deal: 180
  shop stewards: 177
  workers: 62, 191
Chrysler-Rootes (car makers): 29, 154, 215, 330, 350, 396
Civil and Public Service Union (CPSA): 383
Civil service: 272
Class consciousness: 416
Class struggle
  economic, political and ideological levels: 441
  need to link immediate to anti-capitalist: 419
Clause 4: 20, 56, 411
Clegg committee, 1979 (low pay): 387
Closed shop: 95-96, 99, 120, 178, 192, 243, 272, 391, 396

used to discipline rank and file: 272
Collections (strike solidarity): 90, 394-395, 424, 435
Collier: 333, 337
Collieries
  Armthorpe: 377
  Annesley: 377
  Betteshanger: 235-237
  Cadeby: 409
  Gedling: 377
  Grimethorpe: 401
  Maltby: 377
Combination laws (1801-02): 24
Combine committees (see also shop stewards committees): 88-90, 135, 150, 280, 291, 301, 342
  weakness of: 290-291
Common Market (EEC): 28, 332
Communist Party (France): 132
Communist Party of Great Britain: 11, 20n, 68
  factory branches: 343, 366, 411
  position undermined: 140
  rank and file mobilisation: 413
  role in shopfloor organisation: 410, 432, 436, 441
  seeks to influence/win union positions: 140, 411
  support for left officials: 399
Confederation of British Industry (CBI): 155, 199
Conway, Jim (AEU leader): 139, 263
Concorde (aircraft): 249
Convenors (and senior stewards): 370-371, 406, 433
  collaborate with management: 371
  distance from rank and file: 405
  effect of being full time: 404-405
  integration into management structures: 407
  integration into union machine: 399
  numbers of: 405
  provide union bureaucracy with base: 370
Cooling-off periods: 97, 321n, 397
Cooper, Lord (GMWU leader): 270
Corfield, Tony (TGWU leader): 275
Cousins, Frank (TGWU leader): 14, 140, 440
Coventry Blue Book: 170-173
Cox, Roger (AEU): xxi, 404
Cripps, Sir Stafford (Labour Party politician): 23, 33
Craft restrictions: 194

Daly, Lawrence (NUM leader): 281, 321n
Deakin, Arthur (TGWU leader): 13, 69, 276
Dean, Brenda (SOGAT leader): 429

Deflation: 33, 152, 223

De Gaulle, Charles (French president): 32

Delacourt, Lord (Charles Smith, POE leader): 158

Demarcation (of trades): 155, 207, 265
(see also skilled/unskilled workers)

Denning, Lord, 398-399

Deskilling: 155

Desoutter strike (1978): 395

Devlin report: 151, 377

Differentials: 308

Dividends to shareholders: 39-40, 42, 48, 255

Do it yourself reformism: see reformism from below

Dock Labour Board: 198

Dockworker: 337, 361

Docks: 221, 253-254, 327n, 392, 397
liaison committee: 291
productivity deal: 180, 297
strikes: 76, 198, 333-334, 369, 378-383, 408, 439
workers: 7-8, 66, 75, 91, 165, 198, 260, 262, 264, 284, 291, 295-296, 331, 338, 373, 377-380, 384, 397, 401-402, 408, 431-432, 438, 440-441

Donovan commission (1965): 156, 162, 193, 231, 241, 267, 400

Douras, Tommy (TGWU): 418

Downturn in class struggle: 370, 379, 431-432
reasons for: 399

Draughtsmen: 163, 217

Dromey, Jack (TGWU): 434

Dunlop rubber company: 36

Dustmen: 262, 294, 303, 403
strike (1971): 369

Economic struggle
role of: 293
relation to political: 416, 433

Economist: xix, 40, 66, 432

Education (Marxist): 365-367

Electrical industry: 37-38, 51, 55, 60, 83, 94, 116, 158, 161, 217, 400, 411, 438

Electricians: 65-66, 161, 207, 371, 432

Electricity supply: 83, 87, 157, 160, 162, 184, 220, 273, 295, 336, 373

Electrical Trades Union (ETU): 70, 87, 195, 211, 323n

Employers' offensive: 145-146, 156, 294-295, 305, 311, 395-396

Employers support union leaders against rank and file: 279

Engineering Employers' Federation (EEF): 41, 148, 193, 209, 395

Engineering industry: 31, 37, 51, 55, 60, 96,

110, 158, 254, 325n, 380-383

Engineers: 9, 17, 61-62, 65, 73-75, 89, 91, 110, 162, 200, 242, 273, 277, 279, 291, 324n, 338, 369, 371, 384, 408, 431, 441
earnings: 167-168, 380-382
lockout (1922): 142
importance of tea breaks: 190
shop stewards: 79, 87, 91

ENV (Acton): 395

Esso (Fawley and Milford Haven): 86, 147, 153, 157

Etheridge, Dick (TGWU convenor British Leyland Longbridge): 405

European Free Trade Area (EFTA): 28

Evans, Moss (TGWU leader): 281

Exley, Pete (NUM): 401

Export of capital: 48-52

Factory branches: 339-367
Communist Party: 343, 366, 411
difficulty of building: 347
how and when to form: 351-352
innovation for revolutionary socialists: 339
links socialists to majority of workers: 340
main tasks of: 339-340
meetings of: 340, 349
must promote rank and file papers: 358
names of (Albion Motors, BSC Consett, CA Parsons, CAV Acton, Copper Pass Hull, Coventry BL, Chrysler Ryton, Doncaster-Monkbridge Leeds, Edinburgh building workers, Leeds hospital workers, London hospital workers, Merseyside building workers, Oxford hospitals, Reyrolles Hebburn, Rowntrees York, Scottish and Newcastle Breweries, Standard Triumph, Teesside Steel, Woodheads, Ossett, York bus workers): 342-349
needs membership secretary: 351
organises vanguard of class: 340
political education: 349
relation with other IS bodies: 352-354, 360-361
relation with rank and file organisations: 357-359
to win leadership of the factory: 341
trades councils: 359
unites socialists and militants: 340
versus industrial branches: 343-347
work in trade unions: 347-348, 359

Factory bulletins: 340-342, 349, 361-365
advice on summarised: 365
aim to win workers to revolutionary socialism: 362

hated by supervisors and management: 363
written by IS and sympathisers in factory: 364
Factory occupations: 135, 369, 385, 388-389, 403-404, 431, 439
'Fair day's work for fair day's pay': 259-260
Fascism: 142, 412, 436
Feather, Victor (TUC leader): 278, 337
Fenn, Mickey (dock worker): 377-378, 380
Ferranti (electronics firm): 49
Financial Times: 66, 120n
Fine Tubes strike (1970-73): 331, 392
Firefighters: 187, 294-295, 385, 390
    productivity deal: 186-187
Fire service: 186-188
Flexibility: 156, 158, 179-201, 208, 306, 375
Ford: 87-89, 135, 201-203, 215, 385
    job evaluation: 203-205
France
    general strike (1968): 129, 131, 134, 136, 436
    Communist Party: 130, 132, 134
    fragmentation of class: 132
    privatisation: 132
    rank and file: 130
    revolutionary organisations: 131
    revolutionary press: 131-132
    strength of reformism: 132
    strike committees: 130-131
    trade unions: 131
Full employment: 31, 33, 35, 103, 113, 124, 137, 142, 172, 439

Gaitskell, Hugh (Labour Party leader): 3, 15, 18
Gas industry: 370, 438
Geddes, Bill: 383
General Strike (1926): 8, 17, 75-76, 106, 109, 135, 191, 285, 336, 373, 392, 424
    labour leadership attitude to: 5
    miners' defeat: 142
General strike threat from TUC (1972): 408, 431
Generalisation (see also labour movement)
    created by anti-Tory feeling: 370, 372
German Ideology, The (Karl Marx): 414
Germany: 32, 188
Gilliat, Phil: 417
Gormley, Joe (NUM leader): 336, 443
Go-slows: 75, 285
Govan shipyards (Glasgow): 79, 376
Grading: 304
    schemes (see job evaluation)
Grievance procedures: 177-179, 205
Griffiths, Peter (Tory MP): 110

Grimethorpe colliery: 401
Grunwick strike (1977): 392-394
Gunter, Ray (Labour Party leader): 95, 183
Green, Sidney (NUR leader): 270

Hardie, Keir (Labour Party leader): 2, 6
Hargreaves, Leonard (victimised Sheffield engineer): 90, 119n, 293, 326n
Hattersley, Roy (Labour Party deputy leader): 428
Healey, Dennis (Labour Party deputy leader): 50, 439
Health: 258, 438, 440
Health and safety: 177, 217, 249, 281, 305, 309-310, 412
Heath, Edward (Tory prime minister): xix, 330, 337, 370
Henderson, Arthur (Labour Party leader): 4
Hill, Ted (Boilermakers' Union leader): 13-14
Holidays: 245, 247-248, 306, 308, 312
Horner, John (FBU leader): 19
Hospital workers: 272, 344, 369, 371, 383
Housing: 249-250, 258, 437
Hughes, John (academic): 37

Ideological offensive: 244, 313, 418, 440
Immigration: 110, 348, 358
Imperial Chemical Industries (ICI): 12, 29, 48, 135, 149-156, 177, 201, 210
Incentive schemes: 87-88, 433
Incomes policy: 23, 25, 28, 53-54, 57-58, 63, 80, 110, 119, 121, 136, 140, 146, 262, 295, 313, 324n, 329, 337, 369-370, 376, 385-386, 399-400, 402, 407-408, 413, 434
    as alternative to reserve army of unemployed: 33-34
    as wage restraint: 35-43, 65, 100, 145
    failure to stem wage rises: 147, 151-153
    generalising effect of: 137-138
    international phenomenon: 151
    linked to anti-union laws: 92, 100, 231
    prepares way for productivity deals: 151, 153
Industrial Relations Act (1971): 369, 408
Industrial Relations Court: 233, 377
Industrial Reconstruction Corporation: 224
Inflation: 15, 30, 32, 34-35, 45, 47, 93, 100, 108, 145, 152, 165, 301, 313, 331-332, 387, 415-416, 439
Injunctions: 233-234
'In Place of Strife': xxiii, 233, 337, 373
International competition: 28, 30-32, 100, 105, 123, 146, 189, 225
International Harvesters (Doncaster): 208
International Socialists (IS): xx, 327n, 333, 337, 373

factory branches compared with
    Communist Party factory branches: 343
must fight to be stewards: 341
trade union fractions: 355, 360-361
work in unions: 347-348
Investment pattern: 28, 30, 43-45, 48, 50-51,
    56, 105, 250, 252-253

Japan: 32
Jeffreys, Steve: xxv
Jenkins, Clive (ASTMS leader): 140
Job evaluation: 231, 307
    an attack on workers' control: 209
    biased towards management: 205-207
    central to productivity deals: 207
    how to respond to: 206-207, 209-210
    leads to divide and rule: 207-208
    types of: 202
    United States: 209
Jones, Aubrey (Tory politician): 58, 66, 151,
    386
Jones, Gerry (TGWU): 406
Jones, Jack (TGWU leader): xix, 140, 331,
    336, 373, 399
    and Scanlon as example of left leaders: 282
Joseph Lucas (motor components): 157
Journalists: 369, 385, 389 398-399

Keep Left (Young Socialist paper): 19
Kenya: 9
Kinnock, Neil (Labour Party leader): 425, 428
Kirkwood, David (Clydeside Labour MP): 4
Korea: 9

Labour aristocracy: 10
Labour governments
    1924: 4, 425
    1929-31: 5, 425
    1945-51: 14, 59, 103, 437
    1964-70: 37, 41, 51, 92, 100, 112, 126, 153,
        223, 276, 281, 385, 434, 439-440
    1974-79: 369-371, 385-386, 415, 418, 434,
        439
    1997-2001: 437, 440
Labour movement: 1, 100, 102, 106-109, 442
    attack leads to generalisation: 147, 294,
        419
    crisis of leadership: 417
    fragmentation of: 18, 86, 90-91, 109-111,
        132, 134-135, 138, 141-142, 331, 369,
        417
    generalisation in: 110, 135, 138, 140-141,
        333-334, 416, 432, 435
    growth of solidarity: 294
    history of: 2

ideological crisis of: 414-416
loyalty to Labour: 127, 369, 372, 415
move to right in: 425
narrowness of outlook: 91
political apathy: 109, 125, 132, 299
stages in development of: 431
volatility: 332
in Western Europe: 332
Labour Party: 1-20, 37, 426-427, 432
    history of: 2, 7, 10
    leadership: 1, 3, 5-6, 9, 16, 224, 441
    membership of: 107, 132
    rank and file supporters: 1-2, 17, 126
    vote: 6, 107, 425
    youth: 11
Labour Representation Committee: 2
Labour/Tory consensus: 233-234, 439
Lee, Willie (AEU): 376, 406
Lenin, Vladimir Ilyich: 9, 135, 338
Lever, Harold (Labour MP): 336
Lib-Labism: 1
Light, Bob (TGWU): 379-380
Local government workers: 371
Local to national disputes, drift from: 408
Lockouts: 142, 388, 390, 396
London busmen: 159
London Transport Garage, Acton strike
    (1969): 395
Lorry drivers: 91, 199, 291, 295-296, 336,
    369, 385, 390
Luxemburg, Rosa: 293
Lyddon, Dave: 404

MacDonald, Ramsay (Labour prime
    minister): 3, 6, 425
McGahey, Mick (NUM leader): 410
Malaya: 9
Management control of piece-work: 172-174
Mandelson, Peter: 437
Marx, Karl: 33, 111, 190
May 1968 (France): 129
Measured day work (MDW): 145, 167-180,
    186, 217, 210, 221, 229, 294, 297, 304-306,
    342, 433
    defined: 174
    reduces power of shop stewards: 175
Media (capitalist): 81, 99, 112, 149, 244, 313,
    334, 336, 389, 416
Message, Bill: 414
Middle class: 107-109
Militant (RSL paper): 428
Militants, gap with rank and file workers: 337
Miners: 12, 56, 68, 70, 75, 105-106, 162, 236,
    272, 284, 295, 298, 331, 336, 371, 373,
    376-377, 384, 409, 414-415, 424, 436

break incomes policy: 376
strike (1969): 294
strike (1972): 332, 334, 336, 369, 439
strike (1974): 369, 410, 432, 439
strike (1984-85): 424, 428, 430, 433
strikes: 76, 81, 135, 142, 191, 235-236,
    285, 335, 388, 413, 415
Miners' Union: 281-282
    officials not trusted: 176-177
    weakened by productivity deal: 176
Mining industry
    job evaluation in: 201, 227
    measured day work in: 174
    power loading agreement: 162, 174, 176,
        401
    penalty clauses in: 198
Ministry of Labour: 97
Mobil Oil (Coryton): 147
Mond-Turner talks: 416
Montague, Ken: 402-404
Moore, George (bus worker): 262
MUPS (Manpower Utilisation and Payment
    System): 149
Murdoch, Rupert: 424
Murphy, J T: 269
Mutuality: 217, 305-308

National Association of Local Government
    Officers (NALGO): 108, 383
National Board for Prices and Incomes: 38,
    93, 105, 145-151, 160
National Coal Board (NCB): 409
National Economic Development Council
    (Neddy): 105
National Graphical Association (NGA): 163,
    398, 427
National Incomes Commission (NIC): 38
'National interest': 244, 255-256, 295, 415-
    416
National Union of Journalists: 398
National Union of General and Municipal
    Workers (also GMWU): 387, 406
National Union of Mineworkers (NUM): 76,
    281, 410, 413, 433, 436
National Union of Railwayworkers
    [RAILWAYMEN?—PW]: 195
National Union of Teachers (NUT): 383
National Union of Vehicle Builders: 195
National Plan: 26, 51, 54
National Power Loading Agreement (1966):
    174-176
Nationalisation: 14, 48-49, 119, 415, 438
Nationalised industry: 14
'New Realism': 425, 435
New Unions (1889): 7

Nicholas, Harry (TGWU leader): 277
'No redundancy' demand: 303
North, Dick (NUT): 417
No-strike deals: 375-376, 425
Nuclear bomb (see also CND): 125
Nurses: 91, 291, 435

Official strikes: 90, 93, 97, 108, 139, 208, 234,
    285, 332-333, 337, 379
Oil refineries: 83, 157-158, 252
Oppression: 92
Overtime: 75, 83-85, 89, 135, 138, 156, 186,
    197, 229, 241, 285, 308, 310, 376

Pace of work: 194, 241
Paish, Professor F W: 34, 330
Parliamentarism: see reformism from above
Parliamentary democracy: 10
Partnership: 241, 243, 295, 313, 371
    joint union/management courses: 263
Paynter, Will (NUM leader): 321
Penalty clauses/labour discipline: 195-200,
    311
    impact on strikes: 197, 200
Pensions: 56, 91, 97, 103-104, 110-111, 125,
    227, 245, 291, 336, 338, 438
Pentonville: xxiii, 329, 336, 369
Permanent arms economy: 10, 34, 113, 133-
    134, 142
Pessimism of the intellect, optimism of the
    will: 425
Picketing (see also scabbing): 334, 336, 342,
    370, 385, 394, 398, 410, 425
    respect of picket lines: 417-418
Piece-rate: 25, 74, 88, 99, 138, 167, 169-172,
    175, 177, 179-200, 210, 221, 241, 277, 294,
    297, 302, 305, 316n, 326n, 370, 379, 400,
    411, 433
    as weapon of employers: 171-172
    different rates divide workers: 298
Political strikes: 135, 388
Political struggle: 416
Political power, question of: 138
Politics/economics, relationship of: 7-9, 105,
    416, 433
Poll tax: 434
Pompidou, Georges (French prime minister):
    129
Post Office Engineers (POE): 158-159, 162,
    294
Postal workers: 187, 330, 332, 336, 370, 393,
    435
Port Shop Stewards Committee: 333
Poverty: 105-106, 110, 249, 258-259, 314
Prentice, Reg (Labour then Tory MP): 337

Pressed Steel Fisher: 29, 182
Prevailing ideas are ruling class ideas: 414
Prevost, Eddie (TGWU dock worker): 401
Price control: 100, 301, 313
Prices (see inflation)
Printers: 70, 163, 165, 260, 265-267, 334,
    374, 408, 424, 426, 429, 431, 434
Privatisation: 132, 435, 438, 442
Production for profit or use: 244, 261
Productivity deals (see also flexibility,
    individual industries, measured day work,
    shift work, penalty clauses, 'restrictive
    practices', strategy for resisting productivity
    deals, tea breaks, time and motion study):
    83, 137, 138, 147, 166, 260, 262, 329, 370-
    371, 376, 399, 400, 402, 410
  brings in time and motion study: 210
  brought in by threat of redundancy: 220-
    223, 229
  causes unemployment: 226-230
  danger of workers disunity: 298
  designed to weaken shop stewards'
    influence: 145, 156, 177-180
  end job and earnings security: 182
  enhances role of supervisors: 176
  enhances role of union officials: 178
  formal character: 242-243
  generalises workers' experience: 299
  gives management control over workers:
    175-177, 223, 241-242
  ideological implications: 244-261
  key decisions made elsewhere: 125-126
  long time to implement: 153
  main components of: 155
  no-redundancy pledges: 226-227, 229-230
  non-wage benefits lost: 161
  numbers and sections affected: 148, 386
  part of employers' offensive: 145, 149, 295
  partial productivity deals: 157
  provokes greater militancy: 294, 313
  raises issue of wealth distribution: 260
  reverses normal wage negotiations: 296
  shift from piece-work: 85
  soft option alternative to class struggle:
    145, 153, 165, 262, 264-265, 283
  as thin end of the wedge: 200
  union officials' intervention encouraged: 139
  United States model: 283-284
  wage rises associated with: 83-84, 154, 156-
    161, 165, 196, 296, 300, 310-311, 387
  wage rises loses through inflation: 145
  workers' shopfloor unionism: 145
Profits: 48
  nature of: 35-38
  relation to investment: 43-44

Public/private sectors: 56, 59 (see also
    nationalisation/ privatisation)

Racism: 110, 138, 343, 353-354, 358, 363,
    367, 418
Railway industry: 56, 157-158, 211, 220, 438
Rail workers: 63, 65-66, 110, 131, 272-273,
    285, 332, 336, 374, 390, 397, 434-435
Rank and file
  acting independently of stewards: 342
  confidence: 432
  committees: 288
  control: 305, 418
  independence: 282-283
  initiative: 305, 410
  leadership: 304
  movement: 101, 112, 281, 333, 346, 372
    (see also shop stewards' movement)
  nature of: 359
  need for control of unions: 301, 314, 337,
    359
  need for socialist ideas: 418
  newspapers: 337, 340, 346-347, 355, 357,
    360, 366-367
    and strikes: 357-358
  organisations: 301, 358, 411, 413-414, 417
    linking workplaces together: 337
  potential power of: 281, 337, 410
  response to productivity deals: 284
Rank and File Teacher: 333
Rate of exploitation: 161-166, 259-260
Rationalisation: 220, 223-226, 265
    (see also capitalist concentration)
Red Friday (1921): 5
Red Tape (civil service paper): 16
Redundancy (see also unemployment): 208-
    209, 226, 327n, 341, 415
Reformism: 9-11, 17, 19, 27, 104, 132, 141,
    442
  conditions for granting of: 102
  from below: 103-104, 107, 111, 142
  in decline: 140
  parliamentary (from above): 6, 12, 101-106,
    111, 123-124, 126-127, 140, 276, 439
  prevailing ideology in working class: 18, 134
  through official union channels: 103
Regional development grants: 252-253
Reserve army of unemployed (see also
    unemployment): 33, 102-103, 124, 171
Restrictive practices: 83-86, 119, 172, 191-
    193, 288
  examples of: 192
  socialist attitude to: 193-195
Right to Work Campaign: 308, 333
Revolution: 426

need for: 10
Revolutionary
    alternative needed: 442
    movement: 111, 132, 134, 140, 149, 358
        need for: 314
    newspaper (see also *Socialist Worker*): 337-338
        tasks of: 141, 417
        weakness of: 339
    organisation
        as a union of factory branches: 339
        depends on working class initiative: 140-141, 337
    party: 333-334, 358, 418, 428, 430
        has no rank and file: 350, 366
        relationship to class struggle: 429
        strategy: 28, 101, 142, 146-147, 419, 440
        need for network linking workplaces: 436
        need for workers' offensive: 295
        needed on shopfloor: 417
    socialism, prospects for: 102, 129, 141-143
Revolutionary Communist Party (1940s): 11
Revolutionary socialist ideas: 9, 11-12, 134
Right to Work Campaign (1970s): 372
Roberts Arundel strike (1966-67): 272, 392-393
Robertson, Ann (hospital worker): 418
Robertson, Jack: 412-413
Robinson, Derek (TGWU convenor British Leyland Longbridge): 404-407
Royal Commission on Trades Unions (1964): 92, 94
Rolls-Royce (Hillingdon and Derby): 208, 387
Ronan Point disaster: 249
Russell, Bertrand: 19
Russian Revolution (1905): 132, 436, 441
    strikes: 130, 133
    reform through revolution: 133
    revolutionary press: 131
    wages during: 133

Sacking of strikers: 392
Saltley coke works (1972): 336, 415
Sanderson strike: 417
Scabbing: 7-8, 14, 92, 221, 371, 392, 432-434
Scamp commission on low pay (1979): 387
Scanlon, Hugh (AEU leader): xix, 140, 281, 370, 373, 399, 432, 440
Scargill, Arthur (NUM leader): 410, 436
Scientific management: 214
Seafarers: 7-8, 272, 434, 439
Secondary industrial action: 398
Sectionalism: 38, 296, 299, 370, 424
Selwyn Lloyd (Tory chancellor): 23, 151, 223, 370

Shares: 39-41
Shift work: 156, 183-184, 265, 303-304, 309, 327n, 348-350, 364, 367
    physical and psychological effects: 187-189
    trade union and socialist attitude: 189
Shipbuilding industry: 44, 158, 196, 211, 220, 229, 235, 373-376
Shipyard workers (see also UCS): 75, 273, 371, 373, 384, 431, 439
    productivity deal: 175
Shonfield, Andrew (economist): 49
Shopfloor democracy (see workers' control)
Shopfloor organisation (see shop stewards organisation)
Shop stewards (see also individual industries, labour movement, shop stewards organisation): 17, 20, 23-25, 27, 107, 150, 341, 363
    becoming isolated from members: 120, 342, 402
    committees: 1, 24, 72, 86, 88, 101, 112, 139, 142, 150, 288, 301-2, 308, 333, 394
        during Second World War: 90, 119, 283, 293, 326n
    courses for: 211
    drawn into negotiating productivity deals: 155
    election of: 80, 107, 271
    express desire for workers' control: 288
    facility time, etc, provided for: 231, 292, 342, 401 (see also convenors)
    historical background: 79, 90
    incorporation by management: 292, 295, 401
    incorporation by trade union machine: 146, 231, 283, 342, 400
    informal rights of: 242
    key point of contact with union: 272, 292
    losing role of local wage negotiators: 139
    movement: 90-91, 112, 119, 121, 418, 432
    national conferences of: 87, 279-280
    need for coordination of activities: 290
    not more militant than their members: 120, 342, 402
    numbers of: 288
    power of: 85-86, 232, 370-371
    power under attack: 83-84, 111-112, 140, 146, 149, 175, 216, 235, 299, 400, 433
Shop stewards' organisation: 27, 82, 91, 101, 134, 137, 139, 171-172, 180, 200, 242-243, 284, 380, 410-411, 424, 431
    narrow horizons: 291, 293
    role of: 67, 80, 411, 431
    relationship to socialist movement: 91
    strengths and weaknesses: 27, 86-92, 101,

290-294
United States: 139
unofficial strikes: 73, 288-289
weakened by 1979: 392, 400, 402-404, 424
workers' control: 84
Single-union deals: 424
Sims, Lionel: 261
Skilled workers: 7, 64-65, 102, 121, 124, 150, 167-169, 181-183, 266, 374
Slump (1930s) (see also unemployment): 10, 26, 106, 142, 417, 437
Smethwick by-election (1964): 110, 139
Smillie, Robert (Miners' Federation leader): 4
Smith, John (Labour Party leader): 438
Snowdon, Philip: 6
Social Democratic Federation (SDF): 2
Social Contract: xix, 370
Social wage (see welfare)
Socialism: 83, 311, 418
self-emancipation of workers: 111-112
workers' control: 290
Socialist
consciousness: 136, 301
planning: 26, 100
strategy (see revolutionary socialist strategy)
Socialist League (1930s): 11
Socialist Review Group: xx
Socialist Worker: 337
Socialist Workers Party (see International Socialists)
Socialists: 109, 111, 117, 244
influence on strikes: 370
must despise but respect enemy: 424
must raise issue of exploitation: 260-261
realism of: 429
Society of Graphical and Allied Technicians (SOGAT): 266, 398
Soviets: 130, 426
Speed-up: 74, 82, 94, 139, 210, 215-220, 277, 329
causes accidents: 217-219
consequence of productivity deals: 215
effect on staffing 215
psychological effect: 218
Staffing levels: 158, 194, 216, 241, 288, 306, 389
State: 34, 104-106, 137, 295, 313
integration with capitalist class: 32, 136
supports capitalism: 220, 256-258
Steel industry: 29, 55, 252
union: 323n
unions and redundancy: 267-268
productivity deal: 181-182, 190, 220
workers: 184, 219, 273, 349, 363, 390,

434
Steel industry Green Book: 190, 215
Steelworker: 337
Sterling crisis: 51, 53, 125, 332
Stop-go economic policy: 31, 223, 239, 250, 252
Strategy for fighting productivity deals: 146
conditions: 311
demands to place on unions: 301-302, 313
depends on specific circumstances: 299-300
discipline: 311
fight even after introduction: 312-313
fighting from within: 304-305
find demands that overcome sectionalism: 296
first stage demands: 302-304
flexibility: 306-307
health and safety: 309
job evaluation: 307-308
measured day work: 306
mobility of stewards: 307
mutuality: 306
need to educate rank and file: 300
need for fight against incomes policy and anti-union laws: 313
need for offensive: 299-302
need for rank and file initiative: 303
need for socialist policies: 301, 313
procedure: 311
redundancy: 308-309
shift work: 309
staffing levels: 306
start by opposing: 300
tea breaks: 310-311
time and motion: 307
wages: 311
workers' control: 306, 313
Strikes (see also individual industries): 15, 81, 95, 109, 133, 174, 335, 373
defensive: 389
express desire for workers' control: 288-289
express rebellion against system: 137, 289
figures: 9, 74-76, 285-288, 335, 371, 415
'Kill The Bill': 408
pattern of: 284, 388
relation to revolution: 135-136
Students: 135-136, 140-141, 435
Supervisors: 27, 82, 85, 176-177, 179, 182, 242, 363-364, 432
Sysiphus, labour of: 91
Swan Hunters shipyard: 46, 196, 371, 376, 466
Sweden: 238, 240, 321n
Swedish strikes: 238-239
Syndicalism: 81, 138-140

Taff Vale (1901): 8
Taxation: 256
Taylor, Frederick Winslow: 214
Teachers: 295, 369, 435
Technology, impact of: 15, 29-30, 103, 124, 146, 265, 300
Textiles: 60, 74-75, 284, 374
Time and motion study: 145, 156, 174, 186, 200-201, 210-220, 262-263, 294, 307
   biased towards management: 212-214
   dangers of: 214-215
   definition of: 212
   union attitude to: 210-211
Time rates: 85, 169
Thomas, J H (Labour politician): 4
Thorneycroft, Peter (Tory chancellor): 47
Titmus, Richard (academic): 103
Tillett, Ben (dockers' leader): 3
Todd, Ron (TGWU leader): 425
Tolpuddle Martyrs: 337
Tories
   attack on working class: 329
   governments: 14, 68
Trade union consciousness: 12, 136
Trade unions: 7, 93, 146, 233
   activists: 261
   apathy towards: 72, 299
   branches: 72, 80, 271-272, 351, 353, 367
   continental Europe: 33
   democracy: 273-275, 358
   density (comparison of): 374
   disciplining members: 98, 149, 195, 198, 279-280, 331
   elections: 360
   enforcing procedure: 73-75, 277, 324n
   fail to fight redundancy: 265-268
   increasing bureaucratisation: 70-72, 132, 271, 283
   increasing centralisation: 67, 72, 271
   integration with state: 69, 100-101, 105-106, 132, 138, 140, 146-147, 239, 295, 313
   link to labour: 12-16, 71, 276, 426
   membership: 8-9, 106-107, 391-392
   popular support for: 418
   procedure: 73-75, 277-278, 310
   rank and file: 68, 72-73, 80, 93, 98, 413, 418, 435
   rank and file/revolutionary party, interrelation of: 333
   recognition: 139, 268, 389, 392, 395, 417
   resilience of: 424
Trade union bureaucracy: 1, 13, 16, 19, 27, 67-72, 90, 106, 112, 134, 138, 261-284, 295, 331, 370, 372, 418, 427, 432, 435, 441

   ambivalent attitude of: 138-139, 268-271
   fears rank and file struggle: 138
   hold on mass movement: 435
   impotence of: 280-281
   support for incomes policy: 92
   treachery of: 336-337, 409, 417
   wish to control stewards: 277-280
Trade union officials (see also trade union bureaucracy): 15, 27, 70, 85, 93, 117, 138, 150, 235, 273, 301, 323n, 362, 371, 405, 414, 432
   act as unpaid supervisors: 96, 243
   collaborate with management: 407
   control national strikes: 69-74, 370
   criticise employers for conceding to rank and file: 278
   high salaries of: 270
   left wing: 117, 140, 239, 261, 282, 324n, 366, 370, 399, 407-410, 413-414, 432, 440
   make scabbing respectable: 371
   numbers of: 283
   substitute for workers' self-activity: 281-282
   social status: 71, 269-271, 277
   support productivity deals: 149, 262-265, 268, 283, 327n
   right wing: 72, 117, 140, 146, 239-240, 261-262, 407, 409, 433
   smash rank and file organisation: 407
   urge to control stewards: 283
   unelected: 273-274
Trades Disputes Act (1906): 8
Trades councils: 18, 271, 347, 351, 353-355, 357, 359, 403
Trades Union Congress (TUC): 16, 45, 70, 239
Transport and General Workers Union (TGWU): 98-99, 261, 379, 399, 440
Transport workers: 187
Tribune: xix, 321
Trotsky, Leon: 10, 20n, 142.

Unemployment (see also slump): 6, 8-9, 15, 17, 66, 79, 104-106, 113, 220, 223, 244, 249, 251-253, 267, 280, 291, 329-230, 343-344, 370, 376, 409, 415-417, 437
   dampens struggle: 370
   international: 34
Unilever: 48
University College Hospital strike (1993): 435
Unofficial strikes (see also individual industries, strikes): 24, 27, 73-78, 85, 92-95, 99, 101, 107, 110-111, 137, 142, 196,

229, 285, 336-337, 363, 407, 410, 413, 435
anti-union legislation: 97-98, 101, 234
decline in: 433
Donovan commission: 232
duration of: 78
express strength of shopfloor organisation: 284
as proportion of official strikes: 285, 432, 435
in Sweden: 238-239
Unskilled workers: 7, 64-65, 102, 110, 121, 124, 150, 182-183, 208, 266
Upper Clyde Shipbuilders (UCS): 175, 229, 371, 373-374, 431
Upturn: 431

Vassall, Gordon (FBU): 418
Victimisation: 357-359, 363-364, 389
Vietnam War: xix

Wage drift: 61-63, 65, 79, 100, 116, 138-139, 161, 167-171, 288, 374, 381, 383, 431
Wage freeze/control: 260-261, 276, 331, 409, 415, 418, 434
Wage-price spiral: 34-35, 45, 152, 415
Wages (see also bargaining, bonus, incentives, overtime, piece-rates, time-rates): 25-26, 35, 40, 42, 53, 61-67, 72, 109, 142, 311, 332, 423
cuts: 329-330, 439
effect of productivity deals on: 162
how rises are won: 63, 100
international comparison: 45-46, 133, 245-246
key settlements: 66-67, 94, 330
motivation for claims: 82
nature of: 35-37
patterns over time: 385-388
relationship to profits: 43, 55, 57-58, 100, 329
Walsh, Stephen (Labour minister, 1924): 4
Wapping dispute: 424
War of attrition: 426
Warrington, Battle of (1983): 427
Wastefulness of capitalism: 247, 249-250, 253-254, 260
Wealth, inequality in: 40-41, 244, 255, 260, 415
Webb, Beatrice: 4
Weinstock, Arnold (GEC chairman): 255
Welfare: 103-104, 110, 125, 245, 250, 258-259, 386, 437, 439
White collar
unionism: 15
workers: 12, 16, 63-64, 104, 107-108, 141,

170, 371, 383, 391
Willis, Bob (NGA leader): 58
Wilson, Harold (Labour prime minister): xix, 50, 223, 231, 250, 330, 369-370, 374, 415, 434, 438-439
'Winter of Discontent': 439
Women: 341, 353, 355, 370, 404
equal pay: 306
oppression: 207, 418
Woodcock, George (TUC leader): 16, 105, 113n, 281
Work study (see time and motion study)
Workers'
control: 17, 67, 81-83, 111, 137-139, 149, 458, 171-172, 209, 243, 288-290, 305-306, 313, 363, 390
defensive: 290
embryo of socialist society: 290
over unions: 284
participation: 399, 406-407, 418
power: 339
Workers Revolutionary Party (WRP): 429
Working class consciousness: 142, 440
Working class unity: 110-111
Working hours: 306, 308, 312
Workplace divided into two camps (management/ supervisors versus workers/stewards): 290
Works committees (see shop stewards committees)
Working to rule: 75, 285
World War One: 79, 90, 112, 121, 332
World War Two: 13, 33, 67, 79, 103, 113, 124, 172, 238, 299, 410, 415, 439

Young workers: 136-137, 140